SURVEY
OF
SOCIAL
SCIENCE

SURVEY
OF
SOCIAL
SCIENCE

GOVERNMENT AND POLITICS SERIES

Volume 2
445-902

Consumer Politics—Independence Movements and Transitions

Edited by
FRANK N. MAGILL

Consulting Editor
JOSEPH M. BESSETTE
CLAREMONT MCKENNA COLLEGE

SALEM PRESS

Pasadena, California   Englewood Cliffs, New Jersey

∞ The paper used in these volumes conforms to the
American National Standard for Permanence of Paper for
Printed Library Materials, Z39.48-1984.

Library of Congress Cataloging-in-Publication Data
Survey of social science: government and politics series /
edited by Frank N. Magill; consulting editor Joseph M.
Bessette.
    p.   cm.
Includes bibliographical references and index.
    1. Political science—Encyclopedias. 2. United States—
Politics and government—Encyclopedias. I. Magill,
Frank Northen, 1907-   . II. Bessette, Joseph M.
JA61.S88   1995
320'.03—dc20
ISBN 0-89356-745-0 (set)   95-30408
ISBN 0-89356-747-7 (volume 2)   CIP

PRINTED IN THE UNITED STATES OF AMERICA

CONTENTS

GOVERNMENT AND POLITICS

SURVEY
OF
SOCIAL
SCIENCE

CONSUMER POLITICS

Field of study: Politics

The consumer protection movement advocates the interests of buyers of goods and services. It uses education, lobbying, legal actions, and boycotts.

Principal terms

CONSUMERS' RESEARCH: earliest national consumer testing and information service

CONSUMERS UNION: group formed by former staff of Consumers' Research, becoming the largest national consumer testing and information service, publishing *Consumer Reports* magazine

MUCKRAKER: person—typically a journalist—who exposes corruption in public matters

PROGRESSIVISM: social movement started in the late nineteenth century in reaction to the growth of business' power in politics and the marketplace

USURY: exorbitant rate of interest charged on money borrowed

Overview

"Consumerism," "consumer protection," and "the consumer movement"—all these terms have been applied to the primarily twentieth century phenomenon of intervention of buyers to protect themselves from dangerous or inferior goods and services and fraudulent or unfair sales tactics. Although this movement has been most prevalent in the United States, it has spread to many other countries, including several less developed ones.

The earliest societies had measures that aided consumers, such as prohibitions against adulterated foods, regulations governing coins, weights, and measures, and the issuance of charters and licenses, but such rules were primarily instituted to promote efficiency in commerce—benefits to consumers were a by-product. During the Middle Ages, guilds imposed standards of craftsmanship on their members, and laws on usury were instituted. In general, however, the rule governing transactions between buyers and sellers was caveat emptor (let the buyer beware). This system was relatively workable in a nonindustrialized society in which buyers generally had direct contact with the producer. This condition, however, does not apply in an industrialized society.

Among the many profound changes that the Industrial Revolution imposed on society, one of the first was the removal of direct contact between producer and purchaser. Later, many new, technologically complex products were introduced, and advertising grew in scope and sophistication. These factors changed the relation between producers and consumers and contributed to the rise of the consumer movement in the United States and elsewhere.

It is generally agreed that there have been three major cycles of consumerism in the

United States. Each resulted from a combination of dedicated advocacy and lobbying, one or more popular books that called the public's attention to an issue, and often a dramatic incident that focused public attention on the issue. Each cycle was also tied to a national social or political movement.

The first major period of consumerism in the United States began in the late nineteenth century, after such household products as food and textiles had begun to be mass produced, and businesses had begun to concentrate their power both in the marketplace, through monopolies, and in the political arena, through money. Mass production created an imbalance in the buyer-seller relationship by breaking the link between producer and consumer. This period coincided with the Progressive movement, which not only worked for political and business reforms, but also began the move toward consumer issues with its attempts to control the sale of food and drugs. Prominent voices raised in support of greater efforts to ensure the safety of food and drugs included Harvey Wiley (the head of the Department of Agriculture's Division of Chemistry), citizens' groups (such as the National Consumer League and the American Medical Association), and President Theodore Roosevelt, who had had firsthand experience with the problem of adulterated foods causing illness among his soldiers during the Spanish-American War. Nevertheless, laws regulating food and drugs were not passed until after the publication of one of the earliest muckraking books, Upton Sinclair's *The Jungle* (1906). Although Sinclair's intention in writing the book was to arouse sympathy for the horrific conditions under which persons in the meatpacking industry labored, his vivid descriptions of filth and feculence in America's meat enraged the public, and the Meat Inspection and Pure Food and Drug acts were quickly passed. The onset of World War I, however, put an end to this first cycle of the consumer movement.

The second period of intense consumerism began in the mid-1920's. By this time the Industrial Revolution had further affected consumers in their homes, in large part because of the greater availability of electricity. In 1907, approximately 8 percent of American homes had electricity; by 1925, the number had risen to 53 percent. These newly electrified homes provided a ready market for such innovations as electric toasters, vacuum cleaners, and sewing machines. Such technological marvels, however, seemed so mechanically complicated that consumers did not have the knowledge to understand and evaluate their purchases. Having greater disposable income than before, and being presented with mysterious new technologies, consumers began to feel the need for impartial information to make sense of their many choices.

Frederick J. Schlink cowrote two books that ignited the second phase of consumerism in the United States. The first, *Your Money's Worth* (1927), written with Stuart Chase, advocated the setting of product standards by the government, and the establishment of impartial testing laboratories. Public interest was so great that Schlink started Consumers' Research, to do product tests and provide information, and the *Consumers' Research Bulletin* to disseminate the results. Within five years, subscriptions to his magazine had reached 42,000. Schlink's second book was *100,000,000 Guinea Pigs: Dangers in Everyday Foods, Drugs, and Cosmetics* (1933), written with

Arthur Kallet. The title, whether intentionally or not, tapped into the feelings of Depression-battered Americans who felt their lives were being run by forces they could not control.

The rapid early growth of Consumers' Research was shattered by internal dissension among staff members, who began agitating for union representation. A strike was called, and Schlink rejected arbitration. Many of the strikers left Schlink and formed the rival Consumers Union, which was run collectively, made political activities part of its mission, and assessed the conditions under which employees worked as part of its product evaluations. The first issue of *Consumers Union Reports* was published in May, 1936; it quickly surpassed the *Consumers' Research Bulletin* in circulation.

At the federal level, the nature of New Deal programs helped to increase consumer representation in government. The New Deal widened the parameters for government control of the economy, and representatives from business, labor, and consumers were invited to participate in the process. Consumers were consistently less successful than business and labor in making their needs and concerns felt, however, because they are an amorphous group and lacked a focused agenda. It was not until approximately a hundred people died from a new sulfa drug containing a toxic additive that consumer concerns again became a priority at the federal level. The Food, Drug, and Cosmetic Act of 1933 provided several new protections to consumers. Cosmetics and therapeutic devices were regulated for the first time. Proof of fraud was no longer required to stop false advertising claims. Drug manufacturers had to prove their products were safe (although not that they were effective) before they could be sold.

This second major period of consumerism was brought to a swift end by World War II. No resurgence of consumerism followed in the years immediately after the war's end. Consumer demand after years of rationing and shortages, a growing economy providing many workers with extra time and money, and such new luxuries as television all took precedence in the public consciousness over regulation of products.

The third period of consumerism began slowly in the late 1950's. The stage was prepared by several books. Vance Packard's *Hidden Persuaders* (1957) condemned the manipulative effects of political and product advertising; John Kenneth Galbraith's *The Affluent Society* (1958) asserted that advertising promoted the pursuit of private goods to the detriment of public goods; Rachel Carson's *Silent Spring* (1962) exposed the dangers of pesticides and added environmental concerns to the widening focus of consumerism; and *Unsafe at Any Speed* (1965) indicted car safety in general and General Motors in particular. The last book introduced the best known and most durable consumer advocate in the United States, Ralph Nader.

Although each of these books caused much discussion on the issue it raised, and the Great Society programs of the 1960's were creating a climate favorable to more government intervention, it took a tragedy and a scandal before consumer protection legislation again became a federal priority. The tragedy came in the form of reports from Europe of a rash of children born with gross physical defects, which were soon linked to the use of the drug thalidomide (not yet approved in the United States) by pregnant women. This gave impetus to the Kefauver-Harris Amendment to the federal Food, Drug, and Cosmetics Act, which required more stringent testing of new drugs. The scandal involved General Motors' use of a private detective to investigate Ralph Nader, who was scheduled to testify before a Senate subcommittee on car safety. When GM's investigation was discovered and exposed, Nader's invasion-of-privacy suit resulted in a settlement from GM of more than $400,000, with which Nader funded several consumer organizations.

During the 1960's and 1970's, consumer groups and federal, state, and local consumer protection agencies grew rapidly throughout the United States, and the movement began to spread across the world. Federal interest in and financing for consumer initiatives declined, however, under the antiregulatory Reagan Administration.

Applications

Public interest in and campaigning for consumer protection have resulted in the passage of legislation, formation of agencies, funding of research, and other government responses on the federal, state, and local levels. At the federal level, many resources are directed toward consumer protection, but by the mid-1990's no independent agency existed that had a clear mandate for consumer welfare, regulatory power, and a budget sufficient to give it clout. *The U.S. Government Manual, 1994-1995*, has fourteen entries in the index under "consumer," including agencies and offices in the Department of Agriculture, the Department of the Treasury, the Federal Deposit Insurance Commission, and the Interstate Commerce Commission. Three of the main consumer-related offices at the national level are the U.S. Office of Consumer Affairs (OCA), the Consumer Products Safety Commission, and the Bureau of Consumer Protection of the Federal Trade Commission (FTC).

The OCA was established in 1964 as the Consumer Advisory Council and renamed in 1971. It is located administratively within Health and Human Services, but reports directly to the president. It advises the president and the secretary of Health and Human Services on consumer-related policies and programs, analyzes and coordinates implementation of all federal activities in the area of consumer protection, and recommends ways in which government consumer programs can be made more effective. Its effectiveness is limited by its small budget and lack of power.

The Consumer Products Safety Commission, an independent federal regulatory agency, was established in 1973 to protect the public from unreasonable risk of injury from consumer products, assist consumers in evaluating the safety of consumer products, promote unified safety standards for consumer products, minimize conflicting state and local regulations, and investigate the causes and prevention of product-related deaths, illness, and injury. Although charged with ensuring the safety of more than 15,000 types of products, it had one of the smallest budgets of any federal agency and had to rely on voluntary measures from manufacturers.

The Bureau of Consumer Protection exists to ensure that advertising is truthful and not misleading, reduce fraudulent and deceptive marketing practices, investigate telemarketing, business, investment, and franchise fraud, enforce credit statutes and trade rules, and educate businesses and consumers regarding their rights and responsibilities under FTC rules. Despite its name, the bureau is concerned with protecting producers as well as consumers. It is expected to "advocate the consumer interest in a competitive marketplace by encouraging courts, legislators, and government administrative bodies to consider efficiency and consumer welfare in deliberations [supporting] procompetitive means of regulating the nation's economy, including the elimination of anticompetitive regulations . . . and the implementation of regulatory programs that protect the public [while preserving] competitive markets."

Individual complaints are not handled at the federal level. The Federal Trade Commission, for example, records complaints but is mandated not to resolve individual complaints. On the state and local level, the consumer agencies that flourished in the 1960's and 1970's have declined in size, funding, and influence since the late 1980's, despite increases in consumer complaints and requests for assistance. Dallas, Texas, provides one example of the cost to consumers of elimination of consumer protection services. In 1990, cutbacks in the Office of Consumer Protection forced elimination of the Weights and Measures Division, which had checked store scales and gas station pumps for accuracy at least twice a year. The task was transferred to a state agency, which was able to check scales and pumps only once every three years or so. It has been estimated that inaccuracies in food weights and gasoline delivery costs Dallas consumers approximately $1.5 million a year.

Context

As national economies have become more globalized, the consumer protection movement has spread beyond its United States roots, particularly into Western Europe and Japan. Consumerism in industrialized countries generally focuses on eliminating unsafe products through the institution of government regulations and standards. Consumerism usually depends in great part on private organizations that test products and disseminate information to consumers and often is aligned with other social movements, such as labor or environmental groups.

Governmental regulation and consumer organizations vary widely according to the political climate of the country. In Canada and Australia, as in the United States, the consumer movement has come mainly from the concerns of citizens. In Great Britain, the Consumer's Association, founded in the 1950's, is funded by sales of its magazine, *Which?* and engages in lobbying, product testing, and dissemination of information. The British government provides funding for national and local citizens' advice bureaus. In Germany, *Stiftung Warentest*, founded in 1964, receives funding both from private sources and from the government. It engages in product testing and consumer information only. The China Consumers' Association, founded in 1984, had 162 members in 1993—individuals and organizations—promoting consumer rights in the People's Republic of China, and establishing standards for goods and services. In Japan, the consumer movement is fueled by the efforts of homemakers' groups. In other countries, family organizations, cooperatives, or labor unions may form the basis of the consumer movement.

In Scandinavian countries, which have strong social democratic traditions, consumer protection is considered to be part of the social safety net, and is funded by the government. The governments of Sweden, Norway, Denmark, and Finland each employ an ombudsman who investigates complaints against business and, if unable to obtain voluntary compliance with consumer protection laws, brings legal action, not on behalf of an individual, but for consumers as a group. Norway also mandates consumer education in the schools.

The consumer protection movement has begun to influence Third World countries also, although with a different focus than the one it has in highly industrialized countries. In Third World countries, problems are similar to those present in the United States early in the twentieth century—adulterated or poorly preserved food, and lack of quality control in manufactured products—combined with the importation of technologically advanced products that consumers are unprepared to judge or even use properly. A further problem for Third World consumers is the "dumping" on them of products that have been banned or severely restricted in developed countries as being unsafe or ineffective, such as defective medical devices or banned pesticides.

Several multinational consumer protection groups have been formed since 1960, and have been particularly helpful in advancing consumer protection in Third World countries. One of the most significant is the International Organization of Consumers Unions, which represents national and local consumer groups from sixty-eight countries and has 175 branches throughout the world. Among its goals are to advance consumer self-organization, promote international cooperation in testing consumer goods and services, provide consumer information, education and protection, collect and disseminate information regarding consumer laws and practices, and provide a forum for consumer groups to discuss problems and explore solutions. It works with agencies of the United Nations and other international organizations and provides seminars, training, and special working groups. It has demonstrated its commitment to the needs of developing countries in several ways. It opened regional offices in Malaysia and Uruguay, established Consumer Interpol (which works to expose and prevent incidents of product dumping), and was instrumental in the adoption of the United Nations Guidelines for Consumer Protection.

The consumer protection movement has been an important force in enabling buyers to evaluate products, pressuring corporate interests to improve product safety and quality, and prodding governments to take responsibility for setting standards. In most countries, the movement derives its strength from the concerns of general citizens and tends to be less effective when public attention is not focused on a specific use.

Bibliography

Brennan, Shawn, ed. *Consumer Sourcebook*. 7th ed. Detroit: Gale Research, 1991. Guide to approximately eight thousand government agencies and offices, to national, regional, and grassroots organizations, to information centers and clearinghouses, and to other consumer resources.

Brimelow, Peter, and Leslie Spencer. "Ralph Nader, Inc." *Forbes* 146, no. 6 (September 17, 1990): 117. Critical view of Ralph Nader and his various consumer organizations, in a business-oriented magazine.

Buckhorn, Robert F. *Nader: The People's Lawyer*. Englewood Cliffs, N.J.: Prentice-Hall, 1972. Overview of Ralph Nader's early career and pioneering organizations, based on interviews with Nader and his associates, his articles and congressional testimony, and court records from his lawsuit against General Motors.

Griffin, Kelley. *Ralph Nader Presents More Action for a Change*. New York: Dembner Books, 1987. Examination of a grassroots consumer-related movement—the Public Interest Research Groups—a student activist group begun by Ralph Nader.

Mayer, Robert N. *The Consumer Movement: Guardians of the Marketplace*. Boston: Twayne, 1989. Excellent coverage of contemporary consumerism, including its history, structure, economic impact, and global aspects.

Irene Struthers

Cross-References

Activist Politics, p. 7; Aging and Politics in the United States, p. 35; Environmental Protection, p. 617; Grassroots Politics, p. 797; Interest Groups, p. 936; Lobbying and Lobbyists, p. 1130; Political Participation, p. 1479; Populism, p. 1551; Progressivism, p. 1609; Protest Movements, p. 1621; Regulatory Agencies in the United States, p. 1678.

CORPORATISM

Field of study: Economic issues

Corporatism is a system in which government limits economic competition by granting privately owned businesses special privileges in exchange for greater governmental control. Ideally, this will lead to greater national unity and enable government and business to move toward the same goals.

Principal terms

FASCISM: right-wing ideology that advocates dictatorial rule by an elite, stressing nationalism and rejecting individual freedoms

INTEREST REPRESENTATION: group of persons or businesses that organizes to represent members' economic concerns to the government and to seek government support within its area of concern

NATIONALISM: common bond of identity from shared racial, linguistic, historical, or religious ties; in economic terms, a policy to protect domestic businesses and achieve objectives desired by the government

SOCIAL CORPORATISM: form of corporatism that occurs when the government incrementally increases its involvement in economic affairs

STATE CORPORATISM: form of corporatism that occurs when the government makes a revolutionary change in economic policy that results in the immediate control of the economic sector within corporatist guidelines

VERTICAL ECONOMIC ORGANIZATION: labor, management, and others involved in a specific industry form one organization, while those in other industries are in different organizations, as opposed to systems where labor forms one group and management another

Overview

The term "corporatism" is used in a variety of ways. This is partly because this twentieth century phenomenon has been found in countries with both authoritarian and democratic governments. The use of a corporatist economic structure by fascist regimes has led many to dismiss it as something that is only found under repressive regimes; thus it is not often studied independently of fascism. After World War II, however, many Western European democracies structured their economic policies according to interest representation, which is the heart of corporatist doctrine. Further complicating any discussion of corporatism is the fact that—as is true with many political ideologies—the form corporatism takes when implemented generally does not fully fit the definitions of political theorists.

Corporatism is an economic system where the government and privately owned businesses cooperate to limit competition so that a stronger, more unified economy can develop. The goal of corporatism is an orderly economic system that successfully assists government, and the society, to reach nationalistic goals. A business, labor union, or trade association is given a monopoly in a certain economic area and the government is given the right to control the type of decisions that the business, union, or trade association can make. In a corporatist system, the economy is structured by industry: owners, managers, and workers in a single industry are seen as a unit. Programs and decisions are based on the needs of the nation and the needs of the industry as a whole, rather than the needs of a particular economic class. This is a vertical approach to the structuring of the economic system. It is assumed that making industries the focal point for policy formation is a major step toward the goal of making everyone an active part of the social hierarchy and developing a nationalistic orientation.

In theory, orderliness and expertise characterize the focal point of the system as it attempts to move toward national goals. Ideally, this should ensure success in reaching the goals for each industry. The unruly economic competition of capitalism is seen as a wasteful form of conflict and duplication of services. Thus competition is something to be controlled. Although corporatism accepts personal financial gain as an essential ingredient in the motivation of the individual, this is used as a means to a social end. It is asserted that only government will consider the interests of the nation as a whole. Thus, it is the vehicle for drawing up the goals for the nation and for enforcing cooperation among the various sections of the economic community. Because reaching the national goals for the society is considered to be more important than individual goals or freedoms, individual liberty may be sacrificed for the good of the society. When operating smoothly, corporatism allows the government to leave many decisions in the hands of the leaders, or experts, of the various industries.

In 1934, Mihail Manoilesco, a political philosopher, declared that the twentieth century would be the century of corporatism. The social upheaval following World War I gave those advocating corporatism an opportunity to put their theories into practice. The form most often adopted in this period is generally called "state corporatism" or "authoritarian corporatism." Although gaining widespread attention in Italy, in conjunction with the emergence of fascism, it was also tried prior to the mid-1920's in Spain, Portugal, and Austria. In the 1930's, it was adopted by Germany, Spain, and many Latin American nations. In these nations, corporatism was put in place by governments that came to power as a result of social upheavals and that sought to establish a social peace by decree. The economic problems, which were a part of the social upheavals, encouraged the use of corporatism. In order to make rapid economic changes, cooperation between the various labor and business interests was put in place by force. When a government lost power, this authoritarian form of corporatism generally was dismantled by the next government.

After World War II, a new form, often called "social corporatism" or "democratic corporatism," arose. This form of corporatism developed from an incremental evolution of the economic and social system that transformed the competitive, pluralistic system of capitalism into corporatism. Three trends encouraged the rise of social corporatism. First was the expansion of public policy concerns into areas that previously had been the concerns only of business. Second, governments were increasingly called upon to support the nation's industry in the growing economic competition among nations. Third, the ownership and control of private businesses became more concentrated, while a few large companies dominated production within most industries. Thus cooperation between private business and the government came about voluntarily as each sought to gain benefits. Examples of countries that moved in this direction during the 1950's are Denmark, The Netherlands, Norway, Sweden, and Switzerland. Belgium, Germany, and Finland are borderline cases, with some scholars arguing that they adopted corporatist systems, while others insist they maintained capitalist systems.

In its democratic form, corporatism shares ideas with both socialism and capitalism. Capitalism advocates private ownership of businesses with private control. Socialism advocates public ownership of business with public control. Corporatism encourages private ownership but with public control. In "social corporatism," the movement from capitalism begins with the acceptance that the government has a role in setting the limits on what can be done with private property and then evolves, leaving a narrower and narrower range of decisions that the property or business owner can make. It is hard to define exactly when a nation stops being capitalist and becomes corporatist.

Applications

Getulio Vargas, president of Brazil from 1930 to 1945, led a revolution that overthrew the government in Brazil in 1930. Although he began moving in the direction of corporatism in 1930, it was not until he took total control of the country through further military action, in November, 1937, that Vargas established the *Estado Novo*, the first true corporatist state in Brazil.

Fear of communism and the failure of liberal democracy to stem the Depression led Vargas to establish Brazilian state corporatism as an alternative to capitalist democracy, communism, and socialism. Francisco Campos, the author of the constitution of the *Estado Novo*, believed that the class struggles of the traditional capitalist democracy system would lead to communism if strong steps were not taken to stop the process. He saw corporatism as going beyond class interest, allowing private enterprise to continue but directed toward the best interests of the nation. The leaders of the Brazilian corporatist state sought to guide the nation in a less coercive way than was the case in fascist corporatism. They were, however, in total accord with other corporatists in asserting that market forces could not make the best allocation of resources in the economic or the political realms.

The development of domestic industry, which had occurred during the 1930's, had created conflict between labor and management, Although much social legislation had been passed between 1930 and 1937, it was not enough to stem the conflicts. Once in total control, Vargas took mainstream corporatist action to mediate between the groups. He and his advisers believed that technical knowledge would allow the government to do away with conflict and allow cooperation to emerge as the guiding principal of society. Two organizations were established under the ministry of labor: a hierarchy of labor organizations, and trade (employer) associations. Each was structured by the government. For each industry, all the workers within a relatively small geographical area were made members of the local union organization. All the locals in similar industries in each state were made a part of the state labor federation for that industry. Seven national labor organizations were the intermediaries between the ministry of labor and the state federations. The trade associations had an identical structure. The union representatives and the representatives of the trade associations presented their demands to the ministry of labor, and government officials mediated between the two based on the national interest. In reality, however, the trade associations received a much more favorable hearing than did the labor representatives. Nevertheless, the corporatist system established in the *Estado Novo* was enough in tune with society that even after the return of democracy in 1945 much of the structure remained.

Democratic corporatism in Europe has been based on the voluntary cooperation of the leaders of the various economic and social organizations. Within this system, any party is free to withdraw from the arrangement. Economic policies tend to be the focal point for democratic corporatism. Labor and business work together with much less governmental coercion than in the state corporatist system. The corporatist system in Sweden has had strong labor, business, and governmental components. It originated through the cooperation of the Social Democratic Party (which ruled from 1932 to 1976 and 1982 to 1991) and the labor unions. Although the government tended to follow the labor union's agenda, for example, stressing full employment, the business community found it advantageous to cooperate. This gave a stable and predictable environment for economic growth. An example of private-public cooperation was in the area of foreign trade. Various businesses were allowed to accumulate funds to develop the export market; in exchange, the government mandated the use of profits for the development of domestic industry rather than allowing jobs to move out of the country. During the 1980's, when the Social Democratic Party returned to power, the cooperative spirit allowed the government to undertake necessary programs to combat economic problems. In 1982, when the Swedish currency had to be devalued, an action that usually results in labor unrest, the unions granted concessions allowing the businesses to temporarily achieve a high level of profit in order to increase investments and remain competitive in the international market. In 1986 and 1989, when the government needed to raise additional revenue and wanted to moderate union demands, the insurance companies were charged with a one-time tax, and all corporations were charged a one-time tax of 15 percent of their profits. Corporatism in Sweden did not reflect any radical change within the nation; it was a gradual process of cooperation among government, business, and labor. All parties found the economic stability beneficial. The government could move toward national goals of economic strength and stability, while both labor and business found the cooperation useful in achieving a higher level of economic rewards.

Context

Although what came to be called corporatist thought developed in nineteenth century Europe, the ideas were not created in a vacuum. Many of its ideals can be found in earlier economic systems, such as the guild system of the Middle Ages or the economic doctrines of Saint Thomas Aquinas. Guilds were established to limit competition within the various trades and professions as well as to grant credentials to their members. Aquinas believed stewardship of private property included the right to force the owner to use the property for the good of society. The problems resulting from the industrialization of European society caused many to look for a new way of structuring economic forces. Corporatist thought, as well as the foundations of communism and modern socialism, developed during the nineteenth century as alternatives to laissez-faire capitalism. Corporatism emphasizes nationalism, unlike communism, which emphasizes class consciousness. Socialism assumes that public ownership of industry will solve the problems of industrialization; corporatism assumes that this would take away the central economic motivation of personal gain. Capitalism assumes that self-interest will operate in the public interest; corporatism uses the government to guide the economic system toward desired ends.

At the beginning of the twentieth century, most European countries combined capitalism and democracy. In this traditional blend of capitalism and democracy there are two systems that determine the allocation of resources within the nation. Economically, the market system dictates the allocation of certain resources based on the price structure determined by supply and demand. Politically, the electoral system determines the allocation of other resources based on the decisions of the citizens through the mechanism of voting. Corporatism attempts to combine these two systems by allowing the government to establish a supply system, and at times a pricing structure, within which private economic decisions can be made.

Historically, the use of the corporatist framework to support the forceful governing of industry by authoritarian regimes has tended to be short-lived in most nations. What has been more successful has been the gradual transition to corporatism in Western democracies. In all developed nations, there have been increased demands by various economic and interest groups for governmental support and assistance. At the same time, many persons and groups have advocated increased governmental regulation of some industries. Socially, corporatism tends to put the good of the nation above that of the individual and to concentrate power in the hands of technical experts who determine what is best for society. Economically, increased regulation by the government decreases the choices available for the consumer and concentrates power in the hands of a few. Whether the trend will continue depends on whether the citizens of each nation see the changes from a capitalist democracy to a corporatist democracy as social and economic costs, or benefits.

Bibliography

Cohen, Youssef. *The Manipulation of Consent: The State and Working-Class Consciousness in Brazil*. Pittsburgh: University of Pittsburgh Press, 1989. Illustrates how corporatism has been used in Latin American countries to control the working class.

Elbow, Matthew H. *French Corporative Theory, 1789-1948: A Chapter in the History of Ideas*. New York: Octagon Books, 1966. Excellent text dealing with the development of corporatist theory in France from the time of the First Republic. Shows the systematic development and durability of corporatist thought over time.

King, Desmond S., and Bo Rothstein. "Institutional Choices and Labor Market Policy: A British-Swedish Comparison." *Comparative Political Studies* 26 (July, 1993): 147-177. Demonstrates how the social corporatist structure in Sweden allows government programs that cannot be sustained in the noncorporatist United Kingdom.

Nyang'oro, Julius E., and Timothy M. Shaw, eds. *Corporatism in Africa: Comparative Analysis and Practice*. Boulder, Colo.: Westview Press, 1989. Describes the variations of corporatism that have developed in Africa.

Schmitter, Philippe C., ed. *Comparative Political Studies* 10 (April, 1977). Special issue devoted to the discussion of corporatism in post-World War II Europe. Many of the articles have become classics in the description and analysis of social corporatism.

Williamson, Peter J. *Corporatism in Perspective: An Introductory Guide to Corporatist Theory*. London: Sage Publications, 1989. Excellent book with a brief history and a more extensive discussion of the varieties of corporatism.

Zhang, Baohui. "Corporatism, Totalitarianism, and Transitions to Democracy." *Comparative Political Studies* 27 (April, 1994): 108-136. Discusses how the corporatist structure allows corporatist totalitarian states to become democratic more easily than non-corporatist totalitarian states.

Donald A. Watt

Cross-References

Business and Government, p. 177; Capitalism, p. 197; Clientelism, p. 337; Commerce Regulation, p. 357; Fascism and Nazism, p. 656; Individual Versus State Rights, p. 910; Political Economy, p. 1455; Socialism, p. 1865.

COUNTY GOVERNMENT

Field of study: Local and regional government

A unit of its local government, county government is the largest political subdivision of U.S. states. It performs state-mandated functions, such as law enforcement and voting administration, and provides local services, such as water supply and street maintenance, to its residents.

Principal terms

DILLON'S RULE: principle that local government can perform only such functions as are expressly granted by its state government

GENERAL LAW COUNTY: one that does not have home rule powers because it was created by a state general law and not by a special charter

HOME RULE: freedom of local governments to run their own affairs without state interference

MUNICIPAL CORPORATION: legal description of a city, town, or village that is formally incorporated as a municipality through a state charter

PROFESSIONALIZATION OF COUNTY GOVERNMENT: process wherein counties adopt the administrator or elected executive form of government, or adopt a merit system of employment

QUASI-MUNICIPAL CORPORATION: term used to describe the legal status of a county

UNINCORPORATED AREA: section of a county that is not incorporated into a municipality and is thus subject to direct county government control

VETO POWER: authority of an elected county executive to prevent legislative actions from becoming law, (unless overridden)

Overview

In 1994, 3,043 county governments operated in the United States, distributed among every state except Connecticut and Rhode Island—in both of which town governments perform county functions. In Alaska, counties are called "boroughs," and in Louisiana they are "parishes." The average number of county governments per state is about 60, with as few as 3 in Delaware and as many as 254 in Texas. The average population served by a county government is about seventy thousand, but each county serves a dramatically different number of people. For example, county government in Loving, Texas, provides services to a little more than one hundred people, while county government in Los Angeles, California, provides services to more than eight million people.

Since the U.S. Constitution does not mention them, county governments are purely creations of their state. They were formed to administer state laws, unlike other local governments, which are established voluntarily by the local inhabitants to provide local services. Because county governments are political subdivisions of their states, they wield different powers and perform different functions from other local governments. For this reason they are called "quasi-municipal corporations." Like municipal corporations, such as cities and towns, county governments have corporate, governmental, and proprietary powers. Their corporate powers include the right to perpetuate their existence, the legal status to sue and be sued, and the legal ability to buy and sell property. Their governmental powers include such compulsory activities as policing and taxation, which they perform as agents for their states. Their proprietary powers include such enterprises as maintaining public utilities and garbage collection, which may compete with private businesses. County governments act more often as agents of the state than cities and towns do, they are more subject to state legislative control than municipalities, and they may not be liable for civil damages that occur in the process of exercising their governmental powers.

The concepts of governmental and proprietary powers provide a legal basis for the distinction between mandatory and optional functions of county government. Mandatory functions, also known as traditional or basic functions, are those that county governments are required to perform by state laws or state constitutions. Property tax assessment, law enforcement, voting administration, public health, recording of deeds, and public welfare are examples of state-mandated functions. Optional functions, also known as local or urban functions, are those that county governments are permitted by state law to perform for the benefit of their residents. These functions include maintaining parks and recreation facilities, utilities, water supply and sewage, garbage collection and disposal, transportation, parking, and housing. County governments in the early years of the nation served primarily as rural governments and performed mostly state-mandated functions. As populations increased and became more urbanized, many urban and suburban county governments began to provide more optional services along with state-mandated services. The largest and most urban counties eventually offered the widest range of services to their residents. The largest county services in terms of expenditures, however, are still dominated by state-mandated functions, such as health and hospitals, public welfare, education, public safety, highways, and general governmental administration.

To perform this wide range of functions, county governments generate various types of revenues. They collect property and other taxes, including real property, personal property, sales, machinery and tools, cigarette, and transient occupancy taxes. They charge users fees for services such as swimming pools, park admissions, golf courses, and adult education. They also receive a significant amount of state aid and some federal aid. Finally, they can issue tax anticipation notes to cover short-term cash needs, and long-term bonds to finance capital projects, such as sport stadiums and bridges, that require large amounts of capital. There are two types of long-term bonds: general obligation bonds and revenue bonds. General obligation bonds are issued with approval of the voters and are paid back from general revenues, while revenue bonds are issued for a specific capital project without approval of voters and are paid off from revenues generated by the project.

To provide necessary services and generate and manage revenues, county governments elect officials such as sheriffs, treasurers, coroners, and commissioners or supervisors, and appoint many department directors and employees. Who elects or appoints these officials, what they do, and how they work together is determined primarily by the organizational structure of the individual county government. Such governments usually have one of three organizational structures: commission form, administrator form, or elected executive form. These forms are imposed on counties by their states, except in home-rule counties.

Under the commission form, usually three or five commissioners or supervisors are elected by districts, or at-large by the voters, and exercise both legislative and administrative powers. They can hold hearings, enact ordinances, set tax rates, appoint advisory board and commission members, and oversee their appointees. In addition to the commissioners, the voters elect other officers including a sheriff, clerk, tax assessor, coroner, attorney, and recorder of deeds. On the county organizational charts, these officers are listed in a row with the commissioners, and therefore are known as "row" officers. The two groups have different powers and independent constituent bases. Consequently, row officers are not accountable to commissioners and commissioners do not have explicit supervisory powers over row officers, creating diffuse and autonomous power relations between them. Although this diffusion and independence of powers may provide a system of checks and balances, it can also create a fragmented governmental system with a significant power vacuum. Because of the separation of power, no single official can plan for the operations of the entire county, nor be held directly responsible for county policies to the voters.

Under the administrator form, a county administrator appointed by the board of commissioners has supervisory and budgetary powers over the individual departments, such as health, highway, and social services. Formally, the administrator may be called a county manager, chief administrative officer, or administrative assistant. The different names are not incidental: the county manager has the most extensive powers of the three types, and the administrative assistant has the least power. A county manager appoints and supervises most department directors and staff officers, prepares budgets, makes policy decisions, and reviews county programs. Chief administrative officers prepare budgets and supervise staff services, and coordinate county programs, but usually do not directly supervise executive departments and do not appoint department chiefs. Administrative assistants perform mostly administrative tasks without any formal powers. They prepare budgets and draft ordinances at the request of their county boards. They submit reports to their county boards, but do not have appointment powers and do not supervise department chiefs. In counties with the administrator form, the administrators involve themselves in day-to-day operations of county administration, but lack an electoral base of political support and serve at the pleasure of their boards of commissioners.

Under the executive form, county executives and several commissioners are directly elected by the voters. The executives have the power to oversee the operations of county departments, appoint and remove department directors, and veto acts of commissioners; the commissioners have the power to hold hearings on policy matters, pass ordinances, adopt budgets, and override the county executive's veto. Since the executives wield power over the operations of entire county administrations, they can represent the whole county administration, provide strong leadership, and be accountable to residents for county policies.

Traditionally, the commission form was the most common form, but the administrator and executive forms gained popularity in the last part of the twentieth century, particularly in urban and suburban areas. This was partly because of the urbanization of county population, more diverse demands for services from county residents, and the need for professionalization of county administration. Another factor was county reformers' efforts to modernize county administration. For example, the National Civic League in its Model City Charter (1956, 1990) stressed the need for a single official who represents the whole county administration, and for the separation of powers between the executive and legislature. By 1990, about one-fifth of all counties had adopted the elected executive form; the rest were almost evenly split between the commission form and the administrator form.

Applications

Strong state control of county government is one of the most conspicuous aspects of county government operations. County governments are subject to almost unlimited state control. This tight state control of county operations is well expressed in Dillon's rule, which holds that all powers not explicitly granted to local governments belong to the state. An exception to the iron-fist control is found in home-rule counties, which can run their local affairs with little state intervention. Fewer than 10 percent of all counties, however, exercise home-rule privileges, even though about three-fourths of all states grant some form of home-rule authority to their counties. This lack of home-rule among county governments undermines their discretionary authority by limiting their ability to begin new initiatives without state approval.

General law counties (non-home-rule counties) and home-rule counties have significantly different amounts of power in the four major areas: political structure, functional responsibility, fiscal administration, and personnel administration. General law counties must receive state approval to change their own organizational structures, to decide what additional services to provide, to determine what additional revenues to generate, or to change employee salary levels. This lack of home-rule authority is most conspicuous in Texas, Massachusetts, and Missouri, where county governments are subject to especially strict state control. In Texas, both Harris County, with approximately three million residents, and Loving County, with a little more than one hundred residents, are required by the state to operate under the same commission form.

Related to the lack of home-rule authority are ever-increasing state mandates. State mandates are constitutional, statutory, or regulatory actions that place additional administrative or expenditure requirements on county governments, regardless of county preferences. They are imposed on both general law and home-rule counties to assure minimum or uniform statewide service levels, develop professional standards for employees, or implement state social or economic policy objectives. State mandates frequently irritate county officials because they substitute state priorities for local ones, and are often imposed on counties without adequate funding to implement them. Both state mandating and lack of home-rule restrict the powers of county government; the former limits the power of county government to begin new initiatives, and the latter imposes unwanted service responsibilities. State mandating may be a bigger problem for home-rule counties, because it restricts their home-rule activities. State mandating is nothing new to general law counties, because they are administrative arms of the state and are supposed to act as agents of the state in the first place.

County governments in New York are subject to the largest number of state mandates in the nation. After New York state began to grant home-rule powers to counties in 1958, nineteen of fifty-seven counties adopted charters with home-rule powers. These charter counties wield broad powers, including the ability to adopt optional government forms and to supersede state laws regarding local affairs by county law, bylaw, or ordinance. Nevertheless, all counties in New York are subject to mandates in sixty of the seventy-seven broad functional areas defined by the federal Advisory Commission on Intergovernmental Relations. The number of individual mandates in the sixty functional areas is estimated at approximately three thousand. For example, counties are subject to compulsory binding arbitration with organizations representing policemen and firemen, they are required to provide disability pensions to policemen and firemen with any heart ailments, and they must prepare environmental impact statements for every proposed government project affecting the environment. These mandates are often responsible for more than 50 percent of the cost of operating certain departments, and they take a large portion of county expenditure increases each year. Even though some county officials take state mandates for granted and even use them to shift the blame relative to unpopular services to the state, many others contend that mandates significantly limit the ability of county government to manage local affairs, and that they impose additional burdens on financially stretched counties.

Context

American county government was created as an administrative agent of the state, patterned after the English county government, originally called "shire." In the nineteenth and early twentieth centuries, most counties, administered by a board of commissioners or supervisors, provided only a few state-mandated services to their residents. This was particularly true in New England states, where town governments, rather than county governments, were the most important local governmental units. Many county governments at that time were inefficient, corrupt, incompetent, and even chaotic. Consequently, they were depicted by scholars as "the dark continent of American politics," "the lost child of local government," or "the plague spot of American politics."

As more counties became urbanized and the populations within their jurisdictions increased in the late twentieth century, counties became more active in meeting new and diverse service demands from the residents. As a result, the expenditures and functions of most counties increased significantly. Of all local governments, with the exception of special districts, counties grew the fastest during the 1980's. A consequence of this growth is the emergence of megacounties, such as Los Angeles County in California, Cook County in Illinois, Harris County in Texas, and Dade County in Florida. The governments of these megacounties provide services to residents in unincorporated areas, in incorporated cities and towns, and occasionally even outside county lines.

More counties adopted professional forms of government and the merit system of employment to meet the growing service challenges they faced and to eliminate the criticisms directed to their operations. While county governments have become more competent service providers, the need for their services has been increasing. Federal and state governments continuously shift their service responsibilities to local governments, or mandate additional services, sometimes without providing the means to fulfill them. Regional problems, such as air and water pollution, traffic congestion, and lack of environmental preservation, have forced small local governments to ally themselves with other local governments to deal with these problems. Since county governments are the largest political subdivisions of the state, they have an advantage in solving these types of regional problems. If the trends of urbanization of population, professionalization of county government, and regional problems continue, county government could become the primary local government of the twenty-first century.

Bibliography

Berman, David, ed. *County Governments in an Era of Change*. Westport, Conn.: Greenwood Press, 1993. Short essays on county government in the United States. Major topics are county governing structure, legislature and legislation, service responsibility and capacity, and county-state relations. Up-to-date bibliography and an index.

Duncombe, Herbert Sydney. *Modern County Government*. Washington, D.C.: National Association of Counties, 1977. Comprehensive overview of American county government. Includes a history of counties, organizational form, specific functions, and an annotated bibliography.

Jeffery, Blake R., Tanis J. Salant, and Alan L. Boroshok. *County Government Structure: A State by State Report*. Washington, D.C.: National Association of Counties, 1989. Thorough comparison of county governing structures in forty-eight states. Contains information about forms of government, home-rule status, types of officers, electoral methods used, county maps, and information sources for county government structures in each state.

Porter, Kirk H. *County and Township Government in the United States*. New York: Macmillan, 1922. Describes the legal status and the functions of county government; advocates the expansion of county functions, centralization of county administration, and wider use of home-rule powers.

U.S. Bureau of the Census. *County and City Data Book*. Washington, D.C.: Government Printing Office, 1949. Published every five years, this Census Bureau publication has many county statistics, including population, revenues, expenditures, and poverty rates. Most reported data are from the decennial censuses.

Keeok Park

Cross-References

City Government in the United States, p. 266; Courts: State and Local, p. 465; Elected Versus Appointed Offices in the United States, p. 572; Federal Mandates, p. 662; Local Governments, p. 1136; Political Machines and Bosses, p. 1468; Regional Governments, p. 1672; Rural Community Government, p. 1763; State and Local Government, p. 1885; State Government, p. 1891.

COURTS: STATE AND LOCAL

Field of study: Law and jurisprudence

State and local court systems handle most civil and criminal cases in the United States. As the judicial branch of state governments, they issue decisions that control the acts of local authorities, state officials, and all the citizens within their jurisdictions.

Principal terms

APPELLATE COURT: courts that decide matters of law and determine if lower courts acted properly

EQUITY: concept that justice should be administered fairly, even if it means going outside of the strict rule of law

GENERAL JURISDICTION: courts that hear and decide all matters that are presented to them

INJUNCTION: court order that prohibits the execution of certain acts or mandates

JURISDICTION: court's ability to hear and decide cases

LIMITED JURISDICTION: courts that can hear and decide only certain legal issues

OPINION: formal written statement interpreting the law and issued by an appellate court

SUPREME COURT: the highest court within a state

Overview

While no two state or local court systems are identical, most share many common features, such as being separated into three distinct levels. Knowledge of these similarities is critical to understanding how state and local courts function. Each system normally comprises a three-step hierarchy, with courts of limited jurisdiction, courts of general jurisdiction, and courts of appellate jurisdiction. At each level, the specified court provides a service that is important to the functioning of the judicial system within the state. The nature and type of case determines which court will have jurisdiction.

Courts that can hear and decide only certain limited legal issues are known as courts of limited jurisdiction. Typically, these courts hear matters such as certain types of minor civil or criminal cases. For example, they handle traffic tickets, set bail for criminal defendants, resolve small claims matters, and issue rulings on lawsuits dealing with contracts, personal injuries, or other matters where the amounts of money involved are small. In the United States, there are approximately thirteen thousand local courts, which include county, magistrate, justice, and municipal courts. Judges may be either appointed or elected to these courts. In many jurisdictions, these are part-time positions and the incumbents may have other jobs in addition to serving as judges. The fact that these courts handle minor civil and criminal matters does not mean their duties are not important. The only contact many citizens have with the judicial system occurs in such courts.

Courts of limited jurisdiction also may hear certain specialized matters such as probate of wills and estates, divorces, child custody matters, and juvenile hearings. In some states, these matters are heard in local courts; in others, there are courts of general jurisdiction that are designated by statute to hear and decide specific types of cases. For example, in California, a "superior court" is considered a court of general jurisdiction but certain of these courts are designated to hear only juvenile matters; they thus become courts of limited jurisdiction when they sit as juvenile courts.

Courts of general jurisdiction are granted authority to hear and decide all issues that are brought before them. They are known by a variety of names, such as superior courts, circuit courts, district courts, or courts of common pleas. These are the courts that normally hear major civil or criminal cases. As courts of general jurisdiction, they have authority to decide issues that occur anywhere within the state. Larger jurisdictions such as Los Angeles or New York City may have hundreds of courts of general jurisdiction within their city limits. Typically, these courts hear civil cases involving the same types of issues that courts of limited jurisdiction hear, but the amounts of damages are higher and may reach millions of dollars. These courts also hear the most serious criminal matters, including death penalty cases.

Courts of general jurisdiction traditionally have the power to issue injunctions prohibiting certain acts or requiring individuals or entities to perform certain functions or duties. This authority is derived from the equity power that resides in courts of general jurisdiction. Equity is the concept that justice is administered according to fairness, as contrasted with the strict rules of law. In early English common law, such separate courts of equity were known as Courts of Chancery. These early courts were not concerned with technical legal issues; they focused on rendering decisions or orders that were fair or equitable. In modern times, the power of those courts has been merged with courts of general jurisdiction, allowing them rule on matters that require fairness as well as the strict application of the law.

Appellate jurisdiction is reserved for courts that hear appeals from both limited and general jurisdiction courts. These courts do not hold trials or hear evidence; they decide matters of law and issue formal written decisions or opinions. The two classes of appellate courts are intermediate and final.

Intermediate appellate courts are known as courts of appeals. Approximately half the states have designated intermediate appellate courts. These courts may be divided into judicial districts and hear all appeals within their district. They hear and decide all issues of law that are raised on appeal in both civil and criminal cases. These courts accept the facts as determined by the trial courts; since they deal strictly with legal or equitable issues, they do not use juries to decide factual disputes. Intermediate appellate courts have the authority to reverse decisions of the lower courts and send the matters back with instructions to retry the cases in accordance with their opinion. Alternatively, they may uphold the decision of the lower court. In either situation, a party who loses the appeal at this level may file an appeal with the next higher appellate court.

Final appellate courts are the highest state appellate courts. They may be known as supreme courts or courts of last resort. Five, seven, or nine justices generally sit on these courts, depending on the state. Such courts have jurisdiction to hear and decide issues dealing with all matters decided by lower courts, including ruling on state constitutional or statutory issues. Their decisions are binding on all other courts within the state. Once such a court decides an issue, the only appeal left is to file in the federal court system.

State and local courts are traditionally characterized by an absence of supervision, specialization, and geographic organization. Each trait can cause problems within the judicial system.

Since local and state court judges are usually elected to their positions, they can and do claim that they answer only to the general public. Many state court systems have a presiding judge who is elected or appointed by the other judges. This judge may act as a supervisor and regulate the type and amount of cases assigned to all other judges, but can not censure or remove another judge for incompetence or wrongdoing. That function is normally left in the hands of the state supreme court, a state judicial panel, or the state legislature. Therefore, no one person or agency is responsible for the effective administration of the state's court system.

The dividing of courts into courts of limited and general jurisdiction results in specialization and fragmentation of duties. Within each state court system, courts may be further divided into areas of specialization, with one judge hearing all probate matters, another hearing all family matters, and another hearing all juvenile matters. While this system may allow judges to develop expertise in their special areas, it can result in uneven workloads. Many judges cooperate to reduce each other's workloads by accepting cases from colleagues who have heavier workloads, but statutes do not require it.

Geographic organization is a third common characteristic of state and local courts. Courts have established boundaries that have implications for the citizens that reside within their jurisdiction. These courts will reflect the different social values and attitudes of their citizens. For example, a court in a rural jurisdiction may view a certain type of crime as more serious than a court in an urban area.

Applications

Cases heard in state and local courts may be civil, criminal, or equitable matters. The civil justice system of state and local courts punishes private wrongs committed within the state, or wrongs that occurred outside the state that resulted in injuries to citizens living in the state. These wrongs may involve disputes with respect to contracts, personal injury, and statutory or constitutionally created rights. Private parties must litigate such claims, usually represented by attorneys, against their opponent in that dispute. Generally, state and local court actions involving civil disputes request money damages, and the litigants have a right to a jury trial. In order to obtain a judgment against a civil defendant, the plaintiff has the burden of proof: he or she must prove the elements of the case by a preponderance of the evidence—that is, that it is more likely than not that the defendant was at fault. A civil defendant must disprove the evidence against him, or show that he had a justifiable defense, in order to avoid civil liability.

For example, a person might buy a defective appliance, which explodes while being used and causes severe injuries to the individual. She may file a civil action in state court alleging that the appliance was defective and that the defect caused her injury, and requesting money damages to compensate her for her injuries. If she shows by a preponderance of the evidence that the appliance failed to perform in a safe manner and the company is unable to refute the evidence against it, she may obtain a monetary award from the company.

The state and local criminal justice system punishes those who violate state penal statutes, attempts to rehabilitate criminals, and strives to deter criminals and to educate the public. Representatives of the local or state government prosecute claims against those who are accused of violating state or local laws. These attorneys are usually known as district attorneys, county attorneys, or state attorneys general. Most crimes require proof that a physical act occurred, the person committing it had a certain mental state, and there was a concurrence of the act and the mental state. A person charged with a crime is presumed innocent until proven guilty. To obtain a conviction in a state or local court, the prosecutor must prove that the defendant committed the acts beyond a reasonable doubt. This standard does not require the state to prove the case against the defendant is 100 percent certain, only that there is no reasonable doubt as to his or her guilt.

In a murder case, for example, the prosecutor first presents the evidence of guilt. The defendant is then allowed, but not required, to refute that evidence. He may deny that he committed the crime, or contend that although he did commit the crime, he should not be held responsible for his acts because, for example, he acted in self-defense or was insane at the time of the offense. If the jury believes the prosecutor has proved the case beyond a reasonable doubt, it can convict the defendant of murder.

Citizens may ask state or local courts to issue a mandatory injunction. This is a civil action where the legal remedy of money damages is inadequate. This remedy is an equitable remedy, as the court compels the defendant to perform in a certain way or face contempt of court. In equitable proceedings, the parties do not have a right to a jury trial and such cases are decided solely by the judge. To obtain an equitable remedy ordering the defendant to perform or to refrain from certain acts, a plaintiff must show that he or she has no other adequate remedy at law and faces irreparable injury without the remedy being enforced. Injunctions may be temporary, preliminary, or permanent in nature.

For example, a person may sue the owner of a factory that is dumping toxins onto her property, and seek injunctive relief to compel the owner to refrain from further dumping. She will try to show that money damages are inadequate to compensate her, as it would be impossible to calculate the damages the toxins could cause to her property and to her health. She also may contend that if the dumping continues, her property and her health would suffer irreparable injury. If she succeeds, a judge may compel the factory owner to cease dumping his toxins on her property.

State and local courts handle a variety of civil, criminal, and equitable cases every day. These cases affect personal safety, air quality, and many other aspects of daily life.

Context

The state court judicial system is one of the three independent branches of all state governments. In many ways it mirrors the federal government, which also has three distinct branches of government. State courts interpret state constitutions, statutes, and other issues of concern to state citizens. State court decisions normally have a more direct impact on the lifestyle and quality of life of state citizens than do decisions issued by federal courts other than the U.S. Supreme Court.

Most of a state court's time is taken up with criminal cases. Not only are more crimes committed than civil wrongs, but other factors cause the state court system to prioritize criminal cases over civil cases. The Sixth Amendment to the U.S. Constitution requires that a criminal defendant receive a speedy trial, mandating that criminal cases take precedence over civil matters. As a result, it is not unusual for a civil case to languish for five years before it is tried.

Courts and judicial administrators have responded to this predicament by trying a variety of nonjudicial methods to handle civil cases. Some courts are limiting the amount of discovery or pretrial investigation that can occur. Other systems have instituted preprinted forms that all parties must use. Many court systems have encouraged or even mandated that certain civil matters be decided by arbitration or other alternate dispute mechanisms. Alternate methods of resolving civil disputes often are less costly than a court trial; more important, they are faster than waiting for the court to hear the matter. Despite attempts at modernization and use of alternate dispute mechanisms such as arbitration or mediation, the local and state court systems are overcrowded and respond very slowly to most issues.

Bibliography

American Bar Association Journal. Chicago: American Bar Association, 1915-. Monthly publication that addresses all aspects of the legal profession. Up-to-date information regarding modernization of local, state, and federal courts.

Black, Henry. *Black's Law Dictionary*. 6th ed. St. Paul, Minn.: West, 1990. Definitive reference work that defines terms and provides background information and cross-references. Cites cases, statutes, and other reference material.

Criminal Justice 94/95. 18th ed. Guilford, Conn.: Dushkin, 1994. Annual volume providing detailed information regarding various aspects of the court system and its participants.

National Law Journal. New York: New York Publishing, 1978-. Weekly legal newspaper that provides historical as well as current information on state and federal courts. In-depth articles give a detailed description of current issues affecting the legal profession and the court system.

Roberson, Cliff and Max Futrell. *An Introduction to Criminal Justice Research.* Springfield, Ill.: Charles C Thomas, 1988. Explains the structure and operation of the local and state courts within the context of the criminal justice system. Diagrams, pictures, and charts assist in understanding the functions of state and local courts.

Harvey Wallace
Shanda Wedlock

Cross-References

The Constitution of the United States, p. 425; Constitutional Law in the United States, p. 439; County Government, p. 458; Courts: U.S. Federal, p. 471; Elected Versus Appointed Offices in the United States, p. 572; Government Roles, p. 778; Judicial Review, p. 1012; Legal Systems in Anglo-American Governments, p. 1085; State and Local Government, p. 1885; The Supreme Court: Organization and Purpose, p. 1929; Urban Governments, p. 2052.

COURTS: U.S. FEDERAL

Field of study: Law and jurisprudence

As the major components of the judicial branch of the United States government, federal courts operate independently of state judicial systems and are responsible for hearing cases and administering justice respecting federal law. The courts are organized in three levels that include district courts, courts of appeals, and the Supreme Court.

Principal terms

ADJUDICATION: formal giving of a judgment or decree in a court case

CERTIORARI: writ issued by a higher court to a lower court directing that a case be moved to the higher court for review

FEDERAL QUESTION: determination of whether a case concerns an issue of federal law that would bring it under federal court jurisdiction

FEDERALISM: system of government in which powers are distributed between a national authority and constituent units, such as states

JURISDICTION: authority of a court to hear a judicial proceeding and adjudicate concerning its subject matter

PRECEDENT: decision of a court that is used as a model for future decisions in similar cases

Overview

Judicial tribunals established to administer justice, courts are created by governments through constitutions or legislation for the purpose of applying and enforcing the law. In the United States, a national system of courts has been established as the major means to administer justice at the federal level. Federal courts have the power to pronounce judgments, to punish, to rule on the constitutionality of legislative acts, and to interpret laws passed by Congress. In carrying out their work, courts strive to protect citizens from unwarranted interference of government in their lives. The courts were established to be impartial forums for the resolution of controversies between parties. The federal courts exist side-by-side with the courts of the fifty states of the Union. Thus, in the United States there are two distinct court systems, the state and the federal, which were created under different authorities.

The federal courts are based on Article 3, section 1, of the U.S. Constitution: "The judicial Power of the United States, shall be vested in one supreme Court and in such inferior Courts as the Congress may from time to time ordain and establish." In 1789, Congress set up the federal judicial system with trial courts in each state. In 1891, Congress established a set of intermediate courts with appellate jurisdiction. This three-part judicial structure—trial courts, appellate courts, and the Supreme Court—is basically the same today. The jurisdiction of U.S. courts in this three-part system is spelled out in Article 3, section 2, of the Constitution: "The Judicial Power shall extend to all Cases, in Law and Equity, arising under this Constitution, the Laws of the United States, and Treaties made, or which shall be made, under their Authority."

The first level of courts in the federal system consists of district courts. The country and its territories have been divided into ninety-four districts. There is at least one district in every state, and in large and heavily populated states there are several. Almost all district courts have more than one judge available to try cases. District court judges, like other federal court judges, are appointed by the president of the United States. They hold office for life, so long as they are not guilty of judicial misconduct, and their salaries cannot be reduced while they are in office. As the general trial-level courts in the federal system, district courts have jurisdiction over such matters as crimes against the United States, civil actions arising under federal law (if the amount in controversy exceeds a specified dollar amount), and cases involving citizens of different states or citizens and aliens (again, if the amount in question exceeds a certain dollar figure). They also review and enforce actions of certain federal administrative agencies, such as some rules of the Interstate Commerce Commission. The initial trials of almost all cases under federal jurisdiction take place in the district courts, and it is there that trial juries, when they are required, are impaneled. Typically, a single district court judge presides over a trial, but a panel of three judges is required in certain classes of cases involving matters of special importance, such as voting rights. Most cases begin and end in the district courts, but many decisions are appealed to the next level of courts.

The United States Courts of Appeals are the second level of courts in the federal system. Judgments made in district courts are reviewable by the courts of appeals in the judicial circuits in which the district courts are located. Congress has established thirteen federal judicial circuits, twelve of which are organized on a geographic basis. For example, the First Circuit includes Maine, Massachusetts, New Hampshire, Rhode Island, and Puerto Rico. The one circuit court that is not geographically organized, the Court of Appeals for the Federal Circuit, was established in 1982 to handle cases involving subjects such as public contracts, customs issues, and patent appeals. These circuit courts have jurisdiction to review decisions of their district courts and orders of major administrative agencies. The judges of the circuit courts have the same tenure and salary benefits as district court judges. The number of judges on each of the thirteen appellate courts varies depending on the amount of work in the circuit, but most circuits have between ten and fifteen. Each court usually hears cases in panels of three, but when there is sufficient disagreement on questions of law among the judges or when there is a case of special importance, all active judges of the court may sit together to decide the case. Since circuit courts are appellate courts, most cases are decided on the basis of documents submitted from the courts below, but some are selected for oral argument. In theory, decisions at the appellate level are made on the basis of the records, and no new evidence may be presented to the court.

The third level of courts in the federal system is the Supreme Court. The Court has nine judges or justices, but Congress can increase or decrease that number. One of the justices is designated as the Chief Justice of the United States; the others are associate justices. Like other federal judges, justices hold office for life, so long as they are not guilty of judicial misconduct, and their salaries cannot be reduced while they are in office. When vacancies occur, the president nominates new justices, subject to confirmation by the Senate. The Court sits in Washington, D.C., and its annual term stretches from October to June. The Supreme Court has jurisdiction over all federal appellate courts and also over decisions of the highest state courts when those courts have decided a question of federal law. In terms of the Constitution's list of disputes over which the Supreme Court has original jurisdiction, the Court's major work has been with controversies between two or more states, such as the conflict between Arizona and California over water rights. The Court's primary work, however, is appellate, and in that work it is the final arbiter of the meaning of the Constitution.

There are several ways that a case that has been decided by a lower court could reach the Supreme Court, but by far the most important is the Court's granting of a writ of certiorari. A disappointed litigant can petition the Court to consider an adverse ruling from a lower court. In its discretion, the Court can then decide whether to hear the case. If four justices agree that the case merits consideration, certiorari is granted. Briefs will then be filed by opposing attorneys, oral arguments will be presented to the Court, and the case will be decided and reported in written form. If the Court in its discretion chooses not to take up a case, the decision of the lower court stands as the final word on the issue. In a litigious society in which any number of cases and issues may be presented for consideration, the Supreme Court has extraordinary influence in shaping public life in the United States. In fact, it could be argued that every citizen in the United States has been affected by the operation of the federal courts.

In addition to the three levels of constitutional courts in the federal system, Congress has established a number of special legislative courts under its power to constitute tribunals inferior to the Supreme Court. Among these are the U.S. Court of International Trade, the U.S. Claims Court, the Court of Military Appeals, the Court of Veterans Appeals, the Tax Court, the Claims Court, and bankruptcy courts. These courts have specific jurisdictions in the areas implied by their names.

Applications

The power of the federal courts is largely dependent on a principle of law that was established in *Marbury v. Madison* (1803), when Chief Justice John Marshall proclaimed that the judiciary had the power to determine whether particular laws, rules, and regulations conform with the Constitution. This power of the judiciary has come to be known as judicial review, and it has become entrenched in the jurisprudence of the nation. This power gives the courts a major voice in the determination of public policies. This power is especially evident in the field of civil liberties. United States citizens sometimes take for granted the freedoms embodied in the Bill of Rights. That may be largely because of the operation and actions of the federal courts over the years. The freedoms given in the First Amendment to the Constitution, such as the freedoms of speech and religion, are among U.S. citizens' most cherished rights. Constitutional protections against illegal searches and self-incrimination are important to the privacy, safety, and security of all citizens. Challenges to government action that have been adjudicated in federal court have resulted in a number of other amendments to the Constitution. The amendments guaranteeing equal protection of the laws to citizens, prohibiting discrimination in voting rights, and prohibiting age discrimination are just a few examples of the impact of the federal judiciary on American life. The courts also have had dramatic influence in terms of the operation of public schools in the United States in issues of prayer, desegregation, and busing, to name just a few.

Federal courts also have the power to interpret statutes. In many ways, how the courts interpret a law passed by Congress determines who will benefit from the law, as in the case of affirmative action legislation, for example. The federal courts also review the rules and regulations of many federal agencies, such as the Internal Revenue Service. Finally, individual citizens may be affected personally if they are involved in any of the special legislative or constitutional courts in the federal system. Citizens may have dealings with the Tax Court, the U.S. Claims Court, or the bankruptcy courts, and service personnel may have dealings with the U.S. Court of Military Appeals or the U.S. Court of Veterans Appeals.

Context

The United States judicial system is generally considered to be the most complicated in the world. The major reason for this is the simultaneous existence of state and federal systems of courts. With two major legal systems, there is a multiplicity of laws and overlapping jurisdictions. Every citizen of the United States is at all times subject to laws of the federal government and the laws of a particular state.

In the early days of the nation, there was much conflict concerning the necessary power of a central government. The Articles of Confederation in 1781 established a loose union among states that vested little power in a central government. The confederation had the authority to ask states to act, but not to compel compliance. In the face of such difficulties with government under the Articles, a convention was assembled in 1787 and the framing of a new constitution was begun. The central government thereby established was, in contrast to the Articles, given real authority. One of the most important provisions of the new national government was the statement that the Constitution and laws of the United States would be the supreme law of the land and that the judges in every state would be bound thereby. Since 1789, the importance and authority of the national government has continually expanded. The Constitution which set up the Supreme Court went far in establishing the federal judicial system that exists in the late twentieth century.

The Supreme Court has been careful to acknowledge that a state's highest court is the authority on state law so long as no federal question is involved. It also has affirmed consistently that governmental powers beyond those given to the federal government are reserved for the states. The result of this system is a complicated and often overlapping dual system of courts in the United States. The dual system takes account of the need for a strong central government while respecting the values and strengths of states' rights, personal freedom, and self-determination that were so important in revolutionary war days. The name given to such a system of government is federalism.

With certain exceptions as specified by the Constitution, the federal courts can be changed by Congress in order to meet new demands. Congress has made changes in the courts many times in the past. The Federal Courts Improvement Act of 1982, for example, made major changes in the responsibilities of several federal courts. Changes in the organization of the courts are possible, and it is generally agreed that the workload of the courts, which has resulted in severe backlogs and thereby delayed justice, is one problem that needs Congressional attention. Many proposals from interested parties have been made, but the most likely source for substantial reform is a body known as the Judicial Conference of the United States. That body consists of the Chief Justice, the chief judge of the circuit courts, twelve district court judges, and two bankruptcy judges. This distinguished group will in time almost certainly influence the thinking of the legal community and eventually Congress as well.

Bibliography

Abraham, Henry J. *The Judicial Process*. 6th Ed. New York: Oxford University Press, 1993. Detailed coverage of the composition, jurisdiction, and operation of courts in the United States. Extensive list of references.

Barker, Lucius J., and Twiley W. Barker, Jr. *Civil Liberties and the Constitution*. 7th ed. Englewood Cliffs, N.J.: Prentice-Hall, 1994. Detailed summary of the history of judicial concern with Constitutional rights. Specified cases are used for illustration.

Bator, Paul M., and Daniel J. Meltzer, eds. *Hart and Wechsler's The Federal Courts and the Federal System*. 3d ed. Westbury, N.Y.: Foundation Press, 1988. Comprehensive discussion of the structure of the federal court system and its relationship to state courts.

Horowitz, Donald L. *The Courts and Social Policy*. Washington, D.C.: Brookings Institution, 1977. Discusses the role of the courts in determining social policy through the power of judicial review.

Institute of Judicial Administration. *A Guide to Court Systems*. 5th ed. New York: Institute of Judicial Administration, 1971. Complete description of the organization and personnel of the federal court system prior to its publication.

Mayers, Lewis. *The American Legal System*. Littleton, Colo.: Rothman, 1981. Comprehensive discussion of the issue of federalism and its impact on judicial operations. Examines regular state and federal courts, and administrative and military tribunals.

Meador, Daniel J. *American Courts*. St. Paul, Minn.: West, 1991. Accessible guide to the court system and its relationship to the other branches of government. Diagrams show the relationship of courts to one another.

Pound, Roscoe. *Organization of Courts*. Westport, Conn.: Greenwood Press, 1979. Written in 1940 by a former judge, this is a clear but lengthy description of the principles underlying the organization and procedures of federal courts. Proposals for court reform are of historical interest.

R. G. Gaddis

Cross-References

Civil Rights Protection, p. 304; The Constitution of the United States, p. 425; Constitutional Law in the United States, p. 439; Courts: State and Local, p. 465; Elected Versus Appointed Offices in the United States, p. 572; Judicial Review, p. 1012; Jurisprudence, p. 1019; Legal Systems in Anglo-American Governments, p. 1085; The Supreme Court: Organization and Purpose, p. 1929; The Supreme Court: Role in Government and Law, p. 1935.

CULT OF PERSONALITY

Field of study: Political philosophy

A cult of personality develops when a political leader attracts followers because of his or her charisma, rather than because of the leader's views or opinions. Such leaders often have a dangerously strong hold on their subjects, since the public follows them for emotional rather than logical reasons.

Principal terms

CHARACTER: consistent features or traits that form the essential nature of a person

EGO IDEAL: conscious notion of excellence, typically based on a composite image of others, such as parents, with whom one identifies

IDEO-AFFECTIVE POSTURE: a person's characteristic way of experiencing emotion, which is thought to attract one to either the political Left or Right

LEGITIMACY: perception that a person has the right to hold and exercise influence over others

POLITICAL PSYCHOLOGY: area of political science that studies how psychological factors influence human behavior in government

PRIMAL HORDE: small group of people under the domination of the strongest male member; hypothesized by some theorists to be the first form of human society

PSYCHOANALYSIS: theory of human development and personality originally proposed by Sigmund Freud; also a method for examining the possible unconscious origins of troublesome behaviors

Overview

Political theorists have long known that rulers can have power over their subjects for a variety of reasons. In an effort to understand the major types of political leaders, the German sociologist and political economist Max Weber developed a typology of leadership. Weber described three different types of political leaders, who each gain their legitimacy in a vastly different way. According to Weber, traditional rulers, such as monarchs, gain their power because of long-standing custom and the belief that their ancestors have ruled since time immemorial. Rational-legal rulers, on the other hand, obtain their power through the force of laws, statutes, and regulations. In contrast to both the traditional rulers and rational-legal rulers are charismatic rulers. According to Weber, charismatic leaders derive their right to rule from their extraordinary personal qualities and the belief of the ruled in their unique inspiration.

Political psychologists, who study the interplay between the human psyche and the political world, have a special fascination with charismatic leaders. These leaders are often said to attract a cult of personality, in which subjects follow them because of their character, rather than because of their views or opinions. Many theorists have attempted to explain how charismatic leaders often come to exert such a frighteningly powerful hold over their populace.

Sigmund Freud, a Viennese physician and the founder of psychoanalysis, was the first widely regarded theorist to address this question. Although Freud's ideas were based more on speculation that scientific evidence, his theory has had great influence among political thinkers. In *Totem and Taboo* (1913), and *Group Psychology and the Analysis of the Ego* (1921), Freud set forth his major ideas about the advent of political authority. Freud speculated that individuals at the dawn of human society lived in small groups, which he referred to as primal hordes, each of which was under the domination of its strongest male member. This strong male was thought by Freud to be the father of the whole horde; one who used his authority against his sons in a sadistic fashion. The sons were forced by the strong male into sexual abstinence; and had to steal their wives from other tribes. Sons who resisted the authority of the father were killed, castrated, or driven out of the tribe.

Eventually, according to Freud's theory, the sons who were driven out of the tribe organized and overcame the father. After killing the father, the sons ate his body in an attempt to gain identity and strength by incorporating a part of him. When these sons attempted to take over the tribe, they began to quarrel with one another. With the recently acquired knowledge that fraternal aggression was dangerous, these sons formed the first social contract that was based upon mutual cooperation and the renunciation of primitive instincts. The sons agreed not to attack one another and formed a taboo against incest. In this way, the first form of society developed out of the family.

Freud went on to speculate that the experiences of the primal horde left a residue in all humans, which is still experienced. Freud believed that the sons of the primal horde were bound together by the shared memory of their father, and that the same type of emotional tie binds contemporary men and women to a leader. Freud believed that people were especially likely to feel this type of bond in an artificial, but highly organized, social group. As examples, Freud cited the Roman Catholic church and the army, which are both hierarchical in their governance. He suggested that in an army, "the commander in chief is a father who loves all soldiers equally, and for that reason they are comrades among themselves. . . . Every captain is, as it were, the commander in chief and the father of his company."

While Freud acknowledged that factors such as patriotism or the quest for glory also bound soldiers to their commanding officers, he maintained that an unconscious love for the leader was a central force. He thought that military or political leaders often served as ego ideals for the populace, that is, romanticized figures whom the public could admire and strive to be like. By identifying with their leaders, common individuals gained psychic strength and identity. For Freud, the cult of personality represented an unconscious attempt to reconnect with the mythic father of the primal horde and bolster the group's identity through the glorification of a parental figure.

A related, but somewhat different, notion of the cult of personality was developed by Harold Lasswell, a noted political theorist. A serious student of psychoanalysis and

Freudian ideas, Lasswell developed his own notion about the role of character in government. In *Psychopathology and Politics* (1930), Lasswell speculated that three types of individuals seek political influence or power: the agitator, who questions authority and stirs up the existing system; the administrator, who advocates slow-paced, careful, cautious rule; and the theorist, who tries to influence society through the promotion of new concepts or ideas. While these individuals all seek political power, others follow them because of their own emotional needs or difficulties. For example, someone who is suspicious and distrusts authority will be attracted to an agitator, while a fearful and timid individual will support the more conservative stance of an administrator.

No matter which position a person supports, Lasswell suggested that the supporter's motives are likely to stem from emotional deficits. For this reason, Lasswell believed that the more highly disturbed a person is psychologically, the more drastic and extreme their political actions are likely to be. The emptier a person's life, the more he or she must look to a charismatic leader for the fulfillment of their emotional life. Lasswell's theory has been widely criticized, since it implies that mental disturbance motivates nearly all political action, and that the gratification of group pathology is the only source of a ruler's legitimacy. Lasswell's detractors have suggested that surely some political behavior must be motivated by positive factors as well.

Some scholars have turned to U.S. psychologist Sylvan Tomkins for a more neutral view of emotional motives in government. Tomkins speculates that every child is raised to develop a particular type of ideo-affective posture, which is a characteristic or preferred way of experiencing emotion. People's ideo-affective postures attract them to certain types of politicians. Tomkins speculates that people who are more comfortable with positive feelings such as excitement, joy, or surprise, or with the negative emotions of distress and shame, will be attracted to left-wing leaders. Individuals who feel greater comfort with the negative emotions of disgust, anger, and contempt, on the other hand, will be drawn to right-wing politicians. Although Tomkins' work is still controversial, he has conducted several psychological surveys, the results of which appear to support his theory.

Applications

Although the various theorists who have written about the cult of personality may disagree on the mechanisms that draw people to charismatic leaders, these theorists do share a common purpose. These authors all seek to further our understanding of political life, particularly of the factors that bring certain individuals to power. The influence of charismatic leaders on the political process can be seen on both a small, local scale, and the larger national level.

On a small scale, the story of the U.S. clergyman John Humphrey Noyes and the community of Oneida serves as an excellent example of charismatic leadership at work. Noyes was a student of theology at the Yale University Divinity School in the 1830's, when he became attracted to Perfectionism, a radical Christian ideology of his day. Adherents of Perfectionism denied any notion of human depravity, and asserted that people could become perfect both in their relationships with God and with each other. Noyes took this ideology a step further, and declared that he had already attained a state of utter union with God and earthly perfection. His startling proclamation of his own perfection was more than the faculty of the Yale Divinity School could withstand, and he was expelled.

Undaunted, Noyes soon attracted his own small group of religious followers. With them, he founded a utopian commune in rural Vermont based on the principles of Perfectionism. Noyes and his followers eventually became known as the Oneida Community, and for more than thirty years they ran one of the most successful communes in U.S. history. The members of the Oneida Community shared their assets and possessions, and also shared their love in an unusual practice known as complex marriage. Under the principles of complex marriage, every adult was thought to be married to every other adult of the opposite sex. All adult members of Oneida had their own rooms, and any member could request an interview—the euphemism for sexual relations—with any other adult of the opposite sex. Women were thus treated as the sexual equals of men, which was a remarkable idea at the time. Women also worked alongside men in the various trades and occupations of the community.

Eventually, angry neighbors and hostile clergymen in Vermont accused the Oneida Community of sexual immorality, and forced the group to move to upstate New York. Under Noyes's highly charismatic leadership, the group continued to flourish. The Oneida Community founded a successful manufacturing industry, known particularly for its silverware, and by 1875 had attracted almost three hundred members. What is particularly striking is that Noyes managed to control almost every aspect of life at the community, from the investment of the group's assets to the practice of complex marriage. While decisions were officially made through group consensus, Noyes led the community through the power of his emotional influence over others.

Like many charismatic leaders, Noyes apparently provided the glue that held his community together. In 1879, a critical dispute arose over initiation of young women into the practice of complex marriage. While Noyes had previously selected the first partner for each young woman himself, central members began to balk at his authority to make such intimate decisions. At the same time, a group of local clergymen launched a widely publicized attack on the presumed immorality of complex marriage. Faced with dissension from both within and without, as well as the possibility of various lawsuits against him, Noyes fled to Canada. Without Noyes's leadership, the community soon disintegrated. After thirty years as a successful commune and living experiment, the community was reorganized into an ordinary industrial corporation within less than a year.

Although Noyes's leadership reveals the power that one charismatic person can have over a small community, the sinister life story of Nazi leader Adolf Hitler demonstrates the profound influence that one individual can have over an entire nation. Hitler's rise to power also demonstrates how a leader can fulfill the emotional needs of his subjects. Many historians have documented how Hitler came to power during the 1930's, at a time when the German people were suffering from a desperate economic situation as well as the humiliating repercussions of their defeat in World War I. The worldwide Depression of 1929 had left millions of once-prosperous Germans unemployed and impoverished. Germans also greatly resented the Treaty of Versailles, which required them to pay billions of dollars in reparations to other countries for their role in World War I.

Into this era of misery and mass humiliation came Adolf Hitler. Hitler countered the Germans' sense that they had become a second-rate nation by claiming that Germans were actually superior to all other ethnic or racial groups. Hitler's charismatic personality attracted many followers, as he promised to create a German empire that would rule much of the world. Hitler was a gifted orator who was able to win the allegiance of followers by delivering hypnotically powerful speeches at large public rallies. Adolf Hitler represented the cult of personality in its strongest form, since many Germans were attracted to his tremendously charismatic style of leadership, without considering the gruesome specifics of his plans for warfare and genocide.

Context

Viewing Hitler, or any other charismatic leader, as a product of the cult of personality is a relatively recent development in the study of political life. In the history of ideas, the complementary fields of psychology and psychoanalysis are comparatively new arrivals, having both had their birth and development within approximately the last one hundred years. The advent and increasing popularity of modern psychology has slowly led political psychology to become a central aspect of political science. Psychological portraits of leaders have garnered great interest with scholars as well as with the general public.

Such descriptions of a leader's emotional makeup are often referred to as psychobiographies. Two widely read and influential psychobiographies have been *Thomas Woodrow Wilson: A Psychological Study* (1967), by Sigmund Freud and his associate William Bullit, and *Gandhi's Truth* (1969), by psychoanalyst Erik Erikson. While psychobiographies such as these have taken an influential place in the fields of history and political science, controversy about their intellectual function continues. Many prominent psychobiographers, such as Freud and Bullit, and the husband-and-wife team of Alexander and Juliet George, have argued that psychobiographies should not be published when an individual is still living. These authors have argued that a psychobiography is likely to constitute a gross invasion of the individual's privacy, and that living figures are likely to conceal much of the intimate material to which psychobiographers need access. Other scholars have suggested that psychobiographies are too speculative to have a place in a field such as political science, which is focused on observable events.

Despite these objections, psychobiographies, along with other attempts to examine the role of personality in political endeavors, continue to hold significant influence over the fields of history and political philosophy. Only by examining the inner motives of a leader and his or her followers, can the political process be understood in a comprehensive fashion.

Bibliography

Barner-Barry, Carol, and Robert Rosenwein. *Psychological Perspectives on Politics.* Englewood Cliffs, N.J.: Prentice-Hall, 1985. Strongly recommended for the college student or adult reader who wants to know how personality factors fit into the larger field of political psychology. Covers a wide range of topics such as individual personality and group psychology. Includes a useful glossary of the most basic terms in political psychology.

Elms, Alan C. *Personality in Politics.* New York: Harcourt Brace Jovanovich, 1976. This highly readable text contains an excellent overview of how personality factors affect the average U.S. voter, as well as political leaders. Includes an interesting discussion of the controversial art of psychobiography.

Elster, Jon. *Political Psychology.* Cambridge, England: Cambridge University Press, 1993. Clearly written discussion of contemporary issues in political psychology, with a concise account of personality factors in the political process. Well-researched, with an exhaustive list of references and a useful subject index.

Held, Joseph, ed. *The Cult of Power: Dictators in the Twentieth Century.* New York: Columbia University Press, 1983. Fascinating account of despots in contemporary political life, and their eerie sway over the citizens of their respective countries.

Lowenthal, Leo. *False Prophets: Studies on Authoritarianism.* New Brunswick, N.J.: Transaction Books, 1987. Recommended for anyone with a desire to understand more about the hold that dictators often have over their public. Clear and understandable; cites a number of useful examples.

Stone, William F. *The Psychology of Politics.* New York: Free Press, 1974. This extensively researched text is a classic resource in the field of political psychology. Contains a clearly written discussion of the role that personality plays in political life, with lively examples from both U.S. and world history.

Volkan, Vamik D. *The Need to Have Enemies and Allies: From Clinical Practice to International Relationships.* Northvale, N.J.: Jason Aronson, 1988. Applies the knowledge base of psychiatry and clinical psychology to the field of international relations. While the theoretical material in this book can be difficult, it remains a central resource for the college student or adult with a serious interest in diplomacy.

Steven C. Abell

Cross-References

Bonapartism, p. 140; Charismatic Leadership, p. 209; Chinese Communism, p. 223; Demagoguery, p. 507; Dictatorships, p. 546; General Will, p. 745; Heads of State, p. 804; Leadership, p. 1066; Nietzsche's Political Philosophy, p. 1300; Political Machines and Bosses, p. 1468; The Presidency in the United States, p. 1590; Presidential Elections in the United States, p. 1596; Propaganda, p. 1615; Statesmanship, p. 1898; Tribal Government, p. 2027; Utopianism, p. 2084.

DANTE'S POLITICAL PHILOSOPHY

Field of study: Political philosophy

In On Monarchy, *Italian poet and philosopher Dante Alighieri (1265-1321) defended the idea of a universal empire. His defense provided a ground for the Holy Roman Empire to extend its rule into Italy. Dante maintained that the source of the emperor's authority was God, not the papacy.*

Principal terms
AUTHORITY: right to rule
HOLY ROMAN EMPIRE: empire made up of German and Italian territories; regarded as successor to the Roman Empire, it began in 800 and ended in 1806
INVESTITURE: act of confirming in office
PAPACY: office of the pope; system of government within the Roman Catholic church
SUZERAIN: overlord to whom one is bound by oath or duty

Overview

At the beginning of the fourteenth century, much of northern and central Italy was part of the Holy Roman Empire, but for fifty years emperors had neglected this area. The northern and central Italian city-republics were left to devise their own policies, which provoked rival territorial claims and frequent violent discord. The papacy was a major political force, claiming to be the source of temporal authority for the Holy Roman Empire and the temporal authority or the suzerain in large areas of Italy. But the papacy had not been able to bring peace to Italy. There was a bitter rivalry between two Italian political parties: the Ghibellines and the Guelphs. The Ghibellines looked to the emperor to help restore order to Italy and opposed increased political power for the pope. In contrast, the Guelphs wanted the emperor to stay out of Italy and looked to the pope to support their claims.

In the thirteenth century, Dante's own city, Florence, was racked by this rivalry. First one party, then the other, held political sway, sending the opposing party into exile. When the Guelphs finally vanquished the Ghibellines, something like a family feud split the Guelphs into two factions: the Blacks and the Whites. In 1301, the Blacks appealed to the pope to ask Charles of Valois, brother of King Phillip IV of France, to help pacify and reorganize Florence. With Charles's help the Blacks used force to take control of Florence and immediately exiled the leading Whites, including Dante. Dante's exile would be permanent.

Dante's exile distanced him from the pope and put him closer to the emperor. When Emperor Henry VII entered Italy in 1310, Dante addressed letters on his behalf to the kings, senators, nobles, and people of Italy. Dante wrote *On Monarchy*, at least in part, to support Henry's efforts to pacify and unify Italy. *On Monarchy* is divided into three books. The first book maintains that a temporal world ruler is necessary for the well-being of humankind. The second book claims that the Roman Empire was acquired by right and hence that the Holy Roman Empire is based on right. In the third book, Dante claims that temporal political authority comes directly from God, and not through the papacy.

Dante claims that a temporal world governor is necessary for the well-being of humankind because humankind's proper work is to exercise its capacity for intellectual development. This exercise can be done best when there is peace. To bring about peace, there must be a temporal world ruler.

According to Dante, the world is most peaceful when justice is its greatest power, and justice is its greatest power only when a world governor rules. Such a one is not greedy, since he has nothing more to desire. And without greed, he will be guided by justice. Governing all, he can bring about justice more easily. Thus universal peace requires a world ruler.

Book two addresses the question of who the world ruler should be. To establish the legitimacy of the Holy Roman emperor as the world ruler, Dante argues that since the Roman Empire existed by right, then so does its successor, the Holy Roman Empire.

Dante claims that whatever happens according to God's will happens rightfully, and that it was God's will for the Romans to acquire an empire. The ancient Roman historian Livy provides testimony of miracles that God performed to help the Romans, for example, a hailstorm that prevented Hannibal, the Carthaginian general, from following up a victory and destroying Rome. Dante also claims that God's will is revealed in the outcomes of competitions and duels, and therefore, since the Romans achieved world conquest, it was God's will. Finally, Dante claims that those who voluntarily subject themselves to a rule show by their behavior that they regard the rule as just. He concludes that since Christ chose to be born under Roman rule, he regarded it as just.

The third book criticizes the traditional reasons for believing that temporal authority comes from the papacy, and then supports the thesis that such authority comes directly from God. Traditionally, defenders of the papal claim to be the source of temporal authority have said that the pope has this power because Christ gave it to his first vicar, Peter, when he said that whatever Peter bound would be bound also in Heaven and whatever Peter loosed would be loosed also in Heaven. Dante answers in the third book that the scriptural context of Christ's comment made it clear that he meant only that whatever Peter bound or loosed in connection with his office as gatekeeper of Heaven would also be bound or loosed in Heaven. Dante claims that even though Christ held both spiritual and temporal authority, it does not follow that his vicar held both sorts of authority.

Another important ground for papal claims was "the donation of Constantine." Emperor Constantine was supposed to have given imperial authority to the Roman church when he moved his capital to Constantinople. Not knowing that the documentary evidence for this donation was forged, Dante maintains that it was beyond Constantine's authority to renounce imperial authority, being contrary to his office and to human right. Not only was Constantine not a proper donor, but also the Church was not a proper recipient, since Christ's disciple Matthew had prohibited the Church from owning gold and silver. Dante adds that simply because Pope Leo III had crowned Charlemagne emperor that did not mean that the Church was the source of imperial authority.

Dante maintains that one way to show that imperial authority comes directly from God is by showing that it did not have an ecclesiastical source. According to Dante, imperial authority does not come from the Church, since the empire had authority before the Church existed. Therefore, temporal authority came directly from God. Thus the German princes who elected the Holy Roman emperor were only the voice of God.

Further, Dante argues that the power of authorizing governments was contrary to the nature of the Church. When Christ said that his kingdom was not of this world, he renounced participation in temporal government, and he told Peter to follow his example. Thus since participation in temporal government was contrary to the nature of the Church, the Church could not be the source of temporal authority. In Dante's view, a person, as a composite being, has two different goals, eternal bliss for the incorruptible soul, and bliss in this world for the corruptible body. Greed could prevent people from achieving these goals. To prevent this, people need to be guided by the pope to eternal happiness and by the emperor to temporal happiness. Having two guides, each with a separate realm and a separate function, should help humankind achieve heavenly happiness and earthly happiness.

Dante's work was influenced by the *Politics*, a work by the ancient Greek philosopher Aristotle that became available in the West in 1260. Aristotle's idea that humankind, by nature, has a function or proper work gives a basis to Dante's argument for a world ruler. According to Dante, the world ruler is needed not only to keep the peace but also to help humankind realize itself. Aristotle's syllogistic logic also influenced Dante. This logic provided models for reasoning. Throughout *On Monarchy*, Dante formulates one deductively valid syllogism after another to defend his positions.

Nevertheless, Dante's critics raised many questions about his arguments. Would there not be a risk that the world ruler would become a tyrant? How credible were Dante's ancient sources? Might not the stronger party win a duel and still be in the wrong? Might not Christ have subjected himself to Roman rule that was unjust rather than just in the service of a higher purpose, the redemption of humankind? Did not the Church have a special authority in biblical interpretation? Since temporal authority could come from the people, why accept the assumption that it either came from God or from the pope?

Applications

The life of Emperor Henry VII of Luxembourg reflected major doctrines in Dante's *On Monarchy*. Henry was renowned for his virtue, and Dante saw in him a leader destined to bring peace and justice through the institution of empire. When Henry entered Italy, he said that he had come for the sake of all, not for Guelphs or for

Ghibellines. Like Dante, Henry thought that peace depended on empire, and that there was a divine sanction for his world rule.

Henry came to Italy with the blessing of Pope Clement V, who had taken up residence in France at Avignon. A papal commission traveling with Henry was to crown him in St. Peter's Cathedral. Troops from Naples and other papal allies, however, blocked the streets to St. Peter's. Under pressure from the Roman people, the papal commission crowned Henry anyway. Afterwards with no notice, the commission put forward a variety of conditions, such as that Henry must leave Rome that day and not return without the permission of the pope. Henry responded in Dantean fashion: His election was direct from God, and the pope did not have the authority to determine when Henry would leave Rome.

Henry's plan for empire, however, was beset with difficulties that he would not be able to overcome. Papal opposition helped frustrate Henry's imperial ambitions. Pressured by politically powerful French nobles, the pope did not officially oppose Neapolitan resistance to Henry. The pope may have feared losing his suzerainty in Naples if Henry established his rule there, and so Clement threatened Henry with excommunication if he attacked Naples. Clement may have expected that the power, prestige, and autonomy of the papacy would be reduced if Henry united and ruled Italy.

Another obstacle that Henry faced was the dynastic ambitions of the kingdom of Naples. Its king, Robert of Anjou, already held papal territories in central Italy and was influential in Lombardy. He questioned the legitimacy of the empire, maintaining that since it was acquired by force, it was contrary to nature, and so not gained by right. He added that even if the empire had rightfully held its conquered lands, in many of them it had lost its rights because it had not used them for such a long period of time. He used his troops to support his arguments.

A budding nationalist spirit also helped thwart Henry's unification plan. Many Italians disliked the idea of having a foreign ruler. Some questioned whether there was a need for a universal monarch. Echoing John of Paris, the French nationalist writer, they claimed that a national monarchy would be better than a universal one, because of major cultural and ethnic differences across nations.

Partisan politics also played a role in defeating Henry. Henry's desire to be impartial led him to rule that exiles, whether Guelphs or Ghibellines, be allowed to return to their home cities. This rule was unpopular with the exilers, especially with those who had confiscated the exiles' property. And in some cases, exiles returning home created social discord. Old vendettas were rekindled, and the cycle of violence began anew. Many potential allies rejected Henry's rule rather than accept the return of exiles.

Context

Empires have often based their claim to legitimacy on a religious source. Thus the Assyrian empire in the ninth century B.C.E. claimed legitimacy on the ground that its ruler was a god. In the *Aeneid*, the Roman poet Vergil portrayed the Roman empire as destined by the gods. In the fourth century C.E., the Roman emperor Constantine developed an alliance between the Roman Empire and Christianity. One of the first questions for church-state relations was: "Would the Roman emperors be masters of the church?" With the capital of the empire moved to Constantinople, it began to seem that the emperors there were controlling the Eastern half of the Church. Perhaps because of this, in the late fifth century, Pope Gelasius I, the Western pontiff, put forward a doctrine of two swords or two authorities. According to it, two powers rule the world: a spiritual power responsible for one's spiritual well-being and a temporal power responsible for one's temporal well-being. Each power has its own jurisdiction and should respect the jurisdiction of the other power, but there should be a spirit of mutual help between the two powers. The Gelasian doctrine was very influential into the Middle Ages, but its vagueness eventually led to disagreements over boundaries of jurisdiction.

One of the first major disagreements arose in the eleventh century over the practice of lay investiture. Each power regarded the other as infringing its rights. Pope Gregory VII maintained that establishing bishops in office was a religious vocation, and Emperor Henry IV maintained that he had to fulfill this function or lose control over his realm. A compromise was worked out after a long struggle, in which Gregory VII not only excommunicated Henry IV but also decreed that Henry no longer had imperial authority. This was the first time that a pope claimed the right to depose an emperor, but it would not be the last.

Between 1150 and 1250, another major conflict between empire and papacy arose. The point in dispute was whether the emperor had authority to rule Rome and Italy. Two emperors, Frederick Barbarossa and later his grandson Frederick II, King of Sicily, tried to create empires encompassing Rome and Italy. In this jurisdictional dispute, the emperors asked, in effect: "If the emperor of the Romans does not have a right to rule in Rome, where does he have a right to rule?" The papacy responded that the pope was suzerain of the emperor. Allied with the Lombard cities, a series of popes, including Alexander III, Innocent III, Gregory IX, and Innocent IV, successfully opposed the imperial ambitions of the two Fredericks.

The next major dispute between Church and state developed between Pope Boniface VIII and King Phillip IV of France at the end of the thirteenth century. They disagreed over whether the state had a right to tax the clergy. Boniface claimed Church exemption from taxation in virtue of the Church's superior authority. Phillip viewed this as an infringement of French national sovereignty. Eventually, French agents briefly captured the pope and mistreated him. He died within a week of his release. French influence in the papacy increased. The next pope, Clement V, was French, and he moved the papacy to Avignon, where the French king frequently subjected him to political pressure.

At this time—the first decades of the fourteenth century—Emperor Henry VII and Dante entered the historical drama. *On Monarchy* is an attempt to revitalize the idea of universal empire, although the clear trend in Europe from the ninth century on was toward the development of separate national states. Dante's work provided a new basis for world rule: not just that it was needed for order but that it was needed to help humankind realize itself. Dante's work was influential with defenders of the Holy Roman Empire, including Henry VII's successor, Louis of Bavaria.

In 1329, the pope ordered that Dante's book be burned as heretical, perhaps because Dante seemed to make earthly happiness worth having for its own sake or perhaps because he had denied that the papacy was the source of temporal authority. Dante's work provided the basis, at the imperial Diet of Rense in 1338, for German elector princes to deny that the pope was the source of the emperor's authority. *On Monarchy* was placed on the Vatican's index of prohibited reading from 1554 to 1897.

The centuries-long medieval conflict between church and state helped institutionalize in the West the idea of the church and the state as separate powers. The two powers' competing for supporters helped develop the Western ideal of freedom to choose between alternatives. Participants in these church-state controversies often appealed to canonical law, Roman law, general councils of the church, and higher laws. Such appeals helped promote government according to laws and principles.

Bibliography

Armstrong, Edward. "Dante's Political Ideal." In *Italian Studies*, edited by Cecilia M. Ady. Freeport, N.Y.: Books for Libraries Press, 1967. Portrays the historical context of *On Monarchy*, providing insights into the political forces at work in Dante's Italy.

Dante Alighieri. *On World-Government (De Monarchia)*. 2d ed. Translated by Herbert Schneider. Indianapolis: Bobbs-Merrill, Argues in favor of world empire and against the papacy as the source of temporal authority.

D'Entrèves, A. P. *Dante As a Political Thinker*. Oxford, England: Clarendon Press, 1952. Judges the historical significance of Dante's political ideas concerning the city, the empire, and the Church. Also contrasts the church-state views expressed in *On Monarchy* with those expressed in the *Divine Comedy*.

Grandgent, C. H. *Dante*. New York: Duffield, 1916. Shows how Dante's political views are reflected in *The Divine Comedy*, *The Banquet*, and his political letters.

Tierney, Brian. *The Crisis of Church and State, 1050-1300*. Englewood Cliffs, N.J.: Prentice-Hall, 1964. Overview of major conflicts between church and state, interspersed with important documents, such as the donation of Constantine and Pope Boniface VIII's proclamation of supreme church authority.

Gregory P. Rich

Cross-References

Aristotle's Political Philosophy, p. 83; Church and Government in History, p. 230; Empires and Empire Building, p. 597; John of Salisbury's Political Philosophy, p. 1006; Liberal Nationalism, p. 1111; Nationalism, p. 1268; Political Philosophy, p. 1505; Theocracy, p. 1968.

DEBTS AND DEFICITS IN THE U.S. FEDERAL BUDGET

Field of study: Economic issues

The federal government's budget deficit is the shortfall of current revenues against current expenditures. The national debt is the total amount that the federal government has borrowed, and not yet repaid, to cover past deficits.

Principal terms

CYCLICAL DEFICIT: revenue deficits that occur as employment or economic activity varies from full employment levels

CYCLICALLY BALANCED BUDGET: idea that deficits associated with recession would be offset by surpluses during phases of business expansion

DEBT CEILING: maximum amount of money that the U.S. government can borrow, as established by Congress

DEFICIT: amount by which government expenditures exceed revenues within a fiscal year

FUNCTIONAL FINANCE: concept that maintaining full employment should be a greater government concern than balancing the budget

NATIONAL DEBT: amount that the federal government has borrowed, and not yet repaid, to cover past deficits

STRUCTURAL DEFICIT: budget deficit that would occur if the same policies were pursued when the economy is experiencing full employment as when it is not

Overview

The federal budget deficit is the amount by which federal government expenditures exceed its revenues in a given fiscal year. For accounting purposes, the U.S. government's fiscal year runs from October 1 through September 30. The national debt is the cumulative total of all past budget deficits minus all past surpluses. It is customary to examine the national debt relative to the size of the national economy, expressing it as a percentage of gross domestic product.

When the federal government's expenditures exceed its revenues for a given year, several financing options are available. The federal government can increase revenues by raising taxes. Alternatively, it can sell assets it owns, such as land. A third option is to print more money, thereby increasing the money supply. Finally, the federal government can borrow money from U.S. citizens or firms, foreign citizens or governments, or commercial banks. In order to borrow money, the federal government sells bonds, such as savings bonds and treasury notes. This last option results in the national debt.

Although the national debt results from selling bonds in order to finance budget deficits, identifying the sources of the budget deficit leads to a better understanding of the national debt's causes. Budget deficits are structural or cyclical. A structural deficit is one that occurs when the economy experiences full employment; that is, it occurs regardless of cyclical variations, such as a recession, in the economy. Cyclical deficits are the additional deficits that occur as employment or economic activity varies from the levels used to define the structural deficit.

Cyclical deficits are the natural result of changes in economic activity. As the economy enters into a recession, tax revenues fall while government spending increases. As people lose their jobs, the government receives less revenue from income taxes, while spending for social programs such as food stamps and unemployment compensation increases.

Structural deficits can be used to influence the levels of economic activity. In *The General Theory of Employment, Interest, and Money* (1936), John Maynard Keynes argued that deficit spending was necessary to reduce unemployment during a recession or depression. Prior to the Great Depression of the 1930's, politicians and economists had promoted an annually balanced budget. During the presidential campaign of 1932, Franklin D. Roosevelt severely criticized President Herbert Hoover for running budget deficits. After the Great Depression and World War II, many individuals believed that government should play a more active role in the economy. Since the 1960's, the use of Keynesian policy to stabilize the economy at full employment has been supported by both Republicans and Democrats in the United States.

The widespread acceptance of Keynes's ideas after World War II generated numerous questions concerning the need to balance the federal budget. Many economists supported the idea of a cyclically balanced budget. In a cyclically balanced budget, deficits during a recession phase of the business cycle would be offset by surpluses during the expansion phase of the business cycle.

Another group of economists supported the concept of functional finance. They contend that balancing the federal budget is not important; rather, maintaining full employment should be the government's primary concern. Under functional finance, the method of financing federal government expenditures is determined by the level of unemployment. When unemployment is low, federal spending increases would be financed through taxes. With moderate unemployment, increased government spending would be financed by borrowing money through the sale of bonds. During high unemployment, additional spending would be financed by printing and issuing more money.

Finally, a relatively small number of economists and politicians supported the concept of an annually balanced budget. These individuals fear that Keynesian policy results in a deficit bias and increases the relative size of the government sector. Proponents of an annually balanced budget argue that government intervention inhibits market forces, thus retarding economic growth. Therefore, they favor a more laissez-faire economic approach.

Rapid growth in the national debt after 1980 led to increased concern regarding budget deficits, resulting in the passage of the Gramm-Rudman-Hollings Deficit Reduction Act in 1985. This act set annual budget targets that were intended to reduce the budget deficit to zero by 1991. If the annual targets were not met, automatic across-the-board cuts were supposed to occur in most federal spending programs. The Gramm-Rudman-Hollings targets, however, were not met. Inability to cut expenses in popular programs, recessions such as occurred in the early 1990's, and unforeseen crises, such as the Persian Gulf War and the savings and loan bailout, made deficit reduction to the targets virtually impossible.

The failure of Gramm-Rudman-Hollings led to the 1990 Deficit Reduction Act. This act shifted the focus of government policy away from deficit reduction to spending control. Numerous areas of federal spending, including farm subsidies, student loans, Medicare, and military spending, were targeted for spending cuts. As a result of the Deficit Reduction Act, federal spending was grouped under three general areas, military, domestic, and international. When federal spending exceeded the target within an area, automatic across-the-board spending cuts were to occur within that area. Certain emergencies, such as the Persian Gulf War and the savings-and-loan bailout, were not subject to these restrictions. Such exceptions have reduced the likelihood of this legislation's producing substantive deficit reduction.

As a result of the deficit's persistence and the inability of Congress and the president substantially to reduce the deficit, some people have called for a balanced-budget amendment to the Constitution. Such an amendment would require Congress and the president annually to balance the budget. The most common proposals allow exemptions to the annually balanced budget only during times of war, or if three-fifths of both houses of Congress approve an unbalanced budget.

Applications

There is little disagreement among economists concerning the benefits of deficit spending. Foremost among these benefits is such spending's ability to stimulate the economy and reduce unemployment during a recession. The national debt's rapid growth after 1980, however, forced considerable attention on the budget deficit and its broader economic implications. Numerous economists and politicians expressed concern over the tremendous growth in the budget deficit, which deviated considerably from earlier trends, but not all the concerns expressed were equally valid.

A grossly exaggerated concern often mentioned in conjunction with the national debt is that the debt will be a burden to future generations. The burden of the debt typically is borne by the generation that incurs the deficit. For example, the national debt grew substantially during World War II, but subsequent generations have not borne the burden of those deficits. The burden existed when the deficit spending occurred. Government's deficit spending during the early 1940's resulted in a reallocation of resources. In order to produce the materials government required to fight the war, production was diverted from consumer goods toward military goods. People had to do without cars, tires, gasoline, meat, and other goods. They bore the burden of the increased government spending.

In certain situations, however, future generations may bear part of the debt's burden. For example, an economic burden for future generations could result when the national debt is held by foreign investors. In 1993, 13.6 percent of the national debt was held by foreign investors. If the U.S. government borrows from foreign citizens or foreign governments, it is temporarily gaining the purchasing power of those foreign investors. If the foreign investors require repayment of those loans in the future, then the U.S. would have to give up purchasing power at that time. In such an event, future generations would be burdened by a previous debt.

In such a situation, the degree to which future generations would be burdened would also depend on how the borrowed funds were used. If they were used for investment into the capital infrastructure, such as highways, increased economic growth would help enable the repayment of funds with no net loss. If the borrowed funds were used for current consumption, the future repayment of those funds would entail a real loss of future purchasing power.

Another concern associated with deficit spending is its contribution to increasing the size of government. Deficit spending enables politicians to postpone making hard decisions, often throughout their entire tenure in office. As a consequence, the costs and benefits of government programs are not scrutinized as closely as they might be in a pay-as-you-go system. A deficit-financed increase in the size of the government sector may thus not result in the most efficient use of society's resources.

A third concern regarding deficit spending is higher interest rates associated with government borrowing. When a deficit occurs, government must issue bonds in the credit market. These bonds compete with business and household borrowing, driving up interest rates. Throughout the 1980's, the real rates of interest (the actual interest rate minus the rate of inflation) were at historically high levels.

High interest rates have several consequences. Some economists fear that higher rates crowd out private investment into capital. When the cost of borrowing money increases, businesses invest in fewer projects, adversely affecting economic growth. High interest rates also contribute to growing deficits. In 1993, interest payments on the national debt totaled $198.8 billion, while the year's deficit was $254.7 billion. Therefore, the elimination of interest payments would reduce the actual deficit nearly 80 percent, to approximately $56 billion.

In his controversial 1986 book *How Real Is the Federal Deficit?* Robert Eisner took issue with many of the above claims. Eisner contended that the government's deficit figures were misleading, and led to incorrect decisions and economic policies. He concluded that after adjusting for price changes or inflation, the structural deficit was substantially smaller than reported and an excellent predictor of subsequent changes in output and employment. Eisner also concluded, contrary to popular belief, that budget deficits increase investment by stimulating aggregate demand and total output. Finally, Eisner indicated that budget deficits may increase the trade deficit, thereby stimulating economic growth in other countries.

Eisner's views do not necessarily contradict the conflicting concerns raised by others. Rather they emphasize the complexity of the issue: The impact of deficit spending on investment is complicated. Although higher interest rates associated with federal government borrowing may adversely affect investment, increased product demand associated with deficit spending may stimulate the desire for business expansion through investment. Whether investment increases or decreases depends on the relative magnitude of these offsetting effects.

Context

Since the establishment of its political institutions under the Constitution, the United States has had a national debt. Article 1, section 8, of the Constitution grants the federal government the authority to borrow money. At the urging of its first secretary of the treasury, Alexander Hamilton, the federal government agreed to assume responsibility for all debts incurred by the Continental Congress during the Revolutionary War and by state governments under the Articles of Confederation. At that point, the national debt was $79 million.

Until the Great Depression, budget deficits were typically associated with wartime expenditures. For example, in 1914 the national debt was $1.2 billion. By 1919, the federal government ran a $13.3 billion deficit and had a $25.4 billion national debt. This wartime growth in the national debt, however, did generate concern. The Second Liberty Bond Act of 1917 established a ceiling on the total amount of debt that could be outstanding. This debt ceiling can only be raised through congressional action, an event that has occurred with some frequency since 1980.

The expenditures associated with World War I did not institute a debt mentality. By 1921, the federal government had a surplus of $509 million, and through the remainder of the 1920's, the federal government ran annual surpluses. As a result, by 1929, the national debt was reduced to $16.9 billion—equivalent to approximately 16 percent of gross domestic product.

Because of declining incomes and production, the national debt grew during the 1930's. By 1939, it totaled $48.2 billion, 55 percent of gross domestic product. Sharp increases in government expenditures during World War II caused even more rapid growth in the national debt. By 1945, the national debt was $260.1 billion, 122 percent of gross domestic product.

Even though the absolute amount of the national debt increased to $994.3 billion between the end of World War II and 1981, the national debt as a percentage of gross domestic product decreased to less than 34 percent. After 1981, large deficits caused rapid growth in the national debt. By 1993, the national debt was $4,351.2 billion; 69 percent of gross domestic product. That growth increased concern about the national debt and resulted in the Gramm-Rudman-Hollings Act of 1985, the Deficit Reduction Act of 1990, and proposals for a balanced budget amendment.

Bibliography

Blinder, Alan. *Hard Heads, Soft Hearts: Tough-minded Economics for a Just Society.* Reading, Mass.: Addison-Wesley, 1987. Explores the conflict between the goals of efficiency and equity in fiscal policy.

Eisner, Robert. *How Real Is the Federal Deficit?* New York: Free Press, 1986. Argues that accounting methods used to determine the size of the deficit tend to overstate its size, thus contributing to poor policy decisions.

Friedman, Benjamin. *Day of Reckoning: The Consequences of American Economic Policy Under Reagan and After.* New York: Random House, 1988. Examines the causes and impact of growth in the budget deficit and national debt during the 1980's, and concludes with a chapter describing policies that would address these issues.

Lipsey, Richard G., Paul N. Courant, Douglas D. Purvis, and Peter O. Steiner. *Economics.* 10th ed. New York: HarperCollins, 1993. Introductory economics textbook that summarizes the impact of a budget deficit and the national debt within the context of macroeconomic theory. Chapter 34 focuses on budget deficits.

Malkin, Lawrence. *The National Debt.* New York: Henry Holt, 1987. Examines the relationships between deficits, debt, and economic adjustments. Summarizes similarities and differences between government, private, and international debt.

Savage, James D. *Balanced Budgets and American Politics.* Ithaca, N.Y.: Cornell University Press, 1988. Examines the evolution of the federal budget controversy, using a historical and political perspective.

Schier, Steven E. *A Decade of Deficits: Congressional Thought and Fiscal Action.* Albany: State University of New York Press, 1992. Using personal interviews with a large number of legislators, examines the relationship between congressional politics and the budget deficit during the 1980's.

Stabile, Donald R., and Jeffrey A. Cantor. *The Public Debt of the United States: An Historical Perspective, 1775-1990.* New York: Praeger, 1991. Historical examination of the national debt, including sections on debt management and administration. Emphasis on the national debt's growth since 1940.

Robert Charles Graham

Cross-References

DEISM

Field of study: Political philosophy

Especially important as a religious and political philosophy during the seventeenth and eighteenth centuries, Deism holds that the human mind, through the study of nature, can discover the truths needed for a good life. With its emphasis on freedom and natural law, Deism anticipated the English, American, and French revolutions.

Principal terms
ATHEISM: belief that there is no god
NATURAL LAW: principles by which the universe operates
NATURAL RELIGION: knowledge of God and morality obtained by the study of His creation
PANTHEISM: belief that God is the sum of all things and God and nature are synonymous; also, worship of all gods
REASON: human ability to think clearly and accurately and arrive at truth
THEISM: belief in a god, especially one who has revealed himself in some special way

Overview

Derived from the Latin word *deus* (God), Deism was an influential philosophical movement in England and on the European and American continents in the seventeenth and eighteenth centuries. Often called natural religion, it attempted to rediscover the original religion shared by all humans before the rise of particular and divisive denominational creeds. This intellectual adventure was popular for two reasons. On the one hand, the findings of physical scientists suggested the possibility of knowing God directly through nature. The brilliant English scholar, Isaac Newton (1642-1724), asserted in such works as *The Mathematical Principles of Natural Philosophy* (1687) that human reason, reflecting on sensory data, could arrive at fundamental knowledge concerning God and the universe. The world, taught Newton, operated according to predictable and impartial rules. If such things as the mechanics of motion were certain and self-evident, then it followed that the God who created and preserves the cosmos does not need to intervene supernaturally through miracles or in special revelations such as the Bible. As children of nature, all people should be able to use their intelligence and experience to maintain society with the same precision that the Supreme Being sustains creation. This optimistic expectation was revealed in the enthusiastic line of poet Alexander Pope: "Nature, and nature's laws lay hid in night:/ God said, '*Let Newton be*,' and all was light."

On the other hand, political scientists were receptive to natural religion as a moral basis on which to reconstruct society in the wake of the sectarian strife that followed the Reformation and Counterreformation in the mid-seventeenth century. England had been convulsed by a civil war between the Puritans and orthodox Anglicans, while the Continent had been devastated by the Thirty Years' War between Protestants and

Catholics. In an age when religion was politics and politics was religion, it seemed both futile and dangerous to try to base civil law and international relations on any particular denominational belief. Amid the contradictions of creeds, philosophers strove to find a set of common values that could be acceptable to all humans, be they Roman Catholics, Protestants, Jews, Muslims, or adherents of the newly discovered East Asian religions—Hinduism, Taoism, Confucianism, and Shintoism. The social scientist, like the physical scientist, should be able to find values agreeable to all reasonable persons. Deism, a religion without revelation, dogmas, churches, or formal worship, based itself on the self-evident truths of nature as discovered by reason. It would be an alternative to theism—the belief in a god known through a special revelation such as the Bible or the Koran—and atheism—the formal denial of the existence of a Supreme Being. A rational and benevolent first cause had made both nature and human nature, according to Deists, and all humans worshipped him.

While some scholars trace the antecedents of Deism to either the Renaissance Humanists or the left wing of the Protestant Reformation, most regard Edward Herbert (1583-1648) as its real father. A career diplomat and one-time English ambassador to France, Lord Herbert, the Baron of Cherbury, had been an eyewitness to the havoc wrought by religious and political fanaticism in both Europe and England: In 1644 he had had to surrender his own home to the Puritans. For him, it was essential to find a tolerant, rational, moral religion that was not based on any particular sect's teachings. In such works as *On Truth* (1624), *On the Religion of Laymen* (1645), and *On the Religion of the Gentiles* (1663), Herbert propounded the five pillars of Deism. These principles are the existence of a Supreme Being, who created and governs the universe by natural law; the need for humans to worship this deity in whatever fashion their individual consciences dictated; toleration of religious diversity; repentance, the need for each person, using a rationally informed conscience, to try to make good the wrong he had done to others; and a belief in immortality, grounded in the "moral necessity" for each person to be rewarded or punished in the hereafter for deeds done in earthly life.

Applications

Lord Herbert's teachings were elaborated and applied primarily in England, the United States, and France. Although England had a state church, with the sovereign at its head, Deism led to a cry for religious toleration. Matthew Tindal, an eighteenth century British jurist, wrote the so-called Deist's Bible, *Christianity as Old as the Creation* (1730), in which he argued that the true religion of nature, which was eternal, universal, simple, and perfect, was focused in universal duties toward God and man.

John Locke, the celebrated philosopher, was to political science what Isaac Newton was to physics. Locke was secretary to the Earl of Shaftesbury, resident in both England and on the Continent, and participant in and defender of the Glorious Revolution of 1688. In works such as *Two Treatises on Government* (1689), *Essay Concerning Human Understanding* (1690), and *The Letter on Toleration* (1689), Locke profoundly influenced the reshaping of British political life, and advocated the toleration of all religious views, except atheism. England, in the Toleration Act (1689), extended to Dissenters (but not to Catholics, Jews, or Unitarians) the right to worship without political restraint. Locke further insisted that God had given men certain natural rights, such as the rights to life, liberty, and property, that society dare not repeal. The English Bill of Rights, passed by the Parliament in 1689, became "the Bible of English Liberty," upholding the rule of law. It affirmed that only Parliament could suspend or change laws, not the king; the necessity for taxes to be approved by the people through Parliament; and the prohibition of a standing army in the realm in peacetime except by parliamentary permission. This legislation recognized Locke's doctrine of a social contract between the governed and the government, in which, by mutual consent, there were reciprocal obligations. If the state neglected its duties, the people had the right of revolution and the obligation to rise up and redress the wrong done them. As a child of the Age of Deism, Locke worked ardently to bring political and social life back into harmony with the natural laws that Deists believed were implanted in reason and conscience by the Creator.

Several of Locke's contemporaries in Great Britain maintained that happiness would be the chief characteristic of such a natural society. William Wollaston, an English philosopher, said that real religion was the pursuit of happiness by the practice of truth and reason. The "moral arithmetic" by which he measured the respective pain or pleasure generated by each moral act anticipated the utilitarianism of Jeremy Bentham and John Stuart Mill. For Wollaston, the real test of the truth of any teaching was its practical outcome, as measured by its happiness quotient.

John Toland, the Irish intellectual who coined the term "pantheism" ("God is the totality of all things"), insisted that religion and politics, like science, must rest on experience and reason. Such honesty, he felt, would permit the natural goodness of humans to be effective. Anthony Ashley Cooper, the Earl of Shaftesbury, concurred, teaching that humans inherently have a natural sympathy for one another and that self-interest is matched with social interest. Another contemporary author, Bishop Richard Cumberland, agreed that natural laws, or immutably true propositions, could be uncovered by reason, and had authority apart from legal or religious sanctions. Adherence to such natural laws as the "Principle of Universal Benevolence" would bring happiness to all, because no action could be morally good unless it contributed to the happiness of humankind.

American Deism was advocated by such eighteenth century intellectual giants as Benjamin Franklin, Thomas Jefferson, and Thomas Paine. The shared assumptions of these Deists were reflected in such American documents as the Declaration of Independence (1776), the Constitution (1787), the Bill of Rights (1789), and the Northwest Ordinance (1787). One of these values was "the divine right of revolution," the freedom of the oppressed to resist tyranny, so ably defended by Jefferson in 1776. Another was the conviction that governments exist to serve the needs of the governed. In *Common Sense* (1776), Thomas Paine cautioned his readers not to confuse society with government to the extent of making little or no distinction between them, because they were not only different but also had different origins. Paine believed that society was produced by people's wants and government by their wickedness. Society promoted people's happiness but the state impacted people by restraining their vices. This was akin to the Jeffersonian doctrine that government governs best when it governs least. Another ideal was that of the separation of church and state. Jefferson believed that his most important work, after the Declaration of Independence, was the Statute for Religious Freedom (1786) in Virginia, a model for the First Amendment of the United States Constitution. Jefferson taught that all attempts to influence the mind in favor of any particular religion "by temporal punishment, or burdens of civil incapacitations" must cease. Only conscience and reason should guide individuals, not political compulsion. America's Deists also favored the freedoms of speech, the press, assembly, and bearing arms, for, as Jefferson said, "I have sworn upon the altar of God eternal hostility against every form of tyranny over the mind of man."

British and American Deism profoundly influenced France in the eighteenth century. The way had been prepared by François Rabelais (ca. 1494-1533), the witty physician, former monk, and scientist turned humanist, who, in such works as *Gargantua* and *Pantagruel* (1532-1546), epitomized the new man of early modern France: cosmopolitan, widely traveled, tolerant of all "except conceit, torpidity, and violence," flexible, and capable of honoring the truth, even from his adversaries. Those values were embodied in "the prince of French Deists," François-Marie Arouet, or Voltaire (1694-1778). Educated in France, resident in England, exiled to Switzerland and Prussia, Voltaire was a prolific and tireless author, working eighteen to twenty hours a day. From his pen came such works as *Philosophical Letters* (1734), *Candide* (1759), and *Treatise on Toleration* (1764). Living during the *Ancien Regime* (the "Old Order"), when religious minorities were denied civil and spiritual liberties, Voltaire championed freedom of conscience, speech, and the press, allegedly saying, "I don't believe a word you say, but I'll defend to the death your right to say it." Voltaire believed the world was begun by a Supreme Being, governing the natural and moral worlds, whose ways were known by reason and honored by justice. God's natural laws took precedence over those of church and state. If people honored the Creator and his laws, progress would result. Education, for both women and men, would facilitate the evolution of civilization.

Other eighteenth century French intellectuals influenced by Deism were the Marquis de Condorcet, an apostle of the notion of progress; Denis Diderot, whose *Encyclopedia* (1751-1772) disseminated the scientific, technological, and philosophical views of the Age of Deism; and Charles de Secondat, the Baron de Montesquieu, a celebrated political scientist, whose major work, *The Spirit of the Laws* (1748), analyzed comparative governments, favoring that of England. Montesquieu championed a system of checks and balances within the government, facilitated by the tripartite division of powers between an executive, legislative, and judicial branch.

The interrelationship of Deism in England, America, and France is nowhere better illustrated than in the career of Thomas Paine (1737-1809). Born in Great Britain, Paine agitated for liberty there before immigrating to the New World in time to participate as a pamphleteer in the American Revolution. Once independence was won in the United States, Paine journeyed to France to fight for freedom there. In his *Rights of Man*, Paine maintained that by nature humans have four fundamental freedoms: the rights to liberty, property, security, and to resist tyranny. Elected to the French Assembly in 1792, Paine supported the Revolution's Declaration of the Rights of Man and of the Citizen (1789), which articulated such cherished Deist values, already won in Great Britain and America, as freedom of speech, religious toleration, equality before the law, and no taxation or imprisonment without due process of law. In the French Revolution (1789-1799), these beliefs became the common property of Western civilization. Perhaps, as Paine articulated, Deism began as the belief "in one God, and no more" in "a hope for happiness beyond this life," and in the conviction that "my own mind is my own church." By 1789, however, Deism had evolved into an agenda of world revolution, seeking freedom and justice for the majority of humans.

Context

Deism had enormous impact in the eighteenth century by facilitating the Glorious Revolution (1688) in England, the American (1775-1781) and the French revolutions. These democratic movements were generated by Deism's fundamental concepts: belief in the dependability of a predictable, benevolent universe; trust in the reliability of reason; confidence in the possibility of human material and spiritual progress; a feeling of the desirability of freedom, of more personal and social liberty as being a good worthy of sacrifice; and the certainty that these human rights came from nature itself. The entire Atlantic Community feasted at the "table of liberty" prepared by the Deists for more than two hundred years.

During the nineteenth and twentieth centuries, Deism fell out of favor. Critics regarded it as bombast and puerile. Newton's universe of law and logic was replaced by the relative one of Albert Einstein in which absolutes were few and far between. Rene Descartes' easy identification of humanity with rationality ("I think, therefore I am") was thrown into question by the irrationality many twentieth century psychologists found in human nature. In the wake of a Great Depression, two world wars, a Cold War, and the possibility of atomic "omnicide," intellectuals had their doubts as to the inevitability or desirability of progress. The value of liberty was challenged concurrently by a variety of tyrannies: Nazism in Germany, Fascism in Italy and Spain, and Communism in Russia and China. Finally, to some twentieth century minds, the universe seemed indifferent if not inhospitable to the ideals the Deists had believed were guaranteed by the very fabric of the cosmos.

Bibliography

Berlin, Isaiah. *The Age of Enlightenment: The Eighteenth Century Philosophers*. New York: George Braziller, 1957. Excerpts from such great philosophers as Voltaire and Locke, and interpretative comment about them by a well-known American teacher.

Cassirer, Ernst. *The Philosophy of the Enlightenment*. Translated by Fritz C. A. Koelln and James P. Pettegrove. Princeton, N.J.: Princeton University Press, 1951. Classic study, written in 1932. Offers the insight of a celebrated German scholar into the impact of Rationalism on such areas as natural science, religion, law, and aesthetics. Valuable introduction to the age in which Deism flourished.

Commager, Henry Steele. *The Empire of Reason: How Europe Imagined and America Realized the Enlightenment*. Garden City, N.J.: Anchor Press, 1977. Introduces the major ideas and individuals of the Age of Reason. Reliable, enjoyable, and tightly written.

Heer, Friedrich. *The Intellectual History of Europe*. Translated by Jonathan Steinberg. 2 vols. Garden City, N.J.: Anchor Press, 1968. Monumental survey of Western thought, which places Deism and the Enlightenment in the broader context of the rise of modernity.

May, Henry. *The Enlightenment in America*. New York: Oxford University Press, 1976. Carefully reasoned narrative and interpretation, offering an almost-definitive introduction to the Age of Reason in the Western Hemisphere. Well referenced, with a thorough bibliography.

Redwood, John. *Reason, Ridicule, and Religion: The Age of Enlightenment in England*. Cambridge, Mass.: Harvard University Press, 1976. Scholarly study interprets the intellectual climate in which Deism was born as an alternative to both theism and atheism. Excellent bibliography.

Stromberg, Roland. *Religious Liberalism in Eighteenth-Century England*. London: Oxford University Press, 1954. Thorough and insightful introduction to the spiritual environment of England in the Age of Deism. Valuable bibliography, even if dated.

Sullivan, Robert E. *John Toland and the Deist Controversy: A Study in Adaptations*. Cambridge, Mass.: Harvard University Press, 1982. Scholarly biography of the life and times of one of Britain's most influential Deists. First English-language biography of Toland.

Walters, Kerry S. *The American Deists: Voices of Reason and Dissent in the Early Republic*. Lawrence: University Press of Kansas, 1992. Combines primary sources and interpretive text. Among the American Deists introduced are Benjamin Franklin, Thomas Jefferson, Ethan Allen, and Thomas Paine.

Waring, E. Graham, ed. *Deism and Natural Religion: A Source Book*. New York: Frederick Ungar, 1967. Excellent anthology provides, in their own words, an introduction to such leading Deists as John Toland, Samuel Clarke, Anthony Collins, Thomas Woolston, and Matthew Tindal, and offers replies by some of their opponents, such as John Wesley.

C. George Fry

Cross-References

Church and Government in History, p. 230; Church and State Relations in the United States, p. 236; Hobbes's Political Philosophy, p. 836; Locke's Political Philosophy, p. 1142; Montesquieu's Political Philosophy, p. 1228; Religion and Politics, p. 1685; Right of Revolution, p. 1744; Rousseau's Political Philosophy, p. 1756; The Social Contract, p. 1827; Utilitarianism, p. 2077.

DELEGATES

Field of study: Politics

A delegate is an elected or appointed representative of a group of people or a governmental body who acts only according to instructions. Examples of delegates include legislators, political party conventioneers, and ambassadors.

Principal terms

ARTICLES OF CONFEDERATION: charter of government under which the United States operated from 1781 until 1789, when the Constitution was adopted

CONSTITUENCY: people to whom leaders are responsible

PARTY CONVENTIONS: national meetings held every four years by a political party, primarily for the purpose of naming the party's presidential candidate

PRIMARY ELECTIONS: state elections in which registered Republicans and Democrats cast votes to select the party's final candidate

RECALL: procedure, usually a special election, by which a public official can be removed from office before the formal end of his or her term

TRUSTEE: elected official who is free to follow his or her conscience or experience in acting for constituents

Overview

At the end of the eighteenth century, as the United States was developing its democratic system of government, there was much debate about the idea of representation. It was widely agreed that the kind of direct democracy practiced in ancient Greece, in which all citizens of Athens gathered to debate and decide political issues, was impossible in a large, modern nation. Some form of representation would have to be established, a system in which citizens would somehow choose others to act for them in government. There was no agreement, however, about the form representation should take. Should citizens elect their own representatives, or should some body of elites, the better educated or better off, do it for them? Should representatives, once chosen, be given only the narrow power of following instructions from electors, or should they be entrusted to use their best judgment during their term of office?

Dictionary definitions of "representative" and "delegate" are practically interchangeable. Both are persons who act in the place of another. In political philosophy, the two words have more specific and more contradictory meanings. The term "delegate," whether applied to legislators, political party convention-goers, or ambassadors, implies someone who acts under instructions, with little or no free will to make independent decisions. Representatives usually are political leaders with more freedom to act independently, to follow their consciences or use their best judgment on issues.

With the rhetoric and experience of the revolution they had waged and their fear of British monarchy fresh in their minds, most Americans initially wanted a government as close to a direct democracy as possible. They feared a strong, centralized government and distant officials. The first U.S. charter of government, the Articles of Confederation, set up a system under which Congress would be made up of "delegates" sent by state legislatures. The first sentence of the Articles refers to its signers as "we the Delegates of the United States of America in Congress assembled." These delegates were given little independent power. They had one-year terms and could be replaced by the states at any time if they failed to follow instructions.

When economic, social, and foreign policy crises threatened the new nation, state legislatures again sent delegates (and this is what they were called) to a constitutional convention, held in Philadelphia in 1787, with instructions to review and revise the Articles of Confederation, which were blamed for many of the problems. The delegates, acting in secrecy, in effect ignored their instructions. They adopted the representative role and, using their best judgment, abandoned the Articles and wrote the U.S. Constitution. Three men left the convention in anger, denouncing the independent actions of their fellow delegates.

The debate over the meaning of representation persisted. It is usually framed as an argument over whether a representative should act as a trustee or a delegate. English parliamentarian Edmund Burke, in the eighteenth century, and John F. Kennedy, in the twentieth, both argued that legislators should act as trustees. Legislators are at the scene of the action; they better understand problems and their ramifications. Their election shows the trust constituents have in them. Therefore, they should use their own best judgment in deciding political issues. If they err, or if their constituents disagree with them, they can be replaced at the next election.

Other political leaders and thinkers disagree. Legislators are, in essence, stand-ins for their constituents, sent to Congress to express the wishes or fulfill the needs of those constituents. They are under obligation to do their best to discover their constituents' opinions and act on them.

At the national level, this trustee-delegate conflict generally has been little more than an academic debate. Some states and localities, however, have passed measures attempting at least to remind public officials of their delegate status. Thirty-six American states allow for the recall of school board members, city council members, judges, state legislators, and even governors. In most cases, these officials can be recalled not only for corruption or incompetence but also if sufficiently many constituents dislike or disagree with political decisions the officials have made, that is, if they believe the officials to have acted contrary to the desires and needs of constituents. Although representatives could also be subject to recall, such recalls more commonly would be for dereliction of duty than for simple misrepresentation of constituents' interests.

Despite recall provisions, the word "delegate" has been used most commonly in regard not to government itself but to political parties. When the Republican, Democratic, or other political parties gather in their national conventions every four years to choose presidential candidates, the conventioneers are referred to as party delegates, often chosen through primary elections. This is a correct use of the term "delegate," for these people have almost never been independent agents. They are instructed representatives, originally of their state party officials and more recently of the various party candidates.

Applications

Early in U.S. history, presidential candidates were chosen by congressional caucuses, groups of congressmen who shared similar ideological and party preferences. Later, state legislatures forwarded names of likely candidates. By 1832, with the nation growing and political parties becoming more formalized institutions, President Andrew Jackson and others decided that national conventions of party delegates should be held to choose presidential and vice presidential candidates. The convention system that Jackson set up was adopted by both the Democratic and Republican parties, as well as by many minor parties, and it has operated in essentially the same way for more than 130 years.

Although the system for choosing delegates differed somewhat from state to state, it generally worked as follows. Local party supporters gather at district meetings and select one or more of their number to attend a state party convention. The state convention, after several days of public speeches and private negotiations, selects the state's delegation to the national convention. In some states, these delegates are chosen directly by party officials. In others, they are elected by the state convention members, usually after careful coaching by party leaders. The delegations always include the leading public officials of the state belonging to the party in question. The rest of the delegates are longtime, loyal party activists. A trip to the national convention as a state delegate is often used as a reward to someone who has worked faithfully for the party for many years.

State delegates are formally the delegates of their party's supporters in whatever state they represent. In reality, they follow the instructions of their state party leaders. In a classic study of party delegates conducted in 1956, Herbert McClosky showed that both Democratic and Republican convention delegates were not really representative of their party's voters as a whole. In general, the delegates were better educated, economically better off, much more interested and active politically, and more extreme in their views.

The selection and makeup of national convention party delegates began to change in the early 1970's. Civil rights, antiwar, feminist, and student activists pressured especially the Democratic Party to change methods of delegate selection. The parties, activists charged, were too much under the control of a few party "bosses," and the delegates were not a reflection of either the American people or party supporters as a whole.

In 1971, the Democratic Party changed its rules, ordering that state delegations to the 1972 convention must reflect the proportions of women, racial minorities, and young people present in each state's population. Delegates now were to be the agents not only of the state's voters but also of various gender, racial, age, and other groups in American society. This "quota" system, as its opponents dubbed it, along with another rule insisting that delegations must reflect the support that existed in the state for the various candidates running, soon became too difficult to implement fully. Still, the number of African American and other minority delegates rose in the Democratic Party, and the number of women delegates rose in both major parties.

Pressures to open delegate selection and to give ordinary Americans a greater voice in choosing presidential nominees led state after state to adopt the primary election system. By 1976, more than 70 percent of all convention delegates of both parties were being chosen through primaries. National conventioneers became delegates in the full meaning of that word—political servants, not masters. On primary election ballots, delegates are pledged to support one or another of the candidates running. In some states, only the candidates' names appear; in others, the candidates' and their supporters' names are printed. In either case, a particular candidate's delegates attend their party's convention bound by party rules to vote for that candidate at least in the early ballots taken at the convention. Losing candidates in both parties have attempted to overthrow this rule, as Ronald Reagan did at the 1976 Republican convention and Edward Kennedy did at the 1980 Democratic convention. Delegates, they argued, should be "free to vote their consciences." They and others who so argued were unsuccessful.

Political party delegates have never become "trustees." They remain agents of their candidates, carrying out those candidates' (and the primary voters') instructions, supporting their candidates until one of them gains sufficient votes to become the party's nominee. Then, at their candidates' further instructions, usually termed a "request," they cast their vote for the nominee in the name of party unity.

Since 1976, primary elections have determined who will be the Republican and Democratic presidential nominees. The outcome usually is known long before the national conventions are held. Many people, therefore, think that conventions are superfluous and should no longer be held. If that should happen, delegates would virtually disappear from American life, although not from the political vocabulary or from political philosophy or argument.

Context

The American Revolution of 1776 was fought under the rallying cry of "No taxation without representation." British leaders argued in vain that although their angry colonists did not have the right, as they wanted, to send delegates to the British parliament, they were still represented by Parliament, whose members had in their trust all the peoples and lands of the British kingdom. From that time to this, the delegate role has had a complex, contradictory history in the United States. When it was rigidly enforced under the Articles of Confederation, some historians argue, it led to national weakness. It was flagrantly ignored at the convention at which the Constitution was written. As party nominating conventions developed and changed, delegates served first state parties and their leaders and then primary voters (a small minority of all eligible citizens) and candidates.

If party conventions are eliminated, the only delegates left, in the true sense of the term, would be ambassadors. They can give advice to the president, but they are the American delegates to other nations and to the United Nations. They must follow the president's instructions or risk replacement.

The concept of the delegate has a rich historical and philosophical meaning. It will remain important in political, democratic debate, and it saw philosophical revival in the 1990's. In the elections of 1992 and 1994, Americans showed an increased willingness to vote incumbent legislators out of office. Arguments that go back to the country's founding took on a new life. What does representative government mean in a democracy? What should the relationship be between citizens and their representatives? In some ways, Americans seemed again to want representatives to act more as delegates, to remain closely attuned to their constituents' wants and needs and to carry out their wishes. In other ways, however, Americans also seemed to want representatives who were trustees, who would be men and women of conscience, able to ignore narrow parochial interests and act for the general good of the nation as a whole.

Bibliography

Bailyn, Bernard. *The Ideological Origins of the American Revolution.* Cambridge, Mass.: The Belknap Press of Harvard University Press, 1992. An outstanding scholar of American revolutionary thought, Bailyn describes the changing ways in which the Founders conceptualized and argued many great political ideas, including the idea of representation, as they went from being revolutionaries against Great Britain to state builders and constitution writers.

Cronin, Thomas. *Direct Democracy.* Cambridge, Mass.: Harvard University Press, 1989. Discusses the concept of the delegate especially in regard to the debates over the U.S. Constitution and to state legislation establishing the recall. Chapters 6 and 7 are particularly relevant.

DeClerico, Robert E., and Allan S. Hammock, eds. *Points of View.* 5th ed. New York: McGraw-Hill, 1992. Written as a series of staged debates over vital issues in American politics, this book includes arguments regarding the concept of the representative as trustee and as delegate.

Kammen, Michael, ed. *The Origins of the American Constitution.* New York: Viking Penguin, 1986. Includes the text of the Articles of Confederation as well as some discussion of the philosophical and political differences between the Articles and the Constitution in regard to the concept of representation.

McClosky, Herbert, Paul Hoffman, and Rosemary O'Hara. "Issue Conflict and Consensus Among Party Leaders and Followers." *American Political Science Review* 54 (June, 1960): 406-427. Although somewhat dated, this remains the best study of the characteristics of party delegates and the ways in which delegates, a political elite, differ from ordinary party supporters and voters.

Polsby, Nelson. *Consequences of Party Reform.* Oxford, England: Oxford University

Press, 1983. A specialist in the study of parties and elections, Polsby analyzes the effects of the reforms of the 1970's on the parties and their leadership, delegates, and conventions, and how these factors affected the kinds of presidential candidates selected.

Reichley, A. James. *The Life of the Parties*. New York: Free Press, 1992. This thorough, up-to-date history of the American party system contains a good description of the origins of national nominating conventions and of how the role of the conventions and of convention delegates changed from the 1830's to the 1990's.

Mary T. Hanna

Cross-References

The Democratic Party, p. 520; Elections, p. 578; The Media and Elections, p. 1161; Nomination Processes, p. 1312; Political Party Conventions, p. 1492; Political Platforms, p. 1512; Presidential Elections in the United States, p. 1596; Primary Elections, p. 1603; The Republican Party, p. 1699; Technology and Citizen-Government Relations, p. 1949.

DEMAGOGUERY

Field of study: Politics

Demagoguery is a political leader's using strong emotional and personal appeals to call for political action, usually against a scapegoat of some sort.

Principal terms
> CONTROL THINKING: state of mind in which an individual directs his or her mental efforts at obtaining or maintaining control over others for the purpose of being able to manipulate them
>
> GRASSROOTS POLITICS: efforts focused on mobilizing individual voters behind a candidate or policy by making direct personal appeals to them, bypassing interest groups, parties, or other pluralist mechanisms
>
> POPULAR CRISIS PSYCHOLOGY: use of observational evidence or other mental stimuli to create an impression of a pending or present catastrophic social event, regardless of the actual likelihood or existence of the event
>
> POPULISM: political approach that advances both order and equality as desirable political values, and which emphasizes in adversarial terms the interests of the common people over those of the elites
>
> SCAPEGOAT: biblical term commonly used to describe a person or group unjustly blamed for some crime, evil, or social problem

Overview

Demagoguery as a political term emanates from ancient times. Demagogues were the leaders of the common people. The term comes from the ancient Greek words *demos*, meaning "the people," and *agogos*, or "leading." Since those times, however, demagoguery has assumed a much more pejorative connotation. In modern political science, demagoguery is a phenomenon in which a popular leader uses rhetorical tricks, propaganda, highly emotional appeals, and blame of scapegoats to rally the support of significant numbers of people. Not all demagogues were political figures when they began practicing their craft; in fact, many of them have come from outside of the political mainstream. If and when the movement has enough adherents, however, it may become widely recognized as a political force. In such a case, demagogues typically use their political support for personal gain.

Some may ask if demagoguery is necessarily a bad thing, as it is commonly held to be in political debates. In order to be successful, after all, demagogues must have a base of popular support; in turn, the majority rule principle is one of the cornerstones of Western democracy. The logic behind this argument is that people are free to support the candidates and issues of their choice in a democracy, and if a demagogue appeals to a popular enough political perspective, it is only right that he or she might attain a certain amount of political power. This rather straightforward argument is also rather simplistic.

Demagogues are perceived as dangerous because of the nature of their appeal. In addition to the idea of majority rule, democratic principles also hold the notion that persuasion of the public to support candidates, parties, or issues should be based on logic or reason and free from manipulation or coercion. Demagogues generally have little use for these democratic concepts. Rather, they seek to present simplistic solutions—usually based on prejudices, unwarranted fears, and other frailties of human nature—for complex social problems. Demagogues are usually also captivating personalities—attractive, amusing, likeable, articulate—and use such characteristics to get the public to support their political agenda in the absence of any reasonable intellectual force behind their arguments.

Citing earlier criteria developed by author Sterling Fishman, Cal M. Logue and Howard Dorgan describe a telling three-step process in the "control thinking" of the typical demagogue. First, they say: "he identifies a popular 'crisis psychology'; next, he defines the cause of the crisis as being a single and simple abstract or concrete evil; and, finally, he provides an equally simple escape from the crisis, 'a new faith, a new belief,' with himself as the leader." Ironically, demagogues do not seem to care very much about the success or failure of their proposed policies; as devoted as they may seem, history is replete with examples of such figures who, upon riding the support of their adherents into a position of power, quickly forgot or relegated to a secondary status the people's needs and desires in favor of efforts to maintain their own base of power. In other words, once demagogues have attained political power, they tend to devote their energies to attempting to keep it.

In some cases, such as the rise of Adolf Hitler in pre-World War II Germany, demagoguery is relatively easy to identify and there is little doubt about its existence or effects. In many others, however, the line between demagoguery and grassroots political movement is much more obscure. During the 1992 U.S. presidential campaign, for example, Texas businessman H. Ross Perot declared his independent candidacy for president and subsequently financed the organization of a movement which became known as United We Stand. Perot's adherents strongly objected to what they referred to as traditional insider politics of the major parties, and in a number of states they captured enough of the presidential vote to be considered an official political party. Perot's supporters claimed United We Stand, America was a new political movement, but critics of the businessman-turned-politician claimed that he was more interested in using the movement's support for his own personal aggrandizement than he was in enacting serious reform. Was Perot a demagogue or grassroots political protest candidate? Voters' characterizations depended strongly on whether they were for him, in which case he was the latter, or against him, in which case he was the former. While demagoguery is widely accepted as a dangerous and undesirable political phenomenon, it is not always easy to identify. Perhaps it is safest to think of demagoguery in terms of degrees—rather than being able to say it clearly does or does not exist in a given political situation, it may be more accurate to gauge the gray area in between and discuss the frequency with which demagogic behavior is exhibited by a given political leader.

Applications

Of all the demagoguery practiced in modern political times, and by so many leaders in many different countries and cultures, perhaps history's darkest example of the phenomenon is to be found in the rise to power and rule of German dictator Adolf Hitler before and during World War II. In World War I, Germany suffered a devastating defeat, not only on the battlefields of Europe but in an economic and social sense as well. Frustration in post-World War I Germany reached a desperate pitch as its people attempted to come to grips with the humiliation of losing a war, the pain of losing many native sons in combat, and the hardships of an economy left in utter shambles. The conditions in postwar Germany were ripe for exploitation by a demagogue, if only a scapegoat could be found on which to place blame for Germany's misfortunes. Many of these misfortunes could have been directed at the imperialist fantasies and overly-bold projections of power by the old prewar German regime. Such arguments were largely lost on the common German, however, because of their complexity and because to place the blame on Germany's former leaders would amount to placing the blame on Germany itself. Hitler found a scapegoat in Jews. Tragically, Jews in Hitler's Third Reich were persecuted to the point of ultimate sacrifice—millions were executed, in what became known as the Holocaust. While they had nothing to do with Germany's defeat in World War I or the country's subsequent hardships, Jews were a convenient, clearly identifiable target against whom Hitler could direct public anger and frustration. They were also a minority within Germany's Christian population, which added to the ease with which Hitler could mobilize public opinion against them. Using a combination of propaganda, personal charisma, nationalism, and brute force—many of which are mainstays of a typical demagogic rise to power—the German National Socialists came to power in Germany and effected their reign of terror.

The experience of the United States with demagogues has fortunately been less savage, but it has had its share of them, nevertheless. From the time immediately after the Civil War to the early twentieth century, demagogues were particularly common and notable in the American South. In that region at that time, segregation of blacks and whites was a common practice, and southern blacks were a popular target of scapegoatism and abuse at the hands of white demagogues. Southern demagogues used fear of the unknown and common stereotypes about blacks to rail against desegregation and the mixing of the races. In doing so, they became champions of what was called the "white cause" to many voters of the region, who were poorly educated and who had been raised in an atmosphere of bias. Subsequently, these demagogues were elected by the white voters in their respective state or congressional district to high political office—usually the U.S., Senate or the governorship, and occasionally both. Among the more notable of these figures are South Carolina's "Pitchfork Ben" Tillman and "Cotton Ed" Smith, Mississippi's Theodore Bilbo and

James Kimble Vardaman, and father-and-son Georgians Eugene and Herman Talmadge.

One particularly famous character of the times, who became governor and U.S. senator, was Huey P. Long of Louisiana. Long represents an exception to the traditional racism among U.S. Southern demagogues. He was one of the few powerful figures of the era who did not use blatantly racist appeals to fuel his rise to power. Instead, Long trumpeted himself as a "champion of the common man," and formed a society, known as "Share Our Wealth," that was a political outlet for his supporters to protect working men and women from the "tyrannical encroachment of American corporate greed." Whether American corporations were truly or solely dedicated to "soaking the little man dry," is a point of contention among pro- and anti-Long factions, but it is clear that some abuses had occurred. Long built his early career around taking on the powerful Standard Oil Company and weakening its influential grasp on Louisiana state politics.

Instead of using race, as did many of his southern contemporaries, Long artfully found an economic scapegoat and in so doing transformed the typical race-baiting populism of the South into an "us-versus-them, poor-versus-rich" crisis psychology. This tactic disguised his method of attaining power. Although race and religion are clearly not reasons to hate people or blame them for social ills, much honest political debate centers on economic issues. Long still engaged in scapegoatism; his scapegoat, to his credit, was not a largely defenseless minority. He lionized himself as the "political savior of the powerless working man" and oversimplified many complex political problems by blaming big business. Those who criticized Long or attempted to provide alternatives to his plans often met a common fate of those who challenge demagogues; they were ridiculed, harassed, regularly threatened with losing their jobs, and occasionally threatened with the loss of their freedom or their lives.

Even in contemporary Louisiana, decades after Huey P. Long's death, there are many who sympathize with his approach to handling the state's Depression-era problems and who do not think of him as a demagogue. This brings up another important issue surrounding demagoguery and its application as a political term appropriate to a particular person or movement. It is important to identify the criteria for labelling someone a demagogue very clearly and to be sure that the definition applied is specific enough to avoid unfairly labelling a genuine political reform movement as demagogic.

Perhaps the "control thinking" of which Logue and Dorgan speak is a crucial key in identifying the demagogue. If a political leader uses power in such a way as to promote an emotional political cult of support if the leader appears to be more concerned with maintaining his power as the leader of the movement than with the movement itself, if the source of political problems is identified by a stereotype or by a sweeping judgment against a group based on factors beyond its control (race, religion, gender) rather than on specific policies of the group, if the leader seems to be emphasizing in public appearances the existence of a crisis, then citizens should recognize demagoguery in their midst.

Context

Demagoguery does not require a specific political system in which to thrive; it may occur in any type of political system. Rigid, hierarchical political systems, such as the Soviet Union under Joseph Stalin, may be the most obvious place to begin searching for demagogues; they typically tend to flourish in systems in which the means exist to silence critics quickly and effectively. Fledgling democratic regimes may also have their problems with demagogues, as the experience of post-World War I Weimar Germany—which quickly succumbed to Hitler's fascist nationalism—shows. At the first sign of economic or social trouble under a new democratic constitution, there may be a political opportunist waiting to decry the new government as a failed experiment and urge a return to more familiar—if more authoritarian—political norms. Even in more established democracies, such as the United States, demagogues may exploit the great liberties of thought, speech, and political action they are provided under a constitution to convince less educated or less sophisticated citizens that the reason for their plight is some seemingly more advantaged group's sinister scheming against them. Southern demagogues were particularly skilled at turning poor, rural southern whites' post-Civil War frustrations into action against free blacks, who were characterized as inferior beings bent on ruining the white culture that had been built in the region.

Across different types of political systems, demagoguery appears to rely on the same fuel for its fire. First, there must be a significant number of citizens who feel alienated from the political system, or powerless to stop what they perceive as some great and growing social evil. Second, there must be a charismatic individual who is willing to step forward and direct these people's frustration into some sort of political action. Finally, and most importantly for the purpose of separating the demagogue from the more honest grassroots political leader, the person who leads the alienated masses must engage in at least some of the hallmark behavior: identifying scapegoats, presenting emotional, hateful, oversimplified, or narrow answers to complex problems, characterizing oneself as a political messiah (that is, as the only person who is able to lead society out of the identified danger), and the use of physical force or other forms of intimidation to silence enemies of the movement.

Bibliography

Bennett, David Harry. *Demagogues in the Depression: American Radicals and the Union Party, 1932-1936.* New Brunswick, N.J.: Rutgers University Press, 1969. Study of one of the major American third-party movements, and the dire times that gave rise to several demagogues within its ranks. Illustrative of how grassroots movements may be prone to demagoguery.

Black, Earl, and Merle Black. *Politics and Society in the South.* Cambridge, Mass.: Harvard University Press, 1987. A comprehensive look at the traditional populist, one-party politics of the old South and how various social phenomena and economic conditions have changed it over time. Noteworthy for its discussion of the place of racial issues in the politics of the South.

Logue, Cal M., and Howard Dorgan, eds. *The Oratory of Southern Demagogues.* Baton Rouge: Louisiana State University Press, 1981. Outstanding study of the rhetorical devices and habits of some of the American South's most notorious demagogic political figures. Each chapter is devoted to one specific figure, with excellent historical detail.

Dethloff, Henry C. ed. *Huey P. Long: Southern Demagogue or American Democrat?* Lexington, Mass.: D. C. Heath, 1967. Explores the fine line between statesmanship and demagoguery—and identifies a number of the problems of identifying figures in either category—using Long, perhaps the U.S.'s most notable demagogic figure, as the binding figure throughout the work.

Shirer, William L. *The Rise and Fall of the Third Reich: A History of Nazi Germany.* New York: Simon & Schuster, 1981. Penetrating examination of the rise of Adolf Hitler to power in pre-World War II Germany, including his use of demagoguery to attain power, the building of the National Socialist movement, the social conditions which were ripe for demagogic exploitation, and Hitler's increasing fanaticism as the tide of war turned against Germany.

John C. Kuzenski

Cross-References

Charismatic Leadership, p. 209; Citizen Movements, p. 248; The Civil Service in the United States, p. 310; Cult of Personality, p. 477; Grassroots Politics, p. 797; Nationalism, p. 1268; Patriotism, p. 1384; Political Participation, p. 1479; Populism, p. 1551; Propaganda, p. 1615; Protest Movements, p. 1621; Statesmanship, p. 1898.

DEMOCRACY

Field of study: Types of government

The defining aspect of democracy is that political leaders are selected by citizens through free and fair elections. Democracies may be parliamentary or presidential, unitary or federal, and elect leaders by a plurality or through proportional representation. Democracy has become an increasingly common form of government in the last quarter of the twentieth century.

Principal terms

AUTHORITARIANISM: nondemocratic rule, characterized by rigged elections, censorship, and coercion and harassment of political opposition

DEMOCRATIC CONSOLIDATION: process by which a democracy stabilizes and endures

DEMOCRATIC POLITICAL CULTURE: attitudes and values that support democracy

DEMOCRATIZATION: the transition from authoritarianism to democracy and the consolidation of democracy

POWER-SHARING: the accommodation of various groups with guarantees of political influence and autonomy

Overview

The word democracy derives from two Greek words: kratos (rule) and *demos* (people). Although all free societies are democracies, democracies can fail to protect individual freedoms. Countries are generally considered democratic to the extent that they have fair and frequent elections in which nearly all adults have the right to vote, citizens have the right to form and join organizations and to express themselves, and alternative sources of information exist. Democracy may exist without formal written constitutions, as in Great Britain and Israel. It is also possible that a single political party, such as the Conservative Party in Britain or the Liberal Democratic Party in Japan, may govern the country over a long period of time. A country is democratic so long as elections are conducted fairly and the possibility of change exists.

Architects of democracy must determine the constitutional structure that best suits the needs of a particular country. Alternative forms of constitutional democracy include: parliamentary versus presidential forms of government, plurality versus proportional representation systems, and federal versus unitary systems.

In a parliamentary system, the prime minister is elected by the parliament and can be removed from office by a vote of no confidence from the parliament. Executive and legislative powers are fused in a parliamentary system. In a presidential system, the president is elected directly by the people and there is a formal separation of powers.

The United States came close to adopting a parliamentary system at the Constitutional Convention of 1787. The Virginia Plan proposed that the chief executive be chosen by Congress. The proposal at first was unanimously accepted, but later was rejected in favor of the electoral college, whereby electors appointed by the states elect the president. The Founders were concerned that an executive chosen by the legislature, or a collegial executive with two or more persons of equal authority, would be too weak. They wanted what Alexander Hamilton called, in the Federalist Papers, an "energetic executive."

In the twentieth century, there have been powerful prime ministers in Great Britain and Germany. An advantage of a parliamentary system is that the prime minister usually commands a majority of fellow party members in parliament. Members of the prime minister's party are expected to follow the doctrine of collective responsibility, which says that every party member must accept and, if necessary, defend the decisions of the prime minister; otherwise, the member should resign. In contrast, in a presidential system the executive and legislature may be controlled by different political parties, resulting in deadlock. Divided control can prove especially troublesome for a new or fragile democracy.

Proponents of the presidential system respond that a parliamentary system can be unstable. They cite the examples of France's Fourth Republic (1946-1958) and Germany's Weimar Republic (1919-1933). In both cases, parties found it extremely difficult to form majority coalitions. During the Fourth Republic in France, there were twenty governments and seventeen prime ministers. The French constitution of 1958 sought to minimize this instability by setting up the Fifth Republic with a powerful president, Charles de Gaulle. The prime minister who has effective control over the majority in parliament is powerful, but one who heads an unstable coalition of parties is weak.

A second element that varies among democracies is the type of electoral system. In a plurality system, the state is divided into small districts, with each district choosing a single representative. The candidate with a plurality wins. In a proportional representation (PR) system, parties obtain parliamentary representation in proportion to the votes they receive. Seats are allocated according to lists prepared by the political parties before the election. Advocates of this system believe it provides a more accurate representation of electoral opinion. Either type of electoral system may be combined with a presidential or parliamentary form of government. The United States combines presidentialism and plurality; Britain, parliamentarianism and plurality. Latin American countries often have presidential-PR systems; Western European countries, parliamentary-PR systems.

Plurality voting tends to produce a two-party system and greater governmental stability, but it offers voters fewer choices. A voter who favors a small party is often faced with the dilemma of casting his vote for a candidate who is unlikely to win, or casting it for the candidate of the large party he finds least objectionable.

Proportional representation, on the other hand, encourages the formation of small or splinter parties, which can make governments unstable. PR existed under both the

Fourth Republic in France and the Weimer Republic in Germany. Countries that use PR normally have at least four parties of some importance in the legislature. To limit the influence of small parties, Germany requires that a party win at least 5 percent of the national vote to share in the distribution of party-list seats. PR has the advantage of giving minority representation, but this may be at the expense of the ability to govern.

The 1992 British election illustrates how seats could be allocated quite differently under the two systems. The Liberal Democrats received 18 percent of the popular vote and 20 seats, compared with the Labour party, which received 34 percent and 271 seats. Because the Liberal Democrats' support was spread fairly evenly across Great Britain, they would have received 117 seats had proportional representation been used.

A third constitutional choice is whether to set up a federal or unitary form of government. In a federal system, authority is divided between the central government and state governments. Great Britain and France have unitary systems; the United States and Germany, federal systems. In a federal system, each state has its own legislature and executive, and states exercise broad powers. In Germany, these powers include control over education, local administration, law enforcement, and even radio and television stations.

Federalism is especially important for countries that have ethnic and religious divisions. A country that is a model of democracy for multiethnic societies is Switzerland. Switzerland is 70 percent German, 20 percent French, and 10 percent Italian. There are distinctive cultures in different regions, with television stations broadcasting in the regional languages. Switzerland has several important cities, including German-speaking Zurich, French-speaking Geneva, and Italian-speaking Lugano. The Swiss population is approximately evenly divided between Catholics and Protestants.

Several factors have contributed to the peace and prosperity of Switzerland. Switzerland is a federal state, divided into twenty-six powerful cantons. There is a collegial or power-sharing executive: a seven-member Federal Council, elected for four-year terms by the Federal Assembly. The Federal Council has four German-speakers, two French-speakers, and one Italian-speaker, which is proportional to the country's language groups. This arrangement is through custom, not guaranteed by law. In choosing federal councilors, religious denomination and political party affiliation are also considered. The Federal Council includes members of the four leading parties, corresponding to their strength in parliament. The Federal Council has a federal president; the position rotates annually. Each of the seven councilors directs a department, such as defense or interior. Switzerland also has seven three-star generals, who are selected in the same ratio as the Federal Council.

Other countries where power sharing has been successful are Malaysia, Belgium, Austria, The Netherlands, and Canada. Factors have been identified that make it more likely that forms of power sharing (federalism, the joint control of executive power, proportional representation, a veto power for minorities) will work in a multiethnic society. These include the absence of a majority ethnic group; ethnic groups of roughly equal size; rough economic parity among ethnic groups; fewer ethnic groups; a small national population; the existence of a common enemy; some tradition of compromise and accommodation; and ethnic groups that are geographically concentrated, making federalism a possibility for providing group autonomy. Power sharing constitutes a viable alternative to other democratic models for ethnically and religiously divided societies.

Applications

In the late twentieth century, a democratic revolution spread around the world as more countries sought to establish democratic governments. These democratic transitions raised hopes for a better and more peaceful world. In 1989, in the essay "The End of History?" Francis Fukuyama asserted that democracy had triumphed over communism and other competing ideologies. He suggested that democracy would in time become universal.

Will democracy become universal, or will the surge toward democracy be transitory? In *The Third Wave: Democratization in the Late Twentieth Century* (1991), Samuel Huntington examines the history of democracy since its emergence in America. He concluded that there have been three waves of democratization and two reverse waves since democracy first washed up on America's shore. Each successive wave has advanced further, with more countries becoming democratic.

During the first democratic wave (1828-1926), more than thirty countries became democratic. A reverse wave began when Benito Mussolini came to power in Italy in 1922. Between 1922 and 1942, reversals occurred in many new democracies. Countries succumbed to communist, fascist, and militaristic ideologies. A major factor was the Great Depression of the 1930's. By 1942, only twelve countries were democracies.

A second wave of democratization followed World War II (1943-1962), when the United States and Allied occupation promoted democracy in West Germany, Italy, Austria, Japan, and South Korea. The second reverse wave occurred from 1958 to 1975, marked by military coups in Latin America and Asia and the birth of a number of African countries. By 1975, a third of the world's democracies had reverted to authoritarian rule. Reversals occurred in Brazil, Argentina, Chile, Greece, Turkey, India, Pakistan, South Korea, the Philippines, and elsewhere. Virtually all the newly independent African countries were authoritarian. Many social scientists began to think that democracy was not applicable to developing countries.

In the mid-1970's, the third wave of democratization began in southern Europe— Portugal, Greece, and Spain. It spread throughout Latin America, as the military returned to the barracks. It moved into Asia, with India, Pakistan, Turkey, the Philippines, and South Korea restoring democracy. Finally, it spread to the communist countries of Eastern Europe. Between 1974 and 1990, some thirty countries made transitions from authoritarianism to democracy, approximately doubling the world's number of democracies.

The third wave of democratization occurred, in most cases, through negotiations, elections, and nonviolence. As authoritarian rulers lost their support and legitimacy, they negotiated with opposition leaders on arrangements for transitions to democracy.

They called elections and were often surprised when they were defeated. Democratization also usually was accompanied by low levels of violence. In countries where economic progress had produced a sizeable urban middle class demanding democracy, authoritarian rulers were reluctant to use force. Democratic opposition groups in Poland, Czechoslovakia, East Germany, South Korea, and the Philippines pursued democracy through generally peaceful demonstrations.

By the mid-1990's, Nigeria, Sudan, Algeria, Peru, and Haiti had reverted to authoritarian rule. In 1994, United States troops intervened in Haiti to restore the exiled president, Jean-Bertrand Aristide. A number of other democracies appeared to be fragile. India, for example, confronted ethnically and religiously based insurgencies.

Context

Throughout world history, the first attempts to set up democracies in countries often fail, while the second attempts often succeed. Countries with prior experience in democracy have an advantage, because the consolidation of democracy requires the development of a democratic political culture. In other words, the people's political attitudes and values must be supportive of democracy. For example, a major reason why the Weimar Republic failed is that it was a "republic without republicans." Started at a time of defeat and national humiliation, the Weimar Republic lacked the support of many Germans. The lack of appropriate civic education made the Germans especially vulnerable to Nazism.

Fortunately, the legitimacy of democracy depends not only on the performance of the government but also on processes and procedures. The legitimacy of authoritarian rulers depends almost entirely on their ability to solve the country's social and economic problems. In a democracy, however, people may reject their elected leaders without rejecting the system for electing them.

Spain in the last quarter of the twentieth century illustrates that a democracy can survive economic hardship if the country has developed a democratic political culture. Following the death of dictator Francisco Franco in 1975, unemployment increased from approximately 3 percent to more than 20 percent in the early 1980's. Yet public opinion polls showed that the Spanish people continued to support democracy as the best system of government. They were able to distinguish between support for a particular government and support for democracy as a process. In 1982, they swept Felipe Gonzalez and the Socialist Party into power. In 1993, with unemployment again more than 20 percent, Prime Minister Gonzalez lost his parliamentary majority, but he and his party were able to stay in power with the support of two smaller parties.

A second important factor that influences the consolidation of democracy is the country's level of economic development. Most wealthy countries are democratic; most poor countries are authoritarian. Democratic consolidation is more likely to occur in countries that are at the upper-middle level of economic development.

Economic development contributes to democratization for a variety of reasons. It produces a more highly educated society and attitudes, such as trust and tolerance, that are conducive to a democratic political culture. Greater economic wealth facilitates compromise and accommodation among different groups. Power sharing is more likely to work if there is a roughly equal distribution of economic wealth among ethnic groups. Furthermore, economic development usually enlarges the urban middle class. In almost every country that made the transition to democracy in the late twentieth century, the urban middle class was the main supporter of democracy.

Democracy follows, to use Samuel Huntington's phrase, "a two-step-forward, one-step-backward pattern." The consolidation of democracy is influenced by prior experience with democracy, the political institutions that are established, and the level of economic development, among other factors. Democracies that have reached the upper-middle level of economic development have a greater likelihood of consolidating, although the first attempt at democracy often fails. In a democracy, the government and opposition leaders must work together, which often requires learning from the previous experience of others.

Bibliography

Ash, Timothy Garton. *The Magic Lantern: The Revolution of '89 Witnessed in Warsaw, Budapest, Berlin, and Prague.* New York: Random House, 1990. Eyewitness account of the collapse of communism in Eastern Europe.

Barber, Benjamin, and Patrick Watson. *The Struggle for Democracy.* Boston: Little, Brown, 1988. Companion volume to an excellent, ten-part video series. Watson traveled to more than thirty countries to trace the development of democracy.

Diamond, Larry, Juan J. Linz, and Seymour Martin Lipset, eds. *Democracy in Developing Countries.* 4 vols. Boulder, Colo.: Lynne Rienner, 1988-1989. Compares the historical experiences of twenty-six developing nations in Asia, Africa, and Latin America with democratic and authoritarian rule.

Diamond, Larry, and Marc F. Plattner, eds. *The Global Resurgence of Democracy.* Baltimore: The Johns Hopkins University Press, 1993. Twenty-nine essays, first published in the *Journal of Democracy.* Some deal with the relative merits of different types of democratic systems.

Fukuyama, Francis. "The End of History?" *The National Interest,* no. 16 (Summer, 1989): 3-18. Essay that stimulated debate on whether democracy will become universal. Fukuyama argues that democracy and the free-market system have triumphed.

Huntington, Samuel P. *The Third Wave: Democratization in the Late Twentieth Century.* Norman: University of Oklahoma Press, 1991. Examines where, why, and how the resurgence of democracy occurred between 1974 and 1990.

Montville, Joseph V., ed. *Conflict and Peacemaking in Multiethnic Societies.* Lexington, Mass.: Lexington Books, 1991. Essays on ethnic conflict in Northern Ireland, Malaysia, Pakistan, India, Sri Lanka, Sudan, and Nigeria. Emphasizes power sharing as a solution to ethnic conflict.

Muravchik, Joshua. *Exporting Democracy: Fulfilling America's Destiny.* Washington, D.C.: AEI Press, 1992. Evaluates various methods used to promote democracy: military occupation, covert action, crisis diplomacy, foreign aid, overseas broadcasting and exchanges, and the National Endowment for Democracy. Argues that the United States has a special mission to promote democracy abroad.

Harry Caltagirone

Cross-References

The British Parliamentary System, p. 146; Cabinet Government, p. 184; The Canadian Parliamentary System, p. 190; Constitutional Governments, p. 432; Despotism and Tyranny, p. 527; Developed and Developing Nations, p. 533; Dictatorships, p. 546; Fascism and Nazism, p. 656; Federalism in the United States, p. 668; Government Types, p. 785; Invisible Government, p. 975; Legislative Body Types, p. 1091; Legitimacy, p. 1105; Locke's Political Philosophy, p. 1142; Multiparty Systems, p. 1235; Parliamentary Government, p. 1377; Scientific Humanism, p. 1784.

THE DEMOCRATIC PARTY

Field of study: Politics

One of the two major political parties in the United States, the Democratic Party is the oldest political party in the world and traces its earliest origins to the Antifederalists and later to the Democratic-Republican Party.

Principal terms

ANTIFEDERALIST: person who is a member of the party that opposed ratification of the new U.S. Constitution from 1787 to 1789

DEMOCRATIC CONGRESSIONAL CAMPAIGN COMMITTEE: organization of Democratic members of the House of Representatives that provides campaign funds and services to Democratic nominees for House seats

DEMOCRATIC NATIONAL CHAIRMAN: executive official elected by the Democratic National Committee who manages the Democratic national headquarters, manages party funds, and often acts as spokesman of the party

DEMOCRATIC NATIONAL COMMITTEE (DNC): permanent executive council of the Democratic Party composed of members representing all states, U.S. territories, and the District of Columbia

DEMOCRATIC-REPUBLICAN PARTY: political party represented by Thomas Jefferson and James Madison in 1793

DEMOCRATIC SENATORIAL CAMPAIGN COMMITTEE: organization of Democratic members of the Senate that provides campaign funds and services to Democratic nominees for Senate seats

STATES' RIGHTS DEMOCRATIC PARTY: minor party composed of anti-civil rights, conservative Southern Democrats; nominated Governor J. Strom Thurmond of South Carolina for president in 1948

Overview

The Democratic Party is one of the two major parties in United States government and politics. As the oldest existing political party in the world, it traces its origins to the Antifederalists who emerged in 1787, and the Democratic-Republican Party established in 1793.

American citizens eligible to vote may choose to formally affiliate with the Democratic Party when registering to vote. Most states and the District of Columbia require voters to be registered in a specific party to vote in partisan primaries. A primary is a preliminary election in which a party's candidates for public offices are nominated.

In a democracy, political parties exist to nominate candidates for public offices, attract voters, win elections, and govern by developing, enacting, and implementing public policies.

In the late twentieth century, the Democratic Party's efforts to achieve these aims, and to raise and expend the funds required for political campaigns, were conducted nationally by three party committees: the Democratic National Committee, Democratic Congressional Campaign Committee, and Democratic Senatorial Campaign Committee.

The Democratic National Committee, often known simply as the DNC, is the permanent executive council of the Democratic Party. The DNC, established in 1848, is composed of members representing all states, U.S. territories, and the District of Columbia. Its major functions are to elect the national chairman and other executive officers; determine rules for the proceedings at Democratic national conventions, especially the processes by which delegates are chosen by the states, territories, and District of Columbia; and choose the dates and locations of Democratic national conventions. The Democratic national chairman, who serves a renewable four-year term, supervises the activities of the Democratic national headquarters; communicates with state and local Democratic committees; oversees the raising and spending of DNC funds; and serves as a spokesman for the Democratic Party, especially if the president is not a Democrat.

The Democratic Congressional Campaign Committee and Democratic Senatorial Campaign Committee serve more limited and specific purposes than the DNC. They devote their efforts entirely to providing funds and campaign services to Democratic nominees for the U.S. House of Representatives and Senate. The members of each campaign committee are members of that particular chamber of Congress. The congressional and senatorial campaign committees are formally separate from the Democratic National Committee. Thus, the DNC can focus its campaign efforts on the Democratic presidential nominee, instead of the Democratic congressional nominees.

The public policies that the national Democratic Party has developed, supported, and sought to enact into law have changed throughout its long history. This has been especially obvious in the evaluation of its political philosophy as expressed by its presidential nominees and the party platforms presented at national conventions. These changes in ideology have been influenced by the emergence of major policy issues of certain eras, such as slavery and the New Deal, and alterations in the Democratic Party's coalition, that is, the collection of voters and interest groups that support this party.

Many of the Antifederalists who opposed ratification of the proposed U.S. Constitution in 1787 later joined the Democratic-Republican Party established by Thomas Jefferson and James Madison in 1793. Jefferson and Madison later became presidents as Democratic-Republicans. Also known as Jeffersonian Republicans, the Democratic-Republicans opposed a strong, dominant national government, flexible interpretation of the Constitution, creation of a national bank, and high protective tariffs on imported goods favored by the Federalist Party. The party favored a strict interpretation of the Constitution, the continuation of slavery, and strong protection of states' rights so that state and local governments, instead of the federal government, would be emphasized in domestic policy. The Democratic-Republican Party was especially supported by Southern whites of all classes, Northern laborers, and frontier settlers.

With the election of Andrew Jackson, the presidential nominee of the Democratic-Republican Party in 1828, the party became known as the Democratic Party. Like Jefferson, President Jackson emphasized the Democratic Party's ideology and policy goals as representing the interests of the "common man." Besides strengthening its appeal among Southerners and frontier settlers, the Democratic Party became attractive to the growing number of Irish immigrants in the North. Through Jackson's spoils system, many politically ambitious common men received government jobs as rewards for their work in Democratic campaigns.

The issue of slavery divided and weakened the Democratic Party shortly before and during the Civil War. After the Civil War and Reconstruction era ended, the South was a virtually one-party Democratic region. Most Southern whites perceived the party as the protector of states' rights and white supremacy over blacks. In addition to the Irish, other immigrants who lived in Northern cities were attracted to the Democratic Party through the efforts of machine bosses during the late nineteenth and early twentieth centuries. Some farmers in the West were Democrats because they opposed Republican economic policies.

Despite this variety of Democratic voters, the Republican Party, the other major party, won most presidential and congressional elections from 1860 until 1932. Woodrow Wilson, a Democrat, was elected president in 1912 and reelected in 1916. His antitrust policies against big business, bank reforms, and foreign policy favoring U.S. military action in World War I and international cooperation for peace after the war influenced the further development of the Democratic Party's ideology and policy positions.

During the 1920's, the Democratic Party was sharply divided between its Northern and Southern wings on the issue of the national prohibition of alcohol. Many Southern Democrats opposed the presidential nomination of New York governor Alfred Smith in 1928 because of Smith's Roman Catholic faith and his opposition to Prohibition. Smith was easily defeated by Republican Herbert Hoover in the 1928 presidential election.

The election of Democrat Franklin D. Roosevelt as president in 1932 changed the size, coalition, ideology, and policies of the Democratic Party. Roosevelt and the Democrat-controlled Congress enacted the New Deal policies to address the economic suffering caused by the Great Depression and to permanently reform the American economy. Instead of emphasizing states' rights and opposing greater federal power in domestic policy, the Democratic Party, through the New Deal, now supported a bigger and more active federal government in order to provide price supports to farmers, public works jobs to the unemployed, and social welfare benefits to the poor and elderly, to regulate banks and corporations more strictly, and to ensure legal rights to labor unions.

In addition to Southern whites and machine bosses, most Roman Catholics, Jews, African Americans, Hispanics, and union members were Democrats. By 1936, most voters in the United States were registered as Democrats, making the Democratic Party the majority party among voters. The party continued this majority status among voters until the late 1960's.

By the late 1930's, the more conservative Southern Democrats in Congress opposed expanding the New Deal. More generally, they opposed the liberalism of President Roosevelt and many Northern Democrats, which stressed more federal programs and spending to solve social and economic problems. Northern and Southern Democrats especially disagreed on federal civil rights' policies to protect African Americans from discrimination. Conflicts over civil rights continued within the Democratic Party during the 1950's and 1960's.

In the 1960's, Democratic presidents John F. Kennedy and Lyndon B. Johnson supported a liberal identity for the Democratic Party through their civil rights, health care, education, and antipoverty policies. By 1968, however, the Democratic Party was sharply divided over Johnson's policies in the Vietnam War. A seriously divided Democratic national convention nominated Vice President Hubert H. Humphrey for president in 1968, and Humphrey narrowly lost to Republican Richard M. Nixon.

After 1968, more conservative white Democrats left the party as party leaders tried to satisfy liberal activists and interest groups. The election of President Jimmy Carter in 1976 was the only Democratic victory in presidential elections from 1968 until the election of Bill Clinton in 1992. The variety of voters, interest groups, party leaders, and policy positions within the Democratic Party often has made it difficult for the party to unite for victory in presidential elections.

Applications

From July 12 to July 14, 1948, the Democratic Party held its national convention in Philadelphia. Many delegates at this convention either reluctantly supported or actively opposed the renomination of President Harry S Truman. Delegates and party leaders whose support was reluctant thought that Truman would probably lose because of his low public approval ratings. This attitude was especially common among machine bosses and their delegates.

Some delegates, such as those who belonged to Americans for Democratic Action, supported the nomination of General Dwight D. Eisenhower because they thought that Truman was not liberal enough. After Eisenhower firmly denied any interest in running for president in 1948, these delegates switched their support to Truman.

The most determined opponents of Truman's renomination in 1948 were Southern whites who opposed his proposed civil rights policies for blacks. They believed that if these proposals became federal laws, Southern states would no longer be able to segregate blacks and discourage them from voting by claiming states' rights.

After these Southern delegates failed to weaken the Democratic Party's civil rights platform or prevent Truman's renomination, they held a convention in Birmingham, Alabama, on July 17, 1948. This convention's delegates established the States' Rights Democratic Party and nominated Governor J. Strom Thurmond of South Carolina for president. Commonly known as the Dixiecrat party, its platform and Thurmond's speeches emphasized its members' belief that Truman's civil rights proposals were unconstitutional violations of states' rights concerning race relations and voting requirements and a betrayal of the Democratic Party's traditions.

Thurmond received the Electoral College votes of Alabama, Mississippi, South Carolina, and Louisiana. Outside of these states, most Southern whites voted for Truman despite their opposition to a strong, federal civil rights policy for African Americans. After his upset victory, Truman supported the decision of the Democratic National Committee to remove its Dixiecrat members and gave control of federal patronage jobs to Southern Democratic politicians who had remained loyal to him. In general, though, Truman tried to keep anti-civil rights Southern whites loyal to the Democratic Party while maintaining the support of blacks.

The 1948 presidential election illustrates the changes within the Democratic Party's coalition, ideology, and policy goals concerning civil rights for African Americans. After the 1930's, African Americans and their white allies gradually increased their power within the Democratic Party's coalition, while the power of their most determined Southern opponents declined. The result was the defection of Southerners, who had historically been the most loyal Democrats, into the Dixiecrat Party.

Until the 1940's, the political philosophy of the Democratic Party was to allow states to show racial bias regarding jobs, education, public places, and voting requirements. While President Franklin D. Roosevelt was careful not to offend Southern Democrats on race relations, he did order the creation of the Fair Employment Practices Committee (FEPC), a federal agency that prohibited discrimination in hiring by businesses with defense contracts. President Truman went even further: He not only supported the 1948 Democratic civil rights platform, but also ordered the desegregation of the military.

These actions by Roosevelt and Truman, and more aggressive actions later on civil rights by presidents Kennedy and Johnson, changed the Democratic Party's ideology on civil rights. By the 1960's, the Democratic Party, at least at the level of the presidency and national conventions, supported federal laws that banned racial discrimination and segregation and guaranteed voting rights for racial minorities. This significant change in the Democratic Party's ideology and policy actions on civil rights shows how a major party in the American two-party system can gradually transform itself on an issue.

Context

Like any party in a democracy, the Democratic Party can be understood in terms of its coalition, ideology, policy goals, and historical development. Developing from the Democratic-Republican Party, the party emerged during the presidency of Andrew Jackson as a body that identified itself as the party of the "common man." Many Southern whites, frontier settlers, urban laborers, and Irish immigrants were attracted to this egalitarian image, Jackson's party leadership, and the party's ideology and policy ideas that supported states' rights, minimal federal government, and broad political participation for white men, while opposing a national bank and high tariffs favored by Northern business interests. The Democratic Party, though, was divided and weakened by the Civil War and elected only two presidents from 1860 until 1932.

From 1932 until 1968, the party dominated American politics, government, and policy-making. It elected four of the five presidents who served during this period, usually had majorities in both houses of Congress, and was usually supported by most voters. As the party's coalition became larger and more diverse during the New Deal policies of President Roosevelt, its ideology and policy goals now supported more federal programs and spending to solve social and economic problems. This was especially true of the Great Society policies of President Lyndon B. Johnson.

Conflicts within the Democratic Party increased over civil rights, social welfare policies, and foreign policy, especially the Vietnam War. Within the organization of the Democratic Party, DNC members, Democratic national chairmen, and delegates to Democratic national conventions had to settle disagreements on party rules concerning presidential primaries, delegate quotas for minorities, and platform positions during the 1970's and 1980's. The increasing difficulty of uniting the Democratic Party nationally contributed to the defeats of most Democratic presidential nominees during this period. Nevertheless, throughout its history and behavior, the Democratic Party has shown an ability to adapt to political changes and remain competitive in the American two-party system.

Bibliography

Burner, David. *The Politics of Provincialism: The Democratic Party in Transition, 1918-1932*. Cambridge, Mass.: Harvard University Press, 1986. Examination of changes within the Democratic Party from the end of World War I until the election of President Franklin D. Roosevelt.

Cunningham, Noble E. *The Jeffersonian Republicans: The Formation of Party Organization, 1789-1801*. Chapel Hill: University of North Carolina Press, 1957. Study of the efforts to establish the Democratic-Republican Party, the predecessor of the Democratic Party.

Garson, Robert A. *The Democratic Party and the Politics of Sectionalism, 1941-1948*. Baton Rouge: Louisiana State University Press, 1974. Analysis of the political forces that gradually alienated conservative Southern whites from the national Democratic Party.

Lowi, Theodore J., and Benjamin Ginsberg. *Democrats Return to Power: Politics and Policy in the Clinton Era*. New York: W. W. Norton, 1994. Assessment of the 1992 election, Bill Clinton's first year as president, and these events' importance for the Democratic Party.

McCormick, Richard P. *The Second American Party System: Party Formation in the Jacksonian Era*. Chapel Hill: University of North Carolina Press, 1966. Detailed analysis of the development of the Democratic Party under President Andrew Jackson.

Parmet, Herbert S. *The Democrats: The Years After FDR*. New York: Macmillan, 1976. Comprehensive study of changes in the leadership, policies, and electoral strength of the Democratic Party from 1945 until the 1970's.

Savage, Sean J. *Roosevelt: The Party Leader, 1932-1945*. Lexington: University Press of Kentucky, 1991. Analysis of President Franklin D. Roosevelt's influence on the Democratic Party.

Sundquist, James L. *Dynamics of the Party System*. Washington, D.C.: Brookings Institution, 1973. Provides excellent historical, statistical, and behavioral evidence to explain the Democratic Party's dominance among voters and in government from 1932 until the late 1960's.

Wilson, James Q. *The Amateur Democrat*. Chicago: University of Chicago Press, 1966. Study of intraparty conflicts between machine Democrats and reform Democrats in several cities.

Sean J. Savage

Cross-References

African American Politics, p. 28; Civil Rights Protection, p. 304; Delegates, p. 501; Equality and Egalitarianism, p. 630; Liberalism, p. 1118; Political Machines and Bosses, p. 1468; Political Party Roles, p. 1499; Presidential Elections in the United States, p. 1596; The Republican Party, p. 1699; Two-Party Systems, p. 2033.

DESPOTISM AND TYRANNY

Field of study: Types of government

Despotism and tyranny are virtually synonymous terms for governments uncontrolled by law or custom. Power in such governments is typically concentrated in the hands of a single authoritarian ruler. The absence of effective law invariably leaves the rights of citizens unprotected.

Principal terms
> DEMOCRACY: system of government in which the people as a whole directly or indirectly exercise ultimate authority
> EQUALITY UNDER LAW: principle that all citizens are equal before the law
> LIBERALISM: political philosophy that advocates the fullest possible human freedom and equality (not to be confused with the modern use of the term as an opposite of conservatism)
> OLIGARCHY: system of government in which political authority is concentrated in the hands of an elite minority
> POLIS: city or political community; a loose translation of "city-state"
> REGIME: whatever government is in power
> RULE OF LAW: regime in which the law is held to be above those who occupy government offices

Overview

The terms "tyranny" and "despotism" bring to mind notorious figures such as Adolf Hitler and Joseph Stalin. Such rulers are labeled "dictators," "tyrants," or "despots," and their political reigns usually include abuses such as the suppression of dissenting opinions and mass arrests of political opponents. These regimes do not operate under the rule of law, but are instead ruled by one or more rulers; law is based on the satisfaction of their desires and preferences. The general interest of the whole is neglected in favor of the special interest of a part of society.

Tyranny and despotism, like other forms of government, have their place in the history of political philosophy. Four treatments are essential: Greek antiquity, Niccolò Machiavelli's political thought, liberal theory, and early American history. Written in Greece in the fourth century B.C.E., Plato's *Republic* is one of the earliest works of political philosophy, and includes a discussion of the tyrannical regime, as does his student Aristotle's *Politics*. In Greek thought, the notion of human virtue or excellence is of central importance. The pursuit of virtue involves using reason to understand human nature and the human soul, which is the seat of character. The question "What is virtue?" is the starting point for Greek political thought because virtue was held to be the key to happiness. Virtue is a result of a well-ordered soul, and vice is its opposite. Moving from the level of the individual to the polis or city, tyranny is the political equivalent of an ill-ordered soul: the regime where a single individual—the tyrant—rules only to satisfy his own self-interest. This is analogous to the perverted individual soul which—contrary to reason—pursues only the lower pleasures associated with the bodily appetites and does not cultivate its reasoning element. Plato argues that the worst form of rule occurs when an individual with a tyrannical soul—a soul consumed by an immoderate or "lawless" desire for pleasure—actually becomes a tyrant. In such a case the tyrant's soul's lawlessness is imposed on the polis as a whole.

Tyranny, according to Greek thought, is the opposite of the natural, virtuous regime, called "kingship" or "monarchy," in which one individual rules in the interest of the whole polis. The naturalness of the regime results from the ideas that: the polis is necessary for humans to fully develop their individual natures and attain happiness, hence the political community is natural; and that happiness is possible only if the regime educates its citizens to virtue. From this it follows that promotion of happiness is essentially a political matter and requires the direct involvement of rulers in ordering the activities of the city, including citizens' lives. This is done, first and foremost, by the making of good laws. Good rulers and laws must—above all else—look to the happiness of the polis as a whole. If the polis is the only association that can perform the function of promoting complete happiness of its members, then it follows tyranny is unnatural and corrupt, since it acts counter to this end.

As profound and influential as Greek political thought is, it is not ruthlessly realistic. In Niccolò Machiavelli's famous work *The Prince* (1513), there is the first attempt to speak openly of what princes must, not what they should, do if they are to stay in power. Unlike the Greeks, Machiavelli is unwilling to make the distinction between king and tyrant, since the Greek view is based on a belief in how rulers ought to act, not how they must act. Machiavelli goes as far as to say that "a man who wishes to profess the good in everything needs must fall amongst so many who are not good." This points to the radical nature of Machiavelli's project: a lowering of political standards, from a concern with human virtue and the reasoned approach to the best regime, to the way things are. *The Prince* contains many infamous pieces of advice for princes. For example, Machiavelli discusses with cold objectivity how to get rid of enemies, why it is better to be feared than to be loved, and why the ends justify the means. Machiavelli has become notorious; the style of statesmanship based on ruthless calculation of self-interest bears his name. For purposes of this essay, however, Machiavelli represents the starting point for modern political thought. His emphasis on self-interested individuals as the basic unit of politics, instead of the classical emphasis on the organic nature of the polis as a whole, is the beginning of modern political thought.

Without the concept of the self-interest of the individual, it seems unlikely that the liberal idea of the social contract would have developed. The social contract represents the resolution of two conflicting ideas—the sanctity of individual liberty and the necessity of government. Perhaps the most influential political philosopher in this tradition is John Locke (1632-1704), whose *Two Treatises of Government* (1690) was a primary source for political ideology for both the English Whigs of the seventeenth century and the American Founders a century later. Locke is known as the greatest exponent of liberalism, which includes a variety of political theories based on human liberty and equality. Natural equality indicates that no individual or group has a right to rule over others without their consent. For Locke, a law of nature dictates that humans ought not to harm one another, but widespread violation of natural law creates a need for government to provide security and safety. Legitimate governments are, therefore, created to enforce natural law. The elevation of consent as the basis of just government is perhaps the greatest contribution of modern political thought. Today, most people accept as self-evident the proposition that government should be based on the consent of the governed. Locke argues that this consent is given via a social contract, by which people give limited power to government in exchange for its providing them with safety and well-being. Locke argues—as did his intellectual predecessors, such as Machievelli—that fear is at the root of political life, not a desire to be virtuous. Politics comes about because life without some degree of order is subject to the constant fear of harm. From this it follows that the passions or desires are the root of politics.

For Locke, any exercise of political power—or force—beyond proper limits is tyranny and puts rulers in a state of war with the people. The primary concern of Locke—and the American Founders—was the sanctity of private property and the persistent tendency for government to appropriate citizens' wealth. This is evident in Locke's treatment of the evils of excessive taxation and the requirement that government act in a manner consistent with the trust placed in it by the people. If this trust is violated, it is the right and duty of the people to dissolve and replace government. Locke advocates, therefore, a right of revolution. This is a logical conclusion of Lockean consent theory: If the political community exists solely as a result of choice and consent, it follows that it can be dissolved through the withdrawal of that consent.

Tyranny, then, has come to mean any exercise of power without right, as opposed to a specific type of regime. Tyranny is the maintenance by force of a regime that does not have the consent of the governed.

Applications

An explicit application of the ideas of Locke and other political philosophers was made by the Founders of the U.S. government. The birth of the United States was a direct result of the evils inflicted by a tyrannical regime and the conscious effort to found a government based on liberal principles. The Declaration of Independence (1776) justifies and explains the colonies' break from England by citing "a long train of abuses and usurpations" which "evinces a design to reduce them under absolute despotism." Under such conditions, "it is their right, it is their duty, to throw off such government and to provide new guards for their future security." The second paragraph of the Declaration of Independence is a concise statement of modern liberal sensibilities concerning tyrannical government. In addition, the new science of politics utilized by the Founders includes a further extension of the concept of tyranny to include the tyranny of the majority. This notion is discussed most eloquently by James Madison in the Federalist Papers and later by Alexis de Tocqueville in *Democracy in America*. It refers to the tendency, under democratic regimes, for majority opinions and preferences to exercise a tyrannical influence over minorities. This is, in essence, a metaphorical notion of tyranny that refers to a phenomenon that is like tyranny in its effects. By nature, democratic regimes operate under majority rule. Without proper safeguards, majorities tend to usurp the rights of minorities of all sorts (not only racial or economic minorities). The U.S. Constitution, with its system of checks and balances, creates a government based on principles of averting the tyranny of the majority. It is beneficial to remember that the American republic was designed with controlling this form of tyranny in mind. Discussion of the Declaration of Independence brings up the importance of criteria for judging the legitimacy of regimes. Citizens every day are confronted with government involvement in their lives. Whether it be through the taxes they pay, participation in elections and town meetings, or simply mailing a letter, government permeates their lives. Deeply embedded in American political thought is the notion that even the best of governments will—if allowed to—deteriorate into tyranny. Believing in limited government, Americans are always faced with the problem of determining, with some degree of precision, the limits of government authority. A discussion of tyranny and despotism, at the very least, can lead to consideration of the most undesirable alternative to liberal democracy.

Context

Discussion of tyranny should take place within the broader context of political philosophy. Political philosophy is, by its very nature, a practical activity because it aims to improve political life. This separates it, to some extent, from the more speculative goals of philosophy generally. Political philosophy starts with basic questions about human life and political communities, then applies reason to better understand what should be done to improve or reform regimes. Basic questions include: What are humans like by nature? What is a good human life? That is, what is happiness? What role should the political community play in attaining happiness? Who, if anyone, has a right to rule? What form of government is best? Which is best for a particular society?

The history of political philosophy can be characterized as a process by which the answers to these questions change over time, since different opinions about what constitutes human happiness necessarily lead to differing prescriptions for government. A society that holds virtue or excellence in high esteem will likely be ruled by those who are identified as virtuous individuals (aristocracy), and a society organized around the activity of making money will probably result in a regime of moneymakers (oligarchy). A society that values freedom and equality will create a regime of equal participation of every citizen (democracy). Put somewhat differently, the problem of politics is largely reducible to the activity of balancing different—and often conflicting—claims in the name of justice. Justice, simply stated, refers to the proper ordering of social relations, such that each person is treated as he or she deserves. Proponents of the regimes mentioned above would likely cast their arguments in this form: "It is just that (the virtuous or wealthy or the equal) exercise political rule because . . ." Various justifications might follow. The tyrant too is likely to make such a claim: "I have a right to rule because . . ." Again, various justifications are possible: superior strength, courage, valor, wisdom, divine inspiration, racial purity, nationality. Furthermore, tyranny in the modern sense can be exercised by any number of people. Any part of society making a claim to rule based on some uncommon and superior attribute is a potential tyrant. This is why a political conception of justice—that all citizens should be equal under the law—is so appealing. It relies on no claim to superiority based on some exclusive attribute, common only to a few. It is based on the attribute common to all.

It is an ancient and honorable idea that regimes should be in harmony with human nature. If tyranny and despotism result from untenable conceptions of human nature, then the conclusion is that they are untenable regimes. Democratic government is itself highly problematic, but that is consonant with human nature, and makes it the best practicable regime.

Bibliography

Aristotle. *Nicomachean Ethics*. Indianapolis: Hackett, 1985. See Book 1 for his treatment of happiness and its relation to political science.

_____. *The Politics of Aristotle*. London: Oxford University Press, 1958. See Book 1 for a treatment of the nature of the political community, Book 3, chapter 4 for a treatment of regimes in general, and Book 4, chapter 8 for a discussion of tyranny.

Hamilton, Alexander, James Madison, and John Jay. *The Federalist Papers*, edited by Clinton Rossiter. New York: New American Library, 1961. Madison's Federalist No. 10 is a forceful discussion of the tyranny of majority factions and how the proposed Constitution remedies this problem.

Locke, John. *Two Treatises on Government*. Cambridge, England: Cambridge University Press, 1960. The source for much of modern liberal political thought.

Machiavelli, Niccolò. *The Prince*. Prospect Heights, Ill.: Waveland Press, 1982. This remarkable work shows Machiavelli's radical break with classical and Christian thought.

Plato. *The Republic*. New York: Basic Books, 1968. One can get a sense of Plato's understanding of tyranny from sections 571a to 580c.

Tocqueville, Alexis de. *Democracy in America*. Edited by J. P. Mayer and Max Lerner. Translated by George Lawrence. New York: Harper & Row, 1966. What may be the most insightful commentary on American political life yet written. See pages 262-276 for his treatment of the tyranny of the majority.

Matthew Westcott Smith

Cross-References

Aristotle's Political Philosophy, p. 83; Autocracy and Absolutism, p. 127; Colonialism and Anticolonialism, p. 351; Cult of Personality, p. 477; Government Powers, p. 772; Individual Versus State Rights, p. 910; Liberalism, p. 1118; Locke's Political Philosophy, p. 1142; Machiavelli's Political Philosophy, p. 1148; Monarchy in History, p. 1221; Montesquieu's Political Philosophy, p. 1228; Plato's Political Philosophy, p. 1396; Republicanism, p. 1706; Right of Revolution, p. 1744; Separation of Powers: Political Philosophy, p. 1809; The Social Contract, p. 1827; Tocqueville's Political Philosophy, p. 1981.

DEVELOPED AND DEVELOPING NATIONS

Field of study: International government and politics

Developing nations have relatively low standards of living and limited industrial development. Rapid urbanization poses a challenge for these nations. By eliminating excessive legal regulation, they can increase employment and economic growth.

Principal terms

CAPITAL FLIGHT: private capital that leaves one country for another, often by illegal means

GROSS NATIONAL PRODUCT (GNP): total value of all goods and services produced by a nation in a given year

INFORMAL SECTOR: businesses that are illegal in the sense that they lack an official license and pay no taxes

INFRASTRUCTURE: installations or facilities such as paved roads, sewers, piped water systems, and electricity supplies that provide the foundation for economic development

MARKET ECONOMY: an economic system in which businesses are free to compete; also called capitalism or free enterprise

MERCANTILISM: economic system in which the government and influential business groups restrict competition; also refers to the economic system in Europe between the fifteenth and nineteenth centuries

STRUCTURAL ADJUSTMENT LOAN: loan from the World Bank and International Monetary Fund that is conditional on policy reforms, such as currency devaluations and reductions in government expenditures, in the recipient countries

THIRD WORLD: developing nations of Africa, Asia, and Latin America; during the Cold War, "First World" and "Second World" referred to the capitalist and communist systems, respectively

WORLD BANK: international financial institution based in Washington, D.C., that lends money to developing nations for economic development projects

Overview

Economic development is a sustainable increase in a nation's standard of living. It is commonly understood to include improvements in income, material consumption, education, health and nutrition, public services, and political freedom. In *World Development Report 1993*, the World Bank divided countries into four groups according to 1991 per capita gross national product (GNP). These groups are: low-income economies (those with a per capita GNP of $635 or less), lower-middle-income economies ($636-$2,555), upper-middle-income economies ($2,556-$7,910), and high-income economies ($7,911 or more).

Countries with low-income and middle-income economies are considered to be developing nations. They are sometimes referred to as the Third World or "South." The low-income economies are concentrated in sub-Saharan Africa and in South, East, and Southeast Asia. In the early 1990's, some of the world's poorest countries were Mozambique, Ethiopia, Tanzania, Uganda, Somalia, Laos, and Bangladesh—all of which had little industry. Most low-income countries—with the major exception of India—were classified by Freedom House, a human rights organization, as not free: without free elections, a free press, freedom of association, freedom of religion, and so on. Many middle-income countries are located in Latin America, which Freedom House classified as partly free.

High-income countries included the United States, Canada, the Western European countries, Israel, Japan, Australia, New Zealand, Singapore, and several oil-rich countries in the Middle East. These countries were classified by Freedom House as free, except for Singapore and the Middle Eastern oil producers. This indicates that wealth alone is not responsible for democracy and freedom. Economic development contributes to democratization by producing a more highly educated society and attitudes that are supportive of democracy. However, political leaders, such as Lee Kwan Yew in Singapore, may lack commitment to democratic values.

The developing nations have numerous demographic (population related), economic, and social problems. Among the indicators of economic development that are related to these problems are population growth, infant mortality, life expectancy, and adult illiteracy. The characteristics of most developing nations include rapid population growth, high infant mortality, low life expectancy, illiteracy, bad roads, underfunded schools, malnutrition and disease, and inadequate health-care facilities.

The single most important trend affecting the developing nations is rapid urbanization. In 1950, 80 percent of the population of the developing nations lived in rural areas and 20 percent in urban areas. It is predicted that by the year 2020, more than half the people in the developing nations will live in urban areas. Urban population growth results from natural population increases in the cities combined with the migration of people from the countryside to the cities in search of employment.

The United Nations projects that, by the year 2000, the world will have twenty-one "megacities," each with a population greater than ten million. Eighteen of these will be in developing nations. Mexico City will have a population of approximately twenty-five million, and São Paulo approximately twenty-two million. Shanghai, Bombay, and Calcutta will have more than fifteen million. Buenos Aires, Seoul, Beijing, Rio de Janeiro, Jakarta, Tianjin, Manila, Cairo, Delhi, Lagos, Karachi, Bangkok, and Dacca will exceed ten million.

In the 1990's, a large percentage of residents in Third World cities lived in poverty: Calcutta, 60 percent; Karachi, 45 percent; and Manila, 35 percent. Urbanization was not the problem. The incidence of poverty was lower in urban areas than in rural areas, and infant mortality rates were much lower. The problem was the governmental inability to meet the needs of low-income people for employment, housing, and urban services. Sometimes the urban poor face government hostility. For example, in the mid-1970's, the government of Philippine president Ferdinand Marcos evicted over 150,000 squatters in Manila to build a convention center and fourteen hotels for a World Bank conference and the Miss World pageant. In most developing nations, the urban poor were ignored by the government. Municipal authorities collected less than half of all waste generated in large cities. About 40 percent of the urban residents had inadequate sanitation; about 25 percent lacked safe supplies of water.

Economic development depends on the productivity with which a nation's resources (labor and capital) are employed. Government policies can create an environment that is favorable to business with laws that promote economic deficiency, not disrupt it. In most developing nations, however, the government impedes business with excessive legal regulation. The small number of developing nations that have enjoyed rapid economic progress, such as East Asia's Newly Industrialized Countries (Hong Kong, Singapore, South Korea, and Taiwan), have market economies. In these countries, the governments challenge businesses to become more competitive. They shape national priorities, encourage savings or foreign borrowing to generate capital, invest in education and infrastructure, encourage new business formation, and promote exports.

In South Korea, for example, education through the secondary level is almost universal. More than one-third of high school graduates enter college. The South Korean government channels capital from foreign loans to selected industries; promotes exports through tax credits, insurance, and assistance in financing; and supports the establishment of industrial centers built around educational institutions. South Korean industry is characterized by intense domestic rivalry. There are four or more competitors, such as Hyundai, Daewoo, Samsung, and Goldstar, in every major industry. There are more than three thousand textile and apparel companies, which account for about 30 percent of South Korea's total exports. Vigorous competition among domestic industries is important because if stimulates improvement and innovation.

Applications

In the 1980's, most development economists argued that free markets are essential to economic success. In most developing nations, however, governments limited access to markets and were themselves prone to corruption. Many people lived in the informal or underground economy and were called "informals." The informal economy consists of unregistered, illegal businesses that pay no taxes. Informals may work as street vendors, drive taxis and minibuses, or work in factories. Small informal enterprises produce clothing, leather work, furniture, shoes, and housewares. In developing nations, it has been common for 30 to 60 percent of the urban residents to live in slums and squatter settlements.

A major work on the subject is *The Other Path: The Invisible Revolution in the Third World* (1989) by Peruvian economist Hernando de Soto. De Soto chose this title to challenge the ideology of Peru's communist insurgent movement, the "Shining Path." De Soto argues that poverty in Peru and other developing nations is the result of an inefficient, outdated economic system. He refers to Peru's economy as "mercantilist" and compares it with the mercantilist economies of Western Europe between the fifteenth and nineteenth centuries. Mercantilism collapsed in most of Western Europe in the late nineteenth and early twentieth centuries as countries made the transition to capitalism. In a mercantilist economy, access to the market is restricted. Competition is not for markets, but for political influence.

Between the late 1940's and the early 1990's, the government of Peru produced some twenty-seven thousand laws and regulations each year. Only 1 percent were passed by the parliament; 99 percent were produced by the executive branch. Legislation presented in the parliament was debated, and the press could inform the public. Regulations issued by government departments were not subject to public debate. Business therefore could seek favors and privileges from the bureaucracy.

To examine the obstacles to establishing industry, de Soto's Institute for Liberty and Democracy (ILD) assigned a lawyer and several college students to set up a small garment factory on the outskirts of Lima. They sought to register it in compliance with the law. It took 289 days and several bribes before they could operate the factory legally. Eleven permits were required. The cost of complying with the procedures was the equivalent of thirty-two times the minimum monthly wage, prohibitive for an average person. By comparison, it took half a day to get a comparable factory approved in Tampa, Florida.

The ILD also examined the obstacles to obtaining legal housing. For a group of low-income families to acquire vacant land on which to build, it took eighty-three months (almost seven years) to comply with the regulations. The cost of compliance was fifty-six times the minimum monthly wage for each member of the association— the person's entire income, at the minimum monthly wage, for four years and eight months.

The significance of property rights is suggested by two informal settlements on opposite sides of Lima's Rimac River. The settlements were founded about the same time by people with similar socioeconomic characteristics. In the settlement of Daniel Alcides Carrion, the people lived in shacks made of cardboard and plywood, and lacked a sewage system. Across the river in Mariscal Castilla, the people lived in three- and four-story brick houses. They had a sanitation system, sidewalks, and paved roads. Many people lived above their businesses. The value of housing in Mariscal Castilla was forty-one times greater than in Daniel Alcides Carrion. Why did one settlement prosper while the other did not? The difference was that Mariscal Castilla's mayor had worked for six years to procure land titles. With secure property rights, the residents had an incentive to invest in their property. The residents knew that they could not be evicted. In Daniel Alcides Carrion, on the other hand, the residents were still squatters. They had cars, refrigerators, and televisions, which could be moved, but did not invest in their homes.

The result of excessive legal regulation is that hundreds of millions of poor people in the developing nations live outside the law. Informal activities have made an important contribution to employment in Third World cities. Informality, however, has costs. Informals are unable to sell their property, since they do not have legal title. Informal business owners pay out between 10 and 15 percent of their gross income in bribes. While formal business owners get credit from banks, informals must pay exorbitant interest rates on the black market. Informals also cannot get insurance or enforce business contracts in courts.

Excessive government regulation results in a tremendous waste of resources in both the informal and formal sectors. Informals waste resources trying to live outside the law. For them, bribes replace taxes. In the formal sector, businesses waste money and time complying with government regulations in order to stay legal. The ILD found that the profits (and potential investment capital) of Peru's small industrial firms would be four times greater, were it not for government regulations. Administrative employees for legally established companies would save 40 percent of their total working hours.

Excessive government regulation results in an inefficient tax system. Formal business owners resent the fact that informals do not pay taxes. Tax evasion is widespread. Uncertainty or legal instability also produces the flight of capital abroad. In the 1970's and 1980's, as the living standards of the poor declined in the developing nations, wealthy people in these countries deposited billions of dollars in Western banks. According to Morgan Guaranty Trust Company, at the end of 1987, South Americans (mostly Venezuelans and Argentines) held $159 billion in assets abroad, and wealthy Mexicans held $84 billion in assets abroad. The effect of massive capital outflows is pernicious for the developing nations involved. Capital invested abroad reduces funds that are available for investment at home, thus depressing economic growth.

Context

In most Third World cities, up to 70 percent of the workforce is employed in the informal sector. Employment in the urban informal sector is growing faster than in the formal sector. One possible means of increasing economic growth and employment opportunities for the urban poor in developing nations would be to reduce the regulations that force businesses underground so that they can borrow money from banks, get insurance, and enforce contracts in court. Governments could grant squatters titles to their properties so that they can sell them or use them as collateral for loans.

Agricultural subsidies and protectionist trade policies in developed nations place developing nations at a disadvantage in global markets. In most developing nations, however, poverty is the result of the economic policies pursued by their own governments. Much of the countries' wealth is controlled by small elites who want to protect their privileged position. In an African parable, a fat man says to a thin man: "You should be ashamed of yourself. If a foreigner saw you before he saw anyone else, he would think there was a famine here." "And if he saw you next," replied the thin man, "he would know the reason for the famine."

Since they are not popularly elected, leaders in developing nations often make themselves rich at the expense of the poor. Africa has been well known for its corrupt leaders. In Zaïre, President Mobutu Sese Seko had eleven castles in France and Belgium, fifty-one Mercedes-Benz automobiles, and about $4 billion in foreign bank accounts. When the International Monetary Fund (IMF) made a structural adjustment loan conditional on Zaïre's reducing government expenditures, Mobutu dismissed seven thousand teachers from the country's primary schools. He reportedly pocketed twenty cents of every dollar that Zaïre received in development funds.

In Guatemala, the government of General Romeo Lucas in the early 1980's pocketed about $350 million of $1 billion in development loans provided for a giant hydroelectric dam, the Chixoy. To repay the loans, the government raised taxes and increased the price for electricity by 70 percent. The World Bank estimated that between 10 and 15 percent of all development funds received by Indonesia were pilfered.

The recipe for economic growth in the developing nations is a market economy, or capitalism. Developing nations with free markets, such as East Asia's Newly Industrialized Countries (NICs), underwent rapid economic growth in the last third of the twentieth century. In these countries, the government provided the tools necessary for industries to compete. The recipe for poverty is excessive government regulation and rampant corruption. To meet the challenge of rapid urbanization, the developing nations must unleash the energy of the informal sector to create small- and medium-size enterprises. The future of the developing nations will be determined primarily by their domestic economic policies.

Bibliography

Gastil, Raymond D. *Freedom in the World: Political Rights and Civil Liberties 1988-1989*. New York: Freedom House, 1989. Annual reports on the status of freedom around the world, prepared by a human rights organization.

Goldstein, Steven M. *Minidragons: Fragile Economic Miracles in the Pacific*. Boulder, Colo. Westview Press, 1991. Companion volume to a four-part video series on the Pacific Rim countries of Singapore, Taiwan, South Korea, and Hong Kong.

Hancock, Graham. *Lords of Poverty: The Power, Prestige, and Corruption of the International Aid Business*. New York: Atlantic Monthly Press, 1989. Formerly the East Africa correspondent for *The Economist*, Hancock argues that foreign aid rarely benefits the poor in developing nations. He notes that the World Bank's auditors found in 1987 that nearly 60 percent of the bank's development projects had serious shortcomings or were complete failures.

Porter, Michael E. *The Competitive Advantage of Nations*. New York: Free Press, 1990. Presents the findings of a four-year study by research teams in ten leading nations on what makes a nation's industries competitive in international markets.

Soto, Hernando de. *The Other Path: The Invisible Revolution in the Third World*. Translated June Abbott. New York: Harper & Row, 1989. Using Lima as a case study, de Soto argues that poverty in Peru and most of the developing world is the result of an absence of capitalism.

United Nations Development Programme (UNDP). *Human Development Report 1993*. New York: Oxford University Press, 1993. The annual volume emphasizes the need for developing nations to invest in their people. Uses a human development index to determine the extent to which developing nations are making progress.

World Bank. *World Development Report 1983*. Oxford, England: Oxford University Press, 1983. Essential reference on economic development, which includes numerous tables, figures, and maps, and two statistical appendixes containing data on many social and economic indicators. Published annually.

Harry Caltagirone

Cross-References

Africa: Politics and Governments, p. 21; Asia: Politics and Governments, p. 108; Capitalism, p. 197; Comparative Government, p. 384; Food Politics, p. 706; Immigration and Emigration, p. 868; Industrialization, p. 916; International Monetary Fund, p. 963; Mercantilism, p. 1173; Mexico: Politics and Government, p. 1179; National Economies, p. 1248; Nonaligned Movements, p. 1319; Underdeveloped Nations, p. 2039; Urbanization, p. 2071; The World Bank, p. 2153; World Government and Environmental Protection, p. 2167; The World Health Organization, p. 2180.

DIALECTICISM

Field of study: Political philosophy

Dialecticism is the process of resolving opposite concepts into a higher-level resolution. It has been used in political theory to analyze and predict patterns of history.

Principal terms

CONTRADICTION: seemingly incompatible ideas that may express the same thing and each of which may be necessary to understand the other

IDEALISM: in philosophy and religion, the idea that consciousness can exist outside the physical world and may even create the physical world

MATERIALISM: idea that consciousness does not exist outside the physical world, which existed before anyone thought about it

POSITIVISM: philosophy of science that argues that the universe is governed by a set of laws that can be learned by objective observation

THESIS, ANTITHESIS, AND SYNTHESIS: three phases of a process, in which an original condition creates its opposite, which leads to yet a third new state

Overview

Common understanding, especially in Western cultures, sees a world divided into separate things, such as people, rocks, trees, chairs, and wood. A dialectical perspective, however, would not see a wooden chair as a thing with clearly defined boundaries, but rather as a relationship, a system of interactions that are interconnected to other things. Looking at a wooden chair, one could see something to sit on, but one could also think of it as a piece of furniture with which to decorate a room. One could focus not on the chair but on its composition—wood. The wood, in turn, may be seen as something cut by humans, a dead building material for human manipulation, a product of nature, or as the body of a tree, which was a living being, tied into an interactive system involving water, soil, and the sun. Wood may also be seen as the remains of living cells, or a potential source of heat energy, or molecules, or atoms, or electrons and protons. From a dialectical perspective, a wooden chair—indeed almost any object—does not have a fixed definition. Rather it can be viewed in almost an unlimited number of ways, depending upon context. What something is becomes redefined all the time, depending upon how it is thought of at a given moment. To understand a wooden chair, one may be obliged to consider the entire universe.

Common sense, or even scientific forms of reasoning like positivism, accepts a number of concepts, like cause and effect, without much reflection. A dialectical view point would argue what is cause in one context is effect in another; in reality, everything is simultaneously both a cause and an effect. For example, the tree caused the wood, the carpenter the chair, the idea of a chair caused the carpenter to cause the chair, the mother caused the carpenter, and so on in multiplicity. Dialecticism resolves one of the oldest questions in political philosophy: Does the individual create society, or society the individual? They create each other, dialecticism answers. Karl Marx, the founding theorist of international socialism and the person most responsible for bringing dialecticism into political philosophy, suggested that people make history, but under the conditions that history gives them. Opposites such as cause and effect are actually interdependent; one cannot be understood without the other. Together they form a single interactive system.

In positivist logic, contradiction is to be avoided. In dialectical logic, contradiction may be the path to understanding. Dialectical thinking does not separate cause and effect, individual and society, life and death, objects and their environment, objectivity and subjectivity, observer and the thing being observed, theory and practice, quantity and quality, or facts and values. For example, everything a living system does to preserve its existence, such as eating and breathing, brings it closer to its death. Objects are part of the environment of the objects in their environment.

Positivism contrasts fact with personal feelings; the observer and the thing being observed are completely separate. Mao Tse-tung, however, using a dialectical method, noted that the only way to know what an apple tastes like is to bite it. The bitten apple becomes part of the person biting; the thing being observed becomes inseparable from the person observing. As the apple is changed in the process of being bitten, so detached study without involvement and without change is impossible. Theory can hardly exist without practice. Practice can hardly exist without theory.

Dialecticism regards all things as systems, sets of interactions whose members are opposites, clashing, contradicting each other. All things therefore are inherently unstable and forever changing. Accordingly, dialectical social theories focus upon change. Living beings are born, mature, age, and die. There are slow gradual changes of degree, and there are fundamental changes of kind. Degree and kind are another set of opposites that merge into each other. When water decreases sufficiently in temperature (degree), it becomes ice (kind). When feudalism grows increasingly urban and focused upon trade, it becomes capitalism. Georg Hegel the philosopher who first systematically developed dialecticism and from whom Marx borrowed the concept, conceived of systems as evolving through phases, which he termed thesis, antithesis, and synthesis. Systems change; they create their own oppositions. The conflict between the original (thesis) and its opposite (antithesis) is resolved through the creation of a new condition (synthesis).

A dialectical perspective fosters the examination of how things come about and how they are interconnected. It uncovers nonobvious relationships. Common sense and positivist perspectives often take the way things appear to be for granted—an economy organized around private property, most individuals having to work for someone else, nations maintaining military arsenals capable of destroying the world's population—

without asking why such conditions exist or how they came into being. Using the dialectical method, Marx proposed that private property was not something created by nature or God, but that it emerged out of particular historical conditions as a device to allow one class of people to control the lives of others. From this observation, he raised serious questions about whether private property should exist. A dialectical outlook often judges when it describes. It acknowledges in fact, the relationship between judgment and description. Facts and values seldom can be distinguished. To describe things as they are without judging is to accept things as they are, and acceptance is a value judgment. Dialecticism, at least in its Marxist version, seeks to help people understand why they live as they do and to conceive of alternatives.

There are significant differences between the ways Marx and Hegel used dialecticism. Hegel was a political conservative who admired the Prussian state. Marx clearly was a revolutionary. The dialectic, as conceived by Hegel, had mystical, perhaps religious, overtones. He looked primarily at the evolution of the idea he termed the *Zeitgeist*, or world spirit. Changes in the *Zeitgeist* lead to changes in the physical world. Hegel's was an idealist philosophy. Although Marx certainly was concerned with ideas, he believed that ideas emerge from material conditions. For him, material conditions include not only the physical world, as studied in physics, chemistry, and biology, but also the social, economic, and political conditions under which people lived. Marx was a materialist. For him, materialism required that in order to understand how people think, one must understand how they live.

In contrast to Hegelianism, Marxism is sometimes called dialectical materialism. Thinking dialectically, Marx implied that idealism and materialism, seemingly irreconcilable opposites, can merge. Although thought may be a product of material conditions, once ideas emerge they transform the material world. Virtually all physical objects that people encounter in urban settings are there because somebody designed and built them; the objects may be made out of physical matter, but they are products of human thought. People are both the products and the creators of the world in which they live. For Marx, dialectical materialism teaches that people must come to understand how the conditions under which they live have come about. Marx's methodology, however, also indicates that people need not, even that they cannot, passively accept all the conditions under which they live. According to dialectical materialism, people will use their knowledge to change the world in which they live.

Dialectics is useful primarily as a methodology, as a way of understanding and learning, and as a guide to action. Friedrich Engels, Marx's collaborator, went so far as to argue that dialectics is more than a path to understanding; it is the way the world works—not only the social world, but the natural as well. Engels based his claim on examples known to the science of his time, such as the principle that electricity and magnetism are governed by the tension between positive and negative attractions. Had he lived in the twentieth century, he might have argued that relativity and quantum mechanics offered stronger cases for his position. Quantum mechanics, for example, seriously challenges the possibility in both the theoretical and the practical arenas, of separating the observer from the thing observed. It also questions, however, whether people can know nature as it really is. Such a question undermines any exuberant claim of total understanding of any school. Dialecticism clearly offers a tool for understanding. Its own logic threatens the idea of knowing nature or society as they are in an absolute sense, independently of one's position within them.

Applications

Marxist dialecticism has had a profound effect upon world politics. It was the intellectual foundation of the governments under which perhaps a third of the world has lived at one time or another. In countries where Marxism never gained power, primarily the Western capitalist democracies, it served as a worldview among many radical social critics.

Marx used dialectic to develop a critique of capitalism. Capitalism is an economic system based upon competition. To its strongest supporters, this seems to be a point of pride. Contradictions seem, however, to be embedded in competition. Competition implies winners and losers. As capitalism evolves, more and more wealth becomes concentrated into fewer and fewer hands. Winners, once they have won, do not have to risk all their money in every game; the losers do. A capitalist dominant class emerges that is able to redefine the rules of the economy, and society in general, in their own interest. Virtually no one outside this class has the resources to compete with the class. A quantitative change in the distribution of wealth (winning and losing) leads to a qualitative change in capitalism (winners form a group). Competition becomes monopoly; democracy becomes oligarchy. The losers cannot win anymore; competition, essential to capitalism, does not exist. Therefore, capitalism has changed so much that it has ceased to exist. This is the dialectic of capitalism.

A capitalist economy is motivated by profit. Profit means gain, but in order for someone to gain, someone else must lose. Normally, capitalists extract profit by paying their workers less than the value of what the worker makes. The ordinary person is simultaneously in the contradictory roles of producer and consumer. There is also a contradiction between the interests of capitalists as individuals and capitalists as a class. Each capitalist, as an individual, tries to pay his or her workers as low a wage as possible, yet he or she depends upon the ability of other workers to buy his products. The individual capitalist needs the working class, with the exception of his or her own workers, to be well paid. Capitalists as individuals want low wages; capitalism as a system needs high wages.

This tension has lead to periodic cycles of prosperity and recession, the most serious of which was the Great Depression of the 1930's. In perfect capitalism, the market should be self-regulating, with the state playing a small economic role. In the face of the poverty generated by the Depression, the working class could not consume, and the capitalist class could not profit. To save capitalism from itself, President Franklin Roosevelt directly involved the state in the economy, initiating a number of reforms to shift wealth toward the lower classes. Capitalism as a system required that wealth be shifted away from the capitalist class. For the sake of capitalism's survival, the state abandoned the traditional minimal role capitalism assigned it. The state even became a consumer; this became even more the case with the coming of war, when the capitalists produced armaments for the state instead of goods for workers to buy. This resolution of one crisis has produced a new series of contradictions, which presumably will in turn be resolved in the cycle of thesis, antithesis, and synthesis. The U.S. government, in the years since World War II, has faced massive deficits, inflation, renewed disparity between wealth and poverty, and a military absorbing the resources needed by the civilian economy. Marx predicted that one day capitalism would confront a crisis it could not resolve and collapse under its own contradictions; something which had not happened as of the mid-1990's.

Capitalist societies, at least in the West, tend to be democratic. Democracy implies equality and capitalism, inequality—contradiction. The equality that capitalist democracies usually claim for themselves is equality of rights, or equality under law, sometimes called formal equality. Everyone is subject to the same law. If vagrancy is illegal, then rich vagrants must face the same penalty as poor ones. If the law is to protect all private property equally, dollar for dollar, then it gives far more protection to billionaires than to the homeless. Such a law reinforces inequality in the name of equality—a contradiction. For the law to create substantive equality, it would have to end extreme disparities of wealth. It would have to take from the rich and give to the poor. To do so would be to treat the rich and the poor unequally—a contradiction.

Context

Since Marx's time, dialectical materialism has posed the greatest challenge to the authority of the liberal, social contract, capitalist state. The Russian Revolution of 1917, the Chinese Revolution of 1948, and the Cold War attest its impact upon world history. Even if such events had never occurred, dialecticism would still be important because of the new perspectives it sheds upon assumptions that most people living in Western capitalist democracies accept with little reflection. Dialecticism encourages looking beneath the surface to see a reality beyond appearances. The dialectical point of view may reveal what appears to be just, proper, and natural to be unfair and artificial. Mainstream political scientists, for example, speak of "national interests," as if there is one common good in which everyone shares. The national interests may dictate going to war to protect access to oil, or reducing expenditures on education to balance government budgets. Thinking dialectically, one might wonder if such actions in the national interest really serve everyone the same way: oil companies, soldiers facing death on the battlefield, and schoolchildren.

Dialectical thinking not only challenges common beliefs about the social and natural world, but also raises questions about the very process through which people know those worlds. Positivist political scientists usually value their objectivity. Dialecticism, however, argues that it is not possible to separate fact from value. One's view of the world is a reflection of the conditions under which one lives. There may be no universal truth. The truth that a capitalist needs to downsize his labor cost may be the truth that his worker risks losing a living wage. Dialecticism suggests political scientists should not seek universal truth, but instead ask whose truth they are seeking.

To do otherwise is to seek, perhaps unintentionally, the truth of those who pay one's wages.

Bibliography

Engels, Friedrich. *The Dialectics of Nature*. New York: International Publishers, 1960. Engel's presentation of his thesis that dialectical materialism can be used to understand the natural world.

Hegel, Georg Wilhelm Friedrich. *Hegel, the Essential Writings*. Edited by Frederick G. Weiss. New York: Harper & Row, 1974. Contains enough excerpts from Hegel's writing on dialecticism for the reader to gain familiarity with Hegel's original thought.

Mao Tse-tung. *The Wisdom of Mao Tse-tung*. New York: Philosophical Library, 1968. Contains two essays that lay out Mao's reading of dialecticism.

Marx, Karl. *Selected Writings*. Edited by David McLellan. New York: Oxford University Press, 1977. Comprehensive anthology of Marx's writings.

Ollman, Bertell. *Dialectical Investigations*. London: Routledge & Kegan Paul, 1993. A comprehensive, readable introduction to Marxist dialectics.

Smith, Tony. *Dialectical Social Theory and Its Critics: From Hegel to Analytical Marxism and Postmodernism*. Albany: State University of New York Press, 1993. Presents the debate about how important dialecticism is for understanding Marx and how much Marx was influenced by Hegel.

Yale R. Magrass

Cross-References

Anarchism in Marxist Thought, p. 72; Capitalism, p. 197; The Civil Service in the United States, p. 310; Communist Parties, p. 377; Idealism, p. 855; The Left and the Right, p. 1079; Liberation Theology, p. 1124; Marxism-Leninism, p. 1155; Nietzsche's Political Philosophy, p. 1300; Plato's Political Philosophy, p. 1396; Political Economy, p. 1455; Political Philosophy, p. 1505; Positivism, p. 1557; Radicalism, p. 1661; Revolutions, p. 1738; Right of Revolution, p. 1744.

DICTATORSHIPS

Field of study: Types of government

A dictatorship is a political system in which almost all power is held by a single person or group, with few restrictions on the activities of the government. It is one of the principal types of government in the world.

Principal terms
CIVIL LIBERTIES: freedoms or rights guaranteed to all individuals by law, custom, or judicial interpretation
GOVERNMENT: all the people or institutions that administer or control the affairs of a territorial unit, such as a nation
MASS PROPAGANDA: use of television, radio, newspapers, and education to promote the interests of the government
REGIME: type or form of government
REPRESSION: use of the tools of government, including force, to prevent actions or statements contrary to the interests of the government
STATE: political system of a territory, including its rulers and institutions

Overview

Dictatorship is one of the two most common types of political organizations in the late twentieth century, the other being democracy. A dictatorship is a form of government, or a political system, in which a single leader or group possesses almost absolute power, with few effective formal or informal constraints. Political power is concentrated in the hands of the political elite, who rule with little regard for concerns or interests expressed by other groups. In a democratic system, on the other hand, significant political actors and institutions can limit and influence the actions of political elites in terms of their ability to make policy that is binding on the citizens of the nation.

The basic organizing principle of a dictatorship involves the relationship between the state and society. In a democracy, various actors, ranging from individual voters to interest groups to political parties, all have some degree of influence, and often control, over both the selection of rulers and the decisions they make. In a dictatorship, the government and policy-making are controlled by the political elite to the exclusion of all other people or groups. In extreme cases, the state dominates society completely, with power that is almost completely unchallenged.

The first, and perhaps most significant, characteristic of a dictatorship is the exclusive and arbitrary use of power. All significant political power, control of financial, social, military, and foreign policy, for example, is concentrated in the hands of the individual ruler, or a small political elite. This is possible because all restraints on the political power of the ruler(s) are loosened significantly. Constitutions either are eliminated or are created to be instruments of the rulers rather than restraints on their actions. Decisions are made based on the will or interests of the leaders.

This does not mean, however, that all other groups are eliminated. Dictators often tolerate, and sometimes even create, institutions that they do not directly control; unions, churches, legislatures, or political parties, for example. The key is that the leader is not accountable to these groups in any way. Dictators usually argue that there is no need for the trappings of democracy because they and they alone are in tune with the people, the embodiment of the people's collective hopes and desires.

Dictatorships usually are established first by force or fraud, and all are eventually maintained through the elimination or severe restriction of civil liberties such as freedom of speech, the press, and assembly. Control over politics and society is exercised through despotic methods: intimidation, mass propaganda, even terror and harsh repression.

No government, however, can completely and totally ignore its citizens. The consent of perhaps 20 to 30 percent of the population is maintained based on performance, the supplying of material goods and demands, the efficiency of decision making, and the provision of civic order, as well as appeals to nationalism, myth, ideology, religion, or other unifying factors. The Brazilian military dictatorship of the 1960's and 1970's, for example, only began to lose its legitimacy when economic growth began to slow in the mid- to late 1970's.

Dictatorial regimes have been established in a variety of ways. In some cases, charismatic individuals rise to power thanks to the force of the masses who follow and support them, sometimes through elections—which are then subsequently restricted or eliminated—and sometimes by the leadership they eventually drive out. Dictators are often brought in as a response to some danger to the existing regime. Individual citizens or members of the military often take power in response to internal problems, such as the incompetence or corruption of the existing regime, national economic problems, or social instability. Wars, both between and within nations, often have provided opportunities for people or groups to seize dictatorial powers. Internal developmental needs, such as modernization and industrialization, often bring to power dictators who contend they can more effectively and efficiently achieve these goals. Some dictatorships have been established to protect or defend the existing political or social order.

There are also many factors that contribute to the decline and fall of dictatorships. Despite the efforts of the rulers, it is virtually impossible to eliminate all opposition to the regime. Eventually, this opposition may become strong enough to form an organized force that undermines or even overthrows the dictator. Given the lack of effective institutions linking the leader to society, dictators often lose touch with the masses. If the citizens become sufficiently alienated, the dictatorship will not survive. Often dictatorships have proven to be no better at governing than the regimes they replaced, no better at maintaining economic growth, ensuring domestic tranquility, or providing strong leadership, and so they lose whatever support they had in the population.

Applications

Dictatorship, by its most general definition, is the most common form of government established since individuals began coming together in larger communities. For hundreds of years, the predominant type of dictatorship was the autocracy, a government in which the sovereign, or leader, usually a hereditary figure, held absolute power. He ruled without any restraints and considered his subjects slaves as much as citizens. Although these types of monarchies in Western Europe and the rest of the world began to fall in the twentieth century, there are still some examples. Many of the dynastic regimes of the Middle East, such as the Saudi Arabian government established by Ibn Saud, have been governed by individuals deriving their authority from divine or hereditary sources, without any significant independent representative institutions, and who have retained control over much of the wealth of the nation. Because of various customs, understandings, and traditions, these rulers have been often more limited than the autocracies of old, but they clearly have been dictatorial. In Saudi Arabia, for example, political parties remained illegal, and there was no mention of political, civil, or social rights in the Organic Law, the 1992 equivalent of a constitution.

In the twentieth century, new forms of dictatorships were born. One type, directly related to the autocracy in some ways, is the traditional dictatorship. A traditional, or conservative, dictator is committed to maintaining the prevailing societal forces, especially the class structure, in the face of new forces pressing for change. Often this type of regime is established to prevent a revolution. The conservative dictator establishes his authority by referring to history and traditions, rather than to the future and modernization, along with patriotism or nationalism, service, obedience, discipline, and order. These regimes are characterized by the emphasis on establishing a passive populace. General Francisco Franco, Spain's head of state from 1939 until his death in 1975, established a conservative regime, outlawing the leftist parties that had led the government prior to the Spanish Civil War and banning all forms of political participation.

In sharp contrast to the traditional dictatorship are the reforming dictatorships. These dictators are dedicated to transforming social structures, sometimes radically, and mobilizing the population to pursue that goal. Reforming dictatorships arise in response to the demands of new groups and new social classes who wish to replace the status quo powers, calling for land or income redistribution, and industrialization. Kemal Ataturk of Turkey was one such ruler. When he took power in 1922, Turkey was transformed from an Islamic state to a Western-style secular state, replacing Islamic law with European law codes and traditional dress with western clothes, and introducing new secular curricula in the schools.

In the years before World War II, a new type of dictatorship—totalitarianism—was established in Italy, Germany, and the Soviet Union. Totalitarianism involves a sophisticated effort to combine the centralized authority and repressive power of a dictatorship with the mass support and popular cooperation enjoyed by democracies. A totalitarian government is characterized by the extreme concentration of power in the hands of a ruler, particularly a party leader, where almost all organizations in the society are subordinate to the state. The use of censorship, mass propaganda, and indoctrination are heightened, because of the deterministic nature of the leader's ideology. The presence of a comprehensive worldview is a basic feature of this type of regime. Totalitarianism is, therefore, the most extreme form of dictatorship, where the state becomes identified completely with a single mass party, and the party with its single, charismatic leader.

In 1927, Joseph Stalin, as secretary general of the Communist Party of the Soviet Union, began the process of establishing himself as the Soviet Union's supreme leader. He quickly purged the government and party of opponents, and then of potential opponents, leading to arrests and deaths numbering in the millions. He eventually came to control all levers of political power, imposed complete ideological conformity with his own ideas as the center of political and national discourse. Such control is often referred to as the cult of personality, because the emphasis is on the individual leader rather than the party or the state.

In January, 1933, the head of the National Socialist German Workers (Nazi) Party, Adolf Hitler, became chancellor of Germany. He imposed the Nazi Party and its related organizations upon the German state, particularly the secret police. Power was quickly centralized in Hitler's hands, destroying the division of powers inherent in the federal system established by the Weimar constitution. Hitler eliminated all civil liberties, transferred all legislative power from the Reichstag (German parliament) to his government, and arrested all political opponents. Hitler eventually established a Nazi presence in all German social and economic organizations and institutions.

While Stalin and Hitler, as well as Benito Mussolini of Italy, were establishing political control, they were also engaged in extensive propaganda and agitation of the population. The dictators were featured in film and print as the father, defender, and savior of their nations and were supported by youth organizations espousing their values.

Populist dictators have been particularly common in Latin America, where they often are known as *caudillos* (men on horseback). Given the ethnic conflicts, economic underdevelopment, and internal instability of many developing nations, populist dictators are seen as liberators or saviors. They are often military men whose authority is based almost entirely upon their personality. They assert there is no need for democratic institutions because only they are capable of solving the nation's problems, through force of will, charisma, and intuition. Juan Perón of Argentina is a classic example of this type of dictator. Using his appeal to the working class, established while he was secretary of labor, Perón won election to the presidency in 1946, was reelected in 1951, and moved to establish an authoritarian government, eliminating freedom of the press and opposition in the judiciary and the universities.

Similar to the Latin American populist dictator is the founding father dictator in Africa. Many newly independent nations in Africa came under the control of the individual who led the independence party or movement. Jomo Kenyatta, head of the Kenyan African National Union, became prime minister of newly independent Kenya in 1963. In 1964, Kenya declared itself a republic, with Kenyatta as president. Kenyatta, facing criticism from rivals, moved to isolate them by eliminating their political positions, banning their parties, and eventually establishing a one-party state.

The most common type of dictatorship since World War II has been the military regime, which some two-thirds of the nations of the world have experienced at one time or another. The main characteristic of these regimes is direct military rule, where the military chain of command substitutes almost completely for the civilian organization. In some ways the army, or the military in general, becomes the government. In much of the developing world the military sees itself as the institution best qualified to act as an agent of political unification and development, and many citizens agree. Military regimes are often led by a junta, a collegial body of top military officers who make decisions on leadership and policy. From 1964 to 1985, Brazil was a typical military dictatorship. The Brazilian dictatorship was characterized by institutional takeover. All the most significant positions were filled by military officers, and succession was determined by internal military decisions. Consequently, several different individuals served as head of government, while the military as an institution continued to hold power.

Context

Dictatorship is probably the oldest form of government known to humanity. One can trace its existence back to the earliest organized political communities of ancient history in the Middle East and Greece. Political scholars from Plato and Aristotle to Machiavelli have described such regimes.

Many terms have been used to describe the various types of dictatorships and their rulers. One of the most common is authoritarian, a regime that stresses authority and acquiescence to it, as opposed to individual freedoms. Absolutism refers to a government in which the power of the rulers is unconditional. Despotism is a political system in which power is used in an arbitrary, or unlimited and domineering, manner. A tyrant is a ruler who is interested solely in his own welfare.

Although many nations made the transition from dictatorship to democracy in the late 1970's and 1980's, and many communist nations made the transition in the early 1990's, dictatorship has continued to be a predominant form of government, particularly in Africa and Asia. The factors that often lead to dictatorial government have continued to be prominent features of many nations. The military has continued to be one of the most powerful institutions in many nations, often with an interest in maintaining order and stability at all costs. Given that many nations in the developing world still suffered at the end of the twentieth century from severe economic disparities and recurring recessions, from insurgencies and political violence, and from incompetent government and corruption, it is unlikely that dictatorship will soon be removed from the political landscape of the world. Therefore, this form of government will continue to be of significance to policymakers, who will have to deal with dictators in key strategic areas such as the Middle East; to the people of these nations who struggle with the oppression and violence often associated with dictatorial regimes;

and to scholars of political science who seek to explain the existence of dictatorships and learn how they can be transformed into democracies.

Bibliography

Arendt, Hannah. *The Origins of Totalitarianism*. New York: Meridian Books, 1958. While somewhat dated, provides a valuable set of case studies in the degeneration of republican principles into totalitarianism.

Chirot, Daniel. *Modern Tyrants*. New York: Free Press, 1994. A sweeping look at the despotism of the twentieth century. Historical and normative commentary provided. Thorough bibliography.

Crassweller, Robert D. *Peron and the Enigmas of Argentina*. New York: W. W. Norton, 1987. Colorful life-and-times look at Argentine dictator Juan Perón, an example of a populist dictator. Includes a complete and up-to-date bibliography.

Jackson, Robert H., and Carl G. Rosberg. *Personal Rule in Black Africa*. Berkeley: University of California Press, 1982. Well-written volume examining major African leaders and their activities. Includes discussion of the prospects for effective constitutional rule.

Rubin, Barry. *Modern Dictators*. New York: McGraw-Hill, 1987. Effective general analysis of dictatorship in the Third World. Includes a good review of the modern theories of authoritarianism and a useful select bibliography.

Eduardo Magalhães III

Cross-References

Africa: Politics and Governments, p. 21; Aristocracy, Oligarchy, and Plutocracy, p. 78; Asia: Politics and Governments, p. 108; Autocracy and Absolutism, p. 127; Checks and Balances in U.S. Government, p. 216; Cult of Personality, p. 477; Despotism and Tyranny, p. 527; Fascism and Nazism, p. 656; General Will, p. 745; Government Types, p. 785; Irrationalism in Politics, p. 987; Military Governments, p. 1192; Oligarchy, p. 1344; One-Party Systems, p. 1350; Political Violence, p. 1539; Theocracy, p. 1968; Totalitarianism, p. 1987.

DIPLOMACY AND INTERNATIONAL NEGOTIATION

Field of study: International government and politics

Diplomacy is the process by which nations communicate with one another, either through agents or directly. It is the art of managing international relations, primarily through negotiation.

Principal terms

AMBASSADOR: highest-ranking diplomatic representative appointed by one country to represent it in one or more other countries

EMBASSY: permanent mission established by a national government in a foreign country to represent the government's interests in that country

EXTRATERRITORIALITY: one country's political rights over people in another country

FOREIGN POLICY: a nation's goals and actions in global politics

SOVEREIGN STATE: supreme authority over a specific territory, legally equal to other states under international law, and subject to no higher external authority

Overview

Diplomacy is the established method of international discourse, or the art of managing international relations, chiefly through negotiations. It is the process by which governments, acting through their official diplomats, communicate with one another. Diplomats are responsible for carrying out the day-to-day relations between countries.

Diplomacy is possible because, although nations often differ on values or national interests, they also have common interests (preventing massive destruction by war, for example) that provide the basis for negotiation. Although technology has changed diplomacy (allowing for much more direct communication between nations and leaders, for example), it remains an art rather than a science. Personal contact is still of great importance in relations between states. Diplomacy provides the norms, protocols, and practices that make the reconciliation of differences among states possible.

Diplomacy is not foreign policy. Foreign policy involves the establishment of goals and objectives, while diplomacy is simply an instrument of foreign policy, one means of reaching the objectives established by a government. In fact, diplomacy is probably the principal tool with which the broad objectives of foreign policy are implemented. One can also contrast foreign policy and diplomacy by noting that foreign policy generally involves public statements, while diplomacy is often conducted in secret, with the results made public once negotiations are concluded.

There are many practices that are often associated with diplomacy. Many definitions of diplomacy refer to the practice of sending representatives to live in other countries and to work out of an embassy, the headquarters of diplomats living abroad. Most nations have embassies or consulates in all foreign capitals, except for some poorer nations that rely on their United Nations staffs to provide their representation to other countries. The representatives are subject to strict rules of rank and protocol. The ambassador is a country's highest-ranking official in another country. Ambassadors and their diplomatic staffs are responsible for numerous tasks. They protect the rights of their nation's citizens who are travelling abroad. They provide ongoing personal contact with the leadership and economic figures of the host nation. They test reactions from these contacts to new proposals from their home government. They are responsible for the distribution of economic aid to the host country. Sometimes embassies dictate policy to dependent allies, as the United States frequently did to South Vietnam during the 1960's and 1970's.

Foreign diplomats serving abroad are granted special privileges and immunities. Many of these, based on traditions dating back for centuries, were established by the Vienna Convention on Diplomatic Relations in 1961. Diplomats (and usually their families) cannot be arrested by a host country. Their residences, papers, and effects cannot be searched or seized by the host country. Personal belongings cannot be taxed by the country in which the diplomate serves. Finally, diplomats, their families, and staffs enjoy complete freedom of worship.

Another aspect of diplomacy is the unit of government at home that is responsible for the conduct of foreign affairs. It is called variously a foreign office, state department, or ministry of external or foreign affairs. This institution, guided by political leaders, provides instruction for diplomats engaged in negotiation around the world, and collects information on the political, economic, and social situation of host countries, information which is then used by political leaders to formulate foreign policy objectives.

Finally, other aspects of diplomacy include the process of negotiating agreements. The first step in this process is the recognition by each side that they share an interest in bringing about a new arrangement on some issue of conflict, or that they can exchange goods and services they cannot obtain by themselves. There are some reasons (propaganda, for example) that can lead a nation to enter negotiations without expecting to find a common interest, but successful negotiation requires that all parties negotiate in good faith.

Once the conditions of common interest and good faith are met, the sides must agree on the time, place, agenda, and diplomatic level at which discussions will take place. These issues can be surprisingly contentious, as occurred in the Korean truce negotiations, for which the shape of the conference table was debated for years. The early stages of negotiation are characterized by each side's defining the issues and common interests, in order to ensure that all sides are operating on the same assumptions. At this stage it is assumed that each side will present its maximum terms for agreement, so that there will be room for compromise. The process then moves into the bargaining stage, at which each side uses persuasion, promises, commitments, threats, and rewards in order to resolve the differences between the maximum positions and find the point at which each side has received enough to justify what it has given up.

Originally, diplomacy only referred to official relations between states, carried out by professional diplomats. With modern advances in transportation and communications, heads of state have chosen more frequently to act as first diplomats for their nations, making summits (meetings between heads of government) an increasingly important tool of diplomacy. Related to this is the development of personal diplomacy. The secretary of state for the United States in the 1950's, John Foster Dulles, was the first major diplomat to engage in extensive personal negotiations around the world, often bypassing ambassadors and other professional diplomats. Another U.S. secretary of state, Henry Kissinger, developed the practice of shuttle diplomacy after the Yom Kippur War between Israel and the combined forces of Egypt and Syria. In shuttle diplomacy, the agent travels back and forth between foreign capitals, with camera crews in tow, in an attempt to negotiate an agreement.

The growth of international conferences and the role of the United Nations have also changed the nature of diplomatic activity. These forums involve multilateral diplomacy—negotiations conducted simultaneously within a group—rather than diplomacy between two states, as has been traditional. Consequently, negotiations are made that much more complex by the necessity of bringing numerous representatives to a consensus.

There are numerous specific tasks associated with diplomacy. Two of diplomacy's most basic tasks can be contradictory. Diplomats are charged with defending their nation's concerns and interests, but as vehicles of communication they are expected to provide fair representation to their home governments of the interests of other nations. Diplomats are also often responsible for intelligence gathering, acting as the eyes and ears of their government in another nation. When they fail at this task, as occurred in Iran in 1979, when the American diplomatic staff did not recognize how weak Iran's ruling shah was becoming, decision makers will be operating on the basis of faulty assumptions, which can lead to bad policy. Image management (or public relations) also frequently falls within the portfolio of diplomats. The Soviets, in 1983, after withdrawing from various arms control negotiations, launched a diplomatic campaign in Europe to convince North Atlantic Treaty Organization allies of the United States that the deployment of Pershing II and cruise missiles (which the organization had recently ratified) would increase the risk of nuclear war and that therefore they should not allow those weapons to be deployed. The Soviets were attempting to make the United States look aggressive while making themselves look peace-loving.

Applications

When Richard Nixon became president of the United States in 1969, one of the principal foreign policy goals of the United States was removing American troops from the conflict in Vietnam. Nixon wanted, however, to ensure that the North Vietnamese would agree to a cease-fire on America's terms. One way the administration believed it could accomplish this was by isolating Vietnam from its principal backers, the Soviet Union and China. The administration pursued a policy known as détente (lessening tension through arms control and trade agreements) with the Soviet Union. China presented a much more difficult and different problem.

After the communist defeat of the Chinese Nationalist government in 1949, the United States had refused to recognize (that is, accept as the legitimate government of the nation) the communist government of the People's Republic of China. The United States continued to recognize the Nationalist government, which had been driven onto the island of Formosa by the communists, as the only representative of the entire Chinese people. Therefore, American efforts to isolate Vietnam from the Chinese were complicated by the fact that the United States had no direct contact with the Chinese government.

China's foreign policy, on the other hand, was driven by China's deteriorating relationship with the Soviet Union. Several border clashes between Soviet and Chinese troops took place in 1969, generating some fear of war between the two communist giants. Therefore, China was looking to the United States to provide some leverage against the Soviet Union. The Chinese wanted from the United States at least a promise not to support the Soviets in a direct military confrontation with the Chinese.

As early as 1969, the United States sent out diplomatic feelers through the Poles, the French, the Romanians, and the Pakistanis that the new administration might be willing to develop a new relationship with the People's Republic of China. The United States also announced a series of unilateral initiatives designed to indicate a change in attitude: removal of the prohibition against Americans traveling to mainland China, permission for Americans to bring up to one hundred dollars worth of Chinese goods into the United States, and limited permission for grain shipments to China.

Looking to accelerate the process, in December of 1969, the American ambassador to Poland, Walter Stoessel, was instructed by the Nixon Administration to approach the Chinese chargé d'affaires (a diplomatic official temporarily taking the place of an ambassador) at the first social function they both attended and invite him to resume ambassadorial talks, which had been going on for some time but for the most part had provided only an opportunity for each side to denounce the other. After these secret talks proved to be fruitless, the United States looked to some other, more flexible, avenue for pursuing talks toward rapproachment between it and China. Henry Kissinger, the national security adviser to President Nixon, took over these negotiations. In March, 1971, the Chinese sent a signal of their desire for friendly relations by inviting a traveling American ping-pong team to visit China (this came to be known as ping-pong diplomacy). The following July, Kissinger himself went to China (after disappearing in Pakistan, claiming to be sick). During his time in China, Kissinger negotiated a visit of the United States president to China to open relations between the two countries.

The principal complicating aspect of these negotiations was the U.S. relationship with Taiwan (as the Nationalist government on the island of Formosa was known). The United States, through treaty and public statements, was committed to defending the Nationalist government against the People's Republic, and in fact had intervened militarily at various points to defend the island from Chinese shelling. Therefore, the

United States and Chinese negotiators had to develop positions and relations regarding Taiwan that would be acceptable to both parties.

The communiqué (diplomatic statement) which was publicly announced at the end of the summit meeting is a model of diplomatic solutions. After a lengthy description of the conflicting views of the two sides, it indicated that the United States recognized that both Chinese governments claimed that Taiwan was part of China, and acknowledged that the Beijing government was the sovereign power in China. It also affirmed that neither side would seek hegemony (dominance) in the Asia-Pacific region, nor would either allow any other nation to achieve dominance. Furthermore, the Chinese implicitly agreed not to exacerbate the situation in Indochina, which was one of the principal goals of the United States. This communiqué provided the roadmap for Sino-American relations for the next ten years. Despite all that was accomplished in the beginning negotiations, it still took seven years, after President Nixon's trip to China, before the United States formally recognized the People's Republic of China. This delay is revealing of the complexity of the negotiations between the two nations.

This example demonstrates several of the principles of diplomacy noted earlier. Much of the negotiation took place in secret; diplomats at various levels, from embassy staff up to the President, were involved; and numerous tactics, from symbolic gestures to threats and promises, were utilized to reach a conclusion satisfactory for both sides.

Context

Diplomacy is as ancient as politics itself. Human beings organized in groups (whether tribes, kingdoms, nations, or city-states) have always had some kind of relationship with other groups, apart from war. The ancient kings of Babylonia, Assyria, and Egypt sent envoys to negotiate with other rulers as early as 1500 B.C.E. What most scholars call modern diplomacy originated in ancient Greece. The Greek city-states employed heralds as inviolable messengers between warring states. Some time later, envoys came to be chosen for their oratorical skills in conducting diplomatic missions. A special class of envoys was also developed, who were distinct from other envoys by their resident missions.

The Italian states of the middle ages developed the system for exchange of ambassadors that is still followed. By the sixteenth century, resident embassies were common, and the system of diplomatic protocol was developing. The seventeenth century brought the organization of foreign ministries. Many of the features associated with diplomacy in the late twentieth century have their roots in much earlier eras.

Diplomacy will continue to be important because it contributes to an orderly system of international relations and remains the most common political technique for the peaceful settlement of international disputes. According to one study of serious confrontations between great powers between 1815 and the early 1990's, only 10 percent of these conflicts ended in the use of force, meaning that 90 percent of disputes were resolved through diplomacy and negotiation.

While some of the functions of diplomats have been taken over by others (higher-level officials conducting negotiations, for example), the responsibilities of the diplomat continue to be significant. The routine business of international affairs is conducted through the peaceful instrument of diplomacy. In simple numerical terms, the size and number of diplomatic missions have grown significantly in the twentieth century. The growing number of independent states resulting from the end of the Cold War augurs continued expansion of the diplomatic mission. Many of the conditions that made diplomacy necessary in the past (numerous cultures, political ideologies, and interests) are still present. Diplomacy provides the norms, protocols, and practices that make the reconciliation of differences among sovereign states possible.

Bibliography

Craig, Gordon A., and Alexander L. George. *Force and Statecraft: Diplomatic Problems of Our Time*. New York: Oxford University Press, 1983. After looking at three hundred years of history, the authors provide a broad analysis of the tools of international statecraft, including a comparison of the American and Soviet styles of negotiating.

Eban, Abba. *The New Diplomacy*. New York: Random House, 1983. Written by an experienced Israeli diplomat with considerable wit, style, and grace, this work is organized around various major issue areas in diplomacy.

Ikle, Fred Charles. *How Nations Negotiate*. New York: Harper & Row, 1964. Somewhat dated, this work provides a scholar's perspective on the art of diplomatic negotiation, relying on numerous historical examples, interviews, and clinical analysis.

Kissinger, Henry. *Diplomacy*. New York: Simon & Schuster, 1994. Remarkable survey of the craft of international relations from the early seventeenth century to the 1990's.

_____. *White House Years*. Boston: Little, Brown, 1979. With the inside perspective of one of the principal players in American diplomacy at the time, the author discusses with great detail the process of foreign policy in the United States during the late 1970's.

Schulzinger, Robert D. *American Diplomacy in the Twentieth Century*. 3d ed. New York: Oxford University Press, 1994. Examination of American foreign policy since 1898, written in an engaging, colloquial style.

Zartman, I. William, and Maureen R. Berman. *The Practical Negotiator*. New Haven, Conn.: Yale University Press, 1982. Interesting attempt to bridge the gap between social scientists who study bargaining and practitioners who do it.

Eduardo Magalhães III

Cross-References

Alliances, p. 47; Ambassadors and Embassies, p. 53; Arms Control, p. 95; Foreign Relations, p. 718; International Agreements, p. 949; International Law, p. 956; International Relations, p. 969; Realpolitik, p. 1668; Supranational Government Institutions, p. 1922; Treaties, p. 2020; United Nations, p. 2045.

DISASTER RELIEF IN THE UNITED STATES

Field of study: Functions of government

Governmental units at the local, state, and federal levels have an obligation to respond to disaster or emergency situations through an integrated emergency management system as endorsed by the Federal Emergency Management Agency (FEMA).

Principal terms
CATASTROPHIC DISASTER: event or incident that produces severe and widespread damages of such a magnitude as to need significant relief resources from outside the affected area
MITIGATION: elimination or reduction of the degree of long-term risk to human life and property from natural and technological hazards
PREPAREDNESS: actions taken in advance of an emergency to develop operational capabilities and facilitate an effective response to emergencies
RECOVERY: activity to return vital life support systems to minimum operating standards and long-term activity designed to return life to normal or improved levels
RESPONSE: actions taken immediately before, during, or directly after an emergency occurs, to save lives, minimize property damage, and enhance the effectiveness of recovery

Overview

Disasters, which can strike anywhere, at any time, with or without prior warning, are classified by origin into three major groups, including natural, technological, and civil. The major natural hazards include hurricanes, tornadoes, floods, earthquakes, landslides (avalanches), volcanic eruptions, severe winds, tsunamis, and winter storms. Natural hazards have varying characteristics but generally follow a well-understood causal sequence. The major technological hazards include chemical emergencies, transportation accidents (land, air, and sea), and nuclear accidents. These hazards have grown with the proliferation of advanced technology and are believed to pose the most important emergency management problems in developed countries because they present the greatest risks and are the most difficult to manage. Civil hazards include famine, hostile attack (war), and terrorist activities. Hazards are grouped according to whether they primarily affect people, property, or both. Financial loss and loss of life from disasters are significant. It was estimated that by the year 2000 hurricanes striking the United States mainland alone would cause $5.7 billion in damages and loss of life for 250 people. Floods were expected to cause $3.2 billion in damages and result in approximately 160 deaths.

When disaster strikes, what are the expectations and requirements for governmental units to respond? The answer depends on the level of government involved and the degree or size of the emergency management situation. In the United States, governmental units are established at the local, state, and federal, or national levels, each of which is responsible for complying with specific legislation and responding to unique jurisdictions. Depending upon the magnitude of the disaster, the emergency responses may well overlap jurisdictions.

Since the early 1980's, governmental programs at each level have been charged with responsibility for creating comprehensive emergency management programs. These programs are based upon four distinct phases, specifically, preparedness, response, recovery, and mitigation. Although the phases overlap, each has specific aims and also serves as a building block for the next phase.

The goals of emergency management are to preserve life and property and to restore normal activities and routines rapidly. A primary phase of emergency management is that of emergency preparedness. By definition, preparedness includes all actions taken in advance of potential emergencies to develop operational capabilities and facilitate effective responses in the event of actual disaster or emergency. Local officials must address issues such as ensuring the continuity of government functions, emergency communications, mutual aid agreements, and adequate resource management. Efforts must be made to ensure adequate warning systems in the event of an emergency and to provide the capability to maintain an emergency broadcast system. Communities should have facilities capable of operating as emergency operations centers (EOCs) when disasters strike. Local officials should also create emergency operating plans (EOPs) and exercise the plans or systems on a continuing basis.

Another phase of comprehensive emergency management is that of response. Response is defined as those actions taken immediately before, during, or directly after an emergency occurs. Response efforts are intended to save lives, minimize damage to property, and enhance the effectiveness of recovery from the disaster. Local officials are often assigned to man the EOCs and activate the prepared emergency plans. Emergency broadcast systems are activated and emergency information is provided to the public. If the emergency dictates, residents may be evacuated and shelters may be activated to accommodate the disaster victims. The EOC personnel will mobilize emergency resources as necessary and provide search and rescue units as required.

A third phase of comprehensive emergency management is that of recovery. By definition, recovery includes activities intended to return vital life support systems to minimum operating standards and long-term activities designed to return life to normal or improved levels after an emergency or disaster occurs. Recovery efforts are thus intended to provide both short-term and long-term relief to victims of disasters. Activities such as debris clearance, establishing disaster assistance centers to provide food and shelter, damage assessment, crisis counseling, and decontamination are immediate responses. Establishing application processes for disaster loans and grants, building temporary housing, providing unemployment assistance, aiding reconstruction, and reassessing emergency plans are all extended activities.

The fourth phase of comprehensive emergency management is that of mitigation—actions taken to eliminate or reduce long-term risks to human life and property from natural or technological hazards, and civil disorders. Mitigation efforts include such general measures as establishing building and safety codes, promoting disaster insurance, ensuring proper land use management, and conducting hazard analyses. Public officials should initiate adequate emergency management statutes and ordinances, provide risk mapping, promote public education, ensure proper monitoring and inspections, and incorporate tax incentives or disincentives for public land use.

In 1988, a federal law was amended and retitled as the Robert T. Stafford Disaster Relief and Emergency Assistance Act. It created the Federal Response Plan in order to address the consequences of any disaster or emergency situation requiring federal response assistance. The plan applies to natural disasters, such as earthquakes, hurricanes, typhoons, tornadoes, and volcanic eruptions; technological emergencies involving radiological or hazardous material releases; and other incidents. The plan describes the basic process and structures by which the federal government will mobilize resources and conduct activities to augment state and local response efforts. The plan uses a functional approach to group available federal assistance into twelve emergency support functions (ESFs), each of which is headed by a primary agency with appropriate resources and capabilities in its particular functional area. The federal assistance is provided to the affected states under the overall coordination of the federal coordinating officer, who is appointed by the director of the Federal Emergency Management Agency (FEMA). The twelve emergency support functions cover transportation, communications, public works and engineering, fire fighting, information and planning, mass care, resource support, health and medical services, urban search and rescue, hazardous materials, food supplies, and energy.

Applications

In 1987 severe rains, snowstorms, floods, tornadoes, and earthquakes led the president of the United States to sign twenty-three federal disaster declarations that ultimately provided nearly $400 million in federal disaster aid. These funds supplemented recovery efforts in fourteen states, three commonwealths, and two Pacific Ocean trust territories. In contrast, in 1988 the federal financial obligation was less than $32 million. That year severe weather, fires, and other natural phenomena led to only eleven events declared disasters by the president. Such divergence of financial obligation vividly demonstrates the volatility and unpredictability of disasters and emergency situations. Each disaster or emergency situation becomes a learning situation and helps to identify areas of adequate preparedness as well as shortcomings or weaknesses in emergency preparedness. Examples of disasters or emergency situations will help to demonstrate both the advantages of proper planning and preparedness and the problems caused by lack of planning, resources, or education and training.

In August, 1985, the largest single-state peacetime evacuation in the history of the United States was undertaken in response to the threat of "Hurricane Elena" as it approached Florida's Gulf Coast. Local officials in nineteen coastal Florida counties issued mandatory evacuation orders resulting in one million residents moving to safer areas. Pinellas County, one of the heaviest populated counties of the Tampa Bay region, evacuated over 350,000 residents; it also opened seventy shelters and housed 114,000 evacuees during a three-day period. The county suffered four deaths, more than 470 persons injured, more than 250 homes destroyed, and more than 7,700 homes damaged, and it suffered an estimated $100 million in property loss and damage. Although these figures are significant, the losses might have been even worse if local officials had not prepared for such an event. Four surrounding counties had conducted two large, full-scale regional hurricane exercises as part of their formal evacuation planning, the last exercise being completed fewer than thirty days before the hurricane struck the Florida coast.

On April 10, 1979, three tornadoes converged on Wichita Falls, Texas. Winds in excess of 200 miles per hour cut a mile-wide, eight-mile-long path of devastation and destruction. The disaster caused 46 deaths and more than 1,600 injuries; it demolished or severely damaged 6,000 homes, destroyed 80 businesses, and left more than 5,000 families homeless. One entire shopping center was devastated, two schools were wrecked, two fire stations were destroyed, and several churches and a nursing home were leveled. Again, although the statistics are significant, the losses and damages probably would have been worse if local officials had not prepared the public for such an event. During the preceding months, educational public service announcements were broadcast reminding residents of the dangers of tornadoes and what basic precautions they should take. After radio and television broadcasts and sirens issued warnings, the tornadoes knocked out both local television stations and five of the six local radio stations. Earlier the same day, another tornado about fifty miles away had caused Wichita Falls officials to activate an emergency operating center (EOC) at police headquarters. The city's disaster plan was activated about two hours before the tornadoes struck and it had been tested six days earlier in a simulated exercise. Communications from the EOC were adequate within the city area, but severely limited to the outside. Some confusion resulted between city, county, and state officials in that each had different perceptions as to which unit was the lead agency. Officials of the regulated utilities (electric, water, and gas) realized that the destruction went far beyond their emergency contingency plans. Full restoration of utilities took most of the week after the disaster. Meanwhile, the Red Cross provided emergency communications with battery-operated radio equipment and undertook damage assessment and sheltering operations. Overall, the response to the emergency situation proved good coordination across the critical resource systems controlled by emergency managers.

On July 8, 1986, in Miamisburg, Ohio, fifteen cars of a forty-four-car freight train derailed, causing a phosphorus-filled tanker to erupt in flames. Three federal agencies, eight state agencies, and numerous local organizations were involved in the five-day response effort. Coordination between state and city units was excellent; however, both a federal agency and a representative of a private firm challenged the city's authority to manage the response effort, and conflicting information was released to the public. On the second day of the incident, the burning phosphorus car erupted into flames and sent out a huge plume of smoke. Evacuation was ordered and within two hours the entire city was evacuated. On the third day, the U.S. Environmental Protection Agency (EPA) strongly objected to how city officials were managing the disaster. However, their objections were overruled and the city's recommendations were implemented with no problems. On the fourth day, local officials belatedly established an EOC in the city council chamber. Such a delay may have contributed to the problem of releasing conflicting information. The fire was finally extinguished on the fifth day and the evacuation order was lifted. No major injuries were reported.

Context

Comprehensive emergency management is the discipline and profession of applying science, technology, planning, and management to deal with extreme events, or disasters, that threaten the lives of large numbers of people, do extensive damage to property, and disrupt community life. Although little can be done to control extreme natural events such as hurricanes, earthquakes, floods, or tornadoes, improved warning, response, and mitigation efforts have done much to limit their damage. The consensus that the federal government ought to play a consistent and leading role in disaster response has gained increasing strength in the course of the twentieth century. Exactly how that role should be implemented has been less clear, however, and the numerous shifts in federal policy and practice have greatly influenced emergency management at the state and local levels. In addition, population growth and development into earthquake or flood-prone lands, the increasing production, use, and transportation of hazardous materials have all added to the magnitude and complexity of the hazards faced by communities nationwide.

Emergency planners at all levels are subject to continuing change and influences. Disaster events themselves will often dictate emergency management approaches and associated priorities. Emergency management officials must be continually aware of the four major phases of comprehensive emergency management programs, including preparedness, response, recovery, and mitigation. Requirements and resources for each phase must constantly be reviewed, revised, and prioritized.

Legislation approved at the local, state, or national levels continually affects the development of emergency management. As examples, passage of the Resource Conservation and Recovery Act of 1976 assigned the Environmental Protection Agency (EPA) with responsibility for enforcing minimum standards for the processing, storage, transfer, and disposal of hazardous wastes. Passage of the Superfund Amendments and Reauthorization Act of 1986 requires producers of hazardous materials to provide material safety data sheets to emergency planners to incorporate into local emergency planning.

The field of emergency management is fast becoming more technical and complex, requiring managers to gain professional credentials and education. Institutions of higher education are developing both undergraduate and graduate-level degree-granting programs in emergency management. Such university-based programs will complement the continuing training programs offered through FEMA's Emergency

Management Institute and through state emergency management offices.

Emergency management offices within local and state governments continue to evolve and gain greater status as the regulatory requirements and professionalism of the field increase. Emergency management offices are also adopting new technologies, such as the microcomputer programs that have been developed to maintain extensive data bases of information and provide immediate emergency response recommendations.

Public appreciation, perception, and expectations of the field of emergency management are ever increasing. Given the changing environment, technological advances, and uncertainties and unpredictability of natural disasters, the quest to ensure public safety is unending.

Bibliography

Drabek, Thomas E., and Gerard Hoetmer, eds. *Emergency Management: Principles and Practice for Local Government*. Washington, D.C.: International City Management Association, 1991. Excellent collection of writings describing principles and practices of emergency management for local government units. Describes in detail the history and foundations of emergency management. Explains phases of a comprehensive emergency program, including preparedness, response, recovery, and mitigation. Also good discussion of daily operations and legal issues facing an emergency manager and the future of the discipline. Each chapter contains an excellent bibliography.

Drabek, Thomas E., et al. *Managing Multiorganizational Emergency Responses*. Boulder: University of Colorado Institute of Behavioral Science, 1981. Monograph describing in detail search and rescue activities in disasters and major emergencies. The study describes six actual events, including a tornado over water in a Kansas state park, flash floods in Texas, tornadoes in Texas and Wyoming, a hurricane in Mississippi, and the volcanic eruption of Mount St. Helens in Washington.

The Federal Response Plan. Washington, D.C.: Federal Emergency Management Agency, 1992. Complete federal response plan as legislated by Public Law 93-288, as amended. Detailed compendium of the federal government response plan to provide assistance to states to help them deal with the consequences of significant disasters.

Mileti, Dennis S. *Natural Hazard Warning Systems in the United States: A Research Assessment*. Boulder: University of Colorado Institute of Behavioral Science, 1975. Assessment of the effectiveness of hazard warning systems throughout the United States. Examines fifteen natural hazard agents, including avalanches, coastal erosion, droughts, earthquakes, floods, frost, hail, hurricanes, landslides, lightning, tornadoes, tsunamis, urban snow, volcanoes, and wind storms.

U.S. National Committee for the Decade for Natural Disaster Reduction. *A Safer Future: Reducing the Impacts of Natural Disasters*. Washington, D.C.: National Academy Press, 1991. Survey of natural disasters that addresses such factors as hazard and risk assessment, awareness and education, mitigation, preparedness, prediction, and warning. Also provides an excellent hazard reduction checklist that applies to community emergency planning efforts.

John L. Farbo

Cross-References

City Government in the United States, p. 266; County Government, p. 458; Environmental Protection, p. 617; Fire Protection, p. 700; Food Politics, p. 706; Local Governments, p. 1136; Rural Community Government, p. 1763; State and Local Government, p. 1885; Terrorism, p. 1962; World Government and Environmental Protection, p. 2167.

EDUCATION MANAGEMENT

Field of study: Functions of government

From the earliest times, the governing bodies of communities—whether tribes, religions, or states—have had an interest in transmitting their values to the next generations. As cultures became more developed, there was an increasing need to pass on the accumulated knowledge of the wisest members. As a result of this need, education developed as a function of the governing body.

Principal terms
NORMAL SCHOOL: nineteenth century name for a teacher training school
SCHOOL BOARD: elected or appointed group of citizens who administer school districts
VOLUNTARY SCHOOL: in England, a nonpublic school, usually run by a religious group but supported by the local education authority

Overview

Education is the process by which a social group transmits the most valued aspects of its culture to the next generation. It is also the means by which a social group trains its leaders, provides a forum for the development of new ideas, and creates the conditions for adjusting to change. The earliest societies educated children through initiation rites and by the passing of skills from elders to children. Formal education developed in advanced ancient civilizations when societies became able to produce more food than they required to survive. This surplus allowed the development of a small elite class whose time was available for cultural and educational pursuits. Priests and royal officials were the repositories and transmitters of knowledge. The Fara tablets of Mesopotamia, dating from shortly after 3000 B.C.E. are temple accounts that were used as school texts. In Egypt, education began with the training of scribes and clerks. This training was extended to mathematics, astronomy, and medicine, all of which were developed and taught by priests.

In Western civilization, the Greek states provide the earliest example of educational systems designed to train ordinary citizens. Education was tightly controlled by the state in Sparta, but under the control of the home and private schools in Athens. Much of the emphasis in Sparta was on physical education, with the goal of producing warriors whose needs were subordinate to those of the state. At seven years of age, boys were sent to live in barracks. Girls remained at home, but also received physical training. Little intellectual training was given. In Athens, the prescribed training for boys included physical education, reading and writing, and music, until the age of eighteen, when military training was stressed. The aim of Athenian education was to ensure that citizens were physically, aesthetically, and intellectually developed.

Roman education at first stressed practical training for military life and citizenship, mainly through studying Roman history and memorizing the laws of the Twelve

Tables. Later, formal schooling based on the Greek model became more common, and rhetorical schools were established to train future leaders. After the fall of the Roman Empire, however, the formal education system collapsed.

A decline in Western education during the Middle Ages began to be reversed by Charlemagne's (742?-814) establishment of a palace school and his decree requiring clergy to found schools in the cathedrals and monasteries. The eleventh and twelfth centuries saw the beginning of the great universities of Europe, for example at Salerno and Bologna in Italy, at the University of Paris in France, and at Salamanca in Spain. In the sixteenth century, scientific academies devoted to the study of Greek and Roman classics were established; secondary schools shifted from the study of the seven liberal arts (arithmetic, geometry, music, astronomy, grammar, rhetoric, and dialectics) to the study of grammar and literature.

The Reformation produced a revolution not only in religion, but also in education. Martin Luther envisioned translating the Bible into German, and providing instruction in language, history, singing, and mathematics at public expense for children of both sexes and all social classes. John Calvin also promoted the concept of public education, but saw schools mainly as agents of religion. In German cities and states, elementary schools for basic subjects and religion were established by the civil authorities but controlled by the church.

The Reformation's ideals regarding public education were taken to the New England colonies. The Law of 1642 in the Massachusetts Bay Colony, for example, does not specifically mention the establishment of schools, but does dictate that "prudential men . . . take account from time to time of their parents and masters and of their children, concerning their calling and employment of their children. . . ." After 1647, every Massachusetts town with fifty or more families was required to provide an elementary school.

In the eighteenth century, nations began to establish systems of compulsory elementary education, beginning with Prussia in 1763. In 1833, elementary education was made compulsory in France, and Great Britain's Parliament awarded its first education grant, which was divided between two principal groups who provided schooling in the nation. In 1870, the Education Act in Great Britain allowed for the election of school boards and the levying of local taxes for elementary schools. School attendance was made compulsory in England and Wales in 1876. Schools run by school boards were financed by taxes; those run by voluntary societies were to be financed by subscriptions. Unlike the national boards in France and Germany, which prescribed the curriculum to be followed, England's national board, set up in 1899, only made suggestions based on recommendations of its inspectors.

By the 1830's, interest was growing in the United States in improving elementary education, in making schooling compulsory, and in providing more formal education for teachers. Horace Mann's *Seventh Annual Report* (1843), discussing the success of Prussian schools, brought Prussian ideas into the United States, influencing both teaching methods and teacher training. Opposition to replacing church authority with that of the state, and to financing schools through taxes instead of by tuition, however, was strong. In the United States, as in Great Britain, support for public schooling was driven by influential private citizens rather than government action. In the late nineteenth century, two social factors led to the increased provision of public vocational education: the need for skilled workers occasioned by the Industrial Revolution, and the vast numbers of immigrants, often illiterate, who needed training that would enable them to be self-supporting.

Applications

Developed countries generally provide a compulsory elementary education that is financed and administered by the government. The United States, France, and Great Britain typify three distinct national approaches to the provision of education: decentralized, centralized, and a cooperative mixture of national and local control. Other systems of providing education are through political parties, such as was done in the former Soviet Union, and through sectarian systems in which religious groups have control. These varied systems reflect and reinforce a nation's predominant social, political, and cultural forces.

The U.S. Constitution does not mention education; under the Tenth Amendment, therefore, the rights to education, and to administer schools, are reserved to the people or the states. Initially, the responsibility for training or educating children was left to the parents and churches. The first school laws in the United States required parents to see to their children's education. Education in the United States has as a result been seen as an extension of the home. Even before the adoption of the Constitution, however, Massachusetts, Vermont, New Hampshire, Pennsylvania, North Carolina, and Georgia had laws that made these states responsible for education. State constitutions generally mention education as a responsibility to be undertaken by the state but delegate most of the power to local communities.

The federal government has no direct control over education: Federal subsidies to schools—which typically account for only about 10 percent of a school's financing—go there through state boards of education. Education grants do not imply federal control or definition of programs or their administration, other than requiring states to comply with any federal laws associated with the grants, such as those prohibiting discrimination by race or gender. Each state has laws that require it to establish and maintain nonsectarian public schools open to all. A board of education, elected or appointed, oversees curriculum, sets policy, certifies teachers, and determines budget. The board is headed by a commissioner or superintendent, who may be appointed either by the board or the governor, or who may be popularly elected.

Public education in the United States is still considered to be controlled by parents and private individuals through the election of local school boards, or less directly, by the appointment of school boards by elected officials. In the 1980's, more than 16,200 local school districts in the United States handled the daily administration of schools. Approximately 90 percent of the nation's local school boards were elected. The district school boards and superintendents of schools are supported by professional staff. Local boards are autonomous within state guidelines. School boards are, however, agents of the states; court decisions have upheld the principle that education is a function of the state—not of any lower civil unit.

In the 1980's, approximately one-fourth of the schools in the United States, with about 12 percent of the country's students, were private; 60 percent of these were run by the Roman Catholic church. Private schools cannot receive direct government subsidies, but they are eligible for some publicly funded benefits, such as transportation, school lunches, health services, and funds for libraries and nonsectarian equipment.

The tradition of local autonomy and the pluralism of U.S. society have contributed to great diversity in curricula and in methods of teaching. There is no national curriculum, and state departments of education differ greatly in the specificity of their guidelines on curriculum. Local curricula are influenced by teachers and school administrators, public interest groups, subject specialists, professors of education, and commercial interests such as textbook publishers. Requirements for schooling, such as the ages at which schooling is compulsory, vary from state to state. Additionally, there are variations between districts in the same state on issues such as whether to have a two-tiered system of elementary and high schools, or a three-tiered system that includes junior high school.

The French system of education traditionally has been an extreme example of a centralized system in a nontotalitarian society. The French Revolution of 1789 ended the Roman Catholic church's control over education. The constitution of 1791 required free, public, universal education, which was centralized under Napoleon's rule. The Third Republic (1881-1940) made primary education not only free, but also compulsory and secular. The Third Republic also reorganized teacher training for primary and secondary levels and created new higher education diplomas. The new regime, unable to end the antagonisms and philosophical rifts between the supporters and opponents of the revolution and the republic, decided to promote nationalism (and therefore unity) in the schools by creating a highly centralized system, and using textbooks that emphasized the continuity of France since the monarchy.

In France, the smallest unit of educational administration is the *commune*, several of which are under a *département*. Two to eight *départments* are contained in each of nearly two dozen *académies*, each of which is headed by a university. Virtually the entire system of formal education is controlled by the ministry of education; a small number of university-level schools are run by other ministries, such as those of agriculture and the military. Even Catholic schools are subsidized and supervised by the national ministry. The universities and *académies* are headed by rectors appointed by the French president; *départments* are administered by appointed prefects. *Académies*, which are the administrative arm of the ministry of education, have no real power. Rectors and prefects are assisted by appointed advisory councils. *Communes*, of which there are more than thirty-six thousand, are headed by mayors, who serve as school board presidents but have little authority as such.

The minister of education is a political appointee and thus subject to change at any time. Ongoing power over education is held by civil servants. These include the inspectors general, who visit all classrooms regularly to ensure that the official curriculum is being followed, track progress, and identify and report on the schools' needs. Although the 1980's saw a tendency toward more local control of schools, the final responsibility has continued to reside with the national government. Teachers are civil servants; qualifications are national; and school programs are set nationally. One may claim that the intended goal of the structuring of the French educational system—political unity through cultural unity—has been to a large extent achieved.

In England, the development of government-provided public education has a different historical context. The English common law principle is that parents control and direct their children's education. Government intervened, however, with the Education Act of 1870, which required that children attend elementary schools, and that these schools be financed by the government. The Education Act of 1902 created a system of government-supported secondary schools and a national system of education in cooperation with local school administrations. The Education Act of 1944 established the Ministry of Education, later renamed the Department of Education and Science (DES), as the final authority for elementary and secondary education in England, and for the university system throughout Great Britain. The DES, assisted by advisory councils, sets policy in line with legislation passed by Parliament. Her Majesty's Inspectors (HMIs) are civil servants who ensure that educational legislation is complied with and that government funds have been spent appropriately. They also offer professional advice to schools, survey current practices and recent trends, and report back to the DES.

Elementary and secondary schools are administered by Local Education Authorities (LEAs), which have limited power to interpret national policies according to local need, preferences, and condition. LEAs employ teachers, build schools, and purchase books and equipment. They are appointed by elected local officials, and appoint the local education committee, which chooses a chief education officer. This education officer, who is responsible to both the national ministry and the local education committee, has little power; he or she presents proposals to the community and carries out those that are adopted. The headmaster of the school, however, has more authority to formulate and carry out internal policies than a typical school principal in the United States.

There is no national curriculum in Britain. Details of curriculum and methods of teaching are left to teachers. The examination boards for the General Certificate of Education at the end of secondary school, however, impose some standardization upon the system. LEAs not only establish and run the county (public) schools, but also finance the so-called voluntary schools, which are primarily church-run. Only about 5 percent of the schools in England are private, fee-charging schools, run by private individuals, companies, or charitable trusts.

The English system of sharing power between the national and local level, along with the combination of private and volunteer groups running the schools, has created a situation in which responsibility for education is spread throughout the country and society.

Context

In democratic states, it is generally felt that a free public school system is necessary to promote an educated and informed citizenry. On the other hand, totalitarian governments have used the educational system of the state to indoctrinate their citizens. Educational systems change in response to variations in the nation's social and political climate. The recent history of education in Germany, beginning in Prussia in the eighteenth century, is instructive. The goal of Prussian education was to train citizens to be loyal to the state, God-fearing, and self-supporting. In 1806, a new government changed this goal to one of promoting a national revival. After the revolution of 1848, German elementary school teachers were criticized for having promoted liberal ideas; normal schools thereafter were controlled closely. The Weimer Republic, the government that was in place after World War I, again changed the direction of education, providing better teacher training, severely lessening church authority over education, and giving teachers greater freedom to develop courses of study. This liberal trend, the opposite of what had gone before it, stopped with the rise of Nazism. The trend toward intellectual freedom was replaced with rigid control of education and with an emphasis on training children to be loyal to the fatherland. The entire curriculum was saturated with Hitler's racial theories, and physical training was stressed. After the end of World War II, the federal constitution adopted in 1949 made the states sovereign in primary and secondary education. Overall, German states stress developing the particular abilities and interests of individual students, and emphasize democratic values.

Bibliography

Archer, Margaret Scotford. *Social Origins of Educational Systems*. London: Sage Publications, 1979. A sociological approach to the question of how educational systems develop and change. Chapters on the emergence of state education systems.

Husen, Torsten, and T. Neville Postlewaite, eds. *The International Encyclopedia of Education Research and Studies*. Elmsford, N.Y.: Pergamon Press, 1985. More than 1,400 scholarly articles on a wide variety of educational topics. The educational systems of 160 nations are described in individual articles. A supplement to this set published in 1989 adds another 180 articles on the subject.

Postlewaite, T. Neville, ed. *The Encyclopedia of Comparative Education and National Systems of Education*. Advances in Education. Elmsford, N.Y.: Pergamon Press, 1988. Part 1 contains articles on comparative education; part 2 comprises articles describing the educational systems in 159 countries. Articles in part 2 are revised and updated, if applicable. For a student of comparative education, the one-volume format may be preferable to the ten-volume encyclopedia listed above.

Smith, William A. *Ancient Education*. New York: Philosophical Library, 1955. Traces the cultural and educational development of the ancient Mesopotamians, Egyptians, Indians, Chinese, Greeks, Romans, and Hebrews.

Irene Struthers

Cross-References

The Arts and Government, p. 101; Civic Education, p. 278; Communications Management, p. 370; Federal Mandates, p. 662; Government Agencies, p. 765; Government Powers, p. 772; Government Roles, p. 778; State and Local Government, p. 1885; Urban Governments, p. 2052.

ELECTED VERSUS APPOINTED OFFICES
IN THE UNITED STATES

Field of study: Politics

Government systems of the United States comprise both elected representatives and appointed officials. Elected offices are thought to have the greater influence over government affairs, but appointed officials often exert influence equal to or greater than their elected colleagues.

Principal terms

APPOINTED OFFICIAL: person who is appointed to carry out an agenda and execute public policy

ELECTED OFFICIAL: person who is elected to a public office by citizens who reside in a specified jurisdiction (a city, district, county, state, or nation)

NATIONAL GOVERNMENT: federal government and its three branches—presidency, Congress, and the federal courts

PUBLIC POLICY: whatever a government decides to do; usually expressed through laws passed by an elected public body, such as a city council, state legislature, or Congress

SUBNATIONAL GOVERNMENT: government below the federal level—cities, districts, counties, and states

Overview

The United States operates with government at the national level and at the subnational level. Both levels arrange for the election and appointment of public officials. In theory, the distinction between elected and appointed positions generally is that elected representatives enact laws and that appointed officials administer those laws, although variations exist. In either case, elected and appointed public officials exercise power over matters of public policy, which leads to conflict at times.

At the national level, members of Congress are elected by their respective constituencies in the fifty states. Congress consists of 435 members in the House of Representatives and 100 in the Senate. Members of Congress have power, under the first article of the U.S. Constitution, to enact laws governing the country. Congress has no power to appoint officials; the president does. The Senate, however, has the authority to approve or not approve presidential appointments for various offices.

The executive branch, or presidency, also an elective office, functions in an administrative capacity, directing the affairs of the country with the help of numerous appointed officials. The president, who derives his authority from Article 2 of the U.S. Constitution, appoints more than 4,000 individuals to executive positions in the federal government, including members of the cabinet, heads of independent agencies, and members of various boards and commissions.

The president also appoints all federal judges. The federal judiciary is composed of the U.S. Supreme Court, the courts of appeals, district courts, and some specialized courts, consisting of more than 800 justices in all. Presidential appointments to judgeships are made only when vacancies occur. The power of federal judges lies in their ability to render laws unconstitutional, to change previous judicial rulings, and to require remedies for violations of the law. Prescribing remedies has been equated by those who do not like the prescriptions to an act of legislating, something the courts do not have the authority to do, since it often involves setting specific requirements for how remedies must be implemented. Judicial requirements for desegregating school districts is a classic example.

Subnational governments also have arrangements for electing and appointing officials. The arrangements are different from the federal system's in that many executive and judicial offices are elected. For example, offices, including those of the attorney general, secretary of state, and state treasurer, are often elective at the state level. These positions do not carry legislative power but rather executive authority to carry out the responsibilities of the respective offices. These positions, when elective in their own right, are not accountable to gubernatorial direction, so they have a degree of independence. State governors appoint only about half of the major administrative posts of their state governments.

States tend to have a greater preponderance of boards and commissions than the national government. These boards function in advisory, quasi-judicial, or policy directive capacities. Advisory boards make recommendations to governors and legislators and function as forums for citizen input on issues. Their power is often limited by their abilities to persuade. Frequently, board members are appointed based on estimations of what they will decide to say after having investigated a given issue. Quasi-judicial boards work somewhat like courts, rendering decisions that have some adjudicative function. State parole boards are a good example. Finally, most gubernatorially appointed boards serve to direct policy, establishing operational procedures and oversight of state-sponsored institutions. Higher education boards exemplify this role.

State courts parallel the three levels of the national judiciary with supreme courts, appellate courts, and district courts. State judges exert powers similar to those of federal judges, but their powers apply only to state laws. Twenty-seven states elect their judges, and the remaining states use an appointive process to fill judicial vacancies.

Local systems of government, consisting of counties, cities, towns, school districts, and special-purpose districts, follow more complex patterns of operation regarding elected and appointed officials. The majority of county governments have elected officials, called "commissioners," who often play both legislative and administrative roles. Consequently, commissioners can be very influential, as they have the power both to enact and to administer laws. Some county commissions appoint executives, known as "county managers," to handle administrative duties. For the most part, counties serve as extensions of the state, providing for such services as welfare, vital statistic records keeping, revenue collection, and road maintenance. Many counties elect officials for administrative positions such as county coroner, treasurer, auditor, clerk, sheriff, and assessor. Some counties elect additional officers. All but two states, Connecticut and Rhode Island, have counties.

Judicial districts are an extension of state-level justice systems, with elected district attorneys serving as heads of these districts. This system differs from its counterpart on the federal level, in which appointed attorneys serve as chief prosecutors in federal courts. District attorneys receive their powers from states to prosecute criminals. District attorneys are politically elected, so not surprisingly they have been accused at times of taking actions for political motives, and as such, using discretionary judgment in determining law enforcement priorities.

Cities and towns are organized under various arrangements, most having either strong or weak legislative structures. At the municipal level, legislative bodies usually are called "councils." Weak councils relinquish considerable authority to strong mayors, who carry veto power over legislative acts of councils. Strong councils, on the other hand, have weak mayors chosen from among council colleagues. Under strong councils, mayors typically have no veto authority, rather only the same authority as other council members. Strong councils often appoint professional executives, or "city managers," to take care of municipal administrative duties. City managers have considerable influence; they control city budgets, appoint key city department heads, and often propose policy initiatives to councils. Although most large cities have strong mayors, a number operate under a city manager, including Phoenix, Kansas City, Oakland, and Dallas. Approximately 2,700 cities and towns in the United States are classified as council-manager governments.

Finally, special districts, including school districts, are, with some exceptions, governed by elected boards. Other than school districts, special districts are usually established to address specific needs such as water, sewers, recreation, fire protection, and health. Many district boards appoint administrators and delegate them authority, much like council-manager arrangements. Boards of special and school districts are considered legislative, but their legislative powers are restricted to matters affecting the operation of their districts.

Applications

The National Security Council (NSC) serves as adviser to the president of the United States on matters of national security. Staffed exclusively by presidential appointees, the NSC serves as a clearinghouse for national security requests and proposals coming from the different departments of the federal government. The NSC is independent of related agencies like the State Department, Defense Department, and Central Intelligence Agency (CIA), and answers only to the president.

During the presidency of Ronald Reagan, the NSC played an influential role in foreign policy matters. One particular case, known as the Iran-Contra affair, received national attention, with special focus on the exploits of NSC staff member Oliver North. North and his NSC colleagues achieved great power without having been elected—to the extent that they were exclusively in control of clandestine foreign operations in Nicaragua.

The Iran-Contra affair contains a complex, intricate web of details and players in the upper reaches of government. In brief, the story began during the first term of the Reagan Administration. A staunch cold warrior, Ronald Reagan at the start of his presidency approved the Central Intelligence Agency's covert support of the Nicaraguan Contras in their efforts to overthrow the country's Marxist Sandinista government. Congress, fearing the fighting would escalate and more deeply involve the United States, requested that the administration cease further aid to the Contras. Congress eventually enacted legislation making it illegal to aid the Contras.

In response to congressional actions, key NSC staff—in particular Oliver North—devised secret plans meant to circumvent congressional restrictions. North established secret bank accounts that were used to funnel monies to the Contras. The monies came from private sources and from secret arms sales to the government of Iran (thus the Iran-Contra connection). Eventually, the secret operations were discovered, and North, along with the other NSC staff members, stood trial for violating U.S. law against aiding the Contras.

One resulting issue is how the NSC staff was able to rise to its high level of influence. In *The Power Game* (1988), Hedrick Smith describes the factors that gave rise to the NSC's control in dictating foreign policy toward Nicaragua and Iran. According to Smith, President Reagan was a "hands-off" manager, delegating great authority to subordinates once he set a general course for them to follow. For aides, this meant the details were left to them, giving rise to the NSC's opportunity to fix its course for operations in Nicaragua.

The NSC was also the beneficiary of the typical duplication of responsibility and infighting among agencies in the federal government. State Department officials were upset by NSC National Security Advisor Bud McFarlane's solicitation of Israeli support to ship arms to Iran. From the State Department's perspective, McFarlane was engaging in diplomacy well beyond the purview of the NSC. From McFarlane's perspective, he could not get clear consensus or support from the State Department, which was at odds with the CIA, so he moved forward on his own. It was McFarlane's boldness, Smith says, that allowed the NSC to take advantage of confused, bureaucratic dynamics so prevalent at the federal level of government.

Hedrick Smith sees Oliver North's rise to power as a situation of circumstances—of his being in the right place at the right time. The CIA wanted to find a way to continue its operations in Nicaragua if Congress banned further Contra aid. North presented the opportunity for the CIA, who used him and his NSC office to create a way around a ban on aid to the Contras. When Congress finally invoked such a ban on October 14, 1984, North—already well into an independent role in the Contra affair—argued that a congressional ban did not apply to the NSC because the agency was not involved in intelligence activities.

Finally, Oliver North's ascendancy to power owes much to his personality. He understood how to manipulate the power game. Smith describes North's willingness to act when others hesitated, and his White House connection, as crucial to his success. North's position in the White House enabled him to say that he was acting in the name of the president—thereby opening the doors of power.

Context

The Framers of the U.S. Constitution engaged in ample debate over the method of establishing a representative form of elected government. One fiercely argued issue was the system of representation that would be used to represent the people of the different states. The Framers eventually reached a compromise. Each state would elect members of the House of Representatives based on population, while in the Senate each state would be allowed two members. Together these houses of Congress would enact laws. The compromise also established a system for electing a president, who would lead the country.

The U.S. Constitution says little about the appointment of federal executive officials. Article 2, section 2 states that the president "shall appoint Ambassadors, other public Ministers and Consuls, Judges of the supreme Court, and all other Officers of the United States." The first government under George Washington saw only three cabinet departments: State, Treasury, and War. With time, changing circumstances necessitated the addition of new cabinet departments and independent agencies. Consequently, the influence of the president extended through the appointment of more officials.

At the subnational level, the U.S. Constitution (Article 4, section 4) requires only that a republican, that is, elective, form of representation be practiced in the states. This freedom of organizational arrangement has made for a variety of state and local government systems.

The power of the government appointees is derived from many sources: legislation that defines the extent of appointee responsibility, delegated authority from an appointing official, individual persuasive powers of appointees, discretionary authority to determine priorities in executing laws, and finally, knowledge of the intricate processes of bureaucracy. With so much opportunity for appointees to secure and exercise power, elected officials figure only partially into the issue of responsibility and accountability in government. The issue of conflicting powers between elected and appointed officials in governmental systems is constantly being tested.

Bibliography

Dye, Thomas R. *Politics in States and Communities*. 7th ed. Englewood Cliffs, N.J.: Prentice Hall, 1991. Overview of state and local government, focusing on politics, public policies, and differences among states and local communities.

Edwards, George C., III, and Stephen J. Wayne. *Presidential Leadership: Politics and Policy Making*. 3d ed. New York: St. Martin's Press, 1994. Analysis of the workings of the White House.

Smith, Hedrick. *The Power Game: How Washington Works*. New York: Random

House, 1988. Readable analysis of the power, personality, and gamesmanship involved in the federal government.

Michael J. Garcia

Cross-References

Accountability in U.S. Government, p. 1; City Government in the United States, p. 266; Congress, p. 412; County Government, p. 458; Courts: State and Local, p. 465; Elections, p. 578; Executive Functions in U.S. Government, p. 636; Government Agencies, p. 765; Government Roles, p. 778; Legislative Body Types, p. 1091; Legislative Functions of Government, p. 1098; National Security, p. 1261; Political Ethics, p. 1461; The Presidency in the United States, p. 1590; Public Policy, p. 1633; State Government, p. 1891; Term Limits, p. 1956.

ELECTIONS

Field of study: Politics

Elections occur when members of a political unit (country, state, province, city) vote to select their government's personnel or policies.

Principal terms

INCUMBENT: elected officeholder

INITIATIVE: legislation placed on the ballot by the voters rather than by the legislature

ISSUE VOTING: votes motivated by how parties or candidates stand on political issues

PRIMARY: election held to select party nominees for a general election

PROPORTIONAL REPRESENTATION: elections in which several persons are elected to office from a district

REFERENDUM: a popular vote on a proposed change in law rather than to select an officeholder

RETROSPECTIVE VOTING: voting primarily on the performance of a candidate in office

SINGLE-MEMBER PLURALITY ELECTIONS: those in which the single person with a majority or plurality of the vote is elected from a district

TURNOUT: the proportion of those eligible who vote in an election

Overview

Elections are used throughout the world to select executive, legislative, and judicial officials, to express popular opinion on public policy, and to give governments symbolic support. In most of the world, political parties present candidates for office in elections. General elections in the United States usually pit Democratic against Republican party nominees. Those from other parties or without a party affiliation may run, but they rarely win. In most states, registered Democrats can vote only for Democrats in Democratic Party primaries, while registered Republicans can vote only for Republicans. In the United States, party nominees are usually chosen in primary elections held between March and September, and general elections are held on the first Tuesday in November.

A few states do not use primaries, instead choosing party nominees through party caucuses or conventions. In a caucus, the party's registered voters in a local precinct meet to decide which candidates to support. Since this can take hours, relatively few people participate. Those who do so usually care greatly about politics and often have more extreme views than those of the average primary voter. In party conventions, a few thousand party activists (often selected through caucuses) meet together in one place to choose a nominee. Most democratic nations use caucuses, party conventions, or similar mechanisms to select party nominees. Few use primaries.

Most nations have elections, but in many they are neither free nor fair. Incumbent governments can assure victory by outlawing opposition parties, limiting opponents' access to television and other campaign resources, intimidating opposition leaders, refusing to register opposition supporters so they cannot vote, or miscounting ballots. Such repression was practiced in all of the former communist nations as well as in many Latin American, Asian, and African nations. In the United States, party organizations in such cities as Chicago, Philadelphia, and New York once practiced vote fraud and intimidated opponents. Such behavior became rare, in part because the news media and the public are less tolerant of corruption.

American elections have become more open over time. Before the 1820's, most states allowed only property owners to vote. Women were generally denied suffrage (voting rights) until 1920. In most Southern states, African Americans were effectively denied suffrage from the 1890's to the 1960's. The Ku Klux Klan and local police threatened nonwhites who wanted to vote, and local registrars used poll taxes and other mechanisms to limit nonwhite registration. Congress and federal courts ended such practices in the 1960's.

Though such repressive practices are no longer used, electoral turnout has been lower in the modern United States than in the deeper past. In a typical modern presidential election, slightly more than half of eligible adults vote. Fewer still vote in primary elections and in state and local contests. Turnout was higher in the past because parties were better organized to encourage voting, voting registration was easier (for whites), and fraud often inflated turnout figures. In America and in most other nations, wealthier and better-educated citizens are more likely to vote.

American turnout is relatively low for a number of reasons. With divided government and federalism, America has a large number of elections for different offices on the federal, state, and local levels. Many voters find this confusing. Most countries have fewer elected offices, and thus fewer elections. In addition, American elections are usually held on a Tuesday; in many nations, elections are held over a two-day period or on weekends. In most nations registration is automatic. In the United States, would-be voters must complete paperwork at local government offices weeks or months before an election. This discourages vote fraud, but also reduces turnout.

The United States also has low turnout because there are only two main political parties—Democrats and Republicans. For most offices, single-member plurality elections are held. These elections encourage Democrat and Republican candidates to take relatively moderate positions, toward the center of the ideological spectrum, in order to appeal to as many voters as possible. Such moderation means that many Americans are not sure how the two parties differ, and thus have little reason to vote.

In contrast, most democracies use proportional representation, in which several candidates (typically three to eight) are elected to office from each electoral district. Though there are many variations of proportional representation, typically parties win elected offices from a district in accord with their percentage of the vote there. For example, if a district has five seats, and party A wins 60 percent of the vote while party B wins 40 percent, then party A would win three seats from the district and party B would win two. In proportional representation, candidates do not need majority or plurality support to be elected. Rather than moving to the ideological center to appeal to a large number of voters, parties may target their appeals to specific groups of voters, some of whom may be quite extreme. Many political parties form to appeal to different groups in the electorate. This diversity provides many choices for voters and better represents the full range of public opinion, but diversity also makes it difficult to form a coherent government since so many parties are represented in the legislature. Proportional representation also allows racist and other extremist movements to gain representation.

Although most elections are held to select officeholders, some are used to change laws. Voters in many states approve changes to the state constitution in popular referendums. In some states and localities government debts must be approved in the same fashion. Some states also have initiatives, in which voters petition to have new proposals put on the ballot in a general election, even if most elected officials are opposed. Few other nations have initiatives.

Applications

In the wake of the Persian Gulf War in 1991, Republican president George Bush reached historically unprecedented levels of popularity, with approval ratings of 90 percent in some polls. It takes more than a year to run for the presidency, so candidates were deciding whether to run for the presidency at the same time. Politicians are reluctant to challenge popular incumbents. New York governor Mario Cuomo, Tennessee senator Albert Gore, and a number of other prominent Democrats decided against challenging Bush. Lesser-known hopefuls such as Arkansas governor Bill Clinton, former Massachusetts senator Paul Tsongas, Nebraska senator Bob Kerrey, Iowa senator Tom Harkin, Virginia governor Doug Wilder, and former California governor Jerry Brown ran for the Democratic presidential nomination.

Forecasts of Bush's continued popularity proved mistaken. From early 1990 to late 1992 the national economy was in recession. The president did little to address the economy, arguing that the recession was relatively mild and would be short-lived. While perhaps true from an economic standpoint, this view was not politically popular. Conservative journalist Pat Buchanan challenged the incumbent in the Republican primaries. Buchanan won more than 30 percent of the vote in a few states and forced President Bush to embrace more conservative ideological views, which may have hurt Bush in the general election. Still, most Republicans thought Bush a good president, and considered Buchanan too conservative. Buchanan never seriously threatened the incumbent's hold on Republican fund-raising and support. Buchanan's challenge, however, diminished Bush's prestige.

Governor Bill Clinton became the Democratic front-runner by raising the most money and emphasizing moderate stands on many issues, but geographic loyalties played an important role in the early primaries and caucuses. As expected, Iowa senator Harkin won his home state caucus in early February. Then Tsongas, from

Massachusetts, won the Democratic primary in neighboring New Hampshire. Despite allegations of marital infidelity and draft-dodging, Clinton came in a respectable second place. Further, he had enough money to run a strong campaign in all parts of the country.

On March 3, 1992, Tsongas won primaries in Maryland and Utah, while Clinton won in Georgia and Brown narrowly beat Clinton in Colorado. Poor showings in these states caused Harkin and Kerrey to drop out. On March 10, Clinton swept a series of eight Southern primaries while Tsongas won only three Northeastern states and Brown was shut out. By this time Tsongas was nearly out of money and Clinton's front-runner status helped his fund-raising. Campaign contributors are more likely to give money to a likely winner than to a candidate seen as a lost cause. Tsongas was also seen by many Democrats as too conservative on economic issues. A week later, Clinton beat Tsongas in Illinois and Michigan, clinching the Democratic nomination.

Still, Clinton was not as trusted as Bush, and was behind Bush in the polls. The chemistry of the race changed when billionaire businessman H. Ross Perot entered the contest as an independent in late March. Unlike most other independent challengers in the American system of plurality elections, Perot was well known, well funded, and relatively moderate. Perot was soon in first place in some polls, and spent far more time attacking President Bush than Governor Clinton. When Perot temporarily dropped out of the race in July, his tacit endorsement and most of his support went to Clinton, who never again trailed and won a three-way race in November with a plurality of 43 percent of the vote. President Bush won 37 percent and Ross Perot, who had reentered the race, won 19 percent. Perot's was the best showing for a presidential candidate not running as a Democrat or Republican since 1912. Turnout in 1992 was unusually high, partly since voters unhappy with the Republican and Democratic candidates had a third choice in Perot.

Like most elections, the 1988 and 1992 presidential contests were decided by both retrospective and issue voting. In 1988, good economic performance under President Ronald Reagan and the perception that Democratic nominee Michael Dukakis was too liberal combined to give Vice President Bush the victory. In 1992, poor economic performance led voters to negatively evaluate President Bush, and the Clinton campaign capitalized on this. Bush claimed that Governor Clinton was too liberal to be president, but Clinton parried this by emphasizing his conservative positions on the death penalty, welfare, and other issues. The worldwide recession, which damaged President Bush's campaign, also helped lead to the defeat of incumbent governments in Canada, Japan, Greece, Sweden, and a number of other nations in the early 1990's.

The Republicans lost the presidency for the first time since 1976, but they had no net loss of seats in the Senate and gained ten seats in the House of Representatives. At one time, the majority of Americans voted a "straight ticket" of either all Republicans or all Democrats. Large numbers began voting a "split ticket" of Republicans for some offices and Democrats for others in part because the parties inspire less loyalty than before, but it is also because changes in balloting have made it easier to vote a split ticket and because television has made it easier for candidates to run campaigns independent from their parties. In addition, incumbents in Congress today have large staffs and free mailing privileges, which they use to increase their public standing. This enables them to win votes away from the opposing party, even if the opposing party has the presidency.

Context

Elections are not the only means of influencing government. Riots, guerrilla wars, and military coups can also change or influence government. Indeed, in many nations it is more common for government to change through military coups than through free elections. Nonviolent protest and appeals to other governments have had some success in democratizing South Africa, Eastern Europe, and parts of Latin America, although at great cost to the protestors, since nondemocratic regimes often react with repression.

Citizens are more likely to think a government legitimate if they have safe, nonviolent means of changing that government. Further, elected leaders seek to please the public. For this reason, governments subject to democratic elections can change to meet popular demands. Nonviolent change being possible, elected governments are more stable than dictatorships.

Interest groups can influence government through protests, public hearings, the news media, lobbying, lawsuits, and public opinion polls. Indeed, some argue that these methods are more important than elections in influencing government. More Americans vote, however, than belong to interest groups, so elections may be more democratic. In addition, interest group leaders do not always represent their members.

It is possible that in the future, voting for officeholders will be replaced by referenda on public issues, perhaps using home computer terminals. Such direct democracy would require considerable involvement on the part of citizens, perhaps more than most are willing to put forth. For this reason, elections for officeholders are likely to play a vital role in politics for a long time to come.

Bibliography

Abramson, Paul R., John H. Aldrich, and David W. Rohde. *Change and Continuity in the 1988 Elections*. Rev. ed. Washington, D.C.: Congressional Quarterly Press, 1991. Account of presidential and congressional campaigns and voting behavior in the United States.

Ehrenhalt, Alan. *The United States of Ambition: Politicians, Power, and the Pursuit of Office*. New York: Times Books, 1991. Describes the motivations of modern American politicians and how these motivations help the Democrats remain the dominant political party.

Nelson, Michael, ed. *The Elections of 1992*. Washington, D.C.: Congressional Quarterly Press, 1993. Account of the 1992 American presidential and congressional elections.

Popkin, Samuel L. *The Reasoning Voter: Communication and Persuasion in Presidential Campaigns*. Chicago: University of Chicago Press, 1991. Describes how voters make decisions.

Rae, Douglas W. *The Political Consequences of Electoral Laws.* Rev. ed. New Haven, Conn.: Yale University Press, 1971. Empirically analyzes how electoral systems affect the number and composition of political parties.

Riordon, William L. *Plunkitt of Tammany Hall.* New York: E. P. Dutton, 1963. Explains the operation of older party organizations, which often used vote fraud to maintain control of local politics.

Wolfinger, Raymond E., and Steven J. Rosenstone. *Who Votes?* New Haven, Conn.: Yale University Press, 1980. Describes turnout in the United States and other nations.

Robert Maranto

Cross-References

THE ELECTORAL COLLEGE

Field of study: Politics

The electoral college is the body that officially chooses the president and vice president of the United States. Its 538 members, called "electors," are allocated proportionately among the states.

> *Principal terms*
> ELECTOR: one of the 538 members of the electoral college
> ELECTORAL VOTE: vote that actually elects the president, as opposed to the popular vote, which selects the electors
> FAITHLESS ELECTOR: member of the electoral college who does not vote for the candidate he or she has pledged to support
> FRAMER: member of the constitutional convention that framed the U.S. Constitution in 1787
> PLURALITY: more votes but not a majority
> TWELFTH AMENDMENT: section of the United States Constitution that specifies how electors are to vote and the procedures to follow if no candidate wins a majority of the electoral vote
> TWENTY-THIRD AMENDMENT: section of the United States Constitution that gives Washington, D.C., representation in the electoral college
> UNIT RULE: rule that gives all of a state's electoral votes to the candidate that wins the most votes among that state's electors

Overview

The electoral college is one of the genuinely original ideas found in the U.S. Constitution. It resulted from the practical political difficulties faced by the Framers of the Constitution, especially regarding sectional rivalry, tensions between the large and small states, and the Framers' desire to have nonpartisan, politically independent presidents. The Constitution describes how the electoral college system works in Article 2, section 1, in the Twelfth Amendment, and in the Twenty-third Amendment. These short and simply worded passages contain all the basic information about the electoral college system.

In summary, the system works as follows. There are 538 electors for the fifty states and Washington, D.C. The number of electors that each state receives is equal to the number of senators (each state has two) and number of representatives (which depends on the state's population) it has. The 538 electors are the electoral college. The electoral college—not the people's votes—elects the president and the vice president of the United States. What the popular vote determines is who become electors. In every state before the election, political parties and independent candidates draw up lists, or slates, of people who are pledged to vote for their given candidates. In all but two states, the selection continues in the following manner. On election day, the people cast votes for candidates for president and vice president. In each state, the votes are counted and winners declared. The winning candidates then receive all of each state's electoral college positions. Thus candidates who win with 51 percent of the popular vote in a state, or even, as happens sometimes, win a three-way race with less than a majority vote, receive all of that state's electoral college votes. This is called the "unit rule," or the "winner-take-all" system. The winning candidates then place the people they previously put on their list into the electoral college, and these electors vote for their candidates. The candidates with the most electoral votes win. If an elector votes for candidates other than those he or she has pledged to vote for, he or she is called a "faithless elector." Such votes are usually cast as a form of protest and have not had any significant effect on the outcome of an election. This state-by-state system is the reason why, when presidential elections are covered in the news, the results are reported state by state.

This system of selecting presidents, despite being subjected to intense scrutiny and review at the Constitutional Convention, has not worked as intended. The Framers expected the electors to exercise independent judgment in their voting for the president and vice president. Large states would have the most electors and small states would be guaranteed a minimum of three, one for each representative and senator (although federal officials themselves could not be electors). Rivalry among the states was so intense that the Framers believed that most electoral college votes would not succeed in choosing a clear winner, which would result in the election's being settled in the House of Representatives, with each state having one vote. This compromise was intended to protect the interest of both the large and small states. Large states, benefiting from their large representation in the electoral college, would in effect nominate presidential candidates, and small states would have equal say in the final selection of the president and vice president.

It was felt that the size of the country made national campaigns impossible. The Constitution, after all, was written before trains, automobiles, modern highways, telephones, radios, televisions, or computers existed. The Framers imagined, therefore, that states, more than political parties, would choose their candidates, leading to a problem as each state tried to get its own candidates elected. The electoral college system was created in order to solve that problem. With the electoral college, the Framers thought they had achieved the executive independence and federal balance they desired.

The election of 1800 proved them wrong. Thomas Jefferson and Aaron Burr received equal numbers of electoral votes. This threw the election to the House, which, because of intense partisanship, took thirty-six ballots to select Jefferson. The political turmoil involved in selecting Jefferson led to the passage of the Twelfth Amendment. This amendment provided for a separate vote for the president and vice president by each elector. If there was no majority, the House would pick the president from the top three candidates, with each state delegation getting a single vote, and the Senate would pick the vice president from the top two candidates. This amendment, along with the original method of allocating electors, has governed presidential elections ever since.

Forty-eight states have unit rules that specify that whoever wins a plurality of the popular vote wins all of that state's electoral votes. These winner-take-all rules arose in the nineteenth century because of the evolution of national political parties, a development unforeseen by the Framers. Two states, Maine and Nebraska, have abandoned the unit rule. In these states, two electors are selected by the statewide popular vote and the remainder by the popular vote in each congressional district.

By federal law, electors vote on the second Wednesday of December in their state capitals. Each elector must cast one vote for a candidate from outside of his or her own state (which is why presidents and vice presidents are never from the same state). This rule was a consequence of intense state rivalries that existed during the period of the framing of the Constitution. The electoral votes are sealed and sent to the president of the Senate, who opens them during a joint session of Congress in January. In most elections this is a ceremonial formality. Two-hundred seventy electoral votes are necessary to win. If there is no majority, Congress votes immediately to elect a president and vice president, with each state having one vote.

Contrary to the expectations of the Framers, only two elections have been decided in the House. The first was the election of 1800 and the second was the election of 1824, when the House selected John Quincy Adams over William Crawford and Andrew Jackson, who had more electoral votes (though not a majority). It is still possible for a presidential election to be settled in the House, especially if a strong third-party or independent candidate were to run. It is also possible for a candidate to win a majority of the electoral vote without winning the popular vote. This happened in 1824 (John Quincy Adams), 1876 (Rutherford B. Hayes), and 1888 (Benjamin Harrison). There have also been a number of presidents elected with popular pluralities but without a popular majority. In the twentieth century, Woodrow Wilson was elected twice with a plurality, as were Harry Truman, John F. Kennedy, Richard M. Nixon (in 1968), and Bill Clinton.

Critics of the electoral college system describe it as undemocratic and, in the age of modern communications and transportation, no longer necessary. They also cite the danger of faithless electors; although in practice no one has bought the presidency by means of bribing electors, the theoretical possibility exists.

Three different reforms have been proposed. The most popular and simple of these is direct election. This would abolish the electoral college, repeal the Twelfth Amendment, and provide for a direct popular vote for the president. To win, a candidate would need 40 percent (some prefer 50 percent) of the popular vote. If no candidate were to win the required percentage, a second election, called a "runoff," between the top two candidates would be held, with the winner becoming president. Direct election proponents argue that this is the most simple and democratic approach. Critics fear that this would destroy the federal character of the current system, which ensures that sparsely populated states are not as prone to the domination of densely populated ones. It has also been argued that the runoff mechanism would extend an already lengthy election process and thus make elections even more costly.

A second approach is the district plan used by Maine and Nebraska. Most supporters of this plan prefer a joint session of Congress to make the final selection if no candidate receives a majority. This system would preserve the role of the states as electoral units but would make third parties and independent candidates much more viable. Proponents of this plan view this as democratic and desirable. Critics fear that this would undermine the stability of the two-party system and weaken the separation of powers by tying presidential elections to congressional districts. A variation, known as the proportional plan, is advocated by some. This would allocate electoral votes according to the proportion of popular votes in each state, rather than by districts.

A third approach is the bonus plan. This would preserve the current system but would give 102 (two for each state plus Washington, D.C.) additional electoral votes to the winner of the popular vote, thus making it impossible for a president to be elected with a minority of the popular vote, while preserving the states as units. The other features of the current system would be left unchanged. It would preserve the federal features of the electoral college and would not encourage third parties.

A more modest reform, one that does not change the system to any great extent, is aimed at the problem of faithless electors. Called the "automatic plan," it would, by constitutional amendment, eliminate the electors and automatically award each state's electoral votes to the winner of the popular vote within that state. The other features of the system would remain intact. Sixteen states and the District of Columbia already require electors to automatically cast their votes, but these laws are probably unenforceable, even though the Supreme Court ruled in *Ray v. Blair*, 343 U.S. 214 (1952), that electors may be required to pledge themselves to a particular candidate. It is simply not clear how electors can be compelled to honor such a pledge, especially given the theoretical independence the Framers expected of them.

Defenders of the current system point out that each of the suggested reforms would create new problems. For example, the reforms might weaken the stabilizing influence of a two-party system, making it more difficult to govern, by ending the tendency toward decisive electoral vote majorities that the current system encourages. For example, John F. Kennedy won by a tiny margin of 118,263 popular votes in 1960 out of over 68 million votes cast. He received 303 electoral votes, however, a decisive majority. Some say this practice, the unit rule, increases the legitimacy of the outcome, which makes it easier to govern. All reform plans except the bonus plan propose abolishing the unit rule, which some fear would weaken the leverage that minority interests have in close state races to affect the outcome. Many defenders simply think that the problems of the current system are not severe enough to warrant the risks associated with any new approach.

Applications

The electoral college has a profound effect on presidential politics. Presidential elections are not decided by the popular vote but rather by the electoral vote, so candidates must concentrate their campaign efforts in the states with the most electoral votes. Simply put, presidential campaign managers understand that the vote of one Wyoming resident affects three electoral votes, while a single Californian's vote influences fifty-four, nearly a fifth of the total needed to win. While no candidate can afford to ignore the states with small numbers of electoral votes, the unit rule forces candidates to concentrate their efforts in the larger states. Thus the larger states and, more important, the large interest groups within them, become the focus of presidential platforms, campaign strategy, and the candidates' time and money.

In large states, certain geographically concentrated groups become the target of campaigns, because they are able to function as a "swing" bloc of votes, especially if the state is fairly evenly split between the two major parties. For example, candidates may woo the Cuban vote in southern Florida, with which they may hope to tip, perhaps by small margins, the entire state's popular vote to their favor. That candidate then wins all of Florida's electoral votes. Suburbanites, who tend to swing their votes entirely to either one candidate or another, receive more attention, and presumably more representation, from candidates than do groups that do not have a pattern of cohesive bloc voting. This fact is crucial in understanding presidential campaign strategy.

The electoral college system determines the strategy of the major parties and has a similar effect on minor parties and independent candidates. Third-party and independent candidates can obtain electoral votes only by winning majority votes in states. It may be best, therefore, to concentrate a third-party campaign in one region. If third-party candidates are able to win a few states, they may possibly find themselves in a position to throw the election into the House. This was George Wallace's strategy in 1968. If he had prevented the Democratic or Republican party from having an electoral majority, he could have extracted concessions from one or the other major parties in exchange for the vote of his electors or he could have perhaps hoped for victory in the House.

The importance of geographic concentration for independent candidates can also be seen in the case of H. Ross Perot in 1992. Perot won nearly twenty million popular votes, or about 19 percent of the total, but he received no electoral votes. This was because his support was spread over the entire nation rather than being geographically concentrated. He was thus unable to win a plurality in any state in spite of a large measure of popular support nationally. This was also the case for Henry Wallace's Progressive Party in 1948.

Even given a strong, well-organized, and concentrated vote, it is still difficult for third parties to affect the outcomes of presidential elections. While candidates such as Henry Wallace, George Wallace, and Eugene McCarthy may have narrowed the winners' margins, it is not likely that their absence would have produced different outcomes. The last time a third-party candidate clearly affected the final result was in 1912, when former president Theodore Roosevelt and his Bull Moose campaign split the Republican Party, thus leading to the election of Democrat Woodrow Wilson. Third-party candidates in the twentieth century who have won electoral votes include Theodore Roosevelt (eighty-eight electoral votes), Robert M. LaFollette (thirteen), Strom Thurmond (thirty-nine), George Wallace (forty-six), and Harry Byrd (fifteen). None of these candidates won as a third-party candidate. This record shows how the electoral college serves to reinforce the two-party system in the United States. If the district plan reform were adopted, third parties would potentially have a far greater opportunity to elect a president.

Context

The politics of the electoral college, along with the various arguments put forth for its abolition or reform, bring the issue of majoritarianism into sharp focus. At the core of all the reform proposals is the sentiment that the electoral college needs to be modified because it is not democratic. Its critics argue that it does not directly reflect the will of the people because of its structure and its political workings. It discourages alternatives to the two major parties.

This criticism ignores the fact that the system created by the Framers was not meant to be a simple majoritarian democracy. Rather, it was meant to be a system of checks and balances in which no national majority would be able to dominate any region and in which no branch of government would be able to dominate any other branch. All the proposed reforms may upset the delicate balance among the branches of government and the states that has withstood the test of time. The Framers created a system that was meant to be essentially democratic but not majoritarian. The electoral college, for all of its faults and complexity, leads to a majority aggregated through the states, rather than a national majority. This has produced a government that has been extraordinarily stable and accommodating of regionalism and faction. The college's tendency to discourage independent and third-party challenges has contributed to stability and consensus. It has not worked in the way the Framers intended, but it has produced the results they intended. There are periodic complaints about the electoral system, but there is no consensus on an alternative, and there is not much popular dissatisfaction with the current system. Reform of the electoral college is therefore very unlikely.

Bibliography

Abbott, David W., and James P. Levine. *Wrong Winner*. New York: Praeger, 1991. Argues that the electoral college is undemocratic and indefensible. Recommends a direct election system.

Best, Judith. *The Case Against Direct Election of the President*. Ithaca, N.Y.: Cornell University Press, 1971. Argues for preserving the electoral college. Concedes that while no election system can be perfectly neutral, the current system favors desirable outcomes.

Glennon, Michael J. *When No Majority Rules*. Washington, D.C.: Congressional Quarterly Press, 1992. Argues for reform through the district plan.

Longley, Lawrence D., and Alan G. Braun. *The Politics of Electoral College Reform*. 2d ed. New Haven, Conn.: Yale University Press, 1975. Summary of the problems with the electoral college. Makes a case for direct election.

Longley, Lawrence D., and Denny Pilant. "Should the Electoral College Be Abolished?" In *Controversial Issues in Presidential Selection*, edited by Gary L. Rose.

Albany: State University of New York Press, 1991. Longley argues the affirmative, and Pilant defends the current system. Excellent overview for the general reader.

Sayre, Wallace S., and Judith H. Parris. *Voting for President*. Washington, D.C.: Brookings Institution, 1970. Offers a very thorough analysis of the direct election, district, proportional, and automatic plans for reform of the electoral college. Argues for the current system.

Melvin A. Kulbicki

Cross-References

Checks and Balances in U.S. Government, p. 216; The Constitution of the United States, p. 425; Democracy, p. 513; Elections, p. 578; Federalism in the United States, p. 668; Political Campaigning, Planning, and Financing, p. 1427; Political Representation in the United States, p. 1525; The Presidency in the United States, p. 1590; Presidential Elections in the United States, p. 1596; Two-Party Systems, p. 2033; Voting Processes, p. 2123.

ELITISM

Field of study: Political philosophy

Elite theory maintains that there are two major groups in society: a small group of powerful elites and the powerless masses.

Principal terms
CLASS: social position that may be determined by one's economic, educational, birth, or occupational status
ELITISM: concentration of power in the hands of a small number of people
IDEOLOGY: set of norms, values, beliefs, and attitudes
INSTITUTION: social arrangement that directs human behavior in the important areas of societal life
POWER: ability to get what one wants from someone else, by force or by getting someone to think in accordance with one's interests
SOCIAL ORDER: rules of government, law, language, custom, and so on that define people's roles in a society
SOCIAL ORGANIZATION: order of a social group as represented by the positions, norms, and other constraints that control behavior and ensure predictability

Overview

Elite theory can be traced to Europe and the works of Vilfredo Pareto (1848-1923) and Gaetano Mosca (1858-1941), both of whom wrote about the inevitability of a ruling elite's governing in any society. Elites are often viewed as essential and necessary for society. Whenever people come together, there is a need to agree on a set of ordered relationships so that the people may know how others around them will behave. There is an expectation that a few will make decisions about the nature of the ordered relations on behalf of the group. For example, in primitive societies someone has to decide when a hunt will begin, how it will proceed, and what will be done with the catch. In elite philosophy, all societies are elitist. Government is thus always government by the few.

Although there is agreement that only a few people exercise great power, there is disagreement over the nature of elite rule. Pareto and Mosca argued that elites functioned to protect democracy from the authoritarian tendencies of the masses. The irony of democracy is that the masses are often less tolerant of diversity, of democratic notions of individual liberty and freedom, of participatory democracy, and of other democratic principles than the elite are. The masses are also viewed, in elite theory, as more likely than the elite to be responsive toward the demagoguery of totalitarian regimes and leaders. This assessment of elite rule has been called democratic elitism. In U.S. political history, Alexander Hamilton, one of the Founders, took this view.

Hamilton argued that government by elites was preferable to rule by uninformed and apathetic masses.

Contrary to Hamilton's assessment of elite rule is another conception of elite rule that argues that democracy rests upon a concept of maximizing human dignity. Human dignity can be accomplished by enhancing the self-esteem of every individual, resulting in a responsible and knowledgeable citizenry. Although this second view agrees that democracy is not perfect and accepts that a minority will rule society, it does not accept the notion that the ruling elite will be more democratic than the ordinary citizen. Democratic elitism, as this second view is called, rests on the belief that policy-making is too important and too technical to be left to the populace as a whole. It supports a form of rule by those who are presumably intellectually superior, an elite of the ideologically and technically sophisticated. A possible result of such a system of rule, however, is that elites may use their power to serve their own interests rather than the interests of the ordinary citizen. Elite-rule theory takes it for granted that there will be elite rule. The goal of just government, however, is to allow for a high level of participation by the ordinary citizen. This participation requires a sharing of power. The ordinary citizen must have the decision-making opportunities where human dignity and self-esteem are realized.

A critical point in elite philosophy is that elite rule characterizes all political societies. Questions remain, however, about who the elite are, how they come to power, how much power they wield, and what they do with power.

Practically speaking, there cannot be large institutions in a complex society without power being concentrated in the hands of the few at the top of such institutions. Power is organized and exercised through institutions. Individuals do not become powerful as individuals. Certain personal qualities may be helpful in gaining positions of power, but it is the position itself that gives one person control over the activities of others. Power is an attribute of roles in a social system. Elites are the people who occupy institutionalized roles of power in a society. Elites are the people who occupy positions of authority in large institutions. Authority is the right to make decisions. Authority is the ability to direct, manage, and guide programs, policies, and activities of the major institutions of society. Not all power is institutionalized. A gun-toting mugger exercises power when he or she forces another person to hand over money. Great power, however, is found only in institutional settings. People are powerful when they occupy positions of authority in social organizations.

Elite philosophy points out that the few who govern are not typical of the masses who are governed. Elites are drawn disproportionately from the upper socioeconomic class of society. Moreover, elites share a consensus on the fundamental values of the social system and on the preservation of the system. For this reason, the changes that elites in power may support are incremental rather than radical. Incremental changes permit response to events that threaten the social system. Nonelites who have accepted the basic elite consensus have some opportunity to advance into elite circles, but the movement of nonelites to elite positions must be slow in order to maintain stability and to avoid sudden or radical social disorganization.

Elite rule is sustained by maintaining a consensus on basic values. In other words, elite theory suggests that the elite class is unified by a common ideology. The result of common social origins, education patterns, occupational status, and the like, is a shared ideology. Group consciousness and shared objectives follow from a common social background.

Elites not only share attitudes on significant issues and maintain a basic consensus of values but also are aware of this basic consensus. This feature suggests, in turn, that agreement on significant issues allows elites to manage government according to their interests. Simply put, members of an elite must be rational and purposeful in order to maintain their hold on power. This view should not be understood as a conspiracy theory. The scenario is not one in which members of the elite sit behind closed doors privately plotting every political power play. Conspiracies, grown too large, are no longer conspiracies; they become governments. Instead, the elite class is united by its hold on power and by its social background. Power is more than a manifestation of a social category; that is, power is not acquired by virtue of one's class position.

Although there is a broad consensus among elites on fundamental values and future directions of the societies they lead, disagreement within elites occurs. The range of disagreement is relatively narrow, and disagreement is generally confined to means rather than ends. Loyalty to common goals does not preclude conflict over how goals might be realized.

Much disagreement occurs between local, regional, and national elites. For example, the broadly dispersed power in the United States political system results in a government that favors elite interests, because the advantage goes to the people with the money to hire lawyers and lobbyists to influence parties and candidates. Stated differently, at all levels of government, elites have the greatest access to government. The result is a variety of self-interested elites successfully getting different things from government. Elites fill up the agenda of government with particular and often conflicting demands. In the United States, one example of how different elites may conflict is the differences between the "cowboys" of the Southwest and the "Yankees" of the East. The cowboys have acquired their wealth relatively recently (after World War II) in independent oil operations, the aerospace and computer industries, and Sunbelt real estate. These cowboys do not share the liberal values of the established Yankees. They are self-made persons of wealth and power—individualistic, highly competitive, and politically conservative. The Yankees have enjoyed wealth for generations or have slowly climbed the career ladder among the largest corporations, law firms, banks, and foundations. They have acquired a sense of civic responsibility. They wish to exercise power in public affairs, to be respected in Washington, D.C., or in their local communities, and they wish to cultivate a favorable media image. By contrast, many self-made cowboys believe that they best serve the nation or the local community by making their enterprises profitable.

Elite theory of the twentieth century argues for a plurality of elites that may interact or compete in a variety of ways. The belief that a single dominant elite effectively directs all important human functions and activities is too rigid a view. This is not to say that the belief that a higher circle commands all arenas of human society—political, economic, and social—has been irrefutably discredited. Rather the elite theorist looks for verifiable demonstrations of such command over society. The elite theorist seeks to identify who the winners and losers are in the game of politics. The elite theorist tries to describe a method by which one might distinguish between the powerful and the powerless. An example of such a distinction is to say that an elite group is well organized and controls the major economic, social, and political institutions in society, and that while the masses influence government through elections and related processes, their influence is marginal and not a serious challenge to elite dominance. The dominance of the elite is imbedded in socioeconomic institutions and is reinforced by beliefs and attitudes. The elite are the few who have power in society, and their decisions reflect their interests.

Applications

In one sense almost all politics is elitist in that nearly all government decisions are made by the few rather than the many. Elitist theory asserts that it is always the same elite that makes policy, whatever the issue. Elitist theory argues that the elite acts in concert or that it at least has a common social, economic, or occupational background. It also argues that the elite is only weakly influenced, if at all, by popular opinion.

It makes a difference whether a small group has power because it is the direct beneficiary of some policy or because it has general characteristics (wealth, prestige, social standing) that enable it to influence even policies that do not bear on its material interests at all. Elite philosophy suggests that the general attributes of wealth and prestige are the cause of an elite's power.

The U.S. federal judiciary provides a good example for the application of elite theory. Justices are not astonishingly well paid or prestigious but they are drawn from a profession (law) that provides them with influence. Judges make decisions without being closely constrained by interest groups or voters. Judges make decisions that do not bear on their interests. They share a common orientation. Judges are, therefore, an elite. U.S. foreign policy-making is another interesting case of elite influence. In U.S. foreign policy, the power of the elite does not depend on its ability to win votes, mobilize popular opinion, or raise campaign funds. The influence of the elite depends on its members' being part of a group that shares certain ideas and that has acquired experience in managing foreign affairs. At one time the foreign policy elite was also distinctive for its common social background—well-to-do, white, Anglo-Saxon Protestants who had attended Ivy League colleges. This has changed somewhat. Members of the foreign policy elite are unified even more in their ideas than in their origins. Their ideas are formed by experience, academic training, and ideology.

Context

The way that power is concentrated in society raises the question of who benefits. At times nearly everyone does but for the most part the decisions made tend to benefit those who make decisions. In short, government is an institution made up of an elite that seeks to maintain its advantageous position in society. In U.S. political history, for example, the government's policy has primarily, although not exclusively, favored the needs of the ruling elite.

The Framers of the U.S. Constitution were mostly wealthy members of the upper class. The Constitution they wrote gave power to people like themselves—property owners. This bias continued throughout the nineteenth century as bankers, railroad entrepreneurs, and manufacturers joined the landed gentry in the power elite. The shift from local business to large-scale manufacturing during the last half of the nineteenth century saw an increase in government activity in the economy. Business was protected from competition by protective tariffs, public subsidies, price regulation, patents, and trademarks. Throughout the nineteenth century there was unrest by miners, farmers, and workers. The government always took the side of the elite against the masses. Federal troops were used to crush railroad strikes. Antitrust laws, which were not used to stop the monopolistic practices of business, were invoked against labor unions.

During the nineteenth century approximately one billion acres of public land (almost one-half of the United States) were given to private individuals and corporations. The railroads in particular were given huge tracts of land as a subsidy. These lands were and continue to be very rich in timber and natural resources. The active intervention of the government in the nation's economy during the nineteenth century was almost solely on the behalf of business. Little attention was given to unemployment, work conditions, the exploitation of natural resources, or the living conditions of millions of destitute Americans.

The early twentieth century was a time of a large amount of government activity in the economy, which gave the appearance of restraining big business. The actual result of federal regulation of business was to increase the power of the largest corporations. The Interstate Commerce Commission, for example, helped the railroads by establishing common rates, thereby reducing damaging competition. Federal regulations in meatpacking, drugs, banking, and mining weeded out the weaker competitors, leaving a few to control the markets at higher prices and higher profits.

World War I intensified the government's bias toward the elite. Industry was converted to war production. Corporate interests became more actively involved in councils of government. Government actions favored business in labor disputes. The police and military were used against rebellious workers because strikes could be considered efforts to weaken the war effort and therefore treasonous.

The New Deal of the 1930's is typically viewed to be a time when the needs of those impoverished by the Great Depression were paramount in governmental policies. One may, however, after study of the facts, contend that the central goal of the Franklin D. Roosevelt Administration (1933-1945) was business recovery rather than social reform. The federal government, under his direction, subsidized business with credits, price supports, bank guarantees, stimulation of the housing industry, and the like. Welfare programs were instituted to prevent widespread starvation, but even these humanitarian programs also worked to the benefit of the big business community. The government provided jobs, minimum wages, unemployment compensation, and retirement benefits, which aided those in dire economic straits. These programs were actually promoted by the business community because of the benefits that business could realize from them. Government and business favored social programs at the time, one may argue, not because millions were in misery but because of the threat of violent political and social unrest. Scholars have concluded that government institutes massive aid to the poor only when the poor constitute a threat. When large numbers of people are suddenly barred from their traditional occupations, the legitimacy of the system may be questioned. Crime, riots, looting, and social movements bent on changing the existing social, political, and economic arrangements become more widespread. Under this threat, relief programs are initiated or expanded by the government to diffuse social unrest. During the Great Depression the government remained aloof from the needs of the unemployed until there was a surge of political disorder. Such evidence supports the argument that elites run governments and that elites protect their own interests above those of others.

Bibliography

Dahl, Robert A. *A Preface to Democratic Theory*. Chicago: University of Chicago Press, 1956. Classic study of how pluralism serves to maintain and enhance democracy.

Domhoff, G. William. *Who Rules America Now?* New York: Simon & Schuster, 1983. Proposes the idea that a relatively fixed group of privileged people dominate the U.S. economy and government.

Dye, Thomas R., and L. Harmon Ziegler. *The Irony of Democracy*. 9th ed. Belmont, Calif.: Wadsworth, 1993. Applies the concept of democratic elitism to U.S. political institutions and processes.

Mills, C. Wright. *The Power Elite*. New York: Oxford University Press, 1956. Critical of the privileged few who govern America.

Piven, Frances Fox, and Richard A. Cloward. *Regulating the Poor: The Functions of Public Welfare*. Rev. ed. New York: Vintage Books, 1993. Case study of how elitism works in everyday governing of society.

David E. Camacho

Cross-References

Burke's Political Philosophy, p. 171; Democracy, p. 513; Fascism and Nazism, p. 656; Hegemony, p. 817; Imperialism, p. 889; Iron Triangles, p. 981; Machiavelli's Political Philosophy, p. 1148; Nietzsche's Political Philosophy, p. 1300; Plato's Political Philosophy, p. 1396; Pluralism, p. 1402; Political Myths and the Philosophies of Mosca and Pareto, p. 1474; Political Representation in the United States, p. 1525; Power Divisions in Governments, p. 1578.

EMPIRES AND EMPIRE BUILDING

Field of study: Types of government

A form of supranational government, an empire consists of disparate peoples bound by force, but also by a common language, institutions, and laws. Empire builders think of themselves as extending civilization or indoctrinating the masses with a superior ideology.

Principal terms

ETHNOCENTRISM: belief that one's own ethnic group is superior to all others and that one may judge others in terms of one's own group's values

IMPERIALISM: aggressive invasion, occupation, and subjugation of foreign lands, which are then incorporated into a central state or empire

MANIFEST DESTINY: belief that Americans were ordained by God to settle and govern the New World

MILITARISM: readiness to use military means to achieve political goals

SUPRANATIONAL GOVERNMENT: government that is not limited to a single nation's borders

Overview

When governments equate their survival and prosperity with state expansion, they form empires. In the ancient world, empires or supranational governments encompassed disparate peoples. For example, the Chinese empire at various times included the peoples of Southeast Asia such as the Vietnamese; the Roman Empire defeated and incorporated the Egyptian Empire; Persia conquered an older empire, Assyria, and extended its rule into parts of what are today Afghanistan and Pakistan.

All ancient empires had in common a willingness and readiness to use force. War was a common tool to extend and preserve order. The Romans, for example, saw their conquests as a way of establishing the rule of law over large areas of the world they considered "barbarian"—that is, dominated by nomadic peoples who did not have a concept of the state and of civil institutions but instead were governed by arbitrary leaders whose only claim to loyalty was their courage, intelligence, and power to strike fear in their followers and foes. Empire, in other words, was associated with stability and continuity. Empires may have often had arbitrary, even irrational emperors, but they survived the criminal and chaotic behavior of individual leaders because their solid administrative structures provided continuity. Eventually, of course, the ancient empires disintegrated. In the case of Rome, it was because the senate gradually lost the moral and political authority to maintain order and became merely an extension of the emperors' power.

The concept of empire, like the Roman notion of barbarians, entails a form of ethnocentrism, a belief that elevates empire builders above those whom they would conquer. In this case ethnocentrism justifies the domination of lands and peoples by governors who consider themselves wiser and more advanced spiritually and technologically than the subjects over whom they rule. The idea is similar to that of slave owners in the United States, who built what was called a "cotton kingdom," a thriving economy based on the belief that slaves were subhuman property and that the slave owners could control them with impunity.

American empire builders developed a concept of "manifest destiny" to rationalize their settling and exploitation of the North American continent. They established a religious conviction that they were ordained by God to spread civilization westward. The indigenous inhabitants of the land were regarded as heathens who had no right to ownership of the land, and who had no conception of ownership or—as the more religious empire builders called it—"stewardship" of the land. Because the Indians had not improved the land, they could not be its true stewards.

The concept of empire building goes in hand with certain religious and civic beliefs. The Spanish conquerors of Mexico were accompanied by members of Roman Catholic religious orders who believed they were spreading the word of God with the help of the Spanish Empire. By such reasoning, imperialism could serve the glory of God and the glory of Spain at the same time.

Not all empires or empire builders express the same kind of ethnocentrism or conquer other peoples in the same ways or with the same degrees of force. The Roman Empire, for example, expanded through war, but it also kept the peace between warring groups within its realm. Often the Romans granted citizenship to conquered peoples, improved roads, public facilities, education, and gave conquered groups a code of laws and institutional structures that marked progress and instilled peace in their lives. Similarly, the British Empire created a commonwealth of nations that arguably has improved the fortunes of humanity considerably by extending the rule of law, the building of roads and other public works, the irrigation of land, the development of hygiene, and the treatment of disease. Nevertheless, in both the Roman and British empires, subject peoples variously protested imperial rule and embraced it as a boon.

The growth of the Japanese empire in the 1930's is a good illustration of the complexity of the problem of empire. In earlier times, the Japanese looked to China, a much older civilization, as a model for their culture. But the deterioration of China in the late nineteenth and early twentieth centuries, China's inability to repel Western invaders, and its internal disputes between warlords caused the Japanese to lose their respect for this empire. The Americans and the British, with their superior technology and military prowess, encroached on Asia, prompting the Japanese to attack China and occupy large parts of it. Although the Japanese were severely criticized by the West for invading China, others in Asia saw the Japanese as competing with Western imperialists for dominance in Asia.

When Japan first attacked U.S. naval installations at Pearl Harbor in 1941, the initial reaction in many parts of Asia was positive. Finally, an Asian power had asserted itself against the West, and some of the smaller Asian countries looked forward to cooperation with the Japanese. But the Japanese forces were interested not in collaboration but in the subjection of their neighbors—such as the Koreans. As an imperial power, in other words, Japan ultimately acted no better than Westerners. The logic of empire dictated a policy that was both antidemocratic and ruthlessly militaristic.

Applications

The rise and fall of the Soviet empire presents a good case study of the dynamics of empire building. The Bolsheviks, a revolutionary communist political party, came to power in October, 1917. Their stated goal was not only to overthrow the ruling czar, but to create a dictatorship of the proletariat—that is, a society governed by the working class. Vladimir Lenin, the leader of the Bolsheviks, expressly rejected the idea of bourgeois or middle-class democracy which consisted of political parties vying for power in open elections. Instead, the Bolshevik Party itself would represent the interests of the people—not only in Russia, but in the lands adjacent to Russia and, indeed, the rest of the world. The Bolsheviks proclaimed their faith in world revolution and believed the success of their own revolution depended on uprisings in Germany and elsewhere. Consequently, Bolshevik foreign policy was aggressive and professed opposition to imperial powers such as Great Britain, France, and Germany.

Lenin renounced Russia's World War I alliance with Britain and France against Germany, making a separate peace with Germany. Lenin further indicated that Russia would no longer participate in what it considered capitalistic wars fomented by imperial powers looking to generate profits. Lenin's desire not to take part in wars of capitalist expansion, however, did not prevent him from taking part in wars of communist expansion. In 1918, a civil war began in Russia. On one side were the anticommunist "White" forces, supported by Great Britain, France, the United States, and Japan. On the other side were the Bolsheviks, whose Red Army, under the direction of Leon Trotsky, defeated the White forces in 1920. Along with the victory came the reoccupation by military force of Ukraine, Georgia, Armenia, and Azerbaijan, along with a failed attempt to take over Estonia, Latvia, and Lithuania. It was not capitalism, but it did look like empire building. Estonia, Latvia, and Lithuania would fall under Russian control twenty years later, during the rule of Lenin's successor, Joseph Stalin.

Like other empire builders, Lenin and Stalin had an ideology. They believed that communism, as promulgated by its founder, Karl Marx, was the one true form of government adaptable to all societies. It was antireligious, because religion, Marx argued, served to lull people into accepting the status quo and hence was antirevolutionary. The communists justified the overthrow of governments by pointing to what they regarded as the laws of history. All change, all progress in history, came through conflict, through the clash not only of conflicting ideas but of groups vying for power. History showed, in the communist view, the gradual triumph of the working class, the vast majority of the people, who had been downtrodden by kings, the nobility, the middle class, and the capitalists, but who were beginning to assert their power, their control over society's means of production—in other words, over the factories, shops, businesses, and institutions of all kinds that could not thrive without the labors of the masses.

In the 1920's and 1930's, Stalin and his followers established communist parties throughout the world. These parties rarely were able to take power, but even as minority political groups they exerted considerable influence and extended the influence of Soviet ideology, which they championed as the form of government for the future. Many of these parties—as in the case of the German Communist Party—were dealt paralyzing blows with the advent of another form of imperialism and empire building: fascism. Adolf Hitler in Germany and Benito Mussolini in Italy commanded significant respect in the Europe of the 1930's, causing Stalin concern as he saw imperial powers such as Britain and France back away from confrontations with the new fascist regimes.

Stalin decided that the best way to preserve the Soviet empire was through a nonaggression pact with Germany. In effect, two empires formed an alliance of convenience that led to Stalin's grabbing the eastern half of Poland during the German invasion of 1939. The German-Soviet alliance lasted less than two years, however, ending when German forces invaded the Soviet Union in June, 1941. Stalin's only choice was to accept American and British offers of help in turning back the German attack. Eventually more than twenty million Soviet soldiers and citizens died in World War II, but at its end a large part of Central and Eastern Europe was occupied by the Red Army, which had driven out the Germans.

The war provided Stalin's empire the opportunity to expand. It would have been difficult for Stalin's allies to push him out of his newly occupied territory without risking another world war. Furthermore, the Soviet Union had borne the brunt of the fighting, and the allies were not unsympathetic to Stalin's desire never to allow Germany to invade its territory again. But in the guise of achieving security, Stalin swallowed up the Baltic republics, and his followers set up puppet governments in Poland, East Germany, Czechoslovakia, Hungary, Romania, and Bulgaria. These new governments were called Stalinist regimes or satellites because they slavishly adhered to the Soviet Union's policies and their resources were exploited primarily for the Soviet Union's benefit.

Later uprisings in East Germany, Hungary, and Czechoslovakia were crushed as Stalin and his successors brooked no variation on their brand of communism. The answer to political disagreements between the Soviets and their satellites was tanks in Prague, and the presence of the Red Army in Poland and the other satellites. In the United Nations, the satellites voted as a bloc—the only exceptions being Tito of Yugoslavia and Nicolae Ceausescu of Romania, who were semi-independent but followed communist orthodoxy in stifling political dissent and in establishing centralized planning and command economies that allowed little leeway for individual businesspeople or private companies.

U.S. President Ronald Reagan was both praised and blamed for calling the Soviet Union the "evil empire." He was on sound ground insofar as he was criticizing an imperial power that had stifled freedom of human expression and had treated its subject peoples with incredible arrogance and inhumanity. Yet the phrase "evil empire" masked as much as it revealed. For the Soviet satellites had tried to break away from the Soviet Union by various means, and their citizens managed to cultivate under-ground, surreptitious contacts with the Western democracies. The Soviet Union itself thus became an increasingly hollow empire, relying almost exclusively on milita-rism—a huge stockpile of nuclear weapons and security forces that could still intimidate its own people and the satellites.

Like the Roman Empire, the Soviet Union crumbled from within. The last Soviet leader, Mikhail Gorbachev, believed he could reform communism, but as soon as he began to relax its rigid forms of political and economic control, Soviet society began to collapse. Even the most diehard communist leaders seemed to lose faith in their ideology, knowing it could command respect only with the barrel of a gun. Like the last emperors of the Roman Empire, Gorbachev tried to cut his losses, relinquishing the Eastern European satellites that he knew he could no longer control except by force; and force, he well knew, would do nothing to resuscitate the Soviet Union's dying economy.

The astonishing difference between the decline of the Roman and Soviet empires is that the latter dissolved in less than one decade, whereas the former declined for several hundred years before collapsing. The Romans—although they became increas-ingly corrupt and violent—nevertheless established concepts of honor, of law, and even of virtue which they repeatedly violated and yet never quite relinquished as their model of good behavior. Romans genuinely incorporated alien people into the Roman concept of governance. Even slaves were known to have purchased their freedom and to have become outstanding Roman citizens. Romans were capable of turning the very people they vanquished into their allies and over several generations into full-fledged Romans.

In spite of the ideology of a ruling working class, in spite of the concept of world revolution, the Soviet Union never behaved as the Romans did; it never put the Polish communists or Czech communists on the same footing as Russian communists. Although Russian communists proclaimed an end to racism, they purged Jews from the Communist Party. The Soviet imperium, in other words, had neither the flexibility nor the farsightedness to make the expanding Soviet empire synonymous with an expanding notion of what it meant to be a communist. The Roman Empire lasted as long as it did because the idea of being a Roman grew over time and territory, so that even the subject peoples believed they had contributed to the very notion of what constitutes a Roman.

Context

The model of empire for the modern world remains Roman. No empire since ancient times has achieved Rome's degree of success as a world power or made a contribution to world civilization as great as the Roman legacy of law and institution building. The power of the Roman example is particularly vivid in the United States, where the architecture of public buildings is Roman and many of its institutions, such as the Senate, have Roman names. The excesses of Rome have often been recommended for study because the Romans confused the power of rulers with that of the laws they enacted, and the Romans relied too heavily on their leaders such as Augustus to rule for them. It is why American jurists so often like to assert that the United States is a government of laws, not of men.

Since the late nineteenth century, empire and empire building have been soundly repudiated. Critics rightly show how the evils of slavery and the concentration camps, for example, have their roots in an imperial ideology which treats certain peoples as less than human. No democracy—not the United States, Britain, or France—has not acted as an imperial power with colonies or protectorates. Yet not all forms of imperialism are the same, nor should the imperial aspects of a policy be the sole determinant of whether or not a state is an empire. For even those opposed to empire recognize that it is difficult for a state to exist solely within its own borders, never interfering in the internal affairs of other states. Sometimes intervention in another state's affairs is the only way a state can protect its own citizens.

Empire is one response to centralizing power, and to developing a form of governance that creates peace throughout extensive areas of the world. Without a true center, as in the former Yugoslavia, certain parts of the world disintegrate into civil war. Empire, in other words, is one way of binding diverse peoples and of creating larger civic goals. Unfortunately empire has also stood for tyranny; that is, the suppression of minorities and individual points of view. Other forms of government such as federalism—a combination of sovereign states which do not relinquish their sovereignty—is one alternative to empire. But federalism risks the problem of a hollow center and lack of direction, the absence of a Rome to which all roads lead. Empire poses the problem of unity and diversity; to move beyond empire is to express a faith that there can be something that approaches a true unity in diversity.

Bibliography

Achebe, Chinua. *Things Fall Apart*. London: Heinemann, 1958. A modern classic, this Nigerian novel provides insights into an African culture which is invaded by empire builders and imperialists.

Conrad, Joseph. *Heart of Darkness*. Edited by Robert Kimbrough. New York: W. W. Norton, 1963. First published in 1899, this classic novel is a brooding, riveting account of a journey into the Congo Free State (now Zaïre) in search of Kurtz, a white empire builder who has apparently "gone native." This edition includes several essays on the novel, its sources and background.

Gibbon, Edward. *The Decline and Fall of the Roman Empire*. Edited by Dero A. Saunders. New York: Viking Penguin, 1983. One-volume abridgement of Gibbon's massive and classic work, still the best study of the Roman Empire but also a valuable guide to understanding the elements of empire and empire building in other civilizations and periods.

Howard, Michael. *The Lessons of History*. New Haven, Conn.: Yale University Press, 1991. Essays on empires, nation states, imperialism, international relations, war, ideology, and social change by a distinguished historian of modern history.

Johnson, Paul. *Modern Times: The World from the Twenties to the Nineties*. Rev. ed.

New York: HarperCollins, 1991. Well-written survey of the twentieth century, with emphasis on its political aspects, particularly imperialism, empire, and ideology.

Nagle, John D. *Introduction to Comparative Politics: Political System Performance in Three Worlds.* 2d ed. Chicago: Nelson-Hall, 1989. Chapters on communism, imperialism and dependence in the Third World, the quality of life and reactions to imperialism in the Third World. Extensive notes and index.

Carl Rollyson

Cross-References

ENERGY MANAGEMENT

Field of study: Functions of government

Energy, indispensable for industry and development, has become a major preoccupation for most governments. Almost all countries have programs to manage the supply, price, and environmental impact of the generation and use of energy.

Principal terms

DECONTROL: removal of an economic activity from government control, allowing its prices, supply, and distribution to be determined by market forces

EXTERNALITY: cost (such as pollution) that is passed on to the public, workers, or some other third party

FOSSIL FUEL: energy source, such as coal or oil, that comes from the chemically altered remains of plants and animals that died hundreds of millions of years ago

NUCLEAR FISSION: process that produces energy by splitting the nucleus of a heavy atom, such as uranium

RENEWABLE ENERGY: energy that is continuously replenished, coming from sources such as the sun, tides, or wind

Overview

Energy management has become a major preoccupation of most governments, particularly those of the advanced industrial regions of North America, Europe, and Asia. There are many different facets of modern energy policy that often overlap with other areas of government concern.

Nearly all the power for the world's factories, homes, transportation systems, and other power consumers comes from fossil fuels: coal, oil, and natural gas. These resources exist in the earth's crust in vast quantities, but only a fraction of this supply can be extracted economically, and much of that cannot be used because of environmental concerns. These basic facts lie behind virtually all of the energy problems that began to emerge in the 1970's.

Easily reached, environmentally safe energy sources are not evenly distributed around the world. None of the highest energy-consuming nations is capable of meeting its power needs by itself. Japan and France, for example, have virtually no oil, coal, or uranium within their borders. Even the United States—which has substantial coal reserves and is the world's third largest oil producer—relies heavily upon imported oil. In 1949, the United States imported less than 5 percent of the oil it used. By 1970, this figure had risen to more than 30 percent. In 1991, the year of the Persian Gulf War, the United States purchased more than 40 percent of its oil from overseas.

Most of the oil imported by the industrialized nations comes from the Middle East, particularly the region surrounding the Persian Gulf. This part of the world has seen considerable political, economic, and social unrest during the latter half of the twentieth century, which has at times not only threatened to interrupt a significant quantity of the flow of this crucial resource, but has also done so. Given that the economies of North America, Western Europe, and Japan depend upon a continuous supply of energy, such events have serious repercussions.

There has also been a growing concern in many industrialized countries over the environmental effects of different types of energy. Every type of power generation produces some sort of waste product. The burning of fossil fuels by power stations, factories, and especially automobiles produces sulfur dioxide and carbon monoxide, thought to contribute to the creation of acid rain and to the "greenhouse effect," which is said to cause an overall increase in the earth's surface temperature. Nuclear power plants' waste products (their spent fuel rods) are highly radioactive and will remain so for millennia, presenting a serious problem of storage and disposal.

Even the act of producing or extracting mineral and oil deposits leads to significant environmental and health problems. Coal mining causes black lung disease, a leading cause of early death among coal miners. Strip mining, a process by which coal lying close to the surface is dug out by giant mechanical shovels operating above ground, is highly damaging to the land. Drilling for oil and gas presents similar problems.

Finally, accidents in energy industries can have severe environmental impact, and often pose a significant risk to public health and safety as well. In the United States, cave-ins, explosions, and fires in coal mines have killed more than 90,000 people since 1900 and seriously injured nearly 1.5 million since 1930. In April, 1986, operator error during a routine shutdown at the nuclear power station at Chernobyl in then-Soviet Ukraine caused a massive explosion, spewing radioactive debris a mile up into the atmosphere and sending a radioactive cloud over Eastern Europe and Scandinavia. On March 24, 1989, the giant oil tanker *Exxon Valdez* ran aground in Prince William Sound, Alaska, spilling 250,000 barrels of crude oil which ultimately contaminated 800 miles of shoreline.

Externalities—or costs (harm to life, property, and the ecosystem) unwillingly borne by third parties—generally fall to government to resolve. The challenge for modern energy policies, therefore, is to ensure that a nation has a continuous supply of energy at a reasonable price, while at the same time seeking to minimize external impacts on health, safety, and the environment.

As a result of the growing importance of energy policy, many countries now have a high-level ministry or cabinet department devoted to energy. In the United States, energy management was widely scattered across a number of departments and agencies until the creation of the Department of Energy in 1977.

Energy management encompasses many different activities. One of the most important is the effort underway in many nations to develop energy independence, that is, to reduce (if not eliminate) dependence on imported oil. In France and Japan, this has meant heavy investment in nuclear plants and related technologies. France, which imports uranium from its former colonies in Africa, now generates around 70 percent of its electricity from nuclear power.

In the United States, anxiety over dependence on foreign oil has risen and fallen more than once since the 1970's. The country attempted to boost domestic production by decontrolling the price of most types of energy in 1980. Prior to that time, the amount that could be charged for electricity or natural gas was regulated by a complex set of rules. According to some economists, one result of these price controls was a series of shortages (particularly of natural gas) throughout the country in the early 1970's. By allowing the price to rise to its market price, decontrol advocates argued, oil and gas producers in the United States would have a greater incentive to locate and develop new wells.

As crude oil prices fell during the 1980's, however, American concern over imports declined as well. As already noted, by 1991 the United States was still purchasing over 40 percent of its oil from overseas. Public discussion of energy independence increased briefly during the Gulf War, but quickly faded after the fighting stopped. Some observers have criticized this attitude, chiding the country, and by extension its energy policy, for failing to think ahead.

Another role of energy policy is to promote energy conservation. Price increases, such as those resulting from price decontrol, encourage consumers to save fuel by driving less, carpooling, buying more fuel-efficient cars, keeping their home thermostats set lower, and so on. Many countries take this idea a step further by imposing high taxes on gasoline or, conversely, offering tax breaks for energy-conserving acts (such as installing home insulation).

Many nations' energy programs are also heavily involved in research and development. Practically all industrialized countries subsidize research into new ways of producing energy, as well as methods for using it more efficiently. The U.S. Department of Energy, for example, maintains a separate agency, the Office of Energy Research, to oversee this activity. The office maintains a number of major research efforts, including fusion energy (creating power by fusing together the nuclei of lighter atoms like hydrogen or helium), "clean" coal (coal that pollutes less), alternative designs of nuclear power plants, and many others.

In addition, there are numerous public and private programs around the world investigating a wide array of energy options involving solar power, wind, tides, and many others. The supply of these natural sources is constantly replenished, so they are considered renewable energy resources. A major challenge for these technologies is that they are not yet economical; that is, they are presently unable to compete with the more traditional energy sources in the marketplace.

Finally, a large portion of current energy policy is devoted to minimizing the environmental impacts of energy production and use. Most governments regulate how much pollution is permitted from power stations, automobiles, and factories. Moreover, some, such as the United States, go so far as to regulate the kinds of energy sources that may be used. The U.S. Department of Energy began in the 1970's to ban the use of coal that contained high levels of sulfur. This was intended to reduce the amount of sulfur dioxide released into the atmosphere.

Taken together, the major goals of contemporary energy policy—to maximize supply, maintain a reasonable price, and protect worker health, public safety, and the environment—are often in conflict. Initiatives related to safety and environmental quality frequently have the effect of raising energy prices. Proposals that would result in expanding supply, such as allowing the burning of coal with a higher sulfur content, can have adverse consequences for public health. Increasingly, it falls to government to decide how these trade-offs should be evaluated.

Applications

The United States in the 1970's, particularly during the administrations of Gerald Ford and Jimmy Carter, experienced a period of great activity in the field of energy policy. President Ford initiated a program known as Project Independence, designed to reduce American reliance on imported oil. President Carter declared energy policy to be "the moral equivalent of war." The programs that were enacted during this decade illustrate many of the relevant issues in governmental energy management.

A major component of both presidents' energy policies was the promotion of conservation. In 1975, Congress established fuel efficiency standards for U.S. automakers, setting a target of twenty-seven miles per gallon by the year 1985. An additional tax on gas-guzzling cars, those whose mileage fell too far below efficiency standards, was passed in 1978.

The federal government also sought to make use of America's abundant coal reserves by encouraging U.S. industries to switch from oil- to coal-produced energy. The 1978 Power Plant and Industrial Fuel Use Act prohibited all new powerplants, factories, and other facilities from burning oil or gas unless alternative fuels were unavailable.

The 1970's also saw renewed efforts to develop new energy sources. The Carter Administration was particularly active in this regard, devoting major funding increases for research into solar energy (President Carter even installed a solar-powered water heater at the White House), fusion, and processes to develop fuels from coal, solid wastes, and oil shale. These programs ultimately were to have little immediate impact on energy usage, however, because of their lengthy development time, and most were cut back or canceled after 1980 by President Ronald Reagan (who also removed the White House solar heater).

As well as promoting conservation and use of alternative energy sources, the Carter Administration sought to increase domestic production by removing government price controls on oil and natural gas. Acting under the Energy Policy and Conservation Act, the president, in 1978, ordered a phased decontrol of crude oil prices, ending in 1981 when all such controls would be removed. U.S. producers responded to these price increases by pushing domestic drilling for oil to record levels. Congress also passed, in 1978, the Natural Gas Policy Act, which attempted to roll back controls on natural gas, allowing it to reach a rough parity with other fuels.

Finally, the Ford and Carter administrations were responsible for a number of important energy-related environmental initiatives. The 1977 Federal Mine Safety and Health Amendments Act established new regulations for coal mine operation, and created a Black Lung Disability Trust Fund for miners suffering from that disease. That same year also saw passage of the Clean Air Amendments, which mandate the use of low-sulfur coal, and the Surface Mining Control and Reclamation Act, which requires strip miners to restore mined land to its original condition. Unfortunately, these programs tend to work at cross-purposes with the others mentioned above, since they serve to make coal more expensive.

Context

It is commonly believed that modern energy policy began in response to the Middle East oil embargo of the 1970's. In fact, however, governments have been involved in energy management in one form or another since at least the beginning of the twentieth century. During the Great Depression of the 1930's, for example, U.S. President Franklin D. Roosevelt mounted a major effort to provide electricity to rural areas. Similarly, in the 1950's and 1960's, many countries supported the development of the nuclear power industry through tax credits, limits on insurance liability, and even direct subsidy.

Still, the oil embargo of October 1973 has had a profound effect upon the conduct of energy policy. In the wake of that year's Yom Kippur War between Egypt and Israel, the major oil-producing nations of the Middle East met in Kuwait to bring about the first oil embargo. This political act soon evolved into a major economic strategy, as the world's primary oil-producing countries, through a cartel known as OPEC (Organization of Petroleum Exporting Countries), began to force massive increases in the worldwide price for oil. Between 1973 and 1974, OPEC raised the costs of crude oil sixfold.

For citizens (particularly in the United States) who had grown accustomed to relatively cheap energy prices, the impact was immediate and profound. During the first days of the embargo, many parts of the United States experienced shortages of gasoline and diesel fuel. Ultimately, many observers believe, the ongoing price increases triggered a new round of inflation and caused (or at least aggravated) a worldwide economic recession. Matters were made even worse by the Iranian Revolution of 1979, which led to a cutoff of oil from that country (the United States had been importing 500,000 barrels per day), and another doubling of prices. Some analysts believe that the economic dislocations throughout the 1970's, caused by the instability of energy supplies and prices, contributed to the electoral defeat of President Ford in 1976 and President Carter in 1980.

In addition to economic and political effects, a nation's energy requirements can also affect its foreign policy. In response to the 1973 embargo, for example, many countries (including Japan and several in Western Europe) agreed to the Arab states' political demands, particularly regarding Israel. Similarly, issues over who would control the rich oil fields of Kuwait and Saudi Arabia were a cause of the 1991 Persian Gulf War.

Bibliography

Annual Review of Energy and the Environment. Palo Alto, Calif.: Annual Reviews. Up-to-date articles on all aspects of energy policy. Topics vary from year to year.

Cohen, Linda R., and Roger G. Noll. *The Technology Pork Barrel*. Washington, D.C.: Brookings Institution, 1991. Highly critical account of government-funded research and development projects, with separate studies on the solar power, breeder reactor, and synthetic coal programs.

Davis, David Howard. *Energy Politics*. 4th ed. New York: St. Martin's Press, 1993. Clear and concise introduction to the economic, environmental, and political issues surrounding energy policy.

Dorian, James P., and Fereidum Fesharaki. *International Issues in Energy Policy, Development, and Economics*. Boulder, Colo.: Westview Press, 1992. Examines the energy policies and markets of many different countries and regions.

International Energy Agency. *Energy Policies and Programmes of IEA Countries*. Paris: Organization for Economic Co-Operation and Development, various years. Useful overview of the newest developments in the energy management strategies of most of the world's industrialized nations.

Marcus, Alfred A. *Controversial Issues in Energy Policy*. Newbury Park, Calif.: Sage Publications, 1992. Views U.S. energy policy in a larger global context. Also has a few chapters comparing U.S. policy to that of Japan, France, and Great Britain.

Perrow, Charles. *Normal Accidents: Living with High-Risk Technologies*. New York: Basic Books, 1984. Discussion of the risks posed by nuclear powerplants, oil tankers, and drill sites.

U.S. Congress, Office of Technology Assessment. *New Electric Power Technologies*. Washington, D.C.: Government Printing Office, 1985. Looks at trends in U.S. consumption of electricity and the status of several emerging energy technologies.

U.S. Congress, Office of Technology Assessment. *Nuclear Power in an Age of Uncertainty*. Washington, D.C.: Government Printing Office, 1984. Somewhat dated, but still a remarkably thorough discussion of the technical, economic, and political problems confronting nuclear power.

W. D. Kay

Cross-References

Business and Government, p. 177; Commerce Regulation, p. 357; Environmental Protection, p. 617; Industrialization, p. 916; Public Utilities, p. 1640; Regulatory Agencies in the United States, p. 1678; Research, Development, and Planning, p. 1711; Resource Management, p. 1718; Transportation Management in the United States, p. 2006.

ENTITLEMENTS

Field of study: Functions of government

Entitlements are rights, claims, or legal titles to benefits conferred by law to specific members of the population who qualify for these benefits through a process of verifying their eligibility.

Principal terms

ASSISTANCE PAYMENT: money provided to or on behalf of needy individuals and families to help them meet basic needs

FOOD STAMPS: credit slips provided to lower-income families to help finance basic food needs

MANDATED WELFARE FUNCTIONS: government programs, required by law, that provide cash assistance, social services, medical assistance or work incentives to individuals and families

MEDICAID: U.S. federal government medical assistance for the poor

SOCIAL SERVICES: variety of helping services for individuals and families, including public assistance recipients and other low-income persons

Overview

Entitlements are rights, claims, or legal title to benefits. They are conferred by law to specific categories of the population, who must qualify for these benefits through a process of verifying their eligibility, which involves meeting standards established by the government. Generally, entitlements take the form of income maintenance, which provides goods, services, or money from public funds in order to meet the needs of individuals.

As provided by the state and federal governments of the United States, entitlements include income and health maintenance programs for the aged, the blind, and the disabled, aid to families for care of dependent children, medical care to the indigent and aging, and various social rehabilitation services to eligible children, families, and single adults.

The basic responsibility of government for welfare entitlements was established in England in the sixteenth century with the Elizabethan Poor Laws. Relief under the provisions of those laws was a local matter, limited to specialized kinds of categorical need and extending only to those whose claims could not be disputed legally. Historically, the Reformation had established a fundamental change in the system of charities and relief for the poor in England. One of its features was the secularization of the monasteries and hospitals that had been the primary source of relief for the destitute. Other benevolent foundations that had provided aid to the needy no longer did so, and with the confiscation of church property by King Henry VIII, it became necessary to provide for the care of the poor by other means. The Statute of 1536 established the first plan of public relief under the auspices of the government of England. It ruled that paupers could be registered in their parishes only after they had resided for three years in the county. The parish had to maintain the poor by means of voluntary contributions of the parishioners through church collections. "Able-bodied beggars" were forced to work, and idle children from five to fourteen years of age were taken from their parents and indentured. Supplemental statutes required that vagrants and vagabonds be forced to perform hard labor and that unemployed beggars between twelve and sixty years of age be hired out as servants. Voluntary collections, however, proved to be insufficient for the support of the poor. Their ranks had been swelled by monks and nuns and by thousands of families formerly sheltered or employed in monasteries and convents. As work became scarce and the price of food rose, vagrancy and begging increased. By 1563, Parliament had to adopt compulsory measures to finance parish poor relief. Each householder was compelled by law to make a weekly contribution based on property and income.

The compilation of statutes called the Poor Law of 1601, often referred to as "43 Elizabeth," was a codification of the preceding poor relief legislation. Its only new feature was the establishment of liability for support to grandparents as well as to parents in need. The Poor Law of 1601 represented the final form of poor law legislation in England after three generations, in which public opinion had been transformed by political, religious, and economic changes. The law confirmed the responsibility of the parish, or local community, for the maintenance of the poor who were not supported by their relatives. The parish's responsibility to the destitute was limited to persons who had been born there or who had lived in the parish for at least three years. This question of residence or settlement right as one of the important requirements for the receipt of public relief has remained a vital issue in public assistance.

In eighteenth century England, workhouses were established in English cities, and relief was refused to any person not willing to enter the workhouse. The "workhouse test" forced families to give up their homes and to live in the workhouse or in a prison, the men separated from their wives and children. Many paupers preferred to live in utmost poverty with their families rather than move to the workhouse. Workhouses conducted by private contractors attempted to make profits by spending as little as possible for equipment, repair, and the food and clothing of the inmates, but the work of the tired and hungry inhabitants was so inadequate that the contractors still operated at a loss.

Other economic changes in England were a source of increasing poverty. For centuries, the poor had used the common land of the village, where they grew vegetables, potatoes, barley, and wheat for their families, and grazed sheep, geese, pigs, or cows, to supplement meager earnings from work as tenant farmers. The enclosure movement, which began in the fourteenth century, enlarged the holdings of the landed aristocracy, but took away from the poor peasants the livestock and products that enabled them to maintain their families. Many peasants had long lived on the common land and thought they owned it, but with enclosure they became squatters and were forced to move.

Residual elements of these old English laws, such as public responsibility for only certain kinds of need and work and residence requirements, are still found in various services and assistance provisions in the United States, particularly at local levels of government. Although many of these measures are repressive and intended to discourage the use of public assistance, it is well to remember that they at least affirm the principle of governmental responsibility.

The U.S. government's responsibility for the public welfare entitlements started in the earliest days of the republic, when Congress made grants of public lands to states for schools in 1785. Other responsibilities were extended when the people, through elected representatives, added other agencies such as the Federal Office of Education, the Children's Bureau, and the Vocational Rehabilitation Administration. Comprehensive plans for the protections of citizens against income risks, however, did not become an enduring principle of federal responsibility until 1935, with the passage of the Social Security Act. Reinforcement of this principle has been a clear result of the many amendments to the original act legislated by Congress.

Applications

The Department of Health, Education, and Welfare (HEW), created in 1953 with cabinet status, was an outgrowth of the widely held view that the federal government has a responsibility for the general welfare. In 1980, HEW was divided into two cabinet-level departments: Health and Human Services.

The federal government now assumes responsibility to insure virtually all American workers and their families against the loss of income resulting from retirement and disability. Survivors of insured workers are also protected. Risks to employed workers from unemployment for a limited period of time are also assumed as a federal and state responsibility. A system is yet to be developed to protect workers for long periods of unemployment and various work stoppages. A health care system, now the largest human service system in the history of the United States, further affirms the role of government as an instrument of social policy. Medical care, under Social Security provisions, protects retired workers, their families, and certain people with disabilities.

The federal government assumes financial responsibility for the aged, blind, and disabled under the Supplemental Security Income (SSI) program. In cooperation with the states, it also extends protection to families covered under the Aid to Families with Dependent Children program, and to other citizens under other provisions of the Social Security Act. The government's protection includes medical care to recipients of public assistance and to the aged whose income is too low to provide for such care on their own.

The cornerstone of public entitlements in the United States is in the Social Security Act, passed by Congress on August 14, 1935. In general, the act and its many amendments are the chief means by which governments at the local, state, and national levels provide income security to citizens. The general provisions of the Social

Security Act relate to old age, survivors, disability, health insurance, unemployment compensation, aid to families with dependent children, aid to the blind, aid to the disabled, and social services.

The national Old-Age, Survivors, and Disability Insurance (OASDI), popularly referred to as Social Security and administered by the federal government, is the largest and most important of the income and health insurance programs in the United States. Cash benefits from this program are designed to partially replace income lost when a worker retires or becomes disabled. Cash benefits also are paid to survivors of insured workers. The program also provides partial health care benefits for old age and disability under Medicare. Amendments to the Social Security Act in 1965 set up a contributory health insurance plan for nearly all people aged 65 and over: There was a compulsory program of hospital insurance and a voluntary supplemental insurance to pay for health services. Other amendments also extended coverage to certain severely disabled persons under age 65, including disabled workers, disabled widows and widowers, and childhood disability beneficiaries. Since its inception, Social Security has extended its benefits; old age, survivors, disability, and health insurance coverage approach universal dimensions.

OASDI is a contributory system. It is not to be confused with insurance in the private sector. Payments to beneficiaries are based on previous earnings. As such, equity can be claimed for the system. Beneficiaries of OASDI are not subject to investigation or a means test to establish eligibility. They do not have to prove they are poor to receive benefits. Records are maintained accurately and claims are processed and paid with technological efficiency. The system's administration is handled efficiently and nonjudgmentally. Other retirement income, including that derived from interest on savings, stocks, and bonds, and rental property annuities, regardless of the amount, do not limit payments. On the other hand, limits are placed on the amount of income retired workers can earn from employment while receiving Social Security payments, although no limits are placed on the income people can earn after they turn seventy. To understand this constraint, it is helpful to recall that the Social Security Act was passed in 1935, when the country was experiencing the Great Depression. Many workers were unemployed. Retirement was written into the law to encourage workers aged 65 and older to retire to make way in the labor market for younger men and women. In time of high employment or labor shortage the act might well have to be changed to induce workers not to retire, but to continue in the labor force.

Taxes, under the provision of the Federal Insurance Contribution Act (FICA), are collected on an equally matched basis from the employee and employer during the productive working life of the worker to pay for OASDI. Self-employed workers pay the full amount of the tax. In 1935, the tax was only one percent each for the employee and the employer on an income base of no more than $3,000 per year.

In adopting OASDI, the United States radically departed from reliance on the family, the church, private philanthropy, and local government to provide a bulwark against want. Many believe that such a departure was warranted and that for the retired, disabled, and survivors of insured workers, OASDI offers greater security and financial independence than they previously knew.

Context

After the failure of President Lyndon Johnson's "Great Society" programs of the 1960's, Americans increasingly realized that government cannot solve all problems. Failure of the Great Society (also known as the "War on Poverty") did not result entirely from a lack of resources. In some ways, failure resulted from a lack of leadership. Community action programs and the model cities program failed because power was given to some groups not ready to use it properly and because it was not recognized that great social changes cannot be mandated or brought about overnight in a democratic society. Change must be an extension of the past, and the War on Poverty appeared to lack the impulse necessary for its survival.

Social Security expanded after 1965 into a set of programs. The question is raised: Has it promised too much to too many? It is a fallacy to assume that the nation has unlimited resources, and that only money is needed to solve personal and family problems. The fact is that resources do not exist to provide all things for all people. Choices from alternatives will have to be made. A nation that invests in general health care may be unable to provide good pensions, and the assumption of resources that do not exist can lead to colossal failures in national policy.

Funding for Social Security will certainly present problems in the years ahead. Concern has been expressed about the financial soundness of the system. The incredible growth of the system, and its spiraling costs, may wipe out the "savings" in the trust fund. This means that the system will be paying out more than it is taking in. When Social Security was enacted, only workers in commerce and industry were covered. Since then, major changes have been legislated, greatly broadening the range of coverage and types of benefits paid. Medicare was expanded in 1972.

In time of recession and high unemployment, the number of workers paying into Social Security is decreased, thus reducing the money available to pay beneficiaries. Also, inflation forces upward adjustments of payments, making heavier demands on the Social Security tax (FICA). The decline in the birth rate may become a major concern in the future, when the population in an aging society will be disproportionately large as compared to the younger, working population.

The system is a pay-as-you-go arrangement. Wage earners are taxed to pay benefits to retired and disabled workers and their dependents. Resistance to the system might be expected as taxes increase, causing paychecks to shrink. Also, an increasing number of workers believe that the private sector can offer greater benefits than Social Security. While this is undoubtedly true for many workers, for the vast majority of the population, Social Security offers more income security than private plans do for retired workers, the disabled, and their survivors. Social Security is a form of social insurance and a reasonably well accepted mechanism for sharing costs and transferring income.

With vast experience in working with troubled families and individuals, social workers know that some problems defy complete solution. Money is needed, but so are understanding and compassion. Money cannot provide these, nor is the mere desire to help enough. Robert Frost, speaking of the Israelis, justified education because it "raised human pain and suffering to a higher plane of regard." The solution to many human problems calls for widespread regard for the worth of the individual, and this cherished value cannot be legislated or purchased.

It is true that voluntary human service organizations are experiencing some extremely difficult periods and that some national agencies are in trouble. Voluntary agencies most likely will continue to play an important role, however, as a viable alternative to public entitlement programs in the future. Some people have observed that centralized, computerized federal programs, including Social Security, often are not responsive to the special needs of individuals and localities. A tenet of the human services is that the smaller, private agencies have the edge over larger, computerized governmental systems when it comes to unanticipated needs. Volunteerism in general is needed today as never before, particularly in the human service area.

Bibliography

Ball, Robert M. *Social Security, Today, and Tomorrow*. New York: Columbia University Press, 1978. A former commissioner of social security, Ball supports the present funding and operation of the program.

Cates, Jerry R. *Insuring Inequality: Administrative Leadership in Social Security, 1935-54*. Ann Arbor: University of Michigan Press, 1983. Cates challenges effectively most of the operational assumptions of Ball.

Kamerman, Sheila B., and Alfred J. Kahn. *Social Services in the United States: Policies and Programs*. Philadelphia: Temple University Press, 1976. Clear, objective overview of the wide range of entitlement and human service programs available in the United States.

Mead, Eugene, and Fanchon Mead. *Man Among Men: An Introduction to Sociology*. Englewood Cliffs, N.J.: Prentice-Hall, 1965. Clear and readable description of the development of social welfare in England, presented as a social history.

Murray, Charles. *Losing Ground: American Social Policy, 1950-1980*. New York: Basic Books, 1984. Cogent analysis of the dilemmas resulting from the realization that government intervention in social problems is not always effective.

Owen, David. *English Philanthropy, 1660-1960*. Cambridge, Mass.: The Belknap Press of Harvard University Press, 1964. Analysis of the political philosophies underlying English philanthropy since the Middle Ages.

Spindler, Arthur. *Public Welfare*. New York: Human Sciences Press, 1979. Includes the laws and court decisions under which public welfare operates, eligibility requirements for various programs, its methods, and its problems.

Trattner, Walter I. *From Poor Law to Welfare State: A History of Social Welfare in America*. New York: Free Press, 1974. Careful historical study of the common law traditions in British and American welfare legislation.

Turner, Jonathan H., and Charles E. Starnes. *Inequality: Privilege and Poverty in*

America. Pacific Palisades, Calif.: Goodyear, 1976. Describes the operation of policies that offer significant "wealthfare" to the wealthy in our society. Excellent tables on the distribution of assets, income, and wealth.

Robert D. Bryant

Cross-References

City Government in the United States, p. 266; Debts and Deficits in the U.S. Federal Budget, p. 489; The Family and Politics in the United States, p. 649; Funding of Government, p. 724; Government Agencies, p. 765; Government Roles, p. 778; Grants-in-Aid, p. 791; Race and Ethnicity, p. 1654; Social Services, p. 1858; Socialism, p. 1865; Urban Renewal and Housing, p. 2064; The Welfare State, p. 2135.

ENVIRONMENTAL PROTECTION

Field of study: Functions of government

The environment provides habitats, resources, and amenities. It can be damaged or depleted through natural events, production of goods, or accidents. Government intervention has become necessary to provide a socially acceptable level of environmental quality and resource availability. The Environmental Protection Agency is responsible for monitoring and regulating environmental quality and resource supplies in the United States.

Principal terms

ENVIRONMENT: air, water and land that provides natural resources for production, a habitat for survival, and aesthetic benefits

ENVIRONMENTAL PROTECTION AGENCY: the primary U.S. government agency responsible for environmental and natural resource protection

EXTERNALITY: the results of an action that affect people other than those who performed the action

POLLUTION: waste put into the environment above the level that the environment can absorb or recycle

PUBLIC GOOD: a good that is provided to everyone at once, and from which no one can be excluded

Overview

The environment is defined as the existing air, land, water, and resources. The environment serves three basic functions: it supports living species, supplies resources for production, and provides aesthetic benefits. The environment must contain air, land, water, and other resources of sufficient quality and quantity to support the diverse species living on the planet. Natural resources used for production include minerals, foods, and wildlife, from which the goods and services necessary to support life and increase living standards can be produced. Finally, the environment provides aesthetic benefits, such as natural beauty and recreational opportunities.

These three functions are often at odds. Production uses resources and may decrease the quality of the environment's habitat and aesthetic beauty. Maintaining resources for habitat and aesthetic purposes decreases resources available for production and increasing living standards. For example, forests provide a habitat for many species and provide recreational opportunities, but timber is a prime resource for production of many goods. Cutting down trees for production takes away crucial habitats and recreational opportunities.

The environment can be adversely affected by many different influences. Natural disasters, for example, floods, fires, and earthquakes, can dramatically influence the balance of nature. Humans also impact the environmental balance. Activities associated with human society and production can interfere with natural processes. Growing

Government and Politics

crops can erode the soil, and building cities can interrupt the life cycle of wildlife. Economic activities also create waste. Production entails transforming inputs into output, but some of the inputs are unusable and become waste. Waste that can be absorbed into the environment, like food in a compost heap, or recycled, like aluminum cans that are collected and reused, does not severely impact the environment. When more waste is released into the environment than the environment can absorb, however, waste becomes pollution. For example, a manufacturer might create chemical waste. Limited amounts of almost any chemical can be absorbed by the environment without causing significant harm. When the firm releases the chemical in amounts that exceed the environment's ability to harmlessly absorb or recycle it, pollution results.

The amount of environmental damage and resource depletion can be reduced in any of three ways: the amount of production can be decreased, so that fewer resources are required and less waste is produced; methods of production that decrease the resource requirements and creation of waste can be used; or ways to recycle waste and resources can be implemented. Relying on voluntary use of these approaches to protecting the environment may not result in optimal levels of environmental protection. It is often necessary for the government to intervene and provide regulation to achieve resource conservation and environmental protection.

Two economic concepts illustrate why the government often must step in to protect the environment and conserve resources. First, degradation of the environment and use of resources can create negative externalities. In economic terms, a negative externality results when an activity is performed by one individual but the costs of the activity fall on another individual. Pollution is a negative externality because those who do the polluting receive the economic benefit of disposing of their waste, while the costs of pollution fall on everyone who lives in the environment. Hunting a species to extinction creates a negative externality because the hunters get the economic benefit of hunting the animal, while society bears the costs of no longer having the species to use and enjoy. In such cases, the government must step in to regulate pollution and conserve resources by making those who damage the environment bear the costs of their actions.

A second reason for the government to regulate environmental quality is that the environment is a public good. A public good is something that cannot be provided to one person without providing it to all; conversely, no one can be excluded from consuming a public good. The environment is a public good because everyone benefits from having a quality environment. A clean environment and protection of resources, like wildlife, provide benefits for everyone. Whether a person works hard to keep the environment clean and resources protected or pollutes and wastes resources, everyone lives in the same environment. Environmental protection cannot be provided for one person without providing it to everyone.

Because the environment is a public good, like a national park or wildlife, it will not be protected efficiently if the government does not step in. Since everyone will benefit from environmental protection and no one can be excluded from it, not everyone will contribute to it, and the quality of the environment will be below the optimal level. If all people were left to make voluntary "clean environment" or "wildlife protection" contributions, some would contribute but others would not. Government must use its powers to attain the socially optimal level of environmental protection. Contributions to protect the environment are made through the government and taxes.

There are many examples of the government intervening to protect the environment and provide public goods. An early example of what can happen when there is no government intervention to protect a public good occurred in the West in the nineteenth century. Large herds of wild buffalo roamed the plains. Since the buffalo had no owners, they were available to everyone. Native Americans hunted the buffalo for many years without depleting this resource. When white hunters began hunting the buffalo for their hides, however, ever larger numbers were killed, because individual hunters did not bear the cost of their actions although they received a benefit. Society experienced negative externalities and the public good, the buffalo, was almost completely depleted. The government intervened to protect the public good and force hunters to bear the costs of their actions. The government was thus able to save the herds from extinction.

An example of government provision of another public good is the national parks system. Individuals do not have the ability or incentive to provide national parks in socially desirable amounts. Because society values wilderness areas, it is necessary for the federal government to intervene. Only with government intervention can a large system of national parks be maintained, providing wilderness to everyone without excluding anyone.

That the environment is a public good and environmental degradation is a negative externality provides the rationale for government having an environmental protection function. As part of its role, the government must determine what level of environmental quality the public wants, monitor the actual state of the environment, and regulate environmental destruction to protect and to improve environmental quality. The government must protect and conserve the environment as a public good for future generations.

Environmental protection functions are carried out by the Environmental Protection Agency (EPA). It is an independent agency located in the executive branch of the government with an administrator appointed by the president. The agency was established in 1970 to protect and improve the nation's physical environment. Since 1970, additional legislation has added to the powers of the EPA, notably the Clean Air Act of 1990. The EPA is concerned with the purity of air, water, and land, and therefore regulates solid waste, pesticides, toxic substances, noise, radiation, and medical waste. It is also charged with resource conservation and recovery.

The EPA's first role, determining what level of environmental protection the public wants, is difficult. The answer to the question "How clean should the environment be?" might well be different for every person. It is the government's responsibility, through the political system, to decide what level of environmental quality is best for all. People all agree that the environment must provide a habitat that supports life. Most people agree that environmental quality should be high enough that they can live comfortable and healthy lives—but how comfortable and how healthy differs from person to person. On the other hand, life necessarily means consuming resources and creating waste. There is a trade-off between environmental quality and production and consumption. The government, through the EPA, must determine the appropriate level of environmental protection.

The second role, monitoring the state of the environment, is done by scientists working for the EPA. EPA scientists must constantly research the state of the environment and the impact of activities on that state. The size of the task and constantly changing scientific knowledge make it a difficult task.

Finally, the EPA is charged with protecting and improving the environment. The quality of the air, water, and land are all considered. Natural resource conservation and recovery must also be monitored by the EPA. The EPA determines the optimal levels of environmental quality, creates regulations to achieve those levels, and enforces the regulations. The size of the environment, the number of activities that degrade the environment, and the variety of natural resources to be conserved make this a formidable task.

Applications

Government regulation of the environment in the United States began before the creation of the EPA. Legislation in the 1940's and 1950's started some of the preliminary research into national environmental issues and problems. This wave of legislation, including the Air Pollution Control Act of 1955 and the Water Pollution Control Act of 1948, focused on environmental legislation from a federal viewpoint, but left regulation and control of the environment to individual states. During this time, it was noticed that in some cases the environment did not automatically provide a quality habitat and natural resources. It also became clear that in some instances the environment as a public good was not automatic or costless. The environment would not clean itself or provide sufficient resources on its own. Thus, the government began to address environmental protection, though leaving the responsibility for regulation to the states.

In the 1960's, it became obvious to many that the earth was beginning to exceed its carrying capacity. The earth was no longer able to recycle naturally all the waste emitted, and all natural resources were no longer renewed naturally. This realization caused many to become concerned with the issue of environmental protection. On April 22, 1970, the first Earth Day was held. Earth Day was an event designed to raise public awareness and illustrate public concern about environmental issues. Environmental activism and political lobbying for environmental legislation increased around this same time. As a result, much environmental legislation was passed during the late 1960's and early 1970's. The original Clean Air Act was passed in 1970 and the Safe Drinking Water Act in 1974. Other laws dealing with toxic substances, pesticides, and harmful substances also appeared. The federal government changed from passing laws that left responsibility with the states, to enacting legislation that mandated state action.

State action was not swift and certain, and many problems resulted from the states not complying with the federal laws. Tension between federal mandates and state responsibilities to meet these mandates remains. In 1990, Congress passed amendments to the Clean Air Act to reaffirm the federal government's role in environmental protection. These amendments deal with the emissions of toxic chemicals into the air, in particular sulfur dioxide emissions, which come largely from electric power generating plants and automobile emissions. These emissions have been determined to contribute to smog and acid rain. The amendments required sharp reductions in emissions to speed up improvements in air quality.

The justification for this regulation comes from the fact that clean air is a public good while pollution is an externality. Firms that release sulfur dioxide do not bear the cost of the emissions; those who suffer the costs of the acid rain that falls downwind do. Society as a whole loses when the public good, a clean environment, is degraded. The individual firm has no incentive, on its own, to clean up the air. State governments were ineffective in regulating air quality. Often, the cost of sulfur dioxide emissions fell on those in states that were downwind or in Canada. This gave state governments little incentive to address the problem, and a political reason not to, since people in other countries and states do not vote for them. Thus, the federal government became responsible for regulating air quality when costs traveled across state and national borders.

The government also has a role in protecting existing environmental resources. One example is the decision to set aside land in Alaska as a national park. Provided to all Americans who wish to visit them, these park lands are public goods. The creation of parks protects the environment and habitat for current and future generations. Not everyone was pleased with the decision to create these national parks. Some felt that the public good was so valuable that even more land should be set aside. Others felt that the resources given up by not producing on the land were too high a price to pay for a park. Government intervention was required to determine the socially optimal level of land to set aside, based on public opinion and lobbying, and to create the parks.

The extent of the role that government should play in environmental issues is frequently debated. There are those who feel the government should play a larger role in environmental protection. For example, environmental groups spend considerable resources lobbying for stronger legislation to protect the environment. Others feel the government should play a smaller role in environmental protection and leave environmental issues to the states or the market. Almost everyone agrees that the government must play some role in providing public goods and correcting externalities; however, the extent of the role that government should play varies from person to person.

Context

As the environment becomes less able to absorb additional waste and renew natural resources, government intervention to provide the optimal level of environmental protection becomes more necessary. Awareness of the extent and interstate nature of environmental issues was first addressed by federal legislation in the 1940's. Awareness and federal government intervention grew with the scope of the problem through the 1960's and 1970's. Recently, environmental issues have become global. As world population, production, and consumption have increased, environmental quality and natural resource availability have become larger issues. In addition, the issues are becoming more global in scope. The environment does not stop at a country's border: air, water, and wildlife continually cross national boundaries. Dealing with environmental issues will require increasing international cooperation in the future.

Examples of global environmental problems abound. Global warming, acid rain, and ozone depletion are all concerns that affect and must be addressed jointly by the entire world. Our global environment is a public good. The Great Lakes provide an illustration of the necessity of global cooperation in addressing environmental protection. Since the United States and Canada each border the Great Lakes, their environmental quality can only be improved if each country is involved. If the United States tries to improve the quality of the water or quantity of fish in the lakes, it will have no effect unless Canada does so also. As long as one country degrades the lakes, nothing the other can do alone will improve their quality.

A second example involves species extinction. If a species migrates across the territory of several countries, or through common areas such as oceans, only global cooperation can work to stop extinctions. For example, whales swim through the territories of many countries as well as in international waters. Without international cooperation resulting in global solutions, such as the Antarctic whale sanctuary created in 1994, whales cannot be protected.

In June, 1992, the leaders of almost every country in the world met for the United Nations Conference on Environment and Development, commonly known as the Earth Summit. While few concrete results came from the meeting, it illustrates the realization that environmental issues are increasing in importance and have become global issues.

Bibliography

Gore, Albert. *Earth in the Balance*. New York: Plume, 1993. Global environmentalist's view of issues in the 1990's, including acid rain, ozone depletion, and global warming.

Mackenthun, Kenneth M., and Jacob I. Bregman. *Environmental Regulations Handbook*. Boca Raton, Fla.: Lewis, 1992. Summary and history of environmental legislation.

Murphy, Earl Finbar. *Man and His Environment: Law*. New York: Harper & Row, 1971. This volume is from a series that looks at issues of environmental protection during a period when the issue was first becoming politically important.

O'Leary, Rosemary. *Environmental Change: Federal Courts and the EPA*. Philadelphia: Temple University Press, 1993. Detailed explanation of the role and functions of the EPA.

Sharpe, Ansel, Charles Register, and Richard Leftwhich. "Pollution Problems: Must We Foul Our Own Nests?" In *Economics of Social Issues*. Burr Ridge, Ill.: Richard D. Irwin, 1994. Develops the basic underpinnings of the role of government in environmental protection.

Tietenberg, Tom. *Environmental Economics and Policy*. New York: HarperCollins, 1994. Comprehensive coverage of the economics of environmental policy.

Margaret A. Ray

Cross-References

EPICUREAN POLITICAL PHILOSOPHY

Field of study: Political philosophy

The Epicurean philosophy arose in fourth century Athens, having as a basic tenet that pleasure (absence of pain and anxiety) was the highest good attainable by humankind. That this pleasure is obtained after living a life of restraint, temperance, and simplicity has many sociopolitical and religious implications.

Principal terms
CANONIC: explanation of the rules (canons) that identify truth, similar to logic in other Greek philosophies
DIDACTIC: works or actions related to or involved in teaching
ETHICS: basis for morality, according to Epicureans and other Greek philosophers
HEDONISM: devotion to excessive worldly pleasures
NEPOTISM: favoritism granted by persons in high office to relatives or close friends
PHYSICS: Epicurean explanation of the nature of both the world and the gods
PLEASURE: absence of pain and anxiety, obtained by a life of temperance, restraint, and simplicity
PROPAGANDA: systematic propagation of a doctrine, or the defamation of ideas contrary to it, by written or spoken means
UTILITARIANISM: sociopolitical doctrine that utility is the criterion of good or worthy actions, and social or political effort must aim at the greatest good for the greatest number of people

Overview

The term "Epicurean" denotes a member of the school of philosophy that was founded by Epicurus of Athens (342-270 B.C.E.). Epicureanism was started by Epicurus in the fourth century B.C.E. and ended as a distinct sociopolitical entity during the fourth century C.E. Many scholars believe it arose as a revolt against the popular Greek religious forms of the day, Plato's rationalism, and the antiscientific superstition that then pervaded both Greece and Greek thought.

Throughout its seven century existence, the proponents of Epicureanism were many. The first major disciples of Epicurus were Metrodorus of Lampsacus (330-277 B.C.E.) and Hermarchus of Mytilene (325-249 B.C.E.), who succeeded Epicurus as the leader of the Epicureans. Famous Epicureans in the second and first centuries B.C.E. included the moralists Zeno of Sidon and Demetrius of Laconia. At this time, Epicureanism spread to Rome, where its main proponents were the famous Roman poet and philosopher Lucretius (Titus Lucretius Carus, 94-55 B.C.E.), and Rome's great political poet, Vergil (70-19 B.C.E.), author of *The Aeneid*.

Many other famous Romans, even Julius Caesar, are thought to have been sympathetic to Epicureanism. Unlike the other philosophic schools of the time, Epicureanism spread widely throughout the Mediterranean world. Hence, Epicureanism was viewed by many as being the first successful missionary philosophy. It is thought that its disappearance was a result of its being absorbed into Christianity, which at first had abhorred Epicureanism but then appears to have been strongly affected by its philosophy. For example, the Epicureans are credited with innovation of Christian concepts such as peace of mind, hope, and brotherly love, concepts that Christianity adopted from Greek classicism.

Unlike Stoicism, which evolved greatly throughout its history, the teachings of Epicurus were modified very little through the centuries. Succeeding generations of Epicurean masters, such as Lucretius, felt called upon only to expand on the original statements that were found in Epicurus' philosophy, to improve its didactic sense, and to refute the arguments of philosophers Epicureanism dismissed or slandered.

The early Epicureans, who reputedly practiced great moderation and austerity in their personal lives, have been widely viewed in modern times as having been extreme hedonists. Numerous modern scholars believe that the idea that Epicureans sought excessive sensory pleasure is due to slanderous propaganda that was disseminated by competing Athenian schools of philosophy, for example, Stoics such as Cicero, and later by Jews and early Christians.

An aspect of the Epicurean school that helped ancient propagandists to generate this misconception was that from the early days women were allowed as members. Such status for women was unheard of elsewhere at the time and was viewed by many as being highly morally suspect. Also, during Epicurus's time, the Epicurean school both lived and met privately in a secluded garden that the philosopher had purchased. Thus, it would have been difficult to disprove such propaganda, assuming that they wished to do so.

Another component of Epicureanism that promoted the idea that Epicureans were hedonists was the basic tenet by which they lived: that pleasure is the greatest good attainable by humans. Once again, a surface reading of an aspect of Epicureanism is misleading. To Epicurus and his disciples, pleasure is only the absence of pain and anxiety, and almost all Epicureans thought that great pleasure was obtained only by living a life of quiet restraint, temperance, and simplicity.

Epicurus, like the other Greek philosophers, divided all of his teachings into three parts, which he called the canonic, physics, and ethics. The Epicurean canonic was similar to the logic used by other philosophers. It provided an exposition of the rules or canons that are used to identify the truth. The physics and ethics of Epicurus, as was the case in the other Greek philosophic schools, explain the nature of both the world and of the gods, and the basis for human morality, respectively.

The canonic of Epicurus was quite simple. It proposed that there was only one means by which true knowledge could be obtained: the direct physical perceptions based upon the senses, which were always entirely reliable because the senses interacted with exact images of all things that can be perceived. Errors that arise in the explanation of the truth, Epicurus said, are not due to sensual misperceptions but rather to opinions that are formed by the human mind and later contradicted or unconfirmed.

Epicurean physics is a variation and an extension of the atomism that had been described earlier by Democritus of Abdera (460-360 B.C.E.). The atomic theory of Epicurus proposed that nothing exists in the cosmos except for indestructible atoms of various kinds and the empty space (void) in which they move. Humans, universes, and the gods, he said, are all the result of chance arrangements of various atoms. Gods are immortal, according to Epicurus, because the flow of atoms into them balances the outward atom flow into the void. In humans, however, the atom outflow exceeds its inflow, causing eventual human death.

Epicurean ethics arose from the physics and the canonic, and asserted that the highest attainments possible for humankind were the serene enjoyment of life and freedom from the violence caused by desires. This predominantly religious and ethical concept, along with the belief that pleasure is the greatest good that can be attained by human beings, governed Epicurean political philosophy. The two other main aspects of Epicurean theology and psychology are the beliefs that the soul dissolves immediately on death, so human fear of death is pointless because upon death we no longer exist; and the gods should not be feared, because they neither trouble human beings nor are they troubled by human affairs.

Applications

The Epicurean view of politics was that it should be avoided wherever possible, and that honesty is the best policy when such avoidance is impossible. The first position is based on the doctrine of Epicurus, which proposes that the best course of action for a wise human is to withdraw into the security of quiet solitude. This concept led to the first Epicureans segregating themselves in the garden of Epicurus, a similar search for seclusion by most later Epicureans, and relatively infrequent Epicurean participation in politics compared to members of the other contemporary Greek philosophic schools.

Balancing this planned political avoidance was the Epicurean notion that injustice, which was evil because it decreased the extent of pleasure for individuals via the improper action of most citizens, had to be fought by the wise individual. This led some Epicureans into the political arena as a means to assure themselves of the maximum attainment of pleasure. Although for true Epicureans pleasure was merely the absence of pain and anxiety, their political or philosophic foes did not recognize that this was their definition of pleasure, and accused all Epicurean politicians of being hedonistic, self-seeking, and biased. Honest politics, as an Epicurean goal, may be inferred from statements of Epicurus proposing that no one can live pleasantly who does not do so in a prudent, honorable, and just fashion, and that human laws that are not advantageous in human relations lack justice.

Propaganda against Epicurean politicians was helped along by Epicurus' view that friendships should be cultivated and deferred to in all aspects of life, because they lead to both increased pleasure and security for all of the individuals involved. This notion resulted in some apparent corruption in political situations by Epicurean politicians who gave preference to their friends wherever possible. It may also be one philosophic basis of nepotism. A corollary to the Epicurean view on friendship was their notion that all human societies are based on self-interest, meaning that they exist due to the agreement of people to avoid harming each other because of mutual advantages gained.

The Lucretian didactic epic poem *De Rerum Natura (On the Nature of Things)* points out that Epicureans tried to closely follow all the doctrines of Epicurus hundreds of years after his death. The poem, divided into six books, primarily deals with the principles of the Epicurean atomist universe; the nature of the soul, including the belief that death is meaningless and not to be feared; the creation of the world and all things in it, exactly as defined by Epicurus; and the basis for natural phenomena. Associated with Epicurean philosophy—implicitly, not explicitly—are Epicurus' concepts of the evolution of human life and human society, and of humankind unafraid of death or the gods. Lucretius, some sources propose, might have talked more directly about the Epicurean political philosophy had he not died before finishing *On the Nature of Things*.

More modern political philosophers influenced by Epicureanism are Thomas Jefferson (1743-1826), who saw himself as an Epicurean in matters such as the minimization of government, and his contemporary, Jeremy Bentham, the founder and chief exponent of the British sociopolitical doctrine of utilitarianism. Several of Bentham's works show the influence of Epicurus, especially *An Introduction to the Principles of Morals and Legislation* (1789). In that book, Bentham defined the main principle of utilitarianism, that of utility as being a property of objects or actions that produce pleasure or happiness, or serve as a deterrent to pain, evil, or unhappiness in individuals.

Like Epicurus, Bentham believed that humankind was governed mainly by pain and pleasure. He stipulated, therefore, that all human action—including politics and legislation—must produce the greatest good for the greatest number of people, a philosophy clearly influenced by Epicureanism. Bentham's lifestyle was somewhat analogous to that in the garden of Epicurus; Bentham gathered around him a close circle of friends with whom he associated exclusively. Primary among these friends was James Mill (1773-1836), once the director of the British East India Company and then Bentham's successor as the head of the utilitarian movement. Mill's son, John Stuart Mill (1806-1873), author of *Principles of Political Economy* (1848) and *Utilitarianism* (1863), succeeded the elder Mill as the leader of utilitarianism. Both father and son appear to have been influenced by Epicurean thought.

Context

In the twentieth century, many people erroneously view the philosophy of Epicurus as having been a form of hedonism. This is exemplified by the scholars who call it altruistic hedonism, by trivial book titles such as *An Epicurean Cookbook*, and by the idea of the excesses of Epicurean delights. These ideas are refuted by the handful of surviving writings of Epicurus, the faithful representation of his ideas by Lucretius, and the commentary of his later interpreters.

In reality, Epicureanism appears to have been a popular and profound sociopolitical philosophy that has had great impact on the religion, economics, political thought, and ethics of our time. The Epicurean proposal that humans attain pleasure—the absence of pain and of anxiety—by living lives of restraint, temperance, and simplicity was an admirable doctrine, and has been followed by many more recent thinkers. Perhaps that is why Epicureanism was quickly incorporated into early Christianity and into the eighteenth century sociopolitical doctrine of utilitarianism. In addition, Epicurus allowed women into his philosophic school. Hence, he and the Epicurean school may be seen as strong proponents of women's rights, thousands of years before the suffrage movement.

Another relevant aspect of Epicurean philosophy is its view on politics: to avoid it if possible, but to be honest when engaged in it. Not all would agree with the first part of the statement; however, honesty is a trait in politicians that is dearly desired, and seen less often than wished by the public. The basis for such honest policy, according to Epicurus, was that no one can live pleasantly who is not prudent, honorable, and just. This view was complemented by his idea that all just human laws yield advantageous human interactions.

Propaganda against the Epicurean political point of view was advanced by Epicurus' idea that friendships should be cultivated and deferred to in politics, as in all other aspects of life. Such nepotism was probably a minor drawback, however, because it was also common in non-Epicurean politics, and for reasons less idealistic than those proposed by Epicurus. The corollary to that view, the notion that all human societies are based upon self-interest, because people agree to avoid harming each other to obtain mutual advantages, is also sound politics and has lasted into the twentieth century.

Scholars such as DeWitt have attributed to Epicurus some sound sociopolitical aspects of Christian philosophy, including the search for peace of mind, the concept of hope, and the idea of brotherly love. Perhaps one reason that Epicureanism is often erroneously discounted as a philosophy that was never very popular, despite evidence to the contrary, was that it was quickly absorbed into Christianity. This assertion cannot be proved with certainty, but it is clear that Epicurus was a profound sociopolitical thinker whose ideas pervade many aspects of twentieth century society.

Bibliography

DeWitt, Norman W. *Epicurus and His Philosophy*. Minneapolis: University of Minnesota Press, 1954. Relates existing data on the life of Epicurus to the development of his philosophy, explores Epicureanism as a source of Christian beliefs, and proposes that the Epicurean innovation of concepts such as peace of mind, hope, and brotherly love paved the way for the transformation of Greek classicism into Christian religion and sociopolitical ethics.

Long, A. A. *Hellenistic Philosophy: Stoics, Epicureans, Sceptics*. New York: Charles Scribner's Sons, 1974. Traces the main developments of Greek philosophy from

323 B.C.E. to the end of the Roman Republic. Discusses Epicurus' life, works, and philosophy; the concepts of knowledge, atomism, the gods, the soul, and mental processes; freedom of action, pleasure and happiness, justice and friendship. Good bibliography.

Panichas, George A. *Epicurus*. New York: Twayne, 1967. Introductory essay meant to familiarize the reader with the basic tenets of the philosophy of Epicurus. Selected bibliography.

Shapiro, Herman, and Edmin M. Curley, eds. *Hellenistic Philosophy: Selected Readings in Epicureanism, Stoicism, Skepticism, and Neoplatonism*. New York: Modern Library, 1965. Contains two important works of Epicurus, and *De Rerum Natura* by Lucretius. The first two set forth important aspects of the original philosophy of Epicurus; the third is a restatement of portions of the doctrines by one of his famous later disciples.

Strodach, George K. *The Philosophy of Epicurus*. Evanston, Ill.: Northwestern University Press, 1963. Contains a number of the works of Epicurus, and attempts to describe his life and philosophy. Includes Epicurus' leading doctrines and excerpts of material published by Diogenes Laertes, who describes both slander of Epicurus by important members of other Greek philosophic schools and his actual general goodness.

Sanford S. Singer

Cross-References

Mill's Political Philosophy, p. 1204; Plato's Political Philosophy, p. 1396; Political Philosophy, p. 1505; Stoic Political Philosophy, p. 1904; Utilitarianism, p. 2077.

EQUALITY AND EGALITARIANISM

Field of study: Political philosophy

Equality, a word with many meanings, did not become a vigorously contested idea until the eighteenth century. Policies that promote different ideas about equality create some of the major dilemmas of modern politics.

Principal terms

EGALITARIAN: believing in economic, political, and legal equality for all

EGALITARIANISM: belief that attaches first importance to the attainment of equality

EQUAL TREATMENT: equality in practice as well as theory

EQUALITY OF OPPORTUNITY: equal chances to better one's lot in life

PROGRESSIVE TAXATION: taxation that increases with income

REDISTRIBUTIVE POLICIES: policies that take money from one group to allocate to another group

Overview

The phrase "All men are created equal" is the first of the self-evident truths listed in the Declaration of Independence of the United States (1776). Thomas Jefferson, the young farmer and lawyer from Virginia who drafted the document, was not, however, an egalitarian. Egalitarianism never has been part of mainstream political thought in America. By contemporary standards, the author of the Declaration of Independence had a very restricted idea of equality. He accepted male supremacy, racial superiority, and the concentration of economic wealth and political power in the hands of white males with property. Jefferson was not alone; his constricted view of equality was shared by most of the delegates who, from May to September of 1787, gathered in Philadelphia and framed the U.S. Constitution.

Moreover, Jefferson and the Founders were at the end of a long antiegalitarian tradition in the history of Western political philosophy. For centuries, the political, social, and economic inequality of human beings had been taken for granted. Anti-egalitarianism, in fact, is as old as political philosophy. In the fifth century B.C.E., Plato, whom many consider to be the father of political philosophy, viewed the entire cosmos in terms of a hierarchy. Everything in the universe had its proper place and purpose. He believed that in a well-ordered or just society those who by nature are best suited for carpentry will be carpenters, that those best suited for military careers will be soldiers, and that those best suited for rule will be kings. Viewed from his perspective, any attempt to implement a doctrine of universal equality represents a crime against nature. Plato was merely the first in a long line of political philosophers to use the metaphor of a cosmic hierarchy to explain and justify the existence of inequality.

The ideal of equality, on the other hand, was never totally absent from the Western intellectual tradition. For example, the Greek philosopher Protagoras, a contemporary of Plato, advocated granting political rights to women and slaves. In the fourth century B.C.E., the Greek school of thought known as Stoicism envisioned an ideal state void of property, family, and racial distinctions. For the most part the Stoics were indifferent to politics; so too were the early Christians, for whom equality was a prehistorical ideal—a garden paradise characterized by peace, freedom, and equality—and a hope to be realized in the heavenly city. Concerning the inequalities of the earthly city, the message of early Christianity was generally one of passive obedience to the will of God. It was Saint Augustine (354-430 C.E.), the early Church leader and philosopher, who provided the theological justification for the inequalities that result from the dominion of one person over another. He proclaimed them to be the deserved punishment of God for the sins of humanity. By the time Thomas Aquinas (1225-1274) developed his philosophical system, the Roman Catholic church had become a great temporal power, and Aquinas found it necessary to return to a hierarchical metaphor to justify the place of papacy in the grand scheme of Creation. He pictured a cosmic hierarchy with God at the top, and the Church just below directing temporal affairs according to his divine plan.

The development of modern ideas about equality had to await the second half of the seventeenth century, when scientific advances replaced the classical and medieval, earth-centered cosmology with a nonhierarchical cosmology that pictured the universe as a mechanical system operating according to its own laws. These laws of nature applied equally to human beings and planetary bodies. In this new conception of the universe, a kind of cosmic equality prevailed. Political theorists faced the question of how dominion of one person over another could be justified without reference to a natural hierarchy.

Among the first of the political theorists to meet this new challenge was the late seventeenth century English philosopher John Locke. Since it was no longer plausible to provide a rationale for government on the basis of the metaphor of a natural hierarchical order, Locke proclaimed that the only kind of legitimate government was one that derived its authority from the people. This view was a radical shift away from the view that authority descended from God to king to noble to freeman to slave. Moreover, he believed that the primary purpose of government was to protect the people's God-given rights to life, liberty, and property. The fact that Locke placed a particularly strong emphasis upon the right to property is critical to his understanding of equality. In his system, equality meant the equal right of all to accumulate, preserve, and dispose of the fruits of their labor as each saw fit. All people had an equal chance to better their economic condition.

Jefferson and the delegates to the constitutional convention were disciples of Locke. His philosophy shaped and gave form to their thinking about equality. Like Locke, they believed in all people's right to improve their economic circumstances. Unfortunately, what this meant in practice was that white males with property had an equal chance to leave the less fortunate behind, for it was the white males who controlled property in colonial America, and those white males who were most successful in developing their property would gain not only wealth, but political power as well.

Applications

Equality of opportunity, or the absence of barriers to individual achievement, is the idea of equality accepted by most Americans. Two other closely related notions of equality that rank high for most Americans are political equality and equal treatment.

Americans are especially dedicated to equality of opportunity in the marketplace. Consider tax policy. While Americans tend, begrudgingly, to accept that taxation is needed to provide for the common defense and general welfare, they are much less receptive to the policy of progressive taxation, the practice of taxing high-income people at a higher rate to fund social programs for low-income people. The basis of this opposition is the widespread belief that government policies designed to redistribute income penalize success and reward failure. This attitude also holds true for government programs intended to provide a safety net for those who fall off the economic tightrope of the capitalist system. Especially controversial is the program Aid to Families with Dependent Children (AFDC). When Americans talk about "the welfare program" it is, more often than not, this program and its beneficiaries they have in mind. Intended to help needy widows and to provide their children with a chance in life, AFDC has in recent years increasingly come to be perceived as a program that punishes hard-working, industrious individuals in order to support the indolent and undeserving. Although this outlook may not conform with the facts, in politics image is often more important than reality. Critics of AFDC would like to see it replaced by a policy requiring able-bodied adults to follow a program designed to provide recipients with opportunities to become self-supporting.

Many Americans think of political equality in terms of free and fair elections, by which they mean an electoral process in which everyone is allowed to participate. Equality at the ballot box did not come easy. At first, the only eligible voters were white males who owned property or paid taxes. The Constitution left the matter of voter eligibility in the hands of the states, and it took more than a half century for all the states to drop their economic barriers. This change was brought about by pressures exerted by the growing democratic sentiments in the new republic.

The odious institution of slavery did not bend as easily. African Americans were denied the right to vote until passage of the Fifteenth Amendment in 1870. Immediate enjoyment of this right was postponed. Legal barriers to voting designed to keep African Americans from exercising their constitutional rights were quickly erected in many states, especially in the South. For example, the poll tax, designed specifically for this purpose, remained in effect until the Twenty-fourth Amendment was passed in 1964. Three years earlier the Twenty-third Amendment had allowed residents of Washington, D.C., to vote in national elections. Women had already been granted the franchise by the Nineteenth Amendment in 1920. The Twenty-sixth Amendment, ratified in 1971, grants those eighteen years old and older the right to vote. The amendments indicate the long struggle that was fought so that all Americans, rich and poor, white and nonwhite, male and female, might have the right to vote.

Constitutional rights are one thing, equal treatment quite another. Equality of treatment calls for tolerance and inclusiveness. In a pluralistic society, however, respect for differences does not always come easily, and in the course of American history the government has found it necessary to define and implement equal treatment for disadvantaged groups, always in the face of strong opposition.

African Americans did not receive equal treatment at the ballot box until passage of the Voting Rights Act of 1965, which authorized federal registrars to register voters in seven southern states. The significant breakthrough in the long and continuing struggle for the equal treatment of schoolchildren was the Supreme Court's invalidation of racial discrimination in *Brown v. Board of Education of Topeka* in 1954. This decision, together with the Civil Rights Act of 1964, which prohibited racial discrimination in employment practices and public housing, initiated a revolution in race relations.

The movement for the equal treatment of women closely parallels that of African Americans. The Equal Pay Act of 1963 required equal pay for men and women engaged in similar work. The Civil Rights Act of 1964 empowered federal officials to act on behalf of victims of sex discrimination. Then, after the Supreme Court began to take a close look at gender-based distinctions, it proceeded in a series of decisions to strike down distinctions based upon sex. Native Americans have also met with some success in their quest for equal treatment. In the 1970's, they began to reassert treaty rights and to press for greater tribal autonomy. Those living off reservations now have full rights of citizenship. Disabled Americans were the next to benefit from the politics of inclusiveness. The Americans with Disabilities Act (1990) extended equal and fair treatment to people with physical or mental disabilities in employment, transportation, public accommodations, and communication services. Gays and lesbians, who represented the frontier in the movement toward equal treatment, did not fare as well as other minorities. The homosexual rights movement received a severe setback when the Supreme Court ruled in *Bowers v. Hardwick* in 1986 that homosexual relations between consenting adults did not have constitutional protection.

Context

The history of the twentieth century can be interpreted largely in terms of the quest for equality. Few words engender as much passion: People have lived, fought for, and died in its cause. Equality was the ideal that provided the motivation behind the socialist movements that swept through much of Europe in the nineteenth century, and it also inspired the communist movement in Eastern Europe and China in the twentieth century. The pursuit of equality also played an important role in the history of modern Africa, much of which can be read in terms of the determined effort to end the white monopoly on wealth and political power. In America, the Civil Rights movement to end white supremacy is perhaps the most momentous event of the twentieth century. It is followed closely in importance by the rebellion of women against their subordinate roles within male-dominated economic, political, and social institutions. Although it is true that significant gains have been made, marked racial and sexual inequalities remain.

To these issues can be added the gay rights movement, which continuously gained momentum after the 1970's, when gay and lesbian individuals came out of the closet, identifying themselves as homosexuals and demanding that their lifestyles be legitimized. The legal status of homosexuals is unclear. The movement has suffered legal setbacks in the courts, but so too did the Civil Rights and women's movements in the first decades of their existence. Although there seems to be a general liberalization of attitudes toward gay individuals among the American public, in some quarters there is also strong opposition to their movement for equal treatment. This was made clear to President Bill Clinton when he set out to fulfill his 1992 campaign promise to lift the ban on gays in the military. Clinton met so much resistance from military leaders that he was forced to compromise and settle for a policy of "don't ask, don't tell." Military recruits would no longer be asked if they are homosexual, but practicing homosexuals could still be discharged from the military.

Finally, a word must be said about the many problems posed by economic inequality. While most Americans live comfortable lives, roughly one in ten live below the poverty level. Poverty a major contributor to a multitude of the nation's problems, such as crime, homelessness, and the blight of many of the nation's inner cities. In a nation where African Americans, Native Americans, and one-parent families headed by women are disproportionately represented among the ranks of the poor, poverty adds to the gender- and race-based discontent within the political system. Equality of opportunity and economic inequality are closely entwined. So long as Americans continue to subordinate economic equality to the ideal of equality of opportunity, redistributive policies will continue to be at the center of the political debate.

Bibliography

Baer, Judith A. *Equality Under the Constitution: Reclaiming the Fourteenth Amendment*. Ithaca, N.Y.: Cornell University Press, 1983. Argues that the idea of equality embodied in the Declaration of Independence and the Constitution have been interpreted by the courts in ways that consistently deny individuals both equality of treatment and equality of opportunity.

Berger, Raoul. *Government by Judiciary: The Transformation of the Fourteenth Amendment*. Cambridge, Mass.: Harvard University Press, 1977. Takes the opposite approach of *Equality Under the Constitution*, arguing that the Framers of the Fourteenth Amendment had very narrow aims that have been violated through judicial interpretation.

Deloria, Vine, Jr., and Clifford M. Lytle. *The Nations Within*. New York: Pantheon Books, 1984. Comprehensive account of the U.S. government's policies regarding the treatment of Native Americans.

Foner, Philip S. *We, the Other People: Alternative Declarations of Independence by Labor Groups, Farmers, Woman's Rights Advocates, Socialists, and Blacks*. Champaign: University of Illinois Press, 1976. Chronicles how different disadvantaged groups have used the Declaration of Independence in their struggles for equality.

Gilder, George. *Wealth and Poverty*. New York: Basic Books, 1981. A work that has had a great deal of influence on conservative policy makers, this book takes the position that government programs are inefficient mechanisms for creating wealth and alleviating poverty.

Green, Philip. *Retrieving Democracy: In Search of Civic Equality*. Totowa, N.J.: Rowman & Allanheld, 1985. Contends that representative democracy is not real democracy because it is under the control of political elites. Recommends redistribution of wealth as a necessary prerequisite for political equality.

Lakoff, Sanford A. *Equality in Political Philosophy*. Cambridge, Mass.: Harvard University Press, 1964. Tracks the history of equality in political philosophy. Ends with a theory of equality that the author believes to be faithful to the history and language of the Constitution.

Mezey, Susan Gluck. *In Pursuit of Equality: Women, Public Policy, and the Federal Courts*. New York: St. Martin's Press, 1992. History of court decisions affecting women. Among the judicial decisions covered are those dealing with matters of race and gender, age discrimination, the rights of the disabled, and homosexual rights.

Redenius, Charles. *The American Ideal of Equality: From Jefferson's Declaration to the Burger Court*. Port Washington, N.Y.: Kennikat Press, 1981. Historical account of America's attempt to come to terms with the notion of equality.

Williams, Juan. *Eyes on the Prize: America's Civil Rights Years, 1954-1965*. New York: Viking Press, 1987. Dramatic and celebrated account of the violence endured by African Americans in one decade of their struggle for equality.

Thomas J. Mortillaro

Cross-References

Citizenship Rights and Responsibilities, p. 260; Civil Rights Protection, p. 304; Feminist Politics, p. 682; Gender Politics, p. 738; Hobbes's Political Philosophy, p. 836; Locke's Political Philosophy, p. 1142; Mill's Political Philosophy, p. 1204; Neo-Conservatism, p. 1281; Pluralism, p. 1402; Political Myths and the Philosophies of Mosca and Pareto, p. 1474; Political Philosophy, p. 1505; Race and Ethnicity, p. 1654; Rousseau's Political Philosophy, p. 1756; The Social Contract, p. 1827; Social Democracies, p. 1839; Stoic Political Philosophy, p. 1904; Tocqueville's Political Philosophy, p. 1981; Utilitarianism, p. 2077; Woman Suffrage, p. 2141.

EXECUTIVE FUNCTIONS IN U.S. GOVERNMENT

Field of study: Functions of government

Political executives carry out or enforce laws passed by the legislative branches of government. For example, when the president of the United States is sworn in, he promises to "faithfully execute" his office. This pledge means that the president is obligated to put into effect laws and to spend money that the Congress appropriates for certain purposes. Executives at all levels carry out similar duties, and when they put laws into effect, they are exercising the executive function of government.

Principal terms
ADJUDICATION: application of existing laws or rules to situations through case-by-case decision making
BUREAUCRACY: government agencies that help the chief executive carry out the nation's laws and spend appropriated monies for their assigned purposes
CABINET: heads of the major government departments of the U.S. government and principal presidential advisors
CHAIN OF COMMAND: path that orders follow, from the chief executive down to the lowest officers in a bureaucracy
CHIEF EXECUTIVE: top officer in the executive branch of a government
EXECUTIVE ORDER: directive from a chief executive to administrative officials communicating instructions about the implementation of laws
IMPLEMENTATION: process of putting into effect the laws of legislatures and the directives of chief executives
IMPOUNDMENT: choice by a chief executive not to spend certain money that the legislature has appropriated
LAW ENFORCEMENT: the carrying out of statutes by professionals hired for that purpose
RULE MAKING: reading and interpreting the abstract concepts of laws and their application to particular instances, such as filling in details of statutory provisions

Overview

The executive function of any government is carried out by its chief executive, such as the president of the United States, the governor of a state, or the mayor of a city. To meet that responsibility, chief executives rely upon the work of many people in government bureaucracy, from the heads of major administrative agencies (such as a cabinet department in the U.S. government) to a policeman enforcing city traffic laws. Often chief executives are able to exercise influence upon administrators who execute the laws through their appointed power, executive orders, or other techniques of leadership, such as persuasion.

The two major perspectives on how chief executives should exercise their executive functions are illustrated by a debate between two U.S. presidents early in the twentieth century. The first view, most prominently advocated by President William Howard Taft, takes a strict or restricted view of executive power. In Taft's opinion, the powers of the president should be limited to the specific grants of authority listed in Article 2 of the U.S. Constitution—the presidential article. According to Taft, there were no residual presidential powers beyond those specifically listed. By contrast, Taft's predecessor, Theodore Roosevelt, described a chief executive as the "steward" of the people, one who should use his constitutional powers as the basis for an expanded view of presidential influence. According to Roosevelt's version of presidential power, the president should not only "faithfully execute" the laws, but also attempt to shape the impact of laws for the public good. Since the end of World War II, chief executives have generally accepted Roosevelt's definition. Accordingly, the exercise of the executive function in U.S. government has taken on far more than the limited view expressed by Taft.

The executive function begins with the appointment of the major administrative heads of departments, those upon whom the chief executive will rely to exercise his "stewardship." For example, the president's cabinet in the early 1990's consisted of fourteen officials heading the major administrative departments of the federal government. Similarly, governors often appoint significant state administrators, and mayors in strong mayor systems can often select important local officials such as police commissioners. The powers of chief executives at state and local levels vary widely, so any illustrations used are necessarily general. Such high administration officials are essential, for they allow the chief executives to delegate day-to-day decision making to others while maintaining overall responsibility for determining policy decisions. These high administration officials in turn, supervise the implementation of laws by putting into action the requirements of their own departments and by spending the money that legislative bodies have appropriated for their departments or agencies.

Implementation consists of rule making, adjudication, and law enforcement. It also may entail the setting of priorities. Most implementation work is quite routine, since in most cases the intent of legislation is clear. In some cases, however, the ways in which laws are carried out affect the ultimate impact that the laws will have. The cabinet departments, through their use of discretionary decisions, can put the stamp of the president on their departments and actually change the impact of laws through the decisions they make with regard to program priorities. The same principle applies at the local level. If a police chief, acting on the instruction of a mayor, chooses to enforce drug laws vigorously, such enforcement may limit the ability to enforce traffic laws, as all administrative agencies work with limited staffs and budgets.

One way in which some chief executives can affect law implementation is through the practice of impoundment of funds. As a general rule, U.S. presidents must spend all the money that Congress appropriates for particular programs. Under President

Richard Nixon, however, the president began to withhold some program funds in an attempt to control government spending. To curtail Nixon's practice of impoundment, Congress passed the Budget and Impoundment Control Act of 1974, which restricts the impoundment function dramatically by allowing presidents to impound funds only in narrowly defined circumstances. Other chief executives may have more or less discretion, relatively speaking, than does the president.

Chief executives can manage their bureaucracies by issuing directives to those in their direct chain of command in a form known as executive orders, which are passed down through the bureaucracy. Chief executives use them to state their policy priorities and to order their subordinates in the government chain of command to carry out their duties in a manner consistent with those priorities. In this way, they can affect the impact of laws and effect governmental change.

The appointment power of a chief executive can also bring to bear administrative change. For example, by appointing a political conservative as attorney general, a governor of a state may affect the law enforcement priorities of the state without any change in state statutes. If an attorney general were to decide to emphasize collecting child-support money from parents who have been delinquent in their payments, for example, he might reallocate resources from his white-collar crime division, so that laws concerning that problem might not be enforced as vigorously.

Executive functions can also require administrators to cooperate with members of the legislative branch and non-government interest groups to develop new public policies. At times, these three components develop working arrangements that lead to the development of policies outside the normal process of political debate. When such an arrangement occurs, analysts say that an "iron triangle" has developed, and that policies may have been developed in a way that abuses the separation of powers inherent in the Constitution. A classic example of an iron triangle would be an arrangement among the American Cancer Association, a subcommittee of Congress, and the executive Department of Health and Human Services to develop an antismoking program. At the same time, tobacco farmers and another congressional subcommittee might work with the U.S. Department of Agriculture to develop a farm subsidy program for tobacco farmers. Such activities can thus work at counter purposes. They are not a traditional part of the executive function, but illustrate how the function has expanded.

The carrying out of laws is not actually done by chief executives and their direct appointees. Rather, it is usually done by full-time, professional employees. Many times, such employees are career public servants protected by civil service employment laws. Such laws attempt to allow full-time professionals to do their jobs without political influence by protecting them from being fired except through very careful procedures.

One mechanism that such employees use in undertaking the executive function involves rule making. Rule making is practiced by many executive officials, but it is normally limited in scope to the specific grant of authority of an agency, making the rule-making function much narrower than the legislative lawmaking function. Rule making, however, can have a significant impact on the effectiveness of a law, as when the U.S. Securities and Exchange Commission (SEC) governs the buying and selling of stocks "as seems necessary in the public interest or for the protection of investors." The ways in which the SEC interprets its grant of power may have a significant impact on the integrity of stock exchanges. Most administrative rules are communicated to the public in written form, such as in the *Federal Register* of the national government.

Yet another element of the executive function is adjudication, which often involves negotiating a reasonable interpretation of law with individual clients, such as occurs when individual taxpayers reach agreements with the Internal Revenue Service regarding what their tax load for the year should be. Similarly, a local fire inspector might be given the authority to determine whether an individual merchant's business constitutes a fire hazard, even if no specific rule covers the particular situation at hand. The adjudication function, like the rule-making function, is narrow in scope, a distinction that differentiates it from decision making in the judicial branch.

All categories of the executive branch rely on their lowest levels of executives, those who deal with the general public. Examples of such "street-level bureaucrats" might include police, case workers for a welfare program, or agents of the Internal Revenue Service. Their jobs are to apply abstract laws to individual cases. While most decisions made at this level are quite straightforward, even here there is administrative discretion. Policemen may decide not to cite a motorist observed narrowly breaking the speed limit. Welfare case workers must make decisions about client eligibility, often with incomplete or even inaccurate information. Street-level bureaucrats are, in effect, engaged in law enforcement—the most basic part of the executive function.

Applications

The executive function of government entails carrying out the laws of the legislative branch in ways in which chief executives can put their imprints on public policy. Examples of the chief executive's role through impoundment of funds, issuing executive orders, and use of the appointment power illustrate that function.

The power to appropriate funds to be spent by the executive branch belongs to the legislative branch—whether that branch be Congress, a state legislature, or a local legislative body, such as a city council, school board, or county commission. The actual spending of those funds, however, is a matter of executive leadership. If an executive does not wish to spend monies appropriated by a legislature, there might be a battle between the two branches of government over their proper roles. The most dramatic instances of such turf wars came about during the presidency of Richard M. Nixon, who argued that it was within his definition of presidential powers to choose not to spend money if Congress had over-appropriated for a specific program. One example came in 1973, when Nixon ordered the Environmental Protection Agency to spend only half of the funds that Congress had appropriated to it to control water pollution. After that decision by Nixon, the Congress wrote a law that dramatically limits the president's discretion with regard to impoundment. Presidents still use their impoundment power, but usually only to defer spending until the next fiscal year, or to reduce spending on a program with congressional approval. These two forms of impoundment are known as deferral and rescission. While no chief executive has absolute discretion to impound funds, executives at the state and local levels generally have more such discretion than does the president of the United States.

An important tactic for exerting influence over the executive branch comes through the issuance of executive directives, such as presidential executive orders. Executive directives guide administrators in the executive priorities in law enforcement. Not all chief executives have control over all administrators, however, particularly in the case of many regulatory agencies, which exercise control over various aspects of the political economy. The degree to which executives have direct lines of authority through their chains of command to all government administrators determines how much impact executive directives can have on law. For example, it was through an executive order that President Harry S Truman desegregated the American military. Similarly, a governor might insist that a state education commission emphasize basic education skills in the curriculum rather than supplemental skills.

Another important way for executives to exercise the executive function is through appointments. Presidents often come into office with distinct administrative goals. They can attempt to reorder the priorities of the federal government by selecting political outsiders to run agencies. For example, by appointing Robert McNamara as secretary of defense, President John F. Kennedy encouraged a new process of management in that department. In a similar vein, a city council might hire a new city administrator or city manager to bring innovative budgeting procedures to reorganize the city administration.

Appointments can also have symbolic importance. For example, a governor might select an environmental advocate to a state board regulating the use of state-owned lands. Or a mayor might select a woman to head a regulatory agency to bolster the role of women taking positions of importance. Presidents try to balance their advisory groups geographically, ethnically, and by gender.

Context

The executive function is one of the three central functions of government, in addition to the legislative and judicial functions. It is typically overseen by an elected chief executive, such as the president of the United States, state governors, or city mayors. In the twentieth century, however, the executive function incorporated a broader definition of executive power. In addition to carrying out laws, executives use their influence to propose and adopt favorable laws. Many members of the executive branch have as their responsibilities drafting legislation or adjudicating conflicts in addition to simply carrying out laws.

When the U.S. Constitution was framed, it divided power among the three major branches of government and established checks and balances to make sure that no branch overstepped its proper bounds. State governments have adopted similar requirements. Over time, the roles of the three branches blurred, as in the case of chief executives proposing policies to the legislative branch or the judicial branch supervising the enforcement of tax equity issues with regard to state educational finance. The result of such blurring of functions is that the old idea of a separation of powers has given way to a revised understanding of the political system. Rather than seeing powers as "divided" among the three branches, observers now see power as "shared" by the three branches. As a result, although most law enforcement is done by the executive branch, it might also well be said that both the legislative branch and the court system undertake substantial elements of the executive operation of government.

Bibliography

Anderson, James E. *Public Policymaking: An Introduction*. 2d ed. Boston: Houghton Mifflin, 1994. General survey of the policy-making process with explicit description of the specifics of the executive function, including implementation.

Cohen, Jeffrey E. *The Politics of the U.S. Cabinet: Representation in the Executive Branch, 1789-1984*. Pittsburgh: University of Pittsburgh Press, 1988. Discussion of the cabinet's role in advising the president and carrying out the executive function. Also discusses the appointment process for members of the cabinet.

Kennedy, Robert. *Thirteen Days: A Memoir of the Cuban Missile Crisis*. New York: W. W. Norton, 1969. Poignant memoir by the former U.S. attorney general that outlines the crisis decision making in the White House during the Cuban Missile Crisis of 1962.

Morgan, Ruth. *The President and Civil Rights: Policy-Making by Executive Order*. New York: St. Martin's Press, 1970. Best single-volume treatment of the presidential use of executive orders.

Nakamura, Robert T., and Frank Smallwood. *The Politics of Policy Implementation*. New York: St. Martin's Press, 1980. Excellent discussion of the discretion associated with the carrying out of legislation.

Pfiffner, James. *The Strategic Presidency: Hitting the Ground Running*. Homewood, Ill.: Dorsey Press, 1988. Excellent discussion of the administrative problems confronting presidents as they enter office and the approaches they take to accomplish their administrative goals.

James W. Riddlesperger, Jr.

Cross-References

Bureaucracy, p. 164; Cabinet Government, p. 184; Education Management, p. 565; Energy Management, p. 604; Environmental Protection, p. 617; Health Care Management, p. 810; Iron Triangles, p. 981; Law Enforcement, p. 1059; Policy Development and Implementation, p. 1414; Public Policy, p. 1633; Social Services, p. 1858; Urban Renewal and Housing, p. 2064.

EXISTENTIALISM

Field of study: Political philosophy

Existentialism was an important literary and philosophical movement in European thought in the first half of the twentieth century. Its proponents depicted each person existing as an individual in a purposeless universe and stressed the necessity for free choice and action in the face of the inevitability of death.

Principal terms
DASEIN: German word for the human dimension of being
FASCISM: revolutionary right-wing political movement in twentieth century Europe
LEFT, THE: individuals and political groups seeking progressive political and social change; the forces of movement in European history since the French Revolution
NIHILISM: literally means "nothingness"; in existentialist thought it typically has the more general sense of a condition in which all cultural values are challenged
RIGHT, THE: individuals and political groups that tend to oppose change; the forces of order in European history since the French Revolution
SEIN: German word for being

Overview

As a philosophical movement, twentieth century existentialism developed around several key themes. These include the finitude of human life in the face of death; the demand that human beings act freely and hence create authentic lives; the threat to authenticity posed by the pressures toward conformity in the modern world; the tension between the claims of the individual life and commitment to the community. Such concerns recur throughout the work of all existentialist writers.

The key figures in the development of twentieth century existentialism are such thinkers as the philosophers Martin Heidegger and Karl Jaspers in Germany and the philosopher Jean-Paul Sartre and the novelist and essayist Albert Camus in France. It may, however, be more accurate to think of existentialism more as the expression of a widespread mood among twentieth century intellectuals than as a formal branch of philosophy or a fully articulated worldview. Even though some key exponents were philosophers, existentialist themes appear in the work of literary figures such as the novelist Franz Kafka and the dramatist Samuel Beckett, in the painting of the German expressionists, and even in the sculpture of Alberto Giacometti.

Several major existentialist themes were prefigured in the nineteenth century in the ideas of the Danish religious thinker Søren Kierkegaard and the German philosopher

Friedrich Nietzsche. Kierkegaard stressed the risks that commitment to Christian faith entails, the absurdity of life without God, and the dehumanization and isolation of the individual in the face of the anonymity of what he called the "Public." In these views he anticipated later existentialists' concern with the absurdity of life in the face of death and with the human necessity to choose freely and responsibly. Kierkegaard's thought inspired such twentieth century Christian existentialists as the German theologian Karl Barth and the French philosopher Gabriel Marcel.

Nietzsche's powerful critique of Western civilization and his conviction that all traditional Western values—religious, ethical, and political—had lost their validity, also struck resonant chords in existentialist thinking. If such values are no longer valid, then it becomes the individual's responsibility to create new ones—or so one might conclude after reading Nietzsche. This Nietzschean sense of a fundamental cultural crisis in the modern world (what Nietzsche described as a condition of nihilism) was widely expressed in the early twentieth century, particularly in German-speaking areas in Europe, and the rise of existentialism should thus be seen emerging from the background of a crisis mentality. That twentieth century existentialist thinkers did in fact live during a time of crisis is easily seen by remembering the key developments during the period in which they reached maturity and began to make contributions to the intellectual history of their times.

The traumas of two world wars, the rise of Nazism and fascism, the Russian Revolution and the establishment of Stalinist totalitarianism, the economic disruptions of the Great Depression—all cataclysmic historical developments—compelled European intellectuals to reevaluate their sense of themselves and of their role in the world. The weighty impress of the momentous issues of this period 1914-1945—which some historians now call the era of the "Second Thirty Years' War"—demanded acknowledgement in the thinking of the existentialists. This can easily be seen by noting when some of the key figures among them reached the age of thirty: Jaspers in 1913; Heidegger in 1919; Sartre in 1935; and Camus in 1943. Furthermore, all of them lived into the post-World War II era that was dominated by the Cold War division of Europe between the American and Soviet spheres of influence, the end of European colonial empires, an escalating nuclear arms race, and an unprecedented period of prosperity and affluence in the Western world.

Any examination of the key ideas of existentialist thinkers must situate them within the broader historical dimensions of the era in which they lived. They saw themselves as participants in the events of their times, as intellectual activists whose ideas could make a difference—perhaps a fundamental difference—in people's lives. Approaching their intellectual tasks with such intentions necessarily demanded that they address the key political issues of their day. They did so, but no common position emerged among them. Indeed, one of the most striking things about the political thoughts of the existentialists is the diversity of political views they produced. This disparity in political thinking is one of the reasons for calling existentialism more a pervasive mood than a formal philosophical position.

It was during the turbulent years between the two world wars that the existentialists produced their key early texts. In Being and Time (1927) Heidegger presented a view of the human world in which the choice lies between an authentic existence, affirming the self against the world and in the face of death, and submission to the world and hypocritical acceptance of some otherworldly purpose which death will only negate. Dread, or Angst, is the peculiarly human emotion which this choice of alternative (authentic or inauthentic) forms of response to death imposes on humankind. To be an "authentic" human being (what Heidegger called *Dasein*) demanded courageous acceptance of the finitude of human existence.

Notions of authenticity, freedom, and choice pervade the early work of Jean-Paul Sartre as well. His novel *Nausea* (1938) and his major work *Being and Nothingness* (1943) articulate his own version of existentialism. In Sartre's view, human beings are condemned to be free, to face the necessity of choosing a morality and hence of creating themselves. The reality of human consciousness is the ceaseless desire to become what one can never be: a completed essence. This resolutely negative conception of human consciousness is what Sartre means by "nothingness" in his book's title. In *Being and Nothingness* and in plays that he wrote during the 1940's, Sartre emphasizes that authentic human choice is personal choice and that to surrender the freedom to choose to some prescribed code or established institution constitutes what he called the condition of "bad faith." Humans, he argues, are condemned to bestow meaning on an absurd world; there is no being behind human existences, no ordering principle.

Albert Camus followed a trajectory similar to Sartre's early career. His novel *The Stranger* (1942) and his philosophical essay *The Myth of Sisyphus* (1942) both grapple with the notion of Nothingness, articulating a view that the human world is fundamentally absurd in the face of human life's finitude and death's inevitable finality. Camus' vision centers on the limited and imperfect character of all human action. Yet he was able to find a liberating view by arguing that a voluntary acceptance of the absurdist position frees human beings from any fruitless desire for an ultimate meaning and from any thoughtless conformity to convention.

The common themes in the thinking of existentialists such as Heidegger, Sartre, and Camus include notions about human finitude; the inevitability of death and the anxiety and dread experienced in the face of that awesome certainty; and the burden of freedom and the necessity of choice in human life. Despite these commonalities, it is important to note that these thinkers also disagreed among themselves, often quite vehemently. Heidegger's thought after the mid-1930's developed toward a far-ranging critique of all previous Western thought from the pre-Socratic philosophers to those of the present. His concerns increasingly focused on the urgency for human beings to "stand open" to the call of Being.

In his celebrated "Letter on Humanism" (1947), Heidegger criticizes Sartre, focusing on a lecture that Sartre gave in 1946 titled "Existentialism Is a Humanism." While Sartre continued to emphasize his view that existence precedes essence and that human beings are what they do, Heidegger stressed the fundamental difference between his thinking and Sartre's. Each repudiated the other's conception of human existence.

Similarly, in the years after 1945 Sartre and Camus would increasingly distance themselves from each other, especially over the question of political commitment and the relationship of the intellectual to the Communist Party and to the goal of political and social revolution.

Applications

The basic existentialist ideas, especially those of the early Sartre and Camus, point toward a radically individualist position, one in which any claims of a broader community are to be treated with suspicion as a temptation to an inauthentic commitment which would produce the condition of bad faith. And yet, thinkers like Heidegger, Sartre, and Camus confronted social and political issues and articulated responses to them. Not surprisingly, given the interwar period in which their various positions emerged, their political thinking developed in response to the two predominant ideological movements of that time, Nazism and Communism.

Heidegger's public support of Nazism and his brief membership in the Nazi Party have stimulated intense debate over what, if any, the connection might be between his philosophy and his political commitment. Here it is important to recall that during the 1920's Heidegger diagnosed Western culture as suffering a profound crisis in all its fundamental values and that he saw his own thinking as a response to it. At least initially he interpreted the rise of Nazism in the same way, as a legitimate political response (indeed, the solution for Germany) to the crisis of the times. When he accepted the position as rector of the University of Freiburg in 1933 and delivered his acceptance address on "The Self Assertion of the German University," he envisioned himself as the mentor of Hitler and the Nazi movement and voiced his commitment to turn the energies of German higher education to the support of Hitler and his party. By 1935 Heidegger realized how little political impact he had and he increasingly isolated himself from public affairs for the remainder of the Nazi era. Importantly, however, in the years between 1945 and his death in 1976, Heidegger never explicitly repudiated his connections with Nazism. Thus one of the major figures in the development of existentialism made the political choice to support the most pernicious of right-wing ideologies to appear in twentieth century Europe.

The political career of Jean-Paul Sartre moved in the opposite direction. The Nazi occupation of northern France, the complicity of the Vichy regime in southern France with Nazi Germany, and the heroism of the underground resistance to the Nazis all convinced Sartre that intellectuals must commit themselves to a political cause. Thus, to Sartre a key existential decision that an individual must confront as part of being human is that of political choice. For Sartre himself, that choice led to a commitment to Marxism and to decades of outspoken political activism after 1945. He became a vehement critic of Western, especially American, policy through the first decade of the Cold War and he was an outspoken supporter of the French Communist Party and of the Soviet Union. He never joined the Communist Party itself, however, preferring the status of "fellow traveler." After the Soviet suppression of the Hungarian uprising in 1956, he stopped speaking out in favor of the Soviet Union. Sartre was also vigorously critical of France's efforts to preserve its tottering colonial hold over Vietnam and Algeria.

Intellectually the most conspicuous product of Sartre's left-wing political commitment was his unfinished work *The Critique of Dialectical Reason* (1960), an attempt to synthesize the insights of his existentialist philosophy with those of Marxism. The fact that he never published a promised second volume of *The Critique* is probably Sartre's admission that a true fusion between his concept of existential humanism and the leading ideology of the Left was impossible.

Sartre's political and intellectual itinerary took him in the polar opposite direction from Heidegger. Unlike the German philosopher, however, Sartre consistently risked taking publicly critical positions. He eagerly assumed the role of intellectual and political gadfly and—again unlike Heidegger—went out of his way to ensure that his views on what he took to be the most important political and moral issues of his times were publicly known.

If Heidegger was at least for a time persuaded to commit his intellectual energies to the politics of the far right, and if Sartre located himself on the far left during the years after 1945, then Albert Camus can be seen as occupying a position somewhere between them. Even more than Sartre, Camus distinguished himself in the French underground resistance to German occupation during World War II, and he emerged from the war as one of the most impressive moral and political exemplars in French public life. When Sartre and Camus parted company politically (and their friendship was also a casualty of this split), it was over the question of totalitarianism in twentieth century political life. No one opposed fascism and Nazism more fiercely than Camus; however, he—unlike Sartre—came increasingly to see Marxism as the basis for an equally dangerous totalitarianism of the Left, as embodied in Josef Stalin's Soviet Union. For Camus, embracing any totalitarian program would betray the fundamental existentialist insight into the absurd. In his writings of the late 1940's—which culminated in *The Rebel* (1951)—Camus sought to show that every political program based on an absolute ethic fell inevitably into the excesses of nihilism, either of the individualist variety (Nietzsche was his example) or the totalitarian variety, either of the Left or the Right.

Camus's position was based on his distinction between rebellion and revolution. Rebellion, he argued, was a protest against the inhumanity of human beings toward each other, but one which did not result in substituting another false absolute for the one against which one has rebelled. A rebel who remains true to the existentialist sense of the absurd refuses to commit to any political absolute and remains a defender of humanity in its variety and imperfections. The rebel is the political advocate of movements dedicated to reducing violence and to augmenting practical freedom. The rebel wagers on the hope that a more peaceful and less violent world can be built by committed people of good will who recognize the danger of any human aspiration to ultimate meaning—something that the finitude of a humanity living in a universe without meaning precludes. In this sense Camus can be said to have articulated an existential version of Western liberal humanism.

Context

The political views of Heidegger, Sartre, and Camus raise an important question: What is the relationship between philosophy and politics? Did the development of their ideas determine their political commitments? For example, was there a necessary connection between Heidegger's thinking in *Being and Time* and his commitment to Nazism? There is a diversity of opinion on both sides of this question. Likewise does Sartre's far more intensive examination of the specifically human level of existence in *Being and Nothingness* as compared to Heidegger's more metaphysical involvement with *Sein* (being) predispose the Sartrean existentialist to a much more socially activist position? Heidegger's overt political involvement was in fact quite short-lived, while Sartre became his era's best known example of the publicly vocal, politically committed intellectual. Until his untimely death in 1960, Camus also spoke out consistently in defense of the causes to which he felt a strong commitment.

Questioning the relationships between the philosophers and the realm of politics is as old as Plato's *Republic* in Western thought. The careers of Heidegger, Sartre, and Camus reveal a complex, varying pattern of relations between them. This complexity is confirmed by contrasting Heidegger's support of Nazism to the German existentialist Karl Jaspers' opposition. Likewise, one could compare Maurice Merleau-Ponty's rapid post-World War II distancing of himself from Marxism to that of Sartre, even though Merleau-Ponty made a cogent argument for staking one's political commitment on communism and its future, despite the terrors of Stalinism, in *Humanism and Terror* (1947).

Just as the languages of philosophy and politics change over time, so do the voices of philosophers and political leaders. There is an inherent instability in each, as political regimes emerge and disappear and different philosophical questions and issues predominate at different times. The pervasive sense of crisis to which existentialist varieties of thought were a response was itself a response to the dramatic historical movements of the first half of the twentieth century. It is no more surprising that existentialist thinkers, aware of those momentous changes, should try to give their ideas political expression than it is that the political forms their ideas took were so various.

Bibliography

Hughes, H. Stuart. *The Obstructed Path: French Social Thought in the Years of Desperation, 1930-1960*. New York: Harper & Row, 1968. This intellectual history of France in the decades after 1930 contains excellent chapters on Sartre, Merleau-Ponty, and Camus.

Judt, Tony. *Past Imperfect: French Intellectuals, 1944-1956*. Berkeley: University of California Press, 1992. Revisionist, critical account of the twists and turns of French intellectuals' political involvement in the immediate post-World War II years. Vigorously anti-Marxist.

Kaufmann, Walter, ed. *Existentialism from Dostoevsky to Sartre*. New York: Meridian Books, 1964. Anthology of key texts in the existentialist tradition; provides an accessible entry into the major themes of existentialist thought.

Macquarrie, John. *Existentialism*. Philadelphia: Westminster, 1972. Excellent introductory overview of the development of the existentialist tradition in philosophy.

Poster, Mark. *Existential Marxism in Postwar France: From Sartre to Althusser*. Princeton, N.J.: Princeton University Press, 1975. Comprehensive examination of the convergence of existentialism and Marxism in France following World War II.

Sluga, Hans. *Heidegger's Crisis: Philosophy and Politics in Nazi Germany*. Cambridge, Mass.: Harvard University Press, 1993. Excellent detailed inquiry into Heidegger's involvement with Nazism.

Wolin, Richard, ed. *The Heidegger Controversy: A Critical Reader*. Cambridge, Mass.: MIT Press, 1993. Fascinating compilation of articles about Heidegger's political involvement with Nazism; includes key texts by Heidegger.

Michael W. Messmer

Cross-References

Anarchism in Marxist Thought, p. 72; Dialecticism, p. 540; Fascism and Nazism, p. 656; Irrationalism in Politics, p. 987; Liberalism, p. 1118; Marxism-Leninism, p. 1155; Nietzsche's Political Philosophy, p. 1300; Postmodernism, p. 1570.

FAMILY AND POLITICS IN THE UNITED STATES

Field of study: Local and regional government

As a focus of modern American politics, the family has often eclipsed even economic and crime problems as a concern at all levels of government.

> *Principal terms*
> CHILD SUPPORT: court-ordered payments that a noncustodial parent makes to the custodial parent of his or her own children
> CONSERVATIVE: advocate of political philosophies that favor solving social and economic problems through free-market forces instead of through government actions
> FAMILY VALUES: loosely defined set of beliefs in the importance of the family as an institution in modern American society
> LIBERAL: advocate of political philosophies that favor using government action to solve social problems, such as financial assistance to poor families
> NUCLEAR FAMILY: traditional family unit consisting of two married parents and their children
> WELFARE: government programs that provide cash and other assistance to poor families

Overview

The dominant modern American conception of the family unit is that of the nuclear family, which consists of one father, one mother, and their children. This conception has faced growing challenges in recent decades and anxiety about the future of the "traditional" family has become an issue of public debate. The counterculture movement of the 1960's and the subsequent movement for women's rights appeared to challenge the traditional nuclear family, bringing family issues under public scrutiny. Policy debates within government over matters such as welfare programs and no-fault divorce laws directed further public attention to the family, as did the increasing numbers of elderly citizens who were left to live alone.

During the nineteenth century, American households and families had nearly the same organization as late twentieth century families. Residential units primarily comprised parents and their children and three-generation households were the exception. Many households, however, also contained boarders, lodgers, apprentices, or servants in addition to their nuclear family units. Contrary to the contemporary idea of the family as a private retreat, the nineteenth century household encompassed many functions and activities that transcended those of the modern nuclear family. Women, for example, performed a variety of domestic management tasks beyond caring for immediate family members. They took care of boarders, apprentices, and other strangers, such as delinquent youth, orphaned children, or abandoned elderly men or women placed in their homes. Though similar practices still survive among some classes of modern American minority-group families, they have virtually disappeared from the larger society.

Throughout the late nineteenth and early twentieth centuries, the family continued to function as a work unit. Through a process of chain migration, people typically acted as recruitment, housing, and migration agents for other relatives, helping them shift from rural to industrial work, thereby carrying over preindustrial patterns and values, providing buffers against poverty, and creating higher standards of living for later generations. Though people generally did not share their households with relatives outside the nuclear family, they usually maintained close personal ties with such kin.

To the extent that families functioned as work units, husbands and wives, as well as parents and children, shared labor more extensively than in modern industrial society. As long as a family was a production unit, its housework was inseparable from its domestic industries or agricultural work, and it was valued for its economic contribution. Since young children were often part of the labor force, motherhood was valued as much for its economic contributions as it was for its nurturing qualities. As modern industrialization progressed, agencies and institutions outside the family increasingly appropriated educational and other functions. The family then became more specialized, with its primary functions becoming childbearing, child rearing, and socialization. After ceasing to be primarily work units, families limited their economic activities to consumption and child care. Housework lost its economic and productive value. Wages of working women went to their parents, since their work was considered part of the family's work, not an independent career. Despite changes in the nature and place of work, families survived as collective economic units. Husbands, wives, and children were all responsible for the well-being of the family unit.

The separation between the home and the workplace that accompanied industrialization tended to glorify the home as a domestic retreat from the outside world. A new ideology, or cult of domesticity, emerged in the first half of the nineteenth century. It became the staple of a growing middle class to which many in the working class aspired. As custodians of this retreat, women were expected to have attributes distinctly different from those of the working wives who had previously been economic partners in the family. At the same time, attitudes toward children changed with the "discovery" of childhood as a distinct stage of life. Stripped of many paid or work-related household functions, families became more private, more domestic, and more child-centered.

The cult of domesticity kept participation of married women in the labor force at modest, though rising, levels well into the twentieth century. Although many immigrants adopted values associated with domesticity, a majority of working class and ethnic families adhered to a collective view of family and its economy. Nevertheless, the major historical shift in family values has been away from a collective view of the family to one of individualism and sentiment. These values contributed to an increasing emphasis on individual priorities and preferences over collective family needs, as well as to greater emphasis on nurturing, intimacy, and privacy as the major justification for family relations. This shift contributed significantly to the "liberation of individuals," but it also eroded the resilience of the family as an institution and lessened its ability to handle crises.

The most imminent crisis facing modern families is economic. Changing economic conditions have cast doubt on the ability of the family to provide a better life for subsequent generations. In the last quarter of the twentieth century, aggregate American wages stagnated, although the median income of full-time women workers increased relative to that of men. Between 1983 and 1992, the real earnings of married women rose 9 percent. The ratio of what full-time working wives made to what full-time working husbands made rose from 63 percent in 1983 to 69 percent in 1992. The wages of women who were heads of single-parent families and worked full-time, however, increased by just 3 percent over the same period. In 1992, the median weekly earnings of these women amounted to only 64 percent of the median weekly earnings of married men who lived with their wives.

Family behavior patterns also shifted through this period. Most significant is the increase in the number of single-parent households, resulting from either divorce or out-of-wedlock births. The percentage of children under 18 years of age not living with both biological parents increased from 33 percent in 1981 to 43 percent in 1993. After the U.S. divorce rate doubled between the late 1960's and the late 1970's, it stabilized at around 40 percent of first marriages. In addition to the growing number of children of divorced parents, the number of children born to unmarried mothers tripled after 1970, reaching 30 percent of all births in the United States in 1991. Only a third of nonresidential parents pay child support or alimony, and their payments generally fall well below court-ordered levels.

Married mothers in the 1990's were twice as likely to work full time as their predecessors of twenty years before. By 1992, two-thirds of all married mothers were working or looking for work (compared to just over half in 1970), including more than half of those with children under six. Families of these working mothers accounted for almost half the nation's children.

Amid these changes, overall child well-being declined, despite increased educational levels among parents, fewer children in each family, and growing levels of public spending. After declines in the 1960's, the proportion of American children living in poverty increased, from 15 percent in 1970 to 20 percent in 1990. The teen suicide rate tripled, while juvenile crime became increasingly violent and random. School performance declined.

Applications

Many of the government policies and programs affecting families' abilities to cope are state and local. Others have a combination of federal and state funding with local administration. States regulate many institutional aspects of families, such as issuing marriage licenses and defining divorce laws. State and local family courts mediate adoptions and foster care, abuse and neglect disputes, divorce settlements, separation contingencies, and the like. State governments also seek to create a business climate with good-paying jobs so that parents can support their families, while generating tax bases sufficient to ensure quality education and an abundant supply of skilled workers. The changing social problems associated with the decline of the modern family's capacity to function as a collective economic unit make it important to examine government efforts to assist families to achieve self-sufficiency.

The modern political climate in the United States stresses family values and parental responsibility. With the passage of the national Family and Medical Leave Act in 1993, the federal government addressed the needs of middle- and working-class parents by requiring employers to allow time-limited unpaid leave to employees who miss work because of illness, having a baby, caring for a newborn child, or tending an ill parent. The act reduced the likelihood of loss of job, promotion, or salary increase to working parents because of family-related problems, all with little cost to government. States, however, bear the burden of increased costs associated with providing cash, medical care, food stamps, and other services to poor and at-risk families.

Two policies that seek to overcome forces thwarting parents' efforts to become economically self-sufficient have actively involved state governments since 1980. The first, child-support enforcement, is a state-administered service available on a sliding-fee scale to all citizens who need help obtaining court-ordered payments from noncustodial or "deadbeat dads" who refuse to pay child support. The second, welfare reform, examines state efforts to move greater numbers of poor single mothers away from dependency on government and into the labor market.

Local family and domestic courts and administrative agencies handle the establishment and enforcement of child-support obligations according to federal, state, and local laws. Working with separated parents and considering the best interests of the children, the courts decide which parent should have custody of the children, the amount of support the noncustodial parent should pay, the rights of access to the children by the noncustodial parent, and how the support obligation will be enforced. The federally mandated child-support enforcement program provides services aimed at locating absent parents, establishing paternity, and establishing and enforcing support obligation. States are required to designate a single and separate organizational unit of state government to administer the program. Most states have placed their child-support agencies within the social or human services umbrella agencies, which also administer the welfare program Aid to Families with Dependent Children (AFDC) discussed below. The law allows states to administer the program either on the statewide or local level. Ten programs are locally administered. A few programs are state administered in some counties and locally administered in others. Both AFDC and non-AFDC families must be served. States operate a parent locator service to locate absent parents and maintain a reporting system.

To facilitate the collection of child-support payments in interstate cases, states cooperate with one another in establishing paternity, in locating absent parents, and in securing compliance with orders issued by other states. Enforcement tools include the use of the federal income tax refund offset procedure, the imposition of liens against real and personal property, the withholding of state tax refunds payable to parents delinquent in support payments, and making available information about the amounts of delinquent payments to consumer credit bureaus. States also periodically determine whether anyone receiving unemployment compensation owes child-support money. State employment security agencies are required to withhold unemployment benefits, and to pay the child-support agency any outstanding child support obligations established by an agreement with the individual or through legal processes.

Welfare reform efforts also target economically disadvantaged families. States have taken the lead to increase the capacity of these families to achieve economic self-sufficiency. Between 1992 and 1994 alone, more than thirty states requested approval from the Clinton Administration to experiment with the federal-state welfare program known as AFDC. These initiatives encompassed three main issues: women who have babies while on welfare, mandatory employment, and deadlines. State-level reformers sought to discourage pregnancies among poor unmarried teens with a range of new incentives and disincentives to welfare recipients. New Jersey, for example, provides free health insurance, food stamps, and cash payments of $64 per month per child to mothers on welfare; however, the state's "child exclusion" provision limits such support to children born to mothers before they go on welfare. Having additional children thus no longer increases the monthly check. Georgia requires unmarried women under the age of eighteen who are pregnant, or who already have children, to live with a parent or guardian to be eligible for welfare. Georgia also freezes the welfare benefits of mothers on welfare for two years if they have another child. Minnesota withholds child and spousal support from the paychecks of "deadbeat" parents.

State reformers also acknowledged the public's acceptance of women's labor market participation, and they sought to equalize the employment experiences of welfare and nonwelfare working poor mothers. Florida's $30 million-a-year "Project Independence," for example, requires its eighteen thousand single-parent participants to attend orientation sessions and contact at least twelve employers in job searches. Project Independence requires enrollees with at least tenth grade educations or recent work experience to find jobs, and it teaches job-seeking skills, such as resume-writing and interviewing techniques, to those who do not find work immediately. More extensive and costlier training programs are offered to people with less education or work experience. California's Greater Avenues for Independence (GAIN) program spends more than $120 million a year in order to train about sixty thousand participants for from several months to a year before they seek work.

Finally, several state-level welfare reformers launched experimental time-limited programs aimed to reduce the numbers of long-term welfare recipients. Wisconsin's "Work Not Welfare" calls for two counties to require welfare recipients to work for their benefits. In 1995, about one thousand Wisconsin welfare enrollees must find full-time work or job-training programs within thirty days of signing up for assistance. After two years, their cash benefits will be cut off although they would still receive health care and food stamps. Other states have asked to experiment with the federal food stamp program by turning it into a job-subsidy program. Oregon and Missouri programs, for example, convert food stamp and AFDC benefits into wages. Reorienting food stamp money into a job subsidy entices Democrats and Republicans eager to require welfare recipients to work but aware of the money necessary to underwrite such efforts. Converting food stamp grants to cash in part provides those funds.

Context

State-level initiatives and programs such as child-support enforcement and welfare reform are part of the country's larger concern about the ability of families to function effectively as collective economic units. This concern takes its most explicit form in the political context of family values. The appeal to family values reflects public malaise about a decline in morality in general and the direction of the country in particular. Many politicians lament a demise and extol the virtues of the "traditional" American family, a married man and woman with children. Yet liberals and conservatives differ regarding measures government should take to strengthen the family.

Liberals prefer economic assistance and social services that place a floor under family income and promote self-sufficiency. Conservatives argue that cash payments and other assistance encourage undesirable behavior patterns, such as indolence, promiscuity, easily available abortion, casual attitudes toward marriage, and parental indifference to child-rearing responsibilities. They argue that right-minded policies should reinforce "traditional" American patterns and not condone deviations that seem irresponsible. For liberals, government assistance to the family can help to redress historical wrongs to blacks, the poor, and women. They argue that support is necessary in order to relieve the economic and social pressures that threaten family stability. On the contrary, their opponents reply, measures that inject easy money into family services will actually invite family instability.

By the end of the twentieth century, all levels of U.S. government were being asked to create conditions more conducive to helping families function in an increasingly global economy. As new international trade agreements and technological advancements necessitate a more fluid and better-educated workforce of men and women, such forces will strengthen the family's capacity to function as a collective economic unit.

Bibliography

Berry, Mary Frances. *The Politics of Parenthood*. New York: Viking, 1993. Primarily historical examination of such issues as child care, motherhood, and the "myth of the good mother" in the United States.

Frum, David. *Dead Right: The Fall of the Conservatism of Hope and the Rise of the Conservatism of Fear*. New York: Basic Books, 1994. Reviews how the administrations of presidents Ronald Reagan and George Bush allowed their opposition to such matters as gay family rights to eclipse the more traditional concerns of the Republican Party.

Skolnick, Jerome, and Arlene Skolnick, eds. *Family in Transition*. 6th ed. Glenview, Ill.: Scott, Foresman, 1989. Collection of essays examining how American families have changed, with attention to demographic trends, parenting and child rearing, marriage and divorce patterns, gender and equity issues, and other issues. Variations along lines of race, socioeconomic status, and age are also considered.

Steiner, Gilbert Y. *The Futility of Family Policy*. Washington, D.C.: Brookings Institution, 1981. Reviews the advent of the contemporary national focus on the family.

Zill, Nicholas, and Christine Winquist Nord. *Running in Place: How American Families Are Faring in a Changing Economy and an Individualistic Society*. Washington, D.C.: Child Trends, 1994. Report documenting the current state of American families in light of modern economic and social changes.

Richard K. Caputo

Cross-References

Conservatism, p. 419; Entitlements, p. 610; Federal Mandates, p. 662; Feminist Politics, p. 682; Gay and Lesbian Politics, p. 732; Gender Politics, p. 738; Government Roles, p. 778; Neo-Conservatism, p. 1281; The New Right, p. 1293; Public Policy, p. 1633; Race and Ethnicity, p. 1654; The Social Security System, p. 1852; The Welfare State, p. 2135.

FASCISM AND NAZISM

Field of study: Political philosophy

A form of government popular after World War I, fascism, through emphasis on the state, charismatic leadership, dictatorial control, and imperialist expansion, attempted to alleviate the social problems of the time.

Principal terms

CHARISMATIC LEADERSHIP: term describing a leader with great personal magnetism able to attract a large following

DYNAMISM: action merely for the sake of action; a characteristic of the fascist state

FASCES: bundle of bound rods surrounding an axe; symbol of authority and the state in ancient Rome; the term from which modern fascism derives its name

ORGANIC STATE: concept of the state as a living organism destined to grow; popular with Fascists

ROMANTICISM: a philosophy that stresses feelings of emotion and intuition, which became the basis for much fascist thinking; opposed to rationalism

Overview

Unlike Marxism or communism, which it violently opposes, fascism has no definitive political philosophy. It is a cluster of ideas, having some historical antecedents but largely reflecting the thinking of two twentieth century dictators, Benito Mussolini and Adolf Hitler. In order to gain power, they fed on the fears of millions of workers who either had lost or were afraid of losing their jobs; of the young who could not find jobs; of the elderly and those on fixed incomes afraid of losing their savings; and, most important, on the fears of capitalists and industrialists afraid of a communist revolution that would socialize their property.

The major element of fascism is the role of the state, which becomes all-powerful. Parliamentary parties, which tend to divide the state, are to be suppressed. So is individualism. The ordinary citizen is submerged into the state, but is expected to feel a sense of power from speaking as one with millions of others. Rather than the classless society envisioned by Marxism, fascism promotes a structured society in which everyone knows his or her place.

Essential to the fascist state is the charismatic leader, capable through personal magnetism and demagoguery of attracting followers. He or she is a kind of super-individual, capable through intuition of understanding the wishes of the homogeneous masses and acting accordingly. The leader's power is unrestricted.

Fascism sees the state as organic or living, capable of and in constant need of growth. States, therefore, are in an endless struggle for survival, with the strong becoming dominant and the weak expiring. Consequently, fascism glorifies war and constant action. Peace and inertia are identified with decline and decay. The Germans added a racial component to the theory of fascism.

As a political theory, fascism cannot be described best by rational analysis alone. Fascist leaders, through symbols, parades, mass meetings, film, and radio, promote an irrational romanticism that appeals to the emotions and the imagination. To keep this form of thinking alive and prohibit any form of dissident thought, strict censorship is imposed. All forms of public expression, including journalism, literature, theatre, art, and music, must be tightly controlled. Without thought manipulation and control, a fascist society cannot survive. What ideally must emerge in the fascist state is the concept of the "general will," where the masses tend to think alike and the charismatic leader can therefore be their spokesman.

Individualism in any form, whether political or artistic, must be suppressed. Political dissidents are silenced, jailed, or executed; artists' creative efforts must be directed toward serving the fascist state or be suppressed. A common characteristic of the fascist state, therefore, is its lack of original artistic expression.

Applications

Had World War I not occurred, fascism might not have arisen. The disillusionment, the bitterness of defeat, and the ensuing economic hardship caused feelings bordering on revolt among the masses. Although fascism developed in several countries, among them Spain and Portugal, and to a lesser extent Japan and Argentina, the two countries in which fascism developed most fully were Italy and Germany.

Although Italy had been among the victors in World War I, its already shaky economy was devastated by the war. Poverty, unemployment, and illiteracy remained. The educational system was strongly influenced by the Roman Catholic church and was not adapted to a modern industrialized state. When Italy became united in 1871, many Italian patriots expected a return to the glories of ancient Rome, but were sadly disillusioned. Public opinion became ever more sharply divided. Parliamentary government became almost impossible, because of the extreme difference between the ultraconservatives on the right and the growing influence of the communists and socialists on the left. Benito Mussolini, a political opportunist and a skillful orator, saw an opportunity to form a new party supported by those disillusioned with a seemingly nonfunctioning government. Called the Fascio di Combattimento, or "Fighting Group," the party was soon simply known as the *Fascio* or Fascists. Getting financial support from those fearful of a communist takeover, Mussolini formed his own private army to help maintain order. He organized squads of ruffians to intimidate people from voting for rival parties at the polls. By 1922, the party had become so strong that an intimidated king gave Mussolini the premiership.

Once in power, Mussolini organized the political structure to be followed by other fascist states. Italy remained—ostensibly—a kingdom with traditional parties and a legal structure. Parallel to this, and controlling the political life of the country, was the party. Divided into ten thousand *fasci* or cells controlled by loyal party members, the apex of the party pyramid was the Grand Council consisting of twenty members dominated by Mussolini. A party militia was the external form of control; a secret police, the OVRA, was the internal and more terrifying means of control.

The chief of propaganda was raised to cabinet rank. Through control of the media, the party depicted Mussolini as a charismatic leader capable of solving all of Italy's problems. Through increased spending for armaments and public works, the fascists did create a semblance of prosperity. Stressing the need for Italy to grow, and encouraging his countrymen to aspire to the grandeur of ancient Rome, Mussolini embarked on a series of imperialist conquests that were all failures. The catastrophic decision to enter World War II as one of the Axis powers nearly destroyed Italy and caused Mussolini to be assassinated by Italian partisans.

Adolf Hitler had political skills much like those of Mussolini. He too had powers of oratory and an intuitive ability to sense the discontent of the Germans, who were even more disillusioned than the Italians because they had been defeated in World War I and believed an unjust peace had been imposed upon them. The same sharp and growing division that existed in Italy between the conservatives and the liberals and socialists, because of the growing influence of the Communist Party, also existed in Germany. The great difference between Italy and Germany was that Germany was a highly industrialized state with a more literate population and a well-developed media industry that included radio and film.

An astute observer, Hitler studied the communist revolution in Russia, from which he derived the value of terror, and Mussolini, who became his model for the seizure of power. Hitler organized his private army, the *Sturm Abteilung* (SA), soon supplemented by an elite army, the SS. The name of his party, the National Socialist German Workers' Party, was shortened to Nazi. The Nazis had their own newspaper; their sacred text, Hitler's *Mein Kampf*; a national anthem; and a symbol, the ancient swastika.

Hitler had the ability to pick supporters and associates who were as capable and as ruthless as he was. With the onset of the worldwide Depression in 1929, almost a third of Germany's skilled workforce was unemployed. Revolution, backed by the communists, threatened, and Hitler's party gained financial support from the frightened propertied class and votes from the desperate unemployed. In 1933, Hitler was appointed chancellor.

Once in power, Hitler used the same means as Mussolini to give the Nazi party total control of Germany. The traditional forms of government were retained, but were subservient to the Nazi political organization superimposed upon them. The country was divided into *Gaue*, or cells, each with its own leader. Rather than a council at the apex of the power pyramid, there was only Hitler. The Nazis developed one of the most effective secret police systems ever known, the dreaded Gestapo. Because ordinary prisons were inadequate to hold the many dissidents and enemies of the new regime, a new means of confinement, the concentration camp, was organized. Hitler liked to think that his was a government of the elite, although it was largely a collection of thugs.

Another of Hitler's methods of consolidating power was through thought control. Joseph Goebbels, his minister of propaganda, manipulated the media to an extent never achieved before. All forms of public expression, from newspapers and books, to art, and even architecture, were controlled. Great rallies were organized, at which the masses were manipulated through music, spectacle, and oratory. Goebbels made special efforts to reach and manipulate the young. Properly indoctrinated, they became major supporters of the Nazi state.

Hitler knew the importance of terror in maintaining control, but he also used more material means to gain the support of the German people. He appointed capable economic advisors. Through the use of Keynesian economics, deficit spending, currency manipulation, public works, and increased armaments, the unemployment problem disappeared. Hitler's greatest successes, however, were in the field of foreign relations. Ultimately, he carried the fascist idea of dynamism or imperialist expansion to the extreme, creating for a short time the largest European empire known since ancient Rome. As in Mussolini's Italy, Hitler maintained that Germany must grow or die. Facing no organized international opposition, Hitler achieved one bloodless conquest after the other until Poland refused to accede to his demands in 1939, thus igniting World War II.

What distinguished Hitler's fascist state and set it apart from the others was the German dictator's theory of race. No other fascist state developed racism to such an extent as did Germany. It was not that Germany was more inclined toward racism than other states, it was because Hitler developed totalitarian control to such a degree that he was able to put his racist theories into practice with terrifying results. Hitler believed his racist theories would be his imperishable contribution to world civilization—an indication of how irrational the fascist mind can become. According to Hitler, human society was divided into races of varying degrees of ability, with the Aryan or Nordic race the most creative and innovative. Others not so gifted included the Slavs and blacks; at the bottom were the Jews, whom Hitler considered to be degenerated and parasitic. Only the superior races were to be considered human; their purity was to be maintained and furthered. Others were dehumanized, to be enslaved or destroyed. Genocide was the logical result.

Context

Even though fascism is of comparatively modern origins and lacks a developed political philosophy, forms of fascism have existed since ancient times. The danger to the state, the discontent of the masses, and the willingness of a charismatic leader to seize control in response to what is perceived as an emergency have been common occurrences in the past and are likely to be so in the future. One can find elements of modern fascism in ancient history, such as when the Greek city-states of Athens and Sparta embarked on the Peloponnesian War that nearly destroyed Greek civilization. The Roman emperors used the excuse of the welfare of the state and the Roman people to destroy the Roman Republic.

Political philosopher Niccolò Machiavelli is considered to be one of the major theorists on fascism, but with an important difference from its practice by modern dictators: Machiavelli emphasized the state in an attempt to strengthen it, whereas fascism as practiced usually destroyed it.

Catherine de Médicis, the sixteenth century queen regent of France, instituted the practice of political purge by the massacre of religious dissidents. Cardinal Richelieu, the powerful minister to Louis XIII of France, anticipated the political cells of Mussolini and Hitler with a system whereby total internal control in France was achieved through appointed officials controlling specific districts. Dynamism, charismatic leadership, and the imperialist expansion essential to modern fascism were indicative of the empire established by Napoleon I. The Napoleonic secret police served as a model for later dictators. The Second Empire of Louis Napoleon, Napoleon's nephew, with its censorship, leadership cult, vast public works, and dynamic imperialist expansion, is considered by some historians to be the first modern fascist state.

Except where elements of fascism were used to support existing legitimate governments, all historic examples of fascism have been doomed to failure. There is no well-defined political philosophy to legitimatize their existence. More important, since these governments depend almost completely on the ability of one individual, there is no provision for the continuation of power. Consequently, the legacy of these proto-fascist governments is usually disillusionment and increased misery for the masses who initially helped bring them to power.

This is not to say, however, that fascism is to be relegated to the past. Political memories are short. Many forget or overlook the miseries and the near-destruction of France caused by Napoleon, and see him as a conquering hero who spread the ideas of French liberalism. The social ills, dread of revolution, and fear for the sanctity of private property, factors that helped bring fascist dictators to power, still exist. So are the potential promises by cynical and unscrupulous political opportunists to eradicate these social disorders.

Bibliography

Carsten, F. L. *The Rise of Fascism*. 2d ed. Berkeley: University of California Press, 1980. Easy-to-read introduction to fascism. Details the rise of fascism in Europe and Latin America in the 1920's and 1930's, concentrating on the three countries where fascism was most fully developed: Italy, Austria, and Germany. Also discusses its resurgence since World War II. Excellent bibliography.

De Grand, Alexander. *Italian Fascism: Its Origins & Development*. Lincoln: University of Nebraska Press, 1982. Detailed discussion of the rise of fascism in Italy from its beginnings in 1919 until its collapse in 1945. Traces its dynamism in the form of imperialist expansion and the essential role that propaganda played in promoting the charismatic leadership of Benito Mussolini.

Hitler, Adolf. *Mein Kampf*. Translated by Ralph Manheim. Boston: Houghton Mifflin, 1971. Writing in the late 1920's, Hitler gives no details on how he expects to establish his fascist state, but clearly indicates policies he expects to institute once power has been attained. The chapter on "Nation and Race" is particularly revealing.

Laqueur, Walter, ed. *Fascism: A Reader's Guide*. Berkeley: University of California Press, 1976. Series of articles on the various forms of fascism before World War I, between World War I and World War II, and during the postwar period. Of special interest are fascist movements in England, France, Latin America, and Eastern Europe.

Mosse, George L. "Fascism" and "National Socialism and the Depersonalization of Man." In *The Culture of Western Europe*. Chicago: Rand McNally, 1961. The chapter on fascism is probably the best and most easily understood overview of fascism available. The following chapter shows how the theory was incorporated into the Nazi state.

Stromberg, Roland N. "The Strife of Ideologies." In *An Intellectual History of Modern Europe*. New York: Appleton-Century-Crofts, 1966. Covers fascism in the context of conflicting ideologies prevalent at the time. Analysis is short, well-written, and to the point. Observes that the fascist leaders understood the powers of ideas, while their liberal democratic opponents did not.

Nis Petersen

Cross-References

Charismatic Leadership, p. 209; Corporatism, p. 452; Demagoguery, p. 507; Dictatorships, p. 546; Existentialism, p. 642; Force, p. 712; General Will, p. 745; Genocide, p. 752; Irrationalism in Politics, p. 987; Machiavelli's Political Philosophy, p. 1148; Military Governments, p. 1192; Nietzsche's Political Philosophy, p. 1300; Oligarchy, p. 1344; Police States, p. 1408; Political Crimes, p. 1448; Political Myths and the Philosophies of Mosca and Pareto, p. 1474; Political Violence, p. 1539; Propaganda, p. 1615; Terrorism, p. 1962; Totalitarianism, p. 1987.

FEDERAL MANDATES

Field of study: Local and regional government

In the American system of government, federal mandates direct state governments or their subunits to implement laws, regulations, or policies in accordance with guidelines established by the federal government. They also prohibit states or their subunits from implementing certain policies, laws, or regulations.

> *Principal terms*
> BLOCK GRANT: grant given with more general guidelines for its use
> CATEGORICAL GRANT: grant-in-aid for a specific program, usually highly controlled and shaped by the federal government
> FEDERAL PREEMPTION: mandates that exert federal control in policy areas generally reserved to state governments
> GRANT-IN-AID: federal fund to state governments or their subunits, usually for specific purposes—highway funding, for example
> GREAT SOCIETY: series of domestic social programs originated by the Lyndon Johnson Administration
> MINIMUM STANDARD: federal requirement for state agencies to regulate to at least the level established by the federal government
> NEW DEAL: domestic programs of President Franklin D. Roosevelt, designed to combat the effects of the Great Depression
> UNFUNDED MANDATE: mandate that imposes a financial burden upon a state or its subunits and which is not reimbursed by the federal government—the Americans with Disabilities Act, for example

Overview

The relationship between the federal government and the state governments has undergone a steady evolution since the ratification of the Constitution in 1789. Article 6, paragraph 2 of the Constitution declares in part:

> This Constitution, and the laws of the United States which shall be made in pursuance thereof; and all Treaties made, or which shall be made, under the authority of the United States, shall be the supreme law of the land.

The Framers of the Constitution clearly intended that federal laws should take precedence over state laws. The powers of the federal government over the states, however, were strictly limited to those powers enumerated in the document. State governments were to remain the principal governing entities over the day-to-day affairs of average citizens. They retain what are often referred to as the "police powers."

Concern about the autonomy of state governments within the new union led to inclusion of the Tenth Amendment in the Bill of Rights. It states: "The powers not delegated to the United States by the Constitution, nor prohibited by it to the states, are reserved to the states respectively, or to the people." Federal intrusion into the domains of state governments thus remained limited until well into the twentieth century. Two provisions in the Constitution—the Commerce Clause, and the Necessary and Proper Clause—would, in time, provide the rationale for nearly unrestricted federal activity. The degree to which the federal government has become actively involved in day-to-day activities within states may have been unimaginable for the Founders.

The Union victory in the Civil War settled many questions regarding the supremacy of the federal government and gave the federal government the new role of protector of individual citizens from the actions or lack thereof of state governments. The Thirteenth, Fourteenth, and Fifteenth amendments to the Constitution prohibited states from taking steps that would violate the civil rights of the newly freed blacks. Federal mandates concerning voting rights, school desegregation, and employment discrimination all are rooted to the Fourteenth Amendment's guarantee of "equal protection of the laws."

Direct federal involvement in policy areas generally reserved to state governments, such as social welfare and business regulation, did not occur on a large scale until the federal government began to collect income taxes after 1913 and to spend large sums of money on domestic programs. The domestic programs originating from the New Deal of Franklin D. Roosevelt greatly expanded the role of the federal government. Myriad social programs and a previously unknown level of business regulation placed the federal government and its bureaucracy at the center of the day-to-day lives of millions of Americans. The New Deal served to increase not only federal involvement in domestic programs but also state involvement, because many of the programs established by the federal government often required the creation of state bureaucratic structures. Administration of many federal social and regulatory programs devolved upon state governments and their subunits. (The U.S. Constitution makes no reference to local governments. The structure of local governing entities are dependent upon state constitutions and laws.) Federal control over the programs of state agencies derived largely from control over the funds on which state governments became dependent for the maintenance of the programs.

After World War II and until the late 1970's, federal grants-in-aid to state governments increased steadily. In the late 1960's, the Great Society programs of the Johnson Administration launched the federal government on an unparalleled course of domestic spending that would further increase the dependency of state governments on federal funds. Great Society social programs, such as Medicaid and Aid to Families with Dependent Children, spawned huge corresponding state programs and structures that were increasingly dependent upon and answerable to the federal government.

By the late 1960's and early 1970's, many state governments were complaining that federal categorical grants-in-aid were limiting the flexibility and discretion that they needed to resolve problems. Many political leaders at the federal level, President

Richard Nixon included, agreed that the mandates associated with categorical federal grants-in-aid were imposing undue burdens upon state governments. In response, the federal government increased use of block grants and initiated a revenue-sharing program. Block grants are federal grants-in-aid that are broadly specified for various uses but are free of many of the strings attached to categorical grants. Revenue sharing is a program that shifts billions of federal dollars to state governments under the broadest of guidelines, allowing states a high degree of discretion in how the money will be spent.

The respite from federal mandates offered by revenue sharing and block grants was short. By the mid-1970's, the number of categorical conditional grants-in-aid and other federal mandates again mushroomed. The peak of spending-based mandates was reached during the Carter Administration.

During the 1980's and into the 1990's, American federalism took a new turn as the federal government began to retrench from its previous levels of domestic spending. Much to the dismay of many state leaders, however, federal mandates did not dry up along with federal dollars. A new generation of federal mandates, not linked to federal grants-in-aid, came to the fore. During the Reagan and Bush presidencies, the states were still required to carry out many programs, but were given decreasing amounts of money with which to work.

In the view of many scholars of American federalism, the federal government in the 1980's and 1990's undertook a sustained effort to preempt state and local laws and regulations for the purpose of achieving uniformity in regulatory policy and to ensure that state regulations met the standards set by the federal government. Minimum standards mandates allow state's discretion in the regulation of various activities, provided the state regulations meet a minimum levels established at the federal level. State regulation and policy-making in areas such as pollution, occupational health and safety, transportation, labor relations, education, health, and many other areas have been preempted to varying degrees by the federal government.

Many state governments have argued that federal mandates and federal preemption are often beyond the scope of the powers delegated to the federal government in the Constitution. Proponents of expansive federal authority argue that the Commerce Clause and the Necessary and Proper Clause of the Constitution (Article 1, section 8) allow the federal government a very wide range of authority to preempt state laws and regulations. In the 1985 case *Garcia v. San Antonio Metropolitan Transit Authority*, the U.S. Supreme Court issued a decision granting the federal government an almost limitless range of authority to regulate private activity within states and to preempt state policies.

Applications

The Eisenhower Administration (1953-1961) committed the federal government to the massive highway construction program known as the Interstate Highway Act. Highway construction projects, highly prized by all states for their positive impact on economic development, soon became financially dependent upon the federal government. By controlling the purse strings, the federal government was able to mandate many transportation policies that had previously been left to the states' legislatures. For example, the federal government has scant constitutional or statutory power to dictate highway speed limits within states. During the 1970's, nevertheless, all fifty states lowered their speed limits to fifty-five miles per hour at the discretion of the federal government. It was the threat of cutting off highway funding for the states that did not comply with the fifty-five mile-per-hour mandate that led to the reductions in speed limits in every state.

Federal mandates in the form of minimum standards are exemplified by the landmark environmental legislation of the 1960's and 1970's. The Clean Air Act and the Clean Water Act empowered the Environmental Protection Agency (EPA) to establish rules for state regulations to protect air and water quality. The need for uniform state regulations, or at least minimum levels, is apparent in the fact that air pollution and most water pollution are oblivious to state boundaries and political jurisdictions. Pollution control regulations, or the lack thereof, in one state may have a major impact on environmental quality in neighboring states. For example, smoke-stack emissions from Midwestern states can quickly find their way to New England. In addition, the potential financial and administrative burdens of dealing with fifty different sets of pollution regulations made the business community, particularly the automobile industry, supportive of national air quality standards.

The Clean Air Act was amended in 1990. Among the mandates contained in the Clean Air Act Amendments of 1990 are requirements that states implement programs reducing the number of single-occupant automobile trips to businesses with one hundred or more employees in any metropolitan region classified by the EPA as being in severe noncompliance with EPA standards for ozone and carbon monoxide pollu-tion. In other words, the federal government placed itself in the position of deciding how many workers at a given business may drive to work alone and how many must find other means of transportation. Fearing the loss of companies to less polluted or less regulated locations, affected state and local governments had to scramble to assist the business community in establishing programs to comply with the 1990 mandates. Many state officials were incensed at these mandates.

The degree to which federal mandates can impose financial and administrative burdens upon states and local governments can be seen when the Americans with Disabilities Act is examined. This act requires public facilities of all kinds—such as schools, public transit, public buildings, and recreational facilities—be made accessi-ble to wheelchairs and those with physical disabilities. Accomplishing this altruistic goal costs states, local governments, transit operators, school districts, and so on billions of dollars.

Context

Regardless of the type of federal mandate, criticisms usually center on the argument that mandates limit the discretion and authority of state and local policymakers. The argument is often made that Congress and the federal bureaucracy do not understand the complexities and unique conditions that exist at the state level. Generally speaking, opponents of federal mandates are also opponents of an active, expansive federal government, despite the fact that many state governments are more active with regard to regulatory and social policies than is the federal government. This line of thinking is often associated with conservatives; however, grouping is risky as it does not always apply to a specific case and is constantly evolving.

Proponents of an active federal government argue that federal mandates are needed because many state governments have historically been reactionary forces, controlled by local business and financial interests. Those favorably disposed to federal mandates point to civil rights, consumer protection, environmental pollution, and other areas, and argue that federal action is often the possible vehicle for reform. Liberals have been associated with an activist federal government, but this again is not always an accurate categorization.

State leaders across the political spectrum complain bitterly about the burdens imposed by unfunded federal mandates and the loss of discretion and control imposed by almost all mandates. The fiscal retrenchment of the federal government, as a result of the huge budget deficits of the 1980's and 1990's, drastically reduced the amount of federal aid available to state and local governments while at the same time mandates such as the Americans with Disabilities Act and the Clean Air Act amendments of the 1990's arrived with enormous price tags.

It is common for presidential candidates and new presidents to propose dramatic changes in the relationships between the federal government and the states. Republican candidates, especially, exclaim on the urgency of "getting the government off our backs." Ronald Reagan's new federalism was designed to accomplish just such a goal. Nevertheless, even during Republican administrations, federal mandates continued to expand and to permeate most aspects of state governmental administration. It could be argued that, despite partisan rhetoric, American federalism will continue to evolve on its own course and that mandates will continue to remain an irritant for state policymakers.

Bibliography

Elazar, Daniel. *American Federalism: A View from the States*. New York: Harper & Row, 1984. Comprehensive analysis of the evolving relationship between the state and federal governments, valuable for insights into the impact of federal mandates on state governments.

Nathan, Richard, and Fred C. Doolittle. *Reagan and the States*. Princeton, N.J.: Princeton University Press, 1987. Examination of the Reagan Administration's approach to federalism and the consequences, intended and unintended, of federal retrenchment on domestic policy.

Reagan, M., and J. Sanzone. *The New Federalism*. 2d ed. New York: Oxford University Press, 1981. Analysis of the changing nature of federal mandates at a time of federal retrenchment on spending for social programs.

Wright, Deil S. *Understanding Intergovernmental Relations*. 2d ed. Monterey, Calif.:

Brooks/Cole, 1982. Important study on the dynamics of the intergovernmental relationships that shape American federalism, with attention paid to the impact of federal grants-in-aid on the administration of state governments.

Zimmerman, Joseph. *Federal Preemption: The Silent Revolution*. Ames: Iowa State University Press, 1991. A leading scholar of federalism and federal preemption of state authority provides insight into the federal preemptive mandates.

Daniel M. Shea

Cross-References

Administrative Procedures in U.S. Government, p. 14; Budgets of National Governments, p. 158; Civil Rights Protection, p. 304; Congress, p. 412; County Government, p. 458; Environmental Protection, p. 617; The Family and Politics in the United States, p. 649; Grants-in-Aid, p. 791; Local Governments, p. 1136; Policy Development and Implementation, p. 1414; Regulatory Agencies in the United States, p. 1678; Social Services, p. 1858; State and Local Government, p. 1885; State Government, p. 1891.

FEDERALISM IN THE UNITED STATES

Field of study: Political philosophy

A system that divides the powers and responsibilities of government between a national government and smaller autonomous units contained within that nation, federalism is said to be the principal United States contribution to government and politics.

Principal terms

CONFEDERATION: government that states or other units may join, surrendering certain powers, or withdraw from, retaining their authority

DUAL FEDERALISM: state and national governments functioning as equals, each having individual and concurrent authority to act in certain matters

FEDERATION: system in which national and state governments are created by the people through a written constitution that delegates and restricts the powers of the central government

SEPARATION OF POWERS: system of checks and balances in which government power and authority is divided among branches

SOVEREIGNTY: supreme political authority and an absolute right to govern without accountability to another entity

SUPREMACY CLAUSE: Article 6 of the Constitution, which states that federal law will prevail in cases of conflict with state law

UNITARY GOVERNMENT: system of government in which nonautonomous institutions are created by a controlling central government

Overview

Federalism was created in 1787 under the United States Constitution and has been adopted by many other countries of the world. It is estimated that the governments of approximately twenty countries contain certain elements of federalism.

Federalism involves a sovereign national government, created by the people and which may act directly on them, and autonomous states, which may exercise certain specific powers and act within designated areas. While the federalist system of government was conceptualized and created by the Framers of the Constitution, and its basic structure was outlined in that document, beyond broad general powers, its relative spheres of influence and areas of responsibility were uncertain. Federalism, therefore, is considered to be a dynamic and evolving system constantly being defined by ongoing practical experience.

As created by the Framers, federalism was seen as the best means to limit dangerous abuses at the state and local level. That goal was to be implemented by transferring some of the power of the states to the national government, thereby limiting potential abuses; at the same time, the powers of the national government would be limited to those enumerated in the Constitution, and national power would be divided among three coequal branches—legislative, executive, and judicial. A system of checks and balances was instituted in order to curb excessive power of any single branch.

Constitutional guidelines created a national government that was to have exclusive authority over a series of government functions enumerated in the document. The enumerated powers in Article 1, section 8 include power over foreign affairs, military affairs, interstate commerce, commerce with foreign nations and Native American tribes, currency, post offices, and post roads. The enumerated powers defined those matters thought by the Framers to be essential, but at the same time afforded a broad and sweeping grant of power to promulgate whatever additional authority may become necessary through the "necessary and proper" clause—"To make all laws necessary and proper for carrying into execution the foregoing powers."

The U.S. Supreme Court has held that the national government has supplementary implied powers that allow it to undertake whatever policies it deems worthy. Augmenting this additional authority are the "inherent powers," most of which deal with foreign policy. The Court has held that those powers can be inferred from the structure of government itself, even if they are not specifically articulated in the Constitution. The Constitution also prohibits Congress from certain actions; it cannot pass ex post facto laws, that is, criminal laws made applicable to acts committed prior to their passage, or bills of attainder, that is, declaring a person guilty of a crime and imposing punishment without trial; it cannot impose head taxes and taxes on imports from other states; and it cannot grant titles of nobility.

The above structure is sometimes called "vertical federalism." The Constitution also contains provisions regarding the relation between states, or "horizontal federalism." The states are to grant "full faith and credit" or legal recognition to other states' judgments and official acts, such as marriage and divorce. The "privileges and immunities" clause prohibits states from discriminating against nonresidents; the "rendition" or "extradition" clause requires the return of criminals who flee across state lines. States are prohibited from impairing obligations of contracts, depriving persons of life, liberty, or property without due process of law, denying any person the equal protection of the laws, entering into treaties, granting titles of nobility, coining money, taxing goods from other states, or establishing a militia.

States apparently were granted additional authority under the Tenth Amendment. The Tenth Amendment reads: "The powers not delegated to the United States by the Constitution, nor prohibited by it to the States, are reserved to the States respectively, or to the people." The powers reserved to the states may be classified as follows: taxing and spending, regulating persons and property in order to promote the general welfare (police power), regulating intrastate (local) commerce, taking private property for public use upon payment of just compensation (eminent domain), and establishing a republican form of state and local government.

The scope and meaning of the Tenth Amendment have been the subject of much debate and discussion among legal scholars and historians. Some feel that it is purely superfluous and should be given no credence; others feel that it would not have been included unless it was intended to have meaning and significance. The Supreme Court has given different constructions to the federalist scheme as well as the Tenth Amendment at various times in history.

Federalism involves the issues of legitimacy and authority. Questions arise as to whether federal or state government may constitutionally act in the most effective and responsive manner. Critics of federalism say that it is outmoded and inefficient. Its defenders, including James Madison, have claimed that federalism offers numerous advantages and safeguards that make democracy function well. Having attempted another government structure under the failed Articles of Confederation, the Founders determined that an innovative government framework was required. The 1787 constitutional convention invented federalism in response to two elements of political thought in the states at the time: There should be a strong national government with substantial authority, but the states should continue to have major political roles and power.

After federalism went through four complete stages, a fifth began with the advent of the administration of President Ronald Reagan's "new federalism" in the 1980's. Classic federalism began in 1789 and lasted until the Fourteen Amendment was adopted at the end of the Civil War. During that time, there was no strict separation between the powers of national and state governments. The national government gave the states land grants, which were used at the end of the Civil War to build public universities. The issue of sovereignty was unsettled, and, as suggested by Madison in Federalist No. 39, a hybrid government resulted, with federal and confederal elements.

Dual federalism existed from 1867 until 1913. From 1913 until the start of World War II in 1941, the national government was forced to aid state governments in relief efforts and other programs of the New Deal, including public housing, welfare, public employment, and unemployment insurance. The Supreme Court acted as overseer to ensure that the national government did not overstep its bounds.

From 1941 through the 1970's, the focus shifted to issues of race and desegregation in schools, sometimes requiring federal marshals and federal troops to enforce court orders, and civil rights, resulting in the desegregation of public accommodations, commercial establishments, and housing. Cooperative federalism during that period established a link between national and local officials; the state level was bypassed, and "intergovernmental cooperation" became a familiar practice. The national government took the lead in formulating policy goals, and by the 1960's the federal government reigned supreme.

The 1970's, 1980's, and early 1990's brought a mounting national deficit, an increased public distrust of big government, and skepticism about whether the national government was the proper entity to solve local problems. Issues such as state sovereignty and states' rights, were common topics of political discussion, and many sought to roll back the federal system so that states could assume a greater degree of power and perhaps administer programs more efficiently. Government reform plans initiated by the Reagan Administration in 1981 aimed at cutting back the activities of the federal government by reducing or eliminating a vast number of programs, with the principal cuts falling on federal aid to state and local governments. Verbally, at least, presidents George Bush and Bill Clinton continued the trend toward talking about eliminating government waste and duplication.

Applications

The Supreme Court has contributed significantly to the transformation of federalism, beginning with its initial inquiry as to whether the national government had the authority to act in ways that might challenge or compromise states' rights, to a focusing on whether the national government will permit state action in an area of public policy. The Supreme Court's interpretation of federalism has been formulated by decisions on the commerce power, the spending power, the Tenth and Fourteenth amendments, and the preemptive doctrine, under which an area of authority previously within the purview of the states is brought within the exclusive jurisdiction of the federal government through an act of Congress. The Court usually has recognized the extensive authority of the national government in "vertical federalism" disputes. Some notable exceptions are contained in early opinions by Chief Justice John Marshall, which recognized limitations on both national power and state sovereignty. The twentieth century Court, however, decided in favor of the national government in every controversy that arose between the Great Depression and the early 1990's.

The first case to consider the matter of federalism was *McCulloch v. Maryland*, decided in 1819. Congress had established a national bank, which Maryland attempted to tax. The bank refused to pay the tax, and a bank employee was punished for the refusal. The Supreme Court set aside the penalty, holding that Congress had the power to establish a bank, and that the tax was unconstitutional because a state could not tax a federal instrumentality. Although the Constitution does not explicitly mention banks, the "necessary and proper" clause enabled its creation in order to permit the legislature to carry out such explicit powers as coining money and borrowing on the credit of the United States.

In *Gibbons v. Ogden* (1824), the Court attempted to define the commerce power and to decide whether it is exclusive or concurrent. Commerce involves not only buying and selling, but also commercial intercourse between nations and states. An act involving more than one state is included within interstate commerce, and Congress is empowered by the Constitution to regulate it. Commerce that occurs within the boundaries of a single state is a local matter, to be regulated by the state in question under the police power. Later decisions by the Court refined Marshall's definition and clarified distinctions between local and interstate activities.

The tendency toward centralization was halted abruptly in 1976 with the decision in *National League of Cities v. Usery (NLC)*. The Court held that Congress lacked the power under the commerce clause to regulate the wages and hours of state and local public employees engaged in "traditional governmental functions." Despite congressional power to regulate any private activity affecting interstate commerce, the Tenth

Amendment was considered to limit congressional power when the regulation in question interfered with traditional functions essential to a state's integrity and separate and independent existence. In 1985, *NLC* was overruled by *Garcia v. San Antonio Metropolitan Transit Authority*, in which the Court reasoned that traditional and nontraditional state governmental functions were not easily distinguishable and withdrew from resolving federalism questions relating to congressional exercise of the commerce power. According to the Court, it was for Congress to determine the extent of its authority.

In *South Carolina v. Baker* (1988), the Court continued its Tenth Amendment retreat, holding that the federal income tax exemption for interest on municipal bonds issued by state and local authorities was not constitutionally mandated. The Tenth Amendment was also called into question by legal scholars as it related to health reform in the 1990's. It is likely that the Court will continue to refine the intergovernmental relations within the federal system.

Context

Dual federalism has been compared to a layer cake to illustrate the relative independence or autonomy of different levels of government. In contrast, the increasing governmental interdependence that developed during the era of the New Deal and the decades that followed suggest a marble cake, with functions being swirled and mixed together. U.S. government had become more complex and the powers and functions of the nation and the states more interconnected. Clusters of federal, state, and local officials often jointly administered programs in cooperation with private organizations.

Intergovernmental cooperation often involves federal funding for part or all of state programs. Federal grants-in-aid may be categorical grants, the traditional means of administering programs, in which the federal government may require states to produce matching funds; project grants, money given by the federal government to help states or cities construct particular facilities; formula grants, the system preferred by states and cities, in which funds are distributed by automatic formula, eliminating possible political influence; block grants, funds for a broad area such as education or law enforcement, to be used according to the recipient's desires and priorities; and general revenue sharing, a direct sharing of national revenues with states and cities.

Theoretical advantages of federalism include diversity and an ability for each state or region to establish distinct public, social, and economic policies if desired; closer involvement and identification of citizens with state government; strengthened community bonds; uncluttering the national agenda; and reducing the control of government over the lives of citizens by reducing each level of government's power, contrasted with unitary government. Its disadvantages include modern problems that transcend traditional state lines and require joint cooperation, such as pollution and environmental problems; frustration of citizens because different states may make different decisions on certain questions; and inefficient and cumbersome administration.

There are several additional concepts involved in federalism. Fiscal federalism involves economic stabilization through the use of monetary and fiscal policy, distribution of resources to the population, and allocation or division of national resources between the public and private sectors. Fiscal equalization is the redistribution of national income from wealthier regions to poorer ones. Fiscal equalization does not exist in the United States, however, because the wealthier states are also those with large concentrations of the poor and facilities in need of replacement.

A hierarchy is a system of authority in which higher ranks exert control over lower ranks, following directives from the highest authority. One central authority is held accountable and has the power to coordinate, evaluate, and eliminate duplication and inefficiency. A hierarchy also exists at state and local levels. Public choice means fewer bureaucratic solutions to public problems and emphasizes demand as a source of government activity. It justifies government intervention only in cases of market failure.

These concepts, while theoretical, provide insights that allow an understanding of general relationships, but stop short of describing actual patterns of behavior. The practical application of concepts of federalism must be assessed on an ad hoc basis.

Bibliography

Anton, Thomas J. *American Federalism and Public Policy: How the System Works*. New York: Random House, 1989. Focuses on federalism by analyzing patterns of behavior of public officials in order to identify concepts. Written for the sophisticated reader.

Barber, Sotirios A. *On What the Constitution Means*. Baltimore: The Johns Hopkins University Press, 1984. Dealing with the Constitution as a whole, presents a general theory of constitutional interpretation through analysis and commentary.

Elazar, Daniel J. *American Federalism: A View from the States*. 3d ed. New York: Harper & Row, 1984. One of the best general outlines of the historical development and operation of the federal system in the United States.

Glendening, Parris N., and Mavis Mann Reeves. *Pragmatic Federalism: An Intergovernmental View of American Government*. 2d ed. Pacific Palisades, Calif.: Palisades Publishers, 1984. Analysis of intergovernmental issues, including the impact of programs of the Reagan Administration. Readable style with numerous graphs and charts.

Hamilton, Christopher, and Donald T. Wells. *Federalism, Power, and Political Economy: A New Theory of Federalism's Impact on American Life*. Englewood, N.J.: Prentice Hall, 1990. Uses policy concepts and political and social theory and analysis to reinterpret federalism as a powerful and underestimated factor in our politics and economics. This perspective makes the book's focus unique, but it remains difficult to understand.

Scheiber, Harry N. "Federalism and the Constitution: The Original Understanding." In *American Law and the Constitutional Order: Historical Perspectives*, edited by Lawrence M. Friedman and Harry N. Scheiber. Enlarged ed. Cambridge, Mass.:

Harvard University Press, 1988. Historical analysis of the adoption of federalism, the problems that engendered it, and what it attempted to solve. Numerous quotations from historical documents. Contains essays on various subjects within legal and constitutional history, presented in a readable yet scholarly manner.

Marcia J. Weiss

Cross-References

FEDERATIONS

Field of study: Types of government

Federations are political systems based on the flexible federal model, in which political authority is divided between two or more levels of government so that each is independent of the other in the area assigned to it.

Principal terms
CONFEDERATION: arrangement among sovereign political units in which all legal power remains in the hands of the constituent units, and whose central government lacks the ability to make and enforce binding decisions on the member states
COOPERATIVE FEDERATION: federal association in which the central (federal) government and the constituent units collaborate in problem solving
CULTURAL FEDERATION: federation in which there are cultural differences separating the constituent units from one another
DUAL FEDERALISM: form of federal government in which each of the different levels of government is rigidly restricted to the powers explicitly assigned to it; also known as competitive federalism
UNITARY GOVERNMENT: form of government in which ultimate political power is vested in the central government

Overview

Federal government, in its modern form, was created in the United States. Indeed, federal government is one of the nation's two great contributions to modern government—the other being the concept of a written constitution as a higher law specifying the framework of government and rules of the game, itself necessitated as much by the creation of federalism in the United States as by the Founders' desire for limited, constitutional government. Alternately, by the very loose definition of federalism that prevailed as late as the 1780's, federations have existed for thousands of years.

The earliest federations were the leagues of fully autonomous Greek city states (the word "federal" being derived from *foedus*, Latin for league). Composed of political actors loosely, and usually temporarily, bound together for cooperation on a common venture, these leagues possessed a formal council that directed their activities but lacked the means of enforcing its decisions. The most famous of these was the Achaen League (281-146 B.C.E.). Created at the death of Alexander in response to the growing dangers posed by Macedonia and Rome, this league grew to include seventy cities before internal disputes led to its dissolution. It was so effective during much of its existence that it became the model for what we now call confederations, and with only a few minor exceptions the nature of these federations did not alter significantly during the following two thousand years.

From the Achean League through the American Articles of Confederation, the qualitative nature of central authority in federal associations remained unchanged. States formed alliances headed by common councils charged with decision-making responsibilities, but they always reserved to themselves the right to determine which rules they would obey and enforce. Even Alexander Hamilton, writing in the Federalist Papers, defined federalism as broadly as "assemblages of societies" and used the term interchangeably with "confederation" when he bothered to use it at all.

It was not until the ratification of the U.S. Constitution in 1789 that a truly substantive change occurred in the nature of federations, as a result of the compromises necessary in Philadelphia to make the highly centralized Virginia Plan acceptable to the newly independent states jealous of their sovereignty. Only then did the central government acquire the extensive machinery and powers of government necessary to execute the laws it enacted for the community under its jurisdiction. Thereafter, it only remained for the German jurists of the nineteenth century to draw their distinction between a *Staatenbund* (confederation) and a *Bundesstaat* (federation), using the United States as their model for the latter and distinguishing it from the former on the basis of its differences from the leagues preceding it.

Scholars have argued that there is ample justification for viewing the United States as the first modern federation. The modest disclaimers of the U.S. Constitution's Framers aside—they never claimed to have invented federal government, only effective federalism—the Constitutional Convention produced a new form of government, resting on the unprecedented principle that in a federal system each person is simultaneously a citizen in two political communities, that of his or her state and that of the nation as a whole. Once this concept became the legal building block for federations, a qualitative shift occurred in the authority of the government of the whole, from depending on the states for the execution of its commands to possessing its own organs for making and executing those laws pertinent to the power vested in it. Federalism thus emerged as a genuine middle ground of government between confederate and unitary systems in which each level of government (the center and the units) would possess full authority in the substantive areas assigned respectively to them.

Federalism has been widely adopted. In 1960, the year of the great explosion of Third World countries to independent statehood, at least eighteen states could be described as federal. These included Canada, the United States, and Mexico in North America; Argentina, Brazil, and Venezuela in South America; Switzerland, West Germany, Yugoslavia, and the Soviet Union in Europe; Nigeria in Africa; India, Pakistan, Malaysia in Asia; and Australia. The federal principal of dual autonomy was violated in practice in several of these countries, for example, by the centralizing, authoritarian dominance of the Communist Party in the Soviet Union, and by the frequent use of extraordinary constitutional provisions enabling central governments to intervene in the internal affairs of the constituent units in Nigeria, India, and several Latin American federations. On the other hand, during the 1960's and 1970's, federalism not only remained a vigorous form of government in the majority of existing federations but also emerged in a variety of newer states to accommodate territorially expressed centrifugal tendencies.

Given the proliferation of federations in the twentieth century, variations on federalism are found in such critical details as the amount of political power possessed by the central governments, the differences between the units composing them, which may be called states (the United States, India), regions (Nigeria), provinces (Canada), cantons (Switzerland), or other terms, and the nature of the relationship between the constituent units and the central government.

In terms of the power of the center, federations can be distinguished along a continuum flanked by highly centralized systems, in which the preponderance of political authority is exercised by the central government (the United States, India), and very peripheralized federations, in which most day-to-day authority for government is exercised in the hands of the units (the Swiss model). Substantial differences separate federations in terms of cultural diversity. The United States' federalism, for example, is essentially structural. The fifty states each possess constitutionally conferred legislative, judicial, and enforcement autonomy in the areas of decision making reserved to them by the U.S. Constitution; however, state boundaries no longer reflect significant cultural differences between these states. In most of the multinational federations in the late twentieth century, however, crossing state borders may alter the official language of politics (as it does when one travels from Quebec to Ontario in Canada) and mirror a passage from one culture to another.

Perhaps most important, today's federations often vary in terms of the relationship between the units and the central authority. In the relationship between Spain's Basque country and its capital in Madrid, or between Quebec and Ottawa, dual federalism is the mode, with the two levels of government seeing each other as competitors for the primary allegiance of their common citizens and placing the emphasis not so much on how well something can be accomplished as on who gets to provide the service or exercise authority. Much the same tone characterized U.S. federalism prior to the Civil War, when the permanency of the union and the validity of its laws were regularly challenged, and again during the period of "states' rights" federalism dating from the Civil War until the Great Depression of the 1930's. Since the Depression, however, the emphasis in the United States and most older federations has been on collaborative (or cooperative) federalism, in which both the states and the central government have sought collaborative frameworks for administering programs for their shared citizenry, with less attention being given to who provides the service than how well it can be delivered.

Applications

At least in theory, these areas of differentiation are linked. Where cultural differences divide the units, the relationship between the center and the units is likely to be strained on sensitive issues (as on the slavery issue in the United States before 1860). The central government can try to present itself as neutral, probably satisfying no one on matters of great emotion, or favor one side over another, estranging itself from those holding an opposing view. Such potential crises can be minimized, however, by restricting the arena for conflict by creating peripheralized federations. Where the responsibility for decision making on highly sensitive issues is assigned to the units, there is less over which to argue at the center. Unfortunately, it has historically been difficult to follow this prescription in practice. The reason for creating federations has usually been that weaker forms of government, such as confederacies, are not up to the task of providing for common defense or general economic welfare. It seems even less possible to follow the plan in the twentieth century, when central governments are expected not only to build railroads to abet the economy but also to assume direct responsibility for managing national welfare programs, maintaining full employment, fostering real economic growth, and otherwise shaping societies.

At the same time, the social diversity and other factors that make federalism attractive to multinational polities cannot be ignored. Federalism has remained popular because it offers an alternative to innately weak, confederate arrangements, and potentially undesirable unitary government in which all legal authority is in the hands of the center however much it may charter more localized units to operate in its name. Federations have normally reflected a balance at the time of their creation between the forces favoring union and those factors making unitary government unattractive. In *Federal Government* (1964), K. C. Wheare identified six factors that functioned in the four classical examples of modern federalism (the United States, Canada, Switzerland, and Australia) to overcome the reluctance to integrate: a feeling of insecurity from outside threats, a desire for independence of foreign powers, the hope for economic advantage, previous political association, a contiguous geographical setting, and a similarity of political institutions. Based on the experience of these and later federations, other factors could be added: homogeneous ethnic, social, and value structures; a sense of national greatness to be achieved in union; a deep commitment among political leaders to the value of union in its own right; a desire to play a more meaningful role in international relations; and the lure of imitation based on the success of earlier federal experiments.

Some of these factors have proven more propitious to the success of federations than others; even where federations have succeeded, their history has often been turbulent, especially in the multinational world. Of the classical federations, both Switzerland and the United States had to survive civil wars, and the prospect of Quebec's leaving the Canadian federation has been a persistent feature of Canadian history throughout the second half of the twentieth century. Federations created since World War II have had similarly stormy histories. A tribal-based civil war ended Nigeria's 1960 essay in federalism in less than a decade; culturally and linguistically different Bangladesh successfully seceded from Pakistan with the assistance of the Indian Army in 1971; Chinese-dominated Singapore withdrew peacefully from the Malay-dominated Federation of Malaysia shortly after that federation's formation in the 1960's; and the United Arab Republic (U.A.R.), formed briefly (1958-1961) to unite Syria, Iraq, and Egypt, proved incapable of containing the egos and different political ideologies of the leaders of these states, although Egypt continued to retain the U.A.R. designation as its official name. Even the Indian federation, the most durable, centralized, and only continuously operating federation formed in the Third World after 1947, barely survived the presidency of Indira Gandhi, who at one time had the majority of India's states under direct rule from Delhi.

Context

In the long term, the success of any political system depends, as Aristotle noted in his *Politics* more than two thousand years ago, on the "portion of the state which desires the permanence of the constitution . . . [being] stronger than that which desires the reverse." In this context, federalism has historically provided a means of giving the desire for union the chance to develop or consolidate (in the United States, Australia, India, and Spain, for example), or of preventing the drift towards separatism (as in Quebec in Canada) from leading to the rapid dismemberment of the state. The continued utility of federalism in both regards was repeatedly showcased during the last quarter of the twentieth century.

In post-Franco Spain, large parts of the Third World, and disintegrating portions of Eastern and Central Europe following the breakup of the Soviet Union, federalism became the model for democratically holding together nationally diverse regions, especially those suddenly freed from the unity imposed upon them by outsiders or nondemocratic governments at home. The model has not always succeeded. Czecho-slovakia chose to divorce peacefully into two states along the divide between its Slovak and Czech regions, no formula could be found to avoid civil war in Yugoslavia, and only a confederate separatism could be fashioned to halt the rush to complete separatism among the diverse nationalities formerly organized as union republics in the Soviet Union. Federalism's successes have been equally visible: in abetting the democratization process in Spain, in holding the Flemish and Walloon portions of Belgium together in the face of the powerful regionalized nationalism in that country after 1968, in enticing Quebec to remain in a more peripheral Canadian federation at the time of Quebec's 1980 referendum on independence, and in providing India with the flexible institutional framework it has needed for democracy to survive amid the general turmoil of its political process and the assassination of some of its most famous leaders.

Meanwhile, the development of a federation in Western Europe steadily gained ground as first six, then nine, and, by the late 1980's, a dozen countries functionally integrated to form the European Community. Along the way, Europe's unique supra-national institutions in Brussels (the Commission, Council of Ministers) and Stras-bourg (European Parliament, judicial institutions) grew not only in power, but also in political autonomy. Substantive issues originally blocking economic integration and the enlargement of the Community, for example, agricultural policy, were overcome. Decision-making arrangements initially requiring unanimity in the Council of Minis-ters were gradually subjected to qualified majority-rule arrangements; the European Parliament was directly elected and given enhanced budgetary authority. Acknowl-edging its changing nature, in 1994 the European Community officially completed its economic integration phase and became the European Union—a supranational entity evolved well beyond the nation-state in its independent political authority and seeking to continue building that United States of Europe of which its founders (with U.S. encouragement) dreamed in post-World War II Europe, and with an expanding number of states (Austria, Sweden, most of the states of Central Europe) petitioning to join Europe's unique venture in federalism.

Bibliography

Bakvis, Herman, and William M. Chandler, eds. *Federalism and the Role of the State.* Toronto, Canada: University of Toronto Press, 1987. Essays present a good blend of general studies of modern federalism, legitimacy, and democracy with case studies of federal-state relations in established and federalizing systems.

Duchacek, Ivo D. *Comparative Federalism: The Territorial Dimension of Politics.* New York: Holt, Rinehart and Winston, 1970. The 1960's produced a wave of new experiments in federal government and a renaissance of interest in federalism in the literature. This is one of the best of the comparative studies to emerge, particularly concerning multinational federations.

Hicks, Ursula K. *Federalism—Failure and Success: A Comparative Study.* New York: Oxford University Press, 1978. Useful case studies of failed federal experiments in Africa and partly successful ventures in Asia. The sections on the older successful federations are less interesting.

Peterson, Paul E., Barry G. Rabe, and Kenneth K. Wong. *When Federalism Works.* Washington, D.C.: Brookings Institution, 1986. Excellent study of cooperative federalism in an advanced democracy, with particular attention to managing redistributive programs in a federal system.

Pinder, John. *European Community: The Building of a Union.* Oxford, England: Oxford University Press, 1991. Basic reading on the background to the European Union, analyzed from the vantage point of both the historical and policy development of the supranational machinery of federally uniting Europe.

Rudolph, Joseph R., Jr., and Robert J. Thompson, eds. *Ethnoterritorial Politics, Policy, and the Western World.* Boulder, Colo.: Lynne Rienner, 1989. Several fine studies of the contemporary use of federalism and quasi-federal arrangements to respond to recent ethnopolitical demands in such multinational developed states as Belgium, Spain, Canada, and France.

Urwin, Derek W. *The Community of Europe: A History of European Integration Since 1945.* New York: Longman, 1991. Outstanding history of the development of the European Community, with an excellent mix of historical narrative, data, and political analysis.

Wheare, K. C. *Federal Government.* 4th ed. New York: Oxford University Press, 1964. The post-World War II study of the mechanics of federalism: when it is appropriate, how it should be organized, and how federal government works. Published in numerous editions, it is basic research material.

Joseph R. Rudolph, Jr.

Cross-References

Alliances, p. 47; The City-State, p. 272; Commonwealths, p. 364; Confederations, p. 391; The Constitution of the United States, p. 425; Empires and Empire Building, p. 597; Federalism in the United States, p. 668; Government Types, p. 785; Individual Versus State Rights, p. 910; Intergovernmental Relations, p. 942; Leagues, p. 1072; Regional Governments, p. 1672; Secessionism, p. 1790; Supranational Governments, p. 1922.

FEMINIST POLITICS

Field of study: Civil rights and liberties

Feminist politics deals with guaranteeing that women are adequately represented, calling attention to the fact that their interests may be different from men's, and recognizing the validity of women's interests and goals.

Principal terms

COVERTURE: legal term that means that married women are "covered" by their husbands and have no separate legal existence

DISCRIMINATION: unequal treatment of an individual or group based on assignment to a particular category

FEMINISM: advocacy for women

POLITICS: means by which power is distributed and policy decisions are made

REPRESENTATION: standing in for individuals and groups to promote and protect their interests

SOCIALIZATION: conscious and unconscious influences over the formation of opinions and behaviors

Overview

Feminist politics is about promoting equality for women. Advocates for women's issues are feminists. Feminist politics deals with promoting equality for women economically, socially, and legally. Inherent to the concept of feminist politics is the conviction that discrimination is wrong. Feminists also fight to end unequal treatment based on sex, race, color, national origin, religion, age, mental or physical disabilities, or sexual orientation.

The American political system derives in great part from the English political system. Early in American history, the colonists accepted coverture, the legal status of women that was in place in England. The rights of single women were somewhat similar to those of males, even though women were not allowed to vote or hold political office. When a woman married, however, the law considered her to be nonexistent because she was "covered" by her husband. For example, she could not own property, had no right of custody over her children, and could even be beaten by her husband in some states.

The legal system was in part based on beliefs that had been handed down by ancient philosophers, such as Aristotle, who maintained that women were emotional creatures whose function in life was to have babies and to care for them after they were born. Since women were assumed to be emotional, they were thought to be irrational, or incapable of making logical decisions based on an understanding of the consequences of their actions. The ideas of Aristotle and others who agreed with him were incorporated into a system called "patriarchy," which for women usually meant that they had little or no control over their own lives. The patriarch—the father, ruler, husband, god, or god's representative—had ultimate authority; no woman did.

One of the first women to write about women's rights was Englishwoman Mary Wollstonecraft. In *A Vindication of the Rights of Women* (1792), she wrote that education was the key to changing the patriarchal system. Like Wollstonecraft, most modern feminists believe that socialization teaches young girls and boys to act in certain ways. For example, parents give little girls dolls and tea sets and, therefore, teach them to engage in nurturing. Boys, on the other hand, are given trucks and guns and are, thus, socialized into action and aggression. Socialization is both conscious and unconscious and teaches gender roles, or the assignment of certain behaviors to females and males. Feminists believe that the way to offset the negative aspect of socialization (such as rearing girls to believe that they cannot do well at math or teaching boys that they should never cry) is to reeducate or countersocialize toward less restrictive definitions of gender roles.

When the U.S. Constitution was written in 1787, women were not given a voice in designing it or in putting it into practice. There was, however, no real way for women or slaves to protest their exclusion from the political process. A number of men and women soon began to question a political system that promised in its Declaration of Independence in 1776 that "all men are created equal," giving white male citizens the right to "life, liberty, and the pursuit of happiness," but that continued to enslave and subordinate a large part of the population. Those who worked to end African American slavery were called abolitionists. Few women or men questioned the exclusion of women's rights on the abolitionist agenda until women who worked in the movement began to recognize that they were discriminated against when they were denied the right to vote in meetings or were forbidden from giving public speeches on the issue. The first active feminists came from this group of women. Women such as Sarah and Angelina Grimké, who had been born in Charleston, South Carolina, began to write and speak out for both women's rights and an end to slavery.

In 1840, the United States sent a delegation to the Antislavery Convention in London, England, which included both women and men. The women were told that they must sit in a balcony behind a curtain, and they were banned from taking part in discussion and voting at the convention. Two Americans who were incensed at this discrimination vowed to take action. Lucretia Mott, a Quaker minister, and Elizabeth Cady Stanton decided to sponsor the first women's rights convention in 1848 in Seneca Falls, New York. For the conference, Stanton rewrote the Declaration of Independence to include women, listing offenses that women had historically suffered at the hands of men, just as the original lists the abuses of the English King.

The goals of the early women's movement were simple: to gain the right to vote, to gain access to birth control, to provide health care information, to ease access to education and child care, and to secure better working conditions for women. After the goal of suffrage was reached with the passage of the Nineteenth Amendment in 1920, the women's movement lost its momentum until the Civil Rights movement in the 1960's. The women most often credited with launching the contemporary women's movement and with returning feminist politics to the front burner are Betty Friedan and Gloria Steinem. Friedan published *The Feminine Mystique* in 1963 and spoke out on behalf of women who wanted to control their own lives and make their own choices about careers and families. She also founded the National Organization for Women. Gloria Steinem became the editor of *Ms.* magazine, which became the voice of the contemporary women's movement.

In 1972, the Equal Rights Amendment to the U.S. Constitution passed both houses of Congress and was sent to the states for ratification. It provided that neither the United States nor any state could deny equality of law on the basis of sex. The amendment, after a promising start, began to lose support as the right-wing opposition organized against it. At the deadline in 1982, the amendment had been ratified by thirty-five of the thirty-eight states needed for it to become law. It did not pass. The Equal Rights Amendment was later reintroduced in Congress several times, but opponents added so many amendments that its original intent became distorted, and the amendment was each time withdrawn by its own sponsors.

Applications

The American political system is a republic, or an indirect democracy, in which voters elect representatives to protect their interests. Feminists believe that women's interests are often distinct from men's because of the historical influence of patriarchy. The influences of patriarchy will decline as more women—and men who support women's issues—are elected to policy-making positions. Women have never held such positions in numbers proportionate to their place in the total population. For example, from the time Congress was created in 1789 until 1994, 11,096 men served in Congress, but only 135 women. The U.S. presidential election of 1992 took place in the Year of the Woman, but in that election the number of women in the Senate rose from only two to only six, and the number of women in the House of Representatives rose from only twenty-eight to only forty-seven. While numbers of women in office are higher at the state and local levels, they are still far short of fifty-percent representation.

As the women's movement redefined women's roles and economic necessity dictated that women—whether single individuals, single mothers, or part of two-wage-earner families—enter the work world, it became extremely important to elect policymakers who understood the needs of women. For many women, having good, affordable day care determines whether or not they can work. Some companies discovered that on-site day care resulted in increased productivity, and the national government began to subsidize child care for poor women. Many women with small children demanded and received flexible work schedules, job sharing, and the opportunity to work at home. The Family Leave Act, which became law in 1993 after much controversy, allowed both mothers and fathers to take unpaid time off from work to care for newborn or adopted babies or seriously ill family members, including elderly parents.

The Family Leave Act originated from a group that began in 1978. The Congresswomen's Caucus was created to promote women's issues in Congress. The bipartisan group originally included only women, but men were added as nonvoting members in 1982, and the name was changed to the Congressional Caucus for Women's Issues. In the 1980's, the group focused its attention on ending economic discrimination against women.

In 1985, women, on the average, made fifty-six cents for every dollar that men made. By 1994, the gap had closed by only nine cents. This gap between the wages of women and those of men has a long history. Automobile maker Henry Ford, for example, paid male workers a family wage; women, whether heads of households or not, received no such consideration. Congress attempted to end the practice of paying unequal salaries to women and men in the same job with the Pay Equity Act of 1972. The problem was more complex, however, than could be handled with a single piece of legislation.

Since women are socialized into nurturing roles, they tend to cluster in service-oriented occupations such as nursing, teaching, waitressing, and child care. Jobs that are dominated by women tend to pay less than jobs dominated by men. Even within the same professions, women tend to make less than their male counterparts because most women take time out from work to have and care for children. Some feminists advocate comparable worth, a practice that uses a formula to compare skills and educational levels, creating a more equitable pay scale. Comparable worth, they hope, would level out salary inequities between women and men.

Other economic problems center on the feminization of poverty, the phenomenon that results in high numbers of single-parent women and their dependent children living in poverty. The numbers are particularly high for minority women and their children. At the other end of the scale, economic problems result from the "glass ceiling," a point from which professional women are unable to progress further, resulting in fewer women than men at top levels of all professions.

In addition, feminists have worked for all women to be physically and emotionally safe in their homes, on the job, and in the streets. The three issues in this battle are domestic violence, sexual harassment, and rape. In all three areas, women are made victims by their lack of power. Feminists believe that women can become empowered by creating laws and policies that deal more effectively with the crimes of domestic violence, sexual harassment, and rape and that establish and enforce punishments for those who commit these crimes. Feminists also work to call attention to the appalling numbers of these crimes in order to train both women and men to recognize and avoid these crimes and to provide public information so that women know what to do about these crimes.

Context

Even though feminist politics, by definition, tends to concern women more than men, the causes endorsed by feminists often concern the quality, and equality, of all people's lives. With the Family Leave Act and greater availability of good quality, affordable child care, for example, all society benefits. Politicians opposed to the

Family Leave Act, for example, could not say that they were opposed to motherhood. The Act's obvious benefits had to be argued against in other ways—the Act's cost to business, for example. On the other hand, some feminist issues do cause great controversy. No example better illustrates this point than abortion. Since the early days of the women's movement, feminists have actively worked to help women gain control over their own lives. In the latter half of the twentieth century, this battle for control focused on access to birth control information, birth control devices, and the right to end an unwanted or dangerous pregnancy.

In 1965, in *Griswold v. Connecticut*, the U.S. Supreme Court recognized the right to privacy within a marriage and granted the right for married couples to obtain birth control. The right for single people to obtain birth control was granted in 1972 with *Eisenstadt v. Baird*. In 1973, in *Roe v. Wade*, using the right to privacy as a basis, the Supreme Court established a woman's right to obtain an abortion. Controversy ensued, and the right was limited in subsequent court decisions. *Webster v. Reproductive Health Services* in 1989 gave states the right to control access to abortion. *Planned Parenthood of Southeastern Pennsylvania v. Casey* in 1992 upheld the right of states to establish waiting periods and require distribution of literature explaining the development of a fetus and the medical procedures and risks involved in abortions. Also in *Casey*, however, the Court said that no state could place an "undue burden" on a woman's access to abortion.

At the same time the Supreme Court was providing or limiting access to abortion, the U.S. Congress often failed to pass legislation because of the controversy over the language involved in laws about abortion. During the 1980's, Congress often restricted foreign aid to countries that granted access to abortion or promoted any form of birth control other than natural family planning. Views on abortion became a major criteria for selection of Supreme Court justices and helped to elect or defeat candidates for political office.

Women's issues such as abortion are further complicated by the fact that not all women agree on a given issue. On the other hand, women generally do agree that women and their interests need to be better represented. Increased numbers of women in diverse positions at all levels of government and in all professions lend legitimacy to redefining roles along the lines advocated by feminists. Seeing women as members of Congress, as active First Ladies, as members of the president's cabinet, as heads of major governmental agencies, as governors, as state legislators, as doctors, as lawyers, as college professors, as astronauts, as engineers, as truck drivers, and as combat pilots sends a strong message. It tells children—both female and male—that girls can grow up to perform these roles. It also shows grown women and men that women have much to contribute to politics and society.

Feminist politics is about providing choices. As positions advocated by feminists become accepted by mainstream America, women and men will have more choices in their individual lives. Some of these changes have already come about. Women in many countries are now free to decide whether to marry and when and if they will have children. Both men and women are more able to choose a profession without restrictions on their choices. Only when women as well as men have equal choices will all individuals be equal members of society and equal citizens of the United States.

Bibliography

Abzug, Bella. *Gender Gap: Bella Abzug's Guide to Political Power for American Women*. Boston: Houghton Mifflin, 1984. Readable account by a former congress-woman of how both political parties have addressed women's issues.

Cantor, Dorothy W., and Toni Bernay, with Jean Stoess. *Women in Power: The Secrets of Leadership*. Boston: Houghton Mifflin, 1992. Examination of women in power in the 1990's.

Carroll, Susan J. *Women as Candidates in American Politics*. Bloomington: Indiana University Press, 1985. Outstanding account of recruitment, campaigns, and elections of women in American politics.

Evans, Sara M. *Born for Liberty: A History of Women in America*. New York: Free Press, 1989. Detailed look at the history of women in the United States, identifying those who played a significant role.

Ries, Paula, and Anne J. Stone, eds. *The American Woman 1992-93: A Status Report*. New York: W. W. Norton, 1992. Best source of statistical information on women's issues. Updated periodically.

Sapiro, Virginia. *Women in American Society: An Introduction to Women's Studies*. 3d ed. Mountain View, Calif.: Mayfield, 1994. Political, theoretical, and societal explanations for why and how women's roles have been defined as they are.

Elizabeth Rholetter Purdy

Cross-References

African American Politics, p. 28; Aristotle's Political Philosophy, p. 83; Civil Rights Protection, p. 304; Congress, p. 412; The Constitution of the United States, p. 425; Gay and Lesbian Politics, p. 732; Gender Politics, p. 738; Political Correctness, p. 1441; Political Representation in the United States, p. 1525; Postmodernism, p. 1570; Race and Ethnicity, p. 1654; Reproductive Politics, p. 1692; Woman Suffrage, p. 2141; Women in Politics, p. 2147.

FEUDALISM

Field of study: Types of government

Feudalism was a political, legal, and military system in which lords exercised rule over fiefs, and the lords' vassals pledged homage, paid a variety of dues, and rendered military service. Classic feudalism flourished in Western Europe from the ninth to about the fifteenth century, but elements of the system have appeared in many other times and places.

Principal terms

ABSOLUTE MONARCHY: centralized government that gradually eclipsed the powers of the lords

DAIMYO: feudal lords of Japan during the Tokugawa period

FEALTY: fidelity owed by a vassal to his lord

FIEF: domain over which the feudal lord exercised political and legal authority

LORD: titled member of the nobility

MAGNA CARTA: feudal document which recognized the privileges of the English nobility

MANORIALISM: economic base of feudalism, with lords in manors ruling over peasants

PEASANT: owner of a small plot of land, one of low social standing

SERF: member of the servile class, bound to the land and the possession of a lord

SLAVE: person held in servitude to another

VASSAL: one under the protection of a lord and who has sworn loyalty to the lord

Overview

Feudalism was a system of fragmentized government and land tenure in Western Europe during the Middle Ages. Parts of the system began to appear with the fall of the Roman Empire; it reached a mature development after the fall of Charlemagne's empire and declined with the political and economic modernization of the Renaissance. In a period without the security of larger-scale centralized government, the feudal order provided for basic needs of protection from invasion, the maintenance of order, and judicial means to settle disputes.

The core of the feudal system was the relationship between the lord and his vassals. The greater lords granted fiefs to lesser lords with the condition that the latter would serve as vassals. Fiefs normally were assignments of authority over land (organized into farming units called "manors"), but fiefs also included honors and rights. Each vassal would take an oath of fealty and would be required to pay a variety of feudal dues and provide military service when needed. In exchange, the overlord would have the obligation to provide protection to his vassals. Originally, a new contract for a fief would be made at the death of a vassal and could be made with someone outside the vassal's family, but with the advent of succession and primogeniture, the fief became hereditary.

The term "manorialism" refers to the control that a lord exercised over his tenants on a manor, and the manorial system was the economic foundation of medieval feudalism. The manorial lord provided protection, maintained order, and held court; he allowed tenants to use defined pieces of land in exchange for a variety of payments and obligations, such as repairing roads, bridges, or castles, as well as working on the lord's reserved land. A manor would strive for self-sufficiency, but it might include more than one village commune. Typically, a single manor would be the fief of a knight and a portion of a larger fief, although some manors were divided into more than one fief. Manorialism was more ancient and continued much longer than other elements of feudalism.

Feudal society was stratified into hereditary class distinctions. In theory, all land was vested in a king (the first among nobles), and the highest nobles (such as counts, barons, and dukes) held their fiefs directly from the king. Noblemen usually performed only military and political functions, while the drudgery of everyday work was the duty of peasants, who belonged to two categories: the free and the unfree. Those of the second category were serfs, who differed from slaves in that they were bound to the manor and had the hereditary obligation to work the land. A minority of peasants owned land and did not make feudal payments to a lord.

The origins of feudalism can be traced to both Roman and German traditions. During the later years of the Roman Empire, much of the land was divided into large estates, whose holders acquired great powers. Many Germanic war bands that roamed over Europe had a code of honor in which warriors pledged to fight to the death for their leaders. With the breakdown of centralized governments, the components of the feudal system evolved as a means of providing some security and order. The medieval Church also had a great impact on the development of feudalism, because its hierarchical structure gave legitimacy to the practice of feudal stratification.

The components of classic feudalism were first integrated under the Carolingian dynasty of Frankish rulers, and it spread from France to Italy, Spain, and Germany. The Frankish form of feudalism was taken to England by William the Conqueror in 1066, although many elements of feudalism were already there. Feudalism should be understood as a flexible system with a great deal of diversity from place to place. Feudalism at its most definitive was most nearly realized in the Latin Kingdom of Jerusalem, created by leaders of the First Crusade in 1099. In the 1100's and 1200's, the principles of the feudal regime were recorded by legal writers such as Gerard Capagisti, Philippe de Beaumanoir, Ranulf de Glanvill, and Henry de Bracton. The Magna Carta of 1215 outlined many of the traditional privileges of the nobility of England. Feudal practices, however, often continued to be based on oral tradition rather than written codification.

Feudalism did exist in eastern Europe, but with local variation and in a more simple form. In eastern Germany, for example, free peasants owned most of the land and kings tended to have fewer limits on their power. In medieval Russia, powerful noblemen had the power to govern the peasants on their semiautonomous estates, but the concept of the lord-vassal relationship was less elaborate and more dependent upon military coercion. In Russia, moreover, the institution of serfdom was not fully established until after the medieval period.

By the fourteenth century, classic feudalism in Western Europe was clearly on the decline. With the transformation to economies based on money rather than exchanges of services, land became a commodity to be bought and sold and the practices of feudal tenure became less useful. This economic modernization also meant that money could finance large armies. The use of mobile armies with firearms also made it more difficult for regional lords to protect their fiefs. Such changes made it possible for absolute monarchs to centralize their political and judicial powers. At the same time, increased trade, the emergence of more cities, and the rise of a bourgeois class combined to challenge the privileges of the nobility. By the time that Sir Henry Spelman and the Count de Boulainvilliers wrote the first historical accounts of feudalism in the 1620's, most of the political and military elements of the classic model were distant memories.

The manorial aspects of feudalism, however, did continue into the modern age. In eighteenth century France, peasants continued to have the obligations of paying feudal dues to members of the nobility. Voltaire led a crusade against these remnants of the Middle Ages, and Pierre-Françoise Boncerf's pamphlet of 1776, *The Disadvantages of Feudal Rights*, appeared to have much influence. In 1789, the first year of the French Revolution, the National Assembly abolished feudal dues and privileges, while retaining property rights that had their roots in the feudal regime. In Germany, many feudal privileges continued until the revolution of 1848, and in Russia they continued until 1917. In Scotland, some feudal obligations continued to be collected during the late twentieth century.

Applications

The term "feudalism" often confuses readers because it has been applied to a great variety of social and political organizations. Some historians insist that the term should be used only in reference to the classic model of medieval Europe. At the other extreme, Karl Marx and followers use the term broadly to refer to any manorial condition in which rural peasants are exploited by a small group of land owners. To minimize semantic problems, it helps to understand that the adjective "feudal" is commonly used in reference to three realities: the classic model of the Middle Ages; political, legal, and military systems which resemble this model; and economic arrangements that resemble this model.

Outside of Europe, the classic model developed most fully in Japan from the tenth until the nineteenth century. Great feudal landholders, the daimyo, maintained almost unlimited dominion over large estates called *shoen*. When Ieyasu Tokugawa became shogun (military dictator) early in the seventeenth century, his supporters were recognized as hereditary vassals of the shogun. These nobles were required to pay taxes to the central government. On their estates they maintained political and administrative control by means of a military class, the samurai. Analogous to European lords and knights, the daimyo and samurai followed a code that emphasized the virtues of honor, self-sacrifice, and loyalty. For many centuries, Japanese feudalism provided a stable political and social order, helping prepare the country for its later development. With the Meiji restoration of 1868, the daimyo quickly lost their feudal privileges, and the samurai were forced to relinquish their prerogatives as a military elite.

Spanish conquerors in the Americas early established a manorial institution known as the *encomienda*, in which Spanish military leaders were awarded large estates over which they exercised political control. The *encomienda* was essentially a decentralized means of organizing and exploiting the labor of the indigenous peoples, forcing them to pay tribute and render services. First established in the West Indies, the *encomienda* system was brutal and contributed to the decimation of the local population. Hernando Cortés and other holders of estates acquired great wealth and power. Beginning in 1542, the *encomiendas* were formally replaced in a repartition of Indians for forced labor and of land. These repartitions later became great landed estates called *latifundia*. The system of Spanish America differed from classic feudalism in that there was no institution of lord-vassal relationships, there was no emphasis on local custom and privilege, and the crown retained final control over the military. The Spanish model of quasi feudalism was adopted and modified by other colonial powers, especially the Portuguese, Dutch, and French.

Context

Classic feudalism is exemplified in the political and legal institutions of Western Europe in the Middle Ages. The term denotes great diversity in customs and practices. Historical textbooks tend to present an overly schematic description of the feudal system, and to minimize its flexibility and adaptability to changing conditions. Most historians distinguish between feudalism (a political term) and manorialism (an economic term), but the two concepts are intimately connected; both refer to organized power for the collection of taxes, privileges associated with the tenure of land, and reciprocal obligations. Some scholars consider that European feudalism was a unique phenomenon, while others look upon it as corresponding to a stage of political and social development. Marxist theory, which postulates that political superstructures rest upon an economic base, uses feudalism to denote any agricultural system in which the core feature is the exploitation of peasant labor by an elite of privileged landlords.

There is much controversy concerning the linkage between medieval feudalism and the later political developments of Western civilization. While the lord-vassal contract based on military service became irrelevant with the emergence of absolute monarchy and modern capitalism, many privileges of the nobility and obligations of the peasantry continued until much later, with some relics enduring into the twentieth century. The concept of a feudal order was introduced in the seventeenth century, and it has often had a pejorative connotation. This is because feudalism usually has been associated with antiegalitarian values, especially privileges based on social position rather than individual merit. Critics have recognized that the feudal order was created by the nobility in order to protect its interests, often at the expense of the peasants and serfs.

In spite of its negative qualities, feudalism in its classic form represented a system of limited government founded upon the rule of law, and it incorporated respect for customary rights and privileges. With this perspective, many historians believe that the feudal system provided a foundation for the development of modern constitutionalism. The Magna Carta, for instance, was written to defend the interests of the great barons of England, but this feudal document included the germ of the idea that government must respect the rights of all citizens. In a period in which many parts of the world experienced civil unrest and invasion, feudal regimes provided order and stability, laying the foundation for change in the future.

Bibliography

Blackstone, William. *Of the Rights of Things*. Vol. 2 in *Commentaries on the Laws of England*. Chicago: University of Chicago Press, 1979. Originally published in 1776, this famous treatise contains an excellent treatment of land tenure under feudalism.

Bloch, Marc. *Feudal Society*. Translated by L. A. Manyon. Chicago: University of Chicago Press, 1961. Shows how the feudal system affected all aspects of medieval life, especially the roles of the various social classes.

Coulborn, Rushton, comp. *Feudalism in History*. Princeton, N.J.: Princeton University Press, 1956. Collection comparing different feudal systems in many parts of the world.

Duus, Peter. *Feudalism in Japan*. New York: Alfred A. Knopf, 1969. Readable and scholarly introduction to Japanese feudalism, with a comparison to the European experience.

Herlihy, David, comp. *The History of Feudalism*. New York: Harper & Row, 1970. Collection of original sources with useful introductions.

Hilton, Rodney. *Class Conflict and the Crisis of Feudalism*. London: Hambledon Press, 1985. Articles from a neo-Marxist point of view, emphasizing the economic base of feudalism.

Painter, Sidney. *Feudalism and Liberty*. Edited by Fred A. Cazel, Jr. Baltimore: The Johns Hopkins University Press, 1961. Argues that feudal institutions afforded a basis for the growth of constitutional government.

Strayer, Joseph. *Medieval Statecraft and the Perspectives of History*. Princeton, N.J.: Princeton University Press, 1971. Essays on the relationship of feudalism to state building.

Thomas T. Lewis

Cross-References

Aristocracy, Oligarchy, and Plutocracy, p. 78; Capitalism, p. 197; Caste Systems, p. 203; The Civil Service in the United States, p. 310; Clientelism, p. 337; Comparative Government, p. 384; Constitutional Governments, p. 432; History of Government, p. 829; John of Salisbury's Political Philosophy, p. 1006; Modern Monarchy, p. 1209; Social Darwinism, p. 1833; Vico's Political Philosophy, p. 2103.

FILIBUSTER

Field of study: Politics

A form of legislative obstruction, the filibuster is a technique by which a parliamentary minority attempts through continuous talking to defeat or alter a measure favored by the majority.

Principal terms

CLOTURE: procedure used to close off debate so that a legislature can move to a vote on a bill

GERMANENESS: rule general to most legislative bodies that speeches must be relevant to the business on the floor

MAJORITY LEADER: floor leader of the U.S. Senate, elected by the members of the majority party in the Senate, who has little real power and leads through negotiations with fellow senators

QUORUM: minimum number of members of a legislature who must be present for the valid transaction of business

RULE 22: U.S. Senate rule, first enacted in 1917 and since amended several times, that establishes the number of senators who must vote to close off debate

UNANIMOUS CONSENT: practice, common to the Senate, of enacting business only with the consent of all the members of the body—a single senator can block action by refusing consent

Overview

The filibuster, the obstruction of legislation by a determined minority, is a parliamentary tactic almost unique to the U.S. Senate. The U.S. House of Representatives eliminated the practice in 1892. Both the informal customs and the formal rules of the Senate promote its use. The filibuster is philosophically grounded in the Senate's traditional role as the place of unlimited debate and its perceived role as a higher body, designed to check impetuous or flawed legislation passed by the House. Its small size—one hundred senators versus 435 representatives—allows such delaying tactics to persist.

The early discard of two rules observed in most parliaments led to Senate development of the filibuster. Originally, debate could be stopped in the Senate by a successful motion to "call the previous question," that is, a motion from the floor that debate on an issue be halted and a vote taken. This is a common procedural rule followed by most assemblies. When the Senate issued its formal rules of order in 1806, however, the call for the previous question rule was dropped.

Soon afterward, the Senate also first weakened and then abandoned the germaneness principle. This is the principle that debate on a bill or issue must be relevant to that bill or issue. In Great Britain's House of Commons, the speaker has the authority to order a legislator to discontinue his or her speech when what the legislator says is judged irrelevant to the issue on the floor. The presiding officer of the Senate, the vice president of the United States, originally had power under the Senate's rules to exercise the same authority. John C. Calhoun, vice president from 1825 to 1832, insisted, however, that only the Senate as a whole, by vote, could deem a member's speech irrelevant. In 1872, Vice President Schuyler Colfax declared that only the senator speaking could judge the relevance of his own remarks. Lack of a germaneness rule strongly encouraged the filibuster because it allows senators to obstruct action on the floor by sustained speech of any kind. "Reading the telephone book" thus became a common description for filibustering.

The word "filibuster" developed in the sixteenth century and originally meant a freebooter, or pirate. It comes from the Dutch, either from *vrij buit* (free booty) or *vlieboot* (fly boat, a small, swift craft used by sea raiders). It was translated into Spanish as *filibustero* and then into English as filibuster. In the early 1880's, it came to signify not an ordinary pirate but a private adventurer who waged wars against states. As a word for piracy, or a private war against the state, it was first used to describe interminable, obstructive debate in 1853. Congressman Abraham Venable of South Carolina made a speech in which he denounced the actions of American filibusterers (freebooters) who were involved in attacks on Cuba. Angered, Mississippi Congressman Arnold Brown declared that Venable himself was "standing on the other side of the House filibustering against the United States." Its use in this sense had become common in the Senate by Civil War times.

No attempt was made to restrict the filibuster until World War I. Eleven senators talked to death a bill proposed by President Woodrow Wilson to arm American merchant ships crossing an Atlantic Ocean bristling with warships. An angry Wilson publicly denounced the filibustering senators as "a little group of willful men, representing no opinion but their own, [who] have rendered the great government of the United States helpless and contemptible." Stirred by fear of war, the public sided with the president. The filibustering senators were hanged in effigy and newspapers termed them Benedict Arnolds.

Alarmed, the Senate passed Rule 22 on March 8, 1917, after only six hours of debate. Often called the cloture rule, Rule 22 provided for the closing or end of debate on any issue by a vote of two-thirds of the senators present and voting. The measure was largely ineffective. Of the forty-five cloture votes taken between 1917 and 1969, only eight were successful.

In 1975, the Senate was prodded into a second attempt to restrict the filibuster. The Senate was alarmed by what it saw as encroachments on congressional powers by the administrations of presidents Lyndon Johnson and Richard Nixon, and senators came to see the filibuster as harmful to their efforts to strengthen Senate capabilities and efficiency so that it might better combat the encroachments. Liberal senators had also increasingly come to oppose the filibuster because it was so often used to defeat civil rights legislation.

In 1975, the Senate approved a stronger cloture rule. Rule 22 was modified so that three-fifths, or sixty senators could vote cloture rather than two-thirds (sixty-seven senators if all were present and voting). Filibusters on measures changing the Senate's own rules, however, required the old two-thirds majority.

For a short time, the number of successful cloture votes increased. From 1975 to 1977, eighteen of the thirty-two cloture votes taken were passed. However, senators skilled in the use of the Senate's parliamentary rules and procedures soon thwarted the intent of Rule 22 by such tactics as the introduction of countless amendments to bills, each of which was subject to debate and filibuster, even after a successful cloture vote on the bill itself.

In the 1980's, with Ronald Reagan in the presidency and Republicans in control of the Senate, liberal senators began to use the filibuster to delay and defeat Reagan policies they disliked. The rash of filibustering in the 1980's and the increasing press of business in the Senate led senators to approve a third change in the cloture rule in 1986. The 1975 rule change had still allowed one-hundred hours of debate after a successful cloture vote. (Each senator was allowed, if he or she wished, to speak for an hour on the issue at hand.) The 1986 rule limited post-cloture debate to thirty hours. This change was added to a bill providing for the televising of Senate proceedings, which indicates that senators were also concerned about negative public reaction to the spectacle of obstructive debate.

In addition to these formal rule changes, Mike Mansfield, Senate majority leader from 1961 to 1977, attempted informal means to limit the obstructiveness of the filibuster. He began a two-tier system in which the Senate by unanimous consent temporarily set aside a bill being filibustered, in order to proceed to other business. When this business was completed, the filibuster was allowed to resume. This Mansfield system, which later majority leaders adopted, requires the cooperation of all one-hundred senators, including the filibusterers. The bargain cannot always be struck.

Applications

From 1890 to 1965, the most serious filibusters were those opposing bills to protect black civil rights. In the 1930's, for example, several anti-lynching bills were defeated by determined Southern filibusters, even though they passed the House of Representatives and had the support of the president.

In 1957, a civil rights bill that gave some protection to black voting rights was before the U.S. Senate. Strom Thurmond of South Carolina secured the floor. He commenced reading the election laws of all of the states. When he finally sat down, 24 hours and 18 minutes later, he had established a record for the longest one-man filibuster in American history.

The Thurmond filibuster involved several traditional aspects of the Senate filibuster. First, it was aimed at preventing civil rights legislation, one of the major uses of the filibuster during the first half of the twentieth century. Second, it was applauded as a heroic feat even by liberal senators supporting the civil rights bill. Filibusters persisted in part because the public and the senators themselves regarded them as a form of entertainment, a kind of sporting contest. Third, as radio broadcast news of Thurmond's filibuster, Southern senators were deluged with telegrams angrily demanding that they show his spirit in defending segregation. One of the main purposes of a filibuster traditionally has been to publicize and stir public protest against the bill being debated.

Often used against civil rights legislation, the filibuster traditionally was considered a largely conservative weapon. During the 1980's, however, liberal senators began resorting to it to oppose policies of the Reagan Administration. In August, 1982, conservative senator Jesse Helms introduced a rider, a non-germane amendment, to a bill raising the national debt limit. His amendment severely limited federal funding of abortions and abortion research and cast doubt on the validity of the U.S. Supreme Court's abortion rights decision, *Roe v. Wade*. Helms added a second amendment, removing the right of the Supreme Court to hear cases involving school prayer.

Liberal senators Robert Packwood and Lowell Weicker organized a team filibuster, always much more effective than the one-man filibuster, to fight the Helms amendments. From August 16 to mid-September, 1982, they led a marathon talk session by senators who took turns arguing that the Helms amendment would upset the Constitutional principle of separation of powers. Only after the Senate finally voted to table the Helms amendment did the filibuster end.

The Packwood-Weicker action illustrated several factors involved with the modern filibuster. First, by law the debt bill to which Helms had attached his amendments, had to be acted on by October first. Filibusters are always most effective when the Senate is under time pressures. As Senate business vastly increased in the postwar period, time pressures on the Senate also increased. Second, by the 1980's the majority leader had, more than ever, assumed the role of chief negotiator in attempts to limit filibusters. Majority leader Howard Baker tried to forestall the filibuster by getting both sides to agree on a specified debate time. He tried twice to round up cloture votes. He had to negotiate unanimous consent agreements to allow other business to proceed. Third, the filibuster ceased to be a debate in the usually understood sense. Most of the time the Senate floor was largely empty except for the senator speaking and the presiding officer. Other senators listened to the speaker over a broadcast system in their offices, going to the floor only for roll call or when it was their turn to talk in the filibuster rotation.

The threat to filibuster has always been almost as effective as an actual filibuster, especially when the Senate faces a deadline of some sort—legislation, such as the annual budget, that the Senate must pass, or an adjournment date. By 1994, with the steady growth of its legislative responsibilities, the threat to filibuster supplanted filibustering itself. Senate leaders began to pull a bill from the floor whenever a small group, or even one senator, threatened to filibuster it. They turned to other business and kept the beleaguered bill off the floor until they could round up the sixty votes needed for cloture or until the bill's sponsors had agreed to the changes those threatening the filibuster wanted.

Context

Every legislative body has some means of delaying the enactment of legislation. In Great Britain a member of the House of Commons may shout, "I spy strangers." By ancient tradition, the speaker must then call for a vote by the members on clearing the press and public galleries. In Japan, in what is called the "cow-waddle," parliamentarians slowly creep to the podium to cast their votes, stopping to talk to friends and adjust their watches.

These tactics can delay legislative action, but they cannot kill a measure or obstruct it for weeks on end as the filibuster does. No legislature but the U.S. Senate permits this powerful weapon. The House forbade its use more than a hundred years ago. It has also been gradually phased out in the senates of some American states that once permitted it. In the Senate, its use has grown. From 1955 to 1960 only two filibusters were staged. During Reagan's first term (1981-1985), the number rose to twenty-five.

Scholars and politicians have defended obstructionist tactics such as the filibuster. Filibusters, they argue, inhibit a majority from riding roughshod over, and perhaps silencing, a minority. They can spark reconsideration of badly conceived or written legislation. They alert the press and public to legislation that might be widely disapproved of if better understood.

The filibuster, however, has also always had strong critics. They insist that the filibuster replaces democratic majority rule with minority veto, sometimes by a very small group, even a single legislator. It encourages demagoguery, since filibusters are often waged on emotional, divisive issues, often involving racial or religious attitudes and beliefs. It increases public contempt for the Senate, and thus the whole political process, as voters watch vital legislation being obstructed.

In the 1980's, the number of filibusters greatly increased and filibusters began to be directed against all kinds of legislation from school desegregation proposals to gasoline taxes. In the 1990's, the practice of withdrawing bills threatened by a filibuster meant that not even the possibly beneficial results of a prolonged public debate on a bill had anything to do with the filibuster.

Despite criticism, however, the filibuster remains a constant threat in the U.S. Senate. The increasing press of business makes the Senate vulnerable to filibusters. The breakdown of loyalty to party and to the Senate as an institution makes curbing filibustering senators more difficult. Senators more dependent than before on interest group money and influence are more willing to use the filibuster weapon to further their aims.

Under the Constitution, except when Congress overrides a presidential veto, the House of Representatives, the Senate, and the president must all agree on legislation for it to be successfully passed and implemented. The practice of the filibuster obstructs the operation of not just of the Senate but of the entire government of the United States.

Bibliography

Baker, Ross K. *House and Senate*. New York: W. W. Norton, 1989. Describes how the differences in formal and informal rules affect the work of the House and Senate.

Burdette, Franklin L. *Filibustering in the Senate*. Princeton, N.J.: Princeton University Press, 1940. The only book devoted entirely to the filibuster, especially valuable for its early history of the filibuster in the House as well as the Senate and for its detailed analysis of how the filibuster was used to obstruct civil rights legislation from 1890 to World War II.

Congressional Quarterly Almanac. Washington, D.C.: Congressional Quarterly Press. Published yearly; explains the major bills, debates, and votes taken, and includes a description of the year's important filibusters.

Origins and Development of Congress. 2d ed. Washington, D.C.: Congressional Quarterly Press, 1982. Periodically updated, this reference work is a good, short history of the U.S. House and Senate.

Safire, William. *Safire's Political Dictionary*. 3d ed. New York: Random House, 1993. Provides both definitions and anecdotes for thousands of words used in American politics.

Sinclair, Barbara. *The Transformation of the U.S. Senate*. Baltimore: The Johns Hopkins University Press, 1989. Prizewinning analysis of how the Senate has changed in the postwar period, including discussion of filibuster uses and procedures during the 1970's and 1980's.

Smith, Steven S. *Call to Order: Floor Politics in the House and Senate*. Washington, D.C.: Brookings Institution, 1989. Easy-to-follow description of how bills are introduced, debated, amended, and voted in the Senate.

Mary T. Hanna

Cross-References

Accountability in U.S. Government, p. 1; Checks and Balances in U.S. Government, p. 216; Comparative Government, p. 384; Congress, p. 412; Demagoguery, p. 507; Interest Groups, p. 936; Legislative Body Types, p. 1091; Policy Development and Implementation, p. 1414; Political Party Roles, p. 1499; Power Divisions in Governments, p. 1578; Race and Ethnicity, p. 1654; Separation of Powers: Presidential Government, p. 1815.

FIRE PROTECTION

Field of study: Functions of government

Fire prevention and control are essential to the economic health and security of every community. Attempts to prevent destruction and death by fire have led to centuries of regulations concerning building construction and establishment of groups of firefighters. Public education and awareness, however, are equally important in fire prevention.

Principal terms

ARSON: deliberate and malicious setting of a house or property on fire; generally classified as a felony

BUCKET BRIGADE: line of people who pass buckets of water from hand to hand, generally in an effort to fight a fire

HAND-PUMP ENGINE: early fire-fighting cart whose movement and water-pumping operations were both powered by humans

NATIONAL FIRE PROTECTION ASSOCIATION: private voluntary and charitable association concerned with the causes, prevention, and control of destructive fire

STEAMER: second generation of fire engine, in which water is pumped by means of steam pressure

Overview

The first organized fire-fighting effort for which there is historical record was in ancient Rome. In approximately 23 B.C.E., Caesar Augustus stationed six hundred slaves at the city gates to fight fires. Because slaves were slow to respond to emergencies and showed little interest in risking their lives for their masters, they eventually were replaced by companies of volunteers. In the year 6 C.E., after another serious fire, Augustus established a corps of professional firefighters called *vigiles* (watchmen), made up of freedmen, whom he paid with public funds. The city of Rome was divided into fourteen wards, with seven *cohortes* (battalions) of up to one thousand men, each responsible for two wards. The *cohortes* were commanded by a *praefectus vigilium*, similar to a contemporary fire chief, who was directly responsible to the emperor. Fires were investigated; when one was determined to have been caused by negligence, the person responsible was punished.

One of the most famous conflagrations in history was the burning of Rome in 64 C.E. At that time construction of Rome's public buildings was strictly regulated; however, there were no controls on the building of tenements. Whether or not it is true—as some historians believe—that Emperor Nero ordered Rome's burning, it is known that prior to the great fire, Nero had a master plan for redeveloping Rome that prohibited all unregulated construction. From the time of the fire until the fall of the Roman Empire in the fourth century, private buildings as well as public structures were built according to regulations covering construction and sanitation.

Little historical record of fire protection exists for several centuries after the fall of Rome. Beginning in the ninth century, however, there are many documented examples of laws pertaining to fire prevention in England. For example, in 872 it was decreed in Oxford that hearth fires be extinguished by a fixed time each night. Two centuries later, William the Conqueror established a general curfew requiring a bell to be rung in every community during the evenings, when metal fire covers had to be placed over hearth fires. Although the measure was partly designed to maintain control of the populace, it also greatly lessened the number of fires that started from sparks touching off fires on the rushes on which the peasants slept. In 1177, authorities of the cathedral at Canterbury purchased shops that they considered to present fire hazards to the cathedral and relocated them away from the cathedral. In the next two decades, it was required that new buildings have stone walls and slate or tile roofs, and that walls sixteen feet high and three feet thick be erected between houses, although these laws apparently were not enforced consistently. In the sixteenth century, fire prevention ordinances that were not related to construction began to be seen, such as a law in Manchester requiring safe storage of fuel of bakers' ovens and a parliamentary act forbidding the melting of tallow in buildings.

Despite several centuries of attempts to lessen fire hazards in England, one of the worst fires in history occurred in 1666 when London burned for five days during which approximately two-thirds of the city was destroyed. Despite pleas from the great architect Sir Christopher Wren, the London Building Act passed by Parliament after the fire allowed the city to be rebuilt with many of the same problems that were responsible for the severity of the fire, such as narrow streets and combustible construction materials.

In the settlements of the New World, fire was a serious hazard throughout the colonial era. Shelters often were made of wood, roofs generally were made of thatch, and heat often was provided by central brick fireplaces held together with mud or clay, topped by chimneys of stalks or brush covered with mud or clay. Because these combustible dwellings usually were built close together for protection from attack, and were well stocked with whiskey and gunpowder, they posed serious fire hazards. Jamestown, Virginia, the first permanent settlement in New England, was established in 1607 and ravaged by fire the following year. Because of the widespread destruction of dwellings and provisions, many colonists starved or died of exposure.

Peter Stuyvesant, the governor of New Amsterdam, instituted many forward-thinking measures to promote fire safety, including efforts to prevent fires by regulating building construction. Among the measures for which he was responsible in the late 1640's were ordinances outlawing thatched roofs, appointing wardens to inspect houses for fire safety, and prohibiting wooden or plaster chimneys. Stuyvesant also appointed four volunteer fire wardens to check chimneys to see that they complied with the law and were maintained properly. Fines were levied against violators of the chimney laws and the money collected went to purchase fire-fighting equipment, such as buckets, hooks, and ladders. Curfews after which fires must be covered also were enacted. Stuyvesant went a step further by instituting "Rattle Watches"—teams of young men who traveled through the city at night, sounding alarms with wooden rattles when they spotted fires. These crews were perceived as bullies by many citizens, however, and were quite unpopular.

When the British took over New Amsterdam in 1664, renaming it New York, new chimney maintenance laws were enacted. In 1687, New York passed a law determining how many buckets were required for different establishments; this law anticipated modern ordinances requiring specific numbers of fire exits and smoke alarms in various types of establishments. Houses with no more than two chimneys were required to have one bucket, bakers were required to have three, and brewers, six.

Boston, which had the worst record of fires during colonial times, purchased the first fire engine to be used in America in 1678. Boston also had the first firehouse—a shed in which to keep the engine—and it hired the first paid firefighter as its captain. Thomas Atkins, the captain, appointed twelve assistants, creating the country's first paid fire department. Boston also began the practice of exempting firefighters from military service and jury duty.

In the eighteenth century, a well-known advocate of fire-prevention measures was Benjamin Franklin, who influenced city officials to buy fire-fighting equipment and enact fire safety regulations. Franklin also campaigned for official chimney sweeps, started an early volunteer fire company, and founded one of the first successful U.S. fire insurance companies. His Contributorship for the Insurance of Houses from Loss by Fire, begun in 1752, was still operating as the Hand-in-Hand Insurance Company in the twentieth century. His famous aphorism, "An ounce of prevention is worth a pound of cure," appeared in a letter that he wrote to citizens of Philadelphia encouraging them to move burning coals from one place to another in covered warming pans instead of shovels.

Boston's early establishment of a paid fire department was not followed by other cities until the nineteenth century. At that time, the move toward professional firefighters was fueled mainly by the increasingly rowdy behavior of volunteer firefighters. Early volunteer organizations, which typically included many prominent citizens, were important social and political organizations. Over time, rivalries began to overtake professionalism in many companies. Volunteer fire brigades often raced one another to fires, using aggressive means to prevent other companies from arriving first. The rivalries intensified to the point where fights between volunteers from different companies sometimes escalated into riots, while the buildings they were charged with saving burned to the ground. In 1851, a fire leveled a mill in Cincinnati while thirteen fire-fighting companies from Cincinnati and surrounding communities rioted. This event began the demise of volunteer firefighters in large U.S. cities. The riot was one of several that had occurred in Cincinnati during conflagrations, causing citizens who were infuriated by the increase in both fire losses and fire insurance rates to demand action from city government.

At the same time, steam engine technology had advanced to the point that it was becoming a feasible alternative to hand-pumps. Although the steamer was still in a fairly primitive stage, its adoption enabled a reduction in the size of the workforce required to get water to fires, compared to the large numbers of men needed to pull and operate hand-pumps and hose-wagons. After purchasing the first steam-powered fire engine to be used in the United States, Cincinnati's city council voted in March, 1853, to replace volunteer fire companies with a paid department. The lack of discipline of volunteer fire crews and improvements in the steam engine began a shift from volunteers in the larger cities, which was interrupted only briefly by the advent of the Civil War.

Applications

Historically, fire protection in the United States has been a local concern, with state and federal interest coming in response to the trends of urbanization, and to the new fire hazards caused by twentieth century technology. Regulations vary greatly among the states. In 1980, all U.S. states except Colorado, Hawaii, and New Jersey had fire marshals as their state regulatory authorities and the focal points for statewide fire prevention activities. The state fire marshal can issue regulations with the force of law covering various fire hazards and can suggest and influence the passage of laws. Areas of interest to fire authorities include fire prevention; the storage, use, and sale of combustibles and explosives; construction, installation, and maintenance of fire alarms, exits, and escapes in buildings; investigation of fires; suppression of arson; and inspections. Many also review plans for nursery schools, nursing homes, and hospitals, to ensure that appropriate fire protection and suppression measures are incorporated.

At the local level, paid professional firefighters have not totally replaced volunteers, despite the nineteenth century trend toward eliminating volunteer companies in larger cities. In 1980, there were many more volunteer than paid departments in the United States, with approximately 21,000 volunteer companies enlisting more than one million personnel, versus approximately 1,600 fully paid departments with fewer than 200,000 employees. Twentieth century volunteers, however, are generally well trained and dedicated to community protection. Because of the costs of maintaining adequate fire protection, some communities rely on small staffs of paid professional firefighters supplemented by volunteers. In addition to fire suppression, the duties typically performed by fire departments include paramedic services, fire prevention and fire safety education, building inspection, and community relations.

Because communities historically have created fire prevention codes to meet their own local needs often in reaction to calamities, such codes vary widely. Building codes are also instrumental in fire prevention and also vary greatly from one community to the next. Enforcement may be divided between fire and building departments and possibly the police force. Overlapping of responsibilities is common. For example, requirements and specifications for fire exits and fire extinguishing equipment are typically found in building codes, but their maintenance tends to be part of the fire prevention code.

Most municipal fire departments have adopted one of several model fire prevention codes and standards in addition to the local code. National codes and standards are often adopted by reference, meaning that they are referred to by title and briefly summarized but not reprinted in their entirety. One of the more commonly used is the *Fire Protection Code* of the National Fire Protection Association (NFPA), an international charitable, technical, and educational organization. The NFPA has developed more than 250 standards and codes, which are published annually in the multivolume *National Fire Codes*. They cover such topics as appropriate protective clothing for firefighters, organization of a fire department, and numbers and locations of fire hydrants.

Although fire protection is reserved to the states and delegated to local communities, the federal government also plays a role. Research is a particularly important area of federal involvement. The National Bureau of Standards (NBS), established in 1901 as a part of the Department of Commerce, does scientific research on building technology and materials. Additional research projects are conducted by the Department of Agriculture (primarily the Forest Service), the Department of Commerce, the Department of the Interior, the Army and the Navy, the Department of Transportation, and the National Aeronautics and Space Administration, as well as U.S. governmental bodies in Europe, Australia, and Japan.

The report of the National Commission on Fire Prevention and Control, *America Burning* (1973), led to the Federal Fire Prevention and Control Act of 1974, the first federal effort directly concerned with fire services. To administer the act, the National Fire Prevention and Control Administration (NFPCA) was established within the Department of Commerce. The act mandated the development and evaluation of fire-fighting equipment; review of state and local fire prevention codes and public education; analysis and dissemination of fire information through the National Fire Data Center (NFDC); setting up a training academy for fire prevention and control that is similar to the academy of the Federal Bureau of Investigation; establishment of a Fire Research Center as part of the National Bureau of Standards; and setting up research programs relating to burns, burn injuries, and the rehabilitation of fire victims in the National Institutes of Health.

President Jimmy Carter's reorganization of the federal government included moving the NFPCA from the Department of Commerce into the newly established Federal Emergency Management Agency (FEMA) and renaming it the United States Fire Administration (USFA). The USFA remained part of FEMA through the mid-1990's and continued to provide training programs for firefighters. It also prepared and distributed a variety of educational materials targeted to children, homeowners, the elderly, and others, and developed and promoted other public outreach programs relating to fire prevention.

Context

Destructive fires can be unleashed through causes as diverse as lightning, careless campers or smokers, arson, ruptured gas lines from earthquakes or other causes, improper handling or storage of flammable materials, unsupervised children with matches, or faulty electrical wiring. Despite the resources invested in fire prevention and suppression, deaths and injuries, along with destruction of property, have continued to take a heavy toll in the United States. In 1993, according to the NFPA, public fire departments in the United States fought 1,952,500 fires, which caused 4,635 civilian deaths, approximately 80 percent of which were in the home, and the deaths of 77 fire-fighters. Fires in that year caused $8,546,000 in property damage, of which 87 percent was in structure fires.

Firefighting has been one of the most hazardous occupations in the United States. A higher proportion of firefighters are killed in the line of duty than members of any other occupation, and they also have the highest rate of severe injury. Although technological advances, such as radio communications and self-contained breathing apparatus, have aided firefighting, technology has also made fires more dangerous to fight. For example, skyscrapers present unique fire-fighting challenges, and hazardous substances, such as toxic chemicals and radioactive materials, present new dangers to firefighters and the surrounding populace.

Bibliography

Cannon, Donald J., ed. *Heritage of Flames: The Illustrated History of Early American Firefighting*. Garden City, N.Y.: Doubleday, 1977. Surveys firefighting in the United States from the Jamestown fire in 1608 to the War of 1812. Lavishly illustrated, including early maps and copies of original documents.

Ditzel, Paul C. *Fire Engines, Fire Fighters: The Men, Equipment, and Machines, from Colonial Days to the Present*. New York: Bonanza Books, 1984. Very readable discussion of the history of fire-fighting in the United States, with chapters on many famous fires. Excellent illustrations and photographs.

Pyne, Stephen J. *Fire in America: A Cultural History of Wildland and Rural Fire*. Princeton, N.J.: Princeton University Press, 1982. Presents a history of fire in the United States, with a comprehensive discussion of efforts to prevent and suppress forest fires and fires in rural areas of the United States. A different focus than most books on fire, which tend to concentrate on urban fires and firefighters.

Smith, Dennis. *Dennis Smith's History of Firefighting in America: 300 Years of Courage*. New York: Dial Press, 1978. Discusses the development of fire-fighting equipment, fire-related legislation, and fire insurance, in the context of famous fires in the United States. The author, a firefighter himself, also includes stories of ordinary firefighters.

Irene Struthers

Cross-References

City Government in the United States, p. 266; Disaster Relief in the United States, p. 558; Intergovernmental Relations, p. 942; Rural Community Government, p. 1763; Social Services, p. 1858; State and Local Government, p. 1885; Urban Governments, p. 2052.

FOOD POLITICS

Field of study: International government and politics

Food politics in recent years has become one of the most studied issues of international government. Those countries in need of food are always in search of cheaper supplies, while those with surpluses of food understandably hope to extract the greatest possible gains from this most desired commodity.

Principal terms

EMBARGO: order by a government prohibiting the sale of goods to another country

FAMINE: widespread and extreme hunger brought on by the lack of food

FOOD AID: shipment of food to areas where provisions are in short supply

FOOD SECURITY: availability of food supplies in quantities large enough to avoid shortages

MALNUTRITION: absence of proper nutrition because of improper diet or disease

SUBSIDY: government aid, in some form, to private commercial enterprises in an effort to guarantee their financial success

Overview

Food is one of the most basic needs. Without food and water, life would cease to exist. It is to be expected, then, that as a basic necessity, food has been and will continue to be used as a political weapon. The politics of food is inextricably tied to a variety of global concerns, including population pressures, economics, development, natural resources, and nationalism.

In a country requiring more food than can be domestically produced, the acquisition of a readily available, inexpensive supply is a must. Political pressures at home always demand that a country's food supply be reliable and the prices low. Domestic agricultural producers are usually a powerful lobby, and as a result, many governments are forced to subsidize otherwise unprofitable agricultural enterprises. Governments are reluctant to allow the elimination of domestic production not only for political reasons but for practical reasons as well. The elimination of all domestic agricultural production makes a country much more vulnerable.

Unfortunately, many countries cannot produce enough food to feed their populations. It has been estimated that even if all arable lands were used for food production, more than half of all countries would still fail to meet population demands. Roughly a third of the world's countries would not be able to support half of their populations without foreign assistance. Food shortages are not new to many areas of the world. Countries unable to acquire enough food from outside sources continue to experience malnutrition, starvation, poverty, disease, and economic devastation. Finding solutions for the problem of food shortages is not an easy task. There are often a variety of political issues that must be resolved prior to the realization of food security.

In time of famine, the most immediate problem faced by a government or multinational organization is getting food to the hungry. Even when supplies are readily available from outside sources, this is not an easy problem to resolve. In times of war, humanitarian aid in any form to one side is often viewed as hostile by the other. Truck convoys and planes are often attacked or commandeered by warring factions, with little chance of the cargo reaching its intended destination. In times of war, food is simply another weapon. The governments of states trying to carry out humanitarian missions abroad are often criticized for endangering lives of their citizens by trying to assist. The 1992 United States humanitarian mission to Somalia, for example, followed such a turn of events. Even when food relief is welcomed, there are often unwelcome side effects.

The most immediate effect of food aid is, in many instances, the destruction of remaining local or regional markets for agricultural products. The distribution of free or subsidized food reduces demand for locally grown food. The few remaining local producers are put out of production by market forces that further weaken the local economy. The food that is imported is often unfamiliar to the recipients. The end result is that if food security is ever restored, the demand is no longer for domestically produced products but for the imported food for which a taste has been acquired. These potential ramifications of food aid programs are often overlooked by the receiving government, which may be more interested in resolving the immediate crisis. Typically, once the immediate crisis is over, the push for political reforms that would ensure national food security are suspended. Thus, as has been illustrated in history on a number of occasions, food aid programs generally create more problems than solutions.

In the twentieth century, those countries producing a surplus of agricultural goods increasingly used that advantage in order to achieve desired political and economic goals. Food has always been a substantial portion of all international trade. It would be natural to assume that as the world population continues to expand and demand for food increases in proportion, states producing surplus food will increasingly find themselves in more comfortable bargaining positions within the global community. Receiving food aid has a price. One price, already discussed above, is the loss of a local food economy and a dependence on foreign supply, which leaves a nation in need of food aid in a very insecure position. Food is one of the primary weapons used in negotiations between states. Governments may discontinue food shipments to states that refuse to embrace a particular ideology or policy.

The increased potential for the use of food as a tool in international affairs has caused great concern in many circles. The human suffering and loss of life involved is great. Several international organizations have called for the creation of an international food production program in an effort to thwart the threat to human life. The formation of a carefully orchestrated worldwide program for food production, it is believed, would eliminate the potential for the effective use of food embargoes as a weapon. Unfortunately, little has been realized by efforts to formulate cooperative programs for global food production. Those states that have the money and technology to make such programs a reality are reluctant to embrace any policy or program that might threaten their ability to profitably export food products. Food production remains, as a result, almost exclusively a matter of national policy and politics.

Outside the standard national and multinational organizations designed to assist in the realization of adequate food supplies, there has been a marked increase in the number of nongovernmental charitable organizations hoping to fill the gap where others have failed. Groups such as Food for Peace, Grassroots International, and the food division of Church World Service have been successful in getting around the many political pitfalls faced by national and multinational organization relief efforts. Many such organizations, however, often seek to provide spiritual food as well. This often leads to conflict in areas of the world where governments are not prone to allow freedom of worship.

Applications

During the early 1990's, the Somali found themselves facing famine. Relief efforts were interrupted by food politics. In 1991, the Somali government of Mohammed Siad Barre was ousted by a coalition of domestic opposition forces. Soon after his ouster, however, the groups that toppled him began fighting among themselves. The country's fledgling economy was soon destroyed by the factional fighting. Agricultural production in the countryside became impossible. Fighting throughout the African nation disrupted the flow of food and forced many to seek refuge in relief camps and urban areas. A horrific famine engulfed the country by late 1992. As it worsened, the combating factions within Somalia engaged in war over food and weapons. The strategy of the various warring factions was to hoard food to feed supporters and to use as a tool for the acquisition of supplies. Attacks on supply trains carrying food to areas controlled by enemy factions, it was hoped, would weaken the resolve of the enemy. This strategy contributed to worsening conditions within the struggling nation.

Hunger and malnutrition had always been a problem in Somalia, but the extreme nature of the 1992 famine soon captured the attention of international media. As images of the human suffering in Somalia were broadcast around the world, international relief agencies began receiving record donations. The International Red Cross, CARE, World Concern, and numerous other agencies began shipping food and medical supplies into the war-torn country. As the food and medical supplies began arriving in Somalia, however, attacks on relief centers and food caravans accelerated. Relief agencies tried to remain neutral as hostilities expanded the civil war. Many agencies, despite their determination, were eventually forced either to curtail relief efforts or to abandon them entirely as the fighting increasingly endangered relief workers.

Internationally, as relief efforts in Somalia were slowed by the fighting, political pressure was beginning to mount for active United Nations involvement in the matter. Moved by the pressure, U.N. secretary general Boutros Boutros-Ghali began discussing the possibility of dispatching an armed peacekeeping force to Somalia in order to ensure that food could be delivered to needed areas without fear of Somali factions' making off with the supplies. By early 1993, armed forces from the United States, Pakistan, and several other countries had arrived in Somalia to serve as the U.N. peacekeeping force.

The peacekeeping force did not slow the conflict in Somalia. In fact, the fighting accelerated. Several of the fifteen warring factions and some relief organizations in Somalia accused Jonathan Howe, retired United States admiral serving as the U.N. special representative to Somalia, of favoring one faction over another. Some observers accused the United States of trying to establish a government that would serve its own purposes. Rumors abounded that the United States hoped to establish a foothold on the African continent—perhaps a military base, it was said, to counter losses of bases in the Philippines and elsewhere.

Pakistani U.N. peacekeepers were allegedly ambushed by troops of warlord Mohammad Farah Aidid, a critic of U.S. and U.N. involvement, in June, 1993. Twenty-four were killed in the attack. United States troops were also being attacked. One United States soldier, after his death, was dragged though the streets by Somali as the international media broadcast the event. The fighting continued to hamper relief efforts in the famine-plagued country, eventually forcing even United Nations support staff out of the country. Public support for continued United States involvement in the matter began to wane as reports of American deaths continued. Some Americans began to demand a withdrawal of troops from Somalia.

All efforts to bring about a peaceful resolution to the conflict were to prove futile as long as Aidid refused to meet with Howe. Howe was removed in early 1994. All United Nations forces were removed from Somalia by March, 1994. A public reconciliation of the warring factions was not finally realized until four days prior to the removal of the last peacekeeping troops. The various U.N. agencies designed to facilitate the revival of the agricultural sector of Somalia could then return the country.

The situation in Somalia between 1991 and 1994 is not an isolated event in human history. In fact, food is used in most developing countries during periods of political turmoil as a tool for political gain. The most troubling aspect of the entire incident is that thousands died so that fighting for power might continue.

Context

During the ice age, who received what portion of a woolly mammoth at the end of the hunt was probably decided based on some sort of political hierarchy. Organized warfare is believed to have evolved as a result of surplus food. Villages experiencing food shortages attacked well-supplied villages in hope of acquiring food. Food has always been a most valued commodity, and as a result, has been used throughout human history for political gain.

It has only been in recent history, however, that efforts have been made to try to regulate the use of food as a political weapon. Beginning in the early 1900's, a powerful movement called for the creation of organized international efforts to ensure the proper and equitable distribution of food products worldwide. In 1943, at Hot Springs, Virginia, the first conference on food and agriculture was convened with encouragement from the United States government. The primary goal of the conference was to begin dialogue on how to feed the world efficiently. The conference was to serve as the catalyst for the creation of the United Nations agency now known as the Food and Agriculture Organization (FAO).

Since that first organizational meeting, the basic goal of the FAO has not changed. Its primary focus is still the encouragement of dialogue in an attempt to address potential solutions for world food problems. The FAO maintains thousands of international civil servants worldwide, who serve in a variety of capacities. The FAO also maintains close relationships with other U.N. agencies created since 1943 to address concern over world food security. These include the World Food Council (WFC), which was established in Rome to implement the resolutions of the 1974 World Food Conference; the International Fund for Agricultural Development (IFAD), which was created as a catalyst for agricultural development projects; and the World Food Program (WFP), a program to stimulate economic and social development through direct food assistance. Cooperative efforts between these and other U.N. agencies are common.

Bibliography

Balaam, David N., and Michael J. Carey, eds. *Food Politics: The Regional Conflict.* Totowa, N.J.: Allanheld, Osmun, 1981. Region-by-region overview of the world efforts to develop comprehensive food policies.

Castro, Josué de. *The Geopolitics of Hunger.* New York: Monthly Review Press, 1977. First published during the height of the Cold War, this book is a must for the student of food politics.

Cochrane, Willard W. *The World Food Problem: A Guardedly Optimistic View.* New York: Thomas Y. Crowell, 1969. Part of the Crowell Economics Series.

Fox, Jonathan. *The Politics of Food in Mexico: State Power and Social Mobilization.* Ithaca, N.Y.: Cornell University Press, 1993. Describes state involvement in agrarian issues.

Garst, Rachel, and Tom Barry. *Feeding the Crisis: U.S. Food Aid and Farm Policy in Central America.* Lincoln: University of Nebraska Press, 1990. Addresses the politics of food from a U.S. versus Central America perspective.

Johnson, David Gale. *World Food Problems and Prospects.* Washington, D.C.: American Enterprise Institute for Public Policy Research, 1975. General overview.

Norse, David. "A New Strategy for Feeding a Crowded Planet." In *Global Issues 93/94.* Edited by Robert M. Jackson. 9th ed. Guilford, Conn.: Dushkin, 1993. Originally published in the June, 1992, edition of *Environment*, this article contains new ideas on world food problems.

Rau, Bill. *From Feast to Famine: Official Cures and Grassroots Remedies to Africa's Food Crisis.* London: Zed Books, 1991. Examination of the causes of modern Africa's food crisis, with close attention to impact of European colonialism and postindependent policies, as well as African responses to the crisis.

Rotberg, Robert I., and Theodore K. Rabb, eds. *Hunger and History: The Impact of Changing Food Production and Consumption Patterns on Society.* Cambridge, England: Cambridge University Press, 1985. Essays.

Stevens, Charles J. *Confronting the World Food Crisis.* Muscatine, Iowa: Stanley Foundation, 1981. Contains five recommendations to help ease the crisis.

Whiteford, Scott, and Anne E. Ferguson. *Harvest of Want: Hunger and Food Security in Central America and Mexico.* Boulder, Colo.: Westview Press, 1991. Overview of food politics in the region and the social dimensions of food politics.

Donald C. Simmons, Jr.

Cross-References

Agriculture Management, p. 41; Business and Government, p. 177; Consumer Politics, p. 445; Developed and Developing Nations, p. 533; Disaster Relief in the United States, p. 558; Foreign Relations, p. 718; National Economics, p. 1248; Sanctions, p. 1777; United Nations, p. 2045; The World Health Organization, p. 2180.

FORCE

Field of study: Political philosophy

Governments often use violent force, or the threat of force, against domestic and foreign enemies in order to achieve desired objectives. A central question in political philosophy is the extent to which the use of such force by states is legitimate.

Principal terms
AUTHORITY: legitimate rule of a government over its citizens
LEGITIMACY: right of those in power to govern by the consent of those who are governed
STATE: group of persons who govern others within a given territory either through authority or power or both
VIOLENCE: the physical or psychological imposition of power over persons and/or their property against their will

Overview

The ancient Greek sophist Cratylus, a skeptic and relativist, claimed that the law of right is the law of the strongest. In other words, power is right, power is justice. This ethic of force was taken over by the argumentative Greek sophist Thrasymachus. Plato's *Republic* opens with a discussion between Socrates and the aged Cephalus over the meaning of life, which leads to consideration of the question of what constitutes justice. After asking for a definition of justice, Socrates receives a reply from Polemarchus, the son of Cephalus, who argues that justice means giving to each what is owed. In the course of their discussion, a frustrated and impatient Thrasymachus charges into the debate. Justice, the latter argues, is anything that brings an advantage to the stronger or to established rule. The argument concludes with Thrasymachus defending injustice as more valuable than justice because it can be used to the advantage of the stronger. In effect, Thrasymachus defines justice as power—might makes right.

In *The City of God*, Saint Augustine argues for the legitimate use of deadly force. God, the supreme authority, makes exceptions to His commandment against killing that include war and capital punishment. War does not violate God's commandment against killing if it is decreed by the authority of God or the state, nor is the commandment broken by capital punishment if the death penalty is imposed by the authority of state. As Augustine sees it, force may be rightfully exercised by legitimate authority—God and the state.

The use of force, according to Augustine, may also be justified on account of the wickedness of a neighboring nation. In his opinion, honest people do not make war on peaceful neighbors, so it is not legitimate to wage war simply to extend a nation's borders. Increasing territory may, however, be justified as a result of waging war against the wicked. Thus, force may be used if the authority is legitimate and the cause just.

In the thirteenth century, Thomas Aquinas gave fuller expression to Augustine's just-war theory. In reply to the question of whether it is sinful to wage war, Aquinas sets forth criteria for waging a just war. First, there must be a declaration on the part of a legitimate authority, who can only be the ruler of the state. War is not just if it is declared by a private individual because it is not the business of the private individual. Second, there must be a just cause. Those who are attacked must deserve it because of some fault. Third, war should be waged with the right intention so that either good is advanced or evil is hampered. Fourth, the outcome of war must be peace. Finally, a just war should use no more force than is absolutely necessary.

Niccolò Machiavelli wrote *The Prince* in 1513, dedicating the book to Lorenzo de Medici in the hope of gaining an attractive political post. His book has been called a grammar of power—and for good reason. It is a manual of how to acquire and maintain power. Many of the key ideas it contains derive from Machiavelli's larger work, *The Discourses*; these include the imperative of military power, the will to survive, and the use of ruthless measures. Though *The Prince* may be studied within the context of the "Mirror of Princes" genre that flourished during the Middle Ages to depict princely virtues, the book is more important as a signal of a revolutionary turn in political thinking because it rejects ethics and metaphysics in favor of political realism. Instead of using ethical questions about what human beings should be, he employed as his starting point the realistic acknowledgement of human beings as they really are. He believed that ideals and ethics are irrelevant in governing, and he advised the prince to disregard questions of whether his actions are virtuous or vicious. Choices between actions, Machiavelli claims, depend not on ethics but on circumstances. Machiavelli concerned himself not with good or evil, but with effective government, and not with virtue, but with *virtu*, or vitality. Chapter 14 of *The Prince* stresses the primacy and necessity of using brute force for strategic ends in war. For Machiavelli, the ruler has no other aim than war, which he must learn through action and study. To Machiavelli, a nation should always be in a state of war—even in peacetime.

In 1523 the German Protestant reformer Martin Luther wrote a political tract formulating a theory justifying the use of force. His "two kingdoms theory" adapts its principal ideas from Augustine's *The City of God*. Like Augustine, Luther divides society into two realms—the City of God (*Civitas Dei*) and the City of Man (*Civitas Mundi*). Luther's concern is to answer questions regarding the division of powers between church and state such as these: Is the church an earthly power? Can secular rulers claim spiritual authority? Luther recognizes the secular authority of the state and the spiritual authority of the church. Each exercises authority in its own realm. Each realm is in the service of the Kingdom of God (*Regnum Dei*) to fight the realm of the devil (*Regnum diaboli*). The state's weapons are law, power, force, and authority. The church's weapons are faith and the Gospel. In effect, the individual divides into a public person and a private person. As a private person the individual abides by the gospel of love, but as a public person he must serve the state—with the sword, if necessary, in order to punish wrongdoers as a magistrate or a soldier. In modern times,

Germany's Lutheran churches advanced Luther's two kingdoms theory in order to remain neutral in the face of Nazism.

In the seventeenth century Thomas Hobbes defined the nature of political power in strong authoritarian terms in *Leviathan*, a powerful argument for government with far-reaching powers and limited individual freedoms. Hobbes wrote *Leviathan* while exiled in Paris during England's civil wars. The book's subtitle, "The Matter, Form, and Power of a Commonwealth Ecclesiastical and Civil," suggests Hobbes's aim to unite church and state into one powerful structure. Subscribing to a mechanical view of the universe, Hobbes naturally built his theory of human nature on mechanistic principles. His book's thirteenth chapter contains the famous passage called the "Natural Condition of Mankind," which asserts that the original state of nature of early human beings was a state of war because of human equality (even a small man could kill a big man with a rock). Human life in this natural state is "solitary, poor, nasty, brutish, and short." Because humans have a natural rational propensity to seek peace, a commonwealth was necessary in order to provide mutual protection. It would be formed by a compact in which each person agreed to allow as much liberty to others as he expected to enjoy himself. By forming a compact and mutually renouncing individual freedoms and power, the members of society would grant absolute power to the sovereign. Then, only government could assign rights, determine justice, and exercise force.

Applications

Karl Marx, the founder of modern communist thought, was a passionate and ardent revolutionary. His advocacy of the use of violent force emerges from careful reading of his writings as a whole. In his introduction to *Towards a Critique of Hegel's Philosophy of Right* (1844), for example, he claims that the weapon of criticism cannot supplant the criticism of weapons and that material force must be overthrown by material force. On the eve of the French Revolution of 1848, Marx and Friedrich Engels drafted the *Manifesto of the Communist Party*, a French translation of which appeared a few months before the Paris insurrection of June, 1848. The problem was how to bring a quick end to class struggle and the rule of the bourgeoisie. Objectives included confronting the state apparatuses (police, military, courts, and so on) as a prerequisite to seizing state power. Marx and Engels shipped arms to the workers arming the barricades, and Engels himself actually took part in the fighting. Marx clearly regarded the forceful takeover of state power as the ultimate aim of the Communist Party: "The immediate aim of the Communists is the same as that of all the other proletarian parties: formation of the proletariat into a class, overthrow of the bourgeois supremacy, conquest of political power by the proletariat." Speaking in Amsterdam in 1872, however, Marx made it clear that the validity of using violent force varies from circumstance to circumstance. He believed that in some countries, such as the United States, Great Britain, and Holland, workers could achieve their aims by peaceful means. However, in most countries, "it is force that must be the lever of our revolutions."

Marx believed that force may be necessary to effect a socialist revolution, but he was not dogmatic and absolute about the use of violence. Nor was he adamant about the speed of the transformation to socialism. The transformation from capitalism to socialism could be a slow development or a traumatic revolutionary upheaval. Marx saw force as a means, not as an end in itself. What Marx was unbending about was the fact that class struggle exists and involves violence, coercion, and repression. Workers are exploited and alienated. Because they lack property, workers are forced into selling their labor for subsistence. If they try to organize themselves, mobilize, and politicize their interests, they are met with repression. Violence breeds violence. The workers' revolution might therefore require violence.

Mikhail Bakunin, an erstwhile companion of Marx who held a philosophy of dialectics, believed that destruction was a necessary stage of social change. Georges Sorel was a syndicalist Marxist who denied the then-popular theory that capitalism would collapse of its own inner contradictions. He espoused a radical brand of revolutionary syndicalism. In 1906 he wrote *Reflections on Violence*, which defines class war as the very essence of socialism. Acts of violence, he believed, would create a workers' morality, destroy the bourgeoisie, and lay the foundations for socialism.

Vladimir Ilich Lenin believed that the Marxist doctrine of the dictatorship of the proletariat meant the conquest and hold of state power by the use of force. Karl Kautsky argued in *Terrorism and Communism* (1919) that Lenin's concept of the dictatorship of the proletariat was leading away from the democratic essence of socialism. In *Terrorism and Communism* (1920), Leon Trotsky replied to Kautsky that violent revolution was necessary because parliamentary means alone were ineffective. The revolutionary class should attain its end by any means at its disposal—even terrorism. György Lukács also decried Kautsky's peaceful transition to socialism and denied the validity of the question of the legality or illegality of means. For Lukács, what counts is whatever will be most successful in achieving the end of social transformation. Questions of tactics and the ethics of force will be determined only by the proletariat when it acquires a sense of world history and world mission.

Malcolm X, Martin Luther King, Jr.'s contemporary in the leadership of the black Civil Rights movement rejected the nonviolent philosophy of King and advocated his own brand of social revolution that allowed for violence. Malcolm X believed that when the law failed to protect African Americans, they were justified in using arms to protect themselves from harm at the hands of whites. He believed that it was criminal to remain passive in the face of being attacked. He not only encouraged self-defense, he mandated it, saying: "I am for violence if nonviolence means we continue postponing a solution to the American black man's problem—just to avoid violence. I don't go for nonviolence if it also means a delayed solution." Malcolm X did not, however, advocate a violent black revolution against whites; he justified the use of force only in self-defense.

What is so revolutionary about Michel Foucault is his localization of the mechanisms of power in apparatuses outside of the state. He locates power or micropowers at the everyday level of family relationships, kinships systems, and local administrations. In *Discipline and Punish* (1979), Foucault presents power as the force of normalization and the formation of knowledge. Normalization and knowledge invest the body, the individual, the masses, and the body politic. "The soul is the effect and the instrument of a political anatomy; the soul is the prison of the body." Power through knowledge moves to a new level as Jeremy Bentham's Panopticon recognizes the need for authorities to observe prisoners. Knowledge is power over people and ends up normalizing people and standardizing them in the factories, schools, prisons, hospitals, and the military. Panopticism, then, means a principle of political anatomy for organizing rules of discipline, political tactics, techniques and strategies for the exercise of control, and the formation of knowledge.

Foucault corrected the traditional view that power is only repressive or constraining. In fact, what Foucault demonstrated was the insidious ways in which power produces conformity, legitimizes political power, and creates exclusionary forms of knowledge.

Context

States may at times have to resort to the use or threat of force in order to exercise authority over domestic enemies or to dominate foreign enemies. Authority without power makes for weak and unstable governments vulnerable to takeover by subversive groups. It also makes for unenforceable laws. Consequently, authority must have a legitimate recourse to force when necessary.

Power without authority, rule without the consent of the ruled, on the other hand, makes for despotism, tyranny, and dictatorship. Governments that rule without legitimacy govern by brute force alone. Despots rule without the consent of their people and hence resort to force as a matter of policy. Lenin, the founder of Soviet communism, instituted a government known as the "dictatorship of the proletariat," which meant rule based on brutal force unrestrained by laws. China's Mao Tse-tung also made an unqualified identification of power and authority. In his view, authority belongs to those who have the power to rule. One of his most famous statements claims that "political power grows out of the barrel of a gun." In order to be just, however, force must have the backing of a legitimate authority.

Tied closely to the issue of force is that of violence, which is used to deny the rights of others. Ethics concerns itself with the personal levels of violence. By contrast, political philosophy is concerned with institutional violence, usually in the form of war or capital punishment. Institutional violence can, however, be covert, taking the forms of repression, racism, and denial of human and civil rights. It is a task of political philosophy to determine what forms of violence represent legitimate uses of force.

Bibliography

Aquinas, Thomas. *On Law, Morality, and Politics*. Edited by William P. Baumgarth and Richard J. Regan. Indianapolis: Hackett, 1988. Aquinas expounds on the just-war theory more systematically and clearly than Augustine.

Augustine, Saint. *Concerning the City of God Against the Pagans*. Translated by Henry Bettenson. Harmondsworth, England: Penguin Books, 1972. Augustine originally wrote this book as a theodicy explaining the compatibility between the sacking of Rome and the goodness of Christianity.

Foucault, Michel. *Discipline and Punish: The Birth of the Prison*. Translated by Alan Sheridan. New York: Vintage, 1979. Concerning itself with the expression of power in penal institutions, this work shows how disciplinary techniques were developed that converted the body into a docile instrument for the inscription of knowledge resulting in normalization.

_____. *Power/Knowledge: Selected Interviews and Other Writings, 1972-1977*. Edited by Colin Gordon. Translated by Colin Gordon et al. New York: Pantheon Books, 1980. Essays and interviews focusing on issues of power and its pervasive presence in human life, especially its intrusive investment into human bodies.

Michael R. Candelaria

Cross-References

Autocracy and Absolutism, p. 127; Fascism and Nazism, p. 656; Machiavelli's Political Philosophy, p. 1148; Mercantilism, p. 1173; Military Governments, p. 1192; Political Myths and the Philosophies of Mosca and Pareto, p. 1474; Political Violence, p. 1539; Power in Politics, p. 1584; Realpolitik, p. 1668; Revolutionary Governments, p. 1725; Terrorism, p. 1962.

FOREIGN RELATIONS

Field of study: Functions of government

A primary function of a national government is to direct the country's relationships with foreign states. A country's foreign relations can take a variety of forms—friendly or hostile, mutually beneficial or highly exploitive.

Principal terms

ALLIANCE: agreement among states in which each pledges to assist the others in security matters

AUTARKY: policy of minimizing a country's dependence on other countries for security, trade, and important resources

COLD WAR: adversarial relationship between Western capitalist countries and Eastern socialist countries after World War II

DIPLOMACY: means of conducting foreign relations, based on formal agreements, face-to-face negotiations, international law, and other techniques

FOREIGN POLICY: official plans that a government adopts to achieve its goals in the international environment

Overview

The various functions of government can be divided between those that are directed within the country itself (domestic functions) and those that are directed abroad (international functions). The domestic functions of government are many and varied, reflecting the broad areas for which government is responsible. The international functions, however, and more particularly the management of foreign relations, are more centralized in the political leadership and less subject to the conflicts of domestic policies. Yet managing and directing foreign relations is hardly an unimportant function of government; it is through foreign relations that states relate to the outside world, attempting to ensure security and prosperity. Foreign relations involve issues of war, peace, and money. For purposes of discussion, three different spheres of foreign relations can be identified: diplomacy, security, and trade.

Diplomacy is traditionally thought of as the essential conduit of foreign relations. Emissaries, ambassadors, and other representatives bring the somewhat impersonal concept of foreign relations to a more human level. Diplomacy employs face-to-face discussions and negotiations between representatives of different governments to resolve disputes and expand cooperation between states. It seeks to codify the resultant agreements in treaties and protocols. These agreements generally are placed within a framework of international law. Although states are sovereign, that is, not answerable to a higher authority, generally there is an expectation foreign relations be conducted within the parameters of international law.

Diplomacy involves various aspects of intergovernmental relations, from setting borders to coordinating visa policies to establishing procedures for the extradition of fugitives. Although not all interactions between states are conducted through diplomatic channels, diplomacy can be utilized to some extent in all dimensions of international relations—even in warfare, which is often conducted as a means of securing a more advantageous peace. Diplomacy is the broadest and most personalized dimension of foreign relations.

Another sphere of foreign relations is security. The international community of states is, for the most part, anarchical (that is, there is no world government to establish order and enforce laws). States therefore must be concerned with ensuring their own security. States often will enlist the aid of friendly states for the purpose of collective security, creating pacts and alliances. Such states can be viewed as security partners. The North Atlantic Treaty Organization (NATO), created in 1949, has been an especially strong and successful alliance between states in North America and Western Europe. Security relations also can include nonaggression pacts, such as that between Nazi Germany and the Soviet Union in 1939, in which the two countries agreed not to join in hostilities against each other. Germany violated the pact two years later in a massive invasion of the Soviet Union. Such are the dangers of legal contracts in an anarchical system. Realizing this, many states seek to provide for their own security not only by signing documents but also by building large arsenals of weapons and by developing military strategies that aim either to prevent war or allow the country to prevail in a war. Even with such self-defense measures, no state can ignore the effects of foreign relations, whether they be hostile, neutral, or friendly, upon its security.

Governments also focus on the economic and trade sphere of their foreign relations. Trade relations have always been an important responsibility of government. As the global economy becomes more complex and as advances in transportation and communication shrink the distance of international commerce, trade relations have become more important to national economic strength, and thus have come to occupy a greater part of a government's responsibilities. Trade relations, like the other aspects of foreign relations, can be friendly or unfriendly. Governments can employ a variety of tools, from trade treaties aimed at increasing commerce through the mutual opening of markets, to unilateral trade barriers such as quotas and tariffs, as well as more aggressive efforts such as "dumping"—government subsidy of exports. Foreign relations in the area of trade should be thought also to include related economic channels, such as financial and monetary relations. Through these channels, the domestic economies of states become connected, thus diminishing the isolation of domestic economic systems.

In all of these spheres—diplomacy, security, and trade—governments seek to promote their own country's interests through building and directing relationships with foreign countries. Of course, determining what kinds of particular relationships will be of benefit to the country is a process often fraught with controversy. Should the country join in a security alliance? Should it offer favored trade status to a trading partner? Should it intervene militarily in a neighboring country's civil war? Should it extend formal diplomatic recognition to a newly independent state? All of these types of questions require judgments based on a prediction of future events and the probable responses of foreign leaders, as well as assumptions about what is and is not in the country's interests. There is not enough time to consider every detail for every decision for every problem. The government must decide how to make a general structure for its foreign relations.

This is the making of foreign policy. The term refers to specific policies aimed at particular countries and issues, and to a general orientation toward the outside world. The institutional structure of a government helps determine how foreign policy is made. For example, a democracy will be more sensitive to public opinion in the making of foreign policy than an authoritarian regime will be. Other factors which affect a country's foreign policy decisions include the country's geographical position, its relative power in the international system, its history (especially its experience with invasion and occupation), its prevailing ideological disposition, its access to important resources, its standard of living, and its wealth. A country's foreign relations develop from an amalgam of diverse and sometimes conflicting factors, and therefore their course cannot easily be anticipated. Some scholars of international relations associated with the realist school nevertheless downplay the significance of domestic factors in the making of foreign policy, suggesting that the primary determinant of foreign policy is the geopolitical position of the country in the international system.

Overall, the stewardship of foreign relations is one of the most critical functions of government, in that it directly bears upon the wealth and survival of the state. Yet because of its application in an anarchical world system, foreign policy involves some very subjective, ambiguous, and difficult decisions. Unfortunately for governmental decision makers, this situation is becoming only more complex with the increasing number of states in the world and the increasing ability among them to influence one another.

Applications

The changing international orientations of the Soviet Union during its seventy-five-year existence provide excellent examples of foreign relations as a function of government. Foreign relationships were a major—indeed, paramount—concern of the Soviet Union from the moment of its creation in 1917. The leader of the revolution that overthrew the czarist monarchy, Vladimir Ilich Lenin, sought above all to direct the new government's energies inward, consolidating the new regime. This task required that the country extract itself from World War I—a war that the new, communist government had inherited from the czarist regime. Lenin obtained a peace treaty with Germany (Russia's primary adversary) and thus was able to obtain "breathing space" for his new country. That breathing space was crucial, in that it allowed Lenin's Bolshevik Party to prevail over the monarchist forces during the ensuing civil war.

Once the new leadership was able to consolidate its gains in the early 1920's, the government again became preoccupied with foreign affairs. The Soviets found themselves essentially isolated. Many countries, including the United States, were unwilling to recognize Russia's communist government—even a decade after the end of the

Russian civil war. (The United States had aided the monarchists.) Moreover, as a communist state, the Soviet Union had only one communist ally: Outer Mongolia. The ideological underpinnings of Lenin's regime held that noncommunist (and particularly capitalist) states were inherently hostile to communist ones. Thus the Soviet Union from the mid-1920's onward became preoccupied with the notion of capitalist encirclement. Foreign relations for the Soviet government (by this time led by Joseph Stalin) were based on suspicion and fear of the capitalist countries. Without other communist governments with which to develop relationships, the Soviets instead developed relations with communist and socialist political parties in other countries— particularly in Europe. Thus, Soviet foreign relations were based largely upon an ideological affinity with subnational groups. Stalin at this time promoted the doctrine of socialism in one country—the Soviet Union; foreign communist and socialist parties in other countries were to work for the preservation of the Soviet Union as an example of communism in the world, rather than for the immediate development of communism or socialism in their own countries.

By the mid-1930's the Soviet Union and other countries were experiencing renewed threats from Germany, now under the control of Adolf Hitler. Soviet foreign relations took a dramatic turn in 1939 as Stalin's foreign minister signed a nonaggression pact with anticommunist Nazi Germany. It seemed that the pragmatism of addressing a military threat from Germany was more important than ideological consistency. In further illustration of that principle, the Soviets formed an alliance with the leaders of the capitalist world—the United States and Great Britain—after Germany invaded the Soviet Union in 1941.

After the end of World War II in 1945, Soviet foreign relations underwent another dramatic turn. The Soviets established communist, Soviet-allied regimes in most of Eastern Europe. With over a half-dozen ideological allies, "socialism in one country" as the doctrine of Soviet foreign relations was changed to include Eastern Europe. Communist regimes arose also in China, Southeast Asia, Africa, the Caribbean, and Latin America. Far from the autarkic, paranoid foreign policy that shunned intimate foreign relations in the 1920's and 1930's, the Soviet Union in the post-World War II period became highly engaged in coordinating its foreign relations with cooperative allies around the globe.

At the same time that this was going on, however, the Soviet Union became increasingly engaged with an unfriendly government: that of the United States. Militarily, economically, and ideologically, the Soviet Union and the United States defined their respective interests as conflicting. This relationship became known as the Cold War. Foreign relations for the Soviet Union, like those of the United States, became remarkably constant for over four decades; both countries viewed the world as divided into two camps, one communist and one capitalist. This situation would persist until the very last years of the Soviet Union's existence, until Soviet leader Mikhail Gorbachev (who came to power in 1985) sought to increase military and economic cooperation with the West, even while trying to retain his bloc's ideological distinctness.

The case of the Soviet Union illustrates a number of different approaches to foreign relations: from preoccupied isolationism, to self-imposed autarky, to regional hegemony, to global bipolar hostility. That the Soviet Union went through so many phases is not so much illustrative of its uniqueness, but rather is to demonstrate how foreign relations are influenced by changing ideological, developmental, and external factors. The case of the Soviet Union also demonstrates how foreign relations are connected with the very identity of the state. Although there was no shortage of pragmatism in the Soviet Union's foreign policy, the Soviet Union's self-identity as the leader of world communism helped to define how Moscow structured its relations with the various countries of the globe.

Context

Are there conceivable alternative entities, aside from national government, which could carry out foreign relations for a country? In formal, legalistic terms, only states are sovereign in the international system, and therefore only the custodians of that sovereignty can act on behalf of the nations. Yet many other institutions and actors are capable of, and tend to engage in, relations with foreign countries.

Subnational actors, such as regional and local governments, engage in foreign relations in a limited way through sister city arrangements, cultural exchanges, tax incentives to attract foreign business, and other programs. Multinational corporations can have a large impact on economic and trade relations between states through foreign investment, establishing foreign offices, hiring local workers, developing the local infrastructure in host countries, and otherwise becoming involved in foreign economies. Particularly influential private citizens, such as industrialist Armand Hammer and former U.S. president Jimmy Carter, can have a significant influence on foreign relations without holding official office. Even less eminent individuals can be thought of as affecting foreign relations through "tourist diplomacy," taking part in letter-writing and penpal arrangements, and participating in student exchange programs.

Foreign relations also can be affected by international organizations. The United Nations (U.N.) is one of the best-known international institutions designed to structure foreign relations among states. Although the U.N. does not normally have formal, legal authority to override sovereign nations' foreign policies, it does provide an alternative to simple bilateral foreign relations and raw power politics, offering instead a widely embracing, multilateral framework for regularizing the interaction of states. There are also regional international organizations such as the Organization of American States, the Organization for African Unity, and the European Union (E.U.). Whereas the first two of these are focused on coordinating regional policies into a coherent and mutually beneficial package, the E.U. has continuously moved toward integrating the European states that are its members into a confederation of states. As the members of the E.U. have moved closer toward this goal, they have sought to develop a common foreign policy, which in the early stages of development was called "European political cooperation." More than any of the above-cited alternatives to national governments as the custodians of their foreign relations, European Political Cooperation poses a threat to state sovereignty in the realm of foreign policy-making. Not surprisingly, therefore, in the first years after the end of the Cold War, the E.U.'s ability to forge common foreign policies was only partly successful, marked sometimes by sharp internal disagreements and a consequent slowness to respond to such issues as war in the Balkans and the disintegration of the Soviet Union.

What all of this demonstrates is that foreign relations is not solely the purview of national governments. The changes within and among states, as well as the increasing power of subnational and international organizations, is causing governmental foreign policy-making to be more constrained by external conditions and actors.

Bibliography

Kissinger, Henry. *Diplomacy*. New York: Simon & Schuster, 1994. Detailed historical account of international diplomacy, negotiations, and foreign relations.

Smith, Raymond F. *Negotiating with the Soviets*. Bloomington: Indiana University Press, 1989. Analysis of how the Soviet Union's cultural, political, and ideological characteristics influenced its negotiating strategies and tactics—and therefore its foreign relations.

Zartman, William, ed. *Positive Sum: Improving North-South Negotiations*. New Brunswick, N.J.: Transaction Books, 1987. Essays on the relations between the industrialized countries of the North and the less developed countries of the South. The essays are united in an effort to discover ways that countries of both regions can develop foreign relations with positive-sum outcomes, even while pursuing self-interested goals.

Steve D. Boilard

Cross-References

Alliances, p. 47; Ambassadors and Embassies, p. 53; Arms Control, p. 95; Conflict Resolution, p. 397; Diplomacy and International Negotiation, p. 552; Food Politics, p. 706; Geopolitics, p. 759; International Relations, p. 969; Isolationism and Protectionism, p. 1000; National Security, p. 1261; Peace, p. 1390; Trade with Foreign Nations, p. 2000; War, p. 2129.

FUNDING OF GOVERNMENT

Field of study: Economic issues

Public officials have the responsibility of determining the number of dollars that may be claimed from private wealth to support public purposes, which funding types to use, and how much money to raise from each. These choices affect the distribution of wealth and other resources and shape the form and speed of economic development.

Principal terms

BOND: certificate of indebtedness, tendered by a unit of government (the borrower) to a lender, that provides written recognition of the legal obligation to repay the loan plus interest

DEBT LIMIT: constitutional or statutory limitation upon the total amount of debt a government may have, usually stated in monetary terms or as a percentage of property value

FEE: method of funding government in which a charge is assessed to service users

HORIZONTAL EQUITY: goal of tax systems that is met when persons in like economic circumstances pay the same tax

PROGRESSIVE TAX: tax in which people with larger tax bases pay a larger proportion of income or wealth as tax

PROPORTIONAL TAX: tax in which everyone pays the same percentage of their income or wealth

REGRESSIVE TAX: tax that places a proportionately larger tax burden on people of lower income or wealth

REVENUES: dollars collected by government through imposition of taxes and fees for services

TAX BASE: something of value (such as income or property) used as the basis for determining tax liability

VERTICAL EQUITY: goal of tax systems that is met when persons of differing means pay different taxes, with the wealthier paying more

Overview

Governments obtain the funding for their programs and services primarily through taxation, charging fees for services, and borrowing in the form of issuing bonds. Taxation is the oldest and most prevalent means of funding government. Tax laws specify the legal taxpayer, define the base for taxation, and establish a rate structure for each tax. The amount of tax an individual or business is legally obligated to pay is the product of the government's estimate of the value of the tax base and the appropriate tax rate.

Because payment of taxes is compulsory for citizens of a taxing government, citizens of representative governments have taken active roles in ensuring the fairness of levies. One of the earliest known laws permitting yet also limiting taxation is contained within Britain's Magna Carta. In 1217, the twelfth article of the reissued Magna Carta placed important constraints on the purposes for which the king could raise taxes and the burden those levies could impose. The prolonged struggle for parliamentary control of the purse in Britain was in essence a fight for power over taxation. With the Glorious Revolution of 1688 and adoption of the English Bill of Rights the following year, British citizens were assured that "no man [would] be compelled to make any gift, loan, or benevolence, or tax, without common consent by Act of Parliament."

A century later, French citizens asserted their right to control taxation. Beginning with a decree on June 17, 1789, it became an enduring tenet of French constitutional practice that no tax could be levied without the consent of the people.

In the United States, since the time of the American Revolution and its rallying cry of "no taxation without representation," taxes generally have been enacted by popularly elected representatives. The power to levy taxes is granted to Congress through the Constitution in Article 1, section 8: "The Congress shall have Power To lay and collect Taxes, Duties, Imposts and Excises, to pay the Debts and provide for the common Defence and general Welfare of the United States." This section's uniformity clause, that "all Duties, Imposts and Excises shall be uniform throughout the United States," was interpreted for many years as a prohibition against progressive taxes. Use of income taxes also was constrained by the apportionment clause of the Constitution (Article 1, section 9), which requires amounts collected from a direct tax to be apportioned among the states according to population. Enactment of the Sixteenth Amendment in 1913 cleared the way for a federal income tax.

In addition to taxation, governments also finance public expenditures by charging prices in the form of fees for public services. Unlike taxes, which are compulsory, the payment of fees for services usually can be avoided by the choice not to receive a service. A particular fee may not recover the full cost of service provision, as would a price in the private market, because the government wishes to encourage use of the service by subsidizing its cost. Fees are usually proportional to the amount of service used. Some local governments in Europe and parts of the United States earn substantial revenues from the operation of electric power plants, water systems, and other utilities that provide services.

Finally, the use of public debt to acquire resources has increased significantly over the decades. Borrowing enables governments to meet financial obligations not covered by current revenues. The authority to incur debt may be provided through a constitution or statute. Article 2, section 8 of the U.S. Constitution assigns Congress unrestricted borrowing power. Although Congress has imposed a limitation on the total amount of debt that may be owed, it also has increased the limit each time additional debt has been needed. Since World War II, numerous federal deficits have contributed to the rapid growth of the national public debt. Federal debt in the United States is in the form of Treasury bills (short term) and Treasury bonds (long term).

At the state and local levels of government, debt is generally acquired through the sale of financial instruments called municipal bonds. Although the term "municipal" would seem to indicate debt incurred by local governments, all state and local government debt issues are termed municipal bonds. Most state constitutions restrain borrowing authority, and some prohibit debt. Constitutional amendments may permit borrowing for specified purposes or under particular conditions, with voter approval. The borrowing authority of local governments is regulated by states through constitutional and statutory provisions.

Public finance specialists have identified a number of overarching goals of a revenue system that may be used to guide policy choices. First, the revenue system as a whole and any proposed change must be politically acceptable. Second, the sources used should produce an adequate level of funds. Unfortunately, no single revenue type is capable of providing adequate revenues at all times because of their differing sensitivity to economic conditions.

Receipts from taxes on income tend to be responsive to economic conditions when the rate structure is proportional and even more responsive when rates are progressive. Revenues from these sources increase during periods of economic growth but decline with economic downturns. The result is an inconsistency in the funds available to support programs, with revenues falling during economic downturns, when states might choose to increase spending.

Taxes on property value are usually less sensitive than income taxes because the value of property does not change dramatically with changes in economic conditions. Revenue collections from property taxes are comparatively stable across business cycles.

Taxes on consumption—including the general sales tax, value-added taxes, and selective sales or "excise" taxes on particular commodities—range in responsiveness from insensitive to very sensitive, depending on the commodities involved. Collections from taxes on such substances as tobacco and alcohol do not change appreciably with a change in economic conditions because consumption of those goods is stable. In contrast, collections are very responsive when the tax base is limited to items that are not perceived as necessities and whose purchase can be easily postponed with the onset of a recession. Governments often use several revenue sources to allow the strengths of sensitive tax types to balance the weaknesses of the unresponsive types and vice versa.

Another prominent goal of revenue policy is neutrality, which is attained when revenue raising policies do not cause people and businesses to alter investment, purchasing, or location decisions in response to revenue policy. In the United States, this goal has become a fundamental concern of economic development policy-making. States have sought to improve their competitive advantage with regard to business location and retention through tax policies such as offering abatements. They also try to avoid measures to increase revenue that would drive business away.

Almost all tax types used by governments have features that are likely to alter the pattern of production or economic choices. In some cases, tax policy is designed to assist particular segments of the taxpaying public. In the United States, it is common for farmlands and open space to be assessed at a lower percentage of market value for property taxation than are other property types. In Scandinavian countries, agricultural property similarly is appraised lightly for net worth taxation. Sales taxes are not applied to the purchase of materials and equipment used in manufacturing in many U.S. states. In France, some value adding activities are exempted from the value-added tax. In Great Britain, taxes are used purposively to alter consumption and production patterns. High taxes on commodities such as automobiles and household appliances make them more expensive; subsidies or negative taxes on food items make them less costly.

Perhaps the most important and fundamental goal of a revenue system is fairness. The fairness objective has two important dimensions. First, government should not impose an excessive burden upon its own citizens and businesses. Second, government should distribute the burden of financing government equitably.

The determination of the level at which taxes become excessive is always circumstantial. In the United States, many citizens believe taxes are too high. Major taxes in the United States have hovered near 30 percent of gross national product for some time, compared to claims on private resources in Canada of 34 percent and the Organization for Economic Cooperation and Development (OECD) nations at an average of 39 percent. Personal and corporate income taxes on average are 13 percent of gross national product in the United States, with social security payroll taxes adding another 8 percent. In Europe, income taxes claim 16 percent of gross national product and social security taxes average close to 9 percent. Canada and the OECD nations make heavy use of sales and excise taxes, at 10 percent and 12 percent of gross national product respectively, compared to only 5 percent in the United States.

Even when the overall level of taxes is not considered too high, particular segments of the taxpaying population nevertheless may be burdened excessively by one or more taxes. Reducing the burden can be accomplished in several ways. The amount of income or property value subject to taxation can be decreased by granting some or all taxpayers exemptions or deductions. Another option, which can be used alone or to complement other strategies, is to decrease the amount of taxes otherwise payable through the use of tax credits or rebates. An important mechanism for reducing and redistributing tax burdens is for a higher level of government to contribute toward financing a lower government's services, to assume full financial responsibility for a particularly costly service, or to provide financial assistance for specific purposes and beneficiaries.

Deciding on an equitable distribution of tax shares among the paying public is a difficult process. Tax experts generally agree that an equitable division of financing is realized when two conditions are met. First, those with greater means to pay taxes actually contribute more than those with lesser means. This notion that taxpayers of differing means should pay differing amounts of tax, with the wealthy paying more, is known as vertical equity. Second, those of equal means pay the same tax. The goal of equivalent taxes for similar circumstances is called horizontal equity.

Most people agree that a tax is unfair when poor people must pay a higher percentage of their income as tax than do the wealthy. This type of tax is called regressive. In contrast, many people would agree that a tax under which everyone pays the same percentage of income as tax is fair. This type of tax is called a proportional tax. Others argue that to be fair, a tax must take an increasing percentage of income as income increases. This type of tax is known as a progressive tax. Wealthy people sometimes argue against proportional or progressive taxes on the grounds that they should not have to pay more for the same services received by others.

Those who advocate for progressive taxes maintain that an equivalent sacrifice from all taxpayers is achieved only when individuals with higher incomes pay larger portions of their incomes as tax. Proponents of this position reason that as income rises, each additional dollar earned is subjectively worth less, because the most important desires have already been satisfied. How quickly the value of each successive dollar declines and whether the decline occurs at the same rate for all taxpayers is unknown. The issue of how progressive tax rates should be must be resolved through politics.

The process of attaining an equitable distribution of tax burdens is complicated further by the need to ensure adequate revenues. Progressive and proportional taxes are more responsive than some other taxes to economic changes. Although regressive taxes usually are considered unfair, using these tax types in combination with the more sensitive taxes helps to ensure that revenue collections consistently will be sufficient to finance the highest priorities of government.

To achieve an overall tax system that minimizes the tradeoffs between equity and adequacy, public finance experts recommend that governments employ a diversity of tax types. The federal government in the United States has experienced a trend toward less diversity, with more than two-thirds of its revenue provided by income taxes and collections for trust funds, particularly social security. Although state governments in the United States rely most heavily on income and sales taxes, and local governments on property taxes, the combination of state and local taxes within each state is generally diverse. Many states have state and local tax systems that are heavily reliant on only one tax type. Relative to Canada and European nations, the U.S. national government makes little use of sales and excise taxes, but these are important revenue sources for the states.

Applications

Two historical tax policy events, Massachusetts' Proposition 2½ and the enactment of the federal Tax Reform Act of 1986, underscore the significance of government's choices about how to fund public programs and at what level. During the late 1970's, citizen disenchantment with the property tax as a means of government finance began spreading through the United States. In 1980, Massachusetts voters approved the passage of a citizen-initiated referendum known as Proposition 2½. This law limited the amount of property taxes that a community could collect in two ways. First, the total amount of taxes collected could not increase by more than 2.5 percent per year, except with a majority vote at a town meeting or a referendum. Second, Proposition 2½ limited the total amount of taxes collected to 2.5 percent of a community's total property value.

Prior to the enactment of Proposition 2½, Massachusetts had been one of the heaviest users of the property tax in the United States. Over the remainder of the 1980's, property taxes declined from 59 percent of local revenues to about 46 percent by 1989. The reduction in dependence on property taxes as a source of finance was achieved by increased use of other revenue sources, some spending reductions, and the state's decision to redirect more of its tax revenues to local governments as operating subsidies.

The passage of Proposition 2½ illustrates the possibilities of using a variety of revenue types and not becoming overly dependent on any one type. The disproportionately heavy use of property taxes to fund local government in Massachusetts caused citizens to bypass their elected officials and take control of tax policy-making.

At the national level of government, passage of the landmark Tax Reform Act of 1986 by the U.S. Congress addressed several aspects of the fairness objective of a revenue system. One of the most important provisions of the act raised the values of the personal exemption and the standard deduction for couples, which increased the amount a household could earn before any tax was due. This action resulted in the removal of several million poor persons from the personal income tax rolls.

A second component of the act sought to increase horizontal equity, or the tax treatment of persons in similar economic circumstances, by eliminating or reducing the use of a variety of tax "loopholes" or special deductions. The deductibility of interest on consumer loans, sales taxes, business entertainment expenses, and individual retirement accounts was eliminated or greatly reduced. Other deductions from taxable income were changed to be allowable only to the extent they exceeded specified percentages of income, rather than being unrestricted.

The act also affected vertical equity, or the tax burdens of citizens at varying income levels. More than a dozen personal income tax brackets were replaced with only two, at 15 percent and 28 percent. Previously, the highest income tax rate was 50 percent. Many people disapproved of the change to a less progressive income tax structure, arguing that the tax system had been made less fair. Nevertheless, the system retained an element of vertical equity, with the wealthy paying more tax than those of less means.

Despite the closer scrutiny of debt at the state and local levels of government, problems have occurred. Many states became deeply indebted in the eighteenth and nineteenth centuries and defaulted on bonds. During the 1970's and early 1980's, a number of cities and special districts approached the brink of default or actually defaulted on bond payments. As a result, elected officials have enacted laws and citizens have approved state constitutional amendments and local charter changes to more closely regulate the amount of government-backed debt that may be issued, the total debt outstanding, and the purposes for which debt may be incurred.

Rather than curtailing debt, these borrowing restrictions have spawned the use of new debtlike financial instruments that neither require voter approval nor fall under debt limit provisions. The certificate of participation, or COP, is one such innovation. Certificates of participation are similar to municipal bonds but differ in three notable ways. COPs are issued by a financial institution rather than by a government, they do not carry a government's "full faith and credit" promise to repay the debt, and the legislative authorization to repay the debt is given annually, rather than for the term of the debt. Several state courts have ruled that COPs are in fact debt and subject to laws governing debt.

Context

How many dollars should be raised to fund government programs and from what sources are among the most important questions facing designers of tax policy. In the United States, the increasing federal deficit brought these issues to the forefront in the 1980's. Although progress was slow, Congress initiated steps to end the unlimited use of debt and reduce the national deficit.

Since the early 1970's, the United States national government has reformed the federal income tax several times. The potential merits of the value-added tax have received increased attention. This type of tax uses the "value added" to a product at each stage of production as its tax base. Value-added taxes have been anchors of many European and Canadian tax systems for years. The likely regressivity of a value-added tax and the similarities between its base of taxation and that of the states' general sales taxes bode against national enactment in the United States.

Britain, Spain, The Netherlands, Denmark, Germany, and Canada have all faced tax policy problems as the result of their economic situations and, in some cases, escalating budgetary demands. German unification created acute financial difficulties, and the need for support by the majority of state governments to change tax laws or reform entitlement programs hindered progress. In Denmark, where local governments have independent authority to levy taxes, expenditures were successfully restrained during the 1980's. Common strategies for meeting the challenges of resource scarcity in Europe and North America have included privatization, decentralization of responsibilities, reduction of services, elimination of programs, efforts to increase service efficiency, and tax reform.

In the United States, the states and local governments have been diversifying revenues. Fees are being used with increasing frequency to pay for services once financed with taxes. Gambling is becoming an increasingly important revenue source for states. By the early 1990's, more than thirty states had instituted state-run lotteries. Some states selectively allow parimutuel gambling. With the exception of off-track betting, which may have state or local proprietors, governments generally do not operate the gaming facilities, but instead regulate activities and collect taxes from gambling proceeds.

In California and Massachusetts, state governments greatly increased aid to local governments after local property tax revolts. As a result, a higher proportion of public expenditures in those states are now funded with income and sales taxes. Although the tax systems may be becoming "fairer" as a result, the reductions in spending for programs benefiting poor citizens may offset tax equity gains. Such issues of adequacy and equity will always be part of the process of funding government programs.

Bibliography

Aaron, Henry. *The Value-Added Tax: Lessons from Europe.* Washington, D.C.: Brookings Institution, 1981. Provides an excellent overview of the way in which value-added taxation has been implemented in European countries—the principal adopters of the tax.

Lincoln Institute of Land Policy and the National Conference of State Legislatures. *Principles of a High-Quality State Revenue System.* Cambridge, Mass.: Lincoln Institute of Land Policy, 1992. Presents a framework for shaping effective tax policies at the state level. Discusses characteristics of high-quality revenue systems and guiding objectives for choosing among alternative tax types.

Phillips, Kevin P. *The Politics of Rich and Poor: Wealth and the American Electorate in the Reagan Aftermath.* New York: HarperPerennial, 1991. Traces the wealth shift that occurred in the United States during the 1980's as a result of changes in federal tax policies, demographics, and economic trends. Tables and graphs throughout the book and a detailed appendix present substantial supporting data in an easily accessible format.

United States. Advisory Commission on Intergovernmental Relations. *Significant Features of Fiscal Federalism.* Washington, D.C.: Author, 1994. This two-volume publication, issued annually, presents extensive data on government expenditures and revenues of state and local governments in the United States. Describes budget processes and tax systems of the states.

U.S. Department of Treasury. *Tax Reform for Fairness, Simplicity, and Economic Growth.* Washington, D.C.: Government Printing Office, 1984. This report provides a comprehensive view of transforming the U.S. tax system. Includes a discussion of value-added taxes.

Webber, Carolyn, and Aaron Wildavsky. *A History of Taxation and Expenditure in the Western World.* New York: Simon and Schuster, 1986. Presents a comparative and historical perspective on taxation in Western nations. One of only a few publications to consider budgeting in a comparative perspective.

Josephine M. LaPlante

Cross-References

Budgets of National Governments, p. 158; Debts and Deficits in the U.S. Federal Budget, p. 489; Entitlements, p. 610; Government Powers, p. 772; Iron Triangles, p. 981; Keynesianism, Monetarism, and Supply-Side Economics, p. 1032; National Economies, p. 1248; Policy Development and Implementation, p. 1414; Political Economy, p. 1455; Research, Development, and Planning, p. 1711; State and Local Government, p. 1885; Taxation and Appropriation, p. 1941; Treasury Systems in the United States, p. 2013; Voting Behavior in the United States, p. 2109.

GAY AND LESBIAN POLITICS

Field of study: Civil rights and liberties

Lesbian, bisexual, and gay people in the United States and throughout the world have organized to ensure protection of their human and civil rights and to change negative perceptions of their sexuality.

Principal terms

AIDS (ACQUIRED IMMUNE DEFICIENCY SYNDROME): disease weakening human immune systems that is transmitted through blood and bodily secretions

BISEXUAL: one who is emotionally and erotically attracted to people of either sex

GAY: male who is emotionally and erotically attracted to other males

HETEROSEXISM: system of advantages bestowed on heterosexuals that rests on the belief that everyone is or should be heterosexual

HOMOPHILE: "homophile" replaced "homosexual" as the preferred term by movement activists during the years 1945 to 1970

HOMOPHOBIA: fear and hatred of homosexuals

HOMOSEXUAL: one who is emotionally and erotically attracted to people of the same sex

LESBIAN: female who is emotionally and erotically attracted to other females

Overview

Since the last decades of the nineteenth century, particularly in Western countries, gay and lesbian people have organized social and political movements to increase their visibility, win their rights, and reduce the oppression directed against them. Gay and lesbian people come from diverse racial, ethnic, and class backgrounds. Although the problems they face around the world are very similar, their movement for social change has taken a variety of forms, has varied in intensity and strength, and includes groups with different focuses.

In the United States, two major gay and lesbian organizations, with a base in Washington, D.C., and with a national focus, are the National Gay and Lesbian Task Force, founded in 1973, and the Human Rights Campaign Fund, founded in 1980 to support candidates supportive of gay and lesbian civil rights and those in favor of increasing funding for AIDS research, treatment, and education. These groups also organize against right-wing attacks on the rights of gay and lesbian people.

The International Lesbian and Gay Association, founded in 1978, works for gay and lesbian people throughout the world against legal, social, and cultural discrimination, and functions as a clearinghouse, connecting groups worldwide with its newsletter and annual conferences. In addition, the Gay, Lesbian, and Bisexual Student

Caucus of the United States Student Association, founded in 1971 as the National Gay Student Center, supports the creation of campus-based groups throughout the country. Earlier national networks of support groups included the Mattachine Society for men (founded in 1951) and The Daughters of Bilitis for women (founded in 1955).

Other groups concentrate on public education campaigns to improve public perceptions of gay and lesbian people (for example, speakers' bureaus, history projects, and telephone hot lines). There are also professional support groups for lawyers, scientists, school workers, health care providers, social workers, academics, business owners, artists, and military veterans, among others. There are gay- and lesbian-owned businesses of all kinds, gay and lesbian religious groups, and gay and lesbian student organizations on college and high school campuses in virtually every state and in many countries. There are also community political, social, and support groups, for example, Parents, Families, and Friends of Lesbians and Gays, Men of All Colors Together, groups for Asians, Latinos, bisexuals, transgenderists, people with disabilities, elders, and youth. There are recreational and artistic groups, cable television programs, radio programs, magazines, newspapers, journals, publishing houses, and media watchdog groups. Legal agencies, such as the prototype Lambda Legal Defense and Education Fund in New York City, founded in 1973 "to advance the rights of gay people and to educate the public at large about discrimination against gay men and lesbians," also exist. In addition, there are local community service centers.

Some groups choose to work outside the established order through the use of highly visible demonstrations that often involve acts of civil disobedience. These groups include the Gay Liberation Front, Radicalesbians, and the Gay Activists Alliance (late 1960's through mid-1970's), the AIDS Coalition to Unleash Power (late 1980's through 1990's), Queer Nation (early 1990's), Lesbian Avengers (early 1990's), and others. Some of these groups concentrate solely on the issue of gay and lesbian rights. Others join in coalition with other disenfranchised groups to challenge the many forms of oppression. A third set of groups concentrates primarily on the AIDS crisis. Grassroots groups organize in municipalities and statewide on an ad hoc basis to repeal repressive laws, to demonstrate against print and broadcast media accounts that are perceived to be derogatory, to engage in confrontations with elected officials, political candidates, and others taking antigay and antilesbian stands.

Some groups work within the established system of electoral politics for candidates sensitive to their issues and for openly gay and lesbian candidates. They also lobby for statutes that ensure gay and lesbian people the rights and benefits currently enjoyed by heterosexuals, for example, antidiscrimination laws for gays and lesbians in the areas of employment, housing, public accommodation, credit, military service, child custody, and domestic partnership benefits. These groups also campaign against politicians whose policies are contrary to the groups' goals, and work to overturn laws and ordinances that deny them equal rights.

Applications

In the early morning hours of August 3, 1982, in Atlanta, Georgia, police officers entered the home of Michael Hardwick and arrested him for having sex with another man. Hardwick and his companion were handcuffed to the floor of the police car, and at the police station they were subjected to humiliating homophobic slurs from the officers and from other arrestees. Four years later, the U.S. Supreme Court, in *Bowers v. Hardwick*, reaffirmed the constitutionality of the Georgia antisodomy law, dating back to 1816, that gave the state the right to jail Hardwick for up to twenty years for the act of engaging in consensual adult same-sex activity. The court essentially restated its long-held opinion that rights of privacy do not extend to gay and lesbian people.

There is a long tradition of police raids on gay and lesbian meeting places. Teenage street gangs have long engaged in acts of violence against people they perceive to be homosexual. In England, the death penalty for male same-sex behavior remained in force until 1861. In many countries, gay and lesbian people have been purged from government jobs and from the military and scapegoated by the religious and political right wing. They have been denied housing, the right to marry, custody of their children, employment, insurance, public accommodations, and hospital visitation rights. They were exterminated in Nazi Germany's death camps. They have been called many things: from sinners to perverts, from disease spreaders to the destroyers of civilization.

In the face of these grim facts, gay and lesbian people have joined to form an increasingly visible and effective social movement. This movement has won impressive victories in the struggle for gay and lesbian rights. Following Wisconsin's lead in 1982, other states have passed statewide antidiscrimination laws protecting the rights of gay and lesbian people. When Israel passed its gay rights law on January 1, 1992, it joined Denmark, France, Norway, Sweden, and some regions in Canada and in Australia in outlawing discrimination in housing and employment based on sexual orientation. In 1989, the Danish parliament legalized same-sex marriage, the first country to do so. In May of the same year, the San Francisco Board of Supervisors extended partial legal protection to the domestic partnership of same- and other-sex couples, a policy that affects partners' visits in hospitals, bereavement leaves, and other employment benefits. By the mid-1990's there were more openly lesbian and gay elected officials than ever before.

Greater numbers of people are coming out of the "closet" of denial and fear than ever before. In the schools, an atmosphere of overwhelming homophobia has begun to change. Literature on gay and lesbian themes has boomed, and gay and lesbian people have gained a greater degree of visibility in many sectors of society. As a result of the feminist and the gay and lesbian movements, rigid conceptualizations of gender roles (which restrain females and males of all sexual identities) are at last beginning to break down.

Gays and lesbians have gained greater acceptance from the society at large because they have developed a greater acceptance of themselves. Ann Landers, the syndicated newspaper advice columnist, asked her readers in 1992 to respond to the question: "Are you glad you are gay, or would you rather be straight?" When she released the results, she said that she was not particularly surprised that the "glads" won. She was astonished, however, by the sheer volume of responses—nearly 80,000 people had replied, with an overwhelming margin of 30 to 1, declaring: "I'm glad I'm gay." Although she had asked for postcards only, thousands wrote letters detailing their stories. The gay and lesbian political movement was largely responsible for this change in attitude.

Context

Records dating back to earliest antiquity document the existence of homosexuality. It is not clear, however, whether people of ancient times defined themselves in terms of their sexual behavior. Some historians argue that although people have always engaged in same-sex sexual activity, an exclusively homosexual identity and a sense of community based on that identity did not emerge until the latter part of the nineteenth century. This occurred predominantly in the West, as the developing capitalist economy, within urban settings, provided people with more social and personal options outside the home. There is evidence of a few isolated and brief periods prior to modern times in which aspects of a homosexual identity surfaced, but only since the mid-nineteenth century has there been documented evidence of an organized and sustained political effort to protect the rights of people with same-sex attractions. This history begins in Germany.

In 1862, a Hanover lawyer, Karl Heinrich Ulrichs (later to be referred to by some as the Grandfather of Gay Liberation) published two studies describing love between men. Ulrichs called those attracted to their own sex the third sex. Five years later, speaking to a conference of jurists in Munich, he was the first known person in modern times to publicly declare his homosexuality. Karoly Maria Benkert (a.k.a. Karl Maria Kertbeny) coined the term "homosexual" in 1869, from the Greek *homos*, meaning "same," and from the Latin *sexus*, meaning "sex."

The first known gay periodical, *Der Eigene*, was published under the editorship of Adolf Brand in 1896, and one year later the first homosexual emancipation organization, the Scientific Humanitarian Committee (SHC), was founded. Its goals were to influence legislation (specifically, the repeal of the repressive German antigay law referred to as "paragraph 175"), to educate the public, and to support homosexuals. SHC founding member, sexologist Magnus Hirschfeld, theorized that homosexuality is innate, and worked to bring men and women into a unified movement. In 1919, SHC founded the Institute for Sexual Science, an international center for sex research and the forerunner of the Kinsey Institute. By 1922, SHC had about twenty-five branches throughout Germany.

In the United States, Walt Whitman published the second edition of his book of poetry, *Leaves of Grass*, in 1860. The book contains poems that are clearly homoerotic. He lost his job at the Department of the Interior immediately following publication. In 1870, poet Bayard Taylor published the first American gay novel, *Joseph and His Friend*. In 1895, Emma Goldman, feminist activist and anarchist, became the first prominent American to speak out in support of homosexual rights.

The Society for Human Rights, chartered in Chicago on December 10, 1924, was the first documented homosexual emancipation group in America. It was founded by Henry Gerber. The group published two issues of a newsletter, *Friendship & Freedom*, but was short-lived. Police harassed and arrested group leaders.

During World War II, many gays and lesbians who had previously lived in relative isolation in small towns met one another in the military. After the war, many remained to form gay and lesbian subcultures in large cities.

Donald Webster Cory published *The Homosexual in America* in 1951, in which he asserts that homosexuals constitute a minority deprived of rights. About this time, a new phase for gay and lesbian rights began. It was the "homophile" movement, led by such groups as the Mattachine Society, a group for men founded in Los Angeles by Harry Hay. The group began publishing a newsletter, *The Mattachine Review*. The Daughters of Bilitis, a group for women, was founded by Del Martin and Phyllis Lyon in San Francisco; it began publishing the newsletter, *The Ladder*. One Inc. of Los Angeles formed as a civil rights group for homosexuals and published *One*, one of the first openly homosexual-oriented magazines in the United States.

The first gay and lesbian student group was chartered at Columbia University in New York City in 1967. Named the Student Homophile League, it created quite a stir on campus and received a great deal of media coverage. The publicity quickly spurred the formation of similar groups at Cornell University, New York University, Massachusetts Institute of Technology, Stanford University, and elsewhere.

The incident generally credited with igniting the contemporary gay and lesbian movement occurred at a small gay bar, the Stonewall Inn, on Christopher Street in New York City's Greenwich Village, on June 28, 1969. In the early hours of that Saturday morning, eight officers from the Public Morals Section of the First Division of the New York City Police Department attempted to shut down the bar. The bar was frequented by gay street people, drag queens, students, and others. The officers entered the bar on the charge that the owners were selling alcohol without a license. This was a common tactic, for there were frequent police raids on gay bars in that city and others throughout the United States. Patrons usually accommodated the officials. This morning, however, was different. Feeling they had been mistreated long enough, the people in the bar fought back, flinging bottles and rocks at police on that night and on three successive nights.

The response by the Stonewall patrons did not occur in a vacuum but was reflective of other forces working within society at the time. The 1960's was a time of tumultuous social change; growing numbers of people began to challenge basic assumptions about authority and power. In communities and on college campuses, people joined in greater numbers than ever before to press for advances in the area of human and civil rights. People were challenging what they perceived as serious inequities in the distribution of resources, the dangerous and potentially irreversible attacks on the global environment, and most visibly, what was increasingly seen as an unwarranted and illegal U.S. incursion into Indochina.

By the mid-1970's, gay and lesbians had established themselves as a minority category, sharing many commonalities with other disenfranchised groups. Unlike other groups, who for some time had had an awareness of their past and a sense of community, the gay and lesbian minority was constructing a self-identity and experiencing, for the first time in recent history, a visible community.

Bibliography

Adam, Barry D. *The Rise of a Gay and Lesbian Movement.* Boston: Twayne, 1987. Comprehensive introduction to the gay and lesbian rights movement, from its origins in Germany at the end of the nineteenth century to its development as a modern international movement.

Blumenfeld, Warren, and Diane Raymond. *Looking at Gay and Lesbian Life.* 2d ed. Boston: Beacon Press, 1993. One-volume guide to major aspects of gay, lesbian, and bisexual life, including an overview of the political movement.

D'Emilio, John. *Sexual Politics, Sexual Communities: The Making of a Homosexual Minority in the United States, 1940-1970.* Chicago: University of Chicago Press, 1983. Analysis of the homophile movement in the United States within the larger historical context of the time.

Faderman, Lillian. *Odd Girls and Twilight Lovers: A History of Lesbian Life in Twentieth-Century America.* London: Penguin, 1991. Scholarly and fascinating study, drawn from a variety of sources.

Hutchins, Loraine, and Lani Kaahumanu, eds. *Bi Any Other Name: Bisexual People Speak Out.* Boston: Alyson, 1991. Covers the wide spectrum of the bisexual experience, from the forms and meanings of a bisexual community to the psychology and spirituality of bisexuality.

Marcus, Eric. *Making History: The Struggle for Gay and Lesbian Equal Rights, 1945-1990.* New York: Harper & Row, 1992. Oral history of the gay and lesbian movement since the 1940's, as told by its pioneers.

Warren J. Blumenfeld

Cross-References

Activist Politics, p. 7; Civil Disobedience, p. 285; Civil Rights Protection, p. 304; The Family and Politics in the United States, p. 649; Feminist Politics, p. 682; Gender Politics, p. 738; Grassroots Politics, p. 797; Human Rights and International Politics, p. 848; Political Correctness, p. 1441; Postmodernism, p. 1570; Protest Movements, p. 1621; Reproductive Politics, p. 1692; Woman Suffrage, p. 2141; Women in Politics, p. 2147.

GENDER POLITICS

Field of study: Politics

The politics of gender recognizes that there are differences in forms of political expression between men and women that are based, in part, on the gender roles for appropriate masculine and feminine behaviors that society defines and teaches its members.

Principal terms

GENDER: behaviors and cultural values society assigns to femininity and masculinity, which are defined differently over time; what is feminine is by definition not masculine

GENDER GAP: measurable difference in voting behavior between men and women voters

POLITICAL EFFICACY: person's belief that she or he can understand political issues, and that her or his actions can or do affect political policy-making

PRIVATE SPHERE: activities and concerns related to unpaid work done inside the home, the family, and sexuality

PUBLIC SPHERE: activities and concerns related to paid employment outside the home, governing, and politics

Overview

Traditionally, societies have divided the labor of society based on biological differences between the sexes and the gender roles that have been developed for their female and male members. Gender roles are based in part, but not entirely, on biological sex differences. Societies throughout the world, and particularly in the Western cultural world, have relegated women to feminine gender roles and work in the private sphere, and have excluded women formally and informally from the masculine gender roles associated with work in the public world and reserved for men. The gender construction of femininity that women are taught almost universally to aspire to emphasizes the qualities of emotional sensitivity and nurturance, passivity, weakness, and deference to the male; men are taught to aspire to a masculinity that idealizes the qualities of rationality, ambition, strength, and dominance over the female. Almost all societies have assigned a superior value to the masculine and an inferior value to the feminine. These gender role divisions result in differences between women's and men's life experiences in terms of their control over money and resources, and access to decision-making power.

Social and political scientists long have recognized that political behavior was influenced by race, class, occupation, and education. Since the 1970's, and after the revival of a feminist movement for equal rights got under way in the West, the impact of gender role expectations has also been considered a legitimate and important factor influencing all forms of political expression. It has been argued that women's political expression is more evident in nonconventional politics, that is, political participation in social movements, antistate protest movements, and even within the family, than in conventional electoral politics. Most studies comparing women's and men's political expression, however, have focused on identifying and quantifying the differences between women's and men's participation in conventional, electoral politics.

Based on studies of voting activity, political party activities, campaigning for political candidates or issues, or running for office, it appears that women participate less frequently than men do in electoral politics. In spite of criticisms by feminists who object to the assumption that levels of political participation by men should be the norm by which to judge women's levels of participation, comparing the levels of women's and men's participation has been a major area of interest and empirical, scientifically tested research in the study of gender politics. Differentials have been attributed to the effects of socialization of gender roles that occurs during childhood or adulthood. Modern Western societies have defined politics as part of the "man's world" that requires the masculine traits of aggressiveness, competitiveness, independence, and rational, autonomous decision making, and recognizes a certain level of corruption among its participants. These values are taught to both female and male members of society.

Women also have participated less frequently than men in electoral politics because of the situational constraints imposed by their roles as mothers and homemakers, which have kept them out of the paid workforce, made them responsible for the welfare of children, and limited their levels of interest in and energy for involvement in public issues and activities. Structural factors relating to the way that society is arranged to operate as an interrelated system have limited women's access to equal educational opportunities, equal wages, and professional opportunities, which also helps to explain different levels of women's and men's political participation. Studies of political behavior have shown that higher levels of education are causally related to higher levels of political participation. Therefore, if women's levels of education are generally lower than men's, it follows that their political participation will be lower, too.

In the United States, differences in women's and men's political participation at the level of mass electoral politics nearly disappeared after the 1970's. Occupation, education, and income were found to be the most influential factors determining behavior. Within the institution of government, women have held a large majority of the low-level, clerical and support positions, but involvement in elite politics, where political power is concentrated, has been dominated by men. This is true in the United States, and throughout the world. The persistence of a disproportionate number of men in elite politics as elected representatives, heads of state, and ministers, has likewise been explained as a result of the effects of gender role socialization, and situational and structural constraints on women. It also has been recognized that men have consciously sought to preserve their near-monopoly of elite political power; that is, this inequality has been attributed to sexism, whereby one sex seeks to economically exploit or socially dominate the other.

Studies have shown, however, that women have been reluctant to challenge that unequal power arrangement. Through measures designed to test political efficacy, women generally have rated themselves as less competent in their ability to understand and take action on political issues than men have. Gendered divisions of labor and social activities, and the hierarchical values assigned to those divisions, have perpetuated women's feelings of incompetence in areas that have been defined by society as male domains and have therefore discouraged participation. Social and political scientists note that in the past, when exceptional women have attained high positions of political power, they have exhibited "masculine" character traits of ambition, competitiveness, and rationality, to fit into the existing political order, rather than challenging or changing the political order.

Studies addressing the politics of gender also are concerned with determining the extent to which women who participate in electoral politics concentrate on women's issues and express a woman's point of view. Because of the gender roles society has defined for women and men, it has been assumed that women in politics would emphasize political issues associated with their roles in the private sphere, such as health, welfare, and child-care, and would avoid issues of economic policy, defense policy, and foreign relations. Health, welfare, and child-care policy require a regard for nurturance, which society defines as a feminine characteristic. Economic policy requires rational decision-making skills; defense policy requires aggressiveness in certain circumstances; foreign relations emphasizes the protection of national sovereignty and values autonomy—all characteristics that men are believed to possess in abundance.

There is evidence that this conscious gendered division of policy-making, and the belief in essential differences in women's and men's attitudes and public policy concerns, exist in working governments. For example, Marjorie Margolies-Mezvinsky, Democratic congresswoman from Pennsylvania, wrote about the shared commitment to women's issues and to bringing a woman's perspective to male issues through a uniquely feminine style of policy-advocacy in her chronicle of the experiences of the twenty-four freshmen congresswomen elected in 1992. Some feminist social and political scientists, however, argue that these gendered distinctions are socially imposed, that there is no essential woman's voice or man's voice, and that imposed distinctions perpetuate and sanction female-male inequalities.

Various assumptions related to gender role definitions have been circulated as popular knowledge: that a woman's political behavior is influenced by her father's or husband's politics; that women are more conservative, or more liberal, than men in their political attitudes; that women personalize politics by focusing on candidates' personalities rather than issues; that women are moralistic when it comes to policy-making; that women are apolitical by nature; or that women are politically superior to men and would enact wiser policies if they gained power. Studies of gender politics have tried to determine which, if any, of the assumptions about women's political behavior can be proved empirically.

Although the study of the politics of gender has most often considered questions related to women's political behavior, social and political scientists also have explored the ways in which the gender construct of masculinity has affected men's political expression. Grounding their studies in a feminist ideological commitment to challenge gender constructions that perpetuate sex-based inequalities, social and political scientists who study masculinity criticize assumptions about men and politics as well. It has been argued that gender expectations for men encourage violence and aggressiveness in defense and foreign policies, and promote militarization, that is, the glorification of the military spirit, to the point of extending it into the realm of civilian life. Male politicians and government leaders who do not display a certain aggressive toughness are not considered "real men," and therefore are not believed to be legitimate power holders.

Applications

In the United States, the politics of gender entered the popular social debate during the 1992 presidential election and during the subsequent presidency of Bill Clinton because of the measurable gender gap in the election results: Women voted for Clinton by an eight-point margin over men. This was attributed to Clinton's emphasis on health care and welfare issues during the presidential campaign, and to his stated commitment to include women in the governing political elite. The attention of the United States was further focused on gender politics because of the unprecedented political power that accrued to Clinton's wife, Hillary Rodham Clinton.

A Harvard-educated lawyer, she had worked outside the home throughout her married life and had been a partner in a Little Rock, Arkansas, law firm before her husband became president. After he was elected to office, the president appointed her to chair the President's Task Force on Health Care Reform. Political analysts and pundits, as well as the U.S. public, scrutinized every nuance of power and position assumed by the First Lady in a spirited national debate over the so-called "Hillary problem." The debate often devolved to the level of discussing whether or not Hillary Rodham Clinton had ever baked cookies for her husband and their daughter, Chelsea, or why she had waited until after the presidential election to officially resume using her maiden name, "Rodham," as well as her married name, "Clinton." The fundamental issue at the heart of the "Hillary problem," however, centered on the debate over the role of women in the public sphere.

With the appointment to lead the Health Care Task Force, Hillary Rodham Clinton took on a formal political responsibility and power unmatched by previous U.S. presidents' wives. She led the nation in developing a health care proposal that was the largest and most far-reaching piece of social legislation considered by Congress since the passage of the Social Security Act in 1935. In doing so, she overstepped U.S. society's gender role expectations for the First Lady, who traditionally had been responsible for ceremonial duties. In the ensuing social debate concerning a woman's right to have a visible and influential role in the public sphere, critics defined her as an overbearing interloper into the apex of elite politics in the United States, who neglected her husband's and daughter's needs in her overambitious lust for power. Her supporters, however, recognized that gender role expectations in U.S. society were in the process of transformation, and looked to her as a role model for women who were trying to integrate a public and private life. Women around the world who were trying to combine a meaningful family life with a satisfying work life outside the home empathized with Hillary Rodham Clinton's situation, which also focused men's attention on the workingwoman's situation. In 1993, in 59 percent of marriages in the United States, the wife worked outside the home; 21 percent of those working wives earned more money than their husbands did. These social changes have forced society to reconsider its most basic, but increasingly problematic, formulation concerning the separation of public and private spheres, and its expectations about gender roles.

Context

Gender distinctions regarding women's and men's participation in public political life have always existed in patriarchal societies. Although gender definitions of appropriate feminine and masculine behaviors change over time, distinctions generally have been used to exclude women from the public life and politics. Because of common gender definitions of women as irrational and overly sensitive, women were excluded by law from political participation and denied the right to vote until the early twentieth century in Western industrialized societies, and even later in unindustrialized countries around the world.

Nineteenth and twentieth century suffragists, campaigning to extend the right to vote to women, used gender definitions of femininity to argue that women's heightened moral sensibilities would allow them to bring compassion and wisdom to public policy-making. Contrary to the expectations of suffragists and antisuffragists, after women gained the right to vote, studies in the United States and Great Britain uncovered no demonstrable differences in women's and men's voting behavior, when women voted. Only about a third of the women eligible to vote in the first national election in the United States after women became eligible to vote, did so.

In the 1950's, social and political scientists began to study the effects of socialization on political behavior and to propose theories to explain women's low levels of political participation. Initially, those studies exhibited the gender biases of the scientists who conducted the studies, and who concluded, based on little or no empirical evidence, that women's low levels of political participation demonstrated that women were not as politically mature as men and were uninterested in politics. Since the 1970's, with the revival of a feminist movement in the West that has challenged gender biases in all academic fields, political participation data collected during the 1950's and 1960's has been re-examined and re-evaluated. As further studies on the political participation of women throughout the world have been conducted, hypotheses about the effects of gender expectations on women's and men's political expression have been tested, and new conclusions are being drawn.

Bibliography

Baxter, Sandra, and Marjorie Lansing. *Women and Politics: The Visible Majority*. Rev.

ed. Ann Arbor: University of Michigan Press, 1983. Chronicles the changes in women's political roles since 1952 and attributes increased political participation to changing social roles. Includes specific information on African American women's political participation.

Beckwith, Karen. *American Women and Political Participation: The Impacts of Work, Generation, and Feminism.* Westport, Conn.: Greenwood Press, 1986. Documents the impact of gender on women's mass political behavior using voting records from 1952 to 1976, and argues that significant differences in female and male political participation are evident only at elite levels.

Epstein, Cynthia Fuchs. *Deceptive Distinctions: Sex, Gender, and the Social Order.* New Haven, Conn.: Yale University Press, 1988. Epstein's chapter on "Women and the Political Process" argues that there are no fundamental differences in attitudes or behavior between women and men, and that gender distinctions only perpetuate men's privileged power and status.

Kimmel, Michael S., ed. "Researching Male Roles." *American Behavioral Scientist* 29 (May/June 1986). Entire issue is devoted to the state of research on the gender construct of masculinity and its effect on men's behavior.

Margolies-Mazvinsky, Marjorie. *A Woman's Place: The Freshman Women Who Changed the Face of Congress.* New York: Crown, 1994. Interviews with the women who were elected to the 103rd U.S. Congress in 1992, with Hillary Rodham Clinton, and with senior U.S. congresswomen, documenting their interest and activism on behalf of women's issues.

Peterson, V. Spike, and Anne Sisson Runyan. *Global Gender Issues.* Boulder, Colo.: Westview Press, 1993. Includes comparative information on women's political participation throughout the world and argues that gender roles have been used universally to perpetuate inequalities.

Randall, Vicky. *Women and Politics: An International Perspective.* 2d ed. Houndsmills, Basingstoke, Hampshire, England: Macmillan Education, 1987. Documents how public policies in countries throughout the world have significantly affected women's social and political status, which is almost universally lower than men's.

Rinehart, Sue Tolleson. *Gender Consciousness and Politics.* New York: Routledge, Chapman and Hall, 1992. Argues that gender consciousness can motivate women to become involved politically to promote women's issues as legitimate political issues and consequently to raise women's status.

Sapiro, Virginia. *The Political Integration of Women: Roles, Socialization, and Politics.* Urbana: University of Illinois Press, 1984. Argues that women have been only tolerated in politics, but that society's goal should be to integrate women into the public sphere and men into the private sphere.

Karen Garner

Cross-References

Equality and Egalitarianism, p. 630; The Family and Politics in the United States, p. 649; Feminist Politics, p. 682; Gay and Lesbian Politics, p. 732; Political Correctness, p. 1441; Political Participation, p. 1479; Political Representation in the United States, p. 1525; Reproductive Politics, p. 1692; Voting in History, p. 2116; Woman Suffrage, p. 2141; Women in Politics, p. 2147.

GENERAL WILL

Field of study: Political philosophy

The General Will is the concept that collective bodies, such as nations, have a will of their own that is independent of and superior to the individual wills of its citizens. By obeying this Will, people are able to attain true freedom and equality.

Principal terms

ARYAN MASTER RACE: doctrine that regards non-Jewish Caucasians as superior to all other races

CONCENTRATION CAMP: prison outside the normal criminal system for the persecution or execution of persons considered enemies of the government because of their race, religion, political beliefs, or sexual preferences

CONSTITUTIONAL DEMOCRACY: form of government in which the majority is limited by rights included in a codified or uncodified constitution, such as freedom of speech and religion

DICTATORSHIP OF THE PROLETARIAT: according to Marxist philosophy, the stage following a revolution that overthrows capitalism when a communist government comes to power and exercises dictatorial control in the name of the working class or proletariat

DIRECT OR PURE DEMOCRACY: system in which political decisions, including laws, are made by majority vote of the people

ORGANIC INTERDEPENDENCE: view that a citizen of a collective body such as a nation relates to that nation like the organs of the body relate to an individual: Each part is essential and dependent on all the others

REPRESENTATIVE GOVERNMENT: democratic system of government in which political decisions, including laws, are made by a small number of popularly elected representatives

WILL OF ALL: sum of the wills or wishes of individuals who have voted in their own selfish interest and constitute a majority; opposite of the General Will

Overview

The "General Will" is a concept that lies behind any considered examination of government and society, but it is not a term to be found in daily newspapers or conversations about politics. A narrow definition of this term simply recognizes that every political community is based on some sort of minimal agreement about why it was created, how its government should operate, and what its goals are. This basic consensus that holds its people together may be found in its constitution. Beyond this narrow agreement, most governmental decisions should be made by majority vote based on whatever motives those authorized to cast votes choose to follow; these votes may reflect a concern for their own individual advantage or for the welfare of the whole society. Either way, the resulting laws and actions are regarded as legal and proper. While it is not an essential element, the narrow definition is often associated with representative government rather than direct democracy.

Those who favor a broader version of the General Will say that, like people, collective bodies such as nations and their governments have a common Will or mind of their own. This Will operates on a level apart from, even superior to, the lives and wills of the individuals who are its building blocks. It reflects the undisputed common good, the highest public interest, what is best for everyone in the society. Those who obey its directives are thought to be truer to their real individual selves than when they seek their own personal benefit.

One thinker closely identified with the broader idea of the General Will is eighteenth century philosopher Jean-Jacques Rousseau. His *Social Contract* (1762) opposed the narrower definition he found in writings such as seventeenth century philosopher John Locke's *Second Treatise on Civil Government* (1690). Arguing against Locke, Rousseau said that the only government that is owed one's obedience is the government that reflects the General Will. This General Will is by definition moral and ethical: It is good for each individual and expresses a just balance between the needs of all individuals. It is general because it takes people away from enslavement and narrow self-interest, and leads people to think of the happiness of the whole. It is a will, since the choice to obey is a voluntary act.

The parts that voice and enforce the General Will are organically interdependent. People and the collective depend on each other as each individual person depends on the healthy operation of the organs of his or her body. Each member has a place, a role to play, and everyone is considered equal and important for the proper operation of the collective body. The result is the unity of all members in a harmonious community.

Rousseau makes a distinction between the General Will and what he calls the "will of all," the sum of the wills of those individuals who are thinking of their own good and not the welfare of the whole society. To him, the will of all is a false will that reflects enslavement to self-interest, while the General Will is authentic.

Rousseau believed the General Will emerges through a process of continuous consent both when making and obeying the law. It requires complete consensus after the most exhaustive discussion and criticism by completely informed citizens. All meet face-to-face in one place, so the size of the total community must be small. All come to each meeting called to determine the General Will on one or more issues without any prior idea of how they will vote, for to do so would defeat the General Will, which must emerge through full and spontaneous discussion. They are bound only by certain rules of procedure. For example, participants must have fully open minds on solutions and must be wholly informed on the facts of any issue that comes before them. In the meeting, all discussion must be public. The meeting continues until all are satisfied that the discussion was as complete as possible and the General Will has been found.

Rousseau implies that there is one, and only one, correct resolution for any problem, and all others are incorrect. He asserts that only those votes cast with the General Will, or the public interest, in mind are valid, but he is not clear on how many votes are required. The General Will may be expressed by the majority, in which case the minority vote is mistaken: The minority voted selfishly and the true will of everyone was expressed by the majority.

On the other hand, it might be that only a minority, or even one solitary person, voted with the General Will in mind, while all others voted their own selfish interests. Then the voice of the people that speaks for the General Will could be found in this smaller number, and less than a majority vote would express that Will. In any case, the General Will is never the same as the will of all, even if a majority: All particular and selfish votes must be subtracted from the total. Only the remaining votes can be considered to speak for the General Will. Once this calculation has been made, the General Will is then reflected in the majority vote.

The General Will cannot be limited by any law, because it is the source of all law. By definition, it can have no real interest contrary to that of the people who vote and act with it in mind. Therefore, Rousseau says it need give no guarantees to its subjects, no individual rights against the collective.

Since each member has agreed to obey the General Will, this also implies the right of the community to use force on those who violate the law. Rousseau asserted that that disobedient must be forced to be free by preventing them from doing as they wish. Since this merely helps them to obey their own real interest, in opposition to the selfish impulse that led them to break the law, force is not being used against their real will, which promised to obey, but against a false will. Freedom is found in restraint.

All citizens are equal in the fullest sense. As they participate in making the law, their views are treated as equally valid, and all are equal in being subject to obeying the law. All are treated equally when they are restrained from violating the law. Neither strength, nor wealth, nor any other attribute gives anyone an exemption from the requirements of citizenship.

Rousseau's democracy is organic. The individual is subordinated to the collective Will of the community and to the government it establishes. Certain details important to constitutional democracy are left unclear or even omitted in Rousseau's scheme, leading some to the conclusion that Rousseau was hostile to such a democracy. For example, simple majority rule is not clearly made an ironclad requirement, and individual and minority rights are not spelled out. It appears that anything that would run counter to the General Will would not be permitted, and this could include effective guarantees of such civil liberties as freedom of speech or the right to establish political parties.

Applications

The operation of the General Will, bound only by procedure as it seeks to make decisions, resembles a jury deliberating during a criminal trial. When such juries operate at their best, they too are unbiased when they begin their deliberations and work to reach consensus decisions after complete discussion by completely informed members.

The equality Rousseau advocated was political, but it has an economic side as well. He says that for the true General Will to be discovered, the few rich must be prevented from using their wealth to gain illegitimate power by trying to buy, or use economic power to influence, votes. This belief has been shared by those who favor elections and government decision making based on the real views of the voters or their representatives on the issues involved, rather than on "the best outcome that money can buy." In the twentieth century, this has led to calls to reform campaign finance laws and limit or abolish gifts and other favors for members of the government by interest groups in order to lessen the influence of money in the political process as much as possible.

Rousseau also prescribed citizen service rather than taxation to pay for public works. He felt it was better for all citizens to work on the roads for some part of each year rather than to pay taxes for a few government workers to do this full-time. He thought public service by all would make citizens aware of their community responsibilities and the social issues of the day, as well as keeping the execution of the General Will close to those who will it. Numerous governments around the world, such as the political arm of the San Blas Kuna people of Panama and the rulers of mainland China, have enlisted their citizens in public works projects such as road building, not only because it is a less expensive source of labor than full-time government workers might afford, but also to promote public awareness of and a sense of responsibility for socially needed projects.

If Rousseau was a collectivist in his strong advocacy of the General Will and his opposition to individuals or groups that might challenge it and divide the community, he was too incomplete or ambiguous about particular details to be considered a proponent of totalitarian dictatorship. For example, he was unclear about how much of society should be included under the authority of the General Will: Was it to cover every aspect or just some parts? Nevertheless, Rousseau's idea of the General Will contributed to what developed into actual totalitarianism in the nineteenth and twentieth centuries. This contribution began with Rousseau's idea that people must first consent to surrender all their rights to the General Will. When the government enforces the General Will, it cannot be mistaken. This opens the door to one of the essential aspects of totalitarianism, total control over all areas of life by an unlimited government that can do no wrong.

Such a government, through its leadership, promises the utopian goal of full human equality and perfectibility. It seeks this through action that only requires people to follow orders. One or a few leaders best express the General Will, representing in themselves the ideals of all the people. Often there is a personality cult around a leadership that is immune to accountability for its actions, or even to criticism. Typically, the leaders govern through a single political party that rules supreme because it alone speaks for the public interest. The mass of people have no legal or political rights against the government and do not participate in decision making, but are merely bound to obey.

Historically, ideals eventually fade away and all that is left is a surviving totalitarian system. The leadership cult, that supreme political party, and nonparticipation by the masses are all aspects that run counter to Rousseau's ideas, leading to the conclusion that he was not a philosopher of totalitarianism. Still, there are features of his doctrine, such as an unlimited General Will, that open the door to its excesses.

The nineteenth century philosopher Karl Marx introduced the ultimately anarchistic version of the General Will. He agreed with Rousseau that by nature people are made for organic community. Marx held the opinion that only by throwing off corrupt capitalism and creating communism, a community of equals who function without needing government, can people fully realize their true human potential. In such a community, all can work voluntarily and cooperatively to seek the goal of the General Will, the fullest development of all humans. In outlining the transition from capitalism to communism, Marx introduced the idea of the dictatorship of the proletariat, where the leaders of government must be absolute dictators in the name of the people until the final goal of communism is achieved.

Two of Marx's followers were Vladimir Ilich Lenin, who led the Russian Revolution in 1917 and introduced Soviet rule to that country, and Mao Tse-tung, who led a successful Marxist revolution in China in 1949. They both established governments that were called communist, because they said that Marx's version of communism was their ultimate goal. In practice, these governments were firmly totalitarian, using Marx's reasoning that a harsh dictatorship of the proletariat, directed by the leadership of the communist party, was necessary and in the real interest of the General Will, which was unalterably dedicated to achieving communism. The party was composed of those who knew the true will of the people, and they would lead everyone to the future. The use of lies, deception, and secret police terror was just a temporary necessity until communism was realized.

Another version of the General Will as applied to twentieth century totalitarianism is embodied in the views of Adolf Hitler, Nazi party leader and absolute dictator of Germany from 1933 to 1945. Hitler claimed that he had the right to rule because he could divine the real Will of the German people. What the people wanted him to do, he said, was take full responsibility for leading the German nation, using the Nazi Party and government elite to secure the Aryan master race in power over the world, while enslaving all other, inferior races. His tactics included lying, propaganda, outlawing any criticism of the government, and the establishment of a police state, including the use of concentration camps where the murder of millions was justified by his pursuit of the General Will.

Context

Rousseau's General Will was his key to the operation of direct or pure democracy based on popular sovereignty, which places final political power in the hands of all the people. He assumed that citizens have a right to control their destiny and can make the necessary moral judgments and practical decisions in their daily life. The General Will as process can be seen as a continuing search for truth in the sense of seeking improved ways to build more democratic social institutions.

Consistent with these aims, Rousseau advocated a process that enables each individual to achieve the highest level of self-development, the greatest degree of freedom and equality, all placed within a system in which they will cooperate to secure the best possible community for all. In Rousseau's democratic project, everyone, even the most ordinary, uneducated human, was given a new dignity. He assumed that given the right social and geographic conditions, each person could make a valuable contribution to the community. This helped shift the burden of proof so that today anyone who favors, say, appointed rather than elected judges, must demonstrate why such inequality is in the public interest.

The General Will has continued to be a standard by which the progress of democracy can be measured. The danger lies in its capacity to serve as a vehicle for totalitarian dictatorship.

Bibliography

Darby, Tom. *The Feast: Meditations on Politics and Time.* Toronto: University of Toronto Press, 1982. Traces Rousseau's view of history and the General Will through a number of later philosophers.

Dodge, Guy Howard, ed. *Jean-Jacques Rousseau: Authoritarian Libertarian?* Lexington, Mass.: D. C. Heath, 1971. Essays by a number of experts seeking to evaluate Rousseau's contributions, often focusing on the controversy over the meaning of the General Will.

Levine, Andrew. *The End of the State.* London: Verso, 1987. Relates Rousseau's idea of the General Will to the political thought of Marx.

Melzer, Arthur. *The Natural Goodness of Man: On the System of Rousseau's Thought.* Chicago: University of Chicago Press, 1990. Links the General Will to Rousseau's positive view of human nature and shows how it leads to authoritarian, but not totalitarian, results.

Riley, Patrick. *The General Will Before Rousseau: The Transformation of the Divine into the Civic.* Princeton, N.J.: Princeton University Press, 1986. Discusses what the term "General Will" meant to various religious and secular writers, particularly those who wrote in the century before Rousseau.

Talmon, J. L. *The Origins of Totalitarian Democracy.* New York: Praeger, 1960. Examines how the ideals of the eighteenth century were transformed into totalitarianism of the twentieth century.

Donald G. Tannenbaum

Cross-References

Anarchism in Marxist Thought, p. 72; Autocracy and Absolutism, p. 127; Chinese

Communism, p. 223; Civil Rights and Liberties, p. 298; Constitutional Governments, p. 432; Cult of Personality, p. 477; Dictatorships, p. 546; Fascism and Nazism, p. 656; Idealism, p. 855; Legitimacy, p. 1105; Locke's Political Philosophy, p. 1142; Marxism-Leninism, p. 1155; Public Opinion Polling, p. 1627; Rousseau's Political Philosophy, p. 1756; Russian Political History, p. 1770; The Social Contract, p. 1827; Totalitarianism, p. 1987; Utopianism, p. 2084; Voting Behavior in the United States, p. 2109.

GENOCIDE

Field of study: History of government and politics

Genocide is premeditated, state-directed, mass murder of racial, ethnic, religious, or national groups. Although genocidal killings have occurred throughout recorded history, the scale of mass murder in the twentieth century is without historical parallel.

Principal terms

AUTOGENOCIDE: state-sponsored political mass murder in a country, directed against its own population

ECOCIDE: planned destruction of the environment

ETHNOCIDE: destruction of the cultures of minorities

GENOCIDE CONVENTION: United Nations' resolution in 1948 on the prevention and punishment of genocide

HOLOCAUST: systematic mass murder of European Jews by the Nazis during World War II

NUREMBERG TRIALS: trial of major Nazi war criminals after 1945

OMNICIDE: potential total destruction of humankind as a result of a general nuclear war

Overview

The word "genocide," from the Greek *genos* (race) and the Latin *cite* (killing) means the killing of a race or tribe. In contrast to general mass violence, genocide is state-supported annihilation of a specific group, either within or outside of a country. The term was first defined during World War II by Raphael Lemkin, a Polish legal scholar. Lemkin also was partially responsible for the passage of the United Nations Genocide Convention on December 9, 1948. This convention defined violent organized attacks on national, racial, ethnic, and religious groups, whether carried out in war or peacetime, as international crimes.

Evidence of genocide can be found as early as the beginning of civilization in the ancient Near East. This region witnessed numerous conflicts between city-states and empires, often involving competition over fertile land and trade routes. These clashes frequently produced genocidal massacres and mass deportations of the noncombatants and vanquished soldiers. Genocidal terror was also used to intimidate the defeated population and to prevent any future opposition.

The most notorious ancient, state-organized mass murder was practiced by the Assyrians, who gained a reputation as brutal conquerors. In establishing a massive empire between 1000 and 665 B.C.E., they used terror annually to intimidate enemies and deter future opponents. The Assyrians also dispersed entire populations, such as the inhabitants of the kingdom of Israel. At times, ancient cultures disappeared completely after conquest. For example, the Hittite empire in Asia Minor was swept away after 1200 B.C.E. by new invaders. Not until the nineteenth century did archaeologists rediscover the history and culture of these ancient people. The ancient city of Carthage, which was located near modern Tunis in North Africa, suffered a similar fate. After a prolonged conflict between Rome and Carthage (the Punic Wars), the Romans in 146 B.C.E. ordered the destruction of Carthage and symbolically plowed its land with salt.

The ancient pattern of genocidal massacres organized by conquerors continued to be practiced by a succession of leaders. From Genghis Kahn, the thirteenth century leader of the Mongol Empire, to Shaku Zulu, a nineteenth century Zulu king in southern Africa, organized brutal terror was used against targeted groups who stood in the way of imperial ambitions. As Europeans expanded abroad and established colonies in Africa, the Americas, and Asia, indigenous peoples, ranging from Tasmanians to Native Americans, were decimated by disease and exploitation. The destruction of the Hereros (1904) in German South-West Africa illustrates how local military leaders brutally crushed native rebellions and even attempted, at times, to exterminate the colonial population.

Ecocide, the planned destruction of the environment, often resulted in ethnocide, the destruction of native cultures. Ethnocide was practiced not only by the European colonialists but also by the Chinese in Tibet and the Indonesians in East Timor in the twentieth century. Although most of the imperialistic genocides were directed by absolutist governments, democracies were also responsible for ethnocide. During the Trail of Tears, 1838-1839, the United States government forced the Cherokee to leave their cultural homelands in Appalachia and march to Oklahoma, causing massive numbers of deaths.

The impact and pervasiveness of genocides increased dramatically in modern times with the rise of the nation-state. Most modern instances of genocide have been carried out by nation-states. Both the process of creating nation-states and the inability of many nation-states to tolerate ethnic subcultures add new dimensions to historic genocide. In the nation-state, the government defines the victims, whether they represent a real threat or just a convenient scapegoat. Victims may be selected because they belong to a specific race or class, not because they resisted a conqueror or a colonialist. By the late nineteenth century, technological advances in communication and transportation, together with the powers of modern government, greatly extended the potential scope of genocides.

Although most ideological and ethnic genocides are products of the twentieth century, religious genocidal massacres occurred during the Middle Ages. Christian Crusaders murdered Muslims in Jerusalem, and Christian heretics in southern France were exterminated during the Albigensian Crusade in the thirteenth century. Witch hunts in early modern Europe and in the British colonies of North America also represent early models for future scapegoat persecution. In the twentieth century, organized ideological genocide carried out by nation-states has become a reality. Genocides claimed over sixty million victims during the first nine decades of the twentieth century.

Before the twentieth century, usually cities were annihilated, not races, classes, and groups. Furthermore, twentieth century organized mass murders were not always a product of war or conquest. Frequently governments used genocide for political and social restructuring, targeting internal, not external, victims. Particularly after decolonization, genocide was used during power struggles in new multicultural nation-states. African and Asian religious and ethnic minorities became targets after 1960. In Nigeria, for example, the Christian Ibo, who attempted to establish an independent Biafra, faced the wrath of the Muslim Hausa and Fulani people. Between 1966 and 1970, at least one million Ibo perished.

Twentieth century genocidal massacres ranged from the murder of Armenians and Jews to the destruction of class enemies by Joseph Stalin and Cambodian communists. In terms of total victims, the numbers of these genocides vary from at least one hundred thousand to the more than ten million of the autogenocide initiated by the Soviet Union in the Ukraine in the 1930's. The largest mass murder of any single ethnic or religious group was the annihilation of six million European Jews by the Nazis. At least one million and perhaps as many as three million people were victims of genocide, in each case, in Armenia, Nigeria, Bangladesh, and Cambodia.

All genocidal governments have created special murder bureaus and techniques, ranging from Idi Amin's Ugandan murder squads to Heinrich Himmler's SS (*Schutzstaffel*) in Nazi Germany. Larger groups in society have also been used during modern genocides. Turks relied on Kurds, Indonesians and Cambodian communists used peasants, and the Nazis relied on German rail personnel and other bureaucrats to carry out their murderous policies. Unlike the ancient Assyrians, most modern governments responsible for genocide publicly denied or attempted to hide mass murder from the world.

Between 1915 and 1945, genocide was most prevalent in Europe, but after 1960 most of the killing took place in newly independent countries in Africa and Asia. Beginning in 1990, after the disintegration of communism in both Eastern Europe and the Soviet Union, the specter of ethnic genocidal massacres returned to Europe in the Balkans and in Armenia and Azerbaijan.

Applications

The two most notorious twentieth century examples of the almost total annihilation of ethnic or religious minorities occurred during World Wars I and II. Between 1915 and 1917, more than one million Armenians died because of Turkish policies, and between 1941 and 1945, six million Jews were murdered by Nazi officials. These genocides were premeditated and organized by the Ottoman and Nazi governments. In each case, specific groups were selected for destruction during a major war, thus eliminating outside interference. In Nazi Germany and the Ottoman Empire, the Jews and Armenians had been singled out as aliens long before the massacres occurred. The Germans and the Turks reacted to national crises by producing dynamic, xenophobic movements that used ideological scapegoats for their political purposes.

The Armenians, a Christian minority in the Ottoman Empire, had suffered discrimination, and, on occasion, massacres between 1894 and 1909. Ineffective attempts by Western powers to protect the Armenians only resulted in increased harassment of the Armenian minority by a growing Turkish nationalistic movement, the Young Turks. The Young Turk movement gained control of the government and entered World War I on Germany's side in 1914. In April, 1915, Armenian leaders in Constantinople were deported and murdered. The following month, the Ottoman minister of interior, Talaat Pasha, accused Armenians of collaboration with the Russian enemy. At first, the religious and political Armenian elites were murdered. Then 200,000 Armenians serving in army construction units were killed. Finally, death marches were organized for the Armenian women and children, resulting in the death of more than half of the deportees. Although estimates vary greatly, between 50 and 70 percent of the Ottoman Empire's two to three million Armenians perished. The survivors lost their homelands and property.

The Jewish Holocaust between 1941 and 1945 was even more comprehensive than the Armenian genocide. In the Ottoman Empire, some Armenian medical officers were still permitted to serve in the Turkish army during World War I, but because of Nazi ideology, all Jews were potential victims. Between 1933 and 1938, the Nazi government introduced a number of laws that discriminated against Jews and targeted them as aliens. Typical of this process were the Nuremberg Laws, which stripped Jews of German political and civil rights. Before the invasion of Poland in September, 1939, Adolf Hitler had reminded his commanders that no one remembered the Armenian catastrophe. After the invasion, plans were introduced to deport the Jews from Germany, resulting eventually in the creation of massive ghettoes in Eastern Europe. Almost 10 percent of all Holocaust victims perished in these camps. Accompanying the German troops that invaded the Soviet Union in June, 1941, were special SS murder squads (*Einsatzgruppen*), who eventually killed over one million Jews in Eastern Europe. By July, 1941, Hitler apparently gave orders to Heinrich Himmler, the leader of the SS, to prepare a "final solution" for European Jews. At a conference in Berlin on January 20, 1942, plans for the elimination of the Jews were finalized.

The process evolved from mass shootings to mobile gas trucks to permanent extermination camps in Auschwitz-Birkenau and other towns. By the spring of 1943, three-fourths of all Holocaust victims had already been murdered. The Nazi leaders planned to eliminate not only German Jews, but all Jews in Eurasia. Although special SS units controlled much of the killing apparatus, German rail employees and army and bureaucratic officials also cooperated. By 1945, the Nazis had murdered two-thirds of all European Jews. The Nazi government also was responsible for the mass murder of 40 percent of Europe's Gypsies and the euthanasia of one hundred thousand Germans afflicted with physical or mental handicaps. Millions of Slavs and others deemed racially inferior were murdered also.

The two most obvious cases of autogenocide based on an ideology that created class victims occurred in the Soviet Union in the 1930's and in Cambodia between 1975 and 1979. Joseph Stalin, the Soviet dictator, ordered the collectivization of private farms in the Ukraine, resulting in mass famine that killed at least ten million people. While millions of peasants were starving to death, Stalin ordered the export of grain from the Ukraine. Similar social and political engineering took place in Cambodia under the leadership of the communist Khmer Rouge between 1975 and 1979. The Pol Pot regime targeted the urban population, political opponents, religious groups, and the ethnic Cham people, an Islamic minority. These people were forced into labor camps or murdered outright. One-third of the Cambodian population of six million people perished as a result of these government policies.

Context

After 1945, the victorious Allies tried and punished select groups of German and Japanese war criminals for crimes against humanity. Article 4 of the United Nations Genocide Convention established the principle of punishment for perpetrators. No immunity was to be granted to those accused of genocide. The culprits could be tried by the state in which the atrocities occurred or before an international tribunal. Unfortunately, no party has ever submitted a conflict to the International Court of Justice. No Turkish leader responsible for the Armenian massacres was ever officially punished, although three were assassinated after 1918. In 1979, a United Nations Human Rights Commission accused the Pol Pot regime in Cambodia of genocide, but the Cambodian communists were not brought to justice. An attempt in the United Nations to condemn China for its policies of ethnocide in Tibet also failed.

The U.N. Genocide Convention failed to include political genocide in its definition. As a result, autogenocide directed against a nation's own population is not covered adequately by the convention. Nor was the murder of homosexuals by the Nazis covered by the U.N. Convention. A United Nations' study on genocide in 1985 suggested the official U.N. Genocide Convention be extended to include political murder, autogenocide, and ecocide, but was not adopted. The United Nations failed not only to deter genocides or punish the perpetrators, but also to achieve control over the potential danger of omnicide through total nuclear self-destruction during the Cold War era.

On February 19, 1985, the United States Senate finally ratified the U.N. Convention on Genocide. In 1993, the Holocaust Museum was opened in Washington, D.C., as a permanent reminder of man's inhumanity to man. The U.S. Congress passed a resolution on April 19, 1994, commemorating the mass murder of Armenians by the Turks during World War I.

A number of private initiatives have produced international organizations to monitor genocides. In 1982, an international conference on genocide and the Holocaust met in Tel Aviv. Both the Jewish Holocaust and the Armenian genocide were addressed. As a result of that conference, the Institute of the International Conference on the Holocaust and Genocide was created in Jerusalem, Israel. In 1985, International Alert was established in London to direct worldwide pressure against genocides. Nevertheless, in 1994, Tutsi and Hutu ethnic groups in Rwanda continued to kill each other, as did Serbs, Croats, and Muslims in Bosnia-Herzegovina.

Bibliography

Boyajian, Dickran H. *Armenia: The Case for a Forgotten Genocide*. Westwood, N.J.: Educational Book Crafters, 1972. Spirited argument that Turkish actions against Armenians in World War I represented a prototype of the Nazi mass murder of Jews. Includes over six hundred official documents that illustrate Turkish policies.

Chalk, Frank, and Kurt Jonassohn. *The History and Sociology of Genocide: Analyses and Case Studies*. New Haven, Conn.: Yale University Press, 1990. Convenient, scholarly single-volume introduction to the issue of genocide in a historical and sociological context.

Charny, Israel W., ed. *Genocide: A Critical Bibliographical Review*. New York: Facts on File, 1988. Indispensable collection of essays on sociological, historical, and specific case studies on genocide. Each article includes a valuable annotated bibliography.

Fein, Helen. *Accounting for Genocide: National Responses and Jewish Victimization During the Holocaust*. Chicago: University of Chicago Press, 1979. Sociological survey of forces that limited or advanced the Holocaust, and an examination of Jewish responses to Nazi policies in Warsaw, Hungary, and The Netherlands. Includes a valuable bibliography of literature on the Holocaust in all European countries.

Harff, Barbara. *Genocide and Human Rights: International Legal and Political Issues*. Denver: University of Denver, 1984. Short theoretical work attempts to establish a workable legal definition of genocide and human rights violations that would permit international intervention.

Horowitz, Irving Louis. *Genocide: State Power and Mass Murder*. New Brunswick, N.J.: Transaction Books, 1976. Brief thematic monograph argues that genocide, unlike mass murder, is not sporadic and can only occur with the approval of the state apparatus.

Katz, Steven T. *The Holocaust and Mass Death Before the Modern Age*. Vol. 1 in *The Holocaust in Historical Context*. New York: Oxford University Press, 1994. This thoroughly documented study of mass murder from antiquity to early modern times is the first of a projected three-volume study that argues that the Holocaust was a unique event, different from other mass murders.

Kuper, Leo. *Genocide: Its Political Use in the Twentieth Century*. New Haven, Conn.: Yale University Press, 1981. Describes major twentieth century genocides and classifies them according to specific categories, ranging from ethnic and racial struggles to the mass murder of political groups.

Lifton, Robert Jay, and Eric Markusen. *The Genocidal Mentality: Nazi Holocaust and Nuclear Threat*. New York: Basic Books, 1990. Collaborative work by a psychologist and a sociologist examines Nazi behavior during the Holocaust in order to evaluate the impact of psychic numbing on American and Russian nuclear policymakers.

Wallimann, Isidor, and Michael N. Dobkowski, eds. *Genocide and the Modern Age: Etiology and Case Studies of Mass Deaths*. Westport, Conn.: Greenwood Press,

1987. Valuable collection of essays dealing with genocide in general and with several specific case studies. The notes are helpful for further research.

Johnpeter Horst Grill

Cross-References

Civil Wars, p. 325; Demagoguery, p. 507; Dictatorships, p. 546; Empires and Empire Building, p. 597; Fascism and Nazism, p. 656; Human Rights and International Politics, p. 848; Independence Movements and Transitions, p. 896; Indigenous Peoples' Governments, p. 903; Police States, p. 1408; Political Violence, p. 1539; Race and Ethnicity, p. 1654; Secessionism, p. 1790; Social Darwinism, p. 1833; Totalitarianism, p. 1987; World Political Organization, p. 2186.

GEOPOLITICS

Field of study: International government and politics

Geopolitics is a branch of political geography that combines the study of geographical features with other social sciences in order to identify patterns of global political power and conflict.

Principal terms

MANIFEST DESTINY: notion that westward expansion of the United States is inevitable; a prototype of geopolitical thinking

ORGANIC THEORY OF THE STATE: idea, developed mainly by Germans, that the state is a living organism with an inherent need to grow and expand

RAISON D'ÉTAT: fundamental principle of geopolitics that divorces politics from ethics in matters concerning the welfare of the state, leading to the conclusion that ends justify means

SOCIAL DARWINISM: theory primarily associated with Herbert Spencer that regards human society as an environment within which a ceaseless struggle is waged among social components, including states, with only the strongest surviving

Overview

At the beginning of the twentieth century, Europe was at the zenith of its power and influence. A peninsula on the land mass of Asia, called a continent by virtue of its economic, political, and cultural importance, it controlled much of the world and its resources. Two nations, in turn, were leaders in Europe; they were Great Britain and Germany. A relatively small island, Britain ruled an empire on which the sun never set. Newly united Germany, which had been a weak conglomeration of states, had quickly become the most powerful continental nation, whose industrial production surpassed Britain's and rivaled that of the United States. The United States too was a great power. Over the past century, in a policy called "Manifest Destiny," it had expanded from ocean to ocean and from north to south to what it considered its "natural boundaries." It had concluded a successful war with Spain, which made the young republic a colonial power.

The time was also a period of great faith in science, including the social sciences. Social scientists worked on offering explanations for this concentration of power and influence. As is customary in all the sciences, they sought to find general patterns in the specifics of history that might be considered laws. The potential of human societies was more or less uniform, they reasoned, so the answer to the question of why some societies grow strong and others weak must be geographic. Geographic elements to be considered fell into three broad categories: geographic configurations, such as the layout of land masses and the accessibility of waterways, climate and climatic variations, and access to economic resources such as fertile lands, forests, minerals, and fuels.

Political geography, a respectable field of academic study that established the relationship between the geographic and the political, was superseded. It did not incorporate ideas such as the organic theory of the state—important to the Germans—or the lack of ethical scruples of which Germans, the British, and Americans alike were guilty. Social Darwinism, which for many explained the discrepancy between the rich and poor in human society as well as among the nations of the world, also was beyond political geography's intellectual borders. A new direction in political analysis was needed. Swedish political scientist Johan Rudolf Kjellen coined the term "geopolitics" in 1916, creating thereby a new academic discipline as well.

What geopolitics attempts to do is establish a spatial relationship in international politics. Geopolitics studies patterns of international power, both political and military, based on geographic factors. Other social sciences, such as history, political science, and economics, are also involved in geopolitical studies. Individual states are components, and it is the structures they make in combination that is the chief interest of geopolitical investigation.

Applications

The discipline of geopolitics may be used as a framework for examining three theories that emerged before the outbreak of World War I in 1914. The theories are: Manifest Destiny, the Mahan theory of naval supremacy, and the Mackinder-Haushofer theory of the world island.

Manifest Destiny, which may be said to have propelled a small maritime power along the Atlantic Coast into a powerful nation-state in the span of a century, was completed before the discipline of geopolitics was established. This American idea, because of its international ramifications, contained all the elements of geopolitical development. In 1804, President Thomas Jefferson concluded that the Louisiana Purchase with Napoleonic France not only gave the young republic vast lands to the west but also control of the Mississippi River from its tributaries to its outlet. Control of this huge natural drainage and transport system also gave the nation a natural center, which political geographers generally consider essential to any strong state.

Placing Manifest Destiny in a greater global perspective came in 1823 through the Monroe Doctrine, in which President James Monroe declared that any attempt by a foreign power to extend its influence in the Americas could be regarded by the United States as constituting a danger to the peace of the whole of the Western Hemisphere. Later, the young republic used political and military muscle in its settlement of the Oregon territory dispute with Great Britain in 1846; the same assertiveness was demonstrated again that year in a war with Mexico that resulted in large acquisitions of territory. Manifest Destiny ethos (or excuse) came into play again in 1898, with a short and successful war against Spain. Not only had the United States expanded to its natural boundaries and staked out its position as the policeman of the Western Hemisphere, but it was recognized as a formidable international power as well. Even though the political philosophy that the United States professed to have was too rational to admit to the metaphoric concept of an "organic state," and much less to explicitly endorse the amorality of *raison d'état* or Machiavellism, the idea that the new state must grow and expand was widely and enthusiastically supported.

One of the most successful battles of the Spanish-American War was the naval battle of Manila Bay on May 1, 1898, which effectively destroyed Spanish power in the Pacific. The newly powerful U.S. Navy had been brought into form by the energetic undersecretary of the Navy, Theodore Roosevelt, who became president in 1901. Roosevelt's views on the importance of a Navy were strongly influenced by a book by an American naval historian, Alfred Thayer Mahan. Mahan's message is clear: The state that controls the seas controls its own fate. Those states that lacked naval mastery were condemned to defeat or secondary status. The sea was the "great highway" of international communication. Free access and unimpeded usage were essential to national growth and even survival. Mahan's views reflected those of the British, long the dominant sea power. They were seized upon with alacrity by the German emperor, William II, who claimed he had not read but had rather devoured Mahan's book and hoped to commit it to memory. He ordered a copy for every German naval vessel. Mahan's thesis, one of the most enduring geopolitical theories, was probably more than any other factor the catalyst for the fierce naval arms race between Great Britain and imperial Germany in the years before the World War I. The ill feelings engendered led to the formation of the rigid alliances that finally erupted into war.

In the postwar era, the defeated Germans were replaced as a naval power by the Japanese, who had demonstrated their naval prowess in a war with Russia that ended in 1904. Japanese naval buildup continued in the 1920's and 1930's to the increased concern of U.S. president Franklin D. Roosevelt, also a Mahan disciple. Mahan's dictum that world power requires sea power was dramatically acted upon when the Japanese attacked the U.S. naval base at Pearl Harbor in 1941. Although the role of navies in the period after World War II has been altered by factors such as the airplane and the submarine, Mahan's thesis continues to be important. Control of the world's oceans and seas, especially its shipping lanes, remains a source of geopolitical tension.

If for Mahan naval power was the key to success in international politics, the key for Sir Halford John Mackinder, a British geographer, was control of a strategic land mass he called the "world island." Mackinder's monograph on the subject appeared in 1904. He is often considered to be the real founder of the discipline of geopolitics. Mackinder's "world island" or "heartland" was a huge land mass on the northern periphery of the Asian continent, including almost all of present-day Russia, extending south to include oil-rich Mesopotamia and northern India, and north to include most of present-day China.

Viewed on a conventional world map, Mackinder's island or heartland seems meaningless. Viewed, however, from a projection centered on the North Pole, the area does indeed become a "heartland" surrounded by the great land masses and centers of population of the northern hemisphere. Around this heartland, also called the "pivot area," Mackinder establishes two concentric zones that serve the dual purpose of expansion and defense. The inner crescent is partially continental and partially oceanic, and the outer crescent is wholly oceanic. Mackinder maintains that whatever power controls the heartland controls the world. Some of the reasons for this hypothesis are unlimited natural resources, including the rich farmlands of the Russian steppes and the oil of the Middle East, natural defenses that include the Himalaya mountains and the Gobi and Arabian deserts, ease of communication, room for military maneuvering, and room for population growth. Mackinder refers to the occupants of the areas as "tenants" and insists the area should remain under the control of the world's democracies.

Mackinder failed to gain recognition in his native Great Britain, but his theory was received with enthusiasm by many Germans, especially after their humiliating defeat in 1918 and their attempts to reestablish themselves on the world stage. Mackinder's most enthusiastic disciples in Germany were the Germanophilic Swedish political scientist Kjellen, who coined the term "geopolitics," and Karl Haushofer, who founded the Institute for Geopolitics in Munich. Haushofer declared Mackinder's 1904 article to be the greatest ever written. Both Kjellen and Haushofer subscribed to the organic theory of the state, which argues that the state must either grow or die and that the theory that only the strongest, best-organized states will survive is true.

The Germans had a long history of looking to the east, and much German territory had been wrested from the Slavs. Haushofer felt that using Mackinder's theory, the Germans and the Russians could work together to play out Mackinder's theory and that what Germany had failed to accomplish on the seas could now be done on land. Haushofer's theories attracted the attention of the Nazi hierarchy then gaining ascendancy in Germany. After their seizure of power in 1933 the Institute for Geopolitics became identified with the policies of the Nazi state.

Between 1939 and 1941, with comparative ease, the Nazis established one of the largest empires in the history of Europe. In 1941 they moved against Russia and for a time it seemed as if Mackinder's theory and Haushofer's expectations would become reality. Possibly, had the Nazis treated their conquered subjects more humanely, history might have been quite different. Their brutal tactics, however, engendered fierce opposition in what was to become, for the Russians, the great patriotic war. Finally, after millions had died, it proved to be Russia that overwhelmed and almost destroyed Germany, not the other way around. A despondent Haushofer committed suicide in 1946.

Mackinder's theory, however, remained alive. The Russians incorporated into their state territories (taken from the Poles and Germans) that had been part of Mackinder's heartland. They continued their penetration of the Middle East, especially Iran. Then, in what looked like the ultimate realization of Mackinder's thesis, they formed an alliance with the newly established communist state of China. The alliance triggered a response in the West, especially the United States, and was a major factor in instituting the Cold War. What Nazi brutality had accomplished in Russia, the five-thousand-year-old Chinese cultural tradition accomplished in the East. The tug of nationalism, which has often frustrated geopolitical development, proved strong.

The Chinese and Russians drifted apart into mutually suspicious camps.

Mackinder's theory of the power of the world island was once realized in the thirteenth century by the Mongols. It has yet to be successfully resurrected in modern times. But the possibility of such a consolidation of power remains.

Context

From a comparatively modest beginning, geopolitics as a discipline became hugely popular during and after World War I. Its association with Nazi ideology spelled disaster for geopolitics as a legitimate academic pursuit, especially when brutal excesses of the Nazi terror, such as the extermination of populations to create "living space," were justified as part of geopolitical policy.

With time, however, geopolitics has been gaining respectability. The limitations and restrictions geography once imposed in many cases are no longer relevant. There is less emphasis on power politics, on confrontation and the costly excess of war, and on monopoly and selfish exploitation of natural resources. There is more emphasis on mutual respect, cooperation, and the equitable distribution of natural resources. The world is increasingly being regarded as a finite entity, the elements of which are mutually interdependent. Arguments for the existence of great powers, long favored by geopoliticians, are being replaced by models for smaller powers that, though less spectacular, are more workable.

Geographically, the shift is away from a Eurocentric world and toward Asia and the Pacific. Rather than disregarding nationalism, which early geopoliticians were prone to do, modern geopolitics, for the most part, treats the nation-state as the most successful form of political organization over much of the world. Finally, there is a discernible movement away from confrontation and political intrigue and a greater reliance on arbitration using established world organizations such as the United Nations.

Bibliography

Bronowski, Jacob, and Bruce Mazlish. *The Western Intellectual Tradition.* New York: Harper & Row, 1962. Chapter on Machiavelli details how he introduced a revolution in political thinking by separating ethics from politics. Understanding the role played by *raison d'état* or Machiavellism is vital to understanding geopolitics.

Freedman, Laurence. *Atlas of Global Strategy: War and Peace in the Nuclear Age.* New York: Facts on File, 1985. More a book of facts than analysis, the book describes geopolitical conflicts since 1945.

Massie, Robert K. *Dreadnought: Britain, Germany, and the Coming of the Great War.* New York: Ballantine, 1991. Case study of one of the great geopolitical ideas: Alfred Thayer Mahan's thesis that world power requires sea power. A narrative of the naval arms race between Britain and Germany that led to World War I. One is impressed by the futility of the arms race.

O'Sullivan, Patrick. *Geopolitics.* New York: St. Martin's Press, 1986. Describes power politics between the West and the Soviet Union at the time of its greatest strength.

Parker, Jeffrey. *Western Geopolitical Thought in the Twentieth Century*. New York: St. Martin's Press, 1985. Lucidly written book on later geopolitical thought.

Weigert, Hans, Henry Brodie, Edward W. Doherty, John R. Fernstrom, Eric Fisher, and Dudley Kirk. *Principles of Political Geography*. New York: Appleton-Century-Crofts, 1957. Excellent textbook on geopolitics. Establishes a close connection between geopolitics and Nazi strategy.

Nis Petersen

Cross-References

Chinese Communism, p. 223; Conflict Resolution, p. 397; Diplomacy and International Negotiation, p. 552; Empires and Empire Building, p. 597; Foreign Relations, p. 718; Imperialism, p. 889; Islam and Government, p. 994; Machiavelli's Political Philosophy, p. 1148; National Security, p. 1261; Nationalism, p. 1268; North Atlantic Treaty Organization, p. 1332; Realpolitik, p. 1668; Russian Political History, p. 1770; Self-Determination, p. 1796; Social Darwinism, p. 1833; Superpowers and World Politics, p. 1916; World Political Organization, p. 2186.

GOVERNMENT AGENCIES

Field of study: Functions of government

Laws passed by legislative bodies in political systems are rarely self-enforcing. Government agencies perform the executive function: They are responsible for carrying out public policy. Overseeing the details of the laws' implementation, agencies play an important role in their ultimate effect.

Principal terms

AGENCY: any administrative organization, which may be named authority, board, bureau, commission, corporation, corps, council, department, ministry, office, secretariat, system, or service

BUREAUCRACY: administrative organization characterized by a division of labor, specialization of tasks, hierarchical chain of command, standard operating procedures, formal record keeping, and career employees

DEVELOPMENT: status of a nation's political, economic, and social institutions, particularly as they compare to those of other countries

IMPLEMENTATION: process by which laws passed by a legislative body are carried out

PUBLIC ADMINISTRATION: organizations, processes, and people associated with the implementation of public policy

PUBLIC POLICY: course of action followed by one or more government officials

RULE MAKING: an agency's working interpretation of a law for purposes of execution

Overview

The legislative and executive leaders of any national political system are generalists who are responsible for running an entire nation. Government agencies are the specialists of the political system. Each agency devotes its attention to only one category of public policy. Lawmakers, presidents, and prime ministers must rely upon administrative organizations to carry out public policy for two fundamental reasons. First, the leaders' heavy workload allows them to devote only limited attention to any one issue. Second, passing a law requires compromise, and general agreement is easier to achieve if the details of a law's execution are decided later.

In a world of diverse nations, the structure of government agencies and their role in politics and governance vary from country to country. Even so, common patterns can be observed. Scholars often explain similarities and differences among nations using three key factors: characteristics of the political regime, level of development, and local culture.

As for regime, administration is centralized in unitary states such as Great Britain but decentralized among territorial governments in federal systems such as Canada's. The prime minister commands the bureaucracy in parliamentary government but power and control are more fragmented in the United States, a presidential government. The control, performance, and continuity of agency behavior are affected by the level of competition between political parties in any country, ranging from very competitive, as in Venezuela since 1958, to the totalitarian rule of one party, as in Cuba. Interest group access to bureaucratic decision making also varies from open (the United States) to closed (common in Europe).

There is general agreement that government agencies in the developed nations look something like the so-called classic bureaucratic model proposed by German sociologist Max Weber. There are five particular features to the classic bureaucratic model. One is that the bureaucracy is pervasive—public employees make up approximately 10 percent of the population in developed democracies. The second is that government agencies are large and complex, differentiated into highly specialized functional units. The third is that administrative decentralization on a geographic basis is common. The fourth is that staffs are professional, achieved through recruitment based on competence. The fifth is that administration is impersonal, based on the rule of law.

The developing nations of Africa, Asia, Latin America, and the Middle East are considered to share some administrative features in common as well. Many agencies of developing nations have a structure modeled after Western bureaucracies, especially in those states that were former colonies. Administration by territorial overlords is a legacy of the colonial heritage, particularly in what were once British and French holdings. People with management, development, or other technical training available to staff government agencies are generally in short supply. An unrepresentative bureaucracy results if its top posts are staffed exclusively from the small, socio-economically advantaged segment of the population. Additionally, considerations other than merit or program goals may preoccupy bureaucratic activity. For example, public jobs may be distributed on the basis of personal loyalty or to reduce unemployment. Corruption, especially in terms of bribes to facilitate transactions, is widespread and expected.

Whether a bureaucracy can or should be apolitical, a neutral agent of its political masters, continues to be debated. In fact, the role of the bureaucracy in the polity is a significant distinction between the developed and the developing nations. In mature and stable governments, the political position of the bureaucracy with respect to other institutions is reasonably evolved, clear, and restricted. In general, bureaucracies in developed nations practice enforcement and rule making almost exclusively. In many developing nations, however, administration often is clearly politicized. Bureaucratic involvement is observable in all phases of policy-making, including the articulation and aggregation of interests.

There is also debate about the role government agencies play in the process of development itself. One school of thought views administration as the key to nation-building. In fact, this was the faith behind Western efforts in the Third World during the period immediately after World War II. An alternative school of thought, however, attributes the fact that widespread development failed to materialize in many former colonies to the dependent economic position of those countries. Indeed, those who take this alternative view—dependency theorists—view public administration as completely irrelevant to the process of development. Although it is not disputed that a competent bureaucracy is important to a developed political system, it also remains undecided whether an efficient, honest bureaucracy matched with other, weaker political institutions fosters or hinders political development.

Local political, economic, social, and cultural factors account for differences between countries and thereby limit one's ability to generalize. For example, a broad explanation for the fact that a series of imitation Western bureaucracies did not flower in Third World countries is that the necessary conditions were lacking, these being, among other things, well-rooted, legitimate political institutions, an expanding economic base, an open society, and a secular culture. Four major cultural factors may be used to account for national differences in organizational behavior. Sweden's informal, consensual method of regulating workplace safety, for example, is a demonstration of its deferential political culture, in contrast to the self-assertive and adversarial political culture of the United States. French attention to rank and titles is quite the opposite of the relative informality found within American governing institutions. A third variable is the importance of the group relative to the individual, a notable characteristic of the Japanese management style. Finally, contrary to the rule of law in European tradition, administration in Latin America is generally personal.

Applications

The United States provides an example of public administration in a developed democracy with a presidential system of governance. The president sits at the apex of the pyramid of the executive branch. His closest political and policy advisers are located on the level immediately beneath him, called the Executive Office of the President. The next level of the hierarchy is composed of the major functional departments, such as the departments of Agriculture or Defense. Each department is headed by a secretary; as a group they form the president's cabinet. The rest of the American bureaucracy is made up of scores of so-called independent establishments (for example, the Environmental Protection Agency) and government corporations (for example, the U.S. Postal Service).

Political appointees hold the top managerial posts. They are charged with carrying the president's policy agenda forward. The president appoints and dismisses them, so they are reasonably loyal to this task. The balance of the bureaucracy is made up of civil service employees. In the modern era, these employees usually are hired by competitive selection and fired only for cause. The goal of such a policy is to have a public work force composed of competent people, insulated from politics, who have made public service a career.

An agency implements policy through the administrative procedures of rule making, adjudication, and enforcement. Rule making is the process by which the details of legislation are established. Federal agencies provide notice of proposed rules in the

Federal Register, allowing interested groups and individuals the opportunity to express their views. Final rules are adopted into the *Code of Federal Regulations*. This is the way that standards are set after legislation, which is often general or open to interpretation, has been passed. Rule making is quasi-legislative; adjudication is quasi-judicial. In adjudication, an administrative law judge hears disagreements over existing regulations, such as those disputes common between industry and environmentalists. Enforcement refers to application of the law. Audits conducted and penalties levied by the Internal Revenue Service illustrate this concept.

The bureaucracy is a significant source of policy ideas as well. That agencies identify ways to innovate is no surprise, given their intimate daily engagement with the law. The space shuttle was proposed to Congress by the National Aeronautics and Space Administration, for example, not the other way around.

The process by which policy is settled upon in the United States has been characterized as a sort of barroom brawl. It is open to all comers in that multiple points of access are available to any interest group with a stake in the outcome. Informal cooperation between members of Congress and the bureaucracy is common, although political alliances shift frequently. Fragmented political authority leads to a disorderly and often lengthy process.

The federal system of government means that administration in the United States is decentralized. State and local agencies adapt the implementation of federal policy to varying regional conditions. The administration of national programs also involves considerable bargaining between levels, given the political autonomy of subnational governments.

Great Britain provides a more orderly and much respected model of politics, administration, and policy-making. Britain is unitary and parliamentary. In this system, political power is concentrated in the hands of the prime minister. The ministry is the basic administrative unit, headed by cabinet ministers who are typically experienced members of Parliament at the time of their appointment. Immediately below each of them is the permanent secretary, a senior civil servant. The balance of the bureaucracy is made up of three classes: administrative, executive, and clerical personnel. Entry is by competitive examination. Traditionally, the civil service has been the province of persons educated at Oxford or Cambridge, although diversity has increased in the post-World War II period. As a result, a tradition of prestige and status characterizes the British civil service.

Administrators at the highest ranks primarily are engaged in policy implementation. They are also an important source of political advice for the minister, whom they are expected to serve faithfully, and who is ultimately accountable to Parliament. Legislative control of the bureaucracy has declined as the power of the prime minister has grown, as happened during the Thatcher era. Unlike the United States, administration in Great Britain is much more closed to intervention by the courts and by pressure groups.

India, Guatemala, and China provide three different administrative patterns. India inherited its administrative structure from its past under British rule. It is considered to be comparatively advanced, probably because it resembles the classical Western model. Most notably, entry to the Indian Administrative Service is by competitive examination, and policy-making and administration are considered separate by political tradition. The Indian bureaucracy has been criticized, however, for recruitment restricted to a very small, well-educated segment of the population, episodes of rapid expansion to create employment, and increasing politicization.

So-called strongman regimes are common historically in Latin America and more recently in sub-Saharan Africa. In such a regime a single individual, usually with a military background, dominates national affairs but depends upon the bureaucracy for policy continuity. The strongman makes most of the major administrative decisions and scrutinizes bureaucrats carefully, rewarding supporters and punishing detractors. Recruitment to the public service is based almost exclusively on personal loyalty or ideology. For example, General Jorge Ubico Castaneda, ruler of Guatemala from 1931 to 1944, had an electrically operated control panel installed in the National Palace to keep close tabs on when his employees checked in and out. Guatemalan bureaucracy was one of complete obedience, an attribute that continued long after his departure.

Party control of the administrative structure is a defining characteristic of communist regimes such as that of the People's Republic of China. The basic model is one of parallel hierarchies. In China, party, state, and military (the Chinese Communist Party, institutions associated with the National People's Congress, and the People's Liberation Army) interlock. In a manner similar to that of strongman rule, bureaucratic power is distrusted, but the need for its functions is recognized. Administration is completely politicized, given that the top posts are held by party members. Even so, Chinese leader Deng Xiaoping discerned the link between bureaucratic professionalization and national modernization. He sought people who were both communist and expert for the civil service.

Context

Across the world, bureaucracy has expanded over time. One report indicates that the number of central government departments increased, on average, from 9.4 per country in the middle of the nineteenth century to 19.2 by the early 1980's. Most of this growth occurred after World War II.

The increase also indicates expanded responsibilities. Ministries in the primordial fields of foreign affairs, justice, finance, war, and internal affairs can be traced back to the Romans. The modern list also includes such areas as education, transportation, and social welfare. In the United States, for example, George Washington's cabinet contained only three departments—State, Treasury, and War. In the 1980's, there were fourteen departments, scores of independent agencies, and thousands of subunits employing some three million people.

Growth in bureaucratic size and function has occurred for a number of reasons. Increasing technological complexity is a fundamental cause. Government regulation has become steadily more extensive since the Industrial Revolution. New technologies are added to old, from biotechnical engineering to railroads. A second cause is that more government programs foster public expectations that the state will intervene as new problems arise, although debates about the government's appropriate role are continuous.

Control of the bureaucracy is an important matter, particularly as political generalists place greater reliance upon policy specialists. The decisions bureaucrats make about implementation construct public policy. Of significant continuing concern, therefore, is how this delegated authority, or discretion, is to be made accountable to those whom these agencies are intended to serve, whether that be the public or a general.

The evidence from Western nations indicates that political control is typically sufficient to guard against bureaucratic dominance. This control should include mechanisms allowing political leaders to provide policy direction and administrative participation. Government agencies in developing countries are likely to be more autonomous. Expertise and prestige, coupled with unstable elites and underdeveloped political institutions, often make the bureaucracy an important, and powerful, source of continuity in the state.

Bibliography

Dwivedi, O. P., and Keith M. Henderson, eds. *Public Administration in World Perspective*. Ames: Iowa State University Press, 1990. A supplement to Heady's comprehensive text (listed below), this book contains global and local perspectives from experts around the world.

Farazmand, Ali, ed. *Handbook of Comparative and Development Public Administration*. New York: Marcel Dekker, 1991. Attempting to be encyclopedic about theory and geography, this volume is broken into two parts: public administration and bureaucratic behavior in comparative perspective.

Fritschler, A. Lee. *Smoking and Politics: Policymaking and the Federal Bureaucracy*. Englewood Cliffs, N.J.: Prentice-Hall, 1969. Classic case study of the cigarette labeling controversy, with a readable, detailed illustration of agency policy-making in the American political system.

Heady, Ferrel. *Public Administration: A Comparative Perspective*. 4th ed. New York: Marcel Dekker, 1991. Heady is clearly the dean of the comparative public administration scholars, contributing directly or indirectly to every other major text in the field.

Rowat, Donald C., ed. *Public Administration in Developed Democracies*. New York: Marcel Dekker, 1988. With four parts: the commonwealth countries, Nordic democracies, western Europe, and other developed democratic nations.

Subramaniam, V., ed. *Public Administration in the Third World*. Westport, Conn.: Greenwood Press, 1990. Includes essays on countries in Asia, the Middle East, North Africa, sub-Saharan Africa, the West Indies, and Latin America. The introductory essay on development administration is an excellent summary and critique of Western research perspectives.

Weber, Max. *From Max Weber: Essays in Sociology*. Edited and translated by H. H.

Gerth and C. Wright Mills. New York: Oxford University Press, 1946. German sociologist Max Weber is the scholar most closely associated with bureaucracy as a theory of organization. His work on its origins, character, and implications is seminal.

John Patrick Piskulich

Cross-References

Accountability in U.S. Government, p. 1; Administrative Procedures in U.S. Government, p. 14; Bureaucracy, p. 164; The Civil Service in the United States, p. 310; Education Management, p. 565; Elected Versus Appointed Offices in the United States, p. 572; Entitlements, p. 610; Executive Functions in U.S. Government, p. 636; Government Powers, p. 772; Government Roles, p. 778; Health Care Management, p. 810; Iron Triangles, p. 981; Policy Development and Implementation, p. 1414; Postal Service, p. 1563; Public Policy, p. 1633; Regulatory Agencies in the United States, p. 1678; Urban Governments, p. 2052.

GOVERNMENT POWERS

Field of study: Political philosophy

The powers of government are those powers which are necessary for the governmental body to achieve the desired ends of the people being governed.

Principal terms

ASSUMED POWER: power that is taken by the government without the express wish of the people

IMPLIED POWER: power granted to the government directly by the people

INHERITED POWER: government power that stems from the need to accomplish the wishes of the people being governed

RESERVED POWERS: powers held to be exclusive within a specified level of government

Overview

Government powers are those exercised by the government in the course of its normal operation. Each of the several different specific types is used to further the goals of the government. Regardless of the type of government, they all exercise power over all the people under that government. Further, they derive their power from the people they govern. Even the most despotic of governments cannot exercise power without at least tacit approval of the people governed. It must be kept in mind that because governments exist to serve their people, they require sufficient powers to handle certain situations in an efficient manner. A simple example is the need for a road. Suppose that the people of a certain region decide that they need a road to make carrying their products to market easier. Once the people make that decision, they must either make the road themselves or engage others to do it. Since most people do not want to spend their spare time repairing roads, they prefer to let a smaller group of people handle it. This need for common services is at the heart of government functioning. To provide these basic services, the people delegated to provide them (normally the government) must have the power to do the work themselves or to find others to do the work. This ability to accomplish a desired task is called an implied power.

An analogy helps to explain implied powers. Suppose one were asked to go to a store to get milk. Within that instruction, it is understood that one had the power to leave the house, walk or drive to the store, and handle the business of buying the milk. Although the latter functions are not stated, they are understood. If one cannot do any of them, then one cannot go to the store and get some milk. It is therefore implied that one has the power to accomplish the task.

Since it is inefficient to have separate groups of people do the various tasks needed by the people being served, those tasks are normally assigned to a single governing body who then has the ability to parcel them out to the different groups to make sure they are accomplished. One way that the government has of doing this is through the power of contract. The ability to negotiate and enforce a contract on behalf of all the people being served is an inherent power. Although it resembles an implied power, there is a difference. An implied power is one that comes naturally from the task itself, whereas an inherent power is one that is necessary in order to achieve that task. As stated above, if the group chosen to build the road has the necessary expertise, then there is no need to contract with someone else to do it.

The power to purchase the gravel and other materials is an implied power, because without it no one can build the road, whereas the ability to contract with another group to do the work is inherent, and stems from the desire of the people governed to get the road built, no matter who does it.

The result of this understanding between the people and the government is that the government "inherits" the power to delegate the authority to do the work to someone else. The government still has the responsibility of making sure that the road is built, but it has the power to authorize someone else to build it.

Suppose that everyone in a town shared the power to decide where a road should be built. Clearly, the road would either serve only the most persuasive, or it would never be built because everyone would be arguing over where it should be built. For example, one citizen may want the road to go through his property, because he wants to build a hotel on it—even though his property is the most inaccessible in the country, while another citizen might not want the road to go through his property because it would spoil some of his best farmland.

To overcome such problems, the government also has what are called reserved powers that it uses to make certain decisions that affect the entire population. Naturally, the amount of power involved is a function of the matter being decided and the size of the government. For example, a city cannot legally declare war on a foreign nation. Clearly, such a decision would affect more people than reside in the city. Such power is reserved by the national government. On the other hand, a city can reserve the power to determine the speed limits on its roads, the numbers and sizes of houses that may be built within its borders, and other such matters that affect the residents of the city directly.

Another type of government power is called "assumed." This can be the most dangerous of all; if misused, it can lead to many of the abuses seen in despotic governments. When a government decides on its own to enact a law that affects the population, without the direct input of the population, then the power is assumed. There are times when it is necessary for a government to make such laws—such as during a national emergency—however, such times must be closely watched by the people being governed.

Clearly, in a case when a nation is attacked by an outside force or there is a national disaster that affects a large part of the population, there may not be time to put matters up for discussion among the people. At such times, it is necessary for the government to assume the powers required to react to the situation. After the situation is resolved, there is usually time for the people to become involved again in the decision-making process.

Each type of government power has a place in the functioning of the government. They all have the capability of being abused, but for the most part they are essential for the government to operate. It is important that the people being governed become involved in the processes that lead to the use of these powers to ensure that they are used for the benefit of the largest percentage of the people governed.

Applications

Governments apply their powers in different ways, depending on the form of the government. For example, in a monarchy power may be based on edict. A king or queen proclaims that something is to be done, and it is done based on that authority. In a constitutional democracy, the powers of the government are based in law, as proclaimed in the establishing document, the constitution. In either case, the power is exercised based on a perceived need, either expressed by the people being governed or by the head of the government. Ideally, the powers that are used form a circle—stemming from the people and serving the needs of the same people. Within this, several variables play a large part. For example, suppose the people express a fear that a foreign neighbor is going to invade. They tell their government that they want to be free from that fear, so the government decides the best way to approach the problem. How the government exercises power is determined by the approach selected.

By telling the government that they are afraid of being invaded and that they want the government to do something about it, the people being governed are implying that the government has the power to affect the situation. Should the decision be made to prepare to defend the country against an invasion, the powers granted by the people to the government may include raising taxes to pay for a military force. They may also include the power to conscript soldiers. These powers are limited to those actions that are directly related to preparing the country to defend itself against an invader.

Suppose now that during the preparations for the defense of the nation, the government decides that it also needs to improve its highway structure. Although not directly related to national defense, improved roads would make it easier to move soldiers and supplies from one part of the country to the other. If the government decides to improve its highway system anyway, the power it uses would be inherited. The improved highways might not make the military significantly more efficient, but they should help.

In going beyond the strict wishes of its people, the government expands its use of power. Inherited power is often expressed this way. Even though the existing roads are adequate for the purpose desired by the people, the government decides that better roads are needed. In this example, the people are actually served by the expanded use of power, because they can use the better roads as well as the military can, and may well approve the government's use of the power.

Now suppose that the government decided that in order to provide for an effective national defense that everyone between the age of fifteen and fifty should attend military training camp. Theoretically, the government has the power to make such a decision and even to pass a law to that effect, but considering the adverse impact such a law would have on the lives of the people and the economy of the nation, it is not likely that such a decision would be widely supported by the people.

Even though people wish to avoid an invasion, there are limits to what they will do. In this example, it is possible that some members of the nation have strong personal beliefs against using weapons and that some might lose their jobs or businesses by going to military camps. It could also be that many are not physically able to conduct that type of training. A government must therefore use its inherited powers wisely, or it risks losing the support of the people.

Because of the possibility of abuse, governments try to reserve as much power as possible. Normally, the amount of reserved power will be determined by the size of the governmental body involved. A national government, for example, will normally reserve the powers to declare war and to conduct interstate trade, as well as the myriad other powers involved in dealing with issues that affect the entire nation. Within this, there is a very fine line. For example, each state within the United States has a small military force. Even though this military force is maintained by the state and can be called up by its governor during crises, the power to conscript troops is reserved for the national government alone. The states can maintain military forces, but they cannot require their citizens to join them.

Reserved powers are necessary to ensure the efficient operation of the government. Governments of different sizes reserve different powers, determined by their overall needs. Normally, the flow of power in government is from the larger to the smaller, and the exact powers are outlined the same way. In other words, the national government will define those powers held by the state, the state will define the powers held by the counties, and the counties will define the powers held by the cities or towns. Because of this flow, it is much more efficient when the larger government body reserves certain powers.

Governments also reserve powers to eliminate duplication of authority. If there is a chance that a federal law will contradict a state law, the federal law will take precedence. Similarly, a state law takes precedence over municipal laws. Ideally, there will be one authority for each law.

Assumed powers are applied through the desire by the government to extend its influence in areas that are not traditionally covered either by custom or by the founding documents. In most instances, a government will assume a power to protect a majority of the people. For example, a government might decide that it is necessary to regulate speed on highways, even though it is not specifically tasked with doing that either by custom or through legislation. Speed limits are seen as a "good" thing, and they save lives, but they are outside the normal boundaries of government.

A central problem with assumed powers is that often the very people who are supposed to regulate the government and ensure that it stays within the framework of its founding documents or within customary boundaries are the same people who exercise the powers. Because of this, it is important to have an informed and participatory population so that the people being governed remain aware of what their government is doing and take the necessary steps to ensure that the actions taken and powers assumed benefit the people governed.

Context

To be effective, a government must have the power to serve the needs of the people being governed. Without such power, a government would be a useless collection of people that serve no practical purpose. The powers given to a government should be those that are necessary to achieve the desired ends of that government as expressed by the people being governed.

As one can see, it is necessary for the government to exercise its powers wisely. Equally important is that the people being governed become involved in the process of making and enforcing laws and monitoring the use of power by the government. When a government body oversteps the boundaries as defined by the people, it is the responsibility of the people to bring it back into legitimacy.

The people being governed should be aware of the actions taken by their government, so they know when the government is exercising its implied powers, inherited powers, or assumed powers. The people should also ensure that the government reserves only those powers necessary to accomplish its functions, without putting an undue hardship on the people being governed.

The government exists as an extension of the people. It serves to take care of those needs that the people decide need to be met, without going beyond its constitutional boundaries. If it is a cooperative arrangement, the people are served by a government that is sensitive to their wishes, and the majority of the people being governed can conduct their affairs without interference.

Bibliography

Hinckley, Barbara, and Sheldon Goldman. *American Politics and Government*. Glenview, Ill.: Scott, Foresman/Little, Brown Higher Education, 1990. General reference text that covers government structures, processes, institutions, and policies, and how they are designed to work together.

Krock, Arthur. *The Consent of the Governed, and Other Deceits*. Boston: Little, Brown, 1971. Well-written and easy-to-read book full of anecdotes that illustrate the inner workings of the political system in Washington, D.C.

Richardson, Elliot. *The Creative Balance: Government, Politics, and the Individual in America's Third Century*. New York: Holt, Rinehart and Winston, 1976. Well described by its subtitle, this volume discusses how the individual interacts with the government and the effect on the individual of government power.

Smith, Hedrick. *The Power Game*. New York: Random House, 1988. Exceptionally well-written book that portrays the inside workings of Washington, D.C., and the people who work there. Describes the explosion in government power in the 1970's and the interaction among the players as the power shifts among the various agencies.

Wills, Garry. *Explaining America: The Federalist*. Garden City, N.Y.: Doubleday, 1981. An examination of the Federalist Papers, a collection of essays written to urge the ratification of the U.S. Constitution, this book explains how the U.S. government came to be the way it is.

Carl A. Thames

Cross-References

Accountability in U.S. Government, p. 1; The Bill of Rights, p. 134; Checks and Balances in U.S. Government, p. 216; Congress, p. 412; Executive Functions in U.S. Government, p. 636; Funding of Government, p. 724; Invisible Government, p. 975; Labor Relations, p. 1038; Law Enforcement, p. 1059; Legislative Functions of Government, p. 1098; Policy Development and Implementation, p. 1414; Regulatory Agencies in the United States, p. 1678; The Supreme Court: Role in Government and Law, p. 1935.

GOVERNMENT ROLES

Field of study: Functions of government

Questions about what roles government should play are interwoven among contemporary and historical debates about what constitutes the needs of society in general and the economy in particular.

Principal terms

AFFIRMATIVE GOVERNMENT: view that modern society's growing complexity demands that government discharge a wider array of responsibilities fairly, efficiently, and democratically

KEYNESIAN ECONOMICS: school of thought holding that because market economies are not truly self-regulating, government should intervene to act as a stabilizing force

MARKET ECONOMY: economic system characterized by private ownership of resources, a limited government role, and competitive markets for goods and services

MINIMALIST GOVERNMENT: view of government that places primacy on market mechanisms to determine levels of production, consumption, and distribution of goods

PRIVATE ENTERPRISE: freedom of private businesses

Overview

There are two basic views of government's proper role: affirmative and minimalist. Aspects of each view crisscross conservative and liberal ideologies, as well as Republican and Democratic party membership in the United States. The liberal political philosopher John Rawls, in *A Theory of Justice* (1971) and *Political Liberalism* (1993), and the economic conservative Milton Friedman, in *Capitalism and Freedom* (1962) and *Free to Choose* (1980), both advance theories supporting a minimalist view of the government. Each of them believes that the individual actor in the market has primacy. They assert that patterns of production and consumption are the logical outcomes of unfettered individual decisions. These theorists leave open the question of socially constructed ends, in other words, what constitutes a good society.

In *The Morality of Freedom* (1986) Joseph Raz embraces a more comprehensive role of government. Raz argues that the state legitimately seeks to promote the well-being of its citizens in ways that involve it in the business of judging the value of particular ways of life. A good life must be autonomous, that is, one must be the author of one's own well-being and have available a multiplicity of valuable options. Unlike Rawls, Raz and others, such as Amati Etzioni in *The Spirit of Community* (1993), place more responsibility on government to tame individual impulses and promote social solidarity. Historian Arthur Schlesinger also views social solidarity as a proper responsibility of government. In *The Vital Center* (1949), Schlesinger argues that it is essential that government provide what are known as safety net programs to ensure a minimum standard of living in order to safeguard society from disruptions. Frances Fox Piven and Richard Cloward in *Regulating the Poor* (1971) argue that government provision of basic services functions as a social control mechanism, quieting dissent and giving the appearance of social cohesion. Their theory of social control is one of a set of theories about how government works. It and other theories, such as public choice, pluralism, corporatism, and bureaucratic, allude to the more normative discussion of the role of government.

Implications about the role of government derived from theories of political philosophy and political economy fall essentially into two groups: those that turn back to a supposedly simpler world of less government, and those that look for ways to enable governments to discharge their widening responsibilities more democratically, equitably, and effectively. The former approach represents the orthodox wisdom of the Ronald Reagan and George Bush administrations in the United States during the 1980's. This approach followed the tenets of minimalist government, whose principles were laid out by economist Milton Friedman in 1962. According to Friedman, government is the mechanism through which citizens exercise their freedom. Paradoxically, because government concentrates power in political hands, it also threatens freedom. The U.S. Constitution embodies two broad principles meant to preserve freedom. First, government must be limited. It has two major functions: to protect its citizens from enemies outside its borders and to mediate between citizens by preserving law and order, enforcing private contracts, and fostering competitive markets. Beyond this, government may enable its citizens to accomplish jointly that which would be more difficult or expensive to accomplish separately. Such use of government has dangers, so there should be a clear balance of advantages before doing so. Relying primarily on voluntary cooperation and private enterprise in economic and other activities ensures that the private sector will check the powers of the government, effectively protecting the freedoms of speech, religion, and thought. The second broad constitutional principle is that government must be dispersed, devolving to the lowest unit of government whenever possible.

Given these two broad principles, Friedman identifies three roles for government. As the rule maker, government provides a means to modify rules, mediate differences about the meaning of these rules, and enforce compliance with the rules. Government also serves as regulator or owner when action is necessitated either by monopoly, for example, technical efficiency, or by neighborhood effects, that is, when one person's actions affect other persons in ways for which it is not feasible to compensate them. Finally, government is a form of paternalism for those designated as not responsible.

The opposing theories about government advance more positive or affirmative roles, looking for ways to enable government to discharge a wider array of responsibilities fairly and efficiently. Nicholas Rescher in *Welfare: The Social Issues in Philosophical Perspective* (1972), for example, advocates shifting the role of modern government from merely providing the minimum requirements for an adequate life to forging the setting of a satisfying life; from a protective role of defensively endeavoring to safeguard people against various hazards, to a positive role of life enhancement.

Budget deficits and global economies, however, present formidable challenges to an administration that seeks to follow prescriptions derived from a political economy or political philosophy of affirmative government.

Applications

In its efforts to improve productive capacity and output, the Clinton Administration sought ways for government to enhance the competitive aspects of U.S. business and attend to job security in light of technological advances during the mid-1990's. Adhering to a deficit reduction timetable designed to eliminate new discretionary spending unless matched by cuts in existing programs, the Clinton Administration advocated a lower federal budget, value-added industrial policy, health care reform, and expansion of the Earned Income Tax Credit, among other things. These initiatives reflect different aspects of the minimalist and affirmative views of government.

Adopting an industrial policy implies active, coordinated government involvement in the economy, despite portended risks of propping up a bad economy or a bad idea. The Clinton Administration's technology reinvestment project and clean-car initiative were two examples of government efforts to increase the private sector's capacity to create value-added products and high-wage jobs. Technology reinvestment programs apply military-related technologies to improving the nation's infrastructure. A University of California at San Diego initiative, for example, sought to demonstrate how advanced composite materials developed for high-performance military aircraft can offer major advantages for repairing and replacing aging bridges. Forty such projects have been planned. The clean-car initiative involved an agreement among General Motors, Ford, Chrysler, and the federal government to accept a set of research and development goals for automobiles. Its long-term goal was to develop affordable, attractive cars that would be up to three times more fuel-efficient than previous cars and that would meet strict standards for urban air pollution, safety, performance, and comfort. The government agreed to finance projects identified as high-risk by an auto industry-government team.

The Clinton Administration's health care reform proposal, based on the vision that a good society provides insurance to all of its citizens, raised the question of who would set the ground rules for the nation's one trillion dollar health economy. The debate pitted states that wanted significant control over the health system against many of the nation's businesses. Many firms preferred a uniform national system for health reform and feared losing their ability to manage health care costs in a maze of varying state laws. Many states, however, wanted the federal Employee Retirement Income Security Act (ERISA) amended so they could initiate their own health reforms. ERISA, passed in 1974, had preempted state statutes and given exclusive jurisdiction over employee benefits to the federal government. These included health benefits provided by firms that self-insure, that is, that pay workers' health expenses directly. Approximately half of all firms with fifty or more employees do self-insure. Several states, including Washington and Oregon, wanted exemption from ERISA so they could tax self-insured companies' health benefits to fund their portended reforms. One issue was the viability of the principle that lower units of government are more appropriate regulators than the federal government.

The Clinton Administration's 1994 health care proposal also altered the contours of what has traditionally guided the development of social insurance in the United States, thereby expanding further the view of affirmative government. It would depart from more traditional programs designed for people who have, in theory, earned their benefits, for example, veterans; who have funds to which they or their employers have contributed, from which they can draw when they retire or lose their jobs; or who claim benefits because of economic necessity or some other special need. Such legislation stretches Friedman's minimalist paternalism prescription beyond recognition, yet may be necessary to promote social solidarity in an increasingly turbulent economy in which many benefits are linked to jobs.

The Clinton Administration also expanded the Earned Income Tax Credit (EITC), targeted to the nation's nearly twelve million working poor families. Full-time workers with children whose annual incomes fall below the poverty line, can receive a percentage of their annual earnings as an additional supplement. The EITC effectively raises the minimum wage of $4.25 per hour to $6.50 per hour, thereby raising many participating families above the poverty line. Rather than taking affirmative steps to establish a wage policy that may grossly distort market mechanisms, the EITC exemplifies a modified extension of the minimalist view of government.

Context

The role of the government has been at the center of American politics since the origins of the country. From the Jeffersonian tradition, the country inherited the maxim that government was best which governed least. Both Alexander Hamilton and John Quincy Adams conceived of the national government as a purposeful instrument of social progress. Hamilton envisioned a United States driven by a strong central government promoting and enhancing an international, industrial, mercantilist economy. He believed that economic behavior and the affairs of nations were best governed by the enlightened self-interest espoused by the Scottish philosopher Adam Smith. Hamilton's political philosophy approximated that of Thomas Hobbes, who believed that a powerful, centralized state was necessary to control the bellicose passions of individuals struggling for survival. Jefferson, on the other hand, feared a big central government. He saw an agrarian and locally communitarian society with minimal federal involvement in the lives of a virtuous and self-reliant citizenry. The Industrial Revolution eclipsed the Jeffersonian vision as the country became more urban and larger amounts of money were needed to finance the nation's increased productive capacity.

The presidential campaign of 1912 highlighted the contrasts between the Hamiltonian and Jeffersonian traditions. Theodore Roosevelt's "New Nationalism" was based on a philosophy of limited collectivism, with the government's role viewed as essential to regulate large corporations through federal commissions and by taxing their excessive profits. The "New Freedom" of Woodrow Wilson pined for a return to

Jeffersonian localism and crusaded against big business on behalf of small business and labor. In Wilson's view, government intervention should not be to plan for the general welfare as much as to roll back the trend of economic development from consolidation to competition.

Roosevelt's New Deal drew from both the New Nationalism and the New Freedom. The National Recovery Administration reflected the New Nationalism, but its failure to ensure that businesses did not take over the government agency set up to regulate them led the Roosevelt Administration to embrace the New Freedom strategy. At issue was the extent to which government should aim to establish conditions of economic decisions or make the decisions itself. Subsequently, the economic philosophy of John Maynard Keynes came to dominate U.S. domestic policy. According to Keynesian economics, the proper role of government was to lay the ground rules creating an economic environment favorable to private business policies that increase production, while allowing the free market to operate with as little interference as possible. Government could use monetary and fiscal policies to set the level of economic activity stable enough to create an atmosphere favorable to private investment and adequate consumption, yet effective enough to prevent economic breakdown. When spending or demand sags too much, government, through tax reduction and compensatory spending, could maintain high levels of employment and production. Taxation and subsidies were viewed as potent means of directing private investment to underdeveloped industries and regions, while other incentives could be used to draw labor and capital into socially beneficial undertakings.

During the 1960's, the Kennedy Administration proposed and the Johnson Administration enacted tax cuts and applied Keynesian principles to influence the economy. A proliferation of programs such as Medicare and Medicaid, as well as legislation dealing with poverty and employment, voting rights, and the like, increased the size and scope of government activities. In the 1970's, the Nixon Administration used a variety of monetary and fiscal policies in attempts to tame an inflationary-prone economy. It also expanded the size and scope of government by increasing Social Security benefits and indexing them to the cost of living, and providing supplemental security income for specified groups of non-labor-force participants. In 1965, social programs cost $30 billion, 25 percent of the federal budget and 4.5 percent of the gross national product (GNP). By 1980, such programs cost $280 billion, 48 percent of the budget and 11 percent of GNP. In constant dollars, the increase was 310 percent, more than five times greater than the increase of real GNP.

The Reagan Administration sought to slow down, if not reverse, the growth of government. Reagan argued against big government on both technical and normative grounds, asserting that government bureaucracy is incompetent to address many problems better dealt with at the state or local level. Furthermore, government has no right to tax citizens, thereby appropriating responsibility for how they spend their money. The Reagan and Bush administrations sought to repudiate Keynesian economics and amassed unusually high deficits, which set the context within which the Clinton Administration sought to rekindle a spirit of affirmative government.

Bibliography

Caputo, Richard K. *Welfare and Freedom American Style: The Role of the Federal Government, 1900-1940*. Lanham, Md.: University Press of America, 1991. Traces the formative development of the welfare state in the United States in light of diverging views of the proper role of the federal government in the economy and society between 1900 and 1940.

_____. *Welfare and Freedom American Style II: The Role of the Federal Government, 1941-1980*. Lanham, Md.: University Press of America, 1994. Traces the changing role of the federal government in the economy and society between 1941 and 1980. Examines the interplay between traditional U.S. values of welfare and freedom and the development of the U.S. welfare state.

Dolbeare, Kenneth M. *Directions in American Political Thought*. New York: John Wiley & Sons, 1969. Contains source documents of those whose political and economic philosophies addressed the role of government, from Thomas Paine through Stokely Carmichael. Several sections that classify the source material and place each contributor in historical context.

Friedman, Milton. *Capitalism and Freedom*. Chicago: University of Chicago Press, 1962. Discusses the role of government in a free society and represents a main variant of contemporary conservatism in U.S. political thought.

Heilbroner, Robert. *21st Century Capitalism*. New York: W. W. Norton, 1993. Discusses the role of government in light of the breakup of the Soviet Union, and the end of communism as a viable alternative to market-based social organization.

Makin, John H., and Norman J. Ornstein. *Debt and Taxes*. New York: Times Books, 1994. Detailed historical overview of the role of government in light of tax-and-spend policies through the Reagan Administration. Also examines several policies of the Clinton Administration related to deficit reduction. Contains an appendix of related graphs and charts, notes, and an index.

Rawls, John. *A Theory of Justice*. Cambridge, Mass.: The Belknap Press of Harvard University Press, 1971. Argument for redistributive principles based on a minimalist view of state intervention in the economy and society that remains the benchmark of twentieth century liberal political philosophy.

Raz, Joseph. *The Morality of Freedom*. Oxford, England: Clarendon Press, 1986. Challenges the political philosophy of Rawls and emphasizes a more communitarian justification for affirmative government.

Self, Peter. *Political Theories of Modern Government: Its Role and Reform*. London: George Allen & Unwin, 1985. Explains the major theories of how government works: individualist, pluralist, corporatist, and bureaucratic. Discusses the future role of government and assesses the extent to which political reform is realistic.

Richard K. Caputo

Cross-References

Communications Management, p. 370; Confucianism and Government, p. 405;

Education Management, p. 565; Entitlements, p. 610; The Family and Politics in the United States, p. 649; Health Care Management, p. 810; Law Enforcement, p. 1059; National Security, p. 1261; Public Policy, p. 1633; Public Utilities, p. 1640; Public Works, p. 1647; The Social Security System, p. 1852; Taxation and Appropriation, p. 1941; Urban Policy, p. 2057; Urban Renewal and Housing, p. 2064.

GOVERNMENT TYPES

Field of study: Types of government

Government is the institution or body that establishes rules for controlling a community and its members. Classifying, defining, and attempting to improve the forms and workings of government has been the major concern of political theorists from the time of Aristotle.

Principal terms
ARISTOCRACY: government by members of a privileged class; its
    original meaning was government by the best men
COMMONWEALTH: republic or democratic state
DEMOCRACY: government by the people
FEDERALISM: distribution of the powers of government between a
    supreme national government and territorial governments in states or
    provinces
MONARCHY: government headed by a king or queen
OLIGARCHY: government by the few
REPUBLIC: state in which the supreme power belongs to the citizens and
    is exercised by representatives chosen by them
SOVEREIGNTY: supreme power in a state or community
STATE: people exerting control over a fixed territory through an
    organized government
TYRANNY: government by an absolute ruler

Overview

The first important classification and discussion of governmental forms is found in the *Politics* of the Greek philosopher Aristotle, which states that a government is either a monarchy, an aristocracy, or a democracy. The distinction among them has to do with the number of rulers: one, in the case of a monarchy; a few in proportion to the total population in an aristocracy; and many in a democracy. When the governing power seeks the good of the whole community, any of the three forms are good. When the governing power seeks its own good or benefit, the forms become depraved or debased: monarchy becomes tyranny, aristocracy deteriorates to oligarchy, and democracy becomes mob rule. Aristotle believed that some debasement is inevitable. To devise systems or forms that prevent or ameliorate this deterioration is therefore the central concern of political scientists and philosophers. Aristotle's conclusion was that the best practical form of government was a system in which the attributes of democracy and oligarchy are blended in such a way as to conceal the political and economic divisions between rich and poor. The resulting form Aristotle sometimes called a constitutional government. Such a government is more likely to favor the middle classes than either the rich or the poor.

Before modern governments can be discussed, it is important to bear in mind the way in which governmental functions are classified in modern practice. There are three forms of political power: legislative, executive, and judicial. Lawmaking is the legislative function; in democratic societies, it is normally performed by an assembly, parliament, or congress. The enforcement or execution of the laws is the executive function, most often performed by presidents or prime ministers. The decision of cases arising under the laws is the exercise of judicial power, usually exercised by judges. In some countries, such as the United States, the powers are exercised by wholly different branches of the government; in other countries, one or more of the functions may be combined into one branch. In a dictatorship, all the functions may be exercised by one person in practice, in form, or both.

Contemporary governments are usually classified first in terms of the relationship between their executive and legislative branches. Governments fall into two main groups by this classification: presidential systems, and cabinet or parliamentary systems. In presidential systems, the executive and legislative bodies are separately elected, usually under the provisions of a written constitution. Although the president may be removed from office for crimes, this office is not normally directly politically accountable to the legislature. In cabinet systems, the cabinet is usually selected from among the members of the elected legislature and is politically accountable to the legislature. The cabinet exercises full executive authority, though it may be under the nominal or symbolic authority of a monarch or elected president, who acts as head of state. This figurehead may, however, have some important formal duties such as granting authority to a member of the legislature to attempt to form a new cabinet in the event of the resignation or dismissal of the old.

Presidential government as it exists in the United States is characterized by the nearly complete independence of the president from the legislative branch. Members of the cabinet are not important legislative leaders. In fact, by the second half of the twentieth century, presidents no longer even though it necessary to appoint important party chiefs to cabinet positions. The cabinet heads are therefore solely responsible to the president, who may dismiss them at his or her pleasure. They are not politically responsible to Congress; that body may remove them only by impeachment. Impeachment is a rare and cumbersome process that requires that the officer who is to be removed be found guilty of high crimes and misdemeanors under the terms of the Constitution. The president is solely responsible to the electorate and holds office for a fixed term of four years. The president's acts cannot be directly controlled by Congress, and Congress cannot directly control the president. The presidential system has been widely copied in Latin American countries, usually with some modifications from the U.S. model. Under the German Empire (1871-1919), in which the emperor was the unremovable president of the federation, a similar system was tried. Ministers were responsible to the emperor, not to the imperial parliament. The system proved stable and effective until the turmoil occasioned by Germany's defeat in World War I brought about a revolution.

In cabinet or "responsible" governments, the executive power is vested in a cabinet whose members are drawn from the legislative body. They are legally responsible to the parliament or assembly but are politically accountable to the electorate, which can change the party balance in the legislature. In the late twentieth century, variants of the cabinet system were the most common governmental forms around the world. The prototype of the cabinet system is that developed in Great Britain, which has been imitated not only in former British colonies but also in Europe since the nineteenth century. The success of the form depends greatly on the depth of the political cleavages in the society, on whether there is a two-party system, as in Britain, or a multiparty system, as in France and Italy. Another important criterion is whether the prime minister has the power to dissolve the assembly and force an election. Where prime ministers do not have this power, cabinet governments are likely to prove unstable. In spite of this handicap, however, cabinet government has been far more widely copied than the presidential form followed in the United States. Japan, France, Italy, Spain, and many other democratic countries have cabinet systems. France, however, has moved closer to the United States form of government under the Fifth Republic, established in 1958 under Charles de Gaulle, by creating a strong, independently elected president. This mixed system remained stable under de Gaulle's successors.

A second means of analyzing governmental forms is to examine the extent to which power is held centrally or dispersed territorially. A unitary system is said to exist when control over policy is centralized in the national government. In a unitary system, any powers that are granted to states, provinces, or cities are delegated by a supreme central government that can reorganize the territories or change the powers granted at will. In federal systems, substantial powers are vested in local units—states in the United States, provinces in Canada, cantons in Switzerland. These powers cannot be taken away by the central government without amendment of the national constitution. The states themselves must approve such an amendment, usually by means of a special majority. In the United States, a constitutional amendment must be approved by three-fourths of the states.

The distribution of powers is a critical question. In the United States, the states retain all the powers not specifically delegated to the national government. In Canada, which also has a federal system, powers are delegated to the provincial governments, and the national government retains the undelegated powers. Political theory aside, the actual distribution of powers in any federal system tends to be intricate and often hard for outsiders to understand. In the United States, for example, the national constitution does not express the reality that one of the powers delegated to the national government—the power to regulate interstate and foreign commerce—has become the functional equivalent of a general welfare or police power. Technological and other enhancements to communications and transportation in the late twentieth century have tended to force economic and social interests to be organized on a national rather than regional or local basis. Because of this, there appears to be an inevitable drift toward unitary government, although the outward forms of federalism persist.

The same need for national unity seems to have made it impossible for confederations to exist. A confederation is a system in which each member state retains its sovereignty. The central government is normally confined to dealing with defense and sometimes foreign affairs. The organization of confederations or leagues actually rests on the equivalent of a treaty or mutual defense agreement. Confederations have existed and sometimes have been a stage in the creation of a true federal system. The "league of friendship" to which all the American states subscribed under the Articles of Confederation was such a transitional form. The loose confederation established by the former republics of the Soviet Union, in contrast, seemed by 1994 to be evolving in the direction of separate sovereign nations with few political ties among them.

There are many other ways in which governments may be classified, but such analyses tend to be more subjective than inquiries into the form of governments. The chief concern of political analysts toward the end of the twentieth century has been to ask how democratic a society is and how evenly power and wealth are distributed among the population. As there is no general agreement on the optimum distribution of wealth and power, this kind of analysis often degenerates into moralizing.

Applications

At the end of the twentieth century, a broad range of governmental types existed. There were still some instances of absolute, one-person rule, in which the regime maintained its power by brutal suppression of dissidence. The two dominant forms of government, however, were the presidential and cabinet systems. The two systems that stand as models of their type in the 1990's are the presidential system of the United States and the cabinet system of Great Britain. Although similar principles underlie these governments, there are some very significant differences.

The governmental system in the United States is a federal presidential form, founded on six main constitutional principles: popular sovereignty, federalism, representative government, civil supremacy, limited government, and separation of powers.

Popular sovereignty means that the public is the ultimate sovereign in the system. The Constitution is said to spring from "We the people," and there are a number of crucial governmental functions that cannot take place without public participation: charging and trying people for crimes, amending the Constitution, and electing members of the government are the most important.

The state governments in the United States, notwithstanding some drift in the direction of a unitary system, still exercise immense power and have great political influence. In particular, the bulk of the criminal and commercial laws are established by each state individually. Thus the United States is a federal system.

The Constitution requires the election of the president and all the members of both houses of Congress. Members of Congress are politically responsible to their constituencies and are supposed to represent their constituents' interests. Consequently, the United States is a representative government.

Civil supremacy is the subordination of the military to the civilian branches of the government. The president is the commander in chief, and Congress raises and supports armies. There are constitutional limits on the duration of military appropriations and on military jurisdiction over civilians. Serving military officers are barred from political office.

The Constitution is full of provisions that limit the powers of both the federal and state governments. While some of these limits support and define the federal system, many of them, especially the Bill of Rights, guarantee individual liberties against the power of the state. These restrictions are normally enforced by the judicial system.

Separation of powers is implemented by dividing the powers of the government among three branches, each independent of the other two, and each with a separate formal role in the governance of the country. Under normal circumstances, the acquiescence of all three branches of the government is required before anything can be accomplished.

By contrast to the U.S. system, the government in Great Britain operates as a cabinet system without a written constitution. Executive and legislative powers are vested in the cabinet and prime minister; some judicial power is vested in the cabinet as well. The prime minister is the head of government and the monarch is head of the state. The prime minister is politically accountable to Parliament and the people, while the monarch ascends to the throne through inheritance. Although there are few formal constitutional limitations on governmental power, the tradition of individual liberty and the subordination of military powers is guarded quite as fiercely in Great Britain as in the United States. The British system has been widely imitated around the world. For example, the Japanese government under the MacArthur Constitution of 1948 is a constitutional monarchy, but with a written constitution.

Context

So far as is known, all human societies have had governments of one kind or another. Many societies in primitive times had legendary accounts of how their state or government came into existence. In myth, the government of Sparta was supposed to have been the invention of Lycurgus, Rome was supposed to have been founded by Romulus and Remus, and Moses was said to have freed the Israelites from bondage and established the ancient kingdom of Israel. These accounts nearly always attribute the establishment of the government or society to the mind of a single great lawgiver. The existence of these accounts suggests that humanity's oldest social institution is that of the elective kingship or monarchy. Indeed, such governments still existed widely among nonindustrial societies in the twentieth century.

Political scientists attempt to trace governmental forms through various stages of social and economic development in the hope of understanding how to devise forms of government that provide protection, justice, and sustenance for the public. In a large and complex society, there is a great distinction between the government and the remainder of the society, and the internal organization of the government becomes more complicated and harder to understand. The great question is whether the existing forms of government, and particularly those thought of as democratic, will be able to cope with changing economic and industrial conditions.

Bibliography

Aristotle. *The Politics of Aristotle.* Edited and translated by Ernest Barker. New York:

Oxford University Press, 1962. Aristotle's *Politics* is the seminal work of Western political theory. His classification of the types of governments is still in use; his discussion of the forms of constitutions is the starting point for many of the most important works of political theory. Barker's translation is the best available for the general reader.

Austin, John. *The Province of Jurisprudence Determined* and *The Uses of the Study of Jurisprudence*. London: Weidenfeld and Nicolson, 1954. Austin's discussion of the relation between the laws of man—that is, commands of the government—and the demands of morality or religion swept away older notions of governmental infallibility and divine right.

Hamilton, Alexander, James Madison, and John Jay. *The Federalist*. Edited by Benjamin Fletcher Wright. Cambridge, Mass.: The Belknap Press of Harvard University Press, 1966. The eighty-five essays of *The Federalist* were originally published in 1788 to promote ratification of the proposed American Constitution. They are among the most brilliant political theory ever published.

Hobbes, Thomas. *Leviathan*. Edited by Michael Oakeshott. Oxford: Basil Blackwell, 1957. First published in 1651, *Leviathan* is the first and most influential discussion of the idea that government arises from people's mutual need to protect themselves from one another's brutality and selfishness.

Locke, John. *The Second Treatise of Government*. Edited by Thomas P. Peardon. Indianapolis: Bobbs-Merrill, 1952. Originally published to justify the Glorious Revolution of 1688, this immensely influential essay provides a powerful argument for limited government and individual natural rights.

Montesquieu, Charles de Secondat. *The Spirit of the Laws*. Translated by Thomas Nugent. New York: Mafner, 1949. Montesquieu's study of the English constitution is justly celebrated for his defense of separation of powers and for his sense that the English constitution arose as a result of experience and history rather than logic.

Rousseau, Jean-Jacques. *The Social Contract*. Translated by Maurice Cranston. Baltimore: Penguin Books, 1968. Rousseau argues that people have no rights or ethical existence outside the community and that governments are formed to liberate their capacities.

Robert Jacobs

Cross-References

Aristocracy, Oligarchy, and Plutocracy, p. 78; Bureaucracy, p. 164; Cabinet Government, p. 184; The City-State, p. 272; Commonwealths, p. 364; Confederations, p. 391; Democracy, p. 513; Dictatorships, p. 546; Federalism in the United States, p. 668; Federations, p. 675; History of Government, p. 829; Liberalism, p. 1118; Monarchy in Constitutional Governments, p. 1215; Monarchy in History, p. 1221; The Nation-State, p. 1241; Parliamentary Government, p. 1377; Polity, p. 1545; The Presidency in the United States, p. 1590; Republicanism, p. 1706; The Social Contract, p. 1827; Social Democracies, p. 1839; The State, p. 1878; Tribal Government, p. 2027.

GRANTS-IN-AID

Field of study: Economic issues

The grants-in-aid system is a primary means by which the U.S. federal government interacts and works with state and local governments. The dramatic expansion of the grants system has produced a shared responsibility among the three levels of government for addressing social, economic, and political policy concerns.

Principal terms

BLOCK GRANT: grant that specifies a range of activities for which monies may be used, with recipients allowed discretion to spend within these limits

CATEGORICAL GRANT: grant provided for a specific purpose, with recipients allowed little discretion in how funds will be spent

FEDERALISM: formal division of governing authority between a national government and state government

FORMULA GRANT: categorical grant distributed automatically according to a preestablished eligibility formula

GENERAL REVENUE SHARING: grants provided by the federal government to state and local governments with few federal limitations

PROJECT GRANT: categorical grant for which applicants must formally apply, with evaluations and awards made by the granting agency

Overview

The relationship between the federal government and state and local governments in the United States is in constant flux. The U.S. Constitution provides for a federal system, a formal division of authority among levels of government. The relationships among these governments is the ongoing product of tradition, negotiation, rewards, and influence. A major aspect of these relationships, particularly since the 1930's, has been the grants-in-aid system, the array of grant mechanisms by which the federal government provides financial resources to state and local governments.

The size and growth of the grants-in-aid system has been remarkable. Grant expenditures by the federal government rose from less than $5 million in 1915, to $3.2 billion in 1955, to more than $149 billion in 1992. The policy issues toward which the federal government has directed these considerable funds, and the mechanisms employed to distribute them, have varied considerably.

Through the grants-in-aid process, the federal government can identify policy areas of concern, establish guidelines for addressing these concerns, and then rely on state and local personnel to implement or administer the programs. The grant approach allows the federal government to achieve one or more broad policy goals: to provide financial resources that state and local governments could not otherwise realistically raise; to establish minimum standards in a program area that will apply in all communities; to equalize resources across states and communities; and to address national issues without creating new federal bureaucracies. A few of the many policy areas where grants have been employed include health care, employment training, law enforcement, education, transportation, agriculture, community planning, and forest protection. During the twentieth century, the federal government has enacted many hundreds of grants-in-aid programs.

Emphases within the grants-in-aid system are constantly changing. The greatest growth in the system took place in the 1960's and 1970's, and, in 1960, grant programs in the areas of income security or antipoverty programs, and transportation accounted for 80 percent of all federal grant expenditures. By 1992, the share of federal grants in these two policy areas had declined to 35 percent. By contrast, grant programs in the health care area, which took a mere 3 percent of the total in 1960, consumed fully 42 percent in 1992. This represented a dramatic shift in emphasis and priorities for the federal government.

While there has been considerable debate over these issues—how much money to devote to the grant-in-aid system and which policy areas to address—at least as much debate has concerned the forms and mechanisms of the grants provided. The federal government can employ several types of grants, and the differences among them have been of particular concern to governors and mayors.

Of the three broad types of grant mechanisms, the most common is the categorical grant, a grant for which the federal government clearly defines and limits how monies can be spent. One example is AFDC, or Aid to Families with Dependent Children. This is the federal government's principal welfare program, and the federal government establishes the parameters for the program: who is eligible, what the minimum benefits will be, and so on. With categorical grants, therefore, state and local governments have little discretion in designing or adapting programs to meet individual needs. There are two major forms of categorical grants: project grants, for which federal agencies evaluate applications and award grants; and formula grants, for which there are preestablished eligibility requirements, and in which funds are distributed to all who meet these standards.

Second, there are block grants. These are grant programs that specify a range of activities for which monies may be spent, with state and local officials allowed the discretion to decide how to spend the funds within these parameters. Block grants have usually been created by combining a series of existing categorical grants within one policy area. The first block grant, the Partnership for Health Act of 1966, blocked together sixteen categorical grants in the health care area. Prior to this, state and local governments had to complete separate applications for each categorical grant, and could not shift monies from one area to another. With the block grant, only one application was needed, and awarded monies could be shifted among the sixteen areas as community needs and priorities changed.

Third, there have been general revenue sharing grants. These grants were unconditional in that they were monies that state and local governments could spend as they saw fit. General revenue sharing was designed to promote tax fairness by raising funds through the progressive federal system, rather than the generally more regressive state and local tax systems, and to help equalize resources among states and localities. General revenue sharing was proposed by President Richard Nixon in 1969 and enacted in 1972, but was relatively short-lived, largely because of ballooning budget deficits at the federal level. With a strong sense that there was no federal revenue left to share, general revenue sharing was eliminated for state governments in 1980, and for local governments in 1986.

These varying grant mechanisms affected state and local governments differently. From the state and local standpoint, the ideal is a maximum of grant funding with a minimum of federal control and direction. For this reason, general revenue sharing was the preferred mechanism. It allowed state and local governments to draw on federal resources, while fully exercising their own authority in establishing spending priorities. In regard to categorical and block grants, governors and mayors have different preferences. Governors have a distinct preference for block grants, because they provide for greater administrative flexibility than categorical grants. Mayors have tended to favor categorical grants, because they usually are awarded by the federal government directly to the municipality, whereas block grants are usually awarded to states, which in turn decide what money will flow to a particular municipality. These differences speak directly to the nature of the U.S. federal system, that is, the distribution of resources and authority among the levels of government. As such, the changing nature of the grants-in-aid system, the size of the system, and the mechanisms employed have consistently reflected changing conceptions of U.S. federalism.

Applications

The grants-in-aid system has seen alternating periods of growth, stability, and retrenchment during the twentieth century, with these changes corresponding to the changing conception and reality of federal relationships. The period prior to the Great Depression and Franklin D. Roosevelt's New Deal has been characterized as that of dual federalism. The national government and the individual state governments were viewed, and viewed themselves, as largely distinct entities with separate areas of authority and responsibility. In this environment, the grants-in-aid system was minimal. Even after a large expansion of the system with the adoption of the Federal Road Act in 1916, throughout the 1920's grants represented only about 3 percent of the national budget.

With the New Deal, a new set of federal relationships emerged, lasting until the early 1960's, which has been characterized as cooperative federalism. In fashioning programs to address the social and economic difficulties associated with the Depression, the role of the national government was greatly expanded. The federal government took on roles previously dominated by state and local governments, and much this expanded role took form through the grants-in-aid system. Many new grant programs were enacted, with expenditures reaching about 10 percent of all federal outlays in 1940. World War II then imposed a period of modest retrenchment on the grants system. Also important during this period was the enactment of the United States Housing Act of 1937, which was the first case of the national government's providing grants-in-aid monies directly to local governments, bypassing the states.

Between 1960 and the end of the 1970's there was an explosion in the grants-in-aid system. This was the period of President Lyndon Johnson's Great Society and broad domestic policy development. The period has been characterized as that of "creative federalism." Although the Nixon Administration campaigned on and took steps to reinvigorate the authority and responsibility of state and local governments, the period was clearly marked by the growing dominance of the national government. Scores of new grant programs were created during this period. Federal outlays directed to grants-in-aid increased from 7 percent in 1959 to almost 17 percent in 1979. By the late 1970's, more than one out of every four dollars spent by all state and local governments was derived from federal grants. This represented a fundamental shift in the distribution of power and authority among the levels of government.

This expansion of federal authority drew criticism and a political backlash. This was first seen in Nixon's campaign for a "new federalism" in 1969. Nixon's efforts did produce block grants and general revenue sharing, both of which provided for increased flexibility for state and local officials, but the financial role of the federal government, and thus the basis for expanded authority, continued to grow. Indeed, in 1994 dollars, the Nixon years actually saw a doubling of grants-in-aid funding, from approximately $20 billion in 1969, to more than $43 billion in 1974.

What ultimately brought a significant retrenchment in creative federalism and the grants-in-aid system was the combination of the Reagan Administration's renewed effort at creating a new federalism, and the fiscal insolvency of severe federal budget deficits in the 1980's. The Reagan Administration succeeded in consolidating sixty-seven categorical grants into nine new block grants, thereby shifting some authority to the state and local level. It also proposed, but failed to enact, a much more ambitious proposal to delineate more clearly national from state and local responsibilities. The proposal would have had each level of government accept full responsibility in policy areas where mixed degrees of authority had developed. For example, the national government would have assumed complete responsibility for Medicaid, the health care program for the poor, with the state assuming complete responsibility for food stamps and Aid to Families with Dependent Children.

The driving force behind grants retrenchment, however, was clearly budgetary insolvency at the national level. Deficits prompted the gradual elimination of all revenue sharing grants, and limitations on many categorical and block grants. Where grants had reached 17 percent of federal outlays in 1979, by 1989, they had declined to less than 11 percent. This prompted a reallocation of authority, responsibility, and action among levels of government, with the states in particular reasserting themselves, but with the role of the national government remaining much stronger in the 1990's than prior to creative federalism. The primacy of the federal role thus remains a significant point of political contention.

Context

The grants-in-aid system raises significant issues of federalism and political power. The federal arrangements of the late twentieth century are dramatically different from those in place in 1789, when the Constitution was adopted. The breadth and depth of authority exercised by the national government has expanded tremendously. As a result, rather than being marked by distinct spheres of responsibility, most policy areas involve overlapping authority by states, localities, and the national government. Grants-in-aid are a major component of this reality, and they highlight issues concerning the centralization of power, democratic accountability, efficiency, and equity.

There are vocal political arguments both for and against the grants system, and, by extension, cooperative and creative federalism. Those in favor tend to emphasize national problems, efficiency, and equality. They focus on the national character of particular policy problems, arguing that health care for the poor, for example, is a true national concern, not limited to select states or communities. If such problems were left solely to state and local governments to address, inefficient delivery of services and significant inequities would result. Some states would do much, others very little. The grants-in-aid system is thus one way to ensure minimum national standards in areas of general concern.

Political critics have generally been more vocal and focused on issues of centralization, regulation, and accountability. Centralization is the core concern, raising the issue of the best or proper distribution of governing authority. Political conservatives, as a rule, are interested in limiting the authority and reach of the national government. They believe that individual freedom and public responsiveness require the exercise of governing authority in small units, close to the people. This calls for state and local governments to have a stronger position in relation to the national government.

With respect to regulation, critics of the system point to hundreds of grant programs, each with regulations concerning application, compliance, and oversight. They argue that this adds greatly to the complexity, inefficiency, and alienation of modern government. The issue of democratic accountability is also serious, and takes two forms. First, the grants-in-aid system may put unelected federal bureaucrats in positions of authority over elected state and local officials, determining how they will or can act. Second, by creating shared responsibility in so many policy areas, the grants system makes it difficult for citizens to hold any government entity accountable. In cases of policy failure, shared authority enables the various levels of government to blame one another. No one is ultimately and clearly accountable to the general public.

By the 1990's, the explosive growth in the grants-in-aid system was checked and, indeed, the system had undergone some retrenchment. The size of the system remained significant, however, and the implied political issues remained contentious. Public sentiment has generally moved in waves, alternating through periods of support for the expansion of the federal government's role in society, and periods of supporting the reassertion of state and local authority. Within the limitations of the financial resources available to the federal government, the grants-in-aid system is likely to continue to change in conformance with these broader public sentiments.

Bibliography

Aronson, J. Richard, and John L. Hilley. *Financing State and Local Governments*. 4th ed. Washington, D.C.: Brookings Institution, 1986. Readable treatment of the grants-in-aid system in the context of overall funding for state and local governments.

Brown, Lawrence D., James W. Fossett, and Kenneth T. Palmer. *The Changing Politics of Federal Grants*. Washington, D.C.: Brookings Institution, 1984. Three accessible essays on the changing nature of the grants-in-aid system since the Johnson Administration.

Congressional Budget Office. *The Federal Government in a Federal System: Current Intergovernmental Programs and Options for Change*. Washington, D.C.: Congress of the U.S., Congressional Budget Office, 1983. Important review and evaluation by the government of the impact of the grants-in-aid system, with a particular focus on the Reagan Administration's new federalism.

Conlan, Timothy. *New Federalism: Intergovernmental Reform from Nixon to Reagan*. Washington, D.C.: Brookings Institution, 1988. Strong but somewhat advanced discussion of the efforts by the Nixon and Reagan administrations to reform and restrain both creative federalism and the grants-in-aid system.

Derthick, Martha. *The Influence of Federal Grants, Public Assistance in Massachusetts*. Cambridge, Mass.: Harvard University Press, 1970. Detailed examination of the grants system in operation in one case, with a strong presentation of the rationale for creative federalism.

Hale, George E., and Marian Lief Palley. *The Politics of Federal Grants*. Washington, D.C.: Congressional Quarterly Press, 1981. Brief, highly readable overview of federal grants, with useful sections on the impacts of grants on state and local governments.

Zimmerman, Joseph F. *Contemporary American Federalism: The Growth of National Power*. New York: Praeger, 1992. Review of the changing nature of U.S. federal relationships over time, with much valuable and up-to-date data on grants-in-aid funding.

David Carleton

Cross-References

GRASSROOTS POLITICS

Field of study: Politics

Grassroots politics is participation in government by average citizens. This bottom-up approach to involvement includes such activities as petition drives, letter-writing campaigns, marches, referenda, and demonstrations. Grassroots political participation has increased in the United States since World War II.

Principal terms

BOYCOTT: refusal to buy or use specific products or services as a technique of political protest

CIVIL DISOBEDIENCE: refusal to obey a law one considers unjust or unconstitutional

CONSTITUENTS: people who are represented in governmental decisions by an elected official

DIRECT DEMOCRACY: political power exercised directly by the people, rather than exercised for them by elected representatives

EMPOWERMENT: movement encouraging average citizens to take responsibility for and control of actions that occur in the public's name; often applied to specific groups, such as women or the disabled

LOBBYING: contact with public officials for the purpose of persuading them to take a specific course of action

MOBILIZATION: act of bringing individuals together for the purpose of collective political action; usually accomplished through emotion-ladened rhetoric and appeals for unity

PROTEST: expression of dissent from governmental actions or policy

PUBLIC INTEREST: shared or common interests of members of a political society, as opposed to private, or individual, interests

Overview

"Grassroots politics" is a term that describes many situations where the average citizen participates in or exerts pressure on government. Grassroots efforts can involve established political groups, such as parties or interest groups, or can occur outside them. They are characterized by broad public participation, usually at the local level. They represent communication from the bottom up.

Grassroots lobbying is one of many tactics organized groups use to convey their message. Interest group leaders contact their members, who in turn write letters, telephone, or personally visit governmental officials to express the group's views. Political parties also use this approach in their get-out-the-vote electoral activities: Local party activists, supplied with literature from a central location, visit or call potential voters on behalf of a candidate.

In grassroots protests, many persons spontaneously dissent on a government action. The 1989 public outcry about a Congressional salary increase is an illustration. In memory of the Boston Tea Party protest against taxation without representation, thousands of irate citizens sent tea bags to their members of Congress. The tea bag suggestion, first made by a radio talk show host, captured national media attention and the imagination of the public. People responded without the prompting of organized groups.

Grassroots mobilization describes instances where citizens identify an issue and band together to address it; this can be a new issue or one overlooked by more established groups. Grassroots mobilization involves activities that develop group solidarity and identification, as well as activities with a more clearly political purpose. These include rallies, marches, and demonstrations. Grassroots mobilization is typical of many activist groups of the late twentieth century, such as the civil rights, women's, consumers', and environmental movements.

Grassroots organizations may believe that established procedures cannot address their concerns. This may lead them to create alternative arrangements, such as direct provision of public services, for example, free clinics, community banks, or information clearinghouses. They may demand more local participation in decisions about existing government services. This is known as community control.

One characteristic of grassroots actions is their direct nature: There are few intermediaries between those taking action and the targets of that action. The Populist and Progressive reform movements of the late nineteenth and early twentieth centuries introduced three important techniques that enabled average citizens to bypass, and thus curb, the power of corrupt political machines: the initiative, referendum, and recall. The initiative enabled citizens to bypass legislative bodies by proposing laws for a direct public vote. The referendum permitted citizens to vote to nullify a constitutional amendment or law after the legislature had approved it. The recall enabled voters to turn officeholders out of office before their terms expired. Each required that a minimum number of citizens sign petitions to initiate the procedure; once these legal standards were met, state governments could not intervene to stop the action.

Another characteristic of grassroots action is personalized or individual effort; the average citizen takes the initiative for action. Many activities fit this criterion. Conventional types of grassroots actions include petitions, telephone calls, door-to-door appeals for involvement and financial support, mass meetings, letters and telegrams, and meetings with public officials. More confrontational actions include demonstrations, marches, picket lines, strikes, sit-ins, boycotts, refusal to pay income taxes, and civil disobedience.

Grassroots political activities increased dramatically after World War II, encouraged by a number of factors. First, as government expands in size and responsibilities, more citizens are directly affected by government policies. This, in turn, has led to an increase in the number of interest groups at all levels of government. Groups that seek to influence legislative outcomes often find it advantageous to encourage their members to contact elected representatives. Officeholders desire to represent their districts and secure reelection; this inclines them to pay special attention to constituents' concerns. Large interest groups, such as the National Rifle Association and the American Association of Retired Persons, with members distributed throughout all the congressional districts, can enhance their influence by coordinating their Washington lobbying with letter-writing campaigns.

Governmental procedures also have promoted grassroots activity. Many of the social programs of the 1960's and 1970's, such as the War on Poverty, and environmental and consumer protection, required specific types of public participation in governmental decisions. These included the creation of local advisory boards and public hearings in communities affected by government actions. These opportunities for participation often encouraged the formation of grassroots organizations. In some cases, the government even provided resources for grassroots organization. The community action programs of the War on Poverty often hired community organizers to work in poor neighborhoods and develop local leadership skills.

Improvements in communication, especially expanded mass media and computer services, have facilitated grassroots activities. Mass marketing techniques enable political groups to identify and mobilize supporters quickly. Fax machines and electronic mail allow people to communicate across different time zones without delay. Radio talk shows and expanded news coverage bridge regional differences and identify common concerns. Some communities have even experimented with teledemocracy, where citizens participate in town meetings through interactive television. Improved communications lessens the psychological distance between the citizens and government officials and encourages those who do not regularly participate to do so.

A final factor that promotes grassroots activity is a growing distrust with traditional politics, including political parties and established interest groups such as unions. As the federal government grew after World War II, alienation from traditional political institutions also grew. More people reported in public opinion polls that they believed government did not care what ordinary people thought. Rates of voting in national elections declined. Membership in unions fell, and more people reported that they did not identify with political parties. Many activists sought an antidote to this cynicism through community empowerment and direct citizen action. The number of public interest groups increased. The belief that local problems required local action strengthened community action and neighborhood associations. The politics of confrontation fueled such grassroots protest movements as the 1970's Proposition 13 property tax revolt in California, the AIDS (acquired immune deficiency syndrome) activists of the 1980's, and popular support of businessman H. Ross Perot's 1992 presidential candidacy.

Grassroots organizations stay close to their members' concerns, but it is difficult to sustain the interest and involvement of the average citizen. Many grassroots efforts lose momentum and support over time. Mothers Against Drunk Driving, for example, achieved notable successes in raising state drinking ages and penalties for drunk driving, but interest in its cause waned after early victories. Group leaders experienced burnout and some even left the organization. Other groups have found it hard to set broader political goals or form coalitions with other groups. The United We Stand organization, which supported H. Ross Perot's candidacy, had little success in converting support for Perot into a platform of political reforms after the campaign ended.

Applications

Three cases can be used to illustrate the variety of grassroots political movements in the United States in the last half of the twentieth century: the consumer movement, the 1972 presidential campaign, and the bus boycott in Montgomery, Alabama.

In the 1960's, lawyer Ralph Nader organized a consumer protest for automobile safety, which culminated in national requirements for seat belts and the elimination of some models of automobiles. Public Citizen, the watchdog organization Nader founded, has served as an umbrella for projects on consumer safety, public health, workplace safety, government reform, and opposition to nuclear power. Nader pioneered the Public Interest Research Group (PIRG) model of grassroots action. Nader believed that his national organization's approach to research, legislation, and litigation could serve as a model for community efforts, and that new generations of national activists should start their training at the local level. He advocated the creation of local PIRGs, usually based in a high school or university setting and funded and operated by the members.

PIRGs conduct research on local problems and the economic, legislative, and legal solutions possible for that community. Education is followed by mobilization, often in support of new legislation, an initiative, or a referendum. National organizations may provide technical advice, but the local groups determine the political targets and develop the skills and leadership to accomplish their goals.

The 1972 presidential primary campaign of George McGovern, the Democratic Party nominee, illustrates grassroots activism at the national political level. McGovern, an unsuccessful 1968 presidential candidate and strong opponent of the Vietnam War, headed a party reform commission to increase the participation of underrepresented groups—women, minorities, and youth—in the nomination process. McGovern was the underdog in 1972, and faced challenges from more prominent Democrats. The 1972 reforms expanded the number of primaries and required that delegates conform to affirmative action goals. McGovern's campaign, short on funds but strong on volunteers, outmaneuvered local party organizations. By successfully fielding slates of local delegates sympathetic to his platform and by extensive door-to-door campaigning, McGovern's campaign won surprise primary victories and collected enough committed delegates to win the nomination. His campaign also brought a new kind of delegate into the party, people with strong ideological convictions and few ties to the established party organizations. Many of these delegates became party leaders and officeholders.

A third example of grassroots activism, the 1955 Montgomery, Alabama, bus boycott, was one of the seminal events in the effort to end racial segregation. On December 1, 1955, Rosa Parks, a seamstress and National Association for the Advancement of Colored People (NAACP) activist, refused to give up her seat at the front of a bus to a white man and was arrested. Within a week, African Americans throughout the city had announced their refusal to use the public transit system until it desegregated.

The Montgomery transit system had long been the focus of community concern: The majority of the riders were African American, and the policy of relegating them to seats at the back of the bus produced hardship. At mass meetings sponsored by local churches and groups, the community debated the merits and effect of a boycott, developed alternative arrangements for transportation, and trained themselves in nonviolent methods of response. The boycott lasted more than a year, ending only after a 1956 U.S. Supreme Court ruling declared the segregation unconstitutional. This local action elevated Martin Luther King, Jr., and his philosophy of nonviolent protest to national stature. The boycott also demonstrated key tenets of grassroots action: careful selection of targets, education and mobilization of a large number of citizens, and the involvement and coordination of a broad range of community interests.

Context

Grassroots politics is not a new political phenomenon. In fact, the authors of the Constitution of the United States expected that citizens would communicate directly with their government. The First Amendment, which guarantees the right of the people "to petition the Government for a redress of grievances," was a direct reaction to colonial experiences.

The concept that citizens must consent to the actions of government is at the heart of philosopher John Locke's view of the social contract. The Declaration of Independence, modeled on Locke's views, set forth the conditions under which the public could exercise its right to abolish a government; one of these was the failure to address the public's concerns when expressed in a legal and peaceful manner.

The question of how and how often the public should participate in the workings of government, however, soon became problematic for the new nation. The authors of the Constitution expressed severe misgivings about direct democracy. James Madison, fourth president and one of the authors of the Federalist Papers (1787-1788), noted in Federalist No. 10 that the elected representative or republican form of government would refine the public's view: ". . . the public voice, pronounced by the representatives of the people, will be more consonant to the public good, than if pronounced by the people themselves."

Thomas Jefferson, third president and principal author of the Declaration of Independence, disagreed. He believed that representative government over time would become elitist and stagnant unless the average citizen participated in its workings and developed a personal interest in its outcomes. In his 1816 letter to John Taylor, he observed that "the mass of the citizens is the safest depository of their own rights. . . . The evils flowing from the duperies of the people are less injurious than those from the egoism of their agents."

Author and naturalist Henry David Thoreau, in his 1848 essay "Civil Disobedience," took an even more forceful view of the public's responsibility to participate. He maintained that when individuals disagreed with a governmental action, voting was not sufficient to register that dissent. Instead, they needed to repudiate the government's action and be prepared to experience the consequences. Thoreau registered his own dissent from the Mexican-American War by refusing to pay taxes, and going to jail. Thoreau's writings helped to shape King's views on nonviolent protest.

This debate concerning the merits of direct action has persisted throughout U.S. history. At various times, government elitism or distance has been met with calls for expanded participation and more power to the people. The nineteenth century abolition, suffrage, and Populist movements are historical examples. The call for local control and participatory democracy by party reformers in the 1950's, radical and civil rights activists of the 1960's, and the empowerment movement of the 1990's represent contemporary examples.

Grassroots activism is a powerful tool for elevating new social concerns to the political agenda, especially in an era in which the news media play an important role in defining political issues. It also serves an important function by renewing the public's sense of involvement and stake in the political system.

Bibliography

Boyte, Harry C. *Commonwealth: A Return to Citizen Politics*. New York: Free Press, 1989. Provides a historical context for U.S. civic activism through its review of the religious, economic, and political bases for grassroots politics in different eras. Analyzes a number of contemporary cases, including the community action models of the 1960's, and the role of technology in the 1990's. Assumes some knowledge of history and current events on the reader's part.

Encyclopedia of Associations. Edited by Peggy Kneffel Daniels and Carol A. Schwartz. 28th ed. Detroit: Gale Research, 1994. More than twenty thousand descriptions of interest groups, think tanks, associations, action projects, and community organizations across the nation. Updated yearly, and is organized by subject and region. Each entry describes the group's purpose, membership, and general activities, and gives its address. A valuable tool for identifying activist groups.

Hamilton, Alexander, James Madison, and John Jay. *The Federalist Papers*. Selected and with an introduction by Andrew Hacker. New York: Washington Square Press, 1964. Essay number 10 contrasts the dangers of democracy with the merits of a republican form of government; number 39 rebuts Jefferson's call for public referenda on the actions of the national government; number 84 questions whether a Bill of Rights is necessary. A major source of insight into the political philosophy of the authors of the Constitution.

Nader, Ralph, and Donald Ross. *Action for a Change*. Rev. ed. New York: Grossman, 1972. Describes how to organize public interest research groups on high school and college campuses, set goals, and collect information. Many examples.

Osborne, David, and Ted Gaebler. *Reinventing Government*. Reading, Mass.:

Addison-Wesley, 1992. Groundbreaking work considers how government can become more accessible to the average citizen. Examples from federal, state, and local governments highlight ways in which citizens have changed governmental practices, and ways that governments have transformed themselves to serve the public better. The model for federal agency reorganization during President Bill Clinton's Administration.

Williams, Juan. *Eyes on the Prize: America's Civil Rights Years, 1954-1965.* New York: Penguin, 1988. Compelling descriptions of the key events, personalities, organizations, and strategies of the Civil Rights movement. There is also a companion collection of readings and a television documentary.

Carolyn Ann Kawecki

Cross-References

Activist Politics, p. 7; Aging and Politics in the United States, p. 35; Citizen Movements, p. 248; Citizenship Rights and Responsibilities, p. 260; Civil Disobedience, p. 285; Consumer Politics, p. 445; Demagoguery, p. 507; Democracy, p. 513; Gay and Lesbian Politics, p. 732; Government Roles, p. 778; Initiatives and Referendums, p. 923; Interest Groups, p. 936; Lobbying and Lobbyists, p. 1130; The New Right, p. 1293; Political Participation, p. 1479; Political Parties, p. 1485; Protest Movements, p. 1621; Public Opinion Polling, p. 1627; Technology and Citizen-Government Relations, p. 1949.

HEADS OF STATE

Field of study: Comparative government

A head of state is the symbolic leader of a country. In some countries, the head of state plays a purely ceremonial role and has no political power. In other countries, the head of state is also a political leader, possessing immense power as the chief executive of the government.

Principal terms

CEREMONIAL HEAD OF STATE: public official who serves as a national symbol of unity but has no political power

CHIEF EXECUTIVE: political leader of a country, who heads a cabinet of advisers, oversees the bureaucracy, and manages state affairs on a daily basis

CHIEF OF STATE: synonym for head of state, frequently used in the United States

CONSTITUTIONAL MONARCHY: political system that has a royal as ceremonial head of state, but assigns political power to the leader of a majority within parliament

EXECUTIVE HEAD OF STATE: public official who is both the symbolic and political leader of a country

HEAD OF GOVERNMENT: title frequently given to the political leader in a system of government that has a ceremonial head of state

Overview

Virtually every country has a public figure who stands as a symbol of its unity and the pride of its people and who represents the country at official and ceremonial functions at home and abroad. This figure plays the role of head or chief of state for the country.

It is the head of state who hosts formal dinners for visiting dignitaries, makes official visits to other countries, and attends the funerals of foreign leaders. Heads of state often appoint ambassadors, promulgate laws and decrees, and ratify official treaties for their countries. Heads of state also lead parades; dedicate new highways, bridges, and schools; lay wreaths on the tombs of war veterans; open sporting events and congratulate sports champions; issue pardons for criminal offenses; and bestow honors or medals on significant individuals for their contributions to their country or the world.

The role of head of state is often confused with the role of chief executive. The chief executive in a country is the public official who leads the cabinet, oversees the state bureaucracy, and manages state affairs on a daily basis. The chief executive also holds the political power to set policy for the country. In some countries, such as the United Kingdom, the chief executive is referred to as the head of government, and the role is held by the prime minister, while the monarch serves as the head of state. In other countries, the roles of head of state and chief executive are combined in one public official. This is the case in the United States, where the president serves as both chief executive and head of state.

The officials who serve as heads of state in each of the more than 180 countries in the world are selected in many ways and are given various titles. Queen, king, president, chairman, emperor, emir, and sultan are all titles given to heads of state in different countries around the world. Some heads of state claim their role on the basis of their birth into a royal family and their rite of succession. Others occupy their position through the use of force. Still others are elected to their role, either directly by the citizens of their countries or through any number of indirect electoral procedures involving electoral colleges or assemblies. In addition, the head of state may play a variety of other roles, depending upon the system of government used in each country.

Applications

Analyzing and contrasting the political systems of the United States and the United Kingdom illustrates how general concepts and definitions for the roles of head of state and chief executive are applied in different countries.

In the United States, the roles of head of state and chief executive are both played by the president, who is also the commander in chief of the military. A president is elected in the United States every four years. Since the passage of the Twenty-second Amendment to the Constitution in 1951, presidents have been limited to two four-year terms of office each. If a sitting president is assassinated, dies, resigns, or is removed from office through impeachment procedures more than two years into a term of office, the successor is allowed to serve out the remainder of the term and to stand for election for two additional four-year terms. Thus it is possible that an individual could serve ten years in office as president in the United States.

The president is not directly elected by the citizens of the United States but rather is chosen by an electoral college consisting of electors from all fifty states and the District of Columbia. There are 538 electors selected to the electoral college every four years. Of this number, 535 are apportioned to the fifty states based on the size of their congressional delegation. The District of Columbia, which contains the U.S. capital of Washington, does not have any voting members in Congress, but is given three votes in the electoral college.

Every four years, the fifty states and the District of Columbia pledge their electors to a particular candidate for president in the electoral college. A candidate gathers electoral votes by winning a plurality of the popular vote in general elections held by each state and the District of Columbia. In forty-nine states and the District of Columbia, the candidate who receives the most votes in each state's general election is pledged all of that state's electoral votes. The exception is the state of Maine, which apportions its electors to candidates on the basis of the percentage of the popular vote they receive. To win the U.S. presidency, a candidate must receive 270 of the 538 electoral votes in the electoral college.

Although the presidency is one of the most prestigious and highly respected positions of power in the world, the U.S. president is not the only source of power within the U.S. political system. The system is based on the principles of separation of powers, and checks and balances, among the three branches of government: executive, judicial, and legislative.

The checks and balances that Congress and the federal judiciary have over the president illustrate the limitations of the president's power in the U.S. political system. The president can veto legislation passed by the Congress, but that veto can be overridden by a two-thirds majority vote in both the Senate and the House of Representatives. The president can be impeached and removed from office by the Congress for abrogation of the Constitution. The president is allowed to appoint all federal judges, including Supreme Court justices, but those appointments must be confirmed by a majority vote in the Senate. Once confirmed, federal justices and judges are not obligated to support the policy positions of the president that appointed them, because their appointment is for life.

The president is both the executive head of state and the preeminent political leader of the United States. The dual nature of the office can be used for political advantage. When political opponents or the media criticize a president for a particular policy decision or action, the president, in his role as head of state, can appeal to patriotic sentiment among the citizenry to deflect criticism of his political leadership. The president might even suggest that his critics are unpatriotic and are disrespectful of the presidency as an institution in the country.

Political systems in many other countries, particularly constitutional monarchies, assign the role of head of state and preeminent political leader to two different public officials. The logic behind this separation of roles is that the head of state can stand above the fractious debates of politics and serve as a symbol of unity, pride, and continuity for the country as a whole. In these systems, the political leader cannot use the role of head of state for political advantage. Citizens, the media, and political opponents can freely question and criticize the decisions of the political leader without their patriotism and loyalty to the country being brought into question. Proponents of political systems that separate the roles of head of state and political leader point out that in this system all the political leader's time can be spent governing, while ceremonial and perfunctory duties are left to the head of state.

In the United Kingdom, the roles of head of state and political leader are divided between two different public officials: The ceremonial head of state is the monarch; the political leader, or head of government, is the prime minister.

The leader of the political party that holds a majority of the seats in the House of Commons, the lower but more powerful house of the British parliament, is given the role of prime minister. The leaders of British political parties are selected by their membership. A prime minister who remains the leader of the party that commands a majority of votes in the House of Commons can remain in office indefinitely. If a sitting prime minister is replaced as the leader of his or her party, or the prime minister's party loses a major vote on a bill or a vote of confidence in the House of Commons, the prime minister is obligated to resign. A prime minister is also replaced if his or her party loses a majority of seats in the House of Commons in national elections.

Members of the House of Commons are not elected at regular, fixed intervals. Custom dictates that British national elections occur at least once every five years, or whenever the majority party loses a significant vote in the House of Commons. The sitting prime minister is allowed to call for the dissolution of Parliament and new elections. The campaign period for British elections runs for approximately six weeks, very brief by U.S. standards. At the end of that period, a new House of Commons is elected, and the leader of the party that holds a majority of the seats is named prime minister and chooses a cabinet. There is no limit on the number of years any one individual may serve as prime minister.

The British monarch is a member of the royal family, is chosen on the basis of birth, and typically serves for life. The monarch no longer has real political power in the political system. The customs and traditions of British government require the monarch to appoint the prime minister and government ministers, to give approval to all bills before they can become law, to open sessions of parliament, to address the parliament periodically outlining preferred political policies, and to dissolve parliament. While the list of the British monarch's responsibilities may appear formidable, in reality, the monarch is not granted the decision-making power to perform such duties independent of the prime minister and the government. The monarch's address to the Parliament is written by the prime minister's office; the monarch is obligated by custom to approve all bills passed by the parliament; the monarch is required to ask the leader of the political party that holds the majority of seats in the House of Commons to serve as prime minister and name a cabinet; and the monarch can only dissolve parliament at the request of the prime minister.

Context

Recognized leaders of tribes, clans, nations, and countries have existed throughout human history. For most of recorded time, political leaders were all-powerful figures, single-handedly ruling over peoples and territories. Distinctions between the role of head of state and the role of chief executive within a political system, and comparative analyses of the functions of executive, legislative, and judicial branches of government, were not necessary. All political power was held by one or a few individuals within society.

As a new millennium approaches, it is likely that personalized, dictatorial rule will still exist in a number of countries around the world. The likelihood is that such rule will always be present somewhere. What students of politics have seen over the course of the last several centuries, however, is the rise of an alternative to individual rule, namely representative democracy. In this form of rule, no single individual is all-powerful. Different powers, roles, and responsibilities are shared between legislatures and presidents, prime ministers and monarchs.

As a consequence of the rise of alternatives to individual rule, the traditional connotation of a head of state as the all-powerful ruler of a country has undergone revision. As a result, the term "head of state" should not be thought of as a specific position or office within a political system, but rather as a role that is played by an individual within a political system.

In some political systems, the role of head of state is the only one a particular official may play. In others, head of state is just one of several roles that a particular official may play. Applying the defining characteristics of the role of head of state—namely a public figure who serves as a symbol of unity and pride for a country and represents that country at official functions and ceremonies—to the actions of public officials within a country should enable the determination of who functions as the head of state for any given country.

Bibliography

Banks, Arthur S., ed. *Political Handbook of the World*. Binghamton, N.Y.: CSA, yearly. Annual reference work that publishes political information about every country in the world. Includes heads of state and government, cabinet members, leaders and programs of political parties, and representatives to national legislatures.

Blondel, Jean. *The Organization of Governments: A Comparative Analysis of Governmental Structures*. London: Sage Publications, 1982. Comparative study of modern governments. Examines development, structure, political composition, and decision-making patterns of institutions and executive offices in different countries across time.

Chiefs of State and Cabinet Members of Foreign Governments: A Directory. Washington, D.C.: Central Intelligence Agency, bi-monthly. Single best source of names of current heads of state, heads of government, and cabinet members in countries throughout the world. Unclassified; can be found in libraries that are U.S. government document depositories.

Da Graça, John V. *Heads of State and Government*. New York: New York University Press, 1985. Chronologically lists the past heads of state and government of different countries. Entries specify dates of office, family relationships, and political party affiliations.

Longford, Frank, and John Wheeler-Bennett, eds. *The History Makers: Leaders and Statesmen of the 20th Century*. London: Sidgwick & Jackson, 1973. Individual chapters devoted to a diverse group of significant twentieth century political leaders. Most chapter authors knew their subjects personally and provide personal anecdotes and insights.

Neustadt, Richard E. *Presidential Power: The Politics of Leadership with Reflections on Johnson and Nixon*. New York: John Wiley & Sons, 1976. Updated edition of the 1960 classic on the ability of U.S. presidents to wield their personal and institutional power within the American political system.

Rose, Richard, and Ezra N. Suleiman, eds. *Presidents and Prime Ministers*. Washington, D.C.: American Enterprise Institute, 1980. Describes the heads of state and government positions in six European states and Canada. Useful comparisons between the U.S. presidency and the leadership positions presented in the different chapters.

Samuel E. Watson III

Cross-References

Bonapartism, p. 140; Cabinet Government, p. 184; Constitutional Governments, p. 432; Cult of Personality, p. 477; Dictatorships, p. 546; Elections, p. 578; Executive Functions in U.S. Government, p. 636; Hooker's Political Philosophy, p. 842; Impeachment, p. 882; Leadership, p. 1066; Modern Monarchy, p. 1209; Monarchy in History, p. 1221; Parliamentary Government, p. 1377; The Presidency in the United States, p. 1590; Statesmanship, p. 1898; Succession, p. 1909; Veto Power, p. 2097.

HEALTH CARE MANAGEMENT

Field of study: Functions of government

In contrast to the health care systems of other industrialized nations, the U.S. system is a decentralized and predominately free market enterprise. The federal government directly manages only a small part of the national health care system, but uses insurance programs, grants, and regulatory authority to control private health care indirectly.

Principal terms

DEPARTMENT OF HEALTH AND HUMAN SERVICES: executive branch department of the federal government responsible for civilian national health programs

DEPARTMENT OF VETERANS' AFFAIRS: federal department responsible for administering health care programs and facilities for U.S. military veterans

MEDICAID: federal program that provides health insurance to the poor; administered and partially paid by the states

MEDICARE: federal program that provides health insurance to persons sixty-five years of age and older and to others entitled to Social Security benefits

NATIONAL HEALTH INSURANCE: any health insurance program that a national government organizes in order to guarantee coverage to all citizens for private health services

PAYER: organization or individual who provides the funds to pay for the provision of health services

PROVIDER: health care institution, such as a nursing home or hospital (or individual health professional) that provides health services to patients

PUBLIC HEALTH: governmental efforts to prevent disease and to protect the health of the population as a whole by focusing on underlying causes of health problems

REGULATION: rule or procedure made by a governmental agency, and having the force of law

Overview

The United States has one of the world's most decentralized health care systems. Centralization is a function of the extent of government ownership and control of the system's resources. U.S. federal and state governments own and operate only a small part of the system and provide direct services only to special populations. As a result, health care in the United States is predominantly a private enterprise of providers, payers, and patients operating in a free market. This limited government role in health care reflects American cultural and political values that reflect distrust for government intervention in the private sector. Indirectly, government's increasing financial involvement and regulatory authority, in establishing conditions and setting rules to promote social objectives and to protect the public's health, has resulted in considerable and expanding influence over the private health care system.

Health care management as a function of federal, state, and local governments has evolved throughout the entire history of the U.S. government. The basis for any responsibility of government is the Constitution and, because of early beliefs, influenced by the lack of medical technology, that health care is a personal, private, and individual affair, the Constitution does not explicitly mention health nor specify any federal role in health care. Instead, federal authority over health care is indirectly justified by the general powers to regulate commerce and to raise money and spend it. The commerce power enables the federal government to establish rules for the production and flow of goods and services. This power justifies federal regulation of food, drugs, product and occupational safety, and environmental health activities because they move in, or affect, commerce among states or nations. The federal government's spending power enables it to manage health directly by owning and operating health facilities for specific populations, and indirectly, by attaching conditions on money grants to organizations and individuals, enabling it to accomplish indirectly what it lacks constitutional authority to do directly. This power justifies medical research and education grants, Medicare and Medicaid programs, funds for hospital construction, and general health planning.

By contrast, when the states delegated specific powers to the federal government and ratified the Constitution in 1789, they retained for themselves a broad range of authority, known as "police powers," to protect the public's health, safety, and general welfare. Police powers give state governments the power potentially to manage essentially every aspect of the health care systems within their jurisdictions. The rationale for the state's broad interest in the public's and an individual's health as well as the status of the local health care system is to foster healthy citizens who can support themselves, contribute to the economy, and bear arms for the state if necessary. Health management as a function of state government, therefore, includes traditional public health activities as well as regulatory efforts. Traditional public health functions include communicable disease control, maternal and child health services, environmental sanitation, health education, laboratory services, and vital statistics. States frequently delegate several of these functions to local governments. Regulatory activities in state government usually include the licensure of health facilities and professionals, the development and enforcement of health standards, and in some states, the setting of rates, or prices, for hospital and medical services, as well as the regulation of health insurance.

While the role of state and local governments in health care has a longer history and has also developed over time, health care management as a function of federal government has evolved most dramatically as a result of historical changes in technology, economics, politics, social and cultural factors, and patterns of health and disease that identified problems that were not or could not be solved, or were created, by the private sector.

The federal government played a very limited role in the early days of the U.S. government. Early activities included imposing quarantines on ships entering U.S. ports to prevent epidemics and providing direct care, beginning in the late eighteenth century, to merchant seamen, during a time when shipping was a vital economic activity for the nation. States and local governments, however, were regarded as having jurisdiction over the control of communicable diseases within the country. At that time, local boards of health were most heavily involved in health services, and were initially organized to develop and enforce laws on waste disposal and street drainage to improve sanitation, as well as laws on quarantine of homes to prevent the spread of infectious diseases, such as smallpox, typhoid fever, and diphtheria. By the end of the nineteenth century, all states had boards of health to focus on the statewide control of communicable diseases and sanitary control, and at the end of the twentieth century, there were about three thousand state and local health departments in the United States. State and local activities in health have evolved to include direct hospital, outpatient, and emergency services for the poor, immunizations, mental retardation care, mental health and substance abuse services, family planning, prenatal and well-baby care, environmental health, occupational health and safety, as well as traditional public health and regulatory responsibilities.

The federal government's role in health care grew to include direct services for the armed forces, veterans, and Native Americans. After the Depression of the 1930's, the federal government also assumed responsibility for providing financial support to the poor and to the nation's elderly, culminating in a massive enterprise since the 1960's creation of Medicare and Medicaid. Financial assistance to individuals was also supplemented by support for the modernization, construction, and equipment of health facilities, for the education and training of health professionals, and for the development of biomedical research. Because the federal government—along with state governments—became a major purchaser of health care with the implementation of Medicare and Medicaid, financing more than one-third of the nation's trillion-dollar annual health care expenditures in the mid-1990's, cost control has been a high priority and has resulted in greater involvement in and influence over the organization, management, and delivery of private health services.

The principal health agency in the federal government is the Department of Health and Human Services, which is responsible for developing and implementing administrative regulations to promote national health objectives. It is also the main source of regulations affecting the health care industry. Within this department are two operating agencies with specific authority in health care. The Health Care Financing Administration manages the Medicare and Medicaid programs and the Public Health Service includes the National Institutes of Health, the largest biomedical research agency in the world, and the Food and Drug Administration. The latter supervises and controls the introduction of drugs, foods, cosmetics, and medical devices into the marketplace and protects society from impure and hazardous products. The Public

Health Service also administers programs to develop health resources, prevent and control disease, and provide technical assistance to the states and private organizations for planning and delivery of physical and mental health services.

Applications

Health care management is a function of federal, state, and local government. All three levels of government manage health care directly by owning and operating a small number of health care organizations and indirectly by paying for and regulating private health services in the name of protecting and promoting the public's health.

Government directly controls a small component of the health care system by owning and operating hospitals and clinics. At the federal level, medical facilities are provided by the Department of Veterans' Affairs for veterans with service-related disabilities, the Department of Defense for the armed forces and their dependents, and the Indian Health Service, within the Department of Health and Human Services, for Native Americans living on reservations. Most state governments operate mental hospitals, and local governments provide public health programs as well as hospitals and emergency care for the poor or for people without health insurance. Government, by direct ownership and operation, plans, organizes, controls, staffs, and performs all the classical tasks of management to provide health services in these facilities.

The government indirectly exerts economic control over private health care organizations as the largest single purchaser of medical services, since "he who pays the piper calls the tune." Enacted in 1965, Medicare is the federal government's largest health program, providing hospital and medical insurance for persons over sixty-five years of age, the permanently disabled, and people with end-stage renal disease. Medicare has two parts: "A," which is mandatory, and pays for hospital services, and "B," which is voluntary, and covers physicians' services and outpatient care—services that do not require a hospital stay. Medicaid, which was established along with Medicare in 1965, is paid for by a combination of matching federal and state funds and is administered by the states, to provide hospital and medical insurance for the nation's poor, regardless of age.

Although the amendments to the Social Security Act, which established the Medicare and Medicaid programs, forbid federal supervision or control over the practice of medicine or the ways in which health services are provided, the government has in fact mandated conditions of participation in order for providers to receive payment for the treatment of Medicare beneficiaries. In order to participate in Medicare, health care organizations are required to be certified and to meet specific requirements and standards of quality developed by the Department of Health and Human Services, such as specified content and number of hours of training for nurses' aides working in nursing homes. Also, since 1965, policies have been developed to control rising health care costs and to improve the quality of care provided to Medicare beneficiaries and Medicaid recipients, such as changing payment methods and requiring providers to contract with organizations to monitor the appropriateness and quality of care for which the federal government pays. Also, the influence of the federal government has been extended to the rest of the health care system through the adoption of Medicare's payment methods and policies by private health insurance companies.

The federal government also influences the behavior of providers by offering grants for specific purposes to state governments as well as to private health care organizations and individuals. Thus, federal funds have been used to encourage state governments to pursue national goals and interests, such as the provision of maternal and child health services, to offer incentives to the private sector for modernization and construction of hospital facilities, and to develop new methods of health delivery, such as community health centers and health maintenance organizations (HMOs). Individual health professionals, through the National Health Service Corps, have been awarded tuition grants, and educational loans have been forgiven in exchange for serving in medical shortage areas of the country for a specified period of time.

In addition, the government manages both public and private health services through regulation. State and local governments are required by the federal government to provide services or implement various environmental health or occupational health and safety regulations. Private hospitals receiving federal funds can be financially penalized for "patient dumping," discharging or transferring patients for reasons other than medical necessity. Health care facilities are also required to verify and review the credentials of physicians and dentists through a National Practitioner Data Bank, which collects data and requires reporting on professional misconduct, before granting or renewing their privileges to practice in that institution. The federal Medical Waste Tracking Act requires providers in several states to document the disposal of medical waste. The Occupational Safety and Health Administration developed rules for hospitals, as well as dentist and physician offices, to protect health care employees against blood-borne infections, such as hepatitis B and HIV/AIDS. These regulations mandate hepatitis vaccination for health care employees, new laundry requirements for protective clothing, the availability of gloves and goggles, and educational programs for employees. The Patient Self-Determination Act requires hospitals, nursing homes, and other health care organizations to ask all patients upon admission whether they have made advance directives as to their wishes for the use of medical interventions for themselves in case of the loss of their own decision-making capacity. The institutions must provide each patient with written information about advance directives. State governments regulate both individual and institutional providers through licensure and the inspection of facilities to ensure that minimal standards are met. Licensure requirements and other regulations vary from state to state, but they generally include the reporting and publication of both cost and quality data to provide information to consumers and payers of health services. Some states have even required that physicians, as a condition of licensure, accept Blue Cross and Medicare payments as payment in full for their services, banning the billing of balances not covered by these insurance programs.

Context

While government involvement in U.S. health care appears to be extensive and pervasive, other nations provide greater financing and have more control. Examples range from Great Britain's National Health Service (NHS), the most centralized national health care system in the world, completely owned and operated by government, to Canada's national health insurance program, in which government collects and pays for the private health services of all citizens. While Britain has introduced American-style privatization and market reforms in its NHS to make it more efficient and responsive to citizens, the United States has looked to Canada for ideas about increasing health care access while containing costs, as Canada has managed to accomplish.

The United States has debated the adoption of national health insurance throughout the twentieth century. In response to expressions of concern by the public about the high cost of health insurance and medical services, and declining access to care, particularly for the uninsured, the country argued once again about national health insurance during the early 1990's. President Bill Clinton proposed a "Health Security Plan" in 1994 that would guarantee government-organized health insurance to all citizens for private health services. Advocates of national health insurance believe that the nation needs major reform of the health care system, and the "Health Security Plan" envisioned a more centralized organization of health insurance, at the state level, to solve these problems. Opponents of the plan argued that insurance reforms alone were needed to fix the health care system. While public surveys suggested strong dissatisfaction with the health care system, Americans appeared wary of government operation of the health insurance system because of beliefs that choice of providers could be restricted and that care might be less personal.

Bibliography

Graig, Laurene A. *Health of Nations: An International Perspective on U.S. Health Care Reform.* 2d ed. Washington, D.C.: Congressional Quarterly, 1993. Comparative review of several national health care systems and how health care management as a function of government differs among them.

Litman, Theodore J., and Leonard S. Robins. *Health Politics and Policy.* 2d ed. Albany, N.Y.: Delmar, 1991. Collection of articles on the relationships between government and health, including an extensive chronology of the evolution of health care management as a function of government.

Pozgar, George D. *Legal Aspects of Health Care Administration.* 5th ed. Gaithersburg, Md.: Aspen, 1993. Survey of legal issues affecting health care organizations and their management.

Taylor, Robert J., and Susan B. Taylor. *The AUPHA Manual of Health Services Management.* Gaithersburg, Md.: Aspen, 1994. Comprehensive source of information on a broad range of health management issues, functions, and activities, including the role of government in the management of health services.

John F. Racine

Cross-References

Executive Functions in U.S. Government, p. 636; Government Agencies, p. 765; Government Powers, p. 772; Government Roles, p. 778; Regulatory Agencies in the United States, p. 1678; The Social Security System, p. 1852; Social Services, p. 1858; The World Health Organization, p. 2180.

HEGEMONY

Field of study: International government and politics

Hegemony is the preponderant economic, political, and military influence of one state over others in the international system. Because a single state, the hegemon, is perceived as dominant, other states in the system defer to its preferences, reinforcing its political power.

Principal terms

EAST: the territory of the former Soviet Union and most of eastern Europe

INTERNATIONAL SYSTEM: economic, political, and military relationships of all the states in the world

RATIONAL ACTOR: decision maker whose decision is based on an assessment of the costs and benefits of alternative actions

STATE: government whose sovereign authority in a country is recognized as legitimate by other governments in the international system

WEST: the United States and the territory of most of Western Europe

Overview

In world politics, hegemony is the condition in which a single state, the hegemon, is recognized as having superior economic and military capabilities and, hence, predominant political influence as well. The hegemon is at the apex of the hierarchy of states' power in the international system. In the nineteenth and early twentieth centuries, Great Britain was the recognized hegemon, but after the end of World War II, that position was accorded to the United States.

Hegemony in the international system is not achieved through a formalized system; a hegemon is neither chosen by other states in the system, nor does it formally agree to assume a role of leadership. The hegemon is the state that emerges from a major power war with the greatest military and economic capabilities, and to which other states in the system tacitly turn for political guidance.

Conventionally, hegemony in world politics is understood in terms of three characteristics generally attributed to the state that is perceived to be the most powerful: capability, willingness to lead, and a high degree of legitimacy. In some analyses, capability refers to dominant political influence in the international system gained through superior military capabilities. Other scholars, however, contend that economic preponderance is at least as important as military superiority in understanding hegemony. Generally, a hegemon is strong economically to support the credibility of its military power, and strong militarily to protect its economic interests.

A powerful state's willingness to lead is another essential characteristic of the hegemon. As a rational actor, it must perceive that there are net benefits to be gained from a hegemonic role in the international system, and consider itself both diplomatically and strategically competent to lead. If, on the other hand, a powerful state sees only economic and military net costs that it is unwilling or unable to bear, it rejects a leadership role, becoming isolationist and adopting a noninterventionist foreign policy.

Some of the benefits that accrue to a hegemon include a politically stable world order, open markets for global trade, and international capital flows that provide it with disproportionate advantages. Some of the offsetting costs include maintenance of military and technological superiority, leadership and involvement in almost all international events, and balance-of-payments deficits and other means of transferring wealth that redistribute power in the international system.

A powerful state's superior capabilities and willingness to lead are not sufficient to make it the world hegemon: It also must be considered legitimate by other states in the international system. The threat of its economic sanctions and military force should be enough to deter challenges to the powerful state's preferred world order. From the military aspect of state relations, lesser states defer to a hegemon because they fear military retaliation or withdrawal of hegemonic protection. From an economic perspective, lesser states defer to it because they fear reduced access to aid, or sanctions on exports and imports.

These three characteristics form the basis of the theory of hegemonic stability. According to this theory, all states pursue power in the international system in order to protect their self-interests. Since there is no supranational authority to settle disputes, the international system is chaotic, uncertain, and prone to violence. A hegemon effectively brings order to the system by enforcing its own demands through a system of control. Enforcement is possible because of its recognized superior capabilities, leadership, and legitimacy. Order is the result of the creation of tacit international norms about the rules and rights of states in the system, effectively reducing the uncertainty surrounding the expectations and actions of other states in the system.

The benefits that accrue to a hegemon have to do with the system of control in the international system. Three components of control in an international system that help to determine the type of international system are the distribution of power, the hierarchy of prestige, and the set of rights and rules in the system. The most powerful actor in the international system determines, to a large extent, how much and what kinds of power the lesser states have. In a tacit hierarchy of prestige, a hegemon is the most politically influential. The unspoken rules and rights of states largely reflect the preferences of the hegemon. In a hegemonic system, these three components of control belong to a single state and are the sources of opportunities to benefit the hegemon. The capability, willingness to lead, and legitimacy of the hegemon reinforce the components of control in the international system. It protects its self-interests through efforts to preserve and strengthen these characteristics in order to preserve and strengthen its international control. Its efforts to maintain or increase its capability, diplomatic and strategic policy successes, and legitimacy all operate to maintain or increase its control over the international distribution of power, its position at the apex of the hierarchy of prestige, and its control over the rules and rights of the international system.

The economic and military capabilities of a hegemon affect the international system's distribution of power, the hierarchy of prestige, and the rules and rights followed by the system's states. A hegemon can effectively control other states' economic policies, using its own dominant economic power to discourage other states from changing either the distribution of economic power, the hierarchy of prestige, or the rules preferred by the hegemon in the international economic system. For example, a hegemon offers a large market for other countries' exports, a major source of revenue for the governments of these other countries. If it closed its markets to another state, the effects on the target state's economy could lead to domestic political instability, social upheaval, and reduced foreign investment from other countries. Nontargeted states would be affected as well. As the markets for the targeted state's exports were closed, the targeted state would seek other export markets. States that were unable to absorb the increased goods flooding its markets would also experience a damaged domestic economy.

A hegemon's economic capability affects the system's distribution of economic power in other ways. A hegemon is a technologically advanced country that produces, consumes, and exports high-value-added finished goods. The result is a high demand for primary goods imports, especially from less developed countries (LDCs). Some scholars have argued that the heavy reliance of these countries on primary goods exports hinders their economic development. Primary goods are typically low-value-added, labor-intensive products requiring low skills, frequently from the extractive industries. An LDC can become dependent on a hegemon's demand for these goods, diverting labor and capital to these sectors of the economy. The results are reduced potential to develop a skilled domestic labor force, relatively lower returns on domestic investment, potential depletion of the natural resource, and foregone opportunities to develop alternative industries. Because a hegemon typically is reluctant to share advanced technologies, the potential for economic development in a dependent LDC is reduced.

A hegemon's preponderant military capabilities operate in much the same way as its economic capabilities in assuring its control in the international system. It is the threat that a hegemon will use its capabilities that leads other states to defer to a hegemon's preferences in the international system.

A hegemon may use its economic or military power, as well as its political influence with other states, to deter a state from a military buildup and attempts at expansionism. To deter another state from military adventures, it may use a show of force to convey a threat of overt coercion. For example, it might position troops on the target state's borders, conduct joint military exercises with a state adjacent to the target state, or direct naval operations to nearby waters. Its strong economic capabilities also help to convince the target state that the hegemon can sustain a protracted military engagement.

The hegemon also creates dependency among smaller states by offering them military protection. Although this is a costly tool for the hegemon, it is attractive to it as well as to the lesser states. This form of deterrence effectively reduces the military readiness of other states that might otherwise pose a threat to the hegemon, and creates an international alliance that further legitimates it as the most powerful state. Lesser states choosing to accept military protection can put their resources to more productive, nonmilitary use. States under the protective umbrella also benefit from a hegemon's tendency to prefer them in trade arrangements, aid, and foreign direct investment.

Applications

The United States established itself as a major military power during the beginning of the twentieth century. Following its successes in the war against Spain in 1898, the United States continued to demonstrate its military prowess as it annexed Hawaii (1898), intervened in China (1900), conquered Panama (1903), occupied Nicaragua (1912), and intervened in Mexico (1916). By the end of World War II, its military and technological superiority in the world were unchallenged. The United States had clearly demonstrated its economic superiority by the mid-1940's; its involvement in World War II marked the end of its protectionist and isolationist policies.

In the final months of World War II, the United States and Great Britain consulted each other about ways to avert catastrophic global instability in the future. These conversations led to a United Nations conference attended by forty-four countries in 1944 at Bretton Woods, New Hampshire. The agreements that emerged from the conference reflected broad support for global institutions that would provide the framework for a multilateral and liberal economic international system. Such a framework was aggressively promoted by its biggest potential benefactor, the United States, who hoped it would coordinate expectations and reduce the uncertainty among states that had previously set the stage for worldwide war. The Bretton Woods agreements became the springboard for the International Monetary Fund (IMF), the World Bank, and the General Agreement on Trade and Tariffs (GATT), effectively institutionalizing the global economic and ideological preferences of the United States.

By 1947, it was clear that the Bretton Woods prescriptions for achieving global stability could not be accommodated by a Europe on the verge of economic collapse. Fearing the specter of national capitalism or, worse, communism, the United States offered the Marshall Plan in 1947, underwriting billions of dollars in grant aid to Europe. These concessions, it has been argued, effectively saved Western Europe, providing a bridge until it was capable of fully implementing the Bretton Woods agreements. The political leverage and legitimacy that accompanied European reliance on U.S. aid decisively secured the position of the United States as the economic and ideological hegemon of the international system.

Context

The concept of hegemony is useful for understanding behavior in the international system. This is especially true when states expressly formulate their policies with the expectations that other states' policies are based on hegemony as opposed to another theory of the international system. Hegemony is about predominant power, however defined, and the theory assumes that all states respond to the same circumstances in the same way. It assumes that domestic politics, types of leaders, culture, and so forth make no difference in the long term when attempting to understand states' behavior in the international system.

Some have argued that the limiting assumptions that underpin the theory of hegemonic stability operated to prolong the Cold War. By 1945, the United States was very much aware of the benefits of multilateralism and a liberal economic system, as well as the advantages of its position in the hierarchy of such a system. The Soviet Union and the increasing number of communist countries threatened to undermine the tacit rules of an international system that reflected U.S. power and preferences.

In 1947, an article appeared in the journal *Foreign Affairs*, written by a U.S. State Department official, George Kennan, under the pseudonym X. The article described the Soviet Union as an aggressive communist monolith, ever-expansionistic, and seeking to dominate the world. Kennan said that the Soviet state could be stopped only when confronted by a superior force, and he exhorted the West to demonstrate that force wherever the Soviets showed signs of encroaching upon the interests of a peaceful and stable world.

Although Kennan asserted later that his concern was with Soviet power, not communist ideology, and that he had meant economic and political rather than military demonstrations of strength by the West, the "X Article" effectively provided the justification for the U.S.-led containment policy that drove the Cold War. The policy of containing the threat of communism became the primary objective of Western states.

The United States quickly assumed the hegemon's mantle; the arsenal of democracy from World War II became the defender of democracy in the postwar era. All communism was considered inherently expansionistic and Soviet-supported and, therefore, threatening to the free world. Such dogma was the foundation of the Truman Doctrine, and opened previously closed U.S. purse strings to support the Marshall Plan. The United States formed alliances, not the least of which was the North Atlantic Treaty Organization (NATO), committing its troops to possible military action around the world. As the policy of containment continued to drive a wedge between East and West, an arms spiral began as well: Any technological innovation or quantitative increase in military capability by either the Soviet Union or the United States was considered a threat that the other immediately tried to meet or exceed.

U.S. policy reflected a belief in the theory of hegemonic stability. If there could be only one hegemon, any other powerful state was a challenger to peaceful order and it was the duty of the hegemon to provide that order. This policy ignored several facts: that posturing by the United States posed a threat to decision makers in the Soviet Union, provoking a response in kind; that not all communist states were expansionistic; that some communist states did not share Soviet ideology; and that different Soviet leaders throughout the period might have been open to de-escalation if the West's behavior had been less provocative. Soviet policy was merely the other side of the same coin, resulting in provocative behavior and otherwise ignoring opportunities for de-escalation.

Because policymakers viewed the world system in hegemonic terms, they could not risk any attempts at de-escalation. Diplomacy consisted of saber rattling; anything less was considered weak by domestic constituents and exploitable by the adversary. An advance in military capability by one state's adversary was not considered to be a rational response to that state's own military build-up, but an attempt by the adversary to gain the rights and advantages of hegemony.

Nevertheless, one can only speculate as to what might have been the consequences had states' policies been informed by another theory of the organization of the international system. In world politics, the prize of hegemony was too great for the superpowers to imagine alternatives.

Bibliography

Gilpin, Robert. *War and Change in World Politics*. New York: Cambridge University Press, 1981. Considered the authority on the theory of hegemony, emphasizing the economic aspects of the theory.

Goldstein, Joshua S. *Long Cycles: Prosperity and War in the Modern Age*. New Haven, Conn.: Yale University Press, 1988. Thoughtfully considers the concept of hegemony, giving empirical grounding for the integration of both its military and economic aspects.

Keohane, Robert O. *After Hegemony: Cooperation and Discord in the World Political Economy*. Princeton, N.J.: Princeton University Press, 1984. Useful for further investigation of the rise of hegemony, as well as its decline and aftermath.

Kindleberger, Charles P. *The World in Depression, 1929-1939*. Berkeley: University of California Press, 1973. The seminal work on the theory of hegemonic stability.

Organski, A. F. K., and Jacek Kugler. *The War Ledger*. Chicago: University of Chicago Press, 1980. Investigates a theory of power transitions that is useful for understanding the process underlying a hegemonic system.

Rourke, John T., Ralph G. Carter, and Mark A. Boyer. *Making American Foreign Policy*. Guilford, Conn.: Dushkin, 1994. Accessible textbook with several sections relevant to an understanding of hegemony, particularly from a U.S. viewpoint.

Deborah Moore Haddad

Cross-References

Alliances, p. 47; International Relations, p. 969; Leagues, p. 1072; North Atlantic Treaty Organization, p. 1332; Postmodernism, p. 1570; Superpowers and World Politics, p. 1916; World Political Organization, p. 2186.

HINDUISM AND GOVERNMENT

Field of study: Religion and government

Hinduism is the religious customs and practices of the majority of the people of India. The rise of political parties that support the idea of a Hindu India and that advocate lesser rights for members of other religious groups has led to concern about the Hindu revival's effect on the government of India.

Principal terms

BHARATIYA JANATA PARTY: political party that champions the idea of a Hindu India

CASTE SYSTEM: social hierarchy of India in which people are born into one of four castes

COMMUNAL REPRESENTATION: electoral system in which districts are created to represent major religious, caste, and other differences among people

CONGRESS (I): breakaway branch of the Indian National Congress (which helped win Indian independence from British rule), formed by Indira Gandhi (hence the I for Indira).

HINDUTVA: Indian term for the movement by various organizations and political parties to transform India into a Hindu state

RAMAYANA: Indian epic poem detailing the life and exploits of mythical Lord Rama, who in recent years has become the figurehead of efforts to revitalize Hindu sentiments

Overview

The constitution of India describes the state as a secular republic. This reflects the intentions of its framers, who were also members of the Indian National Congress, the party that led India's struggle for independence from British rule. Their primary concern was to create a state that would take account of the religious, cultural, and ethnic diversity of the country. The Indian government committed itself with independence to the ideal of separating religion from politics. The difficulties involved in this ideal became clear soon after independence, when Mohandas Gandhi was assassinated by a Hindu nationalist who blamed Gandhi for having brought about the separation of India and the creation of the Muslim state of Pakistan. India, to the Hindu nationalists, was a Hindu, not a secular, state. The attempt to link the Hindu religion to the Indian state has a long history, going back to the early stages of the Indian nationalist movement. Some leaders of the movement used the information collected by European historians and archaeologists to further their own political ends.

Hinduism, unlike other religions, has no founder, no prophet, and no church. Hinduism encompasses a broad range of sects and religious communities, whose understanding of their religion varies greatly. The beliefs and practices associated with Hinduism can vary from the worship of village and forest deities to highly sophisticated metaphysics. Early European investigators of Hinduism took little note of the diversity of the religion and concentrated on identifying the common threads that were presumed to unite all Hindus. These researchers focused on the ancient Sanskrit texts, the Vedas, as representing the Hindu equivalent of holy books such as the Bible and the Koran. When it became clear that the Vedas are abstract Sanskrit poems in the nature of invocations to the gods, attention shifted to other texts that better fit the nineteenth century definition of scripture. Epics such as the Ramayana, the Mahabharata, and the Bhagavad Gītā were identified by several Western scholars as the unifying thread that bound Hindus across the country. Hindus were also held to be united by the caste system, consisting of Brahmans (the priestly caste) at the top, followed by the Kshatriyas (warrior caste), the Vaisyas (trader caste), and the Sudra (laborer caste) in that order.

In the nineteenth century the idea of a monolithic, unifying Hindu religion became popular among two groups of Indians. In the early nineteenth century, Hindu nationalist scholars, building on the work of Western researchers of Hinduism, wrote about the uniqueness and the superiority of the Hindu heritage. They were followed in the late nineteenth and early twentieth centuries by political leaders who sought power within a system (devised by the British colonial authorities) in which representation was determined by religious and caste affiliation. This form of representation was known as "communal representation." Politicians therefore had an interest in emphasizing the unity, rather than the diversity, of the Hindu faith. By the late nineteenth century, a number of organizations had arisen that promoted the idea of monolithic Hinduism.

These organizations presented two distinct visions of Hinduism. The Indian National Congress, under the guidance of Mohandas Gandhi and Jawaharlal Nehru, supported a secular understanding of Hinduism. This approach emphasized the presence of different religions and communities within India and the important contributions made by these different groups to Indian history and culture. The strength of the Hindu religion, in the Indian National Congress' view, lay in its ability to integrate different beliefs. This secularist vision was rejected by other groups such as the Arya Samaj and the Rashtriya Swayamsevak Sangh (RSS), which advocated going back to the fundamentals of the Hindu faith as represented in the Vedas, and the importance of teaching these texts to the Hindu people. Organized like Christian missions (and formed to counter the effects of Christian missionaries), the Samaj distinguished between believers and nonbelievers, set up schools, and introduced the novel idea of conversion of Muslims and Christians to Hinduism. The RSS took these ideas a step further and identified the need for Hindus to come together as a political, social, and cultural group.

The two conflicting interpretations of Hinduism have created recurring problems for the Indian government in the years following independence in 1947. The fact that independence came on the heels of the partition of the subcontinent into secular India and Muslim Pakistan was a major blow to organizations such as the RSS, which saw the partition as a sign of Hindu weakness. The assassination of Gandhi in 1948 by a former member of the RSS led to the temporary banning of the organization and its activities. In the years since then, the adoption of a secular Indian constitution, which guarantees minority rights, and the passage of legislation to secure these constitutional guarantees, has led to more protests from supporters of activist Hinduism. Activist Hindus have organized politically to gain public recognition of their concerns. RSS members took part in the formation and organization of the Bharatiya Jana Sangh (Indian people's organization) Party, the predecessor of the current Bharatiya Janata Party (BJP), which has mobilized Hindu sentiments. The BJP was formed in 1981, and over the next decade increased its electoral support in many states. In the 1984 elections, the BJP won only two seats in the Indian parliament, but in the 1990 elections the party won 119 seats, making it an influential player in Indian politics. The BJP became an important member of the coalition government headed by the Congress (I) Party.

The success of the RSS/BJP brand of Hinduism, which is called "Hindutva" in India and "right-wing Hinduism" in the West, was facilitated by the domestic and international political environment. First, the creation of a pan-Indian Hindu religious identity became possible after independence as groups mobilized around language, caste, and other differences. These groups sought support, assistance, and sometimes territory from the newly independent secular Indian government. As compromises were achieved with linguistic and tribal minorities in various parts of the country, this added fuel to the right-wing claim that secularism was being maintained at the expense of the majority Hindu community. Second, the growing exodus of people from rural to urban centers in search of jobs in the 1970's and 1980's created a disaffected group of unemployed that was cut loose from its moorings in the relatively stable hierarchy of life in an Indian village. These disaffected people provided the majority of the cadres of the BJP.

Third, the domestic problems of economic and political change were aggravated by the emergence of communal rhetoric in Indian electoral politics. The split in the Congress Party caused by Indira Gandhi in the late 1960's and the subsequent weakening of the party led to the trend of mobilizing voters by appealing to religious, caste, and ethnic differences. As election campaigning focused less on themes of unity and more on mobilizing voters along communal lines, religion became an important tool for politicians. Fourth, the international environment was unstable. Politically, the rise of Islamic fundamentalism in the Middle East and the animosity between India and Pakistan generated concerns about Indian national security. India faced militant Muslim governments all around the region. Fifth, the Indian government's decision to open the Indian market to foreign competition and to encourage the move to a liberal economy led to an opening up not only to Western corporations and technology but also to Western culture, including MTV. This cultural influx increased concern over Indian beliefs and values. As a consequence, the organizations promoting Hindutva generated increased levels of popular support in the 1980's and 1990's.

Applications

The growing importance of Hinduism in Indian government and politics is best illustrated by the conflict over the monument at Ajodhya in the Indian state of Uttar Pradesh. The monument, which is called Ramjanmabhoomi (birthplace of Lord Rama) by the Hindus, and Babri Masjid (Babur's mosque) by the Muslims, was supposedly erected by the Mughal emperor Babur, after he destroyed a temple erected by an earlier Hindu king in honor of Lord Rama's birthplace. Muslims retained control over the building until 1855. In that year, there was a conflict between Hindus and Muslims that left seventy-five dead. As a result, a Muslim sultan and a Hindu king arrived at an agreement by which the Hindus were to take over the shrine once Muslims were given an alternative plot of land on which to build their mosque. The two rulers also agreed to cooperate against the British and were captured and hanged, thus ending an early attempt at settlement.

Hindus and Muslims continued to use the structure until the early decades of the twentieth century, when cow slaughter became an issue that divided the two religious groups. In the 1930's, as a result of Hindu complaints about cow slaughter at the site, the British administration banned Muslims from offering prayers at the mosque. In 1949, a group of Hindus installed idols of Lord Rama, his wife Sita, and his brothers inside the temple. Muslim protests led to a decision by the governments in Uttar Pradesh and in New Delhi to have the idols removed. In fact, however, nothing was ever done about removing the idols. The temple was closed to the public, but a priest was allowed to perform religious services within its precincts.

Another round of problems began in February, 1986, when a district judge ruled that the gates to the monument had to be opened. Congress (I) had been an actor in the decision. Congress (I) hoped to increase its support among voters in a state where its power was being eroded by the militantly Hindu BJP. The result was that the temple/mosque at Ajodhya became the focus of renewed violence between the two religious communities. Hindu organizations called on Hindus across the country to unite in order to free the temple from Muslim control. Sporadic acts of violence followed and culminated in the destruction of the monument on December 6, 1992, by militant Hindus who were supported by the RSS and the BJP, an action that led to Hindu-Muslim conflicts all over the subcontinent.

The organizations in support of Hindutva have pursued a three-pronged strategy aimed at creating support across India for their policy on Ajodhya. First, Hindu organizations, including the RSS and the BJP, have concentrated on bringing together the leaders of various Hindu sects in order to get their approval for Hindutva policy toward Ajodhya. These leaders are important because they lend credibility to the claim that the Ajodhya campaign is part of mainstream Hinduism. Second, the media and new technologies have been used to whip up grassroots support for construction of a Hindu temple at Ajodhya. The message was spread by rented vans and trucks that carried the message on audio and video cassettes. The response was huge. Across the country, people donated bricks or money for the bricks to build the temple. The use of videos, cassettes, and other audio-visual aids to propagate a politically charged reading of Hindu-Muslim relations and of Indian history has served to make Lord Rama and Ajodhya household names in the subcontinent. Third, the fate of the temple/mosque at Ajodhya was made part of the BJP's electoral campaign in the hope that the BJP could unseat the weak Congress (I) government.

Context

The attempt to bring about closer links between Hindu religion and politics is troublesome because it has used hatred as a campaign tool. For example, in December, 1992, and January, 1993, in the aftermath of the destruction of the mosque in Ajodhya, a Hindu political party, the Shiv Sena, seized the opportunity to mobilize against the Muslim community in the city of Bombay. Using stereotypical representations of the Muslim community and alleging that Muslims posed a threat to national security because of their "natural" allegiance to Pakistan (a Muslim country), the Shiv Sena was able to provoke open hostility toward Muslims. In the riots that followed, 550 people lost their lives.

Muslims are not the only groups under attack. Equally disturbing to many analysts is the threat that Hindutva poses to the 75 percent of the Indian population that does not belong to the higher castes. The Hinduism of Hindutva is based on a distinctly upper caste version of the religion that emphasizes the sanctity of the caste system and the religious significance of texts such as the Vedas and the Ramayana. The Hindu faith, as it is practiced across the subcontinent, has many variations that subscribe to very different traditions. Hindutva threatens this diversity. For example, although Hindu organizations such as the RSS focus on Lord Rama, in many parts of India Lord Rama is not even a popular deity.

Temples may be popular, but the Hindu political parties cannot convince lower castes and hill peoples that their interests are best served by supporting a movement that supports the hierarchy laid out in the old Hindu texts. Such texts sanction the lowly and inferior status of the lower castes, hardly a selling point in a democracy. The position of these parties toward lower castes was made clear when the parties used violence to object to a government report that called for larger quotas in education and employment for those castes that had suffered discrimination in past years. An increasing number of Indians have become concerned about the strategies being employed to propagate Hindutva—in particular, the use of violence.

Bibliography

Brass, Paul. *Ethnicity and Nationalism: Theory and Comparison.* Newbury Park, Calif.: Sage Publications, 1991. Collection of essays examining the political forces that drive ethnic, religious, and nationalist sentiments.

Duara, Prasenjit, and James Clad. "The New Politics of Hinduism." *Wilson Quarterly* 15 (Summer, 1991): 45-47. Short and readable piece examining the history and the politics underlying the activities of Hindu political parties.

Juergensmeyer, Mark. *The New Cold War? Religious Nationalism Confronts the Secular State.* Berkeley: University of California Press, 1993. Analysis of the response by the state to the challenges posed by religious fundamentalism in different parts of the world.

Thapar, Romila. "Imagined Religious Communities? Ancient History and the Modern Search for a Hindu Identity." *Modern Asian Studies* 23 (May, 1989): 209-231. Examination of the validity of modern claims to a monolithic Hindu identity in light of Indian history.

Sudha Ratan

Cross-References

Asia: Politics and Governments, p. 108; Buddhism and Government, p. 152; Caste Systems, p. 203; Colonialism and Anticolonialism, p. 351; Islam and Government, p. 994; Nationalism, p. 1268; Political Party Roles, p. 1499; Religion and Politics, p. 1685.

HISTORY OF GOVERNMENT

Field of study: History of government and politics

The organization of the world's people into sovereign nation-states is a relatively recent development in world historical terms; at the same time, the different forms of government of modern states are partly the result of various historical and ideological influences over the centuries. The history of government thus helps explain both similarities and differences among the world's governmental systems.

Principal terms

AUTHORITARIAN GOVERNMENT: government led by an elite whose political power and authority are independent of the consent of the governed

GOVERNMENT: institutionalization of centralized leadership for a defined territory and population

MONARCHY: government whose individual head of state is selected on the basis of heredity

PEACE OF WESTPHALIA: treaty, signed in 1648, that ended Europe's Thirty Years' War and marked the beginning of state sovereignty as a principle of international relations

REPUBLIC: form of government based on representative democracy

REVOLUTIONARY GOVERNMENT: regime that claims authority as deriving from its success in overthrowing an illegitimate regime, and its ongoing efforts to remove counterrevolutionary forces

SOVEREIGNTY: principle that an entity (such as a national government) wields supreme authority over its designated territory

Overview

People in the modern world are grouped politically under a number of distinct, independent governments. The range of governmental forms reflects a variety of historical influences, including the contributions of political theorists, the campaigns of military leaders, the effects of popular rebellions, political and economic control by colonial and imperialist powers, and other factors. In the modern international system, the governments of all countries possess sovereignty; that is, all national governments, by definition, maintain supreme authority within their territory and over their populations.

This has not always been the case. Indeed, the political supremacy of sovereign nation-states (which is a defining element of contemporary international relations) began to be accepted only in the mid-seventeenth century. Over the centuries prior to that time, a variety of political groupings had been dominant.

Identifying the origins of government itself is somewhat speculative. Sometimes the development of society or "civilization" is seen as tantamount to the establishing of government. English political theorist Thomas Hobbes argued that, without government, people would exist in a "state of nature" in which life would be intolerably conflictual, constantly threatened by violence and physical destruction. In other words, without recognized governments, sovereignty (such as it was) would remain with each individual—a definition of anarchy. Hobbes saw this as patently unacceptable to any group of people, and thus some form of social contract would be developed to establish a government.

Hobbes's "state of nature" is merely hypothetical. Most evidence suggests that people always have organized into groups—in the earlier form, kinship groups and clans—with some rough delineation of tasks and roles. Many anthropologists believe that these earliest groups were egalitarian, without clear rankings or stratification of status and authority. When authority eventually became hierarchically ordered and in some way related to territory (rather than simply based on personal relationships), the result was government. The earliest forms of government probably encompassed relatively small groups of people, such as tribes. These "primitive governments" carried out only the most basic functions: defense, conducting religious observances, assigning subsistence tasks, and otherwise upholding the safety, values, and culture of the community. The "governmental leaders" were tribal elders, ritual leaders, or others distinguished as possessing special authority over the rest of the group.

As populations grew and civilizations advanced, and as tribes developed into villages and kingdoms, governments began to take on more extensive and complex structures. Generally governments were able to augment their power and bolster their stability; control of resources combined with technological advancements allowed governments to equip armies with superior weapons. Control over food reserves (grains, in particular) also helped maintain governmental power. With increased power and stability, these "ancient" governments began to develop more formal rules, establish hierarchically defined administrative positions, coin money, and collect taxes, all precursors to the bureaucratic trappings of modern states. Examples of such governments can be found as early as 3000 B.C.E. in Mesopotamia and 1500 B.C.E. in parts of China.

Further advances in defensive technology, as well as in agriculture and food storage, permitted governments to become ever stronger. The Greek city-states of 800-500 B.C.E. are representative. Fortified cities, with high walls, cannons, and other defenses, increasingly enjoyed a large measure of autonomy. Over time, the size of the territories under governmental control grew. Defense requirements, transportation and trade capabilities, improved communications, economies of scale, and other factors tended to reward governments with larger territories. Empires linked smaller governments and cities in various regions of the world. Over time, some of these early empires, including those in China, Japan, and Russia, gave way to feudalism. In Europe after the fall of the Roman Empire, feudalism became the dominant form of political organization. Although the Roman Catholic church had authority and influence over much of the population and control of tremendous financial and military resources, the Holy Roman Empire itself fluctuated for centuries in terms of political strength, geographic reach, and cohesiveness. In short, feudalism caused sovereignty to be diffused among the monarchs, pope, emperor, and other units of medieval Europe.

The Reformation in the sixteenth century posed an especially strong challenge to the power and authority of the Roman Catholic church. The growing conflicts culminated in the Thirty Years' War, whose outcome, institutionalized in the Peace of Westphalia (1648), promoted the distinction between political and religious authority. Doctrines such as "just war," which had provided a rationale for external intervention into other countries' affairs and even the subordination of their governments, were renounced.

Although generally recognized as sovereign, states in seventeenth and eighteenth century Europe largely were the tools of a relatively small number of dynasties and elites. There was little organic connection between a government and the people it ruled, the latter of which stood more as subjects than citizens. Governments were characterized by a "cosmopolitanism" that saw the interests of the state, and perhaps of its rulers, as unfettered by any sense of loyalty to the masses or their cultural heritage. Important governmental offices, including in particular the diplomatic corps, were frequently drawn from foreign nations. Armies made extensive use of mercenaries who served not out of patriotism or obligation, but rather as employees. Indeed, many mercenaries were foreign born.

The French Revolution of 1789 signaled the decline of cosmopolitanism in European governments. The revolution emphasized a special bond between the government and the citizenry, as well as a bond uniting the citizens as a people. In other words, the revolution was a watershed for the rise of nationalism. In the Napoleonic Wars that soon followed, nationalism arose among other peoples as well. In succeeding years, the international system would increasingly be founded upon sovereign nation-states.

As nationalism took hold as a driving force in international affairs, it gave rise to the principle of national self-determination. That philosophy held that nations should be free to govern themselves, and thus that they could (or should) gain independence. The ideal of self-determination reached a new height after World War II, largely in accordance with the Allies' "Atlantic Charter," whereby Britain, the United States, and the Soviet Union proclaimed their allegiance to the self-determination principle. After the war, Britain stepped up the granting of independence to nations within its empire. These advances in the practical applications of national self-determination increased the number of countries in the world, particularly in Africa, the Middle East, and Indochina. Between 1945 and 1975, membership in the United Nations (U.N.) almost tripled, rising from 51 to 144 states. Many of the new states were former colonies that had had no previous experience with self-rule. Indeed, many had not existed as cohesive political units at all prior to their creation by colonial-imperialist powers.

In one sense, then, the global community of states by the mid-twentieth century had developed a remarkable uniformity. All states were, by definition, recognized as sovereign, and most had taken on similar trappings of modern statehood (diplomatic missions, national flags, U.N. membership, highly specialized bureaucracies, and so forth). The governments of these states still reflected a significant diversity of societal values, political philosophies, and domestic power structures. Any number of categorization schemes can be developed for grouping the dominant forms of government. Perhaps the most valuable classification for noting the historical roots of modern government distinguishes the bases of governmental authority: democratic republic, constitutional monarchy, and authoritarian state. Each of these categories can be further subdivided. In many respects, the differences among the dominant categories of government can be traced to the historical developments noted above.

Applications

Modern democratic republics are based upon popular consent, whereby the people, through free elections or other mechanisms, grant to certain individuals the right to govern. This form of government has its philosophical roots in Aristotle's "polity," or, in modern usage, "direct democracy." Close approximations to this ideal can be found in some ancient city-states, such as Athens in the fifth and fourth centuries B.C.E. Because the collective decision making characteristic of direct democracy is best suited only to smaller, homogeneous populations, variations have been derived that accommodate larger, more diverse states while retaining democracy's ideological underpinnings. Drawing upon Greco-Roman republicanism, the representative variant of democracy (that is, the republic) was most famously articulated and developed in the fledgling United States in the late eighteenth century.

Within the broad parameters defining a republic, there are additional variants. The United States government is a presidential system, with a separation of powers, while those of many other countries, such as Germany, are parliamentary systems with fused powers. The particular political structures of different republics accommodate and reinforce the particular political cultures and social stratifications in different parts of the world. They also reflect national apprehensions about past political failures (for example, the rise of Nazism in Germany in the 1930's and 1940's) and bear the imprint of past external influence (U.S. involvement in Japan's 1947 constitution, for example).

Whereas democratic republics claim to derive their authority from popular consent, the monarchical leaders of previous centuries often claimed their authority as sovereign rulers on the basis of heredity. Often the hereditary principles were infused with a sense of divine right to rule. For centuries, many monarchies were considered "absolute," meaning that the authority of the monarch was unquestioned and unhindered. In 1215, however, King John of England was forced to sign the Magna Carta, which established that exercise of certain of the king's powers would henceforth require the consent of the nobility. The English monarchy was further weakened by the creation of Parliament in 1265. In subsequent years, the monarch's authority would progressively be eclipsed by that of Parliament.

Modern Britain is thus a constitutional monarchy, in that the sovereignty of the state continues to be personified by the monarch and governmental powers are carried out in the monarch's name, but actual governmental decision-making powers are wielded primarily by the democratically elected Parliament. Many modern monarchies are limited in this way, owing to the growing sentiment that governmental authority cannot be based merely on hereditary principles. They maintain the trappings of the monarchy largely out of a sense of national pride, history, and conservatism. Monarchies also remain that reserve considerable sovereign power for the monarch. Saudi Arabia and, to a lesser extent, Jordan were two such countries in the early 1990's.

Whereas absolute monarchies are in little evidence in the modern world, other forms of authoritarian states are prevalent. They are led by powerful individuals and groups whose claim of authority is based on neither heredity nor consent. At root these states draw upon the model of Greek Sparta—at least as Thucydides describes it—whereby the government is controlled by a powerful elite that is not subject to practical external or popular controls. Political participation by the masses is discouraged or even prohibited. The rulers often claim to act in the best interests of the state (thus, an "aristocracy" in Aristotle's terms) but sometimes (always?) degenerate into rule based on narrow self-interest ("oligarchy"). These characteristics have been closely associated with the modern authoritarian state.

Authoritarian regimes are among the most prevalent form of government in modern international relations. The power vacuums caused by decolonization in Latin America, Africa, and elsewhere; the resultant societal and economic disruptions; and the lack of established democratic traditions have provided fertile ground for authoritarian governments. In Latin America in particular, "bureaucratic authoritarian" regimes surfaced.

The so-called Second World authoritarian governments of the Cold War era drew (at least rhetorically) upon a traditional of revolutionary regimes. Revolutionary regimes are forged out of a rejection of the perceived lack of legitimacy of the *ancien régime*, as in eighteenth century France. Fundamentally inequitable allocation of resources, systematic abuses of power, oppression of national groups, and other governmental misdeeds have served as the catalyst for revolutions around the world. Some revolutions can produce democratic republics (as with the American Revolution) or even reconstructed monarchies (as with England's "Glorious Revolution" of 1688); sometimes revolutionary forces maintain power as revolutionaries, claiming their legitimacy on the supposed fact that "reactionary" or "counterrevolutionary" forces continue to threaten the society. The Bolshevik Revolution in Russia created such a regime. Mao Tse-tung's regime in the People's Republic of China similarly claimed to be a revolutionary government. Over time, the revolutionary justification begins to lose its credibility, and the authoritarian tendencies of the government become clear. A "party state" results, with one dominant (or sole) party retaining firm control, based on revolutionary or other ideologically defined credentials.

Context

The history of government is to a large extent the history of human civilization. Government has helped direct the course of societal development and has itself been shaped by society. The end of the Cold War in the late 1980's and early 1990's brought dramatic changes in the evolution of government worldwide. The collapse of communism in the Soviet Union, Eastern Europe, and parts of Central America and Africa was seen by some as a triumph of Western liberalism as an ideology and thus a rapid spreading of democracy as a basis for government. Although the world's governments still reflected a broad diversity of structures (parliamentary and presidential republics, constitutional monarchies, traditional and provisional governments, federations and unitary states, and so forth), most at least claimed to be infused with democratic principles, based upon popular consent. Some analysts were even so bold as to claim that this spread of democracy signified an "end of history," with no further major revolutions in terms of ideology or governmental principles. It will be some time before that claim can be substantiated.

Those who believe history has not "ended" continue to speculate about the next steps in the evolution of government. Some Marxists and neo-Marxists still anticipate a genuine socialist or communist revolution, moving toward an inevitable disappearance of government itself. Others envision a fundamentally different scenario, with governments of the world progressively integrating into a united world government. These "world federalists" see the expansion of the European Union and the strengthening of the United Nations as possible evidence of that trend. Still others believe the evolution of government is going in rather the opposite direction, with states increasingly being fractured along ethnic, national, and other lines. The civil wars in the Balkans, in Africa, and elsewhere, as well as less violent cleavages in Canada's Quebec and Spain's Catalonia, lend support to this position. Another view sees a rise not of hundreds of small ethnonational mini-states but of a handful of broad-based "civilizations" that may come to displace nation-states as the primary political grouping in the world.

Technological developments, the transmission of values and ideology, shifts in the global balance of power, redirected trade patterns, demographic changes, and myriad other factors continually influence the strength of governments and even the shape of political systems. Although the long-term prospects for contemporary forms of government remain unclear, history teaches that government is a remarkably diverse and malleable institution.

Bibliography

Fried, Morton H. *The Evolution of Political Society: An Essay in Political Anthropology*. New York: Random House, 1967. Scholarly and authoritative, but witty and readable, book that traces the progression from primitive societies to sovereign states. Balances theory and empirical evidence. Bibliography and index.

Hobbes, Thomas. *Leviathan*. Edited by Richard Tuck. New York: Cambridge University Press, 1991. A classic philosophical statement of why humankind has created government.

McTavish, Hugh. *Ending War in Our Lifetime: A Concrete, Realistic Plan*. Dixon, Ky.: West Fork Press, 1994. Simple, straightforward discussion of why the world should and, the author predicts, will move toward world federalism. Appendices (including a "Proposed Constitution of the Federation of Nations"), bibliography, and index.

Moore, Barrington, Jr. *Social Origins of Dictatorship and Democracy: Lord and Peasant in the Making of the Modern World.* Boston: Beacon Press, 1967. Penetrating study of the transformation from agrarian societies to modern industrial states in various regions of the world.

Rostow, W. W. *The Stages of Economic Growth: A Non-Communist Manifesto.* 2d ed. Cambridge, England: Cambridge University Press, 1971. Rostow's classic presentation of "modernization theory," linking the economic, societal, and political development of states through "stages." Explicitly non-Marxist.

Service, Elman R. *Origins of the State and Civilization: The Process of Cultural Evolution.* New York: W. W. Norton, 1975. Study of the creation of government as a human institution and the development of particular ancient governments around the world. This scholarly work makes extensive reference to established studies from political science, anthropology, and sociology.

Steve D. Boilard

Cross-References

Bonapartism, p. 140; Citizenship in World Governments, p. 254; The City-State, p. 272; Confederations, p. 391; Empires and Empire Building, p. 597; Feudalism, p. 688; Government Powers, p. 772; Government Roles, p. 778; Government Types, p. 785; Imperialism, p. 889; Nationalism, p. 1268; Self-Determination, p. 1796.

HOBBES'S POLITICAL PHILOSOPHY

Field of study: Political philosophy

Thomas Hobbes was a seventeenth century British political philosopher most famous for his account of the origins of society and government and for his contribution to the debate as to what form that government should take. Hobbes believed government arose out of a social contract, and the best form of government was an absolute sovereignty.

Principal terms
ABSOLUTE SOVEREIGN: leader of a government or society who possesses all the power
RATIONAL SELF-INTEREST: tendency of humans to choose those options that they think will be to their long-term benefit
SOCIAL CONTRACT: agreement among people to form a society or government so that they may escape the state of nature
STATE OF NATURE: condition that humans find themselves in prior to the formation of society and government
STATE OF PEACE: condition to which humans aspire in escaping the state of nature; characterized by cooperation
STATE OF WAR: condition humans find themselves in the state of nature; characterized by conflict

Overview

The English philosopher Thomas Hobbes advanced the political philosophy of the social contract to explain how and why people banded together to form society, and how and why governments were formed. He also asserted that the best form of government was one with an absolute sovereign. His political views are found, chiefly, in four of his works: *Elements of Law* (1640), *De Cive* (1642), *Leviathan* (1651), and *De Homine* (1658).

Hobbes began by asking what life would be like if there were no government and no society. This presocietal and pregovernmental condition he called the state of nature. In this state of nature, human beings are completely free to do whatever they want. There is no right and wrong, no justice and injustice, because there is no government saying what can and cannot be done.

In addition to freedom, there are some basic equalities. First, there is an equality of need. Humans all have the same basic needs of food, shelter, and clothing, but there is a scarcity of the things needed. There is also an equality of power. No one is so strong that they cannot be done in by the weakest using guile or cunning.

Hobbes assumed that humans are essentially rational and self-interested; as a result, in the state of nature, there is limited altruism, that is, acting for the interests of others.

Everyone is out for themselves with no concern for others except, perhaps, the immediate family.

Hobbes asserted that life in the state of nature is really a state of war among individuals. There is perpetual conflict, because interests constantly clash. Because humans are self-interested, when two people want the same thing, conflicts inevitably arise. This is why Hobbes said that life in the state of nature was ". . . solitary, poor, nasty, brutish, and short." One's hopes, dreams, and goals, even modest ones, would be thwarted by others by the state of war that exists in the state of nature. On the other hand, since humans are rational, they will recognize that the state of war they find themselves in is not conducive to their pursuit of rational self-interest. They will recognize that their interests could be met in a state of peace, which is characterized not by conflict but by cooperation. Hobbes claimed that the formation of society makes sense to rationally self-interested individuals in the state of nature, since it would allow them to rise out of that state and pursue and achieve their interests peaceably.

Society, according to Hobbes, is formed through a social contract. Individuals in the state of nature enter into a covenant or contract with one another. As rational, self-interested agents, they recognize that the best hope to achieve their interests is through cooperation, which is guaranteed by the contract. In other words, for human beings to accomplish their goals, some network of cooperation is needed. This cooperation is brought about by the social contract.

There is one problem, however. If there is a basic equality of power, how can society guarantee that the contract will be kept? The person who acts first according to the contract is at a distinct advantage. For example, if two persons agree to exchange goods or services, the person who first receives the goods or services has gotten his needs met and may believe it is in his self-interest to keep what was received without reciprocating.

This, according to Hobbes, is why government, or what he calls the commonwealth, is needed. Government exists to set up some mechanism for settling conflicts between individuals when they arise, to ensure that there will be no backsliding into the state of nature. The government will set up a system that ensures that all people keep their part of the contract and those who do not will be brought to justice.

According to Hobbes, to achieve this end, people in the state of nature will surrender something, namely their absolute right to judge and punish, to a central authority; the central authority guarantees that the people who enter into covenants and contracts will honor them, either willingly or by force from the central authority. The resulting system of society and government will ensure that all people may pursue their own interests in a relative state of peace and freedom, with the realization that they have an excellent chance of achieving those interests. People will realize that the costs of escaping the state of nature, namely, surrendering one's rights to judge and punish, are exceeded by the benefits of societal living, namely, the assurance that people will honor their contracts.

The last issue addressed by Hobbes is that of what type of government should be formed. Although in his general account of the origins of government he does not single out one form as being superior to the others, elsewhere, he expresses a preference. It is this aspect of Hobbesian political philosophy that has been the most controversial. Hobbes believed the best form of government is one in which a single person has absolute control over everything. Although the ruler's absolute power is generated by the social contract, the ruler is not bound by the contract. The ultimate basis of the ruler's absolute power resides in the agreement made by the people to escape the state of nature. The people agree to give up their rights to judge and punish unconditionally, and accept the dictates of the ruler because that is in their rational self-interest. The ruler, however, cannot surrender these rights, because there is non one to surrender them to. Therefore, the ruler is exempt from the contract. If the ruler were bound by contractual obligations, the ruler's power would cease to be absolute and the whole system would suffer. The ruler's authority is created by the contract, but because of that power and authority the ruler can ignore the contract.

Hobbes's argument for an absolute sovereign is clever but straightforward. He points out that in governments in which a sovereign has less than absolute rule, individual conflicts among factions will arise. If there is one legislative body with absolute control instead of one individual, conflicts will arise in that body. Even in the simplest scenario, a legislative body with only two members, it is unlikely that conflicts of interest will never arise. This generates a situation that is no different from that which people are trying to escape in the state of nature. In other words, the only sure way to avoid conflict and the state of nature is to have one person with absolute control.

Applications

Hobbes's claim that the best form of government is one with an absolute sovereign has been soundly rejected by political philosophers as an outmoded and outdated concept, but this is not to say that there are no lessons to be drawn from the Hobbesian position. In fact, many aspects of Hobbes's view have value for twentieth century political discussion, particularly his views concerning human nature, the state of nature, and the social contract.

Hobbes was the first modern proponent of the belief that human motivation can be adequately explained by means of rational self-interest. This model of human beings as rational and self-interested has since been adopted by many disciplines. Most economic forecasting models, for example, presume a Hobbesian view of human nature. They refer to individuals in an economic system as rationally self-interested maximizers. Psychologists and sociologists also use this account of human nature when they construct and design studies. Even game theory, a branch of mathematics that began in the middle of the twentieth century, is based on the theory that individuals are rational and self-interested. Many political philosophers use game theory to analyze, study, and test political systems.

The concept of the state of nature has been used not only to describe the state of individuals without society or government, but to describe the conditions of nation-states in the latter part of the twentieth century. The conflict and mistrust that exists among nations seems to be modeled by the Hobbesian account of individuals in the state of nature. This has led some contemporary political philosophers to pose Hobbesian solutions to conflicts. One could construe the existence of the United Nations as an attempt to escape the state of nature and create a state of peace for the countries of the world.

Finally, social contract theory has been put to novel use by ethical theorists in the last part of the twentieth century. The practice of civil disobedience, which is difficult to justify from the traditional ethical perspectives of utilitarianism, can be given a straightforward justification using the social contract. According to this argument, people agree to obey the legitimately established laws of government because they recognize that the legislative aspect of the government keeps them out of the state of nature and allows them to pursue and achieve their interests. In other words, they obey the laws in return for protection from the state of nature. If the legitimately established laws do not protect them from the state of nature, or the government fails to enforce those laws fairly and adequately, the government is not upholding its end of the contract. Thus the people who are not being protected are no longer bound by their end of the contract: They may disobey the laws. Only when the laws are changed or fairly and adequately enforced, must people abide by them. The strategy of civil disobedience by the Civil Rights movement of the 1960's therefore can be rationally justified: Since blacks were not receiving the benefits and protections of society, they were not bound to obey those particular laws that denied them those benefits.

Context

To appreciate fully the content and motive of Hobbesian political philosophy, it is best to place his work in two contexts—the social contract tradition and the political climate of England during his lifetime. Although there were others before him who employed some form of the social contract theory—Thomas Aquinas in the thirteenth century, for example—Hobbes is considered the first major modern philosopher, in a rich and varied tradition that includes John Locke, David Hume, Jean-Jacques Rousseau, and Immanuel Kant, to propose the social contract theory of society and government. In Hobbes's work, there are both modern and medieval components. His position contains forward-looking ideas that his successors found valuable and exploited, for example, his emphasis on equality, rationality, and self-interest. Other elements of his philosophy were throwbacks to an earlier time, for example, his insistence on an absolute sovereign rather than on a democratically elected government.

The English political system was in turmoil during Hobbes's lifetime. In 1605, Guy Fawkes was accused of trying to blow up the House of Lords during James I's state opening of Parliament. James I dissolved Parliament in 1611 and again in 1622. Charles I, James I's successor, dissolved Parliament in 1629; it did not meet again until 1640. The king's chief adviser, Thomas Wentworth, was beheaded in 1641. Civil war between Charles I's forces and those mustered by Parliament began in 1642. Parliament finally prevailed and brought Charles I to trial in 1648; he was beheaded in 1649.

Oliver Cromwell became Lord Protector of England in 1653. Parliament invited Charles II to return from exile in 1660, but required him to surrender power to Parliament.

This turmoil had an impact on the formation of Hobbes's theory. The dispute between the king and Parliament was over power. The king and his royalist followers thought that the powers of government should lie totally within the province of the monarchy and offered a divine-right justification. Supporters of the parliamentary position thought that the powers of government should be shared by different components of government and the king. They offered as justification reference to English Common Law and the fledgling democratic ideals of freedom and equality.

Hobbes's position can be seen as an attempt at a compromise between the two positions. The formation of society and government itself by mutual consent, contract, and covenant certainly is in the spirit of the parliamentary position. On the other hand, Hobbes insisted that for society and government to work, an absolute ruler was needed, although this absolute ruler would not be in place by divine right or by tradition but rather selected by the people.

Bibliography

Copleston, Frederick. *Hobbes to Hume.* Vol. 5 in *A History of Philosophy.* Westminster, Md.: Newman Press, 1966. Good summary of Hobbes's philosophical thought, suitable for anyone who wants to get a dependable perspective on Hobbes.

Hampton, Jean. *Hobbes and the Social Contract Tradition.* Cambridge, England: Cambridge University Press, 1986. Highly technical but extremely thorough analysis of Hobbes's political philosophy. May be beyond the range of the general reader, but gives an excellent discussion of Hobbes's theory and his place in the social contract tradition.

Hobbes, Thomas. *Leviathan, Parts I and II.* Edited by Herbert W. Schneider. New York: Macmillan, 1958. Fullest and most sustained accounts of Hobbes's political philosophy.

Rogow, Arnold. *Thomas Hobbes: Radical in the Service of Reaction.* New York: W. W. Norton, 1986. Full-length biography of Thomas Hobbes, showing the influences his upbringing and the political situation in England had on his thought. Geared toward the nonspecialist.

Sorell, Tom. *Hobbes.* London: Routledge & Kegan Paul, 1986. Places Hobbes's political theory in the context of his overall philosophy. Shows how Hobbes's thought is connected by the common thread of science and deduction.

John H. Serembus

Cross-References

Burke's Political Philosophy, p. 171; Commonwealths, p. 364; Conservatism, p. 419; Deism, p. 495; Equality and Egalitarianism, p. 630; Government Types, p. 785; Hooker's Political Philosophy, p. 842; Idealism, p. 855; Kant's Political Philosophy, p. 1025; Legitimacy, p. 1105; Liberalism, p. 1118; Locke's Political Philosophy, p. 1142; Monarchy in History, p. 1221; The Nation-State, p. 1241; Political Philosophy, p. 1505; Rousseau's Political Philosophy, p. 1756; Self-Interest in Politics, p. 1802; The Social Contract, p. 1827; Spinoza's Political Philosophy, p. 1872; Stoic Political Philosophy, p. 1904.

HOOKER'S POLITICAL PHILOSOPHY

Field of study: Political philosophy

Through an extended examination of law and its applications, Richard Hooker defended the established Church of England from its Puritan critics during the late sixteenth century. Relying on reason and adopting a moderate tone, he portrayed the church as a mean between extremes.

Principal terms

APOSTOLIC SUCCESSION: doctrine that bishops are descendants of the Apostles in an unbroken historical line, representing a divinely sanctioned rank in the order of the ministry

BISHOP: ecclesiastical officer in charge of a region; a successor to the Apostles

CHURCH: the totality of Christian believers headed by Jesus Christ; also a politic society with a temporal head

EPISCOPACY: church organization that places ministers or priests under bishops

NATURAL LAW: observable law of natural objects and living things outside the human order; a basis for positive human law

POLITY: organized society, together with its laws and rules of organization

POSITIVE LAW: human law, although often derived from divine law of scripture or from natural law

SOCIETY: association of human beings in a state, nation, church, or other entity

Overview

During the reign of Queen Elizabeth I, the Church of England adopted an essentially Reformation theology while retaining its traditional episcopal organization. Under the leadership of the queen, the church was overseen by the archbishops of Canterbury and York, with twenty-two other bishops under their jurisdiction. The church and its ministry were influenced by a group of former exiles, ministers, and laymen. They had sought refuge in Europe during the persecutions instituted by Queen Mary I, who had restored Roman Catholicism to the nation during her brief reign in the 1550's. These Protestant exiles, first known as "precisians," later as Puritans, sought to rid the church of practices they considered Catholic and to reorganize it along the lines suggested by John Calvin, founder of the presbyterian system. The Calvinist model of church order eliminated bishops in favor of lay elders and ministers in charge of each congregation. It was especially appealing to Puritans who feared that rule by bishops represented an easy way to return the church to Catholicism in the event a Roman Catholic monarch should ascend the throne. In the 1580's, Puritan spokesmen began a long series of published attacks on the established church.

It became the life's work of Richard Hooker (1554-1600) to produce the most important defense of the English church and its organization. His treatise *Of the Lawes of Ecclesiasticall Politie (1594-1597)*, a tome of half-a-million words, occupied him during the last decade of his life. Born near Exeter, where he attended grammar school, he was recognized early as a gifted student. He attended Oxford University, in part under the patronage of John Jewel, Bishop of Salisbury, an early defender of the church. His well-received *An Apology of the Church of England* (1562), however, was an argument against Catholicism, not Puritanism.

Despite his poverty, Hooker remained at Oxford until he received his M. A., and then became Hebrew lecturer of the university. Later, through the influence of the Archbishop of York, he was appointed to the Middle Temple, the church attended by students and faculty of two London law schools. There he encountered the Puritan controversy firsthand, for his subordinate was Walter Travers, a primary exponent of the presbyterian form of church government. Following a tiring debate between the two clergymen from their joint pulpit, Travers was silenced and dismissed by John Whitgift, Archbishop of Canterbury. From that time forward, Whitgift, whose writings against the Puritans were voluminous, had a hand in Hooker's career. It is generally believed that Hooker's controversy with Travers and his exposure to the legal profession at the Temple Church shaped his role as defender of the established church.

In *Of the Lawes of Ecclesiasticall Politie*, Hooker reveals his profound knowledge of biblical, patristic, and Reformation sources and, more important, his essentially Aristotelian view of reason and government. He makes no attempt to analyze church doctrine nor to resolve theological questions; instead he attempts to justify the outward order and religious rites and practices of the church. In doing so he repeats many of the specific points made earlier by John Whitgift in his own answers to the Puritans. Hooker departed from previous practices in such polemic controversies. Instead of answering the objections point by point, he established a logical order for his discourse, and undertook an extended clarification of general principles before dealing with specific points.

Of the Lawes of Ecclesiasticall Politie was written in eight books, the first four published in 1594. These four concern broad principles of law and its application, the place of scripture in providing rules for living and for church polity, and general ceremonies and rites of the church. Book 5, published in 1597, is longer than the first four combined. It defends specific practices of the Church of England, including public prayer, sacraments, rites, and the ministry. The final three books, dealing with issues of power and authority, were first published after Hooker's death and have long been considered of doubtful authenticity. Book 6, dealing with lay elders, and Book 8, dealing with royal supremacy, appeared in 1648. Book 7, concerning the role of bishops, remained unpublished until 1662. Although questions linger about the books on power, modern scholarship regards them as authentic, although Book 6 is believed to be seriously incomplete.

Hooker laid down broad general principles and applied them to specifics. Nowhere is this better illustrated than in Book 1, dealing with the nature of law. His general concepts emerge from his view of the human as a rational being tending toward three types of perfection—material or physical, intellectual, and spiritual. Like Thomas Aquinas, the medieval scholastic philosopher, Hooker adds a Christian spiritual dimension to Aristotle's teleological view of human beings. For external guidance people turn to laws, those revealed in scripture and those of nature. From people's understanding of natural law, they can derive human laws that are beneficial, natural law being founded on the unexpressed creative principles of the creator. Hooker defines law as "a directive rule unto goodness of operation"; he believes people can establish positive laws based only on what rational understanding discovers to be beneficial. The test of such laws remains their effects, as measured by reason; positive laws often may be judged inadequate. Thus positive laws, unlike those of scripture or of nature, are alterable as need requires or circumstances change.

Concerning the origin of government, Hooker assumes that an original compact for the betterment of humanity established rulers, which people then endowed with power through common consent. Accordingly, government is perceived as an organized society, influenced by numerous types of conventions and laws and designed to promote humanity's general well-being. Laws may be created or altered by common consent or by delegated authority, as in representative assemblies, as the perceived needs of the society require. Just as humanity strives toward perfection in the teleological view, so does human society, and Hooker's writing suggests that law is a major instrument of the progress toward perfection. Custom and tradition had distributed governmental powers among institutions such as the courts, the parliament, and the king, and Hooker partially defines the roles of each. In a properly ordered society, even the king is subordinate to the law of the commonweal, as his oath of office implies. Under the national government, lesser governmental entities exist, with their own laws, limits, and functions. Hooker viewed the state as a complex, overlapping system of organizations, working within a nationalist structure.

The church, in its outward manifestation and practice, is also defined as a society, subject to similar kinds of laws. Hooker assumes that the church is an organization limited by national boundaries, and that the nature of national churches may vary in keeping with differing conditions within nations. Hooker attempts to demonstrate that positive laws of the church, tested by reason, are defensible so long as they do not violate biblical injunctions. In the church as in the state, laws properly are adopted only after the consent of those whom they govern.

Applications

In Book 7 of *Of the Lawes of Ecclesiasticall Politie*, Hooker undertakes to defend the episcopal structure of the church and to elucidate the powers of bishops. His examination of the subject demonstrates his essentially moderate approach, as well as some of its limitations. From the early Christian era, the doctrine of apostolic succession had been promulgated, and earlier in the sixteenth century had been adopted by the Roman Catholic church as official doctrine. The belief holds that bishops are true descendants of the Apostles, in an unbroken line, and that the bishopric is a divinely instituted and ordained office. English clergymen such as Richard Bancroft, Bishop of London, and Hadrian Saravia, Hooker's friend and fellow theologian, embraced the doctrine as a bulwark of episcopacy. Hooker's eclectic and legalistic approach, however, resulted in a different conclusion.

He begins by pointing out that bishop, priest, and deacon constitute the three levels of clergy mentioned in the New Testament. While ignoring textual ambiguities of relevant passages, he argues strongly that they gave the office legitimacy. Citations from the earliest Greek theologians also established that the office had been accepted from ancient times and that its roles and functions were well defined. From a practical standpoint, Hooker explains, it is impossible in a large society of clergy to have discipline without ranked orders, and the bishop represents the office that ensures order. Consequently, the view that bishops are the historical descendants of the Apostles is sound, and Hooker argues vehemently in its favor.

The question of necessity, however, raised another problem. Hooker acknowledged that some reformed churches in Europe, legitimate societies in the sense of being national churches, had eliminated the office. In Lutheran areas, some had retained bishops while others had abolished the office, as Martin Luther himself believed that the office belonged under the category of "things indifferent," or not requisite. From further examination of the New Testament passages, Hooker concludes that Jesus called the Apostles as individuals, neither instituting nor requiring an office or rank. He then concludes that provision for episcopal rule is a positive human law, not a divine law, and therefore the doctrine of apostolic succession cannot stand. As in other instances, his defense of the church rests upon reason rather than an appeal to divine sanction. The episcopacy is justified by its history and its beneficial effects, not by any divine law. This conclusion provided little comfort to the seventeenth century bishops who supported apostolic succession and centralized rule.

Hooker's defense of the monarchy and the monarch as head of the church in Book 8 follows a similar course. He defends kingship on historical and pragmatic grounds, even touching upon the legitimacy of succession, but acknowledges that nowhere in scripture is the office divinely ordained. From historical examples and the practice of contemporaneous nations, he concludes that legitimate republican forms of government exist. Thus he limits monarchical power by placing the monarch under law, and undercuts the institution by classifying the monarchy as being under the concept of alterable positive law.

Context

Any effort to evaluate Hooker's political contributions must begin with the acknowledgment that he had no intention of propounding a coherent system of government. His objectives were to justify the Church of England, defined as a politic society, and to reconcile those opposed to the church. Historically, this purpose failed, because no justification of particulars, however reasoned and conciliatory, could have overcome the Puritans' opposition to the episcopal order. His political ideas are often vague, owing to his inclination to draw on numerous sources, his unwillingness to press his arguments to their full extent, and his occasional inconsistencies. Interpreting his political views has resulted in striking disagreements. Some critics regard him as a precursor of John Locke's social contract theory, an advocate of popular sovereignty, a Whig thinker before the Whigs originated, and a modern liberal political theorist. Others have interpreted his political views as Thomistic and therefore essentially medieval.

Despite their ambiguities and inconsistencies, Hooker's ideas influenced later political thinkers. Before nationalism was well defined, Hooker revealed himself as a nationalist, one who saw the church in its outward form as a national politic society. He argued that any citizen of the nation was by virtue of citizenship also a member of the church. The nation itself was formed by an original compact in which the people surrendered their rights to rulers, principally the monarch.

This original compact implies a popular right to power, yet Hooker's understanding of this is not a modern one. While he pays lip service to the Tudor commonplace that tyrants can be legally overthrown, nowhere does he provide for the people to reclaim the power that their ancestors ceded to government, nor does he accord them the right to reserve certain rights inviolable. His view that the voice of the people, over many generations, is as the voice of God rests on the assumption of natural law, not on a firm concept of popular sovereignty. That is, people derive opinions that are inherently correct through reason, and long experience proves them so. Thus the people's voice represents a principle that can be applied in the support of custom and tradition, not one in support of the popular exercise of power.

Hooker's view of the functioning of government also rests on something resembling a balance of power, with each governing body under the rule of law. This is a forward-looking concept, especially when applied to the monarch. He argues that the king should not raise taxes or enact new laws without consent of the governed, whose spokespersons are their representatives in parliament. In effect, every citizen holds an indirect representative voice in the actions of government. These restraints of law do not apply, however, in the instance of conquest, which endows the conqueror with the right to impose his or her own system.

Hooker's most modern and liberating view of government may rest on a very ancient source, Aristotle. He tacitly agrees with the Aristotelian commonplace that government exists not that people may live but that they may live well. The view does not quite imply modern liberalism, nor does it imply the idea of progress. It does imply a recognition that law is an instrument of change and that positive laws are alterable in accordance with the exigencies of time and circumstance.

Bibliography

Archer, Stanley. *Richard Hooker*. Boston: Twayne, 1983. Surveys Hooker's achievement as a thinker and literary figure. Analyzes *Of the Lawes of Ecclesiasticall Politie*, and Hooker's sermons, tractates, and other miscellaneous writings. Brief biography and an annotated bibliography.

Davies, E. T. *The Political Ideas of Richard Hooker.* New York: Octagon Books, 1972. Davies' popular treatment of Hooker's political thought is useful for its numerous comparisons between Hooker and other political thinkers. General, readable treatment designed for laypeople.

Faulkner, Robert K. *Richard Hooker and the Politics of a Christian England.* Berkeley: University of California Press, 1981. Explores Hooker's ethical views and analyzes his concept of law. Book centers its exploration of government on issues related to monarchical power.

Hill, W. Speed. *Studies in Richard Hooker: Essays Preliminary to an Edition of His Works.* Cleveland: Case Western Reserve University Press, 1972. Among the six essays in this collection, W. D. J. Cargill Thompson's "The Philosopher of the Politic Society" is highly significant. Thompson reviews earlier studies of Hooker's political thought, emphasizes his role as a polemicist whose objective is to defend the status quo, and finds that Hooker embodied little originality and exerted limited influence on succeeding generations. Heavily annotated bibliography.

Hooker, Richard. *Hooker's Ecclesiastical Polity, Book VIII.* Edited by Raymond Aaron Houk. New York: Columbia University Press, 1931. Scholarly edition of the portion of *Ecclesiastical Polity* that deals with the monarchy. Includes a wealth of introductory matter. Houk's discussion of Hooker's view of the monarchy represents a useful introduction to his political thought.

Kirby, W. J. Torrance. *Richard Hooker's Doctrine of the Royal Supremacy.* New York: E. J. Brill, 1990. In clarifying Hooker's view on monarchy, Kirby goes beyond his concept of laws to the theological assumptions that underlie his defense. Carefully relates Book VIII to the earlier books of *Ecclesiastical Polity.*

Marshall, John S. *Hooker and the Anglican Tradition: An Historical and Theological Study of Hooker's Ecclesiastical Polity.* Sewannee, Tenn.: University Press, 1963. Depicts Hooker as a follower of the political and theological ideas of Saint Thomas Aquinas, with some significant departures. Author believes that Hooker sought to produce another Thomistic synthesis.

Pollard, Arthur. *Richard Hooker.* London: Longmans, Green, 1966. Brief and readable explanation of Hooker's contribution to literature and intellectual history.

Stanley Archer

Cross-References

Aristotle's Political Philosophy, p. 83; Burke's Political Philosophy, p. 171; Church and Government in History, p. 230; Church Government, p. 241; Conservatism, p. 419; Heads of State, p. 804; Hobbes's Political Philosophy, p. 836; John of Salisbury's Political Philosophy, p. 1006; Locke's Political Philosophy, p. 1142; Nationalism, p. 1268; Political Philosophy, p. 1505; Thomas Aquinas' Political Philosophy, p. 1974.

HUMAN RIGHTS AND INTERNATIONAL POLITICS

Field of study: International government and politics

Human rights emerged as a potent dynamic of international politics after World War II. Although the concept of universal human rights conflicts with the states' traditional prerogatives under domestic jurisdiction, states themselves have created numerous human rights treaties and regimes. This trend promotes the global development of shared values and common institutions.

Principal terms

APARTHEID: social and political system in which the human right to equality is denied; practiced in South Africa from 1948 until 1991, during which time a white minority held privileged status

DOMESTIC JURISDICTION: internal state sovereignty, the state's exclusive authority over its own people and territory

GENOCIDE: deliberate attempt to destroy an entire ethnic or religious group

HUMAN RIGHTS: held inherently by each human being, identified as individual civil and political rights, group economic and social rights, and peoples' collective rights

UNIVERSAL DECLARATION OF HUMAN RIGHTS: seminal human rights charter passed by the United Nations on December 10, 1948, annually celebrated as Human Rights Day

Overview

Human rights became a prominent part of the world political landscape in the second half of the twentieth century. Conceived as intrinsic to each person, human rights are intended to provide a political, legal, and moral bulwark for human beings against such brutalities as slavery, torture, and genocide. Nazi Germany's genocidal policies against Jews and others inspired the international community to build the post-World War II reconstruction upon the foundations of democracy and human rights.

Human rights are understood to uphold the dignity and fulfill the potential of every human being. The specific content of international human rights, however, has evolved and expanded through three generations. The root concept emerged from the Western tradition of the superiority of natural law over human law, and by the seventeenth century was understood as confirming a person's rights against his or her government. These rights, such as freedom of speech, legal equality, and the right to political participation, are categorized as civil and political rights. The first generation of human rights is highly compatible with supervision by the judiciary.

After the rise of Marxism in the nineteenth century, a growing awareness of the importance of economic and social justice caused a reconsideration of the narrowness of the rights tradition. Human rights came to include group economic and social rights, such as the right to food, the right to work, and the right to an adequate standard of living. Rather than rights held against the government, the second generation of rights looks to the government for fulfillment.

This enlargement of the scope of human rights has been rejected by critics, primarily political conservatives in the West, who claim that, because governmental capacity to fulfill economic and social rights remains relative to its own economic development, they cannot logically be conceptualized as rights. Social and economic rights are actually basic needs rather than standards legally enforceable by judicial supervision. To dilute the moral and legal standing of human rights by adding economic and social content is a mistake, in this view.

Advocates of economic and social rights argue that they are the most fundamental. What is the meaning, for example, of freedom of the press to a starving child? Moreover, economic rights were already imbedded in the original Western version as the virtually sacred right to own property, the very cornerstone of capitalism. Western societies have secured economic well-being and stability for their own societies through "socialistic" policies such as public education and social security.

When the United Nations drafted the Universal Declaration of Human Rights in 1948, both generations of thought were mutually recognized and entwined in the inclusive document. Nevertheless, the tension between the two approaches required a separation into twin treaties: the International Covenant on Civil and Political Rights (ICCPR); and the International Covenant on Economic, Social, and Cultural Rights (ICESCR).

The third generation of human rights emerged as colonialism drew to a close between 1960 and 1975, and nearly one hundred new nation-states from the Third World joined the international community. They asserted the importance of communal or peoples' rights, such as the right to self-determination, the right to development, and the right to peace. The first article in each of the twin Universal Declaration covenants, put forward in 1966, verifies the right to national self-determination. The 1981 African Charter of Human and Peoples' Rights, drafted at Banjul, Gambia, under the auspices of the Organization of African Unity, incorporates all three generations of human rights.

Critics of the third generation argue that, like economic and social rights, communal rights only blur and detract from human rights by espousing ideals rather than enforceable rights. Advocates insist that a narrow Western version of human rights placing the person above her or his community amounts to cultural imperialism, and prevents human rights from being esteemed as universal by the vast majority of the world's people.

Although the Vienna World Conference on Human Rights (1993) declared the total package of human rights to be "universal, indivisible and interdependent and interrelated," the pronounced tendency to view the generations in descending order of importance continued. Especially in the West, the content of human rights generally has been taken by citizens and scholars alike to mean civil and political rights, that is, primarily the first generation.

The best evidence for an emerging consensus on fundamental human rights is that a majority of nation-states, which numbered almost 180 by 1994, have endorsed a series of core human rights treaties. Perhaps the most important are the ICCPR and the ICESCR, which, as the treaty forms of the Universal Declaration, have been joined by nearly two-thirds of the nation-states. In addition, more than one hundred states have become parties to the Convention on the Prohibition and Punishment of the Crime of Genocide (1948) and the Supplementary Convention on the Abolition of Slavery, the Slave Trade, and Institutions and Practices Similar to Slavery (1956). Similar high rates of adherence can also be found for the Convention on the Elimination of All Forms of Racial Discrimination (1966) and the Convention on the Elimination of All Forms of Discrimination Against Women (1979). The international community has directed attention to ratification of the Convention Against Torture, and Other Cruel, Inhuman or Degrading Treatment or Punishment (1984), and the Convention on the Rights of the Child (1989).

Despite this impressive set of treaties, it should be acknowledged that human rights have achieved an honorific status not unlike that of democracy, so that some nation-states may only pretend to support them. Effective enforcement of human rights is a far more difficult matter than attaining nominal adherence.

Compliance with the standards contained in human rights treaties typically relies on self-scrutiny, often through the device of state reports. Some treaties include options to join a separate entity created specifically to oversee the treaty, such as the Human Rights Committee that monitors the ICCPR.

The various United Nations organs, especially the Commission on Human Rights, offer other important forums for evaluating state performance on human rights. The commission, however, has been accused of politicizing its agenda under Resolution 1503, which permits investigations of "a consistent pattern of gross . . . violations of human rights." Under the political domination of the Third World and the Soviet bloc from the late 1960's through the early 1980's, United Nations organs limited their attention to three states as human rights abusers: South Africa, Israel, and Chile. By the mid-1980's the Commission on Human Rights had largely repaired its reputation, especially through the use of a thematic approach to violations such as "disappearances."

Applications

The impact of human rights within international politics can be demonstrated by two case studies. One of them, the stunning Western European regional regime developed under the European Convention on Human Rights (1950), was designed by the states involved. The other, a campaign of sanctions and censure against the apartheid policies of South Africa, directly largely through the United Nations, resulted in the abandonment of apartheid by the besieged government.

The most successful human rights regime of the twentieth century was created under the Council of Europe and based on the European Convention on Human Rights. The treaty permits state-to-state complaints regarding violations of basic civil and political rights. (A subsequent European Social Charter in 1961 added economic and social rights to the Council of Europe's mandate.) The treaty's uniqueness lies in the establishment of a European Commission on Human Rights and a European Court on Human Rights, which together guarantee regional enforcement that supersedes domestic jurisdiction. Each relies upon a separate, optional provision within the treaty itself.

Article 25 permits the European Commission to take complaints from individuals after the exhaustion of domestic remedies, guaranteeing that the state will have the first opportunity to adjudicate the issue. This, in effect, permits the person to reach through domestic jurisdiction to the regional system. The European Commission may then decide to forward the person's case to the European Court, which bears compulsory jurisdiction over those states that have accepted Article 46.

Each of the twenty-two member states of the European Convention had accepted the authority of the commission to receive petitions and recognized the compulsory jurisdiction of the Court, as of 1992. The net result was an impressive case law consisting of nearly 150 cases. Some highly significant and sensitive issues traditionally subsumed under domestic jurisdiction have been decided by the European Court, thereby proving its ability to protect rather than merely promote human rights. Prominent decisions include the *Belgium Linguistics* case (1977), requiring equal opportunity for linguistic minorities in public schools; the *Ireland v. United Kingdom* case, prohibiting the United Kingdom from the five techniques used to interrogate Irish Republican Army suspects; and the *Dudgeon* case (1982), declaring sexual conduct between consenting adult homosexuals to be a private matter.

While the Council of Europe provides an umbrella organization to oversee these institutions, the essential factor is the willing compliance of the states. It has been noted that the most impressive human rights regime has emerged in Western European countries because it is the most compatible with their domestic political culture and laws, and therefore the least needed.

A similar document and set of arrangements exist in Latin America, where the 1980's trend toward democracy coexisted with pervasive human rights violations. Political reality dictates that the Inter-American Commission of Human Rights and the Inter-American Court of Human Rights function more flexibly in Latin America to spotlight the most serious abuses there.

The censure and sanctions directed against South Africa because of its apartheid system offer another example of the influence of the human rights movement. A system of institutionalized racism favoring the minority (15 percent) white population was put in place by the Nationalist Party throughout South Africa in 1947.

Energized by Third World nations using their newly achieved access to the United Nations, an end to apartheid as a grotesque violation of the right to equality became a visible priority within international politics. The U.N. General Assembly called upon member states to treat South Africa as an outlaw state by terminating diplomatic and economic relations. South Africa's privileges in the General Assembly were withdrawn in 1974. The Commission on Human Rights repeatedly used its procedures and authority to condemn apartheid. The International Convention on the Suppression and Punishment of the Crime of Apartheid (1973) provided the foundation for a broad condemnation of South Africa by securing nearly one hundred signatories. Finally, the Security Council established a mandatory arms embargo against South Africa in 1977.

After the United States and other powerful nations instigated selective economic pressure in the 1980's, South Africa began a process of multilateral negotiations in 1991, which culminated in genuinely democratic elections in South Africa in 1994.

One final example of the attention given by the international community to human rights can be found in the establishment by the Security Council of a War Crimes Tribunal on May 25, 1993, the first since the Nuremberg Tribunal. It is authorized to address genocide, ethnic cleansing, systematic rape camps, and crimes against humanity committed in former Yugoslavia.

Context

Because nation-states possess three vital resources—money, military power, and the loyalty of their citizens—international politics is built upon state sovereignty. The external dynamic of state sovereignty is represented by the states' independence in matters of foreign affairs. The internal dynamic, known as domestic jurisdiction under international law, historically claimed the state's exclusive authority over its own people and territory. Clearly, traditional governmental prerogatives under domestic jurisdiction potentially clash with the notion of universal human rights held by their people.

By the treaty process discussed above, topics previously reserved under domestic jurisdiction are progressively being removed to the international sphere. The World Court (Permanent Court of International Justice) denoted a relative relationship between international law and the scope of domestic jurisdiction in the *Nationality Decrees of Tunis and Morocco* case (1923). When nation-states act to endorse certain human rights standards and create oversight mechanisms via a treaty document, these principles then become binding upon the nation-states, given the principle of *pacta sunt servanda* ("treaties must be kept"). Hence, the states themselves, in the exercise of their sovereignty, have eroded the scope of their domestic jurisdiction, and thereby reduced the traditional dominance of the nation-state actors over international politics.

Indeed, as the international community approaches the twenty-first century, most scholars characterize the nation-states as being in a relationship of "complex interdependence," requiring greater collaboration and cooperation. This condition is a result of the mutual vulnerabilities stemming from the shared dangers of the nuclear age, the variable health of the global economy, and the on-going environmental deterioration that threatens the entire ecosystem.

Human rights provides a common denominator that promotes the shared values and common institutions necessary to ameliorate the transformation from a system of state sovereignty to a genuine international community. This process is underway on both the international and national levels.

The continued proliferation of human rights instruments and institutions on the international scene was illustrated by the call at the Vienna World Conference on Human Rights for two new entities: a treaty on domestic violence, and a United Nations High Commissioner on Human Rights. On the national level, if the trends of the late twentieth century continue, constitutional democracies will become more pervasive as human rights values and protective mechanisms infuse local political cultures.

Bibliography

Amnesty International. *Amnesty International Report*. London: Amnesty International, yearly. Annual review of the human rights record of every country by the most widely known human rights nongovernmental organization, and recipient of the Nobel Peace Prize.

An-Na'im, Abdullahi Ahmed, and Francis M. Deng, eds. *Human Rights in Africa: Cross-Cultural Perspectives*. Washington, D.C.: Brookings Institution, 1990. Interesting variety of cultural perspectives on human rights, with a special emphasis on African, Islamic, and Christian views.

Brownlie, Ian, ed. *Basic Documents on Human Rights*. 3d ed. Oxford, England: Clarendon Press, 1992. Classic, comprehensive compilation of human rights documents and materials.

Donnelly, Jack. *International Human Rights*. Boulder, Colo.: Westview Press, 1993. Succinct presentation of the fundamentals of human rights, which includes a discussion of apartheid in South Africa and the text of the Universal Declaration of Human Rights. Includes charts, photos, and cartoons that relate aspects of human rights theory and practice.

Fein, Helen, ed. *Genocide Watch*. New Haven, Conn.: Yale University Press, 1992. Criticizes the limited official definition of genocide as relating only to ethnic and religious groups, because political groups and classes have been the primary victims of mass slaughters since 1945.

Gutman, Roy. *A Witness to Genocide*. New York: Macmillan, 1993. 1993 Pulitzer Prize-winning dispatches, including several remarkable pictures, on "ethnic cleansing" in Bosnia.

Janis, Mark W., and Richard S. Kay. *European Human Rights Law*. Hartford: University of Connecticut Law School Foundation Press, 1990. Background discussion of the European Convention and the roles of the European Commission and Court frame a study of human rights case law emerging from the European system.

Newman, Frank, and David Weissbrodt. *International Human Rights*. Cincinnati: Anderson, 1990. Superb source both for background information about the theory and practice of human rights, with specific illustrations of human rights law under international and regional regimes, as well as for information about United Nations organs and human rights nongovernmental organizations.

Nancy N. Haanstad

Cross-References

Civil Liberties Protection, p. 291; Civil Rights Protection, p. 304; Constitutional Governments, p. 432; Genocide, p. 752; Immigration and Emigration, p. 868; International Agreements, p. 949; International Law, p. 956; Naturalization, p. 1275; Police States, p. 1408; Slavery and U.S. Political History, p. 1821; Totalitarianism, p. 1987; United Nations, p. 2045; The World Health Organization, p. 2180.

IDEALISM

Field of study: Political philosophy

As a formal school of philosophy, idealism is a doctrine asserting that all that exists is mental, nonphysical substance. The doctrine further holds that objects of external perception—in itself or as perceived—consist only of ideas. As a historical body of political and philosophical thought, idealism found its most eloquent expression in the work of Immanuel Kant and Georg Wilhelm Friedrich Hegel.

Principal terms

DIALECTIC: Hegelian process of change wherein an idea (thesis) is transformed into its opposite (antithesis) and is then fulfilled by combining both in a higher form of truth (synthesis)

PHENOMENOLOGY: study of all possible appearances in human experience, during which considerations of objective reality and of purely subjective response are left out of any intellectual account

REASON: thought processes involved in understanding, scientific inquiry, and philosophical argument; to Hegel, the concepts and processes of reason do not merely discover facts about the universe, but help to create them

RIGHT: Hegel's term for the complex of ideas and practices noted by such concepts as individual freedom, privilege, moral duty, and the rule of law

STATE, THE: according to Hegel, the culmination of the "absolute power on earth" on whose actions only history can pronounce judgment

Overview

The European Enlightenment and the French Revolution in 1789 claimed human "reason" as their guiding principle. Napoleon's rise to power and the turbulent events in Europe during the following two decades, however, seemed neither natural nor rational. The gathering pace of the Industrial Revolution put change and development at the center of the age. The idealist movement, particularly strong in Germany led by the German philosophers Immanuel Kant and Georg Wilhelm Friedrich Hegel, laid emphasis on the ways in which humans invest the world with their own meanings. The German idealists considered that human beings collectively and individually created their own reality in response to changing circumstances.

In its Kantian form, idealism insisted upon a sharp distinction between reality as it appeared to the human mind and reality as it truly was. By establishing the role of reason as the centerpiece to his thought, Kant could demonstrate that reason took as its task not only the understanding of the material universe, but also the acquiring of insight into human nature, its limits, its ideals, and its goals. When humans undertake to contemplate the phenomenal world—that is, the world as it appears to be—they are prepared with this kind of understanding to predict the motions of the phenomenal world, though never with certainty. Knowledge of this kind does not give people direct access to the "inner reality" of the material objects of their observations, but only as "representations" of the real world. Knowledge obtained in this manner is always hypothetical, so that humans can make only general propositions about what they perceive.

True knowledge is possible only when reason reveals to human beings the understanding that behind the world of material objects there exists another world of "noumenal" reality, of things as they exist in themselves—a world similar to Plato's forms. The real world of value and meaning is not possible when people experience the noumenal world. They discover an order to "right," and that we perform our duties in accordance with this principle. At that moment they are entirely free and self-determining in their behavior. This positive freedom allows humans to determine their actions by their good will. One's civic duties, in this context, involved discipline, civil order, and allegiance to the state—in short, obedience. Kant argued that it was the duty of the people to bear any abuse of the supreme power, even though it should be considered unbearable. He also argued that a single ruler was justified in taking actions counter to the express wishes of the majority of the people, provided that he had in mind the general welfare.

For Hegel, who tried to give these ideas a systematic intellectual basis, the ideas of a particular age could not claim absolute validity in themselves, for they were relative to changing historical situations. If there is a rationality or meaning to history, it must be found in the whole historical process, rather than in the partial aims of particular individuals and epochs. Hegel attempted to find a new synthesis of Greek ethics and Christian morality. To the ancients, ethics consisted of active participation by the individual in the political life of community, in contrast to Christian morality, which was strictly individual. Influenced by Kant's "principle of moral autonomy," which declared the "will" to be its own laws, Hegel's synthesis marked an important step forward in understanding of man's moral development. In regarding man's rational nature as the ultimate moral norm, it eliminates all external influences that did not originate in the moral subject itself.

For Hegel, it is not material life, but thought that gives history its meaning, shaping force, and essence. From such a perspective, ideas "create" history, so history itself must be seen as the embodiment of ideas realized in events. In history resides a higher reason than the intelligence of any individual. Hegel adopted the notion that historical processes are guided by this "idea" that historical processes go by opposites: Every tendency carried to its limits breeds an opposite tendency that destroys it. Nothing in the world statically "is," but is in the process of continuous change, developing into something else, different from and often opposite to the "being" that it displays at any particular historical moment. Knowledge, or truth, can therefore only be expressed through history's dialectical process of combining opposites. The purpose of the dialectic is to display what Hegel calls "necessity" in history, which shows an orderly unfolding. Each historical period has its own character, which unites all the institutions of the period. For example, the city-state determined the qualities of Greek religion, philosophy, and art, as well as its political character.

If truth is made in individual actions, then there must be an actor to do the making. For Hegel, this is the "mind" or "spirit." Without mind, human experience would have no form or meaning. Whenever we act in the world, it is the processes of "thought" that give form and meaning to events. Looking at the total social process of thought as a historical reality, Hegel discerned a pattern of meaningful change: gradual movement toward greater human self-consciousness, and therefore toward greater freedom of mind to control the world through increased understanding of its laws. Thus, there emerged for Hegel the idea of the "absolute idea"—the mind as the primary reality of the world.

Hegel defines the political state as a sphere in which individual freedom reaches its fullest historical development and individual and particular "wills" become universal will within the state. Thus, only by living within the state can man be completely free. The family and civil society are merely preparatory moments in a historical development that has not yet reached completion. Only when the family and civil society become connected with the state can these agencies receive their proper meaning. Their true reality can be understood only from within the state; subordination is their very existence. Consequently, so long as one has not identified oneself with the state, one has not become a "person" in the full sense of the word. The state is the end of the individual who, as a spiritual being, must develop himself universally in order to become free.

The state constitutes a final end for individuals, who find in it the truth of their existence, duty, and satisfaction. At that moment in history's unfolding, the state constitutes the actualization of the divine in the external world. Through the state individuals take their place in the world; it is only as citizens that they learn what is reasonable in their wishes and claims. This is the stage in which the individual or subjective mind becomes the objective mind or the state as history's final stage.

Applications

Just as traditional idealism criticized the role of social and political thought of its time, it continues to apply its historical concepts to the study of human affairs. Idealism embraces the view that if social analysis is to confront the world in a total way, it does so in order to discover the intellectual and spiritual basis of modern society. Our social and political institutions defy understanding apart from the work of the minds that inhabit them. We can understand behavior only by grasping the nature of human thought.

Idealism had influenced the creation of a fixed philosophical basis for ideas that found a home in liberal democratic states. Hegel's conception of individual freedom and the rights of person has imposed a heavy responsibility on all democratic societies. Liberalism—which in the political field is analogous to idealism in the philosophical—led to the effort to establish a form of political organization expressing the actual contemporary structure of the real life of society. Consequently, the effect of liberalism in politics was to maintain the legal forms of the democratic state, and to use these to transform the actual life of society into a concrete democratic life. Only a blending of the two—state and society—could produce what liberalism intended—the truth of democracy as idea.

That the liberal welfare state requires that political power and authority make real the rights of individuals is an idea compatible with Hegel's thought. One can define a line of intellectual influence, reaching from Hegel through such thinkers as Thomas Hill Green, Ernest Barker, and R. M. MacIver and Americans such as John Dewey to the social reformers who developed the principles of welfare liberalism that culminated in President Franklin D. Roosevelt's New Deal. Thus, individuals are understood to enjoy rights to freedom from want and from fear, freedom to develop as persons. The long list of human rights in the United Nations Universal Declaration of Human Rights, the Nuremberg Principles, and in the U.S. Bill of Rights, together with its judicial interpretation and legislative extension, fit well with Hegelian philosophy.

In spite of the similarity of Hegel's conception of the rights of humankind to that of welfare liberalism, it is also the case that Hegel's influence moved in an antiliberal direction. Hegel's idealization of the nation-state might be said to have paved the way for leaders such as Benito Mussolini, the founder of the Italian Fascist state. Mussolini made the "state" the embodiment of all things good, its force a mode of discipline not only consistent with individual well-being but necessary to achieve the citizen's "true" personality and freedom. The appeal of fascism was to an expansive national pride that glorified war and the collective will to dominate. Fascism's division of state and society, however, defied Hegel's most basic maxims: the commingling of state and society into one. According to Hegel, the state was to be a rational force based on the rule of law and it can limit freedom only through law. In the German conception, law is made by the monarch. Beyond this difference between the Enlightenment conception of law and Hegel's conception, he still insisted that his state proceed according to law.

Hegel's influence on Karl Marx is considerable. Although Marx adopted much of Hegel's thought, he also qualified much of Hegel's philosophy. Marx contended that now that philosophers have interpreted the world it is possible to change the world. Marx thought that German idealism had the necessary conceptual tools, but that it stopped short of penetrating reality in order to change it. Commenting on Kant's legacy to German liberalism, Marx protested against the endless repetition by German liberals who think that they honor liberty by relegating it to the starry heaven of imagination, instead of basing it on the firm foundation of reality.

The revolutionary aspects of Hegel's philosophy got Marx's attention, particularly the notion that no historical state of affairs can ever be considered final. Hegel, because of his political and religious conservatism, refused to accept the revolutionary implications of his own thought. Marx argued that Hegel's philosophy had become an instrument for the preservation of Prussian monarchy and the establishment of the Lutheran church. To the young Marx, philosophy must be critical rather than conservative.

While Marx retained the Hegelian belief in rationality, he reversed Hegel's view that ideas change material conditions. Marx did not view humans as "reasoning" animals who are perfectible through the development of their capacity to reason. Indeed, he rejected such views as "utopian." Rather, Marx saw people as creatures of their material environment, which they are capable of ultimately overcoming through revolutionary action. The process of thought or consciousness does not create life, but life that determines consciousness. Human beings do not discover the truth about the human condition through thought alone; history proves the truth through actual human activity. When people produce their material needs through their labor, they change— along with their real existence, their thinking, and the products of their thought.

Marx's critique of Hegel's philosophy of the state centered on Hegel's conclusion that since the state has a more rational structure than the natural spheres of family and civil society, the latter owe their origins to the state. To Marx, this is ideal mysticism in which family and civil society as mere elements of logical ideas lose their independent reality. Marx countered that the state is the result rather than the cause of the social relations operating within the lower stages of family and civil society. The political state cannot exist without the natural basis of the family and civil society.

Context

Idealism's great contribution is Kant's and Hegel's insights into the essential "activity" of the mind and its attempt to demonstrate that reason rules the world, giving an order to human events that is discoverable through human reason. Also, that reason (Hegel called spirit) can be shown to direct the specific, concrete aspects of history (good and bad), toward an identifiable end. History thus comprises a lengthy process of human development aimed at realizing self-conscious and universal freedom.

Against the background of nineteenth century German history, the Reformation, the peasant uprising, and a series of seventeenth century religious conflicts known as the Thirty Years' War, the conclusion drawn from these events was clear and unmistakable, and no one needed to convince Germans about the necessity of a strong temporal authority to maintain peace, order, and stability. To an age torn by the French Revolution and its perceived excesses of individualism, German idealism seemed to offer a system of order in an all-encompassing state. Idealism held that we are relatively free in nature because we submit to the laws of nature. Similarly, in society, we are free if we accept the laws imposed on us in the name of a higher rationality. German idealism carried this line of reasoning to the extent that Kant and Hegel identified individual freedom with conformity to the will of the state. In considering individual freedom, the starting point was not individuality, but rather the ethical whole that constitutes the state. Only a state governed by an absolute monarch can prevent the destructive tendencies of self-seeking individualism.

Hegel not only defended the rationality of the state against the romantics, who simply turned away from politics, but against the utopians and reformers, who turn away from the "real state" in favor of an ideal state. He saw the function of philosophy as not to teach the state how it ought to be, but to teach men how the state ought to be understood.

The French Revolution had put thought or reason at the very foundation of the state. It represented the harmony of the principle of individual subjective consciousness and, with it, the principle of liberty, equality, and the rights of man and citizen. For Hegel, this principle left no place for organization and government or anything concrete. Moreover, after Napoleon, who had understood the necessity of assimilating the principles of the revolution with the authority of an organized state, French political life remained in the grip of Enlightenment principles proclaiming the rights of nature and citizenship. So long as the people are not organized in and by the state, it is only a collection of particular wills and "does not know what it will."

Bibliography

Avineri, Shlomo. *Hegel's Theory of the Modern State*. Cambridge, England: Cambridge University Press, 1972. Argues that Hegel emphasized the liberating tendencies within the Prussian state. Contains subject index and bibliography.

Friedrich, Carl J. *Inevitable Peace*. Cambridge, Mass.: Harvard University Press, 1948. Places Kant's thought in the context of Western theories of peace and law.

Hegel, Georg W. F. *The Phenomenology of Mind*. Translated by J. B. Baillie. New York: Harper & Row, 1967. Difficult but readable translation of Hegel's philosophical idealism as a foundation for his political thought. Baillie's careful definitions of Hegel's terms is a particularly helpful feature.

Kaufmann, Walter, ed. *Hegel's Political Philosophy*. New York: Atherton Press, 1970. Excellent collection of different interpretations of Hegel's political thought.

Knox, T. M. *The Philosophy of Right*. New York: Oxford University Press, 1952. Excellent jargon-free examination of Hegel's program for the establishment of the German state.

Murphy, Jeffrie G. *Kant: The Philosophy of Right*. New York: St. Martin's Press, 1970. Excellent analytical commentary on Kant's political thought.

Oakeshott, Michael. *The Social and Political Doctrines of Contemporary Europe*. Cambridge, England: Cambridge University Press, 1939. Contains a chapter on fascism that is a readable treatment of Hegel's influence on early fascist thought.

Taylor, Charles. *Hegel*. Cambridge, England: Cambridge University Press, 1975. Readable account of Hegel's influence on a scientific analysis of politics.

Andrew Raposa

Cross-References

Dialecticism, p. 540; Fascism and Nazism, p. 656; General Will, p. 745; Hobbes's Political Philosophy, p. 836; Kant's Political Philosophy, p. 1025; Liberalism, p. 1118; Marxism-Leninism, p. 1155; Neo-Idealism, p. 1287; Plato's Political Philosophy, p. 1396; Political Philosophy, p. 1505; Political Pragmatism, p. 1519; Rousseau's Political Philosophy, p. 1756.

IMMIGRANTS AND POLITICS

Field of study: Politics

The world has been settled and resettled by many diverse ethnic and racial groups. In democratic nations, the incorporation of diverse populations has led to the emergence of systems of government and politics that are called pluralistic.

Principal terms
ASSIMILATION: process by which one cultural group—usually an ethnic minority—adopts the value system of the host culture
MELTING POT: notion that most immigrants will eventually forsake their ethnic heritage and assimilate themselves in the dominant culture
NATIVISM: cultural and political discrimination against newly arrived immigrants in favor of the interests of citizens who have been in the country for several generations
PLURALISM: social system in which distinct racial and ethnic groups retain their own values, beliefs, and customs
QUOTA LEGISLATION: laws that limit or prohibit immigrants from designated regions from entering a country

Overview

The politics of conflict and economic development have been consistently shaped by global patterns of migration throughout world history. From the time that the ancestors of Native Americans crossed the Bering Strait more than 50,000 years ago, to the resettlement of large numbers of workers to the Middle Eastern oil-producing states in the late twentieth century, groups and individuals have always been willing to relocate to new areas. Decisions to migrate are usually influenced by economic factors and the desire to seek out employment or by the desire to escape political repression. According to reports of the United Nations High Commission for Refugees, millions of refugees have migrated since the 1950's because of struggles in the Middle East, Africa, and Latin America. During the war in Afghanistan in the 1980's, for example, more than six million people flooded into Pakistan and Iran. Disorders in Vietnam, Cambodia, Cuba, El Salvador, Haiti, and Guatemala have also significantly increased the number of immigrants to the United States since the 1970's. The rise of transnational corporations has generated additional immigrants, and with the increasing interdependency of the global economy, immigration emerged as one of the most critical political issues in the late twentieth century.

The United States provides an important example of how immigrants affect politics. As a nation founded by several diverse ethnic and racial groups, American political issues have been predominantly influenced by multicultural interests. Operating within a pluralist system, politicians and government officials must invariably consider how policy decisions will affect certain interest groups and whether further immigration is in the national interest. Officials must regularly consider how immigration will affect job opportunities for native-born Americans. They are forced to confront the fact that ethnic and racial diversity often produces violent political conflicts. Moreover, when formulating the nation's foreign policy, the president and Congress are typically pressured to intervene on behalf of various groups' ancestral homelands.

One important way in which immigration contributed to structural changes in American politics was through the rise of urban political machines. From 1865 to 1920, the arrival of millions of new immigrants accelerated the pace of urbanization in the United States and placed new strains on city governments. Faced with unprecedented demands for such services as housing, sanitation, law enforcement, fire protection, and poverty relief, urban institutions proved to be incapable of meeting the essential needs of the immigrant communities. Newly arrived ethnic groups had difficulties with language barriers, finding employment, and learning the customs and laws of a country that differed considerably from their homelands. Local power brokers often recognized the problems faced by immigrants and city governments alike, and these political bosses stepped in and created individual empires in America's cities. They specialized in individual politics by befriending immigrants with such tactics as providing Thanksgiving turkeys, they mediated disputes between ethnic groups, and they guided immigrants through the process of assimilation. These bosses were indeed often corrupt and greedy, but they provided several valuable services and helped ease the transitions that immigrants faced after arriving in the United States. Although most political machines disappeared by the beginning of the twentieth century, some machines such as New York City's Tammany Hall, Kansas City's Pendergast machine, and Richard J. Daley's Chicago cabal functioned well into the twentieth century.

Immigration has also helped generate several political realignments in American history. Following the influx of Irish Catholics during the first half of the nineteenth century, many political and artisan organizations feared that the arrival of approximately three million immigrants threatened to destroy the social fabric of the United States. By the 1850's, most of these immigrants had already endured the necessary five-year waiting period for citizenship and had attained voting rights. Concerned that these individuals would introduce legislation that would enable Roman Catholics to obtain control over predominantly Protestant school districts, many Americans flocked to the newly formed Know-Nothing Party. Between 1853 and 1856, the Know-Nothings achieved considerable success in the northeastern and mid-Atlantic states, dominated political affairs in Massachusetts, and elected more than one hundred members to Congress. Their presidential candidate captured 21 percent of the popular vote in the 1856 election. Although the Know-Nothing Party quickly faded from the political scene, its members helped the Republican Party emerge as a dominant force in American politics.

Ethnic group activity helped engineer another major political realignment during the Great Depression. By the 1920's, most second-generation immigrants—who were for the most part working class—were increasingly disenchanted with the Republican Party's stance on prohibition and its opposition to labor unions. After supporting the unsuccessful Democratic presidential campaign of Al Smith in 1928, ethnic Americans emerged as a major element in the Democratic Party's New Deal coalition. Immigrant votes were crucial to President Franklin Roosevelt's electoral success from 1932 to 1944. African Americans, impressed by Roosevelt's acknowledgment of civil rights issues, also joined his New Deal coalition. This alliance between diverse racial and ethnic constituents subsequently provided the Democratic Party with the strength it needed to dominate American politics until the late 1960's. This coalition, however, was shattered during the Vietnam War era when, in the opinion of many ethnic Americans, the Democratic Party became too liberal. As a result, these individuals began to enter the Republican camp and helped elect Republican presidents Richard Nixon, Ronald Reagan, and George Bush. Consequently, as can be seen from events in both the nineteenth and twentieth centuries, factors related to immigration, ethnicity, and race directly influenced the outcome of numerous political contests.

Market mechanisms have created similar problems for politicians in Europe. During the post-1945 economic boom in Western Europe, approximately 15 million to 20 million people from the Mediterranean region, North Africa, and southeast Asia emigrated to Western Europe. Most of these immigrants stayed, reared families, and established permanent residency. As unemployment returned in the 1980's, politicians were forced to confront growing domestic nativistic demands for restrictive legislation. Some officials even offered to pay travel expenses for the immigrant workers to return home, but this effort produced limited results. As a new multiethnic, multicultural, and multi-religious Europe developed, politicians who had previously escaped the dilemmas associated with immigration and nativism were confronted with problems that had long bedeviled American politics.

These same issues also directly influenced the foreign policy decision-making processes in democratic countries. In the United States during World War I, for example, the Polish-American community exerted considerable pressure upon President Woodrow Wilson to support the creation of a newly independent Polish state. In late 1915, the famous pianist Ignace Paderewski met several times with Wilson's adviser Colonel Edward House. In exchange for Polish-American support in the 1916 election, Wilson agreed to endorse Poland's claims for postwar independence, and in fact, the liberation of Poland was ultimately incorporated into Wilson's renowned Fourteen Points. It seems unlikely that this development would have taken place without the insistence of the ethnic community.

Immigrants have affected other American foreign policy decisions. For example, Latinos have secured concessions for illegal Mexican aliens; Cuban Americans have utilized their political resources to ensure that the United States maintained harsh economic sanctions against Fidel Castro's communist regime; and Irish Americans have persistently lobbied for U.S. support for a unified Ireland. Examples such as these reaffirm the belief that ethnic groups have a direct impact upon U.S. political processes on both the foreign and domestic levels.

Another part of the world in which immigration has played a dramatic political role is the Middle East. Following the Roman conquest of Palestine, the Jews were expelled in 135 C.E.; by the ninth century, the area was populated predominately by Muslim Arabs. In the nineteenth century, however, with the rise of the Zionist movement, Jewish settlers returned to the region and threatened the autonomy of the local Arab Palestinian settlements. Throughout the 1920's and the 1930's, the British attempted to control the region, restrict Jewish resettlement, and partition Jewish and Arab settlements.

The Nazi Holocaust of World War II sparked a new wave of Jewish immigration to Palestine and generated fresh pressures for world recognition of a Jewish homeland. In 1947, the United Nations—with American and Soviet approval—voted formally to partition the region; however, the Arabs refused to accept the plan. The declaration of Israel's independence in 1948 ignited a war between the two groups, and ever since, Palestine has been beset with war. Since 1948, more than a million Jews from Europe, Russia, and other areas have immigrated to Israel. While the region remains volatile, the Palestine Liberation Organization and the Israelis attempted to erect a peaceful resolution during the 1990's. Ethnic tensions remained high as nationalists on both sides refused to accept any agreement whatsoever.

Applications

Xenophobia, or the fear of anything foreign, has often led to nativist legislation and acts of violence against immigrant groups whose cultural habits differ from those of mainstream society. In the 1870's, American citizens in California were becoming increasingly frightened by the arrival of Chinese railroad workers. A California legislative committee subsequently concluded that the Chinese were a racially inferior people, and this led to the passage of the Chinese Exclusion Act in 1882. This bill, which was periodically renewed until 1945, led to the deportation of countless Chinese immigrants. It excluded others from entering the United States, and it closed America's shores to all Chinese except teachers, government officials, students, tourists, and merchants. This bill was eventually extended to Japanese immigrants as well, and by the beginning of the twentieth century, legislative acts had practically eliminated immigration opportunities for all Asian immigrants.

The arrival of millions of Roman Catholic and Jewish immigrants during the nineteenth century Industrial Revolution also caused considerable alarm among Protestant Americans. Founded in 1887 by Baltimore attorney Henry F. Bowers, the American Protective Association attempted to organize workers who were being displaced by cheaper Catholic labor. Although Bowers' star quickly faded, he achieved significant success in the Midwest and the Rocky Mountain states, and his restrictionist rhetoric had a profound impact on American politics. In 1894, Boston's Protestant elite formed the Immigration Restriction League, and they launched an "Americanization" campaign designed to eliminate all remnants of immigrant culture. During the Progressive reform era that followed, new pressures were placed upon immigrants to assimilate and abandon their own cultural heritages. Schools required students to forsake native languages, children's surnames were forcefully changed to more acceptable Anglo-American names, and urban reformers undertook measures designed to eradicate ties to ethnic homelands. This proved to be quite successful and accelerated the process of assimilation for immigrants.

Despite the rapid rate of immigrant assimilation, nativist fears, worries, and anxieties spurred restrictive legislation and violent outbursts during foreign wars. Concerned that German Americans were plotting to undermine the war effort in 1917, Congress passed an Espionage Act, followed by a Sedition Act in 1918. These acts suspended the constitutional right to free speech, outlawed opposition to the draft, and suppressed the publication of antiwar literature. More than two thousand people were prosecuted under these laws, which—despite challenges—were ultimately upheld by the U.S. Supreme Court.

Perhaps the greatest nativist injustice occurred during World War II when approximately 110,000 Japanese Americans were removed from the Pacific Coast and relocated in internment camps. Most of these individuals were native-born Americans, but because of their ethnic origin, they were considered to be a national security threat. The Supreme Court upheld this policy, and thousands of citizens lost all of their property. In 1982, a government commission ruled that these people had been victimized by racist sentiment and were entitled to economic compensation. This admission of national guilt, however, cannot hide the fact that immigrant groups have been unjustly abused throughout American history, and that these attacks have been sanctioned and encouraged by many politicians.

Similar comparisons can be made to events in Europe and the Middle East. In response to the demand for unskilled labor, many immigrants settled in Western Europe after World War II. By the mid-1970's, immigrant workers represented more than 10 percent of the workforces in Great Britain and Germany and almost 25 percent of the labor forces in France, Belgium, and Switzerland. As unemployment increased and Europeans were forced to compete with foreigners for jobs, ethnic and racial tensions escalated. Violent outbreaks of nativism resulted in conflicts between Germans and Turks, Britons and Pakistanis, and French and North Africans. In May, 1993, for example, five Turks were killed in Germany following an arson attack in Solingren. Similar patterns of conflict have emerged in the Middle East, where Arabs compete with workers from India, Thailand, Pakistan, and South Korea. As economic competition continues to increase in the global economy, patterns of immigration will likely continue to generate nativist conflicts among ethnic groups.

Context

Because the United States is a nation founded and settled by immigrants, the nature and structure of American politics has been directly influenced by the contributions of several ethnic groups. Although some people maintain that the United States is a melting pot in which all immigrants eventually become Americanized, the evidence indicates that ethnic identity continues to affect their political behavior. The numbers of immigrants into the United States in the late twentieth century were significantly fewer than the great waves that came during the Industrial Revolution, but the political system nevertheless continues to be dominated by pluralist concerns.

Certain examples indicate that it would be inaccurate to assume that ethnic groups have abandoned their native ancestry. In the 1980's, Cuban Americans financed several political campaigns, and with the help of New Jersey Democratic congressman Robert Toricelli, they were able to secure passage of the Cuban Democracy Act. This bill ensured that economic sanctions against Castro would not be relaxed. Cuban Americans have also secured fifteen million dollars in taxpayer support for the financing of anti-Castro propaganda broadcasts through Radio Marti. Whatever the future course of United States-Cuban relations, foreign-policy makers must confront and appease the volatile Cuban American population if their policies are to succeed.

It is also highly likely that factors related to immigration will continue to influence domestic policies as well. In 1986, Congress passed the Simpson-Rodino Law that granted legal status to all undocumented illegal aliens who had resided and worked in the United States for a number of years. This bill was significantly influenced by the fact that Latinos in California were seeking legal refuge for family members who had recently immigrated into the United States.

As the twenty-first century approaches, the movement of migrant populations seeking work and political freedom will undoubtedly dominate international and national politics. Individuals from the underdeveloped world are steadily relocating to more powerful and prosperous countries such as the United States, Canada, Germany, France, and Australia.

Bibliography

Altschuler, Glen C. *Race, Ethnicity, and Class in American Social Thought, 1865-1919*. Arlington Heights, Ill.: Harlan Davidson, 1982. Discusses the intellectual developments that led to the rise of xenophobia during the formative stages of the Industrial Revolution. It also provides insights into the struggles among Protestants, Jews, and Catholics and reveals how each religious group attempted to cope with the changing religious and political structure of modern American society.

DeConde, Alexander. *Ethnicity, Race, and American Foreign Policy: A History*. Boston: Northeastern University Press, 1992. Historical overview of how immigrants have influenced foreign policy decision-making processes in U.S. history.

Gordon, Milton M. *Assimilation in American Life: The Role of Race, Religion, and National Origins*. New York: Oxford University Press, 1964. Discusses the processes of assimilation, the battle over Anglo-Saxon conformity, cultural pluralism, and the melting pot theory. Should be consulted by any student interested in ethnic subcultures and their impact upon American politics.

Takaki, Ronald. *A Different Mirror: A History of Multicultural America*. Boston: Little, Brown, 1993. Details and outlines how the United States was settled by immigrants. Especially valuable for those interested in Native Americans, Latinos, and African Americans.

Yans-McLaughlin, Virginia, ed. *Immigration Reconsidered: History, Sociology, and*

Politics. New York: Oxford University Press, 1990. Articles by several leading scholars that provide insights into the political activities of immigrant groups. Especially worthwhile for those who are interested in African American studies.

Robert D. Ubriaco, Jr.

Cross-References

Asian American Politics, p. 115; Grassroots Politics, p. 797; Immigration and Emigration, p. 868; Immigration Regulation, p. 875; Latino Politics, p. 1052; Naturalization, p. 1275; Pluralism, p. 1402; Political Machines and Bosses, p. 1468; Political Participation, p. 1479; Race and Ethnicity, p. 1654.

IMMIGRATION AND EMIGRATION

Field of study: International government and politics

All national governments regulate which aliens may enter their countries temporarily or permanently (immigration) through the issuance of tourist cards and visas. Nations may also regulate the international travel of their own citizens, including those who choose to leave permanently (emigration), through the issuance of passports.

Principal terms

ALIEN: person not a citizen or national of the country in which he or she is physically present

CITIZEN: member of a state or nation by birth or naturalization

EMIGRATION: act of leaving one region or country to establish residence elsewhere

GUEST WORKER: alien recruited to work in a country for a limited period of time and who receives a visa and work permit for that purpose

IMMIGRATION: act of entering a region or country of which one is not a native for the purpose of establishing permanent residence

NATURALIZATION: conferring citizenship on an individual who did not have that citizenship by birth

PASSPORT: document issued citizens and nationals by the government, granting permission to travel and authenticating the right to lawful aid and protection as citizens or nationals of the issuing country

VISA: document issued to an alien authorizing legal admission into the country granting the permission

Overview

Migration is a common human way to seek a better life. When people migrate (a permanent change of residence) within a country, the phenomenon is usually called "internal migration." When people leave the country it is called "external migration" or "international migration." Leaving one country to change residence is "emigration," and entering a country in order to establish residency is "immigration."

The English scholar E. G. Ravenstein was among the first to study the emigration-immigration phenomenon systematically. His research in the latter part of the nineteenth century is still the basis for the most widely accepted explanations of the human migration phenomenon. Ravenstein's work remains at the core of what are called "push-pull" theories. These theories explain migration in terms of a people's social, economic, and political difficulties or hardships (being "pushed" out by unfavorable conditions at home) and their urge to resettle in places with favorable conditions (being "pulled"). The push-pull theories assume that migration is best understood in terms of the individual migrant's motivation. The personal conditions in which an individual lives are thought to influence the decision to leave, while the destination is determined by the perceived opportunities, overall attractiveness of the site, and the feasibility of establishing permanent residency there.

Some critics of the push-pull theories believe this focus on the individual ignores the important role that history and social structures play. The "historical-structural" theories emphasize such things as the historical economic relationship between the country of the emigrants and the country of the immigrants, the internal and external pressures on the national economy of the "sending" country, wage differentials, and other factors that could affect labor mobility. In sum, the historical-structural theories explain migration in terms of social rather than individual variables. Some scholars believe it is pointless to attempt to develop a scientific theory of migration because the process is so strongly tied to the volatility and uncertainties of public policy in receiving countries.

International migration usually but not always involves a movement from the poorer, frequently agriculturally based countries to the wealthier, industrial or postindustrial countries. The majority of economically motivated migrants are young, generally under twenty-five. The countries of Northern and Western Europe, North America, Australia, and New Zealand have been the destination of choice for most migrants. In the decades following World War II, most of these countries had guest worker programs to relieve labor shortages. Foreign workers from poorer countries were given visas and work permits, although usually for limited time periods. Many guest workers remained after their initial visas expired and became permanent residents, with or without the permission of the host governments.

Many factors may determine the destination of emigrants. First, bilateral agreements, for example guest worker programs, account for significant movements. Turks and Yugoslavs in Germany and Moluccans in The Netherlands are examples. Second, former colonial ties explain the destination of many. A knowledge of the language and some familiarity with culture and conditions are important. An example of this factor is the Indian population in Great Britain. Geographical proximity is likewise an important factor, as is the case with Mexico and the United States. Third, some migrants receive encouragement from those who have immigrated to a locale earlier. A network of friends and family frequently produces what is known as a chain migration.

International migration within less economically developed regions of the world usually involves movement from poorer countries, particularly those with weak currencies, to states with stronger currencies. This enables immigrants to send remittances home to assist in the support of their families.

International law is also a factor in migration. The 1951 Geneva Convention on the Status of Refugees and the 1967 Protocol Relating to the Status of Refugees have addressed the problem of coerced emigration for reasons of persecution. At the same time, no nation is under any legal obligation to grant refugees permanent asylum. Control over borders is considered a fundamental right of nations. In the 1892 case of *Nishimura Ekiu v. United States*, the Supreme Court asserted that self-preservation is every sovereign nation's right, and accordingly nations are entitled to deny admission or set the conditions of admission to foreigners. The principle continues to generally accepted. Public health, safety, population size, economic opportunities, and national security are all considerations in the determination of immigration policy.

Liberal immigration policies are less common than in the post-World War II period, but most countries continue to accept political refugees. Destinations of choice for asylum-seekers continue to be much the same as for those seeking improved economic conditions, and distinguishing between those seeking better economic conditions and those truly fleeing persecution poses a major problem for many governments.

Temporary or permanent admission into a country is generally regulated by the issuance of visas. Whether an alien is granted a visa depends on the country of origin, the purpose of the entry, the length of stay, the characteristics of the alien, and the number of aliens to be admitted during that year. Some restrictions may be placed on citizens wishing to travel outside the country as well. This is done through the controlled issuance of passports. Ability to obtain a passport usually depends on proof of citizenship in the country issuing the passport, not being a fugitive from justice, and not posing a threat to the native country by traveling abroad (for example, not being a known terrorist or revolutionary).

The basic law governing immigration in the United States is the Immigration and Nationality Act of 1952 as amended. The attorney general has the responsibility of administering and enforcing immigration law. The Immigration and Naturalization Service (INS), which has immediate responsibility for the administration of immigration law, is a division of the Justice Department and therefore is under the direction of the attorney general. The president, the secretary of state, and officers of the State Department, as well as the attorney general and officials in the Justice Department administer the law. The president, in consultation with Congress, sets the annual numerical limits on refugee admissions. The Department of State is responsible for administering the issuance of visas under provisions relating to numerical limitations and adjustments of status. Consular officials throughout the world, operating under the direction of the secretary of state, make decisions on the admissibility of refugees. Domestically, the Justice Department is responsible for administering immigration policy. The attorney general has ultimate responsibility within the Justice Department, but delegates that responsibility to the INS. INS officials conduct initial inspections of individuals (citizens and aliens alike) entering the United States to determine eligibility for admission. Within the INS, the Border Patrol has responsibility for preventing uninspected entries into the country. At various locations in the United States asylum officers interview asylum seekers at the borders or within the country to determine their qualification. Finally, administrative courts may review appeals made by aliens regarding the decisions made by INS officials.

The federal court system may decide to hear cases brought to it by aliens who continue to appeal after a decision made by the Board of Immigration Appeals if, in the opinion of the courts, the INS has improperly applied the Immigration and Nationality Act.

Applications

On November 6, 1986, President Ronald Reagan signed into law the Immigration Reform and Control Act of 1986. The major features of this amendment to the basic Immigration and Nationality Act were sanctions against employers who knowingly hire undocumented aliens, the legalization of status of a large number of aliens in illegal status, and the adjustment of immigrant status of some Cubans and Haitians. The law, which also revised some immigration procedures and numerical limits, is a good example of how domestic and foreign policy considerations directly affect immigration policy. The 1986 act addressed several recurring policy debates associated with immigration, illustrating the complexity of the issue and the range of political interests that attempt to influence policy. The United States is known as a nation of immigrants, but there is rarely national consensus on immigration policy. The 1986 act was the product of a debate that began in the early 1970's on the problem of illegal immigration to the United States. People who enter legally but whose visas expire and who remain without legal status are also illegal immigrants.

Organized labor and other segments of the population argued that illegal (or undocumented) aliens take jobs from citizens and place a heavy burden on social services. Agribusiness argued that illegal aliens take jobs citizens are unwilling to take and that without the presence of these foreign workers the cost of food would be significantly higher. Others opposed tighter restrictions on aliens fearing that such a policy would create a climate leading to increased human rights violations and discrimination against ethnic minorities. The 1986 act ultimately imposed sanctions on employers who knowingly hire aliens without legal status. Further, it authorized some increased border enforcement measures, established a process to legalize the status of many undocumented aliens, and introduced a special agricultural workers (SAWs) category to allow agribusiness to employ alien workers for limited periods of time.

The 1986 act also adjusted the immigration status of many Cubans and Haitians. In 1981, following passage of the Refugee Act of 1980, thousands of Cubans, including some allegedly with criminal records and mental disorders, left Cuba for the United States to seek political asylum. This created a storm of controversy when the Cubans, like many asylum-seeking Haitians, were given temporary admission that would likely become permanent. Proponents of granting asylum to these groups argued that it was a necessary humanitarian measure. Opponents argued that Cuban president Fidel Castro was sending undesirables and making a mockery of United States policy. Many opposing parole for Haitians believed this group sought better economic opportunities, not political asylum. Again, the 1986 act attempted to offer a compromise by adjusting the status of those paroled in the United States while not changing asylum policy. In fact, the new law specifically rejected the future use of parole as a mechanism for granting asylum or refugee status.

The Immigration Act of 1990 was designed to revise the system of legal immigration to reflect the type and source of immigration. Immigration policy will likely continue to evolve as domestic interest groups react to conditions in the world and their perceived effect on the United States.

In Europe, the gradual development of the European Union (EU) influences immigration policy in all member states. The union's goal is to eliminate intracommunity barriers, establish a common asylum policy, coordinate the issuance of visas and rules of extradition, and establish rules governing third-country nationals, that is, non-EU citizens. In 1985, Belgium, The Netherlands, Luxembourg, France, and Germany signed the Schengen Agreement, designed to remove internal borders in Europe gradually. Italy, Spain, and Portugal joined later. The Schengen Agreement also created greater interest in developing a common policy on immigration. In 1990, the Dublin Convention attempted to create a common set of criteria for granting asylum in EU states. Later, the Maastricht Treaty eliminated internal borders within the European Union. In effect, a person entering any EU member state enters all states. Each state thus has a stake in the immigration and refugee policy of all other member states.

Context

International migration is clearly affected by governmental policies in both the sender and receiver states. Passport regulations, visa requirements, prerequisites for naturalized citizenship, refugee policy, numerical limits on the admission of resident aliens, and the social services afforded immigrants are all controlled by governmental policy and thus affect the immigration process.

From the earliest days of the United States as an independent nation, immigration has been a significant topic of policy debate. For various reasons Benjamin Franklin and Thomas Jefferson voiced caution toward an open immigration policy in the United States, leading the Federalists to press for the immigration law in 1798. Nevertheless, the United States maintained a comparatively open immigration policy throughout the first century of its history. The immigration controls that did exist were imposed by the states and it was not until 1875 that federal laws were passed restricting the admission of aliens.

Immigration reform was a plank in the Free Soil Party platform of 1848, the first such mention of immigration in any party's platform in the United States. In 1852 the party endorsed the position of extending a cordial welcome to immigrants and a process to facilitate their naturalization. In 1856 the Democratic Party advocated offering asylum to the oppressed of every nation while the American (Know-Nothing) Party endorsed a restrictive immigration platform.

In the last two decades of the nineteenth century, the door to unrestricted immigration closed. Opposition from labor, a growing nativism, movement and an emerging moralistic tone in national politics influenced immigration policy. Beginning with the Chinese Exclusion Law of 1882, immigration reforms of 1882, 1891, and 1903 created excludable classes of aliens (for example, polygamists, people convicted of crimes of moral turpitude, those with contagious diseases, epileptics, insane persons, professional beggars, and anarchists).

The dramatic increase in the number of immigrants in the first two decades of the twentieth century and the "red scare" resulting from the Russian Revolution contributed greatly to further efforts to limit immigration. The Quota Act of 1921 placed numerical limits on persons by nationality. National quotas were retained in the Immigration and Nationality Act of 1952 and remained until replaced by a preference system in 1965. The 1952 act remains the basic immigration law of the United States although it has been amended frequently over the years to reflect both foreign and domestic policy.

Most of Western Europe had liberal immigration policies in the 1950's and 1960's, and maintained generous asylum policies until the early 1990's. Australia, Canada, and Sweden, for reasons of geography, history, and demography, have all declared themselves to be multicultural societies, and have created a highly favorable environment for immigration at one time or another. Immigration policies among the nations of Africa, Asia, and Latin America vary greatly, but like the major receiver countries, most tend to base their policies on immediate domestic considerations. Less economically developed regions generally do not have liberal immigration policies.

Bibliography

Appleyard, Reginald T., ed. *International Migration Today*. Vol. 1 in *Trends and Prospects*. Paris: UNESCO, 1988. Examines international population movement with focus on migration patterns in Asia, Africa, Latin America, the Pacific, the Caribbean, Arab states, Europe, and North America.

Briggs, Vernon M., Jr. *Mass Immigration and the National Interest*. Armonk, N.Y.: M. E. Sharpe, 1992. Survey of the evolution of U.S. immigration policy and its impact on the economy.

Hammar, Tomas, ed. *European Immigration Policy: A Comparative Study*. Cambridge, England: Cambridge University Press, 1985. Comparative study of immigration policies in six European countries.

Kubat, Daniel, ed. *The Politics of Migration Policies: Settlement and Integration: The First World into the 1990's*. 2d ed. New York: Center for Migration Studies, 1993. Collection of articles comparing national policies by recognized scholars in the field.

McWilliams, Carey. *North from Mexico: The Spanish-Speaking People of the United States*. Westport, Conn.: Greenwood Press, 1990. An early classic on Mexican immigration to the United States.

Moch, Leslie Page. *Moving Europeans: Migration in Western Europe Since 1650*. Bloomington: Indiana University Press, 1992. Good historical overview of European migration over a 350-year period.

U.S. Immigration and Naturalization Service. *Statistical Yearbook of the Immigration and Naturalization Service, 1992*. Washington, D.C.: Government Printing Office, 1993. Annual publication; an excellent source of information on immigration and political asylum in the United States.

Zolberg, Aristide R., Astri Suhrke, and Sergio Aguayo. *Escape from Violence: Conflict and the Refugee Crisis in the Developing World*. New York: Oxford University

Press, 1989. Overview of the dynamics of international population movements and the policy issues associated with demographic changes.

Miles W. Williams

Cross-References

Asian American Politics, p. 115; Citizenship in World Governments, p. 254; Comparative Government, p. 384; Developed and Developing Nations, p. 533; Human Rights and International Politics, p. 848; Immigrants and Politics, p. 861; Immigration Regulation, p. 875; International Law, p. 956; Latino Politics, p. 1052; Naturalization, p. 1275; Underdeveloped Nations, p. 2039; The World Health Organization, p. 2180.

IMMIGRATION REGULATION

Field of study: International government and politics

Immigration regulation is the control and restriction of legal immigration. It is usually enacted to make it difficult for those whose permanent residence is not desired to enter or to stay in a country.

Principal terms

IMMIGRATION: migration into a country

INDENTURE: labor contract system—as practiced it was a form of contractual slavery

MELTING POT: metaphor for a society in which different groups "melt" together into one homogeneous group

MIGRATION: travel across a distance in order to change residence

MULTICULTURAL: describing a society in which various ethnic groups coexist

NATIVISM: anti-immigrant sentiment

PLURAL SOCIETY: society with distinct racial, linguistic, or religious groups

SLAVERY: condition in which one person has powers of ownership over another

Overview

The movement of people from one place to another has been part of human behavior always. The regulation of immigration became important, however, in the middle 1400's, with the rise of mercantilism and capitalism. The means of regulating migration were slavery, indenture, forced migration, voluntary migration (sometimes induced by rewards), and restrictive legislation. Around the middle fifteenth century, Europe was becoming a consumer of global resources. One very popular commodity desired by the English was sugar. By 1750, even the poorest English used sugar in their tea. The English and world demand was so great that regions such as Brazil went to a plantation economy. The need for labor led to the slave trade. In the eighteenth century, the English demand for raw cotton led to rapid settlement in what was later the Southeastern United States, the development of a plantation economy, and the use of slave labor, primarily from Africa. This resulted in the largest forced migration in the world—the shipment of ten million slaves from West Africa to the Americas. When slavery was abolished, indenture labor from China, India, and Japan worked European sugar plantations in the Caribbean, Indian, and Pacific Ocean areas.

During colonization of North America, involuntary and incentive schemes were used to get people to populate the new land. Convicts and demobilized soldiers were sent. Idlers, vagrants, political dissenters, and orphaned children (up to 150,000 orphaned and indigent children, from whom 11 percent of Canada's modern population now claim descent) were also sent. Some extremely religious groups migrated voluntarily. Thus slaveowners, slaves, undesirables, petty criminals, orphans, and religious sects came to establish what is now North America.

Voluntary British migrants went to Canada, New Zealand, and Australia and monopolized political life and many natural resources at the expense of local inhabitants. Voluntary migrants also entered the United States, Rhodesia, and South Africa, but their political hegemony was eroded by other settlers and local people. The Portuguese went to Angola and Mozambique, the French to North Africa and Indochina, and the Dutch to South Africa. Emigration during the colonial period relieved population and social problems in Europe while expanding the resources available to Europe as a result of the colonists' trading with their homelands.

In the colonized areas, labor gangs were needed to build roads and railroads, dig mines, and work plantations. Most of this labor was indenture or slave labor. With industrialization, the free labor market was internationalized. The growth of mass industries, especially in the United States, brought the collapse of serfdom in Europe. The result was that between 1770 and 1914, thirty-five million Europeans migrated to the United States. Also, Poles went to Germany and Irish to Great Britain to work in industry.

Since World War II, four types of immigrants have become prominent: refugees, unskilled labor, skilled and educated labor, and asylum-seekers seeking legal recognition and permanent residence.

Applications

The complexities of immigration regulation are evident in the United States. United States immigration policy falls into five periods: 1609-1775 (colonial phase), 1776-1881 (open-door phase), 1882-1916 (regulation phase), 1917-1964 (restriction phase), and 1965-1990 (liberalization phase).

During the colonial phase, schemes were devised to attract people to the colonies from Europe and the British Isles. The main attraction was the availability of work and property. Also, most areas tolerated different forms of Christianity, although some places, such as Maryland and Pennsylvania, were religious enclaves.

Three important principles were established during this period: Local governments exercised jurisdiction over immigration and settlement; local government and private entrepreneurs were responsible for recruiting immigrants from overseas; and economic developments stimulated an active search for new sources of labor. Policy was directed toward encouraging immigration.

The open-door phase began when the United States declared its independence. These were formative years and immigration was still encouraged. In 1790, Congress passed the law that was interpreted to restrict citizenship to whites; later it included people of African origin—omitting Asians.

Concerning immigration, however, the Alien Act of 1798 was the only federal regulation. It gave the president authority to expel aliens who were a threat to national security. Other restraints on immigration were imposed locally. During this period, immigration was primarily from Northern and Western Europe.

The regulation phase began with the passage of the Chinese Exclusion Act of 1882. Government records correlated immigrants with increased social welfare costs. The methodology for determining these correlations was dubious at best. On the West Coast, labor unions felt threatened by Chinese workers, who did not or could not become union members. In the 1830's, the nativist movement had begun to develop in reaction to Roman Catholic and Chinese immigration. Nativism and labor fears combined to bring about the dramatic shift from open doors to closed ones. Although nativism had originally grown out of anti-Catholic sentiment, those on the West Coast added the anti-Chinese theme. By 1870, a depressed economy resulted in aliens' being blamed for low wages. Politicians succumbed to the anti-Chinese sentiment and Congress passed the Chinese Exclusion Act of 1882. This legislation suspended Chinese immigration for ten years, and prohibited Chinese who were not citizens from becoming citizens.

The Japanese followed after Chinese immigration was stopped. Japan, by the turn of the century, was a world power. The Japanese government felt responsible for the expatriate community in the United States. When public opinion and discrimination was directed against the Japanese in America, an agreement between Japan and the United States was negotiated in 1907-1908. It was an understanding in which Japan would deny passports to laborers intending to enter the United States and the United States would exclude Japanese immigrants holding passports originally issued for other countries. The compromise was intended not to antagonize Japan or the people of California.

The restriction phase developed from rules enacted during the regulation phase. In response to pressures of the Immigration Restriction League on Congress to require literacy tests for admission into the United States, the Immigration Commission was formed in 1907. In 1911, the commission published a forty-two-volume study, *The Dillingham Report*, which found no evidence that a correlation existed between the new immigrants and feeble-mindedness, crime, epilepsy, or tuberculosis. The report concluded, however, that unlimited immigration created social problems. As a result, the commission endorsed a literacy test to stem immigration. In 1913 and 1915 respectively, presidents Taft and Wilson vetoed bills imposing literacy tests, but Wilson's veto was overridden in 1917.

The Immigration Act of 1917 began the restriction phase. The act was a codification of existing immigration laws that had developed up to that time. It retained all the previous grounds for inadmissibility and added illiteracy. It also created the Asia-Pacific Triangle, a zone from which emigration to the United States was barred. The literacy provision was to keep out southern and eastern Europeans because they were believed to be lowering the American standard. The Asiatic barred zone excluded all Asia except Persia and parts of Afghanistan and Russia. The Immigration Act was designed to curb immigration, especially from nations that were considered culturally dissimilar to Western Europe. Non-Western immigrants were alleged to cause the economic and social problems confronting the country at the time. Japanese and

Chinese immigration was already restricted, however, and the legislation did not much curb European immigration. The only people it actually barred were the Asian Indians.

In 1924, the National Origins Act proportioned immigration according to the national origins of the United States population of 1890. This was clearly to give preference to Western Europeans. It set the pattern for immigration regulation for the next four decades. The system was operative by 1930, but with the onset of the Great Depression, the number of people leaving the United States exceeded the number of those coming in.

The McCarran-Walter Act of 1952 was possibly the most significant U.S. immigration legislation in modern times. It tightened the quota system but extended quotas to Asian countries.

The liberalization phase had its origins in the Kennedy Administration's attacking the national origins quota system and attempting to link immigration flow to labor requirements. The result was the 1965 Hart-Celler Act, which took effect in 1968 and which dismantled the national origins quota system. Instead, it placed a ceiling on annual immigration to 290,000. At the same time it removed preferential treatment for Western countries. It was revised in 1976 to give priority to Western immigrants with training, skills, or family ties.

The 1965 legislation had unintended consequences. Until 1980, immigration was dominated by the highly skilled, technically trained, and professionally oriented, who were experienced in urban living and skilled and knowledgeable in dealing with bureaucracies. These immigrants quickly entered the middle and upper level social positions as doctors, engineers, and scientists. These new immigrants were skilled and primarily Asian—the standard of living in Europe was high enough that Europeans did not migrate to the United States. After 1980, these immigrants sponsored family members, and, as a result, the average "quality" of immigrants began decreasing.

Also, illegal immigration and refugee entrants started increasing. People crossed the Mexican border in such great numbers that many concluded that the United States had lost control of its borders. Also, the influx of people asking for asylum and refugee status increased greatly. The Immigration Reform and Control Act of 1986 was instituted to combat illegal immigration by establishing sanctions against employers who hired illegal immigrants or unauthorized workers. The proliferation of bogus documents made the law ineffective and made no difference in the flow of clandestine entries.

It also became apparent that the family reunification clause was causing the quotas to be filled by relatives of immigrants; the relatives were often less productive in economic terms than the first member of the family to arrive in the United States. Proposals were made to eliminate the family reunification clause, but the political force of the Asian American community worked to ensure that family reunification was included in 1990 legislation regarding immigration. The Immigration Act of 1990 raised the ceiling for immigration, excluding refugees, to 700,000 and gave greater emphasis to family reunification. In essence, the law has increased immigration while still maintaining the negative aspects of previous legislation. In the meantime, because of the perceived magnitude of illegal immigration to the United States, especially from Mexico, public opinion against immigration rose.

Context

Modern immigration into the United States is different from that of the past in five respects. First, the welfare system in the United States encourages legal and illegal entrants to stay whether they have a job or not. Second, illegal immigration is of a greater magnitude than in the past. Third, the prominence of highly educated and professionally oriented immigrants is higher than in the past. Members of this group quickly enter the upper levels of American society and become politically influential. Fourth, Asians and Hispanics, rather than Europeans, are more dominant in the immigration population. Fifth, social emphasis is less on assimilation and more on maintaining cultural diversity.

The situation of the United States illustrates the issues concerning research and evaluation of immigration policy. First, it must be kept in mind that legislation does not necessarily bring its intended consequences. This is certainly the case of the 1965 immigration law. No one predicted that the result would be the large Asian and refugee influx. Tactics to reduce the influx included restricting entry at the borders, encouraging sending countries to limit emigration, and employer sanctions.

The issues concerning immigration policy fall into four categories: humanitarian, economic, social, and foreign policy. Concerning humanitarian issues, the view in the past was that the United States was doing people a favor by allowing others of the world to enter. Since the middle 1970's, however, world-system theory has become more prominent in social and economic analysis. World-system theory divides the world into core, semi-periphery, and periphery areas with the affluent core areas, the United States and Western Europe, maintaining their affluence by expropriating resources from the periphery areas such as African countries. This being the case, some, using a world-system perspective, argue that since the wealth of the United States and Western Europe is attributable to the exploitation of the periphery, it is the obligation of the core, rich countries to open their borders to poor people from the periphery regions. Many refugees and asylum seekers are in their position because of the policies of the United States and its allies. Thus, the humanitarian argument runs, it is the moral responsibility of the West to provide a haven for the oppressed people.

Economic issues begin with questions. The questions have different answers, depending on who is answering. Do immigrants pay more or less in taxes than the costs of the services they receive? The Washington-based Urban Institute argues that immigrants pay more than they receive in benefits, even in the case of illegal immigration. California politicians, however, using Immigration and Naturalization Service figures, indicate otherwise. Do immigrants take jobs away from American citizens? Some say "yes, because immigrants work for lower wages." Others say "no, because immigrants take jobs American citizens do not want, and by being productive, immigrants create jobs for citizens." Some argue, immigrants create markets that stimulate the economy. There are truth and distortions on both sides of the debate.

Social issues lead to determining what kind of society and culture the United States should be. Until the 1950's, the melting pot philosophy dominated. It assumed that immigrants would conform to the Western European cultural and social system dominant in the United States. With the advent of the Civil Rights movement, a greater tolerance for other cultures has been part of the American education system. Various groups now counter the melting pot idea with an emphasis on diversity. The result is the debate on multiculturalism and to what degree should diversity be allowed and encouraged.

Another social issue is whether illegal immigrants should be allowed to benefit from social services. Some argue illegal immigrants should not because they are in the United States illegally. Some counter that the illegals help economic growth, and if they are not provided with social services, the long-term costs will be much greater. Their descendants will form a large, unproductive segment of American society. The cost of dealing with their poor health will be much greater later on.

Last, immigration regulations influence foreign relations. If a race or national group is restricted from entering the United States, it perceives that Americans regard it as inferior. Policy may be implemented to give, or to avoid giving, this impression. National groups in the United States exert pressure on Congress and politicians to develop policies favorable to their lands of origin. The United States government may use immigration policy as a facet of broader policy, such as anticommunism.

Immigration regulation is an emotional and hotly debated issue in many countries throughout the world. Different countries have dealt with these issues differently. No good solution is likely until international and local economic and political inequalities are minimized.

Bibliography

Borjas, George J. *Friends or Strangers: The Impact of Immigrants on the U.S. Economy*. New York: Basic Books, 1990. Argues that U.S. immigration policy should favor the skilled.

Briggs, Vernon M. *Mass Immigration and National Interest*. Armonk, N.Y.: M. E. Sharpe, 1992. Argues that legislation on immigration is not concurrent with national interests.

Easterlin, Richard A., David Ward, William S. Bernard, and Reed Ueda. *Immigration*. Cambridge, Mass.: The Belknap Press of Harvard University Press, 1980. Overview of U.S. immigration policy, naturalization and citizenship issues, the economic and social characteristics of immigration, and settlement patterns of immigrants to the United States.

Kritz, Mary M., Charles B. Keely, and Silvano M. Tomasi, eds. *Global Trends in Migration: Theory and Research on International Population Movements*. Staten Island, N.Y.: Center for Migration Studies, 1981. Articles dealing with theoretical issues, patterns of migration, incorporation of migrants into the host society, and return migration.

Kubat, Daniel, ed. *The Politics of Migration Policies: Settlement and Integration, the*

First World into the 1990's. 2d ed. Staten Island, N.Y.: Center for Migration Studies, 1993. Articles concerning the migration policies of countries settled by Anglo-Saxon democracies and by empires.

Miller, Mark J., ed. *Strategies for Immigration Control: An International Comparison.* Thousand Oaks, Calif.: Periodicals Press, 1994. Articles dealing with the different strategies employed by various countries to control immigration.

Simon, Julian L. *The Economic Consequences of Immigration.* Washington, D.C.: Cato Institute, 1989. Argues that freer immigration would benefit the United States.

Tucker, Robert W., Charles Keely, and Linda Wrigley. *Immigration and U.S. Foreign Policy.* Boulder, Colo.: Westview Press, 1990. Articles concerning how U.S. immigration influences foreign policy.

Arthur W. Helweg

Cross-References

Asian American Politics, p. 115; Citizenship Rights and Responsibilities, p. 260; Civil Liberties Protection, p. 291; Civil Rights and Liberties, p. 298; Foreign Relations, p. 718; Immigrants and Politics, p. 861; Immigration and Emigration, p. 868; Industrialization, p. 916; Latino Politics, p. 1052; Naturalization, p. 1275; Race and Ethnicity, p. 1654; Regulatory Agencies in the United States, p. 1678; Social Services, p. 1858.

IMPEACHMENT

Field of study: Politics

Impeachment is part of the legal process by which Congress formally accuses, tries, and removes government officials (such as the president, vice president, federal judges, or federal officials) when the officials are judged corrupt.

Principal terms

ARTICLES OF IMPEACHMENT: formal statements, usually written by the House Judiciary Committee, enumerating why the offending official should be removed

CONGRESS: lawmaking branch of the U.S. government, consisting of the House of Representatives and the Senate

PARTISAN POLITICS: biased behavior of politicians or political parties to support their own agenda, regardless of ethics of the situation

SEPARATION OF POWER: constitutional division of powers assigned to the three branches of government: Congress makes laws, the executive carries them out, and the courts interpret them

WATERGATE: apartment and business complex in Washington, D.C., where a break-in at Democratic campaign headquarters in 1972 nearly led to President Richard Nixon's impeachment

Overview

The United States Constitution and many state constitutions provide a procedure for ousting government officials from their positions that is generally called "impeachment." Technically, impeachment is only part of the removal process whereby the legislature makes formal accusations against suspected wrongdoers. A trial and possible conviction may follow. The U.S. Constitution, in Article 1, section 2, directs the House of Representatives, the lower half of Congress, to be responsible for implementing the impeachment procedure. Article 2, section 4 of the Constitution limits possible impeachments to the president, vice president, and other civil officers, on any of three charges: "treason, bribery, or other high crimes and misdemeanors."

Although the House of Representatives has in the past created special committees to investigate complaints, it usually does so through its Judiciary Committee. This House Judiciary Committee is responsible for gathering evidence, preparing formal written charges, and later, if warranted, managing the prosecution. After the full House of Representatives has deliberated on the matter, a final vote on impeachment is taken, with a simple majority ruling.

The Senate is the upper body of Congress, then tries the impeached defendant (Article 1, section 3). Conviction of the defendant requires a two-thirds majority of the voting senators. Multiple charges may be leveled against the defendant; even if all charges are dismissed but one, the defendant is still considered impeached and convicted. The Senate is limited in regard to punishing impeached officials who are convicted. It can only remove them from office and disqualify them from holding future offices. It is possible that later, impeached officials may be tried in a court of law if criminal charges are appropriate.

John Labovitz, in *Presidential Impeachment* (1978), points out the logic in having the House of Representatives formulate the charges of impeachment and the Senate try the case. Labovitz observes that the House is most directly representative of the people and should initiate procedures to counter any threat to the Constitution. In turn, the Senate, rather than the Supreme Court, is more appropriate in trying the case because the Court might later have to try the defendant on criminal charges after impeachment and conviction. Legally, this would constitute double jeopardy—that is, the defendant's being tried by the Court twice for the same crime or misdemeanor. The Constitution's Fifth Amendment forbids double jeopardy. Congressional members are excluded from the impeachment process because they would be tried by their own colleagues rather than by an impartial body. For misconduct, however, Congressional members may be expelled.

Applications

When national events go awry in the United States, disgruntled voters often cry for the impeachment of an offending president or federal officer. The voters simply want the rascal thrown out, quickly and easily. What they do not acknowledge is that impeachment and conviction in the United States rarely occur. The process is cumbersome, time-consuming, and divisive.

Between 1799 and 1986 only fourteen federal officials were impeached, of which twelve were tried and only five (all judges) were convicted. Overall, 78 percent of the impeachments involved judges. The remaining cases involved one senator (William Blount, 1749-1800), one cabinet member (former Secretary of War William Belknap, 1876) and one president (Andrew Johnson, 1868).

The first threat of impeachment occurred in 1796 against Judge George Turner of the Northwest Territory, who was charged with "arbitrary conduct"; however, impeachment charges were dropped, with the case eventually being turned over to the territorial courts. The first actual impeachment case was that of Senator William Blount of Tennessee, for promoting a military expedition that would take the Florida and Louisiana territories away from Spain and give them to England. The Senate decided that it did not have the authority to try Senator Blount.

The first successful impeachment ending in conviction and removal from office (1803-1804) was that of Judge John Pickering of New Hampshire. Pickering was shown to be senile, alcoholic, and unable to function on the judicial bench. Other judges impeached, convicted, and removed from office included Judge West Humphreys of Tennessee, in 1862, for abandoning the North during the Civil War and joining the Confederacy; Judge Robert Archbald of Pennsylvania, in 1913, charged with speculating in coal properties and misconduct outside the court; District Judge Halsted Ritter of Florida, in 1936, convicted of filing false tax returns and accepting gifts from wealthy cronies; and Judge Harry Claiborne of Nevada, in 1986, charged with evasion of federal income taxes.

Several impeachment trials, detailed below, reveal significant issues about the impeachment process under the U.S. Constitution. These cases involve Justice Samuel Chase of the Supreme Court in 1804-1805 and President Andrew Johnson in 1868. In addition, the near-impeachment of President Richard Nixon (1972-1974) points up other issues about the impeachment process.

In the case of Supreme Court Justice Samuel Chase, a brief history is as follows. During the early years of the 1800's, outspoken Federalists dominated the Supreme Court while the Jeffersonian Republicans controlled Congress. The Republicans feared that the Federalists would obstruct their legislative agenda, so they made a concerted effort to reduce the Federalists' power on the Supreme Court. They attacked vulnerable members of the Court, such as Justice Samuel Chase, in hopes of removing him and getting someone on the Court more sympathetic to Republican views. The House of Representatives drew up eight articles of impeachment against Justice Chase, all involving Chase's conduct while serving as a circuit justice. According to the articles, Justice Chase had verbally prejudged a defendant as guilty before trial began, attempted to discredit the defense counsel, allowed admittedly biased individuals to serve on the jury, and conducted himself in an unbecoming and intemperate manner. During the Senate deliberations, the defense counsel for Justice Chase stressed the risky business of allowing political partisanship to hide behind the business of impeachment for serious crimes. At the trial's end, Chase was acquitted of all articles of impeachment. The case of Justice Chase illustrates the temptation of using the impeachment process for political purposes: to rid oneself of one's political enemies, and in this case, an attempt to stack the Supreme Court with those of one's own political persuasion.

In the case of President Andrew Johnson, there is a similar story of political partisanship dressed as objective criminal prosecution. When Johnson succeeded the assassinated Abraham Lincoln to the presidency, he became embroiled in political battles with the Republican majority in Congress, who wished to punish the South for its part in the Civil War. A Southerner, opposed to secession from the Union but sympathetic with Southern interests, President Johnson vetoed legislative bills detrimental to the South. His veto was repeatedly overridden by a hostile Congress. One such bill was the Tenure of Office Act, which limited the power of the president to remove the then current Republican officeholders. President Johnson ignored the act when on February 21, 1868, he removed Edwin Stanton, Secretary of War, from office because of disloyalty, and authorized an interim secretary of his own choosing. Congress used this violation as the major offense when ten articles of impeachment were drawn up against President Johnson. After the trial (a trial in which President Johnson was never confronted with a specific accusation), the impeachment charges failed, but only by one vote, to get the two-thirds vote necessary to convict. If the conviction had succeeded, it could have undermined the separation of powers, with Congress achieving a dominance over the executive branch of government. According to Raoul Berger, in *Impeachment: The Constitutional Problems* (1973), the presidency could have become subservient to Congress, akin to a chairman of a cabinet responsible to Congress. Berger concludes without reservation that the impeachment and trial of President Johnson was an abuse. If the impeachment had succeeded, no president would be safe from a Congress with the opposition party in the majority. The attempted impeachment of President Johnson also showed how difficult conviction can be, since a two-thirds vote is required, thus acting as a safeguard against partisan politics.

In both cases—that of Justice Samuel Chase and President Johnson—the major issue was that Congress played at partisan politics, attempting to use the impeachment machinery to extend its powers into the judicial and executive branches of government. In Chase's case, the real aim was to manipulate the Supreme Court; in Johnson's case, the real aim was to reduce the power of the president. In neither case did Congress succeed. The principle of separation of power among the three branches of government, as created by the designers of the U.S. Constitution, remained intact.

In the case of President Richard Nixon, who was nearly impeached in 1974, there is further evidence that the cumbersome impeachment process is not without virtues. On June 17, 1972, five men in business suits and surgical gloves, carrying photographic and bugging equipment, were arrested as they burglarized the Democratic National Committee offices in the Watergate Hotel complex in Washington, D.C. Later, investigators linked these men to the Central Intelligence Agency, to important White House aides, and to Nixon's own 1972 Reelection Committee. President Nixon and his camp denied any knowledge, involvement, or wrongdoing in the break-in.

Although Nixon, a Republican, had won his 1972 presidential election by a landslide, both houses of Congress were controlled by Democrats. During the next two years, circumstances surrounding the break-in moved the Democrats of Congress to pursue the matter. Special Prosecutor Archibald Cox investigated the rumors and allegations. The House Judiciary Committee did its own investigation as well, linking Nixon and his Republican allies to such abuses as illegal campaign financing, including financial payoffs for administrative favors; the hiring of goons to harass Democratic candidates; illegal wiretappings of protesters of the Vietnam War; Nixon's making false statements to Congress about the bombing of Cambodia during the Vietnam War; the White House ordering tax audits of its enemies; and even Nixon's home improvements of his San Clemente residence at taxpayer expense, along with his taking income tax deductions to which he was not entitled.

Matters came to a head when it was discovered that Nixon had secretly made audio tapes of all conversations in the Oval Office of the White House. Such tapes would be invaluable in revealing how much involvement Nixon and his associates really had in covering up their alleged misconduct. Immediately, Special Prosecutor Cox subpoenaed the White House tapes, but Nixon refused to deliver them, abruptly disbanding the special prosecutor's office and firing Cox. These events prompted further court appeals until eventually, on July 24, 1974, the Supreme Court ordered President Nixon to turn over the tapes to the investigators. In the meantime, after eight months of hearings, the House Judiciary Committee completed its preliminary work, drawing up three articles of impeachment, accusing President Nixon of obstructing justice, abusing power, and refusing to turn over papers and tapes subpoenaed by the House of Representatives. Just ten days after the House Judiciary Committee approved the impeachment articles, and with the certainty that the House of Representatives itself would impeach him, and with dwindling support from the Republican Party, President Richard Nixon resigned his office on August 9, 1974. President Nixon was not the first to resign because of the serious threat of impeachment and conviction; a number of judges had done so in the past. Nixon, however, was the first president in U.S. history to resign his office.

In the aftermath of the Watergate scandal, more than twenty of Nixon's close associates, including the Attorney General, spent time in prison for their parts in the shameful episode. Nixon's successor, President Gerald Ford, however, pardoned Nixon for all offenses while in office, allowing him to receive his presidential pension. Although Nixon never again held office, he was constantly sought out by politicians and statesmen of various persuasions to provide his expertise on foreign policy until his death on April 22, 1994.

President Nixon's near-impeachment helped clarify the meaning of an impeachable offense, particularly the phrase "other high crimes and misdemeanors" in the U.S. Constitution. The House Judiciary Committee interpreted this to mean a presidential violation of the public trust. More important, the Watergate episode revealed the dangers behind President Nixon and his henchmen's attempt to use the powers of his office to tamper with the investigative process. When Nixon was denied control over the Watergate investigations being conducted by the congressional and the judicial branches of government, the constitutional principles of separation of powers were maintained.

Context

The principles of impeachment are rooted in fourteenth century England. With the emergence of Parliament and its attempt to reduce the often tyrannical and absolute power of the monarchy, impeachment was used during the ensuing centuries as a means of keeping the king's ministers accountable to Parliament as well as to the king.

In 1787, when the Framers of the U.S. Constitution deliberated on how the American government should operate, they vividly recalled how they had just won their freedom from George III, and they did not wish to confront a similar situation in the newly found government of the United States. They feared putting too much power in the hands of the executive branch of government. Hence, the Constitutional Convention of 1787 was very much concerned about how to impeach leaders who abused power. The Framers of the Constitution were familiar with the British system, so they borrowed much of its impeachment machinery to control the executive branch. Under the English system, the House of Commons may initiate the removal proceedings because it is directly accountable to the people; under the American system, the House of Representatives serves the same function. In England, the House of Lords tried such cases; the U.S. Senate served as its counterpart. Even the grounds for impeachment ("treason, bribery, or other high crimes and misdemeanors") were taken directly from British law.

The U.S. Constitution clearly defines the parameters of the impeachment procedures—that is, the responsibilities of the House of Representatives and the Senate, who may be impeached, the grounds for impeachment, and what punishment may be meted out on conviction. Over the years, however, certain questions about impeachment have arisen for which there are no definitive answers. For example, is impeachment a criminal procedure or is it necessarily of a political nature? How can impeachment proceedings avoid being viewed by politicians and the public alike as a partisan weapon, one in which the dominant political party in Congress bashes the offending president or federal officials? How can the president be held legally responsible without making him subordinate to Congress while ensuring the separation of powers of Congress, the presidency, and the courts? In spite of these legal questions, there has been little effort to reform the impeachment procedures originally found in the U.S. Constitution, other than possibly changing the wording in Article 2, section 4, where the grounds for impeachment are given. The final phase, "other high crimes and misdemeanors," taken directly from the British wording on impeachment, is ambiguous. Participants in former impeachment proceedings have taken these words to mean for serious wrongdoing, or for cause, or for violation of public trust. In future impeachment hearings, those involved will again be asked to interpret this ambiguous phrasing.

Bibliography

Berger, Raoul. *Impeachment: The Constitutional Problems*. Cambridge, Mass.: Harvard University Press, 1973. Details the similarities and differences between the British and American views on impeachment, with readable accounts of the impeachment trials of Justice Samuel Chase and President Andrew Johnson.

Breslin, Jimmy. *How the Good Guys Finally Won: Notes from an Impeachment Summer*. New York: Viking Press, 1975. Lively account of the Watergate scandal, from the perspective of members of the House of Representatives hot on the trail of President Richard Nixon's misdeeds.

Bushnell, Eleanore. *Crimes, Follies, and Misfortunes: The Federal Impeachment Trials*. Champaign: University of Illinois Press, 1992. Analyzes the impeachment process and offers detailed case histories of twelve federal officers brought up on impeachment charges.

Labovitz, John. *Presidential Impeachment*. New Haven, Conn.: Yale University Press, 1978. Firsthand account of the procedures that the House of Representatives undertook in 1974 in its investigation of President Nixon.

Rehnquist, William. *Grand Inquests: The Historical Impeachments of Justice Samuel Chase and President Andrew Johnson*. New York: William Morrow, 1992. Uses the impeachment trials of Chase and Johnson to illustrate the importance of maintaining the separation of powers among the three branches of government.

Volcansek, Mary. *Judicial Impeachment: None Called for Justice*. Champaign: University of Illinois Press, 1993. Details three impeachment cases of the 1980's: those of Judge Harry Claiborne, Alcee Hastings, and Walter Nixon. Speculates on why a rash of impeachments occurred during the 1980's.

Richard Whitworth

Cross-References

Checks and Balances in U.S. Government, p. 216; The Constitution of the United States, p. 425; Executive Functions in U.S. Government, p. 636; Legislative Functions of Government, p. 1098; Political Philosophy, p. 1505; Separation of Powers: Presidential Government, p. 1815.

IMPERIALISM

Field of study: International government and politics

Imperialism is a term applied both to the tendency of nation-states to build empires and to the expansionist tendencies of modern capitalist nations. This second sense of the term—popularized by Russian Communist leader V. I. Lenin—has profoundly influenced thinking on international relations, especially among socialists, communists, and nationalists in poorer countries.

Principal terms

CAPITALISM: market-based economic system in which the means of production and distribution are privately owned

CARTEL: collusion of firms in the same industry to suppress competition by fixing prices and limiting each firm's production or sales

COLONIALISM: policy of conquering and governing foreign territories, usually overseas

FINANCE CAPITAL: close alliance of banks and industrial corporations

JINGOISM: extreme national chauvinism advocating expansionist foreign policy

MONOPOLY CAPITAL: business system in which free-market competition among firms is suppressed by the formation of cartels, trusts, and monopolies

NEOCOLONIALISM: domination of underdeveloped nations by imperialist powers after the former have gained formal independence

TRUST: combination of firms governed by a board of trustees through its control of a major portion of the stock of each member firm

UNDERDEVELOPED COUNTRY: nation in which agricultural production predominates over industry, and which is usually poorer and less productive than industrial capitalist countries

Overview

Imperialism is the doctrine or policy of creating empires, especially overseas. Modern international relations uses the term in two related senses, one broad, the other more narrow. Most influential to international relations theory has been V. I. Lenin's identification of imperialism as a particular stage in the development of capitalism. To Lenin and many who followed him, imperialism was both a specific stage in the development and organization of global society and the dominant doctrines and policies that resulted from that pattern of social organization. Others, using the term in a more general sense, have explained imperialism both as a tendency common to powerful nations and as an archaic holdover from precapitalist or feudal societies that disappears as capitalism develops.

International relations theorists known as "realists" believe that imperialism is a common tendency of powerful nations. Realists argue that the tendency of powerful countries to expand and create empires is common to all historical eras, not merely to a particular stage of capitalism.

Joseph Schumpeter, an Austrian social scientist, argued against the Leninist theory of imperialism from a different angle. He contended that imperialist tendencies persisted in the early twentieth century because of the continued influence of the feudal aristocracy in most European nations and Japan. Historian Arno Mayer used a similar argument to explain the origin of World War I. Historically, the aristocracy had been the warrior class. Its social privileges were justified by its military function. By the twentieth century, however, the rapid development of industrial capitalism threatened to displace the aristocracy in favor of the new business elite. The aristocracy could only reassert its social preeminence through vigorous imperial expansion based on military force. Capitalists opposed the militarism of the aristocracy. They favored the fullest possible development of free trade and investment throughout the globe. Imperialism was an obstacle to such expansion; consequently, capitalists opposed it. This theory fails to account for why substantial sectors of business did in fact vigorously support imperialist policies.

The theory of imperialism popularized by Lenin asserted that imperialism was the inevitable product of a new stage of capitalism. Lenin referred to this latest stage as "monopoly capitalism." He argued that the growing prevalence of cartels, trusts, and monopolies in the late nineteenth and early twentieth centuries was forcing capitalist countries into an intensified struggle to control overseas markets and sources of raw materials. This need for economic control led to efforts to secure political control. Lenin contended that the increasingly hostile competition of capitalist powers for control of overseas territories led to the outbreak of World War I in 1914.

Lenin's theory of imperialism was most influenced by two pioneering works, the British socialist J. A. Hobson's *Imperialism* and the Austrian Marxist Rudolf Hilferding's *Finance Capital*. Hobson's book appeared in 1902 as the culmination of a series of studies of the recent overseas expansion of Great Britain and other powers. Hilferding first published his book in 1910. His concept of "finance capital" was closely related to Lenin's later concept of "monopoly capitalism." Although purporting to explain the "latest phase of capitalist development" common to all the great powers, Hilferding's main model was Germany. Lenin followed Hilferding in using Germany as his model, but he also viewed developments in other prosperous capitalist countries, especially the United States, as essentially similar.

All three of these theorists believed that the root cause of the upsurge in imperialist expansion around the turn of the century was the simultaneous transformation of capitalism from an essentially competitive system characterized by small and medium-sized firms to one of huge, highly concentrated firms, trusts, and cartels dominating entire lines of industry within each major country. This growing monopolization of industry stimulated imperialism for several reasons.

Most monopolies and cartels formed during the long depression of the 1870's and

1880's in efforts to restrict production and thereby arrest a chronic decline in prices and profits. Restricting production, however, left many firms with substantial excess productive capacity. Expanding sales overseas provided a way to profit from this excess capacity without undermining domestic cartel restrictions. The most promising avenues for new trade expansion seemed to be in the underdeveloped world, since many industrialized countries were raising their tariffs during this period to prevent lower-priced imports from undermining the high prices of domestic cartels. Thus most of the leading capitalist countries soon began to compete for influence in these poorer countries.

As trade competition grew more ruthless in the effort to secure markets for excess industrial capacity, industries often sought government support to help them acquire control of cheap sources of the raw materials they needed in order to cut their costs and thereby increase competitiveness. Among the most-sought-after raw materials were sugar cane, cotton, silk, copper, coal, metal ores, and petroleum. Political influence and often outright annexation were tools used to gain control of underdeveloped countries that had easily exploitable raw materials.

Excess industrial capacity in developed countries discouraged domestic investment. Finance capital was earning large profits from its many monopolies and trusts, but since those same monopolies kept prices high and restricted output, there were limited opportunities for profitable new investment at home. Thus finance capital sought new investment opportunities abroad, especially in underdeveloped countries. Large-scale investments abroad often both required and facilitated political influence in the poorer countries. The vigorous competition among investment groups from rival imperial powers led to greater and greater efforts to assert political influence. This, in turn, led to each power securing colonies in which their political domination could more effectively exclude the competition.

As cartels, trusts, and monopolies consolidated their control over broad sections of industry, finance, and commerce, they could more easily sway politicians and government officials to support their overseas ventures. Earlier, when industries were divided into dozens of competing firms, governments could not favor one over another without appearing to pander to special interests. With the emergence of "monopoly capitalism," the great cartels, trusts, and investment groups asserted that their own overseas interests represented the broad national interests. Patriotic societies, navy leagues, and other proimperialist organizations were generously funded by businesses interested in overseas expansion. Their imperialist propaganda was reinforced by jingoistic politicians, militarism taught in the armed forces, and government-prescribed textbooks extolling war and patriotism.

Marxist socialists and communists believed that the working class would, under their leadership, pose the greatest opposition to imperialism. They further believed that opposition to imperialism required opposition to capitalism itself, since imperialism was simply the expression of capitalism in its latest stage. For these Marxists, the only real antidote to imperialism was socialist revolution. Wars caused by imperialist rivalries would provide the opportunity for workers to overthrow their imperialist governments, nationalize finance capital, and establish socialism.

On the other hand, Hobson, the theorist who first identified imperialism as a systematic tendency of capitalism, believed that imperialist interests could be curbed by economic reforms at home and international cooperation abroad without expropriating private businesses. Hobson proposed many of the same kinds of reforms that were later implemented in many countries during the Great Depression of the 1930's: policies to curb unemployment and to increase wages and social welfare spending. Hobson argued that such reforms would increase domestic purchasing power enough to eliminate the excess productive capacity that was pushing big business ruthlessly to compete for overseas markets and investments. Hobson also proposed international cooperation to promote free trade and investment. He believed that if all countries traded with and invested in underdeveloped regions on similar terms, who controlled these regions would become economically irrelevant.

Ultimately, Hobson's solution to the problem of imperialism proved more successful than Lenin's. The term "imperialism" is still widely used in the vague sense of attempts by rich and powerful countries to secure influence in poorer, underdeveloped countries, but the essential characteristics of the imperialist system described by Hobson, Lenin, and others (use of political control to create exclusive spheres of economic influence and wars among the great powers to define such spheres) have largely disappeared from relations among capitalist powers since the end of World War II. A long period of relatively free international trade and investment has brought unprecedented prosperity to the most developed countries and eliminated warfare among them.

Applications

The era of the two world wars witnessed both the last great imperialist drives and the simultaneous development of internationalist alternatives. World War I prompted both business and government elites to implement more internationalist policies, especially in the United States and Great Britain. Yet nationalist resistance to international cooperation and free trade frustrated many cooperative efforts during the interwar years. Not until after the Allied victory in World War II did the policies advocated by Hobson a half century earlier begin to triumph. The demise of imperialism was accomplished, not as Lenin had predicted, by socialist revolution, but by the gradual expansion of international cooperation, coupled with domestic reform. International cooperation among governments included new international mechanisms to promote free trade, monetary stability, and investment security. Business also created new institutions of international cooperation, including international investment consortia, cartels, and joint-venture agreements. New business and government institutions began to promote strategic cooperation among the same kind of finance capitalists who formerly promoted imperial expansion. Many former imperialists learned that they could better secure their interests through international cooperation rather than through conquest and conflict.

Late nineteenth century imperialism resulted in the partition of most of Africa and

Southeast Asia among European powers. By the turn of the century, the attention of the imperial powers had shifted to four old empires then in decline: China, Ottoman Turkey, Persia (now Iran), and Morocco. The two decades before the outbreak of World War I were marked by intensified struggle for each of these. By the end of the war all except China had been substantially partitioned among the European powers. China was perhaps the greatest prize, the longest to suffer from foreign contention, but the first place where the imperial powers learned the advantages of cooperation and created new institutions to facilitate it, initiating a pattern that would eventually replace imperialist rivalry.

Japan initiated the new scramble for concessions from China with military victories during the 1890's. Much of the fruits of victory were taken away from Japan, however, when Russia, Great Britain, France, and Germany stepped in to claim their shares of the spoils. China's antiforeign Boxer Rebellion at the turn of the century prompted armed intervention from all those powers plus the United States. Japan started a new round of competition by defeating Russia in a war over control of Korea and northeastern China (Manchuria) in 1905.

About the same time, however, others were beginning to experience the virtues of cooperation. The international scramble for China had so weakened that country that the danger was growing that it would soon be unable to pay its mounting foreign debt. The same capitalists who had financed the scramble for railroad and mining concessions had also financed the Chinese public debt. Any further weakening of China thus might prove to be bad business. Furthermore, the foreign rivalry over investment concessions had given the Chinese government the opportunity to play one national investor group off against another to get better terms. Unless the various investor groups could cooperate, investing would get riskier as each competed to offer better terms to a Chinese government less and less able to pay. Finally, bank-led investment groups from the major powers formed the China Consortium in 1910 to monopolize most major foreign lending and investment in China. This consortium was the ancestor of international investor cooperation that is broadly institutionalized today through such institutions as the International Monetary Fund, World Bank, and London Club of private investors.

Context

The modern imperialist era (roughly the 1880's through the 1930's) taught the world much about the interrelationships between international economics and international politics, and domestic reform and international relations. World War I was an object lesson to both finance capitalists and governments in the terrible costs of unrestrained imperialist rivalries. After the war there were many new initiatives toward international cooperation by both business and governments. Although efforts at cooperation made some progress in the 1920's, social reform of the type Hobson recommended was largely neglected. It was not until after the twin catastrophes of the Great Depression of the 1930's and World War II that durable and effective institutions of international cooperation and domestic economic and social reform were finally put in place. During these same postwar decades, European colonies throughout the world gained political independence.

Since World War II there has been an unprecedented blossoming of international trade and investment. The relative openness of modern international commerce discourages resumption of territorial competition among the industrial powers. If, however, major powers were to revert to the kind of rampant protectionism that was witnessed in the 1930's, the drive to control overseas territories to supply resources not available at home could potentially revive imperialist conflict among the industrial powers.

The domestic pillar of anti-imperialism has been economic and social policies that have stimulated domestic consumption and thus reduced the problem of industrial overcapacity. These policies have been variously known as Keynesianism and the welfare state. Since the 1970's, however, there has been a global trend toward rolling back the welfare state and lowering wages. So long as world trade remains robust, this alone should not revive imperialist tendencies, because exports can often make up for slack demand at home. As concern for high domestic consumption and full employment wanes, international commerce becomes even more important as a barrier to imperialism.

Bibliography

Bukharin, Nikolai. *Imperialism and World Economy*. New York: International Publishers, 1929. The first important treatise on imperialism by a leader of the Russian Revolution of 1917, this book was written in 1915 after Bukharin attended lectures by Hilferding in Vienna.

Darby, Phillip. *Three Faces of Imperialism: British and American Approaches to Asia and Africa, 1870-1970*. New Haven, Conn.: Yale University Press, 1987. This broad study compares various forms of imperialism across time and continents.

Davis, Clarence B., and Kenneth E. Wilburn, Jr., eds. *Railway Imperialism*. New York: Greenwood, 1991. Essays in this collection explore the central role of railroad building and finance in stimulating imperial ambitions during the late nineteenth and early twentieth centuries.

Davis, Lance E., and Robert A. Huttenback. *Mammon and the Pursuit of Empire: The Political Economy of British Imperialism, 1860-1912*. Cambridge, England: Cambridge University Press, 1986. Although the authors argue that Marxists exaggerated the benefits of empire for British capitalism, they agree that the benefits accrued mainly to segments of the upper classes, while the costs fell mainly on the middle class.

Hilferding, Rudolf. *Finance Capital: A Study of the Latest Phase of Capitalist Development*. Edited by Tom Bottomore. London: Routledge & Kegan Paul, 1981. Originally published in German in 1910, this was the single most important influence on the theories of imperialism developed by Lenin and Bukharin. Part five argues why specific forms of business organization promote imperialism.

Hobsbawm, Eric. *The Age of Empire, 1875-1914*. New York: Pantheon Books, 1987.

Probably the most readable history of the heyday of global imperialism.

Hobson, J. A. *Imperialism: A Study*. London: George Allen & Unwin, 1938. The first great study of the economic roots of modern imperialism, first published in 1902.

Lenin, V. I. *Imperialism: The Highest Stage of Capitalism*. New York: International Publishers, 1939. Probably the most influential and widely read book on international relations in the modern era. First written in Russian in 1916, it has been translated into many languages.

Schumpeter, Joseph A. *Imperialism and Social Classes*. Translated by Heinz Norden and edited by Paul M. Sweezy. New York: A. M. Kelly, 1951. Contrary to Marxist theories, Schumpeter attributes imperialism to remnants of feudalism lingering on in capitalist societies rather than to capitalism itself.

Snyder, Jack. *Myths of Empire: Domestic Politics and International Ambition*. Ithaca, N.Y.: Cornell University Press, 1991. Snyder starts from the realist perspective that powerful states have a tendency to expand to create empires, but used ideological myths and special interests to explain why this often leads to overexpansion.

Szymanski, Albert. *The Logic of Imperialism*. New York: Praeger, 1981. One of the most comprehensive surveys of classical theories of imperialism and their recent derivations; this work interprets modern international relations in the light of these theories.

James H. Nolt

Cross-References

Africa: Politics and Governments, p. 21; Capitalism, p. 197; Colonialism and Anticolonialism, p. 351; Commonwealths, p. 364; Developed and Developing Nations, p. 533; Empires and Empire Building, p. 597; Geopolitics, p. 759; Independence Movements and Transitions, p. 896; International Relations, p. 969; Marxism-Leninism, p. 1155; National Liberation Movements, p. 1255; Nationalism, p. 1268; Social Darwinism, p. 1833; Trade with Foreign Nations, p. 2000; Underdeveloped Nations, p. 2039; War, p. 2129.

INDEPENDENCE MOVEMENTS AND TRANSITIONS

Field of study: Politics

Following several centuries of Western colonial dominance over areas of Asia, Africa, and Latin America, a combination of changing international circumstances and emerging militant nationalist movements brought independence to scores of new states in the second half of the twentieth century.

Principal terms
COLONY: country or territory ruled by another country
DEPENDENCY THEORY: idea that former colonial zones will never attain full economic and political independence from developed countries
NATIONAL LIBERATION FRONT: coalition of groups who share the goal of national independence
PROTECTORATE: country or territory that cedes part of its sovereignty to a colonial power
TRUSTEESHIP: called "mandate" under the League of Nations, United Nations trusteeships have involved the temporary assignment of the responsibility of administering a not yet independent state to a designated member nation

Overview

Although the dual phenomena of colonialism and national independence movements have historical roots that extend back at least three centuries, it was during the post-World War II period that the most striking examples of local national demands for independence occurred. Around 1940, much of the less developed world was under European rule. In Asia, Indochina (including Vietnam) was under French control; the East Indies under Dutch; and South Asia, including India, Burma and Malaya, under British. In Africa, all areas north of the Sahara except Egypt were under Italian, Spanish, or French colonial regimes, while south of the Sahara, colonial control was divided between the British (in East African zones such as Kenya and Uganda, as well as West African colonies, including Nigeria and Gold Coast); the French (dominating the regions that would become Senegal, Niger, and Chad, among others, as well as French Equatorial Africa); the Portuguese (Angola, Mozambique, and Guinea-Bissau), and the Belgians (the Congo and neighboring regions of Ruanda and Burundi). In Latin America, small residual colonies existed, including the British, French, and Dutch Guianas, and British Honduras. Many Caribbean islands also remained under European rule.

The impact of World War II on this general colonial setting was substantial. Vast areas of French, British, and Dutch colonial rule were either occupied by enemy powers (as in French Indochina and the Dutch East Indies), or were transformed by wartime circumstances. Vichy France's authority over France's pre-1940 colonies, for example, was repudiated by the Free French forces of General Charles de Gaulle, who rallied whole regions of French Equatorial Africa and North Africa to his cause. Clearly, such "loyalist" Africans looked to local leaders to use their wartime records to make nationalist gains after the war. In Britain's case, the importance of continued dependence on Indian troops to assure strategic and transport security of its remaining holdings in South Asia was also certain to affect postwar relations with expectant nationalist groupings, especially followers of the charismatic nonviolent leader, Mohandas K. Gandhi.

Indeed, from 1945 into the 1960's, the two main colonial powers, Britain and France, had to react to local nationalist independence demands throughout Asia and Africa. The Netherlands, Belgium, and Portugal experienced similar pressures in Indonesia, the Congo and Angola, respectively. Although many independence movements occurred during this same first period of decolonization, the forms they took varied considerably. The results of successful nationalist struggles for independence also differed from country to country.

An essential factor contributing to different patterns in the resolution of colonial-nationalist conflict was the role of international organizations, particularly the League of Nations in the interwar period and the United Nations after 1944. Where international authority came into play, as in the League of Nations mandate regimes (such as Tanganyika) or U.N. trusteeships or other forms of intermediary intervention, transitions from colonial to independent regimes tended to avoid catastrophic confrontations between local nationalists and recalcitrant colonialist powers.

In some cases, however, colonial countries decided on their own that the time had come to relinquish power to national independence movements that had been actively formed decades before. This was Britain's experience in India and Burma in 1947.

Whereas Burma's independence was accomplished largely through bilateral negotiations and occurred without major upsets, India's two main nationalist leaders, Mohandas Gandhi (a Hindu) and Muhammad Ali Jinnah (leader of a large Muslim minority), were destined to face immediate difficulties when Britain's colonial rule was lifted. After disastrous communal strife, Asia's first successfully decolonized giant split into two countries: Hindu India and Muslim Pakistan.

In the 1950's Britain began facing demands for independence from its most important African colonies, such as Kenya, Nigeria, and the Gold Coast. Britain hoped to find common ground for compromise that would allow responsible nationalists to opt for continued Commonwealth status, rather than breaking away completely.

In the same early postwar period two other colonial powers, France and The Netherlands, faced independence demands in Indochina and Indonesia in very different ways. In the Indochinese case, French attempts to reimpose control after Japan's wartime occupation of Laos, Cambodia, and Vietnam met the determined resistance of the communist-founded Viet Minh under Ho Chi Minh. The Viet Minh's guerrilla war against France lasted until 1954, when an international conference at Geneva set up an interim accord that separated Vietnam from Cambodia and Laos. The accord also "temporarily" divided Vietnam itself into northern (communist) and southern (noncommunist) zones until elections could decide the fate of the country. France essentially withdrew in order to deal with independence demands elsewhere.

Rejection of the Geneva Accord by uncompromising parties soon led to Ho Chi Minh's decision to form the National Liberation Front (NLF). The NLF tried to impose a communist regime on the south, but was met by the U.S.-supported noncommunist regime in Saigon. As the Vietnam War escalated in the mid-1960's, it became clear that the struggle had become multitiered. It seemed likely that Vietnam would remain split into distinct countries, each seeking to establish its own version of nationalism despite the looming shadow of the NLF's communist ideology. It was also tragically clear that South Vietnam's own destiny was inextricably tied to the political and military will of a massive foreign power that might be unwilling to pay the cost of a protracted factional war. This destiny was ultimately decided when negotiations between North Vietnam and the United States ended in 1975.

Well before the Geneva Accord tried to end France's violent confrontation in Indochina, The Netherlands in their Dutch East Indies colony had come, after several years of struggle, to recognize that force alone would not dissuade another determined nationalist front, the first elements of which had been organized by Indonesia's future first president, Sukarno, in 1927. Like Ho Chi Minh, Sukarno tried soon after the Japanese defeat to block the return of a colonial regime by proclaiming the independent Republic of Indonesia (August, 1945). The Dutch countered by calling for a "Commonwealth of Indonesia," with a division of various East Indies subregions and ethnic groupings into a federal system that would remain part of the kingdom of The Netherlands. When republican nationalists rejected this, British mediators tried but failed to obtain a compromise. In July, 1947, the Dutch sent military forces to Java and Sumatra. Fighting stopped only after a U.N. Security Council resolution and assignment of an international Good Offices Committee to mediate. Despite serious breakdowns and resumption of fighting in December, 1948, the U.N. efforts proved successful a year later.

Successful resolution of Indonesia's bid for independence involved mutual recognition that an extended armed struggle could be disastrous for all parties. The experiences of both Vietnam and Algeria demonstrated that the presumably benevolent multilateral concerns of the international community could not have an effect where determination to impose solutions through armed rebellion and/or external military intervention persisted. Algeria's armed struggle for independence under its Front de Libération Nationale (FLN) began at about the same date as that of Vietnam's NLF (1954) but attained its ends far earlier (1962). Its experience of the long-term repercussions of violent liberation from colonial rule would, like Vietnam's, fall short of the expectations of its nationalist leaders. Until the postwar period, and after experiencing the bitter cost of defeat in resisting French control throughout the nineteenth century, many Algerians had resigned themselves to the presumed advantages of France's off-and-on promises of either "association" with or "assimilation" into the mother country's political and legal institutions. When these promises proved to be illusory and nationalist demonstrations were put down brutally in 1945, a generation of "freedom fighters" was born. Escalation of violence, as well as domestic political division over the cost of France's last colonial war, attracted world attention between 1954 and 1965. President De Gaulle's government sought a compromise solution and recognized the FLN as the heir to Algerian independence in 1962. Application of the FLN's revolutionary program, however, like that of the NLF in Vietnam after another full decade of struggle, would not prove to be a final answer to the country's bid to enjoy full independence.

Applications

Generally speaking, sub-Saharan African independence movements involved less fighting than was experienced in India, Southeast Asia, and Algeria. To be sure, British colonists faced Mau Mau terrorist violence as early as 1952 in Kenya, and Britain delayed granting Kenyan independence until 1963. After a full decade of tension, however, extensive negotiations paved the way for Jomo Kenyatta to become president in a peaceful transition. By that date, most former French and British African colonies, plus the Belgian Congo, had gained independence by mainly peaceful means. Then, between 1964 and 1975, independence came to the rest of Britain's and Portugal's African colonies.

The first stage of gradualist transition to African independence was already being considered by both France and Britain immediately after World War II. For the French, this took the form of a call, first launched in Brazzaville in 1944, for reforms that would eventually integrate independent African countries into a French Union similar to the British Commonwealth of Nations.

The first sub-Saharan African leader to gain independence for his country was Kwame Nkrumah of the Gold Coast (now Ghana). Nkrumah presented his famous "Declaration to the Colonial Peoples of the World" at the Fifth Pan-African Congress in Manchester, England, in October, 1945. Six years later, he was actively involved, as leader of his country's Convention People's Party, in constructive moves through electoral processes toward independence. In 1955, he became prime minister of a constitutionally established transition government that became formally independent soon thereafter.

A similar pattern, resembling a preparatory stage that could lead to independence, occurred in Britain's largest West African colony, Nigeria. There an attempt was made in 1954 to introduce a federal system to accommodate the distinct ethnic identities of a highly fragmented country. Although encouragement was given to Nigerian politicians to form broadly based parties like those in Ghana, the country's accession to independence in 1960 was soon darkened by an ominous shadow. Tiv riots had to be suppressed in 1960, leading to a Tiv uprising in 1964. Yoruba troubles came in the same year and repression of Southeastern Nigeria's Ibo brought the country to the brink of civil war.

Despite such setbacks, the colonial powers would not hold back the tide of nationalist independence demands. The result of this new climate, described by British prime minister Harold MacMillan in February, 1960, as the "Winds of Change," was that more than a dozen African countries gained independence in the next two years. In most cases, responsibility was transferred peacefully to previously identified moderate local leaders.

A striking exception was the former Belgian Congo (Zaïre), where the precipitous nature of Brussels' decision to grant independence seemed to invite both African and European factions to plunge the country into civil war. The Congo had seen the emergence of several regional or ethnically defined parties in the 1950's. Only one movement (under Patrice Lumumba) claimed support in four out of six provinces. When Belgium suddenly quit the Congo in 1960, the presumed bases for this support were shocked by divisions among followers of Joseph Kasavubu, Moise Tshombe, and Lumumba. The added complication of European colonial attempts to support the mineral rich Katanga's secession would have brought full civil war, had the United Nations not intervened. Nevertheless, before 1960 ended, the independent Congo had experienced its first military coup under Colonel Joseph Mobutu. A year later Lumumba was killed in an obvious conspiracy.

Given the Congo crisis of 1960 and Nigeria's drift toward civil war, the optimistic climate of the 1960's soon became unsettled. By the 1970's another round of winds of change suggested that nationalist activism and independence are only stages in a development that in troubled ethnic or political environments can lead to many disappointments before attaining clear success.

Context

The most obvious tests for successful transition to independence involve political stability and economic vitality. Absence of these two in the postcolonial setting can yield seemingly insoluble dilemmas, including prolonged civil wars. Several cases of latter-day transitions to national independence that occurred from the late-1960's into the 1990's seem to belie this point. Where the stakes were not clearly high, for example, Britain and The Netherlands granted independence to South and Central American countries such as Guyana (1965), Suriname (former Dutch Guiana, in 1975), and Belize (former British Honduras, in 1981) with some assurance that traditional political and economic links would endure.

The situations of Angola and Algeria were very unlike these gradualist examples. Angola's expectations of independence from Portugal began as early as 1959, with the founding of the Union of the People of Northern Angola (UPNA), an ethnically based body that aimed more at reestablishing a precolonial image of the Kongo kingdom than at unifying diverse peoples under an Angolan independence movement. After other African nationalist leaders criticized this, Holden Roberto formed a new movement called the Union of Angolan Peoples. Soon confrontations over Angola's future escalated, and other groups, including the leftist Popular Movement for the Liberation of Angola (MPLA) and Jonas Savimbi's breakaway movement from the UPA, the National Union for the Total Independence of Angola (UNITA), joined in a not altogether united liberation front. The combined movement formed a government in exile, but its internal political divisions gave the Portuguese a "breathing space" for several years. Portugal's home government changed in the mid-1970's, and the new regime granted independence in a single move in 1975 to Angola, Mozambique, and Guinea-Bissau.

This event did not, however, end the divisions among Angolan nationalists. The country's independence was followed by a civil war that lasted through the 1980's. By the 1990's the country's only hope of reconstruction depended on the withdrawal of all foreign forces and ideologies from the scene.

Political independence is not a guarantee of a viable political and economic future. The case of Algeria is instructive. Its independence in 1962 was declared to be the final realization of a social revolutionary struggle; however, the FLN's nearly thirty-year rule as a one-party system proved vulnerable to internal strains that finally surfaced when put to the test of pluralism in the 1980's. Absence of an evolving experience of pluralism cost very dearly when economic conditions in an imposed socialist state deteriorated. A combination of mismanagement and overdependence on petroleum earnings during the 1970's made it impossible for a multiparty division of responsibility to rally to new challenges in the 1980's. Political stalemate led to extremist reactions of two sorts: a reactionary Islamic Front's call for total post-FLN restructuring of the principles of government on the one hand, and, on the other, a military backed reaction to apparent popular support for the Islamic call. Levels of violence between these two groups in France's former colony by the mid-1990's had created a situation of civil war that was comparable to that of newly independent Angola earlier.

Bibliography

Allen, Douglas, and Ngo Vinh Long, eds. *Coming to Terms.* Boulder, Colo.: Westview Press, 1991. History of U.S. involvement in the Indochinese struggles for independence.

Dreyer, Ronald. *Namibia and Southern Africa: Regional Dynamics of Decolonization, 1945-1990.* London: Kegan Paul, 1994. Detailed account of South African and United Nations responses to the growing African demands for the independence of Namibia.

Gibson, Richard. *African Liberation Movements.* London: Oxford University Press, 1972. Examination of the African independence movements, especially in Portuguese colonies, that arose after the negotiated transitions to independence of the early 1960's.

Khilnani, Niranjan. *India's Road to Independence, 1857-1947.* New Delhi: Sterling, 1987. History of the century-long struggle for Indian independence.

Wilson, Henry S. *The Imperial Experience in Sub-Saharan Africa Since 1870.* Minneapolis: University of Minnesota Press, 1977. Broad survey of Africa south of the Sahara, with emphasis on the precolonial cultures, the "Scramble for Africa" in the late nineteenth century, variations in colonial regimes, and the processes leading to eventual independence.

Byron D. Cannon

Cross-References

Africa: Politics and Governments, p. 21; Asia: Politics and Governments, p. 108; Buddhism and Government, p. 152; Comparative Government, p. 384; Empires and Empire Building, p. 597; Imperialism, p. 889; Nationalism, p. 1268; Pacific Islander Governments, p. 1362; Pan-Africanism, p. 1369; Self-Determination, p. 1796; Zionism, p. 2192.

SURVEY
OF
SOCIAL
SCIENCE

ALPHABETICAL LIST

CATEGORY LIST